Streisand

Books by Anne Edwards

Biography
Sonya: The Life of Countess Tolstoy
Vivien Leigh: A Biography
Judy Garland: A Biography
Road to Tara: The Life of Margaret Mitchell
Matriarch: Queen Mary and the House of Windsor
A Remarkable Woman: A Biography of Katharine Hepburn
Early Reagan: The Rise to Power
Shirley Temple: American Princess
The DeMilles: An American Family
Royal Sisters: Elizabeth and Margaret
The Grimaldis of Monaco: Centuries of Scandal/Years of Grace
Throne of Gold: The Lives of the Aga Khans
Streisand: A Biography

Novels
La Divina
The Survivors
Shadow of a Lion
Haunted Summer
Miklos Alexandrovitch Is Missing
The Hesitant Heart
Child of Night
Wallis: The Novel

Autobiography
The Inn and Us (with Stephen Citron)

Children's Books
P. T. Barnum
The Great Houdini
A Child's Bible

Anne Edwards

Streisand

A Biography

Little, Brown and Company

Boston   New York   Toronto   London

First Edition

Lyrics of "As If We Never Said Goodbye" printed by permission of Don Black and the Really Useful Company.

Library of Congress Cataloging-in-Publication Data

Edwards, Anne.
    Streisand : a biography / Anne Edwards.
      p.   cm.
    Filmography: p.
    Discography: p.
    Includes bibliographical references.
    ISBN 0-316-21138-9
    1. Streisand, Barbra.   2. Singers — United States — Biography.
I. Title.
ML420.S915E4   1997
782.42164'092 — dc20
[B]   96-41091

10 9 8 7 6 5 4 3 2

MV–NY

Published simultaneously in Canada by Little, Brown & Company (Canada) Limited

Book design by Jean Wilcox

Printed in the United States of America

For Steve

"Any agent or mother or entrepreneur who believes he has another Barbra Streisand tucked away on a pedestal in the corner, waiting to be unveiled, had better change professions. There is just not going to be another Barbra Streisand, now or ever. What she is, happens once."

— Alan Jay Lerner, 1970

Contents

Streisand

Part I

The MGM Grand Garden

Las Vegas — December 31, 1993

1

_____

She stood outside her dressing room, distanced from the backstage may-hem that existed in the last few minutes before this, her first live concert in years. Her black gown with its deep-cut neckline gracefully framed her slim, curvaceous figure. Circling her neck was a glittering display of diamonds. Her shoulder-length light brown hair, streaked blond, fell loose and was softly styled. With a small wave of her left hand, she motioned the three members of her staff hovering close by — still fussing with her hair, makeup, and gown — to move away. The gesture was regal, immediately obeyed. For a brief moment she stood poised, alone, the famous chalky white undulating hands — lithe fingers like those of a Hindu goddess, elongated nails glossed with lacquer — clasped tightly before her, the only outward sign of her extreme nervousness.

It was December 31, 1993, and Barbra Streisand was preparing to confront the agonizing stage fright that had plagued her since the early, heady days of her extraordinary career. It was as though she were about to go through a belated rite of passage — face the twin demons in her life: an audience that demanded almost more than she had to give and the close friends and loved ones whom she privately feared she had failed and to whom she felt committed to prove otherwise.

The stage manager, a tall, broad-shouldered young man in a business suit and a dark-haired ponytail, moved to her side. He carried a walkie-talkie held close to his mouth. "Give the houselights a flash," he said into it, a signal that the star was ready to appear. People would now be rushing to their seats. A minute later the houselights in the enormous fifteen-thousand-seat auditorium were ordered dimmed.

"Two minutes," he told Streisand.

She stepped forward. The young man at her elbow handed her a freshly lit cigarette, and she took a quick puff as he guided her cautiously across the cable-strewn area to the bottom of the backstage staircase that she would have to ascend to enter the unusual balcony set. Several members of the staff were clustered at the foot of the steps; one held out a paper cup filled with cold tea as she approached. She leaned in close and sipped from it through a straw. She was edgy, in a solemn mood, and silent as she turned aside, poised, waiting. The overture was nearing the end. The sixty-four-piece orchestra, conducted by Marvin Hamlisch, was situated on her right, where it could be seen by her and the audience. Her section of the stage was now concealed by a curtain. Hamlisch, who had been her rehearsal pianist thirty years earlier when she had starred on Broadway in *Funny Girl,* glanced over at her, eyebrows raised, and she nodded that she was ready. The music swelled.

This was the moment she had feared. She took a deep breath, closed her eyes, lifted her chin as though struggling for air.

"To one side, please," Streisand's ponytailed escort said with dispatch as he helped her up onto the rather steep flight of stairs that led to the upper level of the set. "We're on our way to the stage," he announced into his walkie-talkie.

Out front the audience was wild with enthusiasm. Applause filled the air as soon as the orchestra began playing the opening bars of Streisand's great standard "Happy Days Are Here Again." She paused for a moment and then continued up as the assistant helped straighten the skirt of her long gown behind her so that she did not take a misstep ascending to the top.

"Ready?" he asked as she stood prepared to enter.

"Okay," she called over her shoulder.

"Happy Days Are Here Again" came to a rousing finish. The curtain parted and Streisand, head back, a nervous smile on her luminous face, stood pinned in the brilliance of the aureole spotlight on the balcony area to stage left of the giant proscenium, the orchestra visible to her right through tall mock windows of the palatial, columned, two-story living-room set. A fireplace flanked one end, the balcony the other. Chairs, tables, sofas — in the French style — and magnificent sprays of white flowers decorated the stage. Someone in the audience yelled, "Come on, Barbra!" and still smiling, she stepped closer to the balcony rail. The vastness of the Grand Garden was awesome. People were still applauding and calling out to her.

She remained gracefully composed as she looked out on the sea of blurred faces. Hamlisch raised his baton, and as the hesitant opening bars of "As If We Never Said Goodbye" were heard, an anticipatory silence cloaked the arena. The song was from Andrew Lloyd Webber's *Sunset Boulevard,* which had had its American premiere just three weeks earlier, the lyrics having been rewritten specially for her by the show's colyricist, Don Black, "with Andrew's happy compliance"— proof, if any was required, of her position as the world's prima pop diva.

All eyes were focused on her as she stood bathed in light, her nervousness evident, a hesitation in her manner. The entire audience appeared to lean forward as if to let her know that they were reaching out to her.

"I don't know why I'm frightened," she sang in a voice that for a brief moment contained a tremble, the words seeming to express her own thoughts.

I know my way around here:

The band, the lights, familiar sights,

The sound here.

Yes, a world to rediscover

But to stop my heart from pounding

I may need a moment.

She grasped the microphone tightly and breathed into it.

Why, everything's as if we never said goodbye.

Cheers rose from the audience at these last words, but she did not allow them to intrude on her pacing of the song.

I've spent so many evenings
Just trying to resist you.
I'm trembling now
Just thinking how
I missed you,
Missed the fairy-tale adventures
In this ever-spinning playground,
We were young together.

With infinite grace, she slowly started down the steps to the main area of the stage. The emotional response of the audience to the words she sang was almost tangible. People were caught up in thought, remembering. For some, Barbra Streisand had been a presence for most of their lives; others recalled the thirty years that had passed since she burst like a meteor onto the public scene. They had been through a lot with this offbeat, original, feisty Jewish lady — in her life, the country's, and their own. It was difficult to believe that once she had been perceived as homely. She was beautiful in most of their eyes. Her talent made her glow.

She had reached the bottom of the staircase and walked to center stage.

I've been in the wings too long,
All that's in the past
Now I'm standing center stage
I've come *home* at last.

As she reached the high D on the word "home" and held it aloft like a banner, a cheer broke out that swallowed the end of the phrase. It was the combination of the word "home," meaning she had returned to them, coupled with the sheer unequivocal power of her "belt" voice that erased the audience's doubts that she might no longer be as great as their memory told them, that they had foolishly squandered three hundred hard-earned dollars or more on a recollection. It positively brought them cheering and roaring to their feet, misting their eyes.

Shouts of "We love you, Barbra!" rang through the great arena. Streisand was visibly moved. She took a short breath and grasped the microphone tighter while she waited about thirty seconds for the cries to subside. When they did not, she raised her hands and motioned for the audience to sit down; she had more to tell them. They obeyed, as if royally commanded, and she continued her voice clear and strong, filled with driving passion as she promised that

. . . this time will be bigger

And brighter than we knew it,

So watch me fly,

You know I'll try

And do it . . .

Yes, everything's as if we never said goodbye!

The climax of the song had to be negotiated on a perilous high note. Her voice swept up and held it thrillingly. There was a moment of stunned silence and then frenzied applause, bellowing cheers, as the audience rose en masse from their seats. She looked out at the ocean of faces and tangle of arms outstretched toward her. The roar of the crowd washed over her. The careers of other stars who were her contemporaries had come and gone and come and gone again. She alone had sustained her popularity. At this moment of such tremendous adulation, she could not help knowing that this was true. A smile skimmed her face. Her manner eased.

"Aren't you nice. What a wonderful audience," she said slowly, her words so well miked that they were distinct to the people at the farthest reaches of the cavernous arena, where the cheering continued. The Donna Karan dress she wore was split to the knee on one side, and as she walked across the stage, a shapely leg was immodestly exposed. Streisand had long shown pride in the trim shape she maintained. She glanced down over the footlights to the front row and introduced the president's mother, Virginia Clinton Kelley, and Coretta Scott King, Martin Luther King Jr.'s widow, the two widely disparate women taking small bows to enthusiastic applause. Then Streisand continued on with her performance, in essence a one-woman Broadway show, using autobiographical material — her childhood dreams, relationships, family ties, and social positions.

The concert format employed the offstage voices of various fictional analysts (not nearly as many as she had sought out in real life), male and female, allowing her to travel back in memory to her childhood in

Brooklyn, her love affair with movies — and her fantasies about Marlon Brando. On a giant screen his image was projected in a scene from *Guys and Dolls* looking young, vital, *gorgeous.* With the magic of cinematic special effects, an awkward Streisand, age eleven ("Was I a *meeskite!*"), replaced his leading lady, the enchanting Jean Simmons, in the clip and sang with him the engaging Frank Loesser song "I'll Know."

Seated attentively in rows near the stage were her personable twenty-seven-year-old son, Jason; ex-husband, actor Elliott Gould; ex-lover, producer Jon Peters; and on his lap little Caleigh, the golden-haired goddaughter who was so dear to her. An entire page of photographs of herself with the engaging preschooler was featured in the program, and she spoke directly to her from the stage about the bedtime stories they read together. Then Streisand dedicated "Caleigh's favorite song, 'Someday My Prince Will Come,'" to her, and pictures of the two of them together projected on the giant screen behind her.

It was family time, and she followed in the sentimental mood with a moving rendition of Stephen Sondheim's song of maternal protection, "Not While I'm Around" from *Sweeney Todd,* sung to Jason, which was accompanied by home video images from their past — Jason as an infant being held in his mother's arms, as a child gamboling across a lawn, as a boy at his bar mitzvah, as a mugging, toothy teenager, and as a performer on the set of *The Prince of Tides,* a movie directed by Streisand. At the end she blew Jason a kiss and whispered, "I love you."

"I love you, too," he called back. She nodded her head; tears formed in her eyes. Never before had she so publicly revealed her innermost feelings toward her son — and both Jason, who appeared touched with emotion, and the audience reacted to this. From that moment on, there was the rare sense that the performer and the audience had shared private time together; their cheers and their silence, personal gestures of their love. Between songs she sipped herbal tea, fidgeted with her hair, brushed it back from her face, made casual remarks along with the short vignettes that led her from one song to another. But every word she spoke and sang was projected on huge, strategically placed closed-circuit video screens that were visible to both the audience and herself from almost any angle. At one point a startled look gripped her face as she

realized she had mixed up the lyrics to "Evergreen." She had been mis-
cued. Momentarily she froze while Hamlisch and the orchestra vamped
behind her. Then she smiled sheepishly and joked, "And it's my own
song!" She continued on, the orchestra making a seamless continuum
under Hamlisch's baton.

During intermission a security guard was stationed at her door to en-
sure that no one disturbed her as she prepared for the second half of the
program. She took time for a few minutes of meditation, which she often employed to relieve stress. A light tap on the door alerted her that
she had three minutes. She looked somber when she once again made the
long walk across the rear of the stage and up the staircase with the same
young assistant in attendance. Some of the old terror that had gripped her
returned. But she waved it away, managing a slight grin as she patted her
chest in an exaggerated, fluttering gesture. When the curtains opened,
her audience found her smiling. They cheered her entrance in another
provocative Donna Karan ensemble — a white tuxedo jacket and a floor-
length skirt, also split hip-high on one side. It was modeled after the pin-
striped outfit she had worn at Clinton's pre-inaugural gala that had caused
one woman critic to write snidely: "Even a strong, successful woman has
to play the femme fatale role."

As soon as she told this anecdote, Mike Myers, a comedian from
the popular satirical television show *Saturday Night Live,* came running
up onstage cross-dressed hilariously as his "wickedly funny alter ego," a
Long Island housewife with a Streisand obsession, and shouted in a deep,
affected, feminine New York–ese accent, "Barbra, don't listen to *that*
woman!" The act, though cued, had an air of spontaneity, and Streisand
laughed naturally and disarmingly mocked Myers as he described her
skin as being like "buttah" and her nose as "something to die for."

She was highly successful in the closing segment, which she made feel
like encores, with the optimistic philosophies of "Happy Days Are Here
Again," sung while historical clips were shown on the screen; "On a
Clear Day (You Can See Forever)," with its affirmation of a positive and
bright future; and the poignant Bernstein-Sondheim classic, "There's a
Place for Us," from *West Side Story.* Streisand had made the whole program feel as if it were custom-made, as though the lyrics had been writ-

ten for her. This was true, of course, in the case of "As If We Never Said Goodbye" and of Sondheim's "I'm Still Here" ("Sometimes a kick in the rear, but I'm here / One day you're hailed for blazing trails, next day you're nailed for fingernails / Producing, who does she think she is — a man? / I kept my toes and kept my space, I kept my nose to spite my face . . .").

One could carp at the interpretation of some of the songs. She seemed unable to project the deeper meaning of the "doormat" or "victim" songs. "Can't Help Lovin' Dat Man" fell a bit short of total sacrifice, and "Lover Man" missed a young girl's yearning. And "The Man That Got Away," which was superbly sung, eclipsing Garland's notorious mis-accents, lyrically did not feel true as phrased. She had greater success with "My Man."

When she finally left the stage after many bows, the audience continued to shout and applaud for several minutes before accepting the obvious — she would not return. The huge amphitheater, previously filled with the vibrancy of her voice and the power of her personality, seemed empty despite the sounds of the departing crowd milling about. On reluctantly moving to the exits, they called her "divine" and claimed there was "not one wrong note" in her performance; she had, in fact, hit a flat top note in "The Man That Got Away."

There was something historic about being one of those present at that first concert in Las Vegas. Fans had flown in from all over the world: South Africa, Great Britain, Germany, Canada, Australia. "You came all the way from Sydney just for this concert?" one woman was asked by an interviewer covering the concert for a cable network. "Yes," she replied. "She hasn't sung in public in — what is it? — twenty-four or twenty-seven years? What if this is *it* and she never appears again? She is the greatest singer born in my lifetime. There's no one to equal her and never has been."

Seldom before had Streisand interacted with her audience with such immediacy. Pauline Kael had once written in the *New Yorker,* "When Streisand sings, her command of the audience is in her regal stillness; she distills her own emotions. You feel that she doesn't need the audience — that she could close her eyes and sing with the same magnetic power.

Streisand's voice is her instrument." It was true. Yet, this one time she had exposed herself to an audience while at the same time keeping her distance, an ability that great politicians like Roosevelt and Churchill possessed but that is not apparent in many entertainers.

She had always hated New Year's Eve. As a young girl she had never been invited to a party to celebrate the occasion and during her life the holiday had seemed always to hit on the loneliest and most difficult periods. "Good!" she had said when she was offered the engagement at the MGM Grand Garden. "I won't have to spend New Year's Eve alone!" Indeed, she did not. After the show, in a reception she gave in her massive suite filled (as the stage had been) with large bouquets of white flowers, she hosted her own celebration for the friends and family who had attended the concert. There was champagne and a table laden with food. Through the bank of windows in the high-floor suite the garish neon light show of nighttime Las Vegas gleamed. As the gathered guests waited for the first blare of the outdoor fireworks display that would mark midnight, Streisand, dressed now in a simple black gown, her insecurities not dissipated despite the obvious success of her performance, bombarded her longtime associate Marty Erlichman, Marvin Hamlisch, and her good friends Alan and Marilyn Bergman and Cis Corman with questions about the sound system, the TelePrompTer, the visuals, the lighting — all the technical angles that she feared might have been flawed. "There's food. Why aren't you eating?" she asked one guest. And to another, "Was the neckline of my dress too revealing? My mother will have a conniption."

Before and during the concert her one concern had been *Can I do it?* Now, as she seemed always to do, she questioned whether she had done the right thing — appeared too sexily dressed, displayed too much sentiment, embarrassed Jason — and would these remissnesses (if indeed they were) be the cause of more tumult in her life?

She spent most of the next day in her suite, reading the rave reviews, holding meetings with Hamlisch, Erlichman, Cis Corman, and the Bergmans to see what could be improved for the second show. Everyone was in high spirits. Erlichman was now talking about plans for a concert tour. "Your fans want to see you. You owe it to them to show them you're still the greatest" was the theme. She never liked to vocalize before a performance. As showtime drew near, she took a few moments to meditate.

The lines outside the Garden formed early. The house was sold out once again. As she made her way backstage, she seemed less tense than the night before. Onstage she appeared radiant, smiling more easily, laughing more often. For this performance the audience included such celebrities as Michael Jackson, Steven Spielberg, Gregory Peck, Mel Gibson, and television host Jay Leno. If anything, the audience response was even more zealous than the previous evening. "Tonight was the way I hoped it would be," she later told Marty Erlichman. "Everything felt right."

The high she received from the concerts was apparent in her attitude. The financial rewards were awesome. The two shows had grossed over $12 million, topping her own and Erlichman's expectations — and more than twice the revenue of any previous pop or rock star concert. Of course, no singer had ever charged such ticket prices. Then there had been the concert souvenir merchandise, ranging from $100 bottles of Streisand-signature champagne to $25 T-shirts, which had already generated more than $1.5 million.

She knew the crass commercial aspects of the concerts would brand her as greedy. But she had never been ashamed of her ability to make huge sums or felt vulgar in discussing it. To one columnist in the early years of her career she had bragged, "The Beatles have to divide *their* royalties four ways, so I make four times as much as each one of them!"

She had a healthy regard for her earning ability and for having money. The two concerts had helped her not only to deal head-on with her stage fright but to find a viable way to secure herself financially so that she *could,* without too much concern for the future, proceed with the projects close to her, both commercial and charitable. Now she told Erlichman she was ready to go out on the road. He was to solidify plans for a tour that would kick off at the Wembley Stadium in London that April, travel to Washington, D.C., New York City, Detroit, and end at the Arrowhead Pond in Anaheim, California.

It meant being on the road for several exacting months; and there would still be many anxieties, pressures, and demands outside of, and because of, the tour to be confronted: the films she wanted to make; her recording contracts; her private concerns for her mother, who was nearly crippled from arthritis and with whom she had endured a lifelong struggle for approval; Jason, whose love was paramount; Caleigh, so increasingly important in her life; and "the age thing." She was in her fifties and had become that show business cliché — the great star without a man in her life, the star who could not bring her cheering audiences home with her at night.

At the moment, still aglow with the success of the Las Vegas concerts, she was able to keep the demons at bay. The problem was that as soon as she returned to Los Angeles to prepare for the tour, reality reared its head.

2

She was to have three months to organize her life before taking off on tour, a time that would be filled with chaos and self-doubt. "I lost weight and sleep. I thought I would disappoint people, that I wasn't good enough," she later confessed. Despite the overwhelmingly enthusiastic response to the Las Vegas concerts, she still did not feel absolutely at ease onstage, that she "belonged there and deserved to be there, that I could give and receive the love of those audiences." She had never really appreciated her own singing and felt a certain guilt that it was not her love; her love was making movies.

The process of filmmaking — the idea that she could create people and lives, realize *her* visions — had intrigued her since the very first days when she worked with William Wyler on *Funny Girl*. As an actress she had been able to become Fanny Brice, but the vision had been Wyler's. Being able to function as both her own producer and director, as she had in *Yentl* and *The Prince of Tides,* had given her additional power over the script, budget, and production. She made the major decisions, chose material that personally involved her, could make a statement or live out a fantasy, but she had to be strongly motivated — the story and characters had to be absolutely clear to her. She was not alone in the category of actor-director. Clint Eastwood, Mel Gibson, Kenneth Branagh, and

Jodie Foster also starred in major films under their own direction, but none of them had faced the strong resistance from the critics that she had. Recognition and acceptance was of major importance to her; rejection, criticism, cut deeply.

Streisand was never a company- or a studio-owned artist; her obsessive and independent behavior and her feminist activism made her a continual target for the Hollywood "boys' club," that seemingly impregnable male bastion who control the movie industry. She was accused by the establishment of being a perfectionist in a business that necessitates compromise. She hated such accusations. "Perfection is . . . a child when it's born," she once snapped back. "Perfect is too small a word for it, it's a miracle. It's God. It's mind-blowing, it's more than perfect. And yet it shits and pisses. There's no such thing as perfection, because everything seems to fall apart sooner or later."

What she wanted was to be allowed to follow her own convictions, to do the best job she was capable of performing, of turning out a movie in which she had pride. In order to accomplish that, it had to be done *her way*. Hollywood has a company mentality. It is loathe to invest in something not yet proven to succeed at the box office. If they could have done so, they would have made her into an ethnic Doris Day, appearing in the same formulaic musical until time forced her to retire. Streisand refused to let herself be packaged by a studio, frozen and sold like an ice cream bar, and she certainly would not allow the films she chose to direct or produce, or both, be devoured by the system.

Headstrong and as unstoppable now as she had been as a child, she pressed on, choosing subjects as future projects that were controversial and could only create difficulty for her in obtaining full studio backing. On her return to Los Angeles she found herself balancing three major literary properties: Larry Kramer's devastating AIDS play, *The Normal Heart;* Lt. Col. Margarethe Cammermeyer's story of her forced resignation from the Washington State National Guard on her acknowledgment that she was a lesbian; and a screenplay, *The Mirror Has Two Faces,* written by Richard LaGravenese, who had been responsible for the script of the well-received *The Fisher King.*

Streisand saw the Kramer play and the story of Lieutenant Colonel

Cammermeyer as being about people's right to love whomever they choose — about tolerance and acceptance of other people's lifestyles and about not being penalized for being who and what they are.

"Yes! Yes! We must love one another or die!" she told Kramer when she began working with him in 1986 shortly after seeing a performance of the play. "I gotta make the movie," she had insisted. "AIDS is killing all [those] beautiful young people, and your story will wake up America to the crisis, to the fact that nothing *really important* is being done about it." She had been "shaken up from the images" in Kramer's play, obsessed by them, talked about how she must be the one to bring to the screen the story of Dr. Emma Brookner and the men whose lives were in mortal jeopardy with the advent of the plague.

Her relationship with Kramer, an intense dedicated activist, was fraught with emotion. Not since *Yentl* had she struggled so to get financing for a movie or with her own deep-felt, tangled feelings about a project. Kramer, who is HIV positive, was facing the possibility that he might not live to see his strongly autobiographical story, which he sincerely believed would activate more money for AIDS research, brought to the screen. Yet, Streisand seemed incapable of hurrying the process. She had also bonded with Kramer, a charismatic, passionate man charged with anger at the complacency of the American government over AIDS.

Damaged lives and a government turned away from its people in its politics were themes that beat an insistent drum in Streisand's head. She was going through a tremendous change in her own life, becoming more public in her political and feminist attitudes while desperately seeking to ameliorate her relationship with her aging mother and to accept Jason's open declaration of his homosexuality with compassion and love. Kramer believed that Streisand wanted to make *The Normal Heart* "as the ultimate gift of love" to Jason, that she was "torn" in her inability to carry through on this wish as quickly as she would have liked.

Her state of mind was not helped by Elliott, who gave an interview to an English journalist in which he discussed Jason. "I think Jason's being gay is deeply psychological," he replied to a direct question about his son's homosexuality. "It's a result of conditioning, I think. . . . [I blame myself] for not being a more visible father. Barbra won custody when we were divorced. I wasn't fair to him. I left him in that environment without me. I think he was affected by not having love at a vital stage of his life, though the affection and love developed later. Barbra was consumed with her business and career and I just wasn't there.

"I can't fault Barbra for being something she can't be. I can only fault me. I know my intentions were positive, but it has been a great trial for Jason to overcome this lack of love. He's a very worthy, decent guy. I think he and Barbra have a bit more of an adult relationship now. She loves her son and he's as loyal to his mother as he can be."

There was no doubt of Jason's affection for, or his loyalty to, his mother. He quickly came to her defense when someone criticized her either privately or in the press. But Elliott, to whom she had extended her hand in friendship over the years, had both hurt her and heaped more guilt upon her. Had she really been the kind of detached mother he described? Should she have been with Jason more often? Had he felt neglected, his needs overlooked? She tried not to believe that was the case. She loved Jason deeply, unreservedly. She thought he had grown up understanding that she tried to give him priority time, that she was a working mother like so many other liberated women, that it wasn't wrong for women to be ambitious like men or for men to need at times to be soft like women. Her career had consumed much of her energy and attention, demanded that she travel. It wasn't fair of Elliott to expect more of her than he did of himself or to publicly accuse her of not being a good mother.

While she brooded about these private matters, both the Kramer and the Cammermeyer projects moved frustratingly slowly, and she turned her attention to the more commercial project of the three she had under option — *The Mirror Has Two Faces*. The character she was to play bore some similarity to Katie Morosky in Arthur Laurents's *The Way We Were:* the intelligent woman, plain to look at but with inner beauty who eventually wins the love of the handsome hero. For years she had been pressing Laurents, without success, to come up with a story line for a sequel. For a time Robert Redford held the rights and had been equally enthusiastic and had also approached Laurents, to no avail. Now she had a project on a similar theme, and one with the same chance of success.

"I think I'm always drawn to films about the mystery of appearances," she told the press. "*The Mirror Has Two Faces* is a really charming love story. But it has serious overtones about vanity and beauty, the external versus the internal."

The Mirror Has Two Faces was loosely based on a 1959 French film starring Michèle Morgan as an unattractive woman who wins the love of her philandering husband after plastic surgery. LaGravenese gave the story a contemporary twist: a cosmetic makeover raises her low self-esteem and she is metamorphosed into a woman of great desirability. The moral — self-love can physically change people's looks. The story line and characters still required much work, but it was a project that brought into focus some of Streisand's own experience. They had several story conferences, and she believed that LaGravenese could deliver a script that would translate into a successful movie, one that would not have the problems of *The Normal Heart* and would prove to the studios that she could bring in a profitable movie within its budget and on time.

Kramer would not be easy on her if she preempted *The Normal Heart* with *The Mirror Has Two Faces*. She shouldn't care, but she did. Kramer's work represented a cause that she knew was right, one she felt deeply about. She believed it would be easier to make *The Normal Heart* if *Mirror* proved successful. But Larry Kramer had a time bomb ticking away inside him, and although she believed her instincts were right in terms of which project should have precedence, she still suffered guilt from her decision.

This was a period of taking stock of herself. She felt almost grown-up now, although that vulnerable child she was always trying to subdue occasionally gained the upper hand. The wonder was that after twenty-six years of glittering stardom, fame equaled by only a tiny few — Marilyn Monroe, Marlon Brando, Elizabeth Taylor — with a notoriety that never dwindled or showed signs of fading, she remained excited about life, people, ideas. Ambition had once possessed her: being someone, being rich. Now it was accomplishing things that mattered, contributing to a better understanding of a few of the world's problems. But there were always too many distractions, too many demands on her time, energy, and emotions.

She wanted to simplify her life, to "move on," and although she liked "the idea of evolution and change," her acquisitiveness always defeated her. With its exquisite pieces of art nouveau that she had been collecting through the years, the house on Carolwood Drive, high atop Holmby Hills, a short distance from Sunset Boulevard, had begun to look like a museum. Maybe it *was* a museum. Maybe all her homes had become museums: this one, the five-house complex in Malibu, the West Side penthouse in New York. Bitten by the collector's bug early in her life, she had an eye for discovering rare and wonderful pieces. "I didn't grow up with a sense of it around me," she would tell people with a wide flourish of an elegant hand. "My mother used to put newspapers on the floor and plastic covers on the furniture — plastic on the lampshades, plastic everywhere. But it always hurt my eyes in some way."

What she perhaps did not see or understand was that her mother's use of plastic to cover her possessions was a means for someone in her limited circumstances to *preserve* what small beauty she had managed to amass in her home. But the sterility it invoked in her childhood home was to Streisand a painful memory of plastic sticking to the bare legs of a young girl when she sat in a chair, the hostile crunch of paper underfoot, the embarrassment of bringing other young people into her home. And it was this background that had so fed her desire to surround herself with beautiful objects and that was at the heart of her collecting mania, started when she was still in her teens.

Ordinary surroundings depressed her. There had to be unique treasures wherever she looked to help block out the ugly images of her childhood environment, a childhood that haunted her, that would not leave her in peace, that she hated for its pain and its commonness — a childhood whose spell, after years spent in therapy, she had been unable to break. Analysts were always trying to get you to let go of the past, saying that it drags you down, especially avouching that you cannot face all those tomorrows fettered with the past. Maybe, if she started to let go of things, the past with all its pain would go away with them.

Her collecting had started with elegant old evening bags and empty antique picture frames that she filled with interesting, inexpensive prints — often bought for only a few dollars and hung on the walls of the railroad apartment, with its bathtub in the kitchen, that had been her earliest real home in New York City. With the money she had made from her first acting role on Broadway, when she was only nineteen years old, she had acquired the incredible German art nouveau desk that was in her bedroom. Unable to write a check for the full amount, $2,800, she paid it off over a six-month period and then let the antiques dealer, Lillian Nassau, keep it in her shop on Fifty-seventh Street in Manhattan until Streisand had a place to put it. Two years later, *Funny Girl* a big hit and her albums selling in the hundreds of thousands, she fell in love with a Tiffany lamp with a peony shade and a striking red turtleback base "with the mosaics changing colors like the colors of the rainbow," and bought it for $45,000. It was now the centerpiece of the Carolwood Drive living room, which she had designed around it. Even on a rare sunless day, the red glass in the base glowed as if lit by some magic inner fire.

Whenever she saw an object that caught her eye and her imagination, she had to own it. Treasures small and large filled her homes, the overflow contained within giant packing crates in a Manhattan storage company: furniture, stained glass, bronze statues, paintings, china, glass, silver, fine antiques, and twenties kitsch — everything from a glamour-rating penny arcade game to a penny-a-pack cigarette dispenser. A 1926 Rolls-Royce Silver Ghost and a 1933 Dodge customized roadster were kept garaged at the Malibu ranch. Clothes of the twenties and thirties, bought in thrift shops and not worn in more than twenty years, hung as artifacts on display in special closets that held nothing else. The sheer enormity of her possessions, however, had not vanquished the sense of deprivation that had pervaded her since childhood, when her only doll had been a hot-water bottle "dressed" in one of her outgrown sweaters.

It was time, perhaps, to try another approach, to carry through with her decision to "let go," "move on," to sell off a large part of her collection and one of her three residences. Which one to choose was the easiest and yet most painful decision. Easy because it was the most burdensome, and painful because it represented the most intense relationship in her life.

The house on Carolwood Drive had always been *her* house. No, it would be the Malibu ranch complex that she and Jon Peters had built together and where they had spent most of the seven years of their "marriage" (it had always been more than an affair): it had been *their* home. Memories clung to every rafter. Peters's presence still pervaded the place. If she were to divest herself of the past, this would be a natural starting place, and between ever-escalating costs and devastating brush- and forest fires in the Malibu region, it also seemed wise to acquit herself of the responsibilities attached to the property. Before leaving for Las Vegas, she had set negotiations in progress to donate the land and buildings to the Santa Monica Mountains Conservancy for a conservation institute. This would benefit her tax status. Now, she decided she would sell off most of the contents of the five ranch houses — the main house, guest cottages, and studio — as well.

The time before leaving for England allowed her to select what she wanted to put up for sale at Christie's Manhattan. The choices were often difficult. She was attached by memory to many of the pieces. "Sometimes when it's been hard to relate to people, I could relate to inanimate objects," she said about her vast collection. "They didn't give me an argument, they didn't think I was crazy. And therefore we had a good relationship. But I'm at a more whole place now. I can relate to people, have relationships, and have objects. Now they are less precious to me. It has to do with one's growth psychologically and a shifting of priorities."

She did not want to have things in storage, in boxes, and in the basement. "I want other people to enjoy them if I don't have room for them anymore," she said. "It's a good feeling to use these things for a while and pass them on during your own lifetime." However, she would decide to put something in the auction and then a few days later cross it off the list. On a grinding, daily basis she was going over individual possessions, each having a special place, memory, or meaning in her life, and it was wrenching to decide what to sell and what to keep. There were long consultations with the Christie's representative: the value of each item, what it might be expected to bring. Always the good businesswoman, she had kept a record of the prices she had paid for everything she owned, with updated appraisals of the major pieces.

She has a preoccupation with detail and an eye for beauty. Owning the Tiffany peony lamp was like possessing an eternal light. It did not need to be illuminated to be lovely, rare — it just *was*. Owning it had made her feel rich at a time when being poor was not yet far enough in the past to be confined to memory. But its value had grown tenfold, and the auction was really to serve several purposes: to simplify her life, to shore up her financial reserve for the future, to validate her collecting craze — the pieces she had bought to be seen now as investments that had proved her business acumen. So the peony lamp, with its rare beauty that had meant so much to her and was one of the most difficult things to part with, would go under the hammer.

She did not minimize her need to feel not just financially secure but rich enough to do what she pleased in the future, both in her career and in her personal life. She was already consulting experts about buying early American art with part of the money she would realize from the auction, to replace the art nouveau she planned on selling and to create a totally new environment in the Carolwood Drive house. Her relentless need to have antiques and art form a complete and perfect setting was symptomatic of her entire personality. She saw things as a total vision.

"I don't put a black vase in a gray-and-burgundy room," she said. She liked monochromatic rooms, did not wear prints, and was drawn to black-and-white movies. The family photographs on the living-room piano are black-and-white — "color photos would disturb the harmony." Even the wrappers on the candy in her candy dishes had to be color-coordinated.

The two-day Christie's sale was set for March 3 and 4, 535 lots, some containing several items. Every piece was appraised and the lowest acceptable bid agreed upon. If withdrawn or unsold, Christie's would still charge her a fee that had to be taken into consideration. On the other hand, it was a star auction for the company, a coup worth a fortune in publicity, and they traded this off to Streisand's advantage when working out the cost details of the sale. Celebrity sales always brought higher prices for certain objects because of the nature of their provenance.

She gained widely circulated free publicity in an unprecedented arrangement with *Architectural Digest,* whose usual policy was not to feature a photo article on houses or furnishings up for sale. On this occasion they agreed to show the part of the ranch collection that was to be auctioned, and at Streisand's insistence, what she considered her prize piece in the sale, the magnificent Tamara de Lempicka painting *Adam et Eve,* was highlighted with her on the cover. The magazine photographers descended on the property directly following her return from Las Vegas and spent nearly a week on the shoot from early morning until nightfall. Shortly after the photographers were dispatched, Christie's packers arrived. Both operations were closely monitored by Streisand.

Included in the sale with the Lempicka (estimated sale price $800,000 – $1 million) were her cherished peony ($300,000 – $400,000) and cobweb ($800,000 – $1 million), another lead-glass Tiffany lamp that she had bought and paid for on the layaway plan when she was first appearing on Broadway; the two antique cars ($50,000 – $65,000 each); an exquisite diamond-and-jade Cartier clock ($100,000 – $150,000); an amazing assortment of art nouveau glass and furniture; art deco bronzes, silver, dishes, and furniture; and formerly cherished modest china figures, powder boxes, and old clothes.

She remained in Los Angeles during the sale, which received international coverage. When notified of the amount her collection had brought — nearly $6 million, $2 million from the Lempicka alone — she was stunned. The more valuable pieces went for near what they had been appraised at, but the items in the second day of the sale — the memorabilia whose worth depended upon how much the public was willing to pay for something that belonged to Streisand — sold in some lots for ten to fifteen times what was expected.

With the vast sum she had garnered from the auction and the many millions more she was guaranteed to make on her tour, money was no longer a prime consideration. Perhaps it never was. It did very little to lessen the stress of the last few weeks before she was to leave for England for the first engagement of the tour. There were exhausting daily rehearsals, and as the script the Bergmans were writing for the concert relied heavily upon memories of her childhood, youth, and early stardom, she was constantly being forced to look back. Everything that had happened to her in the past three months had demanded this of her — the three film scripts she was working on, the music she was rehearsing for the concert tour (all the songs were either her standards or numbers that reflected important steps in her life), the sale of her possessions. And still she was chasing rather than facing demons, contrary to what she had wanted to do.

"She was in a terrible state the week before she was to fly over to Britain for the kickoff concert of the tour," a member of her entourage said. "Barbra suffers from second thoughts: Should I really be doing this? What happens if I bomb? She gets stomach pains, becomes even more demanding of herself and her performance. The amazing thing is that she never seems to overlook even the smallest detail — something a member of the staff could easily take care of for her — yet, she is terrified that she will disappoint people."

First she flew to New York, where she saw Jason, avoided a meeting with Larry Kramer, had her final fittings on the Donna Karan gowns she would be wearing onstage, and supervised the packing. Suddenly, the evening of her departure arrived. A mountain of suitcases piled up around her, she waited for the limousines that would take her, a select few members of her staff, and her baggage to the airport. She was dressed comfortably, very unstarlike — a thick sweater, loose pants, a funny, beat-up hat. She looked a lot like that "homely" kid from Brooklyn who had once had the chutzpah to think she could be a movie star. She had traveled a long way since then, but Brooklyn and the past seemed always to be there whenever she glanced back over her shoulder.

Part II

Roots

"It'd take a lifetime to know Brooklyn
t'roo and t'roo. An even den, yuh
wouldn't know it at all."
   Thomas Wolfe, "Only the Dead Know Brooklyn," 1935

"Terribly funny, yes, but Brooklyn is also a sad
brutal provincial lonesome human silent
sprawling innocent perverse tender
mysterious place . . . "
   Truman Capote, 1946

"I always wanted to get out of Brooklyn and be someone."
Barbra Streisand, 1970

3

Brooklyn was her universe for the first fifteen years of her life. She was born Barbara Joan Streisand on April 24, 1942, the second child of Emanuel and Diana Ida Rosen Streisand. America had entered the war only five months earlier and already one of Diana's two brothers had been inducted. Several young men in the modest apartment building at 457 Schenectady Avenue, where the Streisands lived, had eagerly enlisted in the service. Boys in Emanuel's English classes at Brooklyn High School for Specialty Trades (later called George Westinghouse Vocational High School), where he taught, were already dropping out to join the service. Aircraft carriers, battleships, cruisers, and destroyers were being built at the 75,000-worker Brooklyn Navy Yard, the largest of its kind in the world. Fort Hamilton, Brooklyn's staging area for the army, was equipped to handle 8,000 men at a time. At night, a blackout was enforced over the entire borough because it was considered a strategic area. Security was diligent. No one was going to forget Pearl Harbor.

At the carefully guarded North River pier, silent lines of men in khaki waited to file aboard transport ships that would take them to Europe to meet the Nazi foe. The last view they would have of their country would be the murky dark waters that bordered the Brooklyn mainland. Wherever you were in Brooklyn, you had a sense of the sea, from the shorefront communities to the many bridges that linked Brooklyn to Manhattan, to the bustling ports, the names of the avenues and parkways — Atlantic, Ocean, Sea Gate, Pacific — to the 197-acre Brooklyn Navy Yard skirting Wallabout Bay, a semicircular elbow of the East River.

When it was first proposed in 1833 that the village of Brooklyn become incorporated into the city of New York, the idea was scoffed at. But geographically and hence commercially, Brooklyn was bound to the island of Manhattan, and in 1898, fifteen years after the completion of the mighty Brooklyn Bridge, incorporation finally took place. Integration was another matter, slower to progress and perhaps never to be achieved. Brooklynites are a people unto themselves. Those raised there speak their own dialect. At the time of Barbara Joan Streisand's birth, the tremendous number of foreign-born, over 900,000, and the ethnic majority of the 2.8 million population (over a million of whom were Jewish) made it quite different from any of New York City's other boroughs and uniquely set it apart from other cities in America.

When war was declared, Brooklyn was one of the greatest maritime and industrial centers in the world. Forty percent of the foreign commerce that moved out of the port of New York was cleared through Brooklyn's thirty-three miles of developed waterfront. There were seventy steamship freight lines, fourteen trunk railways, and a series of huge shipping terminals. Brooklyn was the fifth-largest manufacturing center in the country. Industry, however, was largely concentrated within a few blocks of the waterfront. The rest of Brooklyn was one mammoth residential area, divided into sections by ethnic makeup more than by boundaries. There were twenty distinct and separate Jewish communities. Several might have been classified as ghettos where many of the foreign-born Jews lived and where pushcarts still crowded the streets and where there was a heady scent of sour rye bread fresh from the oven, the smell of fish cooked and stuffed, and the sweet odor of honey cakes. Saturdays the streets were empty, somber as the Sabbath was observed. But the majority of Jewish communities were middle class and upwardly mobile first- and second-generation Americans.

Barbara's parents were both raised in ghettos, but with time, their families had become just slightly removed from these more congested, unrelieved slum areas. Named Ida Rosen at her birth on December 10, 1908 (Diana was a teenage affectation), Barbara's mother was the third child of Louis Rosen, a tailor, and his wife, Esther Etlin Rosen, who emigrated to America during the pogroms in Russia shortly after the turn of the century. Louis was a religious Jew whose joy was derived from his position as a part-time cantor in his shul.* Had his voice and interpretation been more inspired, his prospects might have been brighter, for this was the era of cantorial glory, when great cantors would appear at different shuls as superstars in their field. A synagogue's ability to attract the most famous of these singers drew great respect from other shuls. Jews would walk miles to hear a celebrated cantor.

Louis lacked the vocal talent that was demanded for such a career. His failure embittered him, but it did not stop him from praying or singing. Four times a day he would walk around the Rosen's small, crowded apartment, his tallis draped around his sloping shoulders, and daven in a singsong voice. Sometimes he would sing Yiddish songs that came from the old country. The family spoke Yiddish, but among the younger members, English was preferred. "Speak to me in English," Diana was always telling her mother. And she and her sister, Molly, who was next to her in age, seldom spoke Yiddish between themselves. There was the need to integrate, to become Americanized, and the sooner the better. Diana grew up to the sound of Yiddish music. She had a sweet, untrained soprano voice and liked to listen to operetta on the gramophone that was her father's great pride. At seventeen, pretty, petite, round-faced, and with shining blue eyes, she tried out for the Metropolitan Opera chorus and was rejected. Three years later she went to work in an office, filing and doing light bookkeeping. She met Manny Streisand at a Purim celebration at the home of a friend whose father was the cantor for their shul.

Emanuel's father, Isaac Streisand, a tailor, emigrated from a small Jew-

*The word *shul* is derived from the Greek *schola,* via the German *Schule.* The Hebrew word for a house of prayer is *bet-haknesset,* a house of assembly. Similarly, the Greek word *synagogue* means "assembly." The two words are interchangeable, but often *shul* is used to describe a synagogue with a small congregation.

ish *shetl* in the village of Berezhany in Galicia, a section of Poland on the Ukrainian border, in 1898. On marrying Anna Kessler, who also came from Berezhany, in 1907, Isaac sold the sewing machine he had carried on his back when going from door to door to do small tailoring jobs and used the money to set up a fish stand in the Lower East Side ghetto where they lived. On February 5, 1908, Emanuel, their first child, was born. Three more sons — Murray, Hyman, and Philip — and a daughter, Molly, followed, and in 1920 Isaac opened a proper fish store on Sumner Avenue in the Williamsburg section of Brooklyn. Emanuel, called Manny by friends and relatives, lived with his family in a crowded two-bedroom tenement apartment within walking distance from his father's fish store. Being the eldest son, he helped his father more than his siblings did.

Dealing in such perishable merchandise presented great difficulties for the family. The fish was bought in Manhattan at the Fulton Fish Market, where Isaac had to drive at three in the morning in the erratic, worn-out truck he had bought from the former owner of the fish store. When not in school, Manny would help his father load and unload the fish in their large, heavy boxes layered in ice. When his mother was with his father in the store, he watched over his younger siblings at home, and on Thursday evenings he helped to chop and cut the fish to be sold the next day, the busiest they had, as Jewish households prepared for the Sabbath. After school Manny wrapped fish in newspapers and delivered it to houses in the neighborhood. A work ethic developed that would follow him throughout his life and in future years be inherited by his daughter.

As his business improved, Isaac moved his brood to more spacious accommodations in the Sumner Avenue housing project a few streets down from his fish store — where his older son, an exceptionally gifted student, had no intention of following in his father's footsteps. Yiddish was the first language in his home as well, but Manny was proud of his own mastery of English and had dreams of perhaps one day becoming a writer. With whatever extra money he received as tips, he bought books. When he finished his course of studies at the local yeshiva, which in the United States was a secondary Hebrew school, often with elementary classes as well, he knew that education was the only way he would one day be able to satisfy his ambition.

After graduating from Boys' High School in the summer of 1924, he entered City College of New York that autumn, supported by a small scholarship and part-time jobs as a lifeguard and a Good Humor Ice Cream truck driver. Knowledge, he believed, was the most salable merchandise in the world. He learned that lesson from his mother, who went back to school after her children were in their teens to perfect her English and be able to read books that would open up the world to her. Her firstborn resembled her in looks as well, inheriting her lively hazel eyes and wavy dark hair.

Manny received a bachelor of science degree from City College of New York in 1928. An all-round and well-liked young man, he was active in the drama, math, boxing, fencing, and debating clubs. "Manny is one of those fortunate few who can graduate and say that college work has been easy," it says beside his earnest photograph in the college yearbook. One is struck by the strength of his jaw and the exceptional intelligence in his eyes. His forehead is high, his cheekbones broad, his expression keen.

"There was something about Manny," a fellow student recalled. "It was not just that he was a genius, which everyone thought he was; he had a special quality. We all looked up to him, came to him for counsel." With the help of night classes, he earned a master's degree in education two years later. He and Diana were married by Rabbi Isaac Boomis on December 24, 1930, and spent a weekend honeymoon in Manhattan. On their return they were in an automobile accident. Manny suffered a slight concussion. For a few weeks he had severe headaches. They eased in intensity, and he learned to cope with their frequent return. Manny was not a complainer. His attention was directed on positive action and on his current goal to make something of his life.

After the stock market crash of 1929, jobs and money were scarce. Determined that he would not start a family until he and Diana could have a small place of their own in a more upwardly mobile neighborhood, Manny accepted a position as an English teacher at Brooklyn High School for Specialty Trades. Diana, who had taken secretarial courses, managed to find office work. The newlyweds moved into a three-room apartment in Flatbush, which was where many first- and second-generation European Jews aspired to live once they had achieved some measure of education and advancement. In 1930 fifty percent of Flatbush's 85,000 residents were Jewish.

The newly married Streisands lived frugally, saving their money. In 1935 their son Sheldon Jay Streisand was born. Manny's new responsibility inflamed his ambition. He had a plan. One day soon he would go back to school and work for his doctorate. With a Ph.D. he could teach at a university, which would be more lucrative and prestigious, and he could eventually write — not novels, since he knew he didn't have the imagination that was necessary — but scholarly books. Diana never doubted that Manny had the intelligence and drive to do exactly that.

The students at Brooklyn High School for Specialty Trades tended to be truants on the verge of dropping out or general troublemakers. If the boys were above the age of sixteen, their required classes were strictly nonacademic trades and skills, such as woodworking or automotive work. But younger students had to take general classes — English, mathematics, and social studies — for half a day as well. There were two sets of teachers, the technical staff and classroom instructors like Manny Streisand.

A fellow teacher, Nathan Clark, has retained warm memories of the time when he and Manny were associates. "Many of his students," said his former colleague, "were rough, from bad homes and bad neighborhoods, but they all respected Manny Streisand. He treated them with understanding and kindness, and they weren't used to that. He had no trouble from any student. They revered him, and if there was a student who caused a little trouble, Manny didn't march him down to see the principal; he handled it himself."

Although the emphasis of the school was on vocational arts, Manny seemed determined that the young boys he taught would have an understanding of their language and be able to write it well enough so that their chances for a good life were enhanced. He was a born educator, Clark recalled, a dedicated teacher who was especially endowed with the ability to communicate his thirst for knowledge. He was a man who loved children and who was ambitious not only for himself but to give his son and, once Barbara was born, his baby daughter a good life and a solid education. "He was, I think," Nathan Clark said, "the finest man I ever worked with. Everyone loved him."

When Sheldon, called Shelley by his family, was a year old, Manny enrolled in the doctoral program in education at Teachers College, Columbia University, taking night classes while holding on to his job at the vocational high school. The commute was time-consuming. Columbia is all the way over on the west side of Manhattan on 116th Street, a long journey by IRT subway from Flatbush. The young couple did not have an easy time of it. Diana had to return to work as a file clerk to supplement their income. Shelley was left in the care of a close neighbor. Manny would leave the house just about the time that Diana was coming home. When he returned, Shelley was asleep. Weekends he graded his high-school class papers, prepared his lectures, and then settled down to study for his doctorate, which would take him years with the limited amount of credits he could manage each semester.

Diana's dreams were far more modest than Manny's. Not an intellectual, she did not understand what he was studying or why he was unhappy with being a high-school teacher: the salary of $1,800 a year was low but steady and the job, genteel and respected. There were many things about Manny that she did not comprehend, but she loved him deeply and was awed by the wealth of his knowledge. She still liked to sing, although she long ago had put aside her faint aspirations of a vocal career. Times were hard. Her daily life went on as it had for years, to rhythms set by a depression whose grip remained unbroken. Manny and Diana were the lucky ones. They had weekly paychecks, however small, while jobless men still haunted the streets, pleading for handouts. Neighbors did what they could to help one another by watching children and sharing a soup pot when they knew a relative, neighbor, or friend might otherwise go hungry. The building the Streisands lived in was now half empty, as families, unable to pay the rent, moved into already crowded rooms to live with relatives.

The war came as a feared surprise. For months the stage had been set for a distant but dangerous war. Yet, America was not prepared for Pearl Harbor. Manny was correcting papers on the kitchen table that Sunday afternoon, December 7, 1941, when it was announced over the radio that the Japanese had bombed Pearl Harbor. Doors were thrown open in neighbors' apartments as the occupants gathered in the hallways, stunned but united against "those dirty yellow bastards." Then everybody was screaming. It was bitterly cold that day, but people ran out into the swarming street. Diana was four months' pregnant, grateful that her condition, Shelley, Manny's job as a teacher, and a predisposition to migraines would most probably conspire to keep him out of uniform.

Over 300,000 men left their homes in Brooklyn to fight in the war. A day or two after Pearl Harbor there were air-raid scares that sent people scurrying to shelter areas. More than four hundred sirens were installed at strategic stations throughout the city, nearly half in Brooklyn, and their wail was eerie and piercingly loud enough to strike terror in any heart. Only the most necessary lights were kept on behind blackout shades at night in order to eliminate the sky glow against which ships might be silhouetted and made easier prey for submarines. Manny's subway trips were conducted in near darkness, as sections of the route were aboveground, windows of trains painted black, and dim light used inside the cars. It was all but impossible to read. Blackouts brought into action more than 150,000 air-raid wardens. Manny took a six-week training course based on the experience of wardens in Britain and was certified by the precinct warden commander before being assigned to a post. Two nights a week when he returned from Columbia, he would put on a hard white helmet and an armband and patrol the dark streets of the neighborhood with a protected flashlight before joining his small family.

The onset of Diana's labor came in the midst of an air-raid drill. Manny hailed an emergency taxi driver, one of the few vehicles allowed on the streets at such a time. Barbara Joan Streisand (after Anna Streisand's late sister, Berthe) was born at Israel Zion Hospital on April 24, 1942, healthy and strong-lunged. Family legend has it that her first cries were so loud, they startled the delivery-room staff. Until she was six months old, she slept in a crib in her parents' room; then Shelley was moved to a cot in the living room, and she occupied his former room. With a baby and a seven-year-old son, Diana could no longer work. Money was tight, but she was against Manny's abandoning his work on his doctorate to take a high-paying job at the shipyards, which were now going full steam. However difficult it was, the Streisands survived by living on a rigidly frugal budget. But the strain was hard on both of them.

As the summer of 1943 approached, Manny was offered a chance to help his friend, Nathan Spiro, an industrial arts teacher, as a counselor at Camp Cascade in Highmount, New York, in the Catskills just east of the village of Fleischmanns adjoining New York State's richest farmland. Camp Cascade was set in a protected glade in the foothills of the mountains and boasted a small waterfall and a natural swimming hole. The Streisands' Flatbush apartment, which was at the rear of the building, was stifling hot in the summer. In upper New York State there would be the mountains, cool fresh air, space, and a chance for Manny to relax and be with his family.

A man gifted with entrepreneurial skills, Nate Spiro had rented the camp — which consisted of five large cabins, and a main building with a kitchen, dining room, lounge, and staff quarters — for the season. There was no heat or hot water. Campers took cold showers, but Diana heated water for Barbara's bath on the huge wood cooking stove in the kitchen, which also contained an old-fashioned, commodious icebox amply filled with vegetables and dairy products that came from a nearby farm.

Nate had done a good job of recruiting campers, mostly from Brooklyn's immigrant families. There would be room for both of the men and their wives (each of whom had a young baby) and space with the campers for Nate's four other children and for Shelley. Nate would teach the campers arts and crafts while Manny organized a drama group. A camp cook qualified to cook kosher food was hired to join a staff that also included two cleaners and three more counselors. Diana, Mrs. Spiro, and her teenage daughter, Helene, were to take care of the various other housekeeping chores while the two men supervised the sports with the help of the oldest of the 110 coed campers. Manny would be a great asset to the camp. An excellent swimmer, having once been a lifeguard, he was also proficient in squash and tennis.

Both families set off with great enthusiasm in three rather ancient and dilapidated hired buses crowded with wide-eyed youngsters, most of whom had never before been in the country. Suitcases and equipment were tied to the top of the vehicles. The small caravan moved sluggishly toward its destination, the children led in song by the adults while the older campers comforted the younger members who already were experiencing the first pangs of homesickness.

Manny was in particularly high spirits, happy that he could spend the summer in the country with his family. A proud father, he wanted to see Shelley develop athletic skill. He doted on Barbara, and although she was not a beautiful child — being almost bald as an infant — she had a merry laugh and quick responses that made him certain she was intellectually gifted.

Manny lacked only one year's study for his doctorate in education at Columbia. During that summer he needed to think about his final thesis. The wooded camp setting, removed as it was from the heat and stress of summer in Brooklyn, would be a much better writing environment. The nearest town, Fleischmanns, normally a six-hour drive from Manhattan, but nearly a day's journey with the numerous stops along the way to accommodate weak bladders and the buses' leaky water pipes that caused them to hiss and overheat, had its heyday before World War I. The wealthy Fleischmann family, famous for their yeast product, had constructed a summer home there in the 1860s. A number of rich Austrian-Hungarian Jews followed, building grand estates with elegant verandas, magnificent gardens, and rooms large enough for lavish entertaining. By the end of the century, something like fifty hotels crowded Fleischmanns's borders. The town, however, lost its cachet between the wars when the affluent summer people, whose large homes were generally outside the village, moved to newer, more popular communities closer to New York.

When Manny Streisand came to work at Camp Cascade, Fleischmanns was still suffering from the economic depression. The grand old Fleischmann house had burned to the ground years before and remained a charred ruin. Dotting the surrounding wooded areas were dozens of independent camps like the one that Nate had organized — all very primitive and catering to children of poor, foreign-born families.

The Streisands arrived at the end of June and were contracted for an eight-week stay. Within two weeks it began to look like their work would be more difficult than they had anticipated. After two of the counselors quit, Manny doubled his duties and the number of campers in his care. The exercise was vigorous — hiking through the mountains, swimming in icy water, always having to be alert to danger from wild animals, brambles, insects, or simply the rambunctiousness of his young group. Many campers did not speak English, having recently fled the Nazis. Nights were difficult as those scarred by what they had witnessed awoke with nightmares and had to be reassured that they were safe.

During his fifth week at Camp Cascade, Manny tripped over a rock while out hiking alone, hitting his head in the fall. Dazed, but noting there was no cut, he continued on his way back to camp. The following day he developed a paralyzing migraine and went back to his cabin to lie down. Diana looked in on him a short time later and found him sleeping fitfully. When she returned in an hour, she could not rouse him. Alarmed, she ran to get Nate Spiro. Manny was unconscious, his pulse barely perceptible.

"It was terrible," she recalled. "We were so removed from everything. I suppose that made me . . . frantic."

The nearest hospital was in Margaretville, several miles farther away. With the aid of some of the older campers, Nate got Manny into the one car they had at the camp. Diana accompanied them, leaving Barbara in the care of the Spiros' daughter, Helene. The child cried loudly when the car drove off in a cloud of dust, down the dirt trail to Margaretville. Barbara was never to see her father again.

Twenty-four hours later, on August 4, Emanuel Streisand was pronounced dead. He had never regained consciousness. Respiratory failure was cited on the death certificate as the cause of death. Theories were to circulate in the family for years: Manny had been the victim of hospital misdiagnosis; he had suffered an epileptic fit; he had died from concussion or a tumor on the brain; he had contracted an infectious disease that, because of his close association with so many young people, it was thought better not to disclose. The result of a concussion complicated by his earlier injury and not being treated fast enough or with the right drugs is the more likely explanation. Diana remembered pacing the floor back in their room at the camp, trying as best she could to remain in control for the sake of the children. She had no idea what they were going to do.

She was in shock, unable to believe that she was now a widow and her two children fatherless. Nate Spiro took over immediate arrangements and, through the local Jewish funeral home, contacted the Jewish Burial Organization for assistance in paying for and transporting his friend's body back to Brooklyn. Carrying Barbara in her arms and holding on tightly to Shelley's hand, Diana left Fleischmanns the next morning on the same train as the coffin. Manny was buried almost immediately upon arrival at Mount Hebron Cemetery in Queens.

Barbara, just fifteen months old, could not understand why her mother was crying. But the child's grief for her lost father would very soon form her character, and breed within her such corrosive anger and sense of self-deprivation — *Why me? Why my father?* — that her future happiness would always be compromised.

4

With no insurance money and very little in savings, Diana was forced to leave the middle-class apartment in Flatbush and move into her parents' three-room apartment at 365 Pulaski Street, a four-story building in the Williamsburg section of Brooklyn. As reflected in the spires, campaniles, and domes that rose above the skyline of converted brownstones and small apartment houses, Williamsburg embraced a mixture of religions. A huge black ghetto burgeoned in the northern reaches, where a direct train, which had inspired the Duke Ellington–Billy Strayhorn classic, "Take the 'A' Train," linked it to Harlem. The Pulaski Street area was predominantly old-world Jewish and Irish Catholic, most of the first-generation offspring having recently left for more elite addresses.

To Barbara the area was fascinating. Pushcarts brimmed with a cornucopia of items — ripening fruit, enticing candies, bright fabrics, buttons, threads, mops and brooms, and used clothing. Women in aprons and men in alpaca skullcaps and silkaline coats bargained emotionally with the peddlers. Bed linen billowed out from windows, and on warm days people sat on stoops and fire escapes or by the curb in stiff wooden chairs in the hot sunshine while children in minimal attire played on the sidewalks or on luckier days ran through the gushing cool water of an opened fire hydrant. These were impressions that would color her life. Still, the move to Pulaski Street was not a happy one.

Bubbe and Zayde Rosen, as their grandchildren called them, occupied one room of the apartment; Diana and Barbara shared a bed in another, and Sheldon slept on a folding cot in the third room, which was furnished with a dark wood dining table, chairs, and a china cabinet. There was no living room: the "family" room was the dining room, with no space for a couch. ("Couches to me were, like, what rich people had," Streisand would later say.)

The Rosens were decent, hardworking people, but there was scant love in the house. Zayde Rosen was a cold man, bitter at his failure not to succeed in America and at his unfulfilled cantorial ambitions. Bubbe was asthmatic, and the apartment was filled with the acrid smells of the camphor that she inhaled and of the strong lye soap she used as she hunched over the deep white-enamel sink in the kitchen and scrubbed the family's wash on a ridged metal board while her sprawling breasts shook beneath her cotton housedress and flowered apron.

Diana, depressed, cried a lot. With two young children and a mother who was not well, she felt guilty to be living on the meager army allotment checks her bachelor brother signed over to her, when it rightly should have gone to her parents. As a widow at thirty-four, with no money and two children, she feared she had no future marriage prospects, and in her mind at this time, her life was over. Her own trauma was so all-encompassing that she was unaware, or perhaps insensitive, to what Shelley and Barbara were suffering.

Shelley had lost his father at a crucial time in his childhood. Manny had always been able to communicate with young boys and help them with their problems. Shelley was artistic, and Manny had encouraged his creativity. Never too busy to talk or listen to his son, a great bond had formed. Unable to relate to Diana in her state of depression and never at ease with his grandparents, Shelley keenly felt the loss of his father and during this time drew closer to his little sister, of whom he was protective.

Bubbe Rosen had not been prepared for young children to reenter her household. The tumult they created jarred her nerves and made her irritable. Shelley would run in and out of the apartment banging doors after him. Barbara was all over the place, impossible to keep still, prone to knocking things over as she played. Once she broke a piece of her grandmother's cut glass — Bubbe's most prized possessions, carried with her so many years before on the boat from Russia. Shelley remembers that he and Barbara would scuttle under the dining-room table to avoid a beating whenever their mischievousness caused breakage or disruption. He was more fearful of his grandmother than was Barbara, who treated both her grandparents with measured defiance. She seemed to know just how far to go before Zayde would get out his strap and, although he never hit either one of them with it, crack the leather into a frightening sound that threatened he would.

Barbara simply could not relate to this elderly couple. Bubbe, a short, stout, full-breasted woman with wispy gray flyaway hair, would sit at the dining table and sip a glass of tea through a sugar lump she held between her teeth. She would sigh as she sat there, mumbling things to herself. She seldom had a conversation with either of her grandchildren except to insist that they eat the food she always seemed to be preparing — cabbage soup, *gribenens* (the hard pieces that were left after chicken fat was rendered), *tsimmes,* and honey cakes. She treated her frequent head-aches by wrapping a vinegar-soaked cloth around her head. At those times Barbara knew she had to be especially quiet.

Of her two grandparents, Barbara was drawn more to Zayde. There was something mystical about his appearance, gray-blue eyes that seemed always to be seeing things in the distance that she could not, the move-ment of his oddly graceful stubby hands as he talked, and the singsong ca-dences of his chanting. Wearing a yarmulke on his head, his tallis over his shoulders and his phylacteries (which were strips of parchment inscribed with words from the Torah) strapped to his forehead and left arm, Zayde would daven almost as soon as he awoke, facing east as he said his prayers, for that is where *Eretz Yisroel* is. This ritual intrigued Barbara, who would ask him questions about what he was doing, and he would answer her unpatronizingly. It is doubtful that she understood what he was saying, but she liked being spoken to as if he thought she could.

She and Shelley went to Zayde's small modest shul on special holidays like Succoth and Simchas Torah, when children were given apples to eat. She was envious of the grand appearance of the nearby Catholic church but could well have been proud of the sight of her Zayde as he stood on the *bima* before the Torah scrolls wrapped in crimson velvet embroidered with gold thread and containing the five books of Moses. A short, wiry man, Zayde suddenly took on stature as he held the holy scriptures in his arms.

Diana finally went back to work as a bookkeeper, which aided her strained financial situation but created more responsibility for her ailing mother. Barbara was sent to the neighborhood yeshiva preschool when she was three. During that summer she was shipped off for several weeks to Diana's sister, Anna, and her husband, who had a small house in western Connecticut. These experiences backfired. Parted from her mother, Barbara feared she would never see her again and clung to Diana even more when they were back together.

Shelley was somewhat of a surrogate parent during this period. When he was in school, Barbara played on the stoop of the apartment building or in the hallways, cadging snacks from compassionate neighbors who believed her made-up stories that she had not been given lunch. When her brother came home, she would follow him around, to his annoyance, until he went off to play stickball or other games with his friends. The building was not occupied entirely by Jewish families. There were Irish and Italian neighbors — nonkosher homes — and had Diana or Bubbe Rosen known that Barbara had eaten from these kitchens, they would have been furious. As it was, they never understood why she ate so little at mealtimes and worried that she would grow to be a sickly skinny *marink,* considered a terrible fate for a Jewish girl — for what man would want to marry a scrawny woman? When she was a child, it took two years before her hair began to grow; later she said she looked like a martian. A slight cast in one eye made it turn in at certain times, but the sheer blueness of her eyes compensated for this distraction. Possessing extraordinary energy, she seemed to be a small Vesuvius about to erupt. When Barbara was three or four, Bubbe called her *farbrent,* which in Yiddish means "on fire." She refused to take no for an answer and always had an arsenal of arguments ready to win her point.

One stifling hot day in June when she was four and recovering from the chicken pox, she asked Bubbe if she could go out to play with some of the children from the building. "What kind of *farchadat* idea is that?" Bubbe answered and told her she was to remain exactly where she was. That happened to be on a cot near the fire escape. When Bubbe disappeared into the kitchen, Barbara dressed, climbed out the window onto the fire escape, and descended the treacherous iron staircase several steep flights to the courtyard below. She knew she would be disciplined when she returned. Her actions took a certain amount of bravery and audacity, not caring what the consequences were for herself or Bubbe, who was in a state of shock when she returned to find Barbara gone and the window to the fire escape wide open.

Everyone in these project buildings knew everyone else's business despite the ethnic clannishness of the residents. Pity was generated for the Rosens, who now had their daughter and two grandchildren to take care of. One, the girl, was impossible — her mother should be ashamed. Unsure of what she could do to change her situation, Diana found herself increasingly impatient with Barbara, for as soon as she came in from work, Bubbe would greet her with a list of the child's infractions that day. The beginning of the resentment that her daughter would always have toward her had its roots here. Thrilled to see her after being parted all day, she was greeted by a tearful, angry Diana. "Why do you always make trouble?" Diana would cry, disappearing into her room and shutting the door between them.

Never feeling quite at home on Pulaski Street, Barbara liked to fantasize, often imagining they lived in a grand house with a wide porch and a beautiful garden. She hated the ugliness, the smallness, the claustrophobic atmosphere of the Rosens' apartment. When the windows were open, you could hear voices in anger strained to an ear-piercing pitch, doors slamming, toilets flushing, radios blasting. The daytime soap operas were popular with all nationalities: *Portia Faces Life, Myrt and Marge,* the kindly Papa David on *Life Can Be Beautiful,* and the very popular *My Gal Sunday,* which posed the question: "Can a girl from a small mining town out west find happiness married to a rich and titled English lord?" At night there were *The Goldbergs, One Man's Family,* and the comedy programs: *Duffy's Tavern,* Jack Benny, Bob Hope. Kids liked listening to the adventure and suspense stories like *The Shadow* and *The Green Hornet,* and with only one radio in most families, squabbles arose over who had priority. There was no question about the six o'clock evening news. Everyone gathered around their sets to listen. It brought the war into their homes, their absent family members and friends closer. Many still had relatives in Germany whose fate remained uncertain.

Brooklyn lost over three thousand men in the war, with many more suffering serious injury, but its end in 1945 heralded the safe return of Diana's brother Larry. Families were now reunited. Barbara could not understand why she did not have a daddy when the fathers of the other youngsters on Pulaski Street were returning from the war. She asked Diana questions about her father and refused to accept the truth that she would never see him again. In the intervening years since Manny's death, Diana had gained hope that she would meet a man who could provide for her two children and be a father to them. She felt inadequate to deal with her strong-willed daughter and never did understand what it was that made her so difficult to handle. She was certain that she was to blame for her daughter's unorthodox behavior, her obstinacy, and her lack of friends.

Very much a loner, Barbara did have one comrade in the building, Irving Berakow. Irving's parents had a seven-and-a-half-inch television set, one of the first of the Streisands' neighbors to own such a rare, expensive item. While Mrs. Berakow, a generously built woman named Toby, cooked stuffed cabbage or knitted, the two youngsters watched Laurel and Hardy through a magnifying window placed in front of the minuscule picture screen. This was Barbara's introduction to actors on film. She was entranced, quickly learned the comedians' routines, and attempted imitations. She was able to make Irving and his mother laugh, but the same clowning had no effect on the members of her own family, who found such antics unfeminine and unbecoming.

At five, she entered kindergarten in her yeshiva. Never able to become part of a group, she tried to win the children over by acting crazy or doing something "shocking." When the rabbi went out of the room, she would yell, "Christmas! Christmas!"— a word not spoken in a Hebrew school. But such actions only angered the rabbi and made her look foolish to her classmates.

Thoughts about religion and God aroused her curiosity. She remembered humid summer afternoons and evenings sitting on the iron-railed fire escape of her grandparents' apartment with two other children from the building, one a Catholic girl and one an atheist. "It was so strange being so young, but we used to have debates about God," she recalled. "One night we were sitting there, with our blankets, and I said, 'I'm going to show you there is a God. See that man walking down the street? I'm going to pray that he steps down off that curb.' I never prayed so hard in my life, yuh know what I mean? Just, 'Please show me!' And the man stepped off the curb. That experience was like . . . there must be a God. The guy stepped off the curb!"

She claims she had no toys, only a hot-water bottle that she dressed as a doll. Diana insists this isn't true, but that the toys she had were not to her liking. She had dreidels (a top engraved with Hebrew letters that spins) and picture books. "The children on the street played hopscotch and jump rope. She had stuffed animals when she was little," Diana maintained. The hot-water bottle was used once when she had a chill, and she had refused to relinquish it, filling it every night thereafter with warm water to give it shape and "life," wrapping it in one of her outgrown sweaters and sleeping with it hugged tightly against her body.

The possessor of a vivid imagination, she made up wild stories. To Bubbe's irritation, she would smear Diana's makeup on her face with the edge of a towel or streak it with Shelley's school crayons in grotesque Indian signs that took a lot of scrubbing to remove. Shelley was artistic and loved stories and games about American Indians. He collected feathers from chickens, from pillows and bedcovers, from the street whenever pigeons were molting, and turned them into Indian headdresses. They were sacrosanct, but Barbara would sneak them from his "hiding" place when she knew he was going to be away for a while and wear them as she whooped through the apartment. She liked to play colorful characters, be someone other than who she was.

The summer she was five, painfully underweight and prone to bronchitis and ear infections, she was sent to a health camp in upper New

York State sponsored by a Jewish organization. "I remember their taking off my clothes and dumping me into this bath like I was a piece of dirt," she recalled. "They scrubbed me and washed me and put this lice disinfectant in my hair, then they put me into their uniform." She found the idea of dressing like everyone else intolerable. After nearly drowning in the camp pool, she refused to go back into it. The camp session was six weeks. Parents were allowed to visit twice during this period. With no means of transportation, Diana was unable to get there. Although Barbara was not the only child who had no visitors, the sense of rejection was no less painful.

When she returned home, she found Diana changed, "dressing up" more, wearing new makeup, and having even less time for Shelley and Barbara than before. Diana had finally come out of her depression and was dating. "I hated those men," Streisand admitted. "Once I saw a man kissing my mother. I thought he was killing her. Except she was laughing." Diana had met Louis Kind: attractive, well built, a distinguished profile, thick dark hair flecked with gray, and a certain dash in the way he dressed, fifteen years her senior.

Kind had emigrated from Russia with his family as a child of five and learned tailoring in the small pants factory his father eventually established in Brooklyn. It was a career he detested, and he ventured out on his own as a real estate and used-car salesman. At one point he took over the mortgages of several old rooming houses. A heavy gambler, he soon lost them and the rent money they generated. Recently separated from his wife, Ida, with whom he had three grown children, he seemed genuinely taken with Diana. She was forewarned by friends of his instability and poor reputation. There were stories about the various loose women he had run around with and about his gambling. Still, he was willing to take on the responsibility of another man's family, and Diana found him to her liking.

Barbara was sent back to the detested health camp the following summer and loathed it even more, although she was to remember with lingering fondness the sponge cake the children were served on Friday nights. When Diana drove up with Kind in his car to see how she was doing at the end of her second week, Barbara cried and carried on, insisting on going back to Brooklyn with them. Nothing would stop her. She put together her possessions and crawled into the back of the car and refused to be ejected. "You're not leaving here without me!" she screamed. And they were forced to give in.

Diana became pregnant in the spring of 1950. Kind's divorce was not yet final, and the atmosphere in the Rosen apartment was explosive. To have an unmarried daughter in such a condition was a *shanda,* a disgrace, a terrible thing. Kind was not allowed to come to the apartment. Diana was distraught, crying all the time. Finally, Kind came to her aid and rented a three-room apartment in a vast middle-class building, pretentiously named Vanderveer Estates (a part of the Vanderveer projects), at 3102 Newkirk Avenue near the corner of Nostrand Avenue, a few blocks away from the bustle of Flatbush Avenue. He moved in with Diana and her two children. Barbara attended P.S. 89, which was directly across the street. Diana quit her job, and her neighbors were led to believe that she was married to Kind. He received his final divorce decree on December 19, 1951. Four days later, he and Diana were married in New Jersey by a justice of the peace and on January 9, 1952, their child, Rosalind, was born. Things appeared to be on the upturn for the little girl who had always wanted a father. The problem was that Barbara loathed Louis Kind from the very beginning.

Her stepfather was a man better able to communicate with and charm outsiders than the members of his close family. "He never talked to me except to order me around," Streisand bitterly remembered. "The only thing I can recall him saying to me was when I was riding in a car with my girlfriend. I was talking, and he said, 'Why can't you be more like her? Quiet.'" Kind was in deep financial trouble almost from the beginning of his marriage to Diana. His gambling debts had mounted, and he remained responsible for the support of his ex-wife. For the steady income it provided, he was forced to take a job in a garment company as a cutter, work he had done in the past but felt was beneath him. The atmosphere in the Kind household grew very dark. Kind was moody, hostile. Diana's dream that he would be a father to her children was quickly crushed. Kind had no patience with either Shelley or Barbara. Uncomfortable around a teenage boy whom his wife expected him to counsel and befriend, he had even less tolerance for a difficult, resentful child who did not like him any better than he liked her. Diana expected him to take Barbara to the park or for pony rides on his Sundays off. Kind had places of his own to go to when he had free time, women who did not care if a man was married.

In the beginning, Diana maintained, Kind tried to be nice to Barbara. He bought her gifts: coloring books and crayons, a jump rope, and on her eighth birthday a proper doll with eyes that opened and closed to re-place the homemade water-bottle doll she slept with at night. Barbara pushed the new doll aside. She had wanted roller skates, she claims. She found fault with every offering; it was never right or chosen just for her. Cold and antagonistic toward Kind from the outset, she never warmed to him or allowed herself to see any good in him. He had taken her fa-ther's place, scuttling her fantasy that he would one day return to his family. She would never forgive Kind for this, or her mother for marry-ing him. Yet, down deep, she desperately wanted and needed his ap-proval, but nothing she ever did pleased him.

The first night in their Flatbush apartment she had cried bitterly un-til, over Kind's strong verbal objections, she was allowed to sleep in her mother's bed as she had on Pulaski Street. Kind refused to share the bed with them and stormed out of the apartment. The following morning Barbara awoke complaining of a clicking and buzzing in her ears. Diana, obviously under stress and suspicious that her daughter's complaint was a bid for attention, had her hold a hot-water bottle to her ear and, as Bar-bara had neither fever nor pain, dismissed it. These distressing noises in her head continued without medical consultation throughout her pre-adolescence. She would wrap her head in a woolen scarf in the humid heat of the Brooklyn summer and press her fingers to her ears at other times. The sounds continued, never to disappear, and many years later would be diagnosed as tinnitus aurium, a distressing chronic condition of the inner ear.

At turns she was all dreamer or all realist. She viewed her stepfather with a keen, cold eye surprising in one so young. "Why do you take *his* side?" she quizzed Diana after a confrontation with Kind. "He doesn't need you. *I* do. He doesn't even love you. If he did, he'd be nicer." She could move her mother to injured tears, while she controlled her own emotions.

Her defense was to retreat further into a private world where Kind did not exist. Movies played a large role in her life. When Barbara was very young, Diana or Shelley would take her to the neighborhood movie house on a Saturday afternoon. Shelley liked Westerns and Buck Rogers and Flash Gordon serials; Diana, comedies and romantic dramas. Barbara preferred going with her mother. Shelley was never too pleased to have his little sister tag along, but that was not entirely her reason. Barbara liked not having to share Diana, and she was drawn to the images and the women she watched on the large screen in the darkened theater when she was with her mother. The gamut of her imagination ran from being glamorous like Lana Turner to being glamorous like Rita Hayworth. She equated being loved with being beautiful and decided that one day she would be a movie star — and beautiful. That dream was her touchstone throughout childhood.

Around Kind she remained sullen. It didn't help that Shelley kept telling her how wonderful their real father had been and that her brother had known him, when she had been denied any conscious memory of him. When not daydreaming, she was moody or uncooperative, always the rebel, refusing to do what was being asked of her. One time when Diana had lost her temper and slapped Barbara a glancing blow on the ear, she pretended for the rest of the day that she had been struck deaf and carried it off so well that her mother grew hysterical and was about to rush her to the hospital. Seeing Diana in honest turmoil, Barbara finally confessed the truth.

"Barbra was a very complex child," Diana has said. "She bottled up everything inside her. Perhaps if she could have voiced to me how she was feeling, things might have been easier, but she didn't. She had her own ideas, her own way of looking at life and that was the way she liked things to be. Barbra always saw everything depending on how it affected her, but it was not easy for her as a child.

"I knew that she resented not having a father, especially because Roslyn [Rosalind] had one, but she wouldn't talk about it to me," Diana recalled. "From the age of seven she wanted to be in films. I couldn't fathom why she wanted to be famous, but she did. I was worried that she wouldn't succeed and that she would be hurt, so I tried not to encourage her. But I couldn't break up her ideas and her thinking."

The "grand" apartment in Flatbush allowed little space for anyone. The new baby first slept in a crib in her parents' room. The dinette was turned into a small second bedroom for Shelley, and Barbara slept on the couch in the front room. The fact that they now had a sofa did not make her feel "rich" as she once thought it would. "Ever sleep on a couch night after night?" she asked an interviewer. "All you think about is, 'How can I get a room of my own?' You get to the point where you *have* to make good!" There was at least one benefit. The couch was in the room with the new television set. Barbara quickly became addicted to it and all the early variety programs — Arthur Godfrey, Sid Caesar, Milton Berle — and the various daytime and weekly soap operas and dramas. She especially loved the commercials, committing many of them to memory and then going into the bathroom and locking the door so that she could act them out in front of the medicine-chest mirror without interruption. She would pretend she was a sophisticated young woman smoking a cigarette; Betty Furness, the spokeswoman for Westinghouse, looking glamorous as she opened a refrigerator door; the exotic South Sea Island girl who wore Tabu perfume and undulated seductively.

She prayed one day to be beautiful and famous, as she was in her fantasies. She did achieve a change in her attitude. She held her head up, her back straight. However posed, she nonetheless seemed suddenly not to be just defiant but a bit arrogant. It did not sit well with her stepfather, but Barbara had discovered that she had a fierce desire for survival and that if she had to, she could fight the world alone.

5

Boxed in by his responsibilities, by nature hostile, highly resentful of having to provide for a stepdaughter who was in his opinion ungrateful, Kind increasingly erupted into violence. He became verbally abusive, bullying and threatening on occasion to Diana, and his anger reached out to Barbara. There is no evidence that he ever beat her. He shouted a lot; Barbara shouted back and managed to get out of his way whenever he seemed poised to take a swipe at her. Barbara's strident voice rose shrilly in defiance, and Diana was mortified that the neighbors could hear what was going on in her home. She swore the older children to silence, never to discuss Kind's tyrannizing abuse. Once he told Barbara that she could not have ice cream because she was so ugly. "He was really mean to Barbra," Shelley confirmed. "He taunted her continually, telling her how plain she was compared to Rosalind." With cruelty to Barbara, he referred to the half sisters as "beauty and the beast."

"You're different, that's all, different, and you're smarter than most kids your age," Shelley would tell her to help build her ego. "And being smart is what counts." He defended her against Kind when he could, but he was having his own difficulties in this unhappy home. Currently attending Music and Art High School, his main objective was to move into Manhattan after graduation. He was a good artist (a talent his stepfather held in low regard) and hoped to have a career in advertising. A winsome youngster, Shelley had grown into an attractive and popular young man of medium stature but broad-shouldered and possessing an easy manner and a winning smile. Barbara was greatly possessive of him, jealous when girlfriends called, and dreaded the day when he would no longer be her protector in the house.

At ten, after seeing the leggy, statuesque Cyd Charisse dance with Gene Kelly in *Singin' in the Rain,* Barbara made up her mind that she had to have ballet lessons and badgered her mother for weeks until finally Diana gave in, although it meant a sacrifice on her part. Money was scarce and she did not dare ask Kind for help to finance what even she thought was a frivolous enterprise. Her hope was that the lessons would prove to Barbara how much she cared about her and would make her less difficult. To buy a pair of toe shoes and a leotard and to pay for ballet instruction at a small local dancing school, she scraped together the money by economizing on the table, using cheaper cuts of meat and fewer desserts, walking instead of taking public transportation.

Barbara could not wait to attend her weekly class. Shorter and younger than most of the girls in her group, she applied herself with manic dedication to be just that much better prepared. She showed surprising ability for a youngster who was always considered to be awkward. "When she came home [from dance class] she would practice and practice," Diana recalled. "She spent hours getting up on her toes and walking around the apartment. I was afraid it might hurt her feet — you never know what damage it could do to a child's toes." Barbara pressed for private instruction, which was more costly. Kind was already complaining vociferously that Diana was wasting on Barbara money that should have been spent on the household. Diana found herself in the middle of a dysfunctional family, wanting to appease Kind and at the same time eager to make Barbara happier, less sulky, and more outgoing. Her problem was solved when Miss Marsh, the ballet instructor, moved out of the neighborhood. Barbara continued to bounce around the apartment, doing leaps and turns on her own, but her dream of becoming another Cyd

Charisse was quashed. Not, however, her determination to be recognized, famous. In her mind, her vision of her future set her apart from her Flatbush peers.

There were children of all ages in Vanderveer Estates, in the backyards and on the streets. In good weather mothers wheeled baby carriages up and down the block, stopping and talking with one another. Boys played stickball in the street, and drivers would watch out for them and park their vehicles in places where they wouldn't block the game. Toddlers ran around on the small patches of lawn, an older family member watching from the viewpoint of a folding chair or stretched out on the grass beneath the warm fingers of the sun. Games of hide-and-seek were played where the kids could conceal themselves in the narrow crevices between buildings or in the labyrinth of alleys behind them. Girls played house with their dolls. Sometimes the neighborhood youngsters got together and put on talent shows. Believing these neighborhood productions beneath her, Barbara preferred not to be included.

Newkirk Avenue had trees, and in summer the pavements were dappled with shade. An ice cream truck came by in the afternoon. A white uniformed driver sold Dixie cups with pictures of movie stars on the inside cover. Kids collected and traded them and would lick off the ice cream to see who they got — Betty Grable, Alice Faye, Tyrone Power, Judy Garland, Mickey Rooney, Clark Gable. Barbara bought pink, sweet-flavored bubble gum for a penny at the corner market, chewed it, and stored it nightly in a glass of cold water until its elasticity was gone. Chewing gum relaxed her, made her feel less tense.

Despite all the young people in the building and in the neighborhood, she had trouble making friends. Louis Kind had told her she was ugly so often that she felt ugly deep inside. She had the habit of trying to outstare kids when they turned to look at her, or she would make faces. "When I was nine years old, sometimes the girls would gang up on me in my neighborhood, make a circle around me, make fun of me, and I'd start to cry," she remembered. They called her "Crazy Barbara" and "Big Beak." Barbara attributed these attacks to the shape and length of her nose. However, in Flatbush — with such a high percentage of Jewish, Italian, Polish, and other ethnic groups who often inherited prominent noses — Barbara's was not that unique or oversized. The popular nose-bobbing operation that shortened, dehumped, and remolded an ethnic nose into the pert, snub, all-American profile of movie star Doris Day was seldom performed before a girl was sixteen. In Barbara's preteens, her nose was in the ethnic majority and should not have incited the ugly epithets she claims, but she had a commanding, defiant look, too solemn an expression for a child and she was standoffish. Because her astonishing blue eyes were set close together, her forehead high, and her mouth wide, greater attention was drawn to her nose, perhaps prompting the taunting she received from the kids on her block.

The ridicule she suffered cut deeply and, added to Kind's cruel comments, would mark her for life. Kind — his very name a bitter reminder of his converse nature — became the enemy within her home, the children on the street and in school the enemy outside. She was constantly on guard and adopted an aloof attitude. Her peers at P.S. 89, where she attended grammar school, thought she was conceited and resented her natural intelligence, which she could not refrain from displaying. She used words she had learned from the movies or from television, corrected other children's grammar, stopped them if they had a fact wrong, gloated if they did not know an answer to a question. Much more daunting, she perceived herself as ugly, a *meeskite,* and transferred this impression to others.

Louis Kind had undermined her self-esteem, and Diana had done very little to counter his effect on Barbara. "She was critical of me and never believed in me," Streisand said of her mother. "She used to say, 'I never want you to get a swelled head.'" The youngster was riddled with self-doubt. It did not help that her straight hair was allowed to hang in an unflattering style. Because she was so thin, her head and hands looked too large for her small frame, an effect that was emphasized by the poor fit of her dresses, which Diana chose to buy large enough for her to grow into and then kept her in until she had outgrown them.

Barbara's fear became reality when, in the autumn of 1952, Shelley went off to City College of New York, lived with cousins in the East End, and supported himself with the help of a scholarship and part-time job. She envied his having escaped from Brooklyn and their unhappy home, but her anger at him grew for "deserting" her. Rosalind, a chubby round-faced child with a sunny disposition, commanded most of Diana's attention. Barbara bitterly resented her half sister for having a father when she did not. The truth is, she would have welcomed Kind's paternal interest. A large part of her wanting to succeed had to do with proving to Kind how worthy she was of his admiration. In many families where there is a frustrated and abusive parent, one child is singled out to be on the receiving end of this abuse. Barbara, with her airs and her try-ing disposition, was a ready victim for Kind.

Coinciding with Shelley's absence, the violent scenes between Louis and Diana accelerated. He had a vicious temper and a cruel tongue and spoke demeaningly to Diana in front of the girls. She was stupid, a leech, unattractive, a nag. His face contorted, his voice threatened. Doors slammed. He would leave the house and not return until early the next morning or, sometimes, several days or a week later. Life at the Kinds was painful, crushing. To break out, at the age of ten, Barbara would sneak a forbidden cigarette from Kind's bedside hoard and go up to the rooftop of their building to smoke. There, she slipped into fantasy and became the glamorous star of her dreams.

Vanderveer Estates was within walking distance to Loew's Kings Theater on Flatbush Avenue, and on Saturday afternoons her world brightened. Diana gave her twenty-five cents for a movie ticket and a Melorol, a vanilla ice cream confection of which she was fond. Enter-ing Loew's Kings was like walking through a celluloid screen into an MGM spectacular. Built during the days of opulent movie palaces, it had a vaulted French baroque grand lobby with brightly painted murals of exotic foreign vistas, mystical castles, and lushly costumed men and women. There were mock gaslights attached to the walls, a magnificent crystal chandelier, and brightly polished brass railings on the sides of the massive curved marble staircase, a deep red carpet down its center.

At the back of the lobby was the refreshment stand with its tempting smell of buttered popcorn and spicy frankfurters impaled on a revolving grill, which, as they were *traif* (nonkosher), she was forbidden to eat. The auditorium seated close to 3,800; there was a gigantic four-manual pipe organ referred to as the "Wonder Morton," after its creator, that filled the house with heavenly music when the lights were up. Barbara's refuge was the balcony nearest the starlit ceiling. She fell in love with Marlon Brando when at thirteen she saw him woo Jean Simmons in *Guys and Dolls.* As soon as THE END flashed on the screen, she rushed to the bathroom so that she would not be told to leave. When she knew the film was being shown again, she left the rest room and made her way in the dark to an available empty seat to see her idol again, imagining herself in Jean Simmons's place as the recipient of his affection.

"I was a character in the movie," she said. "Not the actress, but the character. Not Vivien Leigh, but Scarlett O'Hara. It was *me* up there, and those attractive men were pursuing *me!*" She was greatly impressed by *Gone With the Wind* when in 1954 it was rereleased for the wide screen and in stereophonic sound. Just turned twelve, she nonetheless identified with Scarlett — the determination, the fight for independence, the woman invading a man's world and being more exciting for it. The movies were more than a form of escapism, they were a higher form of reality for her. She judged the humdrum experiences of her everyday life and the people she shared them with by what she saw in the movies. Those celluloid images were movers and shakers, not observers and naysayers. She thought less of Diana for letting herself be a doormat for Louis Kind's bullying. The mother-daughter conflict was made all the more tense by Diana's inability to see Barbara as anything more than an unattractive girl with an aggressive and wildly imaginative nature. But in movies and her fast-growing dream of becoming a star and a part of that celluloid world, Barbara found what others sought in religion.

None of this could Diana comprehend. Mother and daughter were of two vastly different temperaments. Diana lacked Barbara's avid curiosity, her quick intelligence, and ability to dream. Very much a pragmatist, when Barbara talked about becoming famous one day, Diana could not see that such a thing would ever occur. It was impossible, she would tell Barbara: "You're not pretty enough." She believed that to be true and felt she had to get her daughter to concentrate on a more reasonable goal. Barbara would come back with a cutting remark about Diana's lack of motivation, her allowing herself to be mistreated by Kind. The two women knew how to hurt each other most effectively.

Barbara entered Erasmus Hall High School in September 1955. Diana wanted her to take typing as an elective course her first term, to get all the nonsense about movies out of her head, to consider a sensible career, like being a secretary. Barbara would not hear of it and let her nails grow to ward off the dreaded prospect of typing lessons. She spent hours painting her lips a dark magenta and shadowing her eyes with blue makeup bought surreptitiously with her lunch money. "Somehow," she said, "it made me think I was attractive." She was hungry a lot of the time and skinnier than ever, but it seemed important for her to prove to her mother and to Kind that she could be pretty. She remained a loner during her first year at Erasmus. It was not that she didn't want friends — she did — it was that she found it difficult to make the overtures. She had an unfortunate manner of putting off potential friends with what one schoolmate called "a smart-ass remark, just something that made you feel she thought she was smarter than you, like she was saying, 'You dumb ox, don't you know *that!*'"

Erasmus Hall High School was one of the compensations for the many Jewish families living in Flatbush, for it held the highest scholastic rating of any public high school in Brooklyn or Manhattan. Founded in 1786 as a private academy by the venerable Dutch Reformed Church and on gifts from Aaron Burr, John Jay, Alexander Hamilton, and other intellectuals, it became part of the public school system one hundred years later. The original academy building, with its hand-carved beams and clapboards, was left standing in 1905 during the construction of a three-story stone castellated building. The new edifice — a massive stone complex that took up a full city block, collegiate Gothic in design — was constructed around and separated by a grassy courtyard from the original building. The school's enrollment exceeded seven thousand when Barbara, troubled and antisocial, entered at age thirteen, a year ahead of most of her peers.

The principal, Dr. James McNeil, had been an air force colonel during the war and was an English educator of some repute. Straitlaced and unapproachable, he dressed in dark suits, conservative ties, vests, white shirts, and pointed collars and operated the school like a flight squadron during wartime maneuvers. His administrative assistant was Miss

Grace L. Corey, who would dock teachers for being a minute late. One student recalled, "That's the kind of school they ran. Nobody stepped out of line."

It was the only high school in New York that taught classical Greek, and it did not have girl cheerleaders. "In every other high school, the kids went to study hall. In Erasmus, they went to 'chapel'— which was the auditorium, but it had stained-glass windows. The Erasmus kids who were in government wore shirts and ties. They were college-bound," a classmate of Barbara's remembered.

The building resembled a medieval castle with an endless crisscrossing of corridors, and the walk from one classroom to another was exhausting and often difficult to make by the bell. "I never knew how big Erasmus was," another student recalled. "I just walked in a door and stayed inside, going from classroom to classroom. I was a senior before I found out about the quad [the grassy square around the original structure] in the middle of the building." Every day Barbara went from an apartment she loathed to a school that was a fortress, huge, intimidating. She almost always walked through the forbidding corridors by herself, posture haughty, diverting the glances of fellow students, always, *always* feeling the outsider.

Erasmus Hall serviced a large district with a variety of neighborhoods, and there was a dichotomy "between the kids from the poor part of Flatbush . . . and the ones from the rich." Barbara lived in a lower-income, but not an economically impoverished, section. It was true that a student's background often dictated the group with which he or she socialized. Yet, in a school the size of Erasmus, with its highly diversified enrollment, taking in many ethnic roots and economic strata, there certainly was a niche for Barbara. But to find it she needed counseling, and there was none to be had. Male students paid her little attention. Diana warned her never to hold hands with a boy, an idea that made her laugh.

"I was never asked out to any of the proms, and I never had a date for New Year's Eve," she has said. "I was pretty much of a loner. I was very independent. I never needed anybody, really." This seems far from the truth. A classmate of hers recalled that Barbara often did do things to try to win friends and attention. "Some of the kids wanted to set up a surprise for a teacher we liked who was celebrating his birthday. Barbara came up with a plan. She would 'faint' in the hall adjoining the classroom. The teacher was called and ran to her side. A gift was then put on his desk. Barbara remained in a 'faint' until all was clear. The teacher was completely fooled by her act. For a few days she seemed one of us. Then something happened. I don't know exactly what it was. But I think it had something to do with class elections. Her name was submitted for some office. But she wasn't elected; in fact, she came in last."

"She often appeared lonely," a neighbor was later to claim. To counteract this feeling of separateness, she dug into her studies and was consistently in the top 10 percent of her class. Knowledge excited her, was the only thing that made her feel exceptional. She liked knowing the answers, being the first one to raise her hand in class, finishing a test.

Still forgoing lunch in order to have an extra dime or quarter in her pocket, she would pose after school behind the curtains in photo booths, imitating her screen favorites. She had the voluptuous Mae West down pat — except for the swiveling hips, which seemed to elude her, not surprising since she had so little flesh on her bones. She had seen a number of old Mae West movies and was fascinated by the ex-Brooklynite who had gone on to become a legend. To amuse her classmates, she would do a takeoff of West spouting some of her most famous movie witticisms: to George Raft playing a gangster, "Is that your gun in your pocket or are you *really* glad to see me?" Or her oft-quoted philosophy: "It's not the men in my life that count, it's the life in my men." Yet, Barbara never bothered to audition for school plays. "Why go out for an amateurish high-school production when you can do the real thing?" she later commented. Of course, she was *not* doing "the real thing," and it is much more likely that she was simply fearful of rejection.

One afternoon in 1956 when Barbara was fourteen, Louis Kind left the house on Newkirk Avenue, ostensibly to buy a pack of cigarettes. He never returned. Once again, Diana found office work and relied on neighbors to look after Rosalind. Although the apartment no longer had a tyrannizing man at the helm, Kind's absence did not make Barbara's relationship with her mother any easier.

Without a man's presence, Diana lost interest in keeping the apartment attractive. Rather, she was concerned with minimizing her workload. The couch and chairs in the living room were now covered in clear plastic, and a girl's bare legs stuck to it on hot days. Lampshades were also covered, light switches had protective shields, and the kitchen floor was littered with newspapers after it had been washed. Barbara hated the pungent smell of the plastic and the absence of flowers, plants, and bright toss pillows that she saw in other people's apartments. She seldom brought children home and Diana never entertained. They lived an insular life. Their occasional visits to Pulaski Street were never happy ones. From time to time they saw Manny's brother Phil and his wife, Sylvia, but Aunt Anna, who Barbara liked, lived in Connecticut and was too far away to visit often.

For many months after Kind's desertion, Diana had only the small income she made from her office job. Finally, on May 7, 1957, she obtained a legal separation on the grounds of Kind's verbal abuse and was awarded $37 a week in support. Too often Kind fell far in arrears and never made up the deficit. This was the most difficult time in Barbara's childhood. There was not always enough to eat, and Diana took on a second job, selling women's undergarments from a small valise she carried with her to the office or from apartment to apartment in her building.

In her freshman year Barbara took chorus and was a member of the Erasmus Choral Club, an interest she kept up throughout high school. She was aware that she possessed a good, clear voice but had not given it much serious thought. Surrounded now by other singers of her age, she realized just how good her voice was and how fast she was able to grasp her part. Because her voice was stronger than those of other members of the chorus, Cosimo De Pietto, the choral director, placed her in the rear so that she would not overpower them. This disturbed her, but she did not sing more softly to oblige. Solos, to Barbara's disappointment, usually went to Trudy Wallace, a pretty blonde with a pleasant soprano voice. Barbara had an unusual range, being able to sing both in the chest and in the head. She could reach and hold a high B-flat. But she preferred the lower register that was used in popular and show music. She was therefore placed in the alto section of the Choral Club, where few female solos were required in the music that was performed.

She claims she had no thoughts of ever becoming a singer, although she had been singing to herself for years in the hallways of the apartment building, listening to the "great echo sound . . . thinking, 'Oh, that's pleasant. It doesn't sound bad.'" She knew an enormous number of songs from Broadway shows, films, and records. In winter she would often sit on the stairway with other kids in the building and lead them in the current popular songs. This won her new admiration. She was looked at for the first time in a different, positive light; unlike her later experience at high school, it was *because* she had a strong voice, "the loudest in the neighborhood." Conversely, she placed little importance upon this talent. Singing, she felt, was no big deal. "It's only wind and noise. I open my mouth and the sound comes out," she would say later. Much of this philosophy came from Diana, who thought popular music and the ability to sing it were of little worth.

Despite her own doubts and Diana's dismissal of her singing talent, back in 1951, when she was only nine, Barbara had suddenly become consumed with the idea that she could be another Joni James, her favorite singer at the time, and badgered Diana into taking her into New York and up to the studio of MGM Records, her idol's record label. As Diana had some errands to do in the city, she had finally agreed to go with her to the recording studio. Barbara found out where the offices were and insisted on being heard once they got there. Mother and daughter had come in cold, without an introduction, agent, accompanist, or musical arrangement. This took great chutzpah on Barbara's part and shows the tenacity of her will and her ability, even at that early age, to overpower her mother, who was certain her daughter's efforts would fail. When Barbara wanted something, she jumped in, pushing aside all obstacles. In this instance, she also revealed a private need to prove that she had talent as a singer, belying her future denials that she considered her singing voice of no consequence.

For her audition she sang Joni James's "Have You Heard?" inside a glass booth, without accompaniment. Being caged in was a terrifying and claustrophobic experience that was to take years to overcome. Told to go home, study, and practice more, she did exactly that, but without benefit of professional help. Instead, she spent more time in the hallways and in the lobby of their apartment house, letting her voice bounce off the walls and echo back to her. When a neighbor complained, she would take herself to another part of the building or go up to the roof to practice.

In the summer of 1955, the year she entered Erasmus Hall, Diana and the two girls had vacationed for a week in the Catskills, a gift paid for by Diana's family, who were concerned about her health. They became friendly with a piano player from Brooklyn. Diana and Barbara sang some songs with him, and he told them about Nola Studios in Steinway Hall on West Fifty-seventh Street in Manhattan. The idea of recording her own singing voice appealed to Diana. The pianist agreed to go into New York with them. The Steinway showroom was on the ground floor; above it were studios occupied by theatrical teachers — dancing, piano, drama, voice — professional photographers, and agents. Steinway Hall had several recording studios used mainly by fledgling singers and composers to make records to disperse to booking agents and producers. Anyone with four dollars to spend was welcome to cut two sides of a record. A sound engineer was supplied. You were given ten minutes to rehearse before the needle cut into the acetate to make the record. There were no retakes; what was recorded at that time was what you got.

In birdlike sound bites, Diana sang "One Kiss," an operetta favorite. Barbara chose "Zing Went the Strings of My Heart," a Judy Garland standard, and the 1930s ballad "You'll Never Know," made popular by Alice Faye.

"My mother went first," Streisand later recalled. "She could hardly get a chorus in edgeways because the piano player kept launching into endless, elaborate refrains. As soon as he started that with me, I told him, 'No, no, we'll just do a *little* interlude and then I'll come back in.' I had planned a simple ending for 'You'll Never Know,' but got carried away. Those last few notes, '. . . if you don't . . . *know-oh-oh* . . . now,' took me by surprise. I guess it was my first musical improvisation. . . . [After I listened to the record,] I wondered, Who was that? Where did that come from? It was like *The Exorcist*."

The making of this acetate record was one of the rare occasions where mother and daughter shared a creative experience. Diana, in hopes of earning some extra money, had renewed early aspirations to pursue a stage career. Any such hope was shattered when she heard the playback. Her voice was ordinary, and she knew it. The amazing thing is that she did not recognize her daughter's talent. The record, preserved lovingly by Barbra into her adult life, displays not only a burgeoning talent but a rare individuality of style, but Diana told Barbara to put aside any thoughts of a singing career. She believed she was being protective but was motivated by her own low esteem, fear of venturing into unknown directions, her background that preached a woman was nothing without a man and that a *career* was something *he* had while *she worked,* mainly to support herself until she married, and then to supplement the family income.

The following year, without Diana's knowledge, Barbara auditioned with a group of other girls from her school for a radio show. She did a speech from Shaw's *Saint Joan:* "He who tells the truth shall surely be caught." ("I always felt that about myself," she later said.) She was rejected, but one Saturday afternoon in April 1956 she took the five dollars she had been given as a gift from Diana for her fourteenth birthday (meant for her to purchase a blouse or a sweater) and made her first solo trip out of Brooklyn by subway. The local paper had printed a story that the Hollywood producer-director Otto Preminger, on a massive talent search for a young girl to play the title role of Saint Joan in his next film, was having his staff conduct preliminary interviews in New York on that day. It seemed fated. She went back to *Saint Joan,* studying it at home and on the subway into New York. By the time she reached the United Artists offices where the interviews were being held, she could almost feel the fire that had consumed Joan of Arc. When she filled out her application, she was told she was too young. Mr. Preminger was looking for a girl in her late teens, nearer the age of Joan of Arc when she raised the siege at Orléans. Barbara argued with the assistant to give her a chance and began to recite some lines from Shaw's play.

"I'm sorry," the assistant said and turned away. "Next!" he called.

She left the building feeling cheated, angry. She had not been given a fair chance. The film company's offices were midtown. She walked over to the Cort Theater on Forty-eighth Street and bought a ticket for the matinee performance of *The Diary of Anne Frank,* a poignant story about a sensitive young Jewish girl who grows into womanhood while hiding from the Nazis in an attic with her family. She had chosen this particular play because it had been discussed in her English class at school. "At first, I was awfully disappointed, looking at the dreary setting," she later commented. Then she became deeply and emotionally involved.* Seated at the rear of the second balcony, she recalled thinking that she could go up on the stage and play any role "without any trouble at all." Perhaps Saint Joan would have been a stretch, but Anne Frank and her family were people she could identify with: they were Jewish and had suffered. She had found a more accessible target for her unfocused ambitions — the stage.

"It was a thrilling experience," she said of that time, "sitting in the last seat of the balcony — I think the ticket was $2.85 in those days. There was something wonderful about not being able to afford to sit very close, because when you sit far away you see the whole stage, you know. You don't see the reality of the actor's pores, you don't see the make-up. You get swept along with the illusion, with the make-believe truth."

When she returned home late that day, she told her mother about her disappointing interview with Preminger's assistant and about her excitement when she saw *Anne Frank*. "I've decided that no matter what, I'm going to be an actress," she announced. Diana tried again to discourage her. "I was so sure Barbara would be a fiasco," she said later, adding that she wanted to "save her from utter humiliation."

Certain that Barbara would fail, that she was not pretty enough, talented enough to make a success of it, Diana did everything she could to talk her out of it. She was placing herself in her daughter's shoes. She had been too terrified, too insecure to compete in the world, to fight for anything. She thought it was love that guided her in discouraging what she saw as her daughter's futile dreams. Barbara was sure it was the opposite. She would always doubt the depth of Diana's love, suffer resentment for her stultifying attitude toward anything she set out to accomplish.

---

*Nearly thirty years later, Streisand visited Amsterdam and the tiny attic where Anne Frank had lived before being discovered by the Nazis and sent to a concentration camp, where she later died. Streisand was overcome with emotion, shaking with sobs when she came back outside. It took several minutes for her to control herself.

It would form the basis of her lifelong struggle to come to terms with her past.

Right now she had too much she wanted to accomplish in what she thought would be a very short time — her last high-school years — to let her mother's negativism place obstacles in her path.

6

Barbara was determined, possessed. No one had ever been able to stop her from doing what she wanted to do, but with Louis Kind's departure, when she was fourteen, she became a freer spirit. At school she began to make friends, to laugh more easily, and to wisecrack. She was outspoken in class, never shy about asking questions. She wanted reasons for everything.

In a high school noted for its allegiance to propriety, she stood out. "I was this absolute misfit," she confessed. Believed to have been the first girl in Erasmus Hall ever to wear mascara to class, she also accented her eyes with blue shadow; bleached blond streaks into her hair; painted her daggerlike nails blood red, gold, or black; and remained razor-thin. Yet, the overall effect was not cheap; it was theatrical. Many of the girls in her class admired her individuality and thought she was attractive. Classmates remember her beautiful eyes, expressive hands, and the bravura way in which she carried herself. "If only looks mattered, she could have been cast as Cleopatra," one friend commented.

Cleverly, she played up these attributes. Her intense interest in offbeat fashion was not simply teenage rebellion. It was a means of personal expression, of setting herself apart from the rest of the girls at Erasmus. She liked the idea of being exotic, foreign, different; but it never gained her popularity with the boys in her school. She had a crush on Bobby Fischer, who was in the class below her and already an international chess champion. They would have lunch every day, and "he would sit there, laughing hysterically, reading *Mad* magazine. Right? And he wore these earflaps on his ears. He was always alone and very peculiar. But I found him very sexy," she recalled. However, this relationship never flowered into a romance because Fischer seemed to regard her as little more than a lunchtime buddy.

Holidays and school dances threw her into a state of agitation. There were no invitations. Teenage boys found her too threatening. They were more comfortable with girls who fit into neat categories; she was smarter than most of the boys and not afraid to let them know it. She fought disdain with disdain and developed what would one day become the famous Streisand shrug: left shoulder raised and angled forward, head turned sideways, chin up, one eyebrow arched. Thought to be arrogant by her male peers, she was merely being defensive. If she encountered a boy in the hallways or rooms of Erasmus who seemed to be smirking at her or who she had heard pass a rude remark, she would slow down as she neared him, then give him an exaggerated shrug. She developed various expressions — boredom, happiness, sophistication — in front of the bathroom mirror or while aping cigarette commercials. One expression that she captured and used as a protective mask for her true feelings was a cool, detached smile that she would adopt whenever she was in a public situation — at school gatherings or when she had to wait in line. She had the uncomfortable feeling at such times that everyone was looking at her critically.

Saturday afternoon movies remained a ritual. She would return home grumpy for the rest of the weekend because after the glamorous settings and sophisticated clothes she had seen in the films, the Newkirk Avenue apartment, with its bargain-store furniture covered in plastic, and her limited wardrobe depressed her. She would read the *New York Times* apartment ads in the hopes of convincing Diana to move to Manhattan. "Ma, look, it's $105, why can't we afford it?" she would ask her mother, who was having trouble making ends meet at half that rent on the small income from the office job she held in a New York City public high school. Rosalind was now attending school, and Barbara was expected to watch her in the afternoons, but there was always someone in the building who would help out. Louis Kind remained perpetually late with his support payments, often missing them entirely.

Diana had no money for extras. Barbara was given only what was essential. Small luxuries were supplied by her deftly performed shoplifting. "I wouldn't take just stuff," she once said, laughing in a high trill as she revealed her petty adventures in crime. "I would walk around the store until I found a receipt on the floor and then go get that item — a compact, a lipstick, books, and candy — cinnamon hots, jujubes — they were my favorites, and even salt shakers. I love salt shakers, especially those fancy ones . . . whatever — and return most of what I took for the money." She never got caught, and Diana was unaware of her daughter's transgressions.

A small inheritance came her way in the late spring of 1957. Her grandfather Streisand had died and left her $150, a stroke of good fortune of which her mother did not immediately inform her. To Diana, her daughter's windfall was a mitzvah, a godsend. Two of Barbara's bicuspids became abscessed about the time of the funeral, and the dentist insisted they must be pulled and replaced. Diana had not known how she was going to pay for the work. The two infected teeth were pulled before Barbara heard about her small legacy; she had quite a different idea on how she would have spent it.

An older girl who lived in the neighborhood had spent the previous summer with a stock company in Malden Bridge, New York, a small town in the Adirondacks, twenty miles east of Albany, the state capital. Barbara questioned her endlessly about the experience. It sounded like the most exciting place in the world if you were looking forward to a career in the theater. Not only was stagecraft and acting taught, but the students performed in well-known plays before a paying audience. Intrigued, she planned to do anything so that she could attend the following summer. She would wash dishes, wait on tables — anything to pay her tuition. A battle of wills between mother and daughter was fought.

Barbara refused to part with what remained of her $150 to have the missing teeth replaced. "You can't go around with gaps in your teeth!" Diana shouted. "You'll look ridiculous!"

"I'll do something so that I won't have gaps!" Barbara hollered back. She bought some Aspergum (because the color was close to that of tooth enamel), chewed it to make it pliable, molded two teeth from it, and pressed them into the empty spaces in her mouth. Diana finally gave in, as she usually did, and up Barbara went to the Malden Bridge Playhouse, with a supply of gum for false-teeth replacements.

Conditions were primitive. The playhouse was reached by a dirt road. Rough-hewn cabins offered bare essentials, nothing more. Water ran icy from the taps. Except for in the main building, toilets were housed in outside structures. The scenery was, however, picturesque, with a stream to one side of the heavily wooded property. The theater was a converted farm building, but the enthusiasm of the group made up for what else might have been lacking. Barbara pitched in without complaint to do the most menial of tasks, sweeping the stage, helping to build and paint sets, even cleaning toilets.

Two of the plays staged that summer were John Patrick's *Teahouse of the August Moon* (based on a book by Vern J. Sneider) and William Marchant's *The Desk Set*. Streisand has been quoted as saying her first stage role was riding a goat in the John Patrick play, a tremendous Broadway success that had been recently transferred into a popular film. "Incidentally," the late John Patrick (who everyone knew as Pat), confided to me, "the report that Streisand rode a goat in *Teahouse* must be wrong. You can't ride a goat. I know this as when I had a farm I had a hundred and fifty milk goats. In the play, however, I did have three goats riding in the back of a jeep and this is where the kids [the young characters in the play] rode. Perhaps this is where Streisand fit in."

The stage at Malden Bridge Playhouse was not large enough to accommodate a jeep. Patrick suggested that a cart loaded with two or three young performers and pulled by a defiant goat across the creaking boards of the stage marked the theater debut of Barbara Streisand. Next, she had a small role as a man-crazy receptionist in *The Desk Set*. "Can't you just see me at fifteen coming on the stage, sitting down on a desk, swinging my legs and playing sexy?" she asked an interviewer once. The weekly local newspaper obviously had not found this difficult. "The girl who plays the office vamp is very sexy, and her name is Barbara Streisand. *Down boys,*" its reviewer wrote.

The years of studying the walk, posture, the come-on looks, and seductive smiles of sexy movie stars had contributed to a facile ability to project sexuality onstage. When she was acting, she could be anyone she wanted to be. She liked the idea of being the vamp, of being desirable to men. Sex was a subject never discussed by Diana except in the form of a warning: a nice Jewish girl doesn't even think about such things. Barbara, and most of the girls she knew, thought constantly about it despite such admonitions. Onstage she could live out her fantasy: she was beautiful and sexy enough to win Marlon Brando, her favorite actor. She had, in fact, developed a sensuality that she incorporated into her personality even at this young age, a flirtatious way of crossing her legs, holding her head, pulling back her shoulders and thrusting her small but well-formed bosom forward. She has said that a young man in the stock company took an interest in her. He was eighteen, Christian, with blond good looks and a glib tongue. They remained after rehearsals, sitting in the empty theater talking. He was off to university in the fall. But after college he claimed to be Hollywood-bound. He told her he thought she had real talent; all she needed was the experience. They went for private walks along the wooded path of the narrow river that ran along one side of Malden Bridge. She claims Diana's warnings were heeded, but attraction to and for the young man was obvious to her colleagues.

The summer sped by. She had found what she was certain would be her life's work — acting. Determined to pay to get her teeth fixed — and to go back to Malden Bridge the following summer — on her return to Brooklyn she took a job evenings at the New China Restaurant, managed by her neighbors, Muriel and Jimmie Choy. Good at computing change, she became a cashier. Her nails were now Fu Manchu–long and vividly lacquered, but she developed a way of punching the cash register keys without harming them. She also had acquired a working Chinese vocabulary and, she says, Muriel gave her a textbook explanation of the art of having sex, along with her introduction to another culture.

"I loved the idea of belonging to a small minority group," she professed. "It was the world against us in the Chinese restaurant." Diana was constantly lecturing her not to eat the *traif* served at the New China. Barbara brought home shopping bags of day-old vegetables, which were acceptable and helped Diana stretch her small budget, but at work she ate forbidden moo shi pork.

Diana could not control her daughter's dietary habits once she had gained her first taste of independence, nor could she keep her at home. On the nights that she was not at school or working at the New China, Barbara would take the IRT subway (which cost fifteen cents) at the corner of Nostrand Avenue and go into Greenwich Village to hang out at the Cherry Lane Theatre, where an acquaintance from Malden Bridge was working. Finally, the manager let her help backstage. One of the young performers, Anita Miller, who was married to Allan Miller, a drama teacher and member of the Lee Strasberg's Actors Studio (where Marlon Brando had once studied), took an interest in her. Barbara went to the New York Public Library on Forty-second Street and immersed herself in the plays of Ibsen, O'Neill, Williams, and Inge. She would discuss a character with Anita and, when the stage was not in use, try out a speech or two, always by memory, never with script in hand, and often — because she said it made things seem more real — with footlights or a spot. "There's *something* about her," Anita told her husband. "You should talk to her. You should teach her."

Anita Miller recognized that Barbara's was a charismatic personality that projected extremely well onstage. Rough and as untutored as she was, she seized one's attention with her inimitable speaking voice: natural, low, and rushing, but not in any way stagy. She had a special way of suddenly stopping to stress key words that gave fresh insight into the lines she delivered, an eye-catching grace in the way she moved her exotic, elongated hands with their amazing fingernails, and an uncanny instinct in how to stand in the stage lights to create the proper mood.

Allan Miller had her read for him. He agreed with his wife that she had potential but did not like the idea of encouraging a fifteen-year-old offbeat-looking girl to go into the theater, where there were so few roles for anyone of her age and appearance. He told his wife to forget it. Anita persisted. One night, following a matinee performance, she brought Barbara back to their apartment for dinner. After they had eaten, Barbara did a scene for him. "It was the single *worst* audition I think I've ever seen in my entire life," he recalled, although unable to remember what scene she did. But he was struck by something raw and compelling in her. "She didn't even try to imitate other actors. There was something striving in her to be really genuinely available to herself, but she didn't know how to put it together. . . . She was so full of this young, raw eagerness that I finally said, 'Okay, listen. I'll give you a scholarship to [one of my classes].'. . . And she said, 'I'll take them *all*.'"

She managed as many classes with Miller as she could fit into her difficult schedule, which included daily attendance at Erasmus, homework, and cramming for midterm finals. Battles ensued almost every time she left the house. Diana felt that she was going wild (Greenwich Village was filled with free-spirited youths and depraved elders in her mother's view) and would get a bad reputation. Neither her mother's pleas nor her tears could keep Barbara at home. She refused to be a baby-sitter for Rosalind. Her resentment of her little half sister had not diminished with Louis Kind's departure. Rather, it had grown as Rosalind occupied more and more of Diana's time and attention.

"I never meant to neglect Barbara," Diana mused later in life. "She was very independent, and when she was in her teens Rosalind was a little girl, half her age. I thought I could do for her what I had failed to do with Barbara — be more involved in her life. The truth was, Barbara never let me be that. She never wanted advice, only approval. She frightened me a little. She was so smart, had an answer for most things. And what questions she did have, I never knew how to answer."

Like her father before her, Barbara was living a dual life, scuttling back and forth on the subway between Brooklyn and Manhattan as he had once done and, with his inherited energy, coping with everything. Always a top student, her grades were in the nineties. She excelled in Spanish. She had a natural talent for languages and liked to experiment, speaking with a French, Spanish, German, or Russian accent with much overkill. Her regard for the all-girl Choral Club held despite her inability to win the director's favor and her difficulty in singing Christian carols containing the word "Jesus." The sound of female voices in harmony attracted her. She still preferred to sing popular to semiclassical music, and she never asked to move from the alto to the soprano section. There was a good reason for this. Better clarity of diction could be achieved in the lower voice register, and the words of a song meant almost more to her than the music did. Unless she could convey the meaning of the words she sang, it seemed an empty exercise and one that did not interest her.

Occasionally she would see Erasmus Hall friends after classes, but she wasn't like the other girls who hung out at Garfield's Cafeteria to meet their girlfriends and mingle with the neighborhood boys. Her years at Erasmus Hall could not end too soon for her. She was to graduate the following June, 1959, but she had accrued enough credits to allow her to do so six months earlier. Being an actress and going on the stage was all she could think about. She barraged Allan Miller with questions about what she was doing wrong or right and whether he had seen this actress or that one and what he remembered most about their performances. She was working hard to get rid of her Brooklyn accent but was intent on keeping her own personality. Her years as a movie fan had taught her one thing: the actresses who became stars were unique and memorable characters. She told Miller she wanted to play all the great women's roles — Juliet, Desdemona, Ophelia — but she thought if she did, she should come up with a new approach.

Working at the New China in the few spare hours she had each week, she earned enough money to have her two missing teeth replaced and to return to Malden Bridge in the summer of 1958 as well. This time she immediately found her niche. Cast as the tomboy sister, Millie, in William Inge's *Picnic,* she split the skirt of her costume (to the director's fury) so that she could place her leg on a table in comedic imitation of Marlene Dietrich, a piece of stage business that was cheered by the audience and then was left in. Her next role was as the uneducated, oversexed ingenue in Erskine Caldwell's lusty hit play *Tobacco Road.* She had the ability to uncover the humor in her lines and to speak them as if they were ad-libbed, fresh, giving the character greater humanity.

A small part as a French maid in Sandy Wilson's musical pastiche of the twenties, *The Boy Friend,* the first time she would sing on a stage, came next. "She was extraordinary," recalled actor Ron Rifkin, who also was performing at the theater that summer. "She made up this crazy accent — French from the moon — and during the rehearsal lunch breaks, she wouldn't eat but would stay in the empty theater practicing a song, 'A Sleepin' Bee.' She was obsessed by it. There was a single-mindedness about her, a drive that I had never seen before."

Rifkin appears to be the only coworker to have recognized her singing ability. Nonetheless, her brief appearance in *The Boy Friend* was a momentous step in her life. The short song she sang was a throwaway, of little importance in the score. She had tried out for the show with much trepidation, unsure that her voice was really any good. Although she had no chance to display any true vocal ability, the idea that she *could* sing well enough to land a job in a musical, however small the part, began to brew. She knew if she were to attempt to try something along that line, she would have to have an audition piece. So, she had chosen "A Sleepin' Bee," from the 1954 Broadway show *House of Flowers* (music by Harold Arlen, lyrics by Truman Capote), an odd, noncommercial ballad — but very beautiful — that required as much acting as singing and that seemingly no other job aspirant would use.

Her work with Allan Miller continued. On her return from Malden Bridge, the first scene she did for him in his class was an earthy one of female seduction from Tennessee Williams's *The Rose Tattoo.* The character was a mature widow who finally puts aside the memory of her dead husband when she meets a robust truck driver. Barbara thought she couldn't do it, but Miller convinced her that she could if she kept the right image in her mind as she played it. "A week or two later," Miller recalled, "she comes in with this scene. Within one minute, the boy in the scene with her was beet red with embarrassment. It was the sexiest scene I think I have ever seen in my life."

"It was a scene of sexual exploration," Streisand herself explained. "All I did was pick a technical task, which was just physically touching the actor I played the scene with. At one point, he stood up and I stood on his feet; one time I jumped on his back; one time I pretended I was blind and while I was talking, I was touching his face. It was this awkward sexuality. I didn't know what I would do next. . . . It's what they call inspiration."

"The poor guy in the scene with her couldn't deal with it," Miller continued. "He could hardly put his hand on her without her turning it into a red-hot iron."

Her talent for displaying an almost raw sexuality was the end result of all her self-practice in looking sexy. She now knew how to internalize the feeling by concentrating on something that could make her sexual temperature rise. In the scene from *The Rose Tattoo,* it had been the need to touch and be touched. Once she mastered this technique, it seemed to free her as an actress, enabling her to begin to dredge up her own deeply felt emotions in performance, although offstage, she kept the same trained cool detachment caused by her fear of rejection. Among the Cherry Lane players, and in and out of the Millers' apartment and Allan Miller's teaching classes, were many attractive young actors, but Barbara was not ready for a relationship that might interfere with her dedication to her purpose of becoming a professional *and* famous actress. After all, Susan Strasberg was seventeen when she played Anne Frank on Broadway, the same age as Jean Seberg, who had won the film role of Joan of Arc during Preminger's talent search.

The Millers had two small children, and Barbara traded off lessons by baby-sitting. Within a few weeks she was staying in Manhattan with them and commuting to Erasmus Hall to attend classes. Unable to get Barbara to return to Brooklyn, Diana called Miller and accused him of keeping her underage daughter from her mother and her home. Miller left the decision to Barbara, who chose to remain with him and his wife. This was a wounding response that caused a deeper chasm between mother and daughter. Barbara was only sixteen at the time, and it would have been possible for Diana to seek a court order to make her return home. She did not, knowing that it would only make matters worse between them. Despite her anger and resentment, she was also confident that the Millers were good, respectable people.

Streisand has claimed that until this time, the only books she had read other than those assigned in English classes were Nancy Drew mysteries, but her work with the Millers fired her with the need to read plays by great writers. The dramas she most liked were the ones that had once starred the likes of Bernhardt and Duse: those by Dumas *fils,* Greek tragedies, Russian novels. Tolstoy's *Anna Karenina,* she says, changed her life.

"I had never been exposed to literature, to painting. I remember hearing Respighi's *Pines of Rome* that summer; *The Rite of Spring* by Stravinsky. Can you imagine what that's like? To hear that music for the first time? . . . It was a very vivid experience, that first hearing of classical music when I was sixteen."

A school paper written by her father at the same age had been the motivation for her cultural baptism. "At sixteen, he wrote about all the things he loved, and I read it, and it was all the things I loved — I read Tolstoy for the first time, heard classical music for the first time. I went to the Forty-second Street library and read Victorien Sardou, Alexandre Dumas," she said later, ticking off the similarities. "Even though I never knew him, I am very much like my father." She paused dramatically. "That was the most exciting time of my life, I think."

Her tendency was to dramatize her life, to reinvent certain periods of the past, to place an emphasis on events and nonevents that altered their importance. Her English classes at Erasmus before she was sixteen certainly introduced her to literature — Hawthorne, Poe, Melville, Henry James, George Eliot. Diana liked to listen to light classical music and operetta on the radio. Shelley was an art major. Barbara, too, had been exposed to the arts; she simply had not pursued them further until the age of sixteen.

Her passion for consuming new foods, culture, education, was enormous. She was not satisfied to limit her acting lessons to Allan Miller. She wanted to work with the man *he* had learned from, Lee Strasberg, the master of theater technique. She wrote letters to him that she was yet too insecure to mail. In them she detailed her reactions to Miller's classes. The late fifties in New York was an exciting time for young performers. Lee Strasberg's Actors Studio was the center for method acting, a technique inspired by Stanislavsky's teaching, which stressed the importance of the actor's inner identification with the character and the actor's natural use of body and voice. The Studio (as it was called) exerted considerable influence on the American theater and cinema during that decade, having nurtured the talents of Marlon Brando, Montgomery Clift, James Dean, Eli Wallach, Paul Newman, Joanne Woodward, and even Marilyn Monroe, who had fled Hollywood in 1955 to study what she termed "serious acting" with Strasberg.

Suddenly, off Broadway was burgeoning, bustling, electrifying — the place for serious theater that found its home in vast empty warehouses, small raftered attics, vacant manufacturing lofts, the back rooms of bars, and unused storage cellars, and the Village was the teeming heart of it all. Cabarets sprang up like wild flowers, and a great army of struggling, unknown young performers lived on the edge of poverty and did so with willing enthusiasm while either auditioning or appearing in one of the dozens of lilliputian venues. There was a sense of being in at the beginning of something terribly exciting. Unless you were in a Broadway show or you were a cabaret artist who could play the great clubs and hotels, your pay as a performer was nominal, if you received any at all. You acted because you loved the theater and because you believed in the American dream of sudden stardom, a life in which *you* were one of the specially anointed rich and famous.

Struggling neophytes like Streisand shared digs and mooched off friends. You learned to create a cup of free soup at the Automat by taking the tomato ketchup that was supplied with a paid-for meal and pouring some into a cup of boiling water provided for tea drinkers. "Making it" meant eating in real restaurants where you were served and having your own apartment in a building with an elevator and a doorman out front. The lucky ones were few, and Streisand's wish was to be among them as soon as possible.

Whereas she had hated being poor in Brooklyn, she was energized by her early days of being nearly penniless in the Village, sleeping on someone's couch in a four-flight walk-up or a cold-water flat, gorging herself whenever she was invited out for a meal. The Village was young, experimental. There was the whiff of newness in the air — fresh, brash, biting. Barbara was drugged with the exhilaration of it, and who could blame her? This was her time of self-discovery. She believed she could do anything. Nothing daunted her — empty purse, rejections, or her mother's harassment. She never sacrificed her work at Erasmus Hall. "I learned a lot in Brooklyn," she later acknowledged. "Out there you couldn't be dumb and survive."

Equally aware that you had to make your own luck, she never turned down a chance to audition for a good role, however ill-suited it might seem for her looks, age, and talent. At the same time she nurtured an unconcealed contempt for producers and casting directors. This perverse and imperious attitude did not endear her to the prospective hirer, but it did provide her with a ready excuse for failure to win a part. "I would read magazines like *Show Business* in which they announced casting calls," she recalled. "I used to look like a real beatnik. I wore black stockings and had this trench coat and they wanted walk-ons for a beatnik. Now, you don't have to be Sarah Bernhardt to do a walk-on as a beatnik! I remember going to this audition and they said, 'Well, we have to see your work.' I said, 'Why do you have to see my work? It's a walk-on; I don't even have to say anything.'. . . It was so nuts . . . people in these powerful positions. That's when I got so angry and said, 'Screw you, 'cause I ain't comin' back and asking you for no work.'" She added, "I was feeling this strange power of struggle. I felt that it was a very undignified position to ask anyone for a job. I decided I would design hats before I begged anyone for a job. That was when I started to sing."

The first person to whom she confided her decision to try her luck at singing was Carl Esser, a young acting hopeful and guitarist who had befriended her. He found her naturally musical, and sometimes when the Cherry Lane was deserted, they would use a corner of the stage where Barbara would sing to his accompaniment. It was also about this time that she met Cis Corman, a slim, vital young woman five years her senior. Married to a man who was just starting out in practice as an analyst, the more sophisticated Cis was taking acting classes and became Barbara's confidant and advisor. Yet, many months were to pass before Cis even became aware that Barbara had any vocal talent or thoughts of becoming a singer. One day Barbara asked her to stay a little later at the theater. They were joined by Esser.

"I want to sing something for you," Barbara told Cis, "but you have to turn around so that I can't see you, or I won't be able to do it."

Cis did as she was asked. Barbara sang "A Sleepin' Bee." Cis was overwhelmed. What she heard was a voice and interpretation that was natural, yet highly professional, and lyrics that were phrased so meaningfully that the singer seemed to be inventing them. She encouraged her new young friend, and this new confidence bonded them further.

But aside from Cis and Esser, she kept this part of her talent to herself for the time being, practicing a cappella or with Esser whenever she had a private place to do so. Suddenly, she discovered something within herself when she sang. There was an involuntary connection between her throat and her heart. "When I sing, something happens, and I can't even tell you what is in that process," she later said. "[It's] a certain musicality to the voice that is not even verbal. Speaking, it's sometimes harder to connect the heart and the throat." She chose ballads, show tunes, emotional songs. "I don't know how to sing on the beat," she explained, "and I think you have to sing on the beat, in pop music."

To her despair, she developed a serious case of acne. Her insecurities intensified. She took a part-time job as a theater usher to help with her expenses and later claimed that she would turn her face away when people spoke to her, "so that they wouldn't recognize me [when she became famous]." The reality was more moving. She was self-conscious and embarrassed that she had acne. The skin eruptions could be partially masked with the use of thick makeup, but the problem remained and caused her much angst. She took to wearing no makeup whenever possible, hoping it would help eliminate the condition. It became a daunting problem.

In October 1958 she was cast in a play called *Seawood* by the author-producer Armand de Beauchamp. Joan Rivers, then using her family name, Molinsky, was also in the cast. "'It's not the best production you'll ever be in and no money [I was told], but it can be a showcase.' I said fine," Rivers remembered. "*Showcase* is the talisman word which electrifies actors, enticing them into all kinds of absurdities in the hope that some agent will materialize and see gleams of talent."

Armand de Beauchamp conducted his School for the Theater in an old sixth-floor brownstone walk-up. The attic above these quarters, named appropriately the Garret Theater, was where he staged his plays and it seated — at full capacity — no more than twenty people. De Beauchamp was a tall, pale, fleshy young man with flowing blond hair who was in the habit of wearing heavy, knee-high, storm trooper boots. He would stare at his cast with faded, incurious blue eyes.

Readings and rehearsals were held in his living room. "The place seemed furnished by an eccentric, impoverished maiden aunt with no taste and too much proximity to a Salvation Army store," Rivers recalled. There was a broken-down sofa. Tables held lamps with "shades mottled black from burn spots." A coffee table, once on someone's lawn, rusted and peeling, was littered with dog-eared *Theater Arts* magazines. On the blotched beige-papered walls "were photographs of his grateful students . . . not one of them recognizable except Tab Hunter,* prominently displayed and frequently mentioned by Armand," Rivers continued.

Rivers also remembered "a skinny high school girl with a large nose and a pin that said GO ERASMUS" on her blouse. "We had immediate rapport, maybe because she seemed a tough little hustler . . . but still obviously vulnerable. . . . Despite being the youngest person by far, she was very outgoing and at the first rehearsal came right over to me and said, 'Hi, what's your name? My name's Barbara Streisand.'"

What impressed Rivers most was that Barbara was "carrying at her age a full theatrical makeup kit with greasepaint in *tubes* and an Equity card earned in summer stock [Malden Bridge]." Barbara did not befriend Rivers. She was always judgmental about the actors and directors with whom she worked. If she felt she had nothing to learn from them — a snap decision she often made — she did not encourage familiarity. Rivers was a complete novice at this time, and Barbara felt more knowledgeable. She was not cold or indifferent, just self-involved. Cast in the play as lesbian lovers, they rehearsed their parts for two weeks. This was during a record January cold spell and de Beauchamp could not afford heat, so during rehearsals the cast wore coats and gloves. The play was set in a

*Tab Hunter (born Arthur Gelien) had made his movie debut in 1950, at the age of eighteen, in *The Lawless*. His all-American, blond, athletic good looks made him a teenage and homosexual idol during the 1950s. He has appeared in many films, on television, and in recent years on Broadway and in three campy movies pairing him with female impersonator Divine.

cottage in the heat of summer and on opening night they almost froze in their skimpy beach-style costumes. To ward off frostbite, they waited for their entrances in front of the kitchen stove in the apartment while the small audience filed up the rickety stairs past them to the unheated attic theater.

"The actual performance is a blur — the mind protects itself," Rivers joked. "I do remember I had a big love scene where I told Barbra I loved her very much and she rejected me and I had a knife in my hand and tried to kill her and then myself. I also remember a horrendous lot of coughing [from the audience] like a tubercular ward. . . ." A review in the next issue of *Show Business* proclaimed that the acting could not be evaluated because the material was so bad. De Beauchamp was undaunted, and the play continued to run for six weeks to near-empty houses. One evening, about fifteen minutes before curtain, Rivers, descending the staircase of de Beauchamp's apartment, met Streisand on her way up. "It's closed," Rivers said. "There's no play."

Streisand shrugged. "That's just as well. I got midterms."

She graduated Erasmus two weeks later, at the end of January 1959, with a ninety-three average and a medal for special achievement in Spanish. Trudy Wallace, who was in the Choral Club with her, was voted class singer. Streisand was so disturbed over this that years later resentment edged her words as she spoke of the still unknown opera hopeful: "*She* was going to be a big star, they said."

Shelley, now working in Manhattan, kept an eye on her and tried to steer her toward furthering her education, but to no avail. It does not seem that she applied to any colleges or cared about taking the college boards. True, money was short, but her grades were high enough for her to have applied for a partial scholarship. The reality was that she was driven by one, and only one, aspiration — to become a rich and famous actress. To do so, she would have to make enough money to tide her over until she found employment in the theater. Her goal was $750. Shelley was an assistant art director at Ben Sackheim Advertising and he secured her a job as a receptionist for $90 a week. Reluctantly, she agreed to a plan that her mother and brother devised. She would return to Newkirk Avenue, commute back and forth to Manhattan, and put away half her salary until she had saved enough money. The arrangement was not a happy one. She now had to contend with Rosalind, an overweight child of eight who felt some resentment at the return of her older half sister into a household that was now her domain. Nor was the arrangement an easy one for Diana, either. Her two daughters bickered constantly, and Barbara would shout at her mother, "Why do you keep pushing food in her mouth? She's fat and at this rate she's going to be obese."

Actually, Barbara herself had a voracious appetite. She loved to eat and having often denied herself lunch as a young woman to buy makeup, food was the greatest reward she could give herself. She remained pencil-sharp thin because of her tremendous nervous energy, chewed gum when she wasn't smoking a cigarette or eating, and kept up a steady flow of conversation if she felt so inclined. She hated her job and paid little attention to the way she dressed for work.

Ben Sackheim, her boss, had an eye for pretty girls and Barbara resembled none of the attractive women among his fifty or so female employees. "She was waiflike, her hair pinned carelessly on top of her head. She wasn't attractive, well-dressed, or even kempt," Milton Mensch, an account supervisor with the agency, recalled. "Her dresses looked as if they needed to be pressed. And she had a terrible complexion — adolescence, I thought.

"Shelley and I used to have lunch together, and two or three times Barbara joined us at a small restaurant near the office in midtown Manhattan. Barbara spoke about her ambitions in the theater and I thought, 'How is this girl going to make it?' She had a mouth like a truck driver and used four-letter words comfortably. She quit after three or four months; shortly after she left, Shelley asked me to see if my brother-in-law Ralph Mann, an agent, would represent her. She went to see him and Ralph, as graciously as possible, said no. He told me she didn't look like she could get an audience to rise to its feet."

Again she departed Diana and Brooklyn. For a short while she shared an apartment with Marilyn Fried, a friend from the Cherry Lane Theatre. "We lived in total poverty on Forty-eighth Street," Fried recounted. "Each of us was getting thirty-two dollars a week on unemployment checks. It barely covered the rent and our fees for acting classes. Once a week when it really got bad each of us had to go to see Mama, to get the bread and the margarine and the soup. Barbara would go to Brooklyn to her mother and I'd go to the Bronx to mine. We'd both come back with the groceries and we'd take everything out of the boxes in the kitchen and put it in the refrigerator. That is how we survived.

"[Once] Mrs. Kind came down to Miller's workshop. She did not say a word after the performance. . . . There was this terrible silence. Then, when we got upstairs to our apartment, it began. Her mother said that Barbara should get a job . . . because she did not have the ability to be an actress. We spent half an hour in the bedroom listening to this nonsense. I was heartbroken because she was not encouraging Barbara. . . . One night Barbara and I sat together wondering what we would like most to do if ever we made it as actresses and she said, 'First of all, I want to buy my mother a mink coat.'"

This shocked Fried, who did not feel she should comment on how strange she found this wish in view of Diana's negative attitude toward Barbara's career. However, this was exactly what motivated Barbara's desire to give her mother such an extravagant gift. "I'll show you!" she was saying. "You thought I could never become rich and a star!"

Diana urged her to return to Newkirk Avenue. Shelley offered a small loan if Barbara changed her mind about college, but she was consumed with the need to make her mark as quickly as she could. She had dreams — big dreams: nothing less than stardom would be acceptable. She intended to show Brooklyn, her family, her classmates, that they were wrong about her. She was a winner. Not quite seventeen when she graduated Erasmus Hall, she expected to be on her way to her goal in a year's time. Meanwhile, she continued to usher during Saturday matinee and evening performances in Broadway theaters. When there was no job, she would go back on unemployment.

Thinking perhaps that her own ethnic roots were a deterrent, she took the name Angelina Scarangella from the New York telephone book. Newly named, her hair dyed red, and dressed in black tights, feathered boas, and 1925 hats found for little money in Village secondhand stores, she went out unsuccessfully on auditions and finally dropped the stage name. Without telling Allan Miller, she started acting classes simultaneously with Eli Rill, also a disciple of Lee Strasberg. Her ability to make the other students laugh infuriated Rill. "I kept telling her that she had to develop what she had and not try to be somebody else," Rill remembered. "She would make it clear that my role was to make her a tragic muse."

She was still working on songs with Carl Esser and, except for Cis Corman, had not yet sung in front of anyone else. One evening Marilyn Fried was in the bedroom of their small apartment and Barbara was in the living room with Esser. "He was strumming a guitar," Fried recalled. "I suddenly heard this remarkable voice coming out of the living room. My immediate reaction was to go to the radio and find out who was singing so marvelously. But the radio was not on. I realized there must be someone in this tiny apartment who had this magnitude, this power. [I went into the room] and asked Barbara, 'Who was singing?' She said, 'I was.'" Fried insisted that she must do something about it.

"Yeah? You really think so?" Barbara mused. Esser agreed with Fried that it was time she did. "I don't know. What's it mean to be a singer?" she shrugged, appearing to Fried, at least, to think it was something demeaning.

Nonetheless, the enthusiastic approval she had received did not go unnoticed, nor had it been so innocently solicited. Privately, she had been honing her talent on the assumption that it might help pave the way to getting a role on Broadway. She had hoped that Marilyn Fried would react to her singing in the same way that Cis Corman had; she needed that affirmation before she tested herself in a professional situation. Now she had it.

7

In the summer of 1959, Barbara circulated a résumé to casting directors stating that she was both an actress and a singer. Attached was a highly idiosyncratic eight-by-ten glossy. Her features could hardly be discerned, and certainly not her chronic skin condition, as she was "swathed in cloaks and veils and earrings and chatchkalas, looking like Ruth Draper [the modern dancer] in a moving moment." Eddie Blum of the Rodgers and Hammerstein casting office was so intrigued by the photograph that he called her and asked her what she really looked like.

"What part are you asking me to audition for?" she shot back.

"It's for the Rodgers and Hammerstein musical *Sound of Music*," he replied.

"Yeah?"

"Do you know the story?"

The show was about to go into rehearsal starring Mary Martin as former nun Baroness Maria von Trapp, who had escaped from the Nazis over the Alps with a brood of singing stepchildren. Three years earlier a German film, never released in the United States, had been made about the von Trapp family. Rodgers and Hammerstein had bought the rights to adapt it to the stage. There had been articles about the von Trapp's adventure, but Barbara had not read any of them.

"Sure!" she lied.

"Well, it's the oldest von Trapp child, Lisl; the one who falls in love with the boy in the Nazi youth movement. She's blond, Christian, and sixteen years old," he told her.

"I'd be perfect!" she exclaimed. She went right down to his office to read for the part. Lisl was a singing role requiring a sweet soprano; her one solo was "I Am Sixteen Going on Seventeen" and was germane to the character, who had to convey girlish naïveté. Barbara went over the music a few times with the rehearsal pianist and then gave it an admirable try. Blum knew from the moment she entered his office, dressed in an outfit that could only be described as "*Baby Doll* camp" (referring to the Tennessee Williams play about a seductive child-wife in the Deep South), that she was entirely wrong for the role, and he warned her of this almost immediately. Her determination made him curious enough to allow her to audition. After she sang Lisl's song, she sensed he was going to turn her down.

"You should see me with blond hair," she pressed. "I bleached it once and even my mother thought I was gentile." Impressed with her voice, Blum suggested she apply her efforts more to singing.

With the few dollars she had, she began voice lessons. Her teacher, found through an advertisement in a theater magazine and who had once sung minor roles in a small opera company, spent entire lessons on vocal exercises and voice production. "I feel that singing is a natural thing," Barbara said, recalling those lessons and how she was being taught to form sounds. "It is an extension of speaking on a heightened level." The singing lessons, which proved to be disconcerting because of her chronic ear problem, came to an abrupt end.

The clicks and buzzing that she had once heard in her ears had evolved into a high-pitched noise, a ringing that was no longer sporadic but continuous. She never heard silence. She had her ears examined and was told about her condition and that she had supersonic hearing. "I hear high-range, high-pitch noises off the machine," she explained. "But I also hear this noise. There were periods in my life when I was very unhappy and it would drive me nuts. . . . I had this secret. I never told anybody. I didn't want to be different. I felt totally abnormal. . . . It made me listen very carefully to life. I would listen like nobody listened. But it's not good, it's not fun. I'm like inside my body, I hear my body. I'm very aware of my body's functions. It's very frightening."

This distressing affliction played a critical role in how she interpreted lines, lyrics, and music. She could feel the cadences, the changes in rhythm, the silences between beats. She could move effortlessly from the deeper chest sounds to the higher-pitched head sounds, an ability that usually took years of musical training to achieve. At the same time, since she heard things more clearly and sharply than most musicians, when she sang she was conscious of every small imperfection in her voice. She seldom played the radio because on the simple machines to which she had access, the fidelity was poor and caused her to concentrate on the defects.

Shortly after being turned down by Eddie Blum, she cashed her last unemployment check and joined the Actors Co-Op, which consisted of a group of somewhat desperate out-of-work performers all hoping for an appearance in a legitimate theater where they would be seen and reviewed. They leased the small off-Broadway Jan Hus Theatre in Yorkville, Manhattan's German center, and mysteriously chose the brothers Karel and Josef Čapek's play *The Insect Comedy,** a satire on human society and totalitarianism. It was written in 1921, and all the roles were citizens of an insect world. Streisand had four parts: a butterfly, a moth, Apatura Clythia, and a messenger.

Also in the company was Barry Dennen, a slim, dark-haired, charismatic young actor from Los Angeles who was cast as a cricket and a snail. "The whole production was slapped together," Dennen remembered. "It was unspeakable, tacky, awful, and Barbara was hysterically funny. She was young, endearing, and exceptionally serious about becoming an actress."

The two were drawn to each other. Dennen, who had attended UCLA and was several years older than Barbara, came from a well-to-do West Coast Jewish family. Lean, lithe, bronzed by the sun, which he loved, Dennen was most appealing. He was also well educated and pos-

---

*Called *The Insect Play* in Great Britain, in its original 1923 London production it had John Gielgud cast as Felix, a small role. This was Gielgud's first West End appearance.

sessed innate style. He was to be Streisand's first grand attraction and her mentor. Multitalented, he could do mime, comedy, or drama; had a unique singing style; was dedicated to theater; and dreamed eventually of becoming a director.*

They shared a sense of far-out humor and began to create short skits that had nothing to do with the Ĉapeks' play. In one, Barbara was Mae West and Dennen was an unscrupulous diamond smuggler who has forced a poodle to swallow the gems so that he can get them past customs. "Whatsa matter with your animal?" Barbara would ask in her most seductive Mae West voice. This double entendre would be accompanied by a provocative sway of her shoulders and a raised eyebrow. They never got to Dennen's reply because they would be laughing so hard.

The Insect Comedy closed on May 11, 1960, after three performances. "No one [in this play] claimed to be anything like a pro," wrote the reviewer from the *World Telegram & Sun*. This was Barbara's first major press notice, and it did nothing to get her career off to even a slow start. Her financial situation was desperate. She and Marilyn were about to be evicted from their apartment. She refused to go to Diana and Brooklyn. "If I could sing like you, I'd know what to do," Marilyn prodded. "I'd try to get a singing job. All you need is a demo tape to give to an agent." In view of their dire circumstances, Streisand agreed that singing might be preferable to sleeping on a park bench. The problem was that making a tape would cost money that she did not have. Then she recalled that Dennen, suggesting they might record their comedy routine, told her he owned an excellent Ampex stereo tape recorder and two good mikes.

The next day she appeared at his apartment with Carl Esser in tow. "We spent the afternoon taping [the song "Day By Day"], and the

*Barry Dennen would go on to create the show-stopping role of Pontius Pilate in the original Broadway production, film, and the first double album of *Jesus Christ Superstar.* He also starred as the evil emcee in the London company of *Cabaret,* for which he won the *Evening Standard* Award for best actor in 1968. He stayed in England and appeared in the BBC's series *Oppenheimer, Beau Geste,* and *Pictures.* On returning to the United States he had supporting roles in numerous films and on television. More recently he has toured as Max Detweiler in *Sound of Music.* In 1992 he won the Dramalogue Award for his performance as the major general in the Santa Barbara Light Opera Company's production of *Pirates of Penzance.* He has also written for theater, film, and television.

moment I heard the first playback I went insane," Dennen later related. "I knew here was something special, a voice the microphone loved. . . . But I thought she had a better chance of getting an agent if she were performing somewhere. There was a club across the street from where I lived [on West Ninth Street in the Village], called the Lion. They had a talent contest on Thursdays. If she would actually walk in there and sign up, I would work with her on a set of songs, help her choose the material, and direct her act." Her terms reversed the order. If she thought she had a chance *after* his coaching, *then* she would sign up. Dennen agreed.

Barbara used a microphone for the first time. Transfixed by the experience, she spent hours experimenting with it, learning how to shade her voice, to project it without strain. Under Dennen's fevered tutelage she mastered microphone technique in a matter of days, adding her own instinctive touches, never pausing to breathe in the middle of a lyric, bringing the instrument closer to her lips to enhance the intimacy of a phrase. Her phrasing — good to begin with — improved even more. Dennen pushed her as hard as he could, and she responded with more questions, repeating a song dozens of times before she was satisfied with her interpretation.

At the end of a week he accompanied her to the Lion, standing over her as she inscribed her name as *Barbra* Streisand on the audition sheet. It was not an accident, she told him later. There were too many *Barbara*s, and she wanted to be different. She did, however, want to keep her last name so that everyone in Brooklyn would know it was her *when* she became famous. Dennen had recorded her practice sessions and played them back for her to study. The newly named Barbra Streisand was confident she was on the road to stardom, a belief that drove her to rehearse at fever pitch for the audition, not stopping until both she and Dennen were too exhausted to continue.

Dennen had made her arrangements of "A Sleepin' Bee" and "Lover, Come Back to Me" a "switch" (that is, a song usually sung in slow tempo but given an up-tempo driving beat). He conceived "A Sleepin' Bee" as a set theater piece, evolving the character of the girl in the lyric story through various moods. It was a perfect choice, enabling Streisand to watch an imaginary bee who sleeps in the palm of her hand. Dennen told her the Jamaican legend of the insect who won't fly away, who won't sting you if you have found true love. Under his direction her graceful hands created a unique stage picture as she acted and sang to this tiny fantasy creature, which somehow seemed unbelievably real.

Demanding and tough, Dennen worked her hard, phrase by phrase, "trying this, trying that, shaping gestures, timing, the kind of effect Barbra and I wanted." She lent herself willingly to his strict instruction, picking up on everything he told her, adding her own improvements both musically and interpretatively — an unexpected change of key, a word given surprising stress. He warned her not to interact with the audience while she was performing, as this would destroy the reality she was creating in her song. He taught her how to be still and yet commanding as she waited to begin her act, what to do with her hands, how to stand, how to sit, how to hold a microphone, how to look out at an audience without seeing them. He insisted she treat each song as if it were a short, crucial scene in a drama, to play a part with music and lyrics. She was a voracious student and by the end of the week had progressed from amateur to the threshold of professionalism. Clearly, they were a good creative team.

Dennen was falling in love with her, but he also recognized her distinctiveness and her vast untapped talent. There was something almost obsessive about his need to develop her into a professional performer, which she had *not* been when they first began to work together. He later said in an interview, "Barbra *was* my creation; at least, I created her musical taste and gave her support, confidence, and the direction she needed to be able to do anything."

Although she recognized just how much Dennen could contribute to her future, she never appeared grateful. Dennen did not expect her to be. She had become obsessed with herself, and he believed that quality was one that would have a positive effect on her performance. Whatever satisfaction he gained from helping her metamorphose into an exciting performer was her repayment. To Barbra, Dennen's considerable help and encouragement were deemed a small measure of compensation for all the years of being put down by Diana and something that she considered was due from someone whom she loved.

Although Dennen had not yet found a theater job that could pay his rent, he lived on a considerably higher standard than other struggling actors in a "small, but modern, clean cockroachless apartment at Sixty-nine West Ninth Street," which he paid for with help from his parents. In Barbra's eyes, the flat — with its paisley fabric walls, black leather chairs, and massive plants in containers made of bamboo — was the essence of sophistication. Dennen had flair, and his two rooms, plus kitchen and bathroom, had been smartly turned out on a modest budget. He also had quality hi-fi equipment and an amazing collection of more than a thousand records of the great entertainers of the twentieth century, which he had shipped from his family home on the West Coast.

Dennen's parents owned an estate in the fashionable stretch of Coldwater Canyon off Sunset Boulevard. His brother and he each had their own small house set a short distance from the main building, with a swimming pool between them. Barbra never tired of hearing him describe the glamorous decor of his home, what the staff were like, the parties the family hosted, movies shown in a private projection room, cocktail parties by the pool, and the huge barbeques, all attended by the rich and sometimes famous. She was impressed.

Dennen now proposed she move in with him. The decision was not difficult, for they had developed an unusual closeness and she had been evicted from her former apartment. Not only was she dependent upon his emotional and financial support, she was in love. While preparing for her audition at the Lion, they entered into a physical relationship. Although she had been attracted to several young men during her early Village days, Dennen was her first real affair and the first man she lived with. She had not given up her prime ambition to be an actress, but she was now convinced that goal would be attainable if she could make a name for herself as a singer who *was* an actress. Phrasing, choice of material, putting together a class act, were what was needed, and her instincts told her that Dennen could expedite the process.

Always together, in what free time they had he dragged her to thrift shops and costumiers to get together some outfits to wear in her act when she won the contest — he was sure she would. He had an unerring eye for spotting the one elegant scarf, pair of gloves, or shoes in a pile of junk, and Barbra was a fast learner who instinctively knew how to put together the bits and pieces of old-world elegance they found to make an intriguing and fashionable ensemble. The finished result, if somewhat bizarre, was a look that would be remembered.

This was at the time of the midcalf hemline ushered in by Dior, with skirts worn over several full petticoats, of wholesome vocalists such as Doris Day and Dinah Shore, of nightclub singers gowned in glitzy gold and sequins. By contrast, Barbra combined a short 1920s dress with colored stockings and T-strapped twenties shoes with four-inch heels. For another costume, a boa in bright crimson was slung around the shoulders of an oyster white Victorian negligee. Together, Barbra and Dennen found extraordinary paste necklaces, dangly earrings, and Venetian glass bracelets that she wore as she walked around the Village so that they became comfortable, old friends. She was costumed rather than dressed, but she had gained a new persona. To some she looked kookie in her flea-market attire, but there was no doubt that she stood out from the crowd and that if she was viewed with a fashion-trained eye, she was more avant than derriere garde.

At the end of this frantic week of transformation, she was ready. The talent contest, they both believed, would lead to her debut as a cabaret performer. The contest was held on July 2, 1960, a muggy, airless evening. Barbra had celebrated her eighteenth birthday the previous April. She looked older by a few years.

The Lion was a "crummy" back room with tables where they served a limited menu. Summers, when their customers liked to go to Fire Island or various other beach areas, were slow. To stimulate business, the owner had inaugurated a Thursday night talent contest, the winner to receive fifty dollars a week for a two-week engagement and all the food and drink he or she could consume. The food offer was a great incentive to the hard-up young actress who loved to eat. The Lion was not the hottest small club in town, but it was a good showcase for performers and was frequented by agents and scouts looking for new talent.

Among her six or seven competitors that evening was a comedian, a black blues singer, and a duo who sang Broadway show songs. The room was dimly lit. There was no stage, just a dark area in front of the piano like a small dance floor. The comedian went first. Then came Barbra. Dennen handed her music to the accompanist and then held her back for a moment and asked for a spot. A few moments went by and a pink light came on. She stepped up to the piano looking like a bird of paradise, eyes outlined in blue, a silver-and-gold blouse with large Elizabethan sleeves worn over a shocking-pink fuchsia skirt a daring inch above the knee, chocolate brown stockings and her T-strapped 1927 gold-and-silver vamp shoes with accents of red. A bang hid part of her forehead, the rest of her dyed auburn hair piled up atop her head with an added hairpiece for extra height.

Glasses were lowered to study this apparition as she stood behind the microphone in the pink light. She should have looked simply weird. Instead, she was startling, breathtakingly unique. She boosted herself onto the seat of a stool. She was chewing bubble gum and as she waited for silence (as Dennen had told her she must), she took the gum out of her mouth and stuck it under the seat — her own innovation. The audience laughed and immediately warmed to her.

Seated out front was a young, struggling actor named Dustin Hoffman, who had been attending acting classes with her. "I thought: What a smart girl," he recalled, reflecting on that night. "It was a seemingly natural act but it had method to its madness. It was quite provoking, and suddenly, out of this amiable anteater, came this *magic.*" She sang "A Sleepin' Bee" in a melting, completely original voice, nasal at times, that rose to the ceiling, circled the small, crowded, smoke-filled room, and in the end brought the house to its feet (so much for agent Ralph Mann's dour prediction that this would never occur). The acts that followed had lost before they began.

Barbra Streisand had arrived.

Now that she had unleashed her voice, she realized its power and range. Despite her youth, it was a mature woman's voice with a certain nasal urgency that was nothing like the youthful yearning, the throaty vulnerability, that was so recognizably Judy Garland's at the same age.

And when Barbra sang, Brooklyn was lost — unless she chose to incorporate it for fun into a line. She became whomever she chose to be.

The amazing thing was how she learned so quickly to turn a song into a vignette, to create an entire scene. To broaden her limited knowledge of vocal styling, Dennen played her countless records and tapes — Ruth Etting, Helen Morgan, Lee Wiley, Ethel Waters, Mabel Mercer, Shirley Temple, Fanny Brice, and Fred Astaire — all performers who possessed strong individual styles. They would analyze and study the songs these artists sang. He recorded Astaire and Rogers dances from televised reruns of their old films, and — a fine dancer — Dennen would whirl around the room with her, jumping on and off the furniture in imitation of that great dance team.

A friend of Dennen's from California, Ira Levy, also lived in the Village and would join them with another friend, Stan Gurell. "We would do an entire review in Barry's living room. All of us singing — but mainly Barbra — songs starting from the turn of the century and continuing on pretty much to the present. Barbra's voice was amazing. You could tell she had a future. And it was incredible how fast she got the period sounds — pre–World War One, the twenties, the thirties. She was terrific."

Dennen welcomed with fond approval the fans, feathers, costume jewelry, and vintage clothing that kept closet doors from closing; the Tiffany-style lamps that she had seized upon and that he had bought for her at a good price in their scavenging through the back rooms of thrift shops; the idiosyncratic collection of period bibelots, additional recording equipment, and the dozens of candles that she lit for their private dinners that she cooked. His modest-sized flat was crowded and overflowing with things that evoked her eclectic personality. "Barbra had fully moved in and made the apartment her home," he says.

Still, it was not truly hers, and the life she led with Dennen was filled with humiliations as well as exciting highs. Believing his father would cut off his support if he knew he was living with Barbra, Dennen insisted she not answer the telephone and introduced her to the doorman of the building as his cousin. This charade was kept up, although it is doubtful that the apartment staff were ever fooled.

Streisand was convinced she was deeply in love with Dennen. He possessed a prodigious memory, and she was learning from him about music, history, politics. Ideas bounced back and forth between them. An eager pupil, she challenged him at every turn. She trusted and believed in his taste in clothes, decor, and — above all — music, consuming and squirreling away everything he had to give her. She had found that she had learned more about acting from interpreting the lyrics of songs than she had in most of her combined acting classes.

During her two-week run at the Lion, Dennen was there every evening taking notes on her performance and on the reaction of the audience. And he would work with her on new numbers. "I would pick material that was excellent musically," Dennen explained, "that would show off her voice and also songs that were unusual, forgotten, or outrageous. It was my idea to have her perform "Who's Afraid of the Big Bad Wolf?" in front of New York's cleverest and sharpest [cabaret] audience."*

Her affair with Dennen was something quite apart from first love. It was the beginning of learning to love herself. He was intelligent; possessed tremendous energy, talent, originality of thought, and good taste; and had chosen her, believed she had the potential of becoming something special — *a star.* He also found her sexy, appealing. More unsure of himself at the time than his bravura indicated, Dennen benefitted greatly from the knowledge that he had discovered someone original, bound for success, and that her trust in him validated his own worth. His most important lesson to her as an artist was to show her that she could display her acting ability within the framework of a song; his greatest contribution to her as a woman was to help her feel beautiful, desired, and confident.

Her engagement at the Lion ended on July 16. The best cabarets in New York would be closed for the month of August. Impatiently she waited while the scorching late summer days stripped Manhattan of much of its glamour. Heat steamed up from the sidewalks, trapped between the tunnels of high-rises. Streets smelled pungently of burning

---

*The original arrangement for "Who's Afraid of the Big Bad Wolf" was done by Peter Daniels.

rubber and baked-in waste matter. The fire department turned on the fire hydrants in the poor sections so that the kids could dart in and out of the water to cool off. Those who could packed their weekend bags for the country. Barbra remained in the city, barely leaving Dennen's apartment, hoping and waiting for a call from the William Morris Agency, who she was told might be interested in representing her.

And Dennen was also preparing her for an audition at the Bon Soir, one of the most sophisticated and popular cabaret rooms in the Village. He was very strict with her, working on the act for hours on end. Dennen's good friend, Bob Schulenberg, arrived in the city from Los Angeles on the last day of the Lion engagement. Dennen met him at the airport and brought him down to the Village.

"The first time I saw her we were walking down Sixth Avenue," Schulenberg remembered. "Barbra approached us with two shopping bags in each hand, and out of them were coming feathers, sequins, net, all sorts of accessory stuff, lots of it. . . . She had little wisps of eyeliner and darkened eyelids under her brow. Her wide and generous mouth was accentuated with mahogany-purple lipstick. . . . Her earrings were glass balls that seemed to hang all the way down to her thorax, and she had an assortment of necklace chains with glass interspersed and she had a dozen exquisite Venetian-glass bracelets on one arm, plus rings on practically all the fingers of her two hands. Outside of *The King and I,* no one had looked that way ever, even on the streets of Greenwich Village."

Schulenberg, an illustrator, makeup man, and designer, was not so much taken aback as he was impressed. "I found her extraordinary from the beginning. She was just so amazing. I never encountered someone with so many ideas and so many wishes, so many desires. We three became a kind of trio. We would terrorize the town, do numbers at the various clubs [to call attention to themselves], even tried to steal pottery from tables at restaurants.

"[She and Barry] talked about getting married, and I was shocked. I was just really stunned," Schulenberg said. "They were very young. As I remember, Barbra was only eighteen and Barry, twenty-one." Dennen was rehearsing a role in *Measure for Measure* in a Shakespearean series being presented in Central Park. When Streisand was on her own,

Schulenberg would see that she was occupied. They became good friends. "I think she was the most intelligent person I'd ever met. She had a great understanding of what she read and tremendous curiosity. If you were introducing a new topic to her, she pelted you with questions. I don't recall her ever putting me off with a feminine tract. She was just her own person. There are certain women who don't act like men but are people without any of the constrictions. Barbra was the first woman I had met that was like that. At the same time an intriguing aura of naïveté clung to her.

"I think I took her to the first [elegant] restaurant she'd ever been to . . . a chic midtown smorgasbord restaurant. She was fascinated by this huge table full of strange food. She would feel the texture of everything with her fingers. There was this marvelous orgiastic tactile experience of touching all the food. . . . 'Look at this,' she'd sigh. It was wonderful to watch. It was also poignant because you realized it was such a thrill for her. Doing things with Barbra in those days was like the first time it had ever been done."

Streisand was beginning to feel somewhat more secure and sophisticated. She was recognized now on the streets of the Village, and she liked that; but waiting for something to happen was depressing her. Finally, she received a call from the William Morris Agency, one of the most powerful in the industry. She was to bring her music, and the agency would supply an accompanist.

Enter Peter Daniels, who would play an enormous role in the next stage of her career. Daniels was a fine musician — accompanist, arranger, and coach — who often helped out the agency when it was auditioning. The son of a Jewish mother and an Irish father, he had grown up in London during the Blitz, worked as a song plugger for Chappell Music and come to the States as a pianist on the Cunard Lines. Once in New York he was loath to leave, worked as a pianist in small clubs, and then began to arrange and to coach Broadway performers in musical roles. A slight man, about five foot eight, with startling, bespectacled sky blue eyes, Daniels was a bit of a character with a winning English accent and wit.

He was sitting at the piano in the office where William Morris conducted its singing auditions when Streisand, a few minutes late, rushed in, dressed in a bizarre fashion and hair going every which way. There was an agent and a couple of assistants present, and they exchanged arched glances. "Whew! It's hot in here!" she complained. "Maybe you could open a window, something?"

She handed Daniels the music. Familiar with the song, he was surprised at the good taste this strange creature had shown in the selection of her material and apprehensive that she would botch it. When she started to sing, he was stunned. She was pure magic. There was an awkward silence in the room when she had finished. Finally, the auditioning agent thanked her for coming in and told her they would be in touch. The group left and Streisand, impressed at the marvelous accompaniment Daniels had provided, asked him if maybe he could help her get ready for the Bon Soir audition, adding that she was dead broke. He had been so impressed with her talent that he agreed.

"Great talent but a dog! We'll never be able to sell her," the agent at William Morris had later decreed, and so Streisand was still without representation. But she now had a brilliant musician who knew people in the business and was willing to help her without expecting to be paid.

Over the next few weeks she worked with Daniels at his apartment on Riverside Drive, also shared by his wife, Anita, and their infant daughter, on refining the musical presentation of her repertoire; Dennen had already done a masterful job of coaching her in her phrasing and dramatic approach. She auditioned for the Bon Soir on a humid Sunday evening in late July. "This is the beginning of something," she remembered thinking on the way to the club with Dennen, Schulenberg, and Burke McHugh, an older off-Broadway producer Dennen knew who was also a scout for new cabaret talent and who had arranged the audition. When a cool breeze suddenly rose, she felt a chill through her entire body. She has recalled that she felt different, surer of herself that evening. She walked so fast, the men had a difficult time keeping up with her. Daniels was waiting for her when she arrived.

The Bon Soir was a Mafia-owned cellar club. The gay bar at the rear of the one large room it occupied existed through police payoffs. The club was known for its all-black company of regular performers, who included Mae Barnes, "a five-by-five singer with dark saucer eyes, a grainy powerhouse voice, and the sassiest good-time spirit ever to haunt a nightclub stage," as well as the Tiger Haynes Trio, each member a spectacular solo musician. It was also an important showcase for up-and-coming white performers — Kaye Ballard, Phyllis Diller, and Dick Cavett among them.

With the club closed on Sundays, Streisand and her supporters entered through a rear door that led down a steep, dimly lit flight of stairs. The place was almost entirely in darkness. Only a few tables were occupied by the management and some employees. One overhead spot was illuminated. The respected guitarist Tiger Haynes watched her from across the room as she paused at the piano to say something to Daniels and then went up on the narrow stage and positioned the microphone. A sense of command pervaded her attitude. The Bon Soir was several times larger than the Lion and, although it was in the Village, had a reputation that brought New York's most sophisticated uptown cabaret-goers to its cellar doors on Eighth Street.

Her usual "bizarre" attire was abandoned (because of the intense heat and advice from Daniels) for a simple, sleeveless brown cotton dress. Her hair was piled high on her head. She insisted on a blue rather than a pink spotlight, and the effect was startling. She looked like a Modigliani painting. A shock rang through the darkened, silent room the moment she started to sing "A Sleepin' Bee" — a spine-tingling urgency behind every note. The sound was pure, commanding; her phrasing, remarkable. It was an astonishing performance. She played to that nearly empty room as though every chair were filled and the phantom occupants raptly listening to her. The magic in her voice was tangible. "It looks good," Burke McHugh told Dennen when she had finished. Tiger Haynes's girlfriend, a diminutive woman named Bea, came over to Streisand and said, "Little girl, you got dollar signs written all over you!"

"Yeah? You really think so?" she grinned. "Maybe you can tell the management."

Her salary was $108 a week for a two-week engagement. She was to be only the featured artist. Comedian Phyllis Diller was the headliner.

"Hey!" she told one friend. "This is only the beginning. Next time the stakes will be higher, and the place classier."

"It's curious," Bob Schulenberg confided, "I always thought Barry would be the legend and Barbra, the cabaret performer." The two men had first met on a set of an amateur film that Dennen had written when they both were attending UCLA. "He was a brilliant performer, very clever. He did performances of *Les Faux Billis di Scapin* that I designed at UCLA, and his French was so impeccable that everyone thought he was French. He's an amazing performer. A perfectionist, a visionary. He always brought something new to the character he played."

Schulenberg, who was himself extremely talented at makeup and design, had been an assistant art director for Berman Costumes in Hollywood and had designed for the Ice Capades. He had arrived in New York to start a job as art director for the firm of West, Weir and Bartell, which was where — as coincidence would have it — Shelley was now employed. "I liked him very much, but I had the sense that he was a little embarrassed by Barbra, at least at that point in time." A great fan of both contemporary and legendary cabaret artists, Schulenberg had been overwhelmed with admiration for Barbra when he first heard her sing. He also felt that proper makeup would add much to her appearance.

"She was very young and she — well, she didn't look bad, but I think she thought that she did," Schulenberg recalled. "That was kind of heartbreaking because I knew how much she wanted to look beautiful and simply did not know how to bring it off. She really had a striking face, marvelous eyes, and a profile that was pure Egyptian. I thought she could be really stunning and that I could help her, but it was a difficult, sensitive point. I thought about it a long time and in the end I made a simple drawing of her without any makeup so that I could study her face structure."

In the month of August, while Dennen was rehearsing in the Central Park production of *Measure for Measure,* Schulenberg saw Barbra more frequently. During their wanderings about the Village, he gradually convinced her that she needed a makeup makeover. They were to attend Dennen's opening night together, and this seemed to present itself as the perfect occasion. Schulenberg came early to the apartment, armed with a theatrical makeup kit. "She had great eyes, a wonderful face. What I did was make cheekbones where there was still baby fat, and I contoured her eyes and feathered some false eyelashes shorter than her own and extended the line at the corner of her eyes. With each step I explained to her what I was doing and why. She didn't have deep-set eyes, and so she had to enforce it. The double layer of eyelashes helped that effect. I used heavy greasepaint to hide the scars of her skin condition.

"She kept staring at herself in the mirror, turning her face at different angles, mumbling excited comments. 'I see! I see! Hey! Not bad, huh?' She was very pleased, thrilled with the transformation."

Streisand and Schulenberg had been so involved with Barbra's makeover that they arrived too late to see Dennen perform. He was deeply hurt, and although they continued to live together, there was now an edge to their relationship. Dennen helped her with the act she was soon to present at the Bon Soir, concentrating on the dramatic presentation. Streisand had a clear concept of how she wanted to sound and what she wanted to sing — great Harold Arlen songs such as "When the Sun Comes Out," Fats Waller's "Keepin' Out of Mischief Now" (sung by her in a breathless, seductive voice), and the childlike "Who's Afraid of the Big Bad Wolf," which she turned into a campy, lively, and raunchy interpretation. They were all included in her new act that worked around the theme of a young girl's transition from tease to love awakening to lost love and maturity — every song performed under Dennen's direction as a minidrama. Strong-willed, always striving to be at the top of her form, Barbra was clever enough to accept outside ideas when she recognized their worth, and she worked tirelessly to take in and adapt all he could contribute to her performance.

She practiced her "look" with equal concentration. Schulenberg made a portrait of Barbra with half her face made up as he designed it, and the other side untouched. She would then take the drawing and all the makeup into the bathroom and patiently attempt to make up the side of her face that was blank in the picture so that it matched the other side in the picture. When it did not, she would scrub her face clean and start over again, sometimes four or five times, a process that often took several hours before she got it right.

Streisand was the center of a curious trio, badgered and disciplined by two young men who were determined that she succeed — a Brooklyn Eliza Doolittle. But things are not always as they appear. Barbra Streisand's wish to succeed was even greater than her mentors' wish for her. Had they been less talented, had they not been able to help her advance her aims, she would have had little time for them. It was not that she was ungrateful. Streisand was in a desperate hurry to arrive at her planned destination, and she accepted all that Dennen and Schulenberg could contribute to her growth as a performer, as she did Peter Daniels's musical assistance.

She believed she loved Dennen, but she had no other experience with a close male-female relationship other than her mother's disastrous marriage to Kind. She was seeking love and approval, an alliance in which she was the center of attention, and Dennen gave this to her. What more could she ask of a man or of an affair?

8

Opening night at the Bon Soir, Friday, September 9, 1960, Streisand walked onstage to a packed house wearing a very tight fitting thrift-shop dress of brown wool jersey, a matching cloche from the twenties, and a pair of spike-heeled, ankle-strap shoes. Ice cubes clinked in glasses, and people engaged in conversation as she tiptoed across the darkened stage to the microphone set up before a high stool. When the spotlight picked her up already seated, the audience took one look and concluded that she was a comedienne.

A wave of terror washed over her. Unlike the audiences at the Lion, these were tough uptown types who would judge her against the current top cabaret entertainers: Julie Wilson, Anita Ellis, Felicia Sanders, Portia Nelson, and the sultry-voiced Julie London. She took a deep breath, glanced over to Peter Daniels at the piano, and began "A Sleepin' Bee" in a hushed throb of a voice, the microphone no more than an inch from her mouth. It was a brave opening. Most cabaret acts started with a spirited number to catch the audience's attention. A few moments into the song, her voice grew louder and she extended her arm and opened the palm of her hand to show where the bee was supposed to lie sleeping. Heads turned toward her. People leaned forward in their chairs. She could feel the crowd's enthusiasm. They exploded with applause when she finished the song and were entirely hers as she cut their response short and swept into "When the Sun Comes Out" as if "she were announcing the eclipse of Western civilization."

"When she got off the stage," remembered comedian and impressionist Larry Storch, who was also making his way in the cabaret world, "Barbra was in a kind of a daze. I went to congratulate her. I think I said something like, 'Kid, you are going to be a very great star!' Then they pushed her back onstage, and after singing those serious songs, she performed 'Who's Afraid of the Big Bad Wolf?'* How well planned that was! What a master stroke! It just killed everybody. They made her sing it three times. It was incredible. It was really like a scene from *A Star Is Born*."

Streisand was overwhelmed by the reception she received. There were tears in her eyes as she finished her set; she appeared feverish. More than her talent had been validated. Barbra Streisand had just discovered her power over an audience.

"I knew that this was a STAR! It was all there," Phyllis Diller, who had the top billing that night, emphasized. "On her third note, every hair stood up all over my body. . . . She was a disciplined, devoted worker, a brilliant genius — and she was a child!"

When Diana came to see her on the second night, Barbra had changed her first outfit for a white lace Victorian morning coat and pink satin shoes from the 1920s. Diana was horrified, certain that her daughter was singing in her nightgown. To Barbra, the outfit was beautiful. "A few days later I realized people were talking about this girl who sings in these weird clothes. They thought it was a gimmick, so I went back to the thrift shop. . . . I used to get lovely dresses at resale shops where rich ladies got rid of their stuff. What's to be ashamed of? Those ladies were clean. . . . Then Phyllis Diller said, 'You can't wear that stuff,' and took me shopping for a [contemporary] cocktail dress, and I actually put on

---

*A future reviewer would write that "Who's Afraid of the Big Bad Wolf?" is "the same song that children sing. But in her version, it seemed new, tripping perilously along the edge of probability, its innocence in doubt [in the dark room] which had suddenly become the dripping jaws of some unruly canine." *Time*, April 10, 1964.

one. I didn't want to make her feel bad, but I could never wear it again. It wasn't me."

Diana admitted feeling a thrill with her daughter's auspicious reception. She recognized, perhaps for the first time, the enormity of Barbra's talent. She was proud and not hesitant in telling Shelley, who had accompanied her, that she didn't know Barbra could sing so well. Yet, when Diana greeted her later, she could only criticize what her daughter had worn. "Did you like the way I sang, Mama?" Streisand finally asked.

"Yeah, you did good," Diana conceded.

The two women were unable to break their pattern. Diana would always find one thing that she disapproved of, Streisand would continue to seek her mother's approval and feel abused when she did not wholly receive it. Despite her ongoing conflict with her mother, with her twice-nightly engagement at the Bon Soir, her confidence grew. She sang five songs in her set; when people would ask afterward if they could buy her a drink, she would order a baked potato with "hard crust and lots of butter."

"At the Bon Soir I got special satisfaction out of performing," Streisand said. "Well, in life I felt, you know, people paid no attention to me. When I would talk, it came out so enthusiastically that they would disregard it. All of a sudden, singing, I could say what I felt and I was listened to."

She battled to overcome nightly sieges of stage fright before she performed. The cabaret's regulars were a boisterous group, a mix of gays who packed the bar to "shop" for a pickup and high-toned, uptown nightclub habitués who came to Village boîtes to listen to new talent with an arrogant "show me" attitude. When a performer did "show them," they could be fervent in their response. They could also be tough, daunting, and clangorous.

"What do I do?" Streisand asked Dennen backstage one difficult night when a group in the audience seemed determined to continue laughing and talking during the act that preceded her. "They're making a lot of noise."

"Stare them down," Dennen told her. "Stand there and think, 'Shut up! Listen to *me!* Look at *me!*'"

She went out front. The room was clouded with smoke and, except for one light over the cash register, in total blackness. Peter Daniels began the introduction to "A Sleepin' Bee." Conversation whirred, laughter trilled and cackled. Streisand stood there while Daniels repeated the introduction. This happened twice before someone could be heard saying, "Shh! Shhh!" and she started to sing.

After a few performances, she grew easier and would talk to the audience between songs — not much, just to introduce her musicians. "Weighing in at one hundred eighty-three pounds in black trunks . . . ," she would say in the seductive Mae West voice that Dennen had always thought was so funny. Before the end of her engagement a distinct group of devotees began to form. The word had gotten around. There was this odd-looking creature, clearly a misfit, who sang "songs of unrequited love or the sudden, surprise discovery of romance" in an inimitable voice. Her choice of material was unexpected, and there was simply no one else around who sounded or looked like her. Still, her first reviews were not all raves.

"At the Bon Soir, Barbra Streisand, singer — file and forget," wrote Roger Whitaker in the *New Yorker.*

"That old fart! What does he know?" she snapped defiantly to Dennen, adding that there was standing room only in both the table section and the gay bar at the back of the room for her twice-nightly performances.

"She would just *do* things that you had never heard anybody ever do," one regular remembered. "She was a hurricane of a certain kind of unbridled passion. She would just hold notes until she would turn blue. And she would just gasp at the end of words, you know, like *uuuhhh!* There was always a sort of edge, the sense that she was giving you so much more than you deserved, as opposed to Liza Minnelli who was just begging you to love her. Streisand never did that . . ."

The Bon Soir raised her salary to $125 a week and extended her engagement for eleven weeks. Streisand was determined to use the time to improve her performance. Her lifelong obsession with perfection in whatever she did had begun in earnest, along with the dedicated work ethic she had inherited from her father. During the first two weeks

Dennen brought in his tape recorder and fastidiously taped her act. Later they would go over every number and change phrasing, the position of certain songs, the backup sound. When he left to visit his family in California, he delegated Bob Schulenberg to look after her, issuing as a final instruction that she was never to call him there because he had not yet discussed their situation with his parents.

Streisand was injured by his dictatorial manner but agreed to his terms. "He really cares about me," she told Schulenberg. "He'll tell his parents about us in his own time."

"There was a certain date when Barry was coming back," Schulenberg recalled. "That night Barbra got all the things he loved to eat and we set up a beautiful table with a floral arrangement. We even had champagne in the refrigerator. We went to the Bon Soir and left him a note saying, 'Eat up, we'll be back after the show.' We ran back and he was not there. Barbra was really upset. She wondered if he'd missed the plane, but she couldn't call his family. . . . We sat up until about three in the morning but Barry didn't call."

The next night they went through the same procedure, and when they returned to the apartment, Dennen had still not returned. Days passed without any word from Dennen. She was at turns anxious, tearful, and furious. "After a week," Schulenberg continued, "I think Barbra ate up all her emotion for Barry. Finally he came back and she was very cool. . . . She just said, 'Hi, how was your trip? Is your family well? Great! [And by the way] I'm still singing at the Bon Soir.'"

She remained at Dennen's apartment, controlling her anger and her growing hostility to him. The flame was gone, and she blamed him. He had humiliated and rejected her. In a short time she would manage to obliterate all conscious awareness of his great contribution to her development as a performer and hang on to the injury she believed she had suffered at his hands. She could not let go completely, because in truth she still needed Dennen's direction, but she began to rely more on Daniels, who had helped her to have a growing respect for her own taste, perhaps shaped by both Dennen and Daniels but, nonetheless, a reflection of herself.

Before her eleven-week engagement at the Bon Soir ended, she agreed to be represented by Ted Rozar, a talent agent who had gone backstage after hearing her sing and had told her he wanted to be her manager. The arrangement lasted only a few weeks.

"They never hit it off," Schulenberg explained. "I saw him sometime later when they had parted company and he told me that 'my little friend' would never make it because she thought she was hot stuff but was too undisciplined for big-time show business."

She then tried to find another agent, without much luck at first. "They were very short-sighted," said Irvin Arthur, who booked acts at Associated Booking Corporation at the time. "Her appearance kind of turned them off. But I had no doubt at all that she was going to be a star." He had come down to hear her sing at the Bon Soir and then took her to a nearby coffee shop.

"I hired my first agent because he took me out for dinner. I could be bought for an avocado," she later joked.

Every night about midnight she called to ask what he had lined up for her the next day — an intrusion into his home life that wasn't appreciated by Mrs. Arthur.

"So, who's this dame who's calling you every night?" his wife would ask him.

He would reply, "Just a *star*."

Barbra finally moved out of Dennen's apartment after a serious argument over the tapes he had made of her voice, rehearsals, and performances — dozens of them over the six months they had been together. She wanted the master tapes, and Dennen refused. Streisand felt they belonged to her — they were of her voice. Dennen disagreed. He had initiated, directed, and recorded the tapes. Neither would give in, and there was a bitter, unpleasant parting. "The tapes were like children in a divorce," Dennen said. "They represented a lot of things. We broke up as lovers who both felt hurt and misunderstood."*

---

*Dennen never sent Streisand the controversial tapes. In 1994 Marty Erlichman approached Dennen about the possibility of including a number from the tapes in Streisand's *Just for the Record . . .* album. "He never followed up," Dennen told me. "Consequently, I never played them for him."

Streisand had nowhere to go and very little money. Packing what she had collected during her time with Dennen in boxes and shopping bags, along with a folding cot she acquired, she moved from one nightly "safe haven" to another, refusing to go home to Diana and Brooklyn. She would spend a night or so with Schulenberg, on the couch at Peter Daniels's apartment, at Irvin Arthur's office, with the Millers — anywhere she could hang her hat. Her calls to Arthur became more intense, and he was relieved to inform her that he had arranged a tour from March to April, 1961. The salary was $250 a week, out of which she had to pay her own road expenses, which would eat up almost the entire amount. But she would be seen, accumulate reviews, and perhaps interest a record company; so she agreed.

Before she left, Shelley took her to lunch. "I made her walk three feet behind me because of her clothes [she was wearing one of her more colorful outfits]," he vividly remembered. "People stared at her. She had these horrible rips in the back of her stockings. I offered to buy her a new pair. She said, 'They're not ripped in front and I don't see them in back, so they don't bother me,' and refused to change them." Shelley, who had recently married, remained as close to her as she would let him. He was in constant touch with Diana, and Streisand did not want things she might say to Shelley to get back to their mother. But he was still her big brother, the only immediate male relative she had, and there was a genuine fondness between them.

The tour would take her by train to Detroit, Cleveland, and Saint Louis, among other cities. "She was half exhilarated, half scared," Schulenberg recalled. "It was to be her first time out of New York. Finally [the day she was to leave] we packed her bags into a taxi and rode to the train station. Suddenly she asked if she could stop the taxi to get something at a drugstore. . . . She was late and I knew she would miss the train if we stopped, so I asked her point-blank what it was she *had* to get. She blurted out, 'Do you think they have toothpaste in Detroit?'" exposing her fear of the unknown she faced, perhaps hoping to delay or postpone it.

Once in Detroit and wanting to make herself seem more interesting, she developed an exotic story to tell the press: she was born in Turkey. The local newspaper hailed her as "the Turkish-born, Brooklyn-raised songstress in a big hurry, with a totally untrained but remarkably true voice."

An appearance on one of the popular television talk shows, she believed, would speed up her ascent to heady stardom, so she began to call and haunt the various program bookers. "I said no to Barbra Streisand," bragged Bob Shanks, a talent coordinator for the *Jack Paar Tonight Show,** which aired nationally every weeknight. Streisand refused to accept his negative response and kept calling. "Everybody in the business says you're so sensitive and understanding about talent that I've got to talk to you," she told him. "I need your advice."

She then explained in a most dramatic fashion that her mother was gravely ill in Cleveland and anxious for her to return home to marry a childhood sweetheart, whom she did not love. "If you could give me only one chance so that she could see me on *The Tonight Show,* it would keep me here and launch my career," she begged in such a poignant manner that Shanks was taken in.

"Paar [who thought she was too overtly Jewish in looks and manner] didn't think she was right for his show," Shanks said. But as fate would have it, Orson Bean — who had seen her at the Bon Soir and been overwhelmed by her talent — was to take over as guest host for Paar on April 5 and agreed with Shanks's suggestion to book her. She interrupted her engagement in Detroit and flew — half terrified, she had never been on a plane before — to New York to appear on her first national television show. Phyllis Diller was also on the program. Looking fresh and young in a short, slim black dress with spaghetti shoulder straps — an outfit counseled by Schulenberg, who told her that *simple* and *elegant* were also attention grabbers — Streisand sang "A Sleepin' Bee" and then somewhat nervously walked over to sit down between Diller and Bean.

"This is so exciting," she beamed, wide-eyed, her modish dress hiked

---

*Successive hosts have been Steve Allen, Johnny Carson, and Jay Leno. *The Tonight Show,* which is still on the air, is the longest-running talk show in the United States.

several inches above the knees of her curvaceous crossed legs. "All these people and cameras and lights and *people!*" She came off as this naive, natural Brooklyn kook, and the audience loved her.

Her television debut bolstered her self-confidence. She felt natural performing before the camera and not having to concern herself with a judgmental cabaret audience. This eased her tension, and she talked glibly, sounding a bit oddball, but very likeable. She was, in effect, playing herself. This allowed her to capitalize on only the parts of her personality that she thought would create an interesting character, and she was right.

Immediately after *The Tonight Show,* she flew back to Detroit and then went on to Saint Louis, from where she wrote Barry Dennen a business-like letter asking him to send her the guitar chords he had arranged for "A Taste of Honey." She added that maybe he could come up with a substitute for "Lover, Come Back to Me" as the closing number of her act.

He answered her request and suggested "Cry Me a River," a plaintive song that Julie London had successfully recorded. She returned to New York with tapes of the local radio shows on which she had appeared during her tour. "We went over them as we had at an earlier time," Dennen said. "I told her how to improve her performance, what songs to include in her repertoire: they were basically the ones she would later do on her first album. In May 1961 she came to my apartment one afternoon and we recorded 'A Taste of Honey.'" The reunion was not an easy one. "We both felt bitter, misused, sad," Dennen said. The love affair was over. They saw each other occasionally over the next few months, the meetings initiated by Streisand, who continued to seek his advice on musical arrangements. Then she simply stopped calling.

"Barbra loved Barry, but it was much more than that," Schulenberg insists. "She respected him as a teacher, a driving force. When it didn't work out between them, she was terribly hurt. She reacted by refusing to take advice from anyone."

She appeared again at the Bon Soir shortly after her tour, including "Cry Me a River" in her act, twisting the original concept of "a repentant lover who had come back for a second chance" into a story about a once-scorned woman demanding tears of loss from the man who had involved her in a hurtful relationship. "When I sang that," she admitted later, "I was thinking of one particular person; I tried to recreate in my mind the details of his face." Barry Dennen.*

Unquestionably, Streisand owed a great deal to Dennen, but she was also driven to succeed. No doubt she would have landed on top without Dennen's coaching. Nonetheless, he helped speed her progress. Once her metamorphosis had occurred, she no longer needed him, and she did not treat him kindly in the future when they happened to meet. "When she's done with you, she's done with you," another close associate observed. "When her need for you is over, so is the relationship."

Although she expected otherwise, neither the tour nor her one appearance on national television catapulted her to stardom. She was nervous, anxious, once more insecure. What had happened? What had she done wrong? Why hadn't she been offered a recording contract, a Broadway show, a screen test? "Here I am! Look at me!" had been her attitude. Each day that passed without something spectacular happening in her career seemed a rejection. She suffered mood swings, ate compulsively, and *still* lost weight. She did, however, undertake a three-week, highly successful return engagement at the Bon Soir, which counteracted some of her depression. But she was broke.

"Usually at the end of an engagement," Tiger Haynes mused, "the performers gave the musicians a gift. I got tons of cuff links and cigarette lighters from [other acts]. Streisand was so poor that she gave each of us a package of cheese in little wedges. Stamped in purple on the back was the price — ninety-nine cents." But to Streisand giving food was giving love, and it would remain one of her favorite gifts for many years.

With no immediate work in sight and refusing to return to Brooklyn, she once again dragged her portable army cot around, from a cousin's sublet for a night or two to one acquaintance's pad to another. Diana

*Eight years later she told a *Life* reporter, "The song no longer works for me as well, mostly because I don't feel that way about that person anymore."

would call Shelley frantically when she could not locate her. "Do something, Shelley! Do something!" she would scream.

"I never questioned Barbra," he said. "I admired her spunk; I thought she should be left alone, she should be allowed to do what she wanted."

Although she had no money, she did have a new manager, Marty Erlichman, a dark, husky man, about a decade her senior. Erlichman, raised in a predominantly Jewish section of the Bronx, was a determined, outspoken man who exuded sincerity and knew how to win over people's trust. Like Irvin Arthur, he had come backstage to meet Streisand after her show at the Bon Soir. Did she have representation? he asked. Yeah, she replied, she did. He gave her a card with a telephone number at which he could be reached and told her to call him if one day she thought she might like to make a change. She liked the way he looked her straight in the eye, direct. "Yuh got many people you represent?" she asked.

"You'd make it two," he replied honestly, his one other client at the time being the Clancy Brothers, an Irish folksinging group.

Unhappy with the financial arrangements made by Arthur for the second tour, she telephoned Erlichman from Detroit. "You still want to represent me?" she asked. He flew at his own expense to her side and renegotiated the last two weeks of her contract, getting her free meals along with a twenty-five-dollar-a-week raise. What Streisand did not know was that Erlichman paid the extra money out of his own pocket, secure that he would find her a high-paying club date or a role in a Broadway show on her return to New York. But even Erlichman's fired-up enthusiasm did not land her a job right away.

"I was pretty hard to reach in those days because I didn't have a phone," Streisand later recalled. "Neither did my manager, Marty Erlichman. . . . All he had was a roll of dimes and a phone booth on Fifty-third Street. He really believed in me, because he sure went through a lot of change."

She still was living like a vagabond, without an apartment of her own. "I can't stand it when I read in [a book] that someone has said she was *dirty,* which is so much the opposite of the truth," Schulenberg said angrily. "She always had beautiful nail care, her hair was clean, and so was she! I remember a whole evening with her when she was occupying [her friend] Don Goftness's office for the night and had to be out before the cleaning crew arrived in the morning — a whole evening she spent steaming and carefully wrapping her clothes in tissue paper — just like every teenager, right?"

She would put all the clothes she did not need in boxes and store them in the apartments of friends, along with treasured items collected while living with Barry Dennen. "When Barbra left an accommodation she had borrowed for a night or two," a former host declares, "it didn't even *need* a cleaning crew. She was immaculate and always left charming little thank-you notes. If this had not been the case, people would not have been so willing to put her up."

She never gave up auditioning for the theater and was eventually offered a part in an off-Broadway revue, *Another Evening with Harry Stoones,* with music and lyrics by Jeff Harris. The title was a takeoff on the proliferation at that time of recent solo-star Broadway appearances such as *An Evening with Marlene Dietrich,* but the revue has no character named Harry Stoones. The title was a gimmick, meant as a satirical comment. The show opened on October 21, 1961, at the Gramercy Arts Theatre, a small house that did not even have a marquee. In the cast were two other newcomers, Dom DeLuise and Diana Sands. Streisand contributed her own short and highly imaginative biographical notes for the playbill.

"I wrote that I was born in Madagascar and reared in Rangoon, and attended the yeshiva in Brooklyn," she later said. "I didn't want people to read, 'Streisand, Brooklyn, yeshiva,' and say to themselves, 'Oh yes, I see who she is.'" She was required to do a great deal of ensemble work, which she did not feel was right for her. By the end of rehearsals, she had two solos, "Jersey" and "Value" (also known as "I'm in Love with Harold Mengert"). She bombarded the director, G. Adam Jordan, with complaints: the lighting was wrong, the costumes cheesy, the orchestrations too thin. She turned to Peter Daniels for help, with pleas of "I'm trapped, I'm trapped," and he arranged the music on her solos. She felt that it was important for New York audiences and critics to see her as more than a cabaret singer.

Another Evening with Harry Stoones closed after its opening night, but it gave her a taste of appearing in theater, which she liked. Next time, she told Erlichman, she wanted to move uptown to Broadway and do a full-scale, well-financed musical. Meanwhile, as she was in between engagements at the Bon Soir, she agreed with him that it was important for her to continue to be visible. She made a series of television talk show guest appearances on the late-night theatrically oriented *Joe Franklin Show* and then was asked to audition for the low-budgeted *PM East,* hosted by Mike Wallace, which "generally had to scrape pretty close to barrel bottom when it came to booking talent."

Preinterviews were conducted with the show's lesser-known guests. "I remember [Barbra] was calling from a bar because not only did she not have a phone but she had no apartment," said Al Ramus, one of *PM East*'s writer-producers.

"When I find a place that's not being used or that has extra room, I go there," she told him. "I carry around a bunch of keys my friends gave me so I can get in anywhere. I don't make much money singing in little places but I have a typical Jewish mother. She waits outside wherever I'm singing till one or two in the morning with frozen steaks" — an apocryphal story. Diana did bring containers of chicken soup to the Bon Soir but came backstage to give them to her. Streisand went on to tell him a fanciful story about her father: He was a genius who had traveled around the country, a wanderer on a bicycle. As a teenager Manny Streisand had hitchhiked through New Jersey and Pennsylvania one summer and for a brief time had delivered telegrams on a bicycle.

"The voice was pure Brooklyn . . . full of *chutzpah.* . . . But there was something about her, even over the phone, that was unique. She was like the *essence* of every confused, not-very-attractive girl who wanted extravagantly more out of life than birth or circumstances could possibly give her. Her voice, her life-style, were almost fictional, they were also so right for the role that I told her — by now it must've been past 1 A.M.— that whether she could sing or not she was going to be a star." Ramus also arranged for her to audition the next day for the show at the Dumont Studios in midtown Manhattan.

She arrived about twenty minutes late, clutching her music and shedding her coat on the floor as she hurried across the empty, unlighted stage. "Hey," she yelled to the lighting man. "Over here! Yeah!" She grabbed a stool and sat on it, her back broomstick-straight, her legs gracefully posed, her head raised to catch the spot when it flashed on. Her voice soared as she sang "A Sleepin' Bee" to a rehearsal pianist's accompaniment.

"[What happened] sounds like a bad Twentieth Century-Fox musical," Ramus commented, "but virtually everyone on the set, sound men, lighting men, secretaries . . . they all stopped and listened. The night before, I told her she'd be a star. Now I was sure of it."

PM East had no studio audience (applause came from the technicians), and it was videotaped, both helpful in making a neophyte television performer feel relaxed. However, the show was built around a theme, which for this particular program was glamour. Two ravishing models who also happened to be sisters, Theodora and Suzy Parker, were to be guests along with model agent Candy Jones and photographer Milton Greene, famous for his pictures of Marilyn Monroe. "Those models were dressed to kill," Streisand later recalled. "Every hair in place as if they'd been carried on a stretcher from the beauty salon to the Dumont studios."

Wearing a sleeveless black dress, with a large silver Indian thunderbird pin, her hair piled up in a beehive topped by her "Danish pastry" postiche, she sang "A Sleepin' Bee" seated on a stool and then climbed onto the top of the piano, legs crossed, skirt hiked so that her thigh was seductively visible, and gave a scorching up-tempo rendition of "Lover, Come Back to Me."

Then she sat down and talked in nasal Brooklynese to Wallace and his guests about her vagabond lifestyle. She was funny, far-out, unabashed — and an instant hit. Wallace, a charismatic personality who would go on to become American television's most outspoken and highest-rated interviewer on *60 Minutes,* knew he had found a rating-booster and booked Barbra over a dozen times during the next few months. And he was right. Ratings went up as "this kook on t.v. with the knock-out voice" became more and more outrageous each week.

"The part I liked best [about appearing on the show]," Streisand said, "was the talk segment. They never knew what I was going to say. Although sometimes I would suggest a topic — like nutrition, Zen Buddhism, or the business about my key ring."

One evening it would be the evils of drinking milk, which drew an angry response from the National Dairy Council; another night she infuriated volatile television producer David Susskind, a guest on the show, by confronting him with a story about the time she had come into his office for an audition and he kept her waiting for hours and then didn't see her. "People like you are ruining show business because you don't let new talent emerge, you think it's your duty to squelch them." Susskind was stunned and seemed unable to reply to her. "I scare you, don't I?" she smirked. "I'm so far-out, I'm in."

The attack on Susskind, who was fairly powerful in the entertainment world, was bold and foolhardy at the same time. It was not likely that he would want to hire Streisand for one of his productions after this assault, but she was getting to enjoy the power such confrontations on live television gave her. When host Mike Wallace told her his show could help her be seen by Broadway producers, she snapped, "Now, let's be honest. Those people don't watch television, not the ones that do the hiring. A show like this gets the public interested in paying the minimum to see me at places like the Bon Soir."

After completing her appearances on *PM East,* she accepted a club tour to New Orleans, Miami, and Chicago, this time with a considerable pay hike that enabled her to put some money aside. When she returned, she began yet another engagement at the Bon Soir. One night Michael Shurtleff, who worked as a casting director for the powerful Broadway producer David Merrick, visited the club. Merrick, the producer of such stage hits as *Fanny, Gypsy, Do Re Me, Carnival,* and *Irma La Douce,* was in preproduction of the show *I Can Get It for You Wholesale,* based on the 1937 bestseller by Jerome Weidman about the New York Garment District. A minor role in the original script was that of a fifty-year-old Jewish secretary. The character had been given one song about her psychosomatic abhorrence to the drab appellation with which she was continually addressed, "Miss Marmelstein," but the character and the number had been cut. When Shurtleff heard Streisand sing at the Bon Soir, he was determined to give her an audition; he hoped that when Merrick heard her, he would reinstate the song, which Shurtleff greatly liked — with Streisand singing it.

There was one hitch. Merrick liked only beautiful women in his shows. Shurtleff took a hard look at Streisand and knew it might be difficult to convince "the abominable showman," as Merrick was called by his many detractors, to make an exception this time. No less pushy than the lady he wanted to sell to his boss, Shurtleff had made up his mind the previous year that he would work for Merrick, writing him once a week for seven months to discuss what was good and bad with each of Merrick's many former Broadway shows. Next, he had mutual friends write to the producer to plead his case. Finally, piqued by curiosity, Merrick agreed to see the offensive letter writer. Shurtleff kept the meeting going for four hours and ended up with a job as casting director.

Streisand's audition was scheduled by Shurtleff for late the next afternoon, a chilly day in November 1961, to follow several other singers trying out for minor roles. He hoped that as the final auditioner of the day, Barbra would so outshine her predecessors with her extraordinary voice that Merrick would not say — as he had so often before —"Too ugly."

That morning she had moved into her first apartment, three rooms over Oscars, a fish restaurant in the Sixties on the Upper East Side and, in her words, was "excited and *furtumphed*." She dashed out on the stage of the St. James Theatre on West Forty-fourth Street, where the auditions were being held, just as the final singer turned to leave. "Hey, I'm sorry," she said, staring at her unseen audience beyond the blinding footlights of the stage. "On the way over, I saw some things in a thrift-shop window on Second Avenue near where I just rented my first apartment and I just had to go in and buy them — to celebrate, you know?" She did a model's turn to show off the forty-year-old amazingly stylish raccoon coat that she was wearing along with an unidentifiable-fur commissar's hat that was perched precariously on top her beehive hairdo.

"Do you like it?" she asked. When there was no reply, she stepped forward as far as she could without falling into the orchestra pit. The glare of the footlights made it difficult for her to see out into the otherwise vast, darkened 1,600-seat auditorium, and she cupped her hands above her eyes attempting to see better. "Is there anyone out there?" she asked in a thick Brooklyn twang.

"Is this girl sane?" Merrick asked Shurtleff, who was seated next to his boss about midway up the center aisle of the orchestra section.

"No," Shurtleff replied.

"Then, why are you putting us through this?" Merrick barked.

"Miss Streisand, would you sing?" Shurtleff called out.

She glanced uncomfortably around. Behind her was the backdrop, a New York skyline from Merrick's current musical offering, *Subways Are for Sleeping*.

"I had never seen her until she walked onto the stage for the audition," *Wholesale*'s director, Arthur Laurents, said. "She had on what I call her 'calculated' look. Her thrift-shop look. She looked like an antique. And she did something right at the beginning that impressed me. I hadn't seen this done before — or since. She had the pages of her music taped together. She put it on the piano stage right, an upright piano. And then, with a flourish, flipped it like an accordion onto and across the stage. A great trick. And I thought, 'She knows what she's doing.'"

She glanced at the music spread out in front of her, unsure which of the three songs she had brought with her would be the most appropriate. Apart from Merrick, Shurtleff, and Laurents, the small, select audience that she could not see included among others: Herbert Ross, the choreographer; Jerome Weidman, the author/playwright; and one of Hollywood and Broadway's most successful composer/lyricists, Harold Rome, who leaned forward and asked, "Have you got an 'up song' you can sing?"

"If I didn't have an 'up song,' would I be auditioning for a musical?" she replied.

Merrick bristled.

"I can't sing without a stool," she complained. A stool was found and placed before the microphone. She removed her coat. "Someone could maybe hold this while I sing?" she called out, looking around her. A stagehand took it from her. Merrick was about to walk. Shurtleff placed a restraining hand on his arm.

She shuffled through her music, picked it up, and then conferred in a whispery voice with the rehearsal pianist.

"We're waiting, Miss Streisand," Merrick yelled out.

"I'm coming! I'm coming!" she shouted back and lifted herself onto the stool.

She sang "Value." There was no response from the darkened theater. She started across the stage to reclaim her coat. "Could you sing a ballad for us?" Rome shouted.

"Sure, sure," she said and came back to the piano. A few moments later she was reseated on the stool and sang the lovely, lyrical "(Have I Stayed) Too Long at the Fair" by Billy Barnes. Again there was no response other than some mumbling among her unseen audience. "Well, did you like it or not?" she asked into the microphone.

"We liked it. But we need to be convinced," Rome replied.

The third song she had brought with her was her favorite audition piece, "A Sleepin' Bee." "When she sang that song," Laurents said, "I didn't care about anything else. I had never heard anyone sing like that. I just kept her singing. And it was extraordinary. Now there was no part for her in the show at the time. At nineteen what one looks like depends on fashion. She was unattractive — and emphasized it, making herself look deliberately gawky. I think she sort of invented a character for that audition — this loose-limbed girl out of the woodwork. [I was so taken with her,] I said to the authors, 'Why does Miss Marmelstein have to be fifty? Why do we have to say her age?'"

"I sang," Streisand later remembered, "and then I sort of ran around the stage yelling my phone number and saying, 'Wow! Will somebody call me, please! Even if I don't get the part, just call!' I yelled out the number and then repeated it. I'd gotten my first phone that day, and I was wild to get calls on it." She was also admittedly excited and nervous over auditioning for a role in a major Broadway show.

She folded up her music and headed into the wings. Merrick turned sharply to Shurtleff and complained, "How many times have I told you I don't want ugly girls in my shows?"

"You can get her for scale," Harold Rome intervened, thinking much as Laurents had and hoping that he could reintroduce "Miss Marmelstein" into the score.

"You're the most anti-Semitic guy I know," Merrick countered. "You've hired every ugly Jew in town for this show, and now you want me to hire this *meeskite.*"

Finally, in view of the zeal of the show's creators, Merrick agreed to give her a chance *if* Miss Marmelstein was reinstated. She was asked to come back onto the stage, where Shurtleff introduced her to Merrick, Laurents, Ross, Rome, and Weidman. She was given the music to "Miss Marmelstein" and told to return for a second audition in a few hours. She immediately called Peter Daniels, dashed over to a new small studio he had on West Fifty-seventh Street, and ran through the number a few times. Although she did not read music, she had the ability to hear a song once and record the music in her head. She also possessed the gift of perfect pitch.

"When I returned to the theater that afternoon," she recalled, "I wanted to sing the number sitting down for two reasons. One — because I was nervous, and two — because I thought it would be funny to have a secretary moving her chair around the stage with her legs, like a wall-flower on wheels. So I sat down, took my gum out of my mouth, stuck it under the chair, and sang."

Arthur Laurents claims that there was never a secretary's chair on the stage for the audition and that Streisand sang "Miss Marmelstein" on an ordinary chair. "After the audition was over and she had left, I had my assistant check the bottom of the chair: there was no gum," Laurents insists. That night Laurents went down to the Bon Soir and after her performance told her that she was hired. The next day she signed a contract for $165 a week on conditional terms, which gave Merrick the right to fire her with a week's notice.

Slouched in the back of the darkened theater on the cold November day of Streisand's audition, Elliott Gould, the young man just cast as the romantic lead, was fascinated by "this strange-looking, skinny creature with long, spiky hair, spidery hands, two-inch nails and purple lipstick."

"A freak — a fantastic freak!" Gould thought at the time. That evening before she left for her stint at the Bon Soir, he telephoned her. "You said you wanted to get calls, so I called," he said. "You were brilliant." Then he hung up.

Part III

Broadway Baby

"She was the most innocent thing I'd ever seen, like a beautiful flower that hadn't blossomed yet. But she was so strange that I was afraid."

Elliott Gould, 1970

9

Barbra Streisand had made it to Broadway at the age of nineteen. Her initiation was not going to be easy. Almost the entire company of *I Can Get It for You Wholesale* were seasoned performers. It is the story of a brash, opportunistic young Jew, Harry Bogen (Elliott), who uses a strike in the firm of Maurice Pulverman (Jack Kruschen) to his own advantage. Miss Marmelstein is Pulverman's secretary. Except for Kruschen, who had been an Oscar nominee for best supporting actor the previous year for his role in Billy Wilder's *The Apartment,* most of the other cast members were counting on this show to mark either their rise to stardom or their comeback.* It was an intense, make-or-break situation not ameliorated by the tough treatment Streisand met at the hands of her producer and director.

Kruschen, a bear of a man always younger than the roles he played, felt "bad for Barbra. She had poise. But she didn't have the worldliness to know how to handle some of David Merrick's or Arthur Laurents's brusque, hard knocks. One morning during rehearsals she arrived a little

---

*In the other main roles were Sheree North (femme fatale in the show), old-timer Lillian Roth (as Bogen's mother), Harold Lang (star of the 1952 revival of *Pal Joey* about another twenty-four-karat heel), Bambi Linn (who had made her debut sixteen years earlier in Rodgers and Hammerstein's *Carousel*), and Marilyn Cooper (as the ingenue lead).

late. She liked to shop at places like the Goodwill, and she was wearing this 1920s diaphanous kind of day dress — foamy, filmy — kind of odd. Arthur, fresh from his success as the librettist of *West Side Story* and *Gypsy,* told her to go change her clothes." (Laurents denies that this ever occurred. But Kruschen stands by his recollection of the incident.)

"I thought she was going to cry. He had chosen to tell her this in front of the entire company. There was nothing she could have done but go home and change her clothes. And he said, 'I don't care what you put on, but don't put on stuff like this and don't come to work like this again.' I felt, how dare he. His rough treatment of her endeared her to me. She knew very little about the stage. Sometimes she'd hit a mark [where she was supposed to stand on stage] and sometimes she wouldn't. That caused problems for the rest of the cast. As Spencer Tracy once told some young performers, 'Learn your lines and, for God's sake, don't bump into each other.'"

Arthur Laurents said, "I was tough on Barbra because she wanted to do what she wanted to do, and as director I couldn't have that. I can remember one time I staged a scene so that when a character entered, everyone had to turn their backs on him, he was ostracized, but she didn't. She said she didn't feel like it. She didn't realize that unless you're [a monologist], you cannot play alone. You have an obligation. You have to be there for your fellow actors. A musical has to be carefully blocked. You can't decide suddenly to go here or there."

Laurents was firm with her, but he also recognized her potential and was one of her staunchest enthusiasts. "Shortly after her audition for the show, I sent her to Goddard Lieberson, then head of Columbia Records. She thanked me." He smiled with an appreciative look on his intelligent face. "Then I got a note from him: 'Thank you for sending me Barbra Streisand. Indeed, she has a spectacular voice, but she is too special for records.' I also dragged Stephen Sondheim down to the Bon Soir before the show opened. He didn't like the way she sang.* Then, at the time of

---

*Laurents wrote the book and Sondheim, the score for *Anyone Can Whistle*. They had also worked together on *West Side Story* (1957) and *Gypsy* (1959), for which Sondheim

Anyone Can Whistle, I sent her some of the songs and she didn't like his songs. [Much later she would have a change of heart.]

"I thought she had an extraordinary voice and was very talented as an actress, but she was really so inexperienced and more concerned with what she was doing with her *nails* than with the other players. I told her, 'When you cut your nails I'll know you really want to be an actress.'"

Laurents is, and was at that time, one of the American theater's finest playwrights as well as a director, and Streisand quickly recognized that there was much she could learn from him. "I began fattening her part because it was obvious that she was a phenomenal talent, which she knew and told us she was. She had no doubt she was going to be a star. It was not shared [by Merrick and others], I think because of what she looked like."

Elliott, on the other hand, thought she looked just dandy and was intrigued by her eclecticism. They did not actually meet until the first day of rehearsals, which she attended in a man's tattered black coat, circa 1930, that reached her ankles, the sleeves turned back so that her hands could show, a turn-of-the-century, black medical satchel bag serving as a purse. Outside, February winds blasted through the tunnel-like streets of New York, wintry blue-gray skyscrapers rising like steel traps on either side. Her face was red with cold. "She looked like a young Fagin," Elliott remembered. "She scared me, but I really dug her. I think I was the first person who ever did."

This, of course, was not true, but Elliott saw her with new romantic eyes. She was not a woman he wanted to change or a performer he wished to mold. He loved her kookiness, her naturalness, her hunger to devour food, people, new experiences. She was drawn to him almost immediately. He was distinctive but did not look like her idea of a leading man. Tall (six foot three), chunky, with dark bushy hair and ethnic features, his clothes — whether custom-tailored or ready-made — never

---

wrote only lyrics. Laurents's nonmusical plays include such dramas as *Home of the Brave, The Time of the Cuckoo, A Clearing in the Woods,* and *Invitation to a March.* He also wrote the screenplays for *The Snake Pit, Rope, Anastasia,* and *The Way We Were,* among many others.

quite fit. He managed to execute a dance with surprising expertise when required to, but he was constantly stumbling on- and offstage.

Born in 1938 and four years older than Barbra, he was the product of a frustrated, confused childhood with an overbearing mother, an overshadowed father, and all the tensions that go with being an only male child in a middle-class Jewish household. Until the age of eleven he had shared a small bedroom in a cramped two-and-a-half-room flat in the Bensonhurst section of Brooklyn with his parents, Lucille and Bernard Goldstein. Bernard was a bookkeeper in the Garment District. From an early age, Elliott recognized that his intrusion into Bernard's otherwise ordered life was resented.

Bensonhurst was Jewish and Italian and only a short distance from the slightly more affluent Flatbush area, where Streisand lived after her mother's marriage to Louis Kind. It was said that the slain bodies of infamous ex-members of Murder Inc. were buried near the school he attended, but neighbors looked after one another's kids, and the streets were kept reasonably safe.

"We'd play things like Ring-o-leevio, Three Feet to Germany, Johnny on the Pony," Gould recalled. "But I excelled at flipping trading cards bought by the fistful down at Irving's Candy Store. There were Smilin' Jack cards, baseball cards, World War II cards with General MacArthur and the bombing of Tokyo on them," he added fondly. He was, he insists, "terribly conscious of a degree of vulnerability, of not wanting to make a fool of myself. I didn't feel abnormal, but I certainly didn't feel normal."

Lucille's memories were sharper. "This child was too good to be true. He was too well-behaved. He wanted to please so desperately. I was too strict with him," she quickly admitted. "Yes, mama watched over him perhaps too closely. But it was done out of love. I wouldn't leave any stone unturned as far as this child went. I'd cut off my arm for this child." Alone with her somewhat bumbling son, when Bernard went off to fight in World War II, Lucille decided he must have drama, singing, and dancing lessons to help him gain self-confidence. She took him to Charlie Lowe's Broadway Show Business School for Children.

"He'll never dance," she firmly told Charlie. "Just fix up his diction and the way he walks." Instead, Charlie Lowe put Elliott through the regular routine that he taught.

"That meant everything," Elliott claimed. "Blow-your-nose lessons, dance lessons, wipe-yourself lessons, masturbation lessons, bunko. Compulsions for a dissatisfied mother. Why did I go? Because I loved my mother a lot. That's why I did it." Within a year Charlie Lowe had placed Elliott on local TV shows to sing and dance. As Elliott was about to go on camera for the first time, Lowe asked him if he would like to be announced as Gold, instead of Goldstein. Elliott said, "No, Gould," thinking of the well-known composer and orchestra leader Morton Gould.

He went on to Professional Children's School in Manhattan, and when his father returned from the war, the family would vacation each year in the Catskill borscht belt, where Elliott won dance contests doing the mambo with his mother.

"When an entertainer needed a stooge," his father remembered, "Elliott would be the one they'd choose. [At the age of fifteen] he could do a dozen dialects — German, Italian, Jewish, all of them." After he graduated from high school, Gould spent three weeks in summer stock. This was followed by a second lead in a pre-Broadway show at Woodstock, *Some Little Honor* (1955), which never made it into Manhattan.

"He was always doing bits," one friend added. "He would go into a diner, sit next to a little old lady and calmly make a meal out of his paper napkin — complete with salt, pepper, and ketchup. He also liked to knock on strangers' doors and inquire politely, 'Is this the party?' Or walk in one door of a Checker cab stopped in traffic and out the other, apologizing to the passenger as he made his exit."

In 1957, when he was eighteen, he won his first Broadway job, in the chorus line, by telephoning one of the producers, impersonating a well-known agent and selling the talents of "a kid named Elliott Gould." The show, *Rumple,* closed after forty-five performances — which was fortunate because he was plagued with bursitis from lifting the rather hefty chorines in the dance numbers. Despite this experience, he went on to dance in the chorus of the Jule Styne show *Say, Darling* (1958) and a revival of *Hit the Deck* at Jones Beach. Then came odd jobs, such as a speed-punching-bag demonstrator at Bloomingdale's and a toy salesman and elevator operator at both Gimbel's and Macy's.

A loner, not terribly popular with the girls, he began to place bets on the horses. By the time he was eighteen, he had run up debts he could not pay; he "borrowed" his father's jewelry to pawn and used the money to pay off the bookies. He also had the Goldstein's home telephone disconnected when hoods started calling to demand the rest of their payment. His parents were furious but, fearful he might end up in the East River with a cement block attached to his feet, helped him out of his predicament. Elliott was screaming out for attention, no matter how negative, and he gambled as many habitual bettors do — ultimately to lose because failure validates their theory that fate does not look well upon them, that they hold no responsibility for what has happened in their lives.

A job in the chorus of the David Merrick musical *Irma La Douce* in 1960 led to his being hired first as the understudy to the lead in *I Can Get It for You Wholesale,* which originally was to have featured British actor Lawrence Harvey. When Harvey backed out of his contract, the role went to the surprised Elliott. Open, friendly, funny, he was well liked by the members of the company, but it was Streisand to whom he paid the most attention. Once rehearsals began, he thought she was even more brilliant than he had first believed. He treated her deferentially and often spent the little free time he had, for he was in a large percentage of the show's scenes, listening to her practice.

"I used to hear her warm up," Jack Kruschen remembered. "She had the most beautiful vocal acrobatics . . . perfect pitch. She just blew my socks away the first time I heard her sing. Everyone in the cast was impressed. Arthur built one group number around her, and, of course, Barbra had the only solo in one [in front of the curtain], 'Miss Marmelstein.' She had her own ideas about how she wanted to sing it, and Arthur did not always agree with her. It was a running battle."

Streisand later confided to journalist Joe Morgenstern, "I spent weeks trying to convince Arthur to let me use my secretary's chair, which had a movable seat that you could twist and tilt. I was told, 'You've got no discipline, you can't do anything twice the same way.' They yelled at me because I didn't do the song with the same gestures each time I sang it. I kept asking for my chair. Finally Arthur said, 'All right, use your chair if you want to,' and when we opened in Philadelphia, I stopped the show. I can't tell you how I felt stopping that show. I felt *guilty*."

Laurents countered, "Nobody remembers the same thing. There are stories that start out an anecdote, then become columnists' grist, and then they become fact. It is curious to me how they creep and spread. A recent book on Barbra has several lies in it about *Wholesale*. In fact, the author told one lie three times. The basic lie is, I never staged 'Miss Marmelstein'; Herb Ross did."

This would imply that Streisand's fight for the moving chair was with Ross, not Laurents; but whoever her adversary, the struggle had not been in vain. She had managed to convert the solo number she had into a star turn that called attention to herself and away from the rest of the cast. And she had approximately four minutes of her own onstage in which to wheel and twirl her secretary's chair, contorting her legs and arms and never allowing any of this action to disrupt the flow and clarity of the comedic story she sang in thick Brooklynese. She gambled in a different way than Elliott did — with her talent, her creative ability, her driven ambition that pushed aside all other considerations. She played for higher stakes — her career, which was to say *her life*. And she knew how to gamble only one way — to win.

In November, shortly before her audition for *Wholesale,* Streisand had made an unexpected one-night appearance at the Blue Angel, an elite cabaret at 152 East Fifty-fifth Street. The front-room lounge wrapped you in a cloak of sophistication as soon as you walked into its gleaming black-and-white cocktail lounge with its black bar, booths, and patent-leather walls. The back room held the small stage — a plaster angel suspended over it — which was lit by a fixed spotlight; the room was decorated in a deep lush pink, with leather on the banquettes, fabric on the walls. The long, narrow room was difficult to play and yet it was a launching pad for top artists (Dorothy Louden, Carol Burnett, and Harry Belafonte had all sung there), a place where you came expressly to hear the entertainer. On the night Streisand first appeared, Felicia Saunders was the star performer, but there was also a comic. He got violently ill just before the show. Desperate for someone to fill in and recalling things he had heard about Streisand's being a funny lady, Herbert Jacoby, the co-owner, called her to come in for the single performance.

"Two singers were never billed on one show," Arthur Gelb of the *New York Times* said. "Jacoby must have thought Barbra was a comic. I was there to review Saunders and was overwhelmed when this strange-looking girl in a beaded dress took to the stage. Everyone was spell-bound. I went back to the paper and wrote about this great new talent. I think it was the first review she ever got in a major paper, and it brought her to the attention of a lot of people."

While *Wholesale* was in rehearsal, she went back to the Blue Angel as the headliner. The club's audience was far more conservative than the habitués of the Bon Soir. Frightening though it might have been to play to such an urbane group, Streisand liked being able to sing songs differently, to experiment. She sang an exquisite arrangement by Peter Daniels of the Harvey Schmidt / Tom Jones song from *The Fantasticks* "Soon It's Gonna Rain" and an upbeat rendition of Leonard Bernstein's seldom-performed "I Hate Music."

Her reviews were glowing, but a generally laudatory one in the show business bible, *Variety,* included an indelicate suggestion that she get a "schnoz bob." Erlichman was furious. "I couldn't believe that a guy like Abel Greene, the respected publisher of *Variety,* whose entire life had been devoted to the business, would use an expression like 'schnoz bob' for a nineteen-year-old girl," he said. "Against the advice of the press agent for the Blue Angel, who was worried about a possible backlash, I called Abel Greene and really yelled at him. 'Would you do that to your own daughter? You can say nose job or have the nose fixed, but where do you come off saying, 'schnoz bob'? It's vulgar and tasteless.' And he apologized to me." The remark, however phrased, was inappropriate in a review of a singer.

To compound this painful jibe, Radie Harris, a columnist for the *Hollywood Reporter,* described her as having, "mousey-colored hair which hung straight and looked unwashed, a nose that a plastic surgeon would have loved to use his scalpel on, and she wore a black blouse and skirt that looked as though they'd been bought in Klein's bargain basement." Unwittingly, she validated Diana's concern when she wrote near the conclusion of her review: "'Why would anyone who looks like that think she has a future in show business?' I thought, as she sat nervous and uneasy beside me." But she added, "And then she got up to sing, and I knew why. Barbra Streisand was suddenly beautiful."

For weeks Streisand talked about nothing but whether she should or should not have a nose job. "Can you become a new person with a new nose?" Elliott asked her. They were seeing quite a lot of each other. One night he took her to a horror movie about giant caterpillars that ate cars. Later they went to a Chinese restaurant. About 2 A.M. it began to snow.

"We were walking around the skating rink at Rockefeller Center when Elly chased me and we had a snow fight," she remembered. "He never held me around or anything, but he put snow on my face and kissed me, very lightly. It sounds *ookhy,* but it was great. Like out of a movie!"

A few weeks after the snow fight, she thought he was paying too much attention to Marilyn Cooper, the ingenue in the show, and refused to talk to him. That night he wandered the city and used up a pocketful of change telephoning her. Each time she hung up. Finally he went home to his small apartment on Morton Street in the Village. "About four A.M. my bell rings, and Barbra's standing there like a little orphan child, in her nightgown, some kind of crocheted thing over her shoulders, tears streaming her face. I wrapped her up in a warm coat and took her home but when we reached her building, which housed a fish restaurant on the ground floor, the hallway stunk so that I refused to go upstairs."

"I didn't care about the smell," Streisand once said. "For the first time in my life I had my own apartment." A connection might well be made with the fact that Manny Streisand had spent his early years in a flat over a fish market. Her father figured frequently in her conversations with Elliott and with Shelley. Her reverence for his reported intelligence and his ambition to make something of his life that might have taken him and his family out of Brooklyn had grown to mythic proportions. Living over a fish restaurant perhaps gave her a sense of familiarity with something he had experienced. The sixty-two-dollar-a-month rent was also cheaper than for most other apartments of its size and location, and one she could afford. Money was always a consideration. She did not mind sacrificing something others might think a necessity for what was important to her. As a youngster she had forfeited lunch to buy cosmetics. Now she endured the odor of fish so that she could have some extra money for the purchase of clothes, furniture, or items that caught her eye, and a telephone so that she did not have to hang around someone's office or a telephone booth to receive a call.

Although he kept the Morton Street apartment, Elliott managed to overcome his olfactory objections and was soon sharing the flat a good part of the time with her. "The only window looked out on a black brick wall," he recollected. "A big rat named Oscar [in dubious honor of the restaurant below] lived in the kitchen." They were very private about their relationship. At this point no one in the cast knew they were living together. Their combined income after taxes was modest (his salary in *Wholesale* was not much larger than hers). They entertained themselves on the cheap. Besides seeing horror movies, they played pokerino in penny arcades, saving up coupons from his winnings to supply their flat with dishes and glassware. She filled the apartment with scented candles and perfumed Chinese incense to overcome the odor of fish, but there was still the hallway to conquer. Elliott took the steps three at a time without breathing.

Diana did not know that her daughter and Elliott were cohabiting. She would come by the theater during rehearsals bringing large containers of chicken soup. "All those stories she tells about her mother," Laurents said, "it's odd because her mother was very much there. When she introduced me to Mrs. Kind, very fleetingly, it reminded me of Sandra Church when she was [starring] in *Gypsy*, introducing me to her mother, whose name was Rose [also the name of Gypsy's mother]. It seemed to me that they had a similar attitude, 'Well, here's Rose,' meaning — pushy, and the daughter wanted to dismiss the mother. It may be that what Barbra has said about her mother is true. But she did bring chicken soup, and it was very good and we all had it!"

She continued to experiment with ways to play Miss Marmelstein, attempting to get a deeper understanding of the character. She was all over the place, making a mess of Laurents's careful blocking. Then there was the matter of her chewing gum onstage.

"Get rid of it," she was told one day in rehearsal.

"Why?" she argued. "If you ask me, Yetta Marmelstein would've chewed gum in the office."

The business with the chewing gum was a leftover from her nightclub appearances, and she soon abandoned it. But she still had problems to overcome.

She had difficulty in ensemble playing and, except for her sensational delivery of "Miss Marmelstein," did not seem to get the right nuances of the character she had been cast to portray. She was playing for comedy, but in rehearsal and on the road, her timing seemed to be off.

Laurents recalled, "In Boston Merrick wanted her fired." He continued, "He felt she wasn't funny enough. And she wasn't. Audiences really didn't get her until we got to New York. She wasn't that successful on the road, and she was madly in love with Elliott, who Merrick also wanted to fire. He wasn't happy with Elliott. He wasn't attractive and he had an unfortunate problem. Elliott is a sweater. He sweat so much that when he did a dance scene, the sweat blew over the first three rows of the audience. Merrick had him call Dr. Miracle Max Jacobson [who was known to push drugs on many Hollywood and New York celebrities] to get something to stop it. Whatever he gave Elliott worked — but it closed his vocal chords, and he had to stop taking it.

"I never saw anything quite like it. She wanted Elliott and she got him. But they were sweet together, really sweet. Romeo and Juliet. Besides Elliott, her close friend in the show was Sheree North. She had been around [a bride at fifteen, mother at sixteen, married four times] and had been having a rough time [after being dropped by Twentieth Century-Fox in 1958]. But Barbra recognized that there was a real purity in Sheree North. Sheree was going through a very, very bad patch, and Barbra was good to her."

Sheree North was also the first movie star — albeit one on her uppers — with whom Streisand had ever had close contact. North had starred opposite Dan Dailey, Gordon MacRae, and Robert Cummings and once had been considered Betty Grable's replacement at the studio. Streisand bombarded her with questions about Hollywood — what it was like to be under contract to a studio, how pictures were made — and North, pleased to be asked, answered in detail. But Ellie Stone, who was Streisand's understudy, and several of the other female members of the cast say Streisand was cold and sometimes cruel to them. "She knew how to cut you down," one of them said, "make a stabbing remark about something you missed in your performance. She could use Sheree but she was a regular Eve [a reference to the overly ambitious character in the film *All About Eve*] with the other young women in the cast. You just knew she would go on half dead before she would let an understudy go on for her. I had the feeling she considered Marilyn Cooper her archenemy — maybe because of Elliott, but more likely because she had a larger role and was onstage more often."

Displaying amazing chutzpah, during rehearsals she went to Arthur Laurents and asked him to recast her in Marilyn Cooper's role. "I told her, 'It's better to steal the show than play that part.' It just shows you that Barbra's eye was on the brass ring all the time." The creative team were finding her abrasiveness and strong mind-set difficult to take. "I have dealt with revolting people all my life," Jerome Weidman, the author, was quoted as saying. "I began my career working in the Garment Center, after all. As far as I'm concerned she has not earned the right to act that way." He was referring to her continued lateness to rehearsals and her determination to play a scene her way. Even her champion Harold Rome found her cold and overbearingly self-absorbed.

But Elliott was smitten. They were always together. Both of them loved to shop. In Philadelphia, where the show was called anti-Semitic, they combed the city's thrift shops. In Boston, where the reviews were lukewarm, they discovered Filene's Basement, which was stocked with marked-down merchandise. She was redoing the walk-up apartment to better accommodate the two of them, and she sent parcels back daily, containing anything from bits of fabric and lace to an old sewing-machine table with wrought-iron legs. They could not be apart for more than half an hour. When she couldn't be found during rehearsals, a chorus of voices would shout out, "Try Elliott's dressing room!"

The show opened in New York on the blustery night of March 22, 1962, at the Shubert Theatre. An air of nostalgia pervaded the audience, many of whom had come to see veteran performer Lillian Roth or who had personal ties to the garment industry. "This could have meant they would be user-friendly or coldly critical," one cast member said. "We were all exceptionally nervous backstage, especially after the rather cool reception we received in Philadelphia and then in Boston."

Streisand, who occupied a small dressing room of her own, arrived early at the theater and remained cloistered behind closed doors until curtain time, although Elliott was seen to enter, remain about fifteen minutes, and then leave. She was shaking as she stood in the wings preparing to make her entrance. "Once she was onstage," a coworker recalled, "she was in total control. I never saw anything like it."

"She really hit her stride with 'Miss Marmelstein,'" an investor who had seen the out-of-town performances said. "This was *her* kind of audience — New Yorkers, predominantly Jewish or of some ethnic culture. Not Boston Brahmins or Philadelphia socialites. It was thrilling to watch as she twisted and twirled in her secretary's chair, her voice startling in its uniqueness. She had the audience in the palm of her hand, and you had the feeling that she knew it. When she finished her number, they went wild."

As she came off the stage into the wings, Elliott gave her a bear hug. She was flushed with excitement.

"The evening's find is Barbra Streisand, a girl with an oafish expression, a loud irascible voice and an arpeggiated laugh," wrote Harold Taubman, the theater critic for the *New York Times*.

"Miss Streisand possesses nothing short of a Chekhovian brand of heart-breaking merriment," John Simon enthused in *Theater Arts*. "Gifted with a face that shuttles between those of a tremulous young Borzoi and a fatigued Talmudic scholar . . . she can also sing the lament of the unreconstructed drudge with the clarion peal of an Unliberty Bell."

Most of the reviews had very little to say in favor of the show, although Elliott, Kruschen, Roth, Lang, Cooper, North, and Linn received good personal notices. But it was Streisand who was lauded as a star discovery. Photo articles in *Life* and *Look,* the two picture magazines with the largest national circulation, and a two-page profile in *Time* appeared shortly after the opening of the show. She was portrayed as a startling new discovery, but her first name was occasionally spelled with three *a*s and interviewers mispronounced "Streisand."

Merrick still had her on a week-to-week contract. He was now forced to renegotiate with Marty Erlichman to make certain she remained with the show for six months. Merrick offered her much the same terms. She refused, which left him with a new star who could leave at a week's notice. Furious at her "attempted blackmail," he had all her out-front theater photographs taken down and killed her publicity. "So she came to me crying, puzzled," Laurents recalled, "and I said to her, 'Why should he build you up if you're going to leave?' She said 'Oh' and signed an extended contract, but it was renegotiated with better terms for her." She was to receive a fifty-dollar-a-week raise, a sum that seemed rather grand at the time.

During the rest of their time in the show,* she and Elliott holed up in the cluttered, "remodeled" flat over Oscar's, the small rooms littered with her thrift-shop scavenges, including a battered dentist's cabinet filled with old shoe buckles and an apothecary jar of faded beauty patches. They would still go down to Elliott's apartment in the Village to keep up the facade.

They loved to play games — Monopoly, chess, checkers, cards — and made wild plans. "Barbra decided we should speak a secret language nobody else could understand," Elliott explained. "We swore never to be

---

I Can Get It for You Wholesale closed after eight and a half months and three hundred performances on December 8, 1962. In the last ten weeks of the run, Barbra Streisand was replaced by Louise Lasser. Elliott Gould was replaced by Larry Kert about the same time.

apart on our birthdays, and we shopped for special presents." He gave her a blue marble egg that she cherished. She presented him with a gold cup inscribed "First Annual Alexander the Great Award," since he was a great admirer of the indomitable Greek conqueror.

Barbra Streisand had not only made it onto Broadway, she had a lover for whom she cared deeply. This should have made her ecstatically happy, but it was not enough. Perhaps nothing ever would be.

10

They existed in a romantic aura. Hurtful memories of Barry Dennen were assuaged by Elliott's honest love and affection. There was something childlike in their relationship, artless, natural. They did not have to put on airs with each other. Both were Jewish and from Brooklyn. She never had to prove herself to Elliott as she had felt obliged to do with Dennen. They shared the same far-out humor; they were conspirators; it was them against the world. She thought that he was an intuitively gifted actor, that all he had to be was himself — a funny, crazy person — and he would succeed. She felt safe with him, protected, small, feminine. She liked watching him pull his big mittlike hands through his thick, dark, curly hair; she was touched when he gazed endearingly at her with his enormous velvet brown eyes; she found the deep cleft in his chin sexy. He had a cuddly teddy-bear quality about him, and yet he was this enormous *fella,* six foot three inches tall, weighing 206 pounds. She believed she loved Elliott.

Elliott never doubted the depth of his feelings for her. "It was my love that powered the relationship," he confessed. "I don't think Barbra knew how to love me back. She was incapable of real love because she never had it from her father, and I don't think she ever came to terms with that. So I gave her something she had never had before: a true, normal, natural love. But I never was able to accept that she didn't know how to love me back. I felt it was my fault. . . . I told her once, 'Your mother thinks affection is something people use to get something.' Barbra replied, 'That's why I am the way I am.'"

She was, he admitted, self-involved, happiest when *he* was concentrating on *her* problems. He was convinced he could change all that. He had never had a strong man-woman relationship before. He loved her unreservedly and thought she was beautiful when she awoke all rumpled in the morning. He considered her the smartest person he had ever known, and the most talented. He found it difficult to keep his hands off her — she was incredibly sexy to him. He wanted to get married and move into an apartment that did not stink of fish. She wanted to wait.

"I don't think she even wanted to marry me," Elliott said in retrospect. "I dwelled on it and insisted. I sublimated my own personality in my quest to please Barbra. . . . I so needed attention that I overcompensated by being good to Barbra, believing I would get it that way, overly trying to please. I *really* loved her. My love for her was pure and never exploitive or opportunistic. She once said she thought I loved her more than anyone else could. Maybe that's right."

He was understanding and supportive of the long hours she worked during the show's run — as she was "doubling out" after the show, appearing late at night, first at the Bon Soir and then at the Blue Angel and then back again at the Bon Soir. Her stamina was tremendous. She would go straight from final curtain to a waiting taxi and on to the cabaret where she was performing. During the days when there wasn't a matinee she would often tape guest spots on TV. On May 29, not long after *Wholesale* opened, she created a sensation on *The Garry Moore Show*. Every week Moore celebrated a particular year in music. For the show with Streisand's segment it was 1929, remembered always as the year the stock market crashed. For Streisand's appearance, the Emmy-winning writer and musical director of the show, Ken Welch, chose to use "Happy Days Are Here Again," an upbeat Depression-era song that was Franklin D. Roosevelt's 1932 campaign theme song and has been sung at every Democratic convention since.

When Streisand expressed her discomfort with singing the number as

written, Ken Welch and his talented writer-wife, Mitzie Welch, wrote a
new verse for it and created a scene in which a woman has lost all her
money and most of her jewels in the crash. Adding to the irony of the
song, they had Streisand seated alone in a plush nightclub. She splurges
and orders champagne. A smartly turned-out waiter presents her with
the check; she slowly removes her diamond earrings and places them on
his tray. A haunting vamp by Ken Welch that telegraphs the rhythm to
come sets the tone for what has — perhaps more than any one of her
numbers — become Streisand's musical signature. The Welches slowed
down the tempo of the song and added some lush, moving chords. The
difference was startling. They had given an old standard a fresh and moving new life.

Her rendition of "Happy Days Are Here Again" was memorable. The
lyrics no longer connoted the past, nor did they seem to have anything
to do with politics, as they once had. The familiar words and tune took
on a poignant irony. Streisand had personalized them; here was a woman
who had lost in love and security, a model with whom everyone could
identify. Immediate interest in her as a recording artist was generated.
She cut an audition demo for RCA Records — ten songs from her
cabaret repertoire — with Marty Gold, the staff accompanist. Included
was an arrangement by Barry Dennen of "At the Codfish Ball," an old
Shirley Temple number. RCA was convinced she was uncommercial and,
to her great disappointment, did not sign her.

Then the cast recording of *Wholesale* was released and sold well, and a
record she made along with several other artists as a twenty-fifth anniversary edition of Harold Rome's 1937 revue *Pins and Needles,* in which
she gave a "gorgeously funny performance" of "Nobody Makes a Pass At
Me," a forerunner to "Miss Marmelstein," netted her good reviews.
Both records were produced by Columbia. Erlichman tried to convince
them to sign her. The executives there thought she was too removed in
style from the commercial scene of pop records.

Her hopes soared once again when record and cabaret revue producer
Ben Bagley approached her to join Carol Channing and Jerry Orbach
on an album featuring rare songs of the late lyricist John Latouche, who
with composer Vernon Duke had written the score to *Cabin in the Sky*

and with Jerome Moross, *The Golden Apple*—both shows critical stand-outs. Streisand, a tremendous fan of Latouche, was to sing "Takin' a Chance on Love" from the former and "It's the Going Home Together" and "Lazy Afternoon" from the latter.* The rights to the songs, however, were withdrawn shortly before the recording session was to be conducted, and the album was abandoned.

A jazz label, Atlantic Records, that issued mostly singles now offered her a contract, but Erlichman decided they should hold out for an album-producing company. "It was a difficult thing to do," he confessed, "turning down an offer after we had waited so long. And neither of us had much money. But we both thought it would be better not to jump at the first offer just because we were hungry."

Early in the run of *Wholesale* Streisand and Sandy Dennis (for *A Thousand Clowns*) tied for the New York Drama Critics Circle Award for best supporting actress of 1962. Streisand's hopes were high that she would win the coveted Tony for the same category in a musical, but she was severely disappointed when it went to Phyllis Newman from David Merrick's *Subways Are for Sleeping*. Barbra found it difficult to be a good loser. It wasn't that she doubted the other person's right to win, rather it made her worry about *why* she had not won, what was wrong with her performance. On the taxi ride home, up the stairs to their apartment, and in the kitchen as they shared a late-night snack (assorted deli meats, pickles, and ice cream), she kept up a running inquisition with Elliott of why she had lost the award, finally deciding that she had not had a strong enough speaking role. In the next show — and there would be a next show, she insisted — her part would have to be considerably larger and more central to the story.

Toward the end of the New York run, Arthur Laurents often accompanied Elliott and Barbra on antique outings in Greenwich Village. She was a compulsive collector, loved the texture and feel of objects and

---

*John Latouche (1917–56) was a brilliant lyricist, considered by current musicologists to be the precursor of Stephen Sondheim. He was noted for his original rhyming talents and the depth of feeling his lyrics expressed. Streisand later recorded both "Lazy Afternoon" and "Takin' a Chance on Love" again.

fabrics, and could indulge in an orgy of touching — the curves of a vase, the soft pile of velvet, the cool, hard feel of marble. Elliott shared her enthusiasm, although not with the same consuming passion.

"I never had much as a girl," she told him. "I like to own beautiful things. It makes me feel rich, even if I'm not." She made a habit of keeping a record of what she paid for each item. "Well, I might want to sell something one day," she said, "and it would be dumb if I didn't remember how much it cost."

Wholesale closed on December 8, 1962. "I was very friendly with Lena Horne and with Anita Ellis, the jazz singer," Arthur Laurents recalled, "and I gave a small party and invited these two ladies and Barbra. I remember Christmas tree trimmings. It was at my house in the Village. Well, Barbra was afraid to even walk into the room. She was odd that way. Obsessed by her own fame at the time, timid of the fame of others. She was in awe of Lena; if you listen, you will hear some of Lena in her voice — and why not? We take the best we can from the artists we most admire, whatever our field of art. You have to have the taste and good sense to pick up the right things from the right people, and she certainly did."

Erlichman did not want her to lose the momentum she had gained from her Broadway debut. She appeared on three segments of the new *Tonight Show Starring Johnny Carson,* which was filmed in New York. She then flew out to California to tape an appearance on the popular weekly *Dinah Shore Show.* It was the first time she and Elliott were separated. "It was hell," Streisand admitted. "I had to be out there for seven days and I cried every day."

Within a short time she grew more accustomed to their separations, as Erlichman secured an engagement for her at Mr. Kelly's in Chicago and the Hungry i in San Francisco. Erlichman was commanding $5,000 a week for her by the time she returned to New York for an engagement at the extremely popular upscale cabaret Basin Street East. Her new wealth gave her a sense of independence. With her ability to demand this kind of money had come power, and she liked the feeling.

Then the moment that she and Marty Erlichman had been waiting for suddenly happened. Goddard Lieberson had been following her career ever since Laurents had first sent her to him. One of the problems, he claimed, was that in listening to an in-performance cabaret tape she had made at the Hungry i,* he could not tell if she was black or white. Erlichman persuaded him to come to the Blue Angel and hear her live. Lieberson liked what he heard and agreed to sign her to a five-year contract with Columbia Records.

By forfeiting an even larger up-front payment — she received $20,000, which seemed a fortune to her — Erlichman gained her complete artistic control, most unusual for all but well-proven and top-selling recording artists. But Lieberson believed she was going to be a big asset to his company. Hers would be the final say, from the quality of studio recording to the design of the album cover, a precedent that would influence all her future business contracts. *Power* was the operative word, and with artistic control she had it.

Before recording her first album, she cut a 45 in the Columbia studio on Thirtieth Street: "Happy Days Are Here Again" on the A side, "When the Sun Comes Out," the Harold Arlen classic, on the back. The record went nowhere. This was followed by a second release, Kander and Ebb's "My Coloring Book" on one side, "Lover, Come Back to Me" on the flip side; it did not sell either. Erlichman met with Columbia executives to discuss the album Streisand was to make. She did not feel comfortable recording in a studio, he explained. She needed a live audience and familiar surroundings. Columbia agreed to have her record in performance at the Bon Soir with Peter Daniels on the piano and the Tiger Haynes Trio as backup.

The record company transported its engineering crew to the Bon Soir on Monday evening, November 5. "They brought in a paid audience," Tiger Haynes remembered, "and recorded her first show for the rest of the week, through Saturday. Same musicians, same songs, every night, so that they had six tracks of every number." After listening to the playback of the edited tape, she insisted that they record another live per-

---

*A bootleg album of this cabaret tape entitled *Barbra Streisand — Life, 1963* surfaced in 1985. Streisand sued the company, and the album was withdrawn.

formance. This one had flaws in the musical accompaniment and in her performance. She had sung the wrong lyrics at one point, not gone for an obligatory high note at another. "I can do better," she kept urging. "Let's try again."

"Columbia scrapped the whole bunch of tapes," Haynes continued, "but Streisand made sure we got paid." This setback only fired her drive to make a commercial record. She needed a musical director, a professional who (like Dennen) could put together a solid, cohesive set of songs. Through composer Harold Arlen, many of whose songs she sang and whose advice she sought after he had seen her and come backstage following a cabaret performance, she met musical director and arranger Peter Matz. Matz would create the musical backup that would help Streisand transform herself from a cabaret performer with a limited audience into a wildly successful commercial recording artist.

Matz brought a rhythmic vitality to her recording performance that she did not have in the early singles and the aborted Bon Soir album.* At that time many singers, including Sinatra, were backed up on recordings by a sweeping string section. For Streisand, Matz brought the brass and the winds into play, and when he needed the music to weep, he swept in the strings. This gave her records a fresh sound and brought out an urgency to her voice. The intimacy she had as a live cabaret performer was replaced by a startling voice on record: full-bodied, soaring, able to move an audience even though disembodied, conveying action solely through the voice of the singer. Matz had given her the commercial sound that would make her a recording success.

An innovative musician in his early thirties, Matz was raised in Los Angeles, where (like Barry Dennen) he had attended UCLA, but it had taken a year in France and several more in New York for him to develop his talent. He was of medium stature, wiry, with penetrating eyes and an enthusiastic manner of speaking, but it was his keen intelligence and

*Eight songs from this aborted album were included in Streisand's 1989 four-disc collection *Just for the Record*. "At the Codfish Ball" was excluded, and another recording of "A Sleepin' Bee" included.

immense energy that captured Streisand's attention. She liked him immediately, respecting his opinions and advice and the way he matched her industry in preparing the material for what would be her first released album.

"You could smell the air of desperation about her," one associate observed. She was determined to become a star but so far had been only a supporting player and a cabaret performer, however highly praised or well paid. Matz understood what it was besides her amazing voice that set her apart from other singers. The very thing that Barry Dennen had known instinctively. At heart she was more actress than singer. Each song became a solid, complete scene — a musical soliloquy. What had to be done was to put all these segments together to form a whole. That unity could be achieved by placing the songs correctly and then using daring and fresh orchestrations to unite them. Streisand recognized what Matz could contribute to her growth as a major artist.

With Matz conducting, Streisand began to record on January 23, 1963. She was in the hands of ultimate professionals and she knew it. She came dressed in an old, loose sweater and a pair of khaki pants — no eccentric clothes. She approached making a record as an almost private matter between herself, the musical director, and the technicians. There was no audience, no one to play to. It didn't matter that her hair needed washing and hung limply. Except for a smudge of lipstick and the habitual pencil lines extending the width of her eyelids, she wore no makeup. The acne had greatly subsided since *Wholesale* and her relationship with Elliott, but in the photographs taken during these sessions the marks from it are plainly visible on her chin and right cheek. She usually masked this evidence of her adolescence with makeup. However, she was here to work, not to impress, and the only people present were Matz, the recording producer Michael Berniker, the engineers, and the musicians. She badgered all of them into excessive overtime to try "just one more" take.

Obsessed with the need to get it right, as perfect as she could, she worked on this album as she would on every subsequent endeavor of her career. She would listen to a replay over and over, hearing things others often did not — a breathiness in her voice that she did not like, a word in a lyric not emphasized to its best advantage. She refused to settle, to compromise, to consider the time and effort this was costing other people. This was *her* record. She would be the one to be judged.

In three days she recorded eleven songs for *The Barbra Streisand Album,* most of them numbers she had performed in cabaret but with new arrangements: "Cry Me a River," "My Honey's Loving Arms," "I'll Tell the Man in the Street," "A Taste of Honey," "Who's Afraid of the Big Bad Wolf?" and "Soon It's Gonna Rain" on one side; "Happy Days Are Here Again," "Keepin' Out of Mischief Now," "Much More," "Come to the Supermarket (in Old Peking)," and "A Sleepin' Bee" on the other. "Come to the Supermarket (in Old Peking)," a comic number, was written by Cole Porter for a television production of "Aladdin." It presented her most difficult problem. She seemed unable to get a proper handle on the lyrics, which were not Porter's best (it was his last show, and his usually trenchant wit had failed him). But "Soon It's Gonna Rain" and "Cry Me a River," sung with a full, rich vocal quality, were so moving that even the experienced technicians who worked on the final cut (with Streisand standing over their shoulders), claimed they got goose-bumps each time they heard the songs.

Columbia executives, however, were mixed in their opinions, uncertain about the marketability of a concept album with no new songs that might take off and help the record hit the charts. Making the album even more chancy was her insistence on using as a cover photograph one of herself singing at the Bon Soir, her face half concealed in darkness (even her bright china-blue eyes look brown in this picture), and wearing a white blouse with a Peter Pan collar, a bow at the neck, and a loose-fitting herringbone vest. Where was the sex?

Ten years later she was to say, "I hear that first record of mine, where I'm *geshreying* and getting so emotional, I think, Oh, my God, how did they ever like me? I'm embarrassed by it. The ending was totally wrong. It was the end of the world, *Happy Days.* It went Oooooo, aaaaaay, my voice cracked. It was nuts. In a sense, that was the purest me. I was yearning for just so much that you hear it in my voice. It's very young, very high, very thin, like a bird. I think my voice has actually gotten better, warmer, mellower. But I probably lost some of my high notes. I don't think I can sing as high."

On the record's release, February 25, 1963, Streisand was sent on a promotion tour that began with a return engagement at the Blue Angel and was to end with an appearance at the Eden Roc Hotel in Miami Beach on March 27. "Her nose is more evocative of moose than muse, and her eyes at best could be called Nilotic only by way of mascara, but about 2 A.M., when she sings 'Any Place I Hang My Hat Is Home,' she's beautiful, if home is only Brooklyn," wrote Robert Rourk, a respected critic, reviewing her Blue Angel opening. "She has a three-octave promiscuity of range, she packs more personal dynamic power than anybody I can recall since Libby Holman or Helen Morgan. She can sing as loud as Ethel Merman and as persuasively as Lena or Ella. . . . She is the hottest thing to hit the entertainment field since Lena Horne erupted, and she will be around 50 years from now if good songs are still written to be sung by good singers."

By the second week in March *The Barbra Streisand Album* made the charts. She was a recording star with huge revenues from royalties almost within her grasp. On the other hand, Elliott was having a tough time getting cast in another Broadway show. "My mate was making it and was very happy about it. I had to deal with it and I did," he says. They were both offered roles in the first London production of the Leonard Bernstein, Betty Comden, and Adolph Green musical *On the Town:* Streisand in the part created on Broadway by Nancy Walker, and Elliott to play the clownish sailor Ozzie, one of the three male leads in this ensemble piece. Erlichman advised her against leaving the country at such a critical time in her career. She was singing at the Eden Roc Hotel in Miami Beach at the time, and a jobless Elliott was with her.

Insecure at leaving her behind with the buzzards of success circling her, he kept up a running argument on why they should get married right away. She wouldn't have to deal with Broadway wolves, and — more important — it would give them both a purpose in what they were doing. He had signed to appear in the production of *On the Town* only for the first three months of the show, and, hey, she could come over to be with him during that time if only for a few days or a week.

"How would it look in a piss-elegant place like London for us to stay together and *not* be married," he asserted.

Elliott was actually proposing in a backhanded manner. Streisand, not yet ready to make such a commitment, only agreed that it might be a problem and with her usual flair for fictionalizing her past life to the press, issued a story that they had just been married in Florida by a justice of the peace. The news hit all the columns. Friends and associates sent congratulations. Even Diana, who had met and liked Elliott, believed her daughter was now Mrs. Gould. Two days after the fraudulent wedding announcement, Elliott left for London.

Streisand was to follow shortly thereafter. She had been invited to sing at the Kennedy White House on May 17, at a gala in honor of the foreign press correspondents and at which she wore her first-ever genuine ball gown, a glamorous white satin affair with miles of material in the skirt and a provocative neckline that exposed her well-divided cleavage. The gown was a great change from her flea-market wardrobe, but this was a special occasion. She was in genuine awe of President Kennedy — whom she had been too young to vote for — of being a guest at the White House, of the First Lady, whose style and class she greatly admired.

"You're a doll," she told the president when they were introduced.

He laughed and she instantly liked the crinkles on his face. "How long have you been singing?" he asked.

"About as long as you've been president," she replied.

She had just celebrated her twenty-first birthday (April 24, 1963), and she had made it big enough to meet the president and the First Lady of the United States. Pretty good for a girl from Brooklyn who everyone thought was too homely to go on the stage.

On the Town was to open in London in a week's time. Streisand and Elliott had spoken for an hour or longer daily since their parting. Whether it was neediness or longing, motivated by a fear of losing him or by a love that she knew neither how to express nor how to control, she could not bear to be away from Elliott. It made her crazy and terrified at the same time. More and more she was asserting her independence in her career, gaining a sense of power and the feeling of exhilaration that came from her success. And yet she longed to be with Elliott and missed him dreadfully. She wanted to be loved and to love, but she was driven even harder by her need to concentrate all her efforts on her career. She was torn, but two days after her appearance at the White House, she flew to London to join Elliott. London was swinging. A spirit of rebellion had swept over this once conservative society. Skirts were up, restrictions down. She trusted Elliott, but not her ability to hold him with a vast distance between them.

1. Barbara Joan Streisand—age seven.
She yearned for love and struggled to
meet the hurtful insults of her peers and
her stepfather with dignity.
Time-Life Inc./CBS Records

2

2. Emanuel (Manny) Streisand, whose
death when Barbra was still an infant
created a lifelong void never filled.
Brooklyn Historical Society

3. Her dreams at age eighteen were centered on becoming a great actress.
Craig Simpson

3

4

4. Her unconventional looks and a serious case of adolescent acne deterred
casting directors. *George Silk/Life
Magazine*

5. Barry Dennen was her first love, coach,
and advisor. He thought her fortune was
in her voice and worked tirelessly to
teach her technique.
Barry Dennen

6. One of her earliest publicity stills
(circa 1960)—making the most of her
dramatic profile and hands.
Craig Simpson

6

7

7. In performance at the Bon Soir—
the cabaret she called her "own
room."
Craig Simpson

8. Singing "Miss Marmelstein" in *I Can Get It for You Wholesale,* her first Broadway show. She kept a wad of bubble gum under the seat of the infamous chair on wheels and overnight became a sensation. *AP/Wide World*

8

9. Elliott Gould, Jack Kruschen, and Streisand. All the cast of the show knew she and Elliott were lovers. Whenever she could not be found, a cry went up, "Check Elliott's dressing room." *AP/Wide World*

9

10. She was by now a successful recording artist. Left to right: record producer Thomas Z. Shepherd, composer Harold Arlen, Streisand, Jonathan Schwartz, Ed Jablonski, and Peter Matz, at Sony Recording Studios. *Thomas Z. Shepherd*

10

11

11. With Elliott Gould, her leading man
in *Wholesale,* in the kitchen of their new
penthouse apartment. They fell in love
during the run of the show and soon
were married.
Henry Grossman/Life

12. Her obsession with shopping for antiques became full-blown once she won the role of Fanny Brice in the Broadway-bound *Funny Girl*. *Time-Life*

13. Costar Sydney Chaplin started out disliking Streisand. They ended up a romantic item. At a story conference, clockwise from right: Streisand, Garson Kanin, author Isobel Lennart, and Chaplin. *Garson Kanin*

14

14. At the party for her birthday before
she left for London. The cast gave her a
small dog she named Sadie.
AP/Wide World

11

On the Town opened to cool reviews on May 26, 1963, just a few days after Streisand joined Elliott in London. Elliott received almost no personal notices; "long, lean and galvanically fit" was all the *Daily Telegraph* said about his performance. Elliott, his hopes unrealized, fell into frequent gloomy moods. Streisand's antidote was to keep him busy when he wasn't appearing onstage. On Saturdays before his matinee, she dragged him down the many side streets off Portobello Road to weave in and out of the myriad displays of antiques, oddities, plain junk, and souvenirs.

One Sunday she hired a car and they drove out into the country, sampled bangers swilled down with beer at a pub, and stopped at every antique shop on the way. She had discovered that the best values were Victoriana and 1920–30 art deco; as these periods had always appealed to her, she sent a large number of packages back to New York. With the huge sales of her album she could afford almost anything she wanted. "A new apartment," she promised Elliott, ready for them when he came home. Given the poor ticket sales of *On the Town,* that time looked as if it might be sooner than anticipated.

They were inseparable during her stay. "Elliott even looked happy despite the half empty houses we played to at the Prince of Wales Theatre," one member of the cast recalled. "I think he wanted the show to be over so that he could go back to the States and be with Barbra. They were always touching and camping around. No one in Britain knew much about her yet. I remember some small mention of her in the London papers. Her first record was not yet released in Britain. They said they were married, and no one had any reason *not* to believe it. Nor do I believe that anyone truly cared. She seemed to be gone almost as soon as she had arrived."

In fact, she had been booked to appear on the June 9 *Ed Sullivan Show,* the most popular television variety program in America. "I liked Ed," she later carped, "but one thing that makes me crazy is how many people mis-pronounce my name. He was no exception. All during dress rehearsals I kept hearing him say, 'And now let's hear it from the Columbia recording star Barbra Streis-*land!*' It made me so nervous that during the actual broadcast, when it was my turn, I stepped behind the curtain whispering, 'Streis-*sand!* Streis-*sand!* Like sand on the beach!' He ended up doing it right."

Three weeks later she was on her way to Las Vegas for an appearance as the opening act for Liberace in the massive showroom at the Riviera Hotel. Streisand knew it was a mistake from the moment she stepped into the flashy lobby filled with slot machines and the jangling sound of coins. Las Vegas is a gaudy Disneyland for middle-aged and retired people. It is not so much a place as an upside-down world where reality is checked at the front desk of garish hotels. People came to enjoy the desert heat, the gambling tables, and a chance to see in person the sophisticated old pros such as Liberace, Frank Sinatra, Dean Martin, Tony Bennett, Sammy Davis, Jr., Noël Coward, and the great stand-up comedians — Milton Berle, Sid Caesar, Joey Bishop, and Jerry Lewis — who had won early fame in the Catskills and went on to radio, films, and television. Vegas audiences liked ostentation; the beautiful, long-legged showgirls in glitzy, sexy costumes; and the great female entertainers like Lena Horne, who knew how to razzle-dazzle her fans.

Mid-June temperatures were in the nineties when Streisand arrived, her suitcase packed with the simple muted brown and tawny gray gowns she had chosen especially for the engagement. She had decided to dress "down" for Vegas — elegantly, she believed, to create a stark contrast with the surroundings, to focus attention on herself. She chose slow ballads to sing to an audience to whom she was little known and who had paid a high price to see Liberace's outrageous costumes and hear his flamboyant piano arrangements. Her act backfired; the audience was tepid in their response. The hotel threatened to fire her. Liberace, who thought her voice and phrasing brilliant, prevailed.

A meeting was called with the management. He would open the show, dressed in a red sequin tuxedo, with a big, upbeat number. Then he would introduce her as his discovery, make a big thing about it, play on his fans' great love for him, and promise to be back to play and sing all their favorites. Her act was cut from six to four songs, and she was coerced into wearing a gold dress and some showy earrings that came from the hotel's expensive boutique. She did not receive a standing ovation, but the crowd, responding to the new theatricality of her appearance, were far more receptive, and she won a host of fans. Still, her first-night experience had been jolting. She had never previously appeared before a hostile audience. Liberace's support had helped her through, but her life-long struggle with stage fright was born.

She went on to the Coconut Grove, situated in the luxurious Ambassador Hotel and perhaps the most glamorous dinner nightclub room in Los Angeles, able to seat over a thousand people and frequented by Hollywood's famous and elite who kept up with who was new and hot in show business. This time she was the solo attraction, her material to include numbers from her hit album, and "Miss Marmelstein" as an encore. This was her dream, to come to Hollywood and be so sensational that she would be signed to a movie contract on the spot, an event that would show Diana that she *was* attractive enough to be in pictures. Once again, she gave great thought to what she would wear.

Clothes had become an important disguise for her. What she wore helped to define the person she wanted to be at a particular time. After her miscalculation in Vegas, for this engagement she had designed a red-and-white-checked gingham jumper worn over a white cotton top with voluminous long sleeves — meant to be a parody of the kind of Swiss peasant dresses worn on Broadway by Mary Martin in *The Sound of Music,* which had been bought by Twentieth Century-Fox and would soon star Julie Andrews in the screen version. She thought it made a statement, showed how "with it" she was, and that it would catch the audience's attention in a positive way.

Both she and Marty Erlichman had been given accommodations at the Ambassador. Although she had a successful rehearsal on the afternoon before her opening, by the time she was due to appear, stage fright had enveloped her. It was nearly an hour before Erlichman managed to persuade her to leave her room on the fifth floor, step into the elevator, and ride down to the Grove.

A rumble of unrest and disapproval at being kept waiting had spread between the giant palm trees that grew incongruously in huge pots that rimmed the vast interior of the legendary room, three stories high with a ceiling painted to look like a sky with sparkling stars. Her entrance was made from the back, a spotlight lighting her way. She was wide-eyed at seeing so many famous stars — Kirk Douglas, Henry Fonda, Ray Milland, and Edward G. Robinson were in the audience. As she went past a well-known producer and his heavily jeweled companion, she overheard the woman say as she stared at her gingham dress, "And I've had to wait all this time to hear some *farchadat* [dopey] country singer?" Never able to forget a detractor, she would comment sharply years later, "*I'm* still here! I wonder where *she* is!"

"At first I guess they thought I was some kind of kook. I thought, 'Gee, they're going to hate me for being so late.' I made some cocka-mamie reason for it and they laughed. Henry Fonda even stood up and applauded after one song. Henry Fonda!"

Her reviews were sensational. The critics all commented wryly on her outfit. Hollywood enjoyed jokes on themselves. But no one was interested in her for movies. Producers and agents in Hollywood spoke another language —"bankable" (a star who could get financing for a film), "big at the box office," and "a power to deal with." Still, she liked the place, declared that one day soon she would be all three, that she and Elliott would set the town on its ass. Long distance, Elliott cheered her on, soothed her nerves, told her how much he loved and missed her. The overseas calls were the highlight of his day. Every evening he expected to walk into the Prince of Wales and see a closing notice posted to the stage door, disappointed that it wasn't there. He wanted to go home, to see Barbra, to make sure that she was all right, that *they* still had a future together.

He seldom went back to his digs after a performance. Gambling clubs were at the height of their popularity in London; members (or guests of members) could dine sumptuously and then go upstairs to the gaming rooms. Each club had select memberships. Theater and film people were mostly concentrated at the White Elephant, the Curzon, and the River Club, all three boasting elegant interiors. There was an excitement, an edge that permeated such establishments. Hit once again by the gambling bug, Elliott managed to run up several hundred pounds in debts, a significant sum considering the state of his finances.

"I didn't have it to pay," he admitted later. "Five hundred dollars, and I think this was a larger sum, was enormous to me then. I went through some of the best acting I've ever done to escape; made up great inventive tales of why I was temporarily without funds." Fortunately, the show's closing notice in early August spared him further humiliation. In Los Angeles Streisand was ending her Coconut Grove engagement, having just finished recording sessions with Peter Matz on *The Second Barbra Streisand Album,* which included several Harold Arlen songs and some newer material like Billy Barnes's dramatic piece "(Have I Stayed) Too Long at the Fair," already a favorite of hers, and Matz's own "Gotta Move." After all, she had just been named Entertainer of the Year by *Cue* magazine and the Top-Selling Female Vocalist by the National Association of Record Manufacturers. It pleased but did not satisfy her. She wanted to be recognized by her peers for a Grammy. Her contract terms settled, she accepted Liberace's proposal to appear with him in Lake Tahoe, a short distance from Los Angeles. After that engagement, she would return to New York to start work on her third album for Columbia, which wanted to cash in as quickly as possible on her success.

Elliott could not wait that long. He flew directly from London to Los

Angeles, where she was still appearing. The day after he arrived was his birthday. They were eating in the coffee shop of her hotel. The waitress set down a piece of cake with a flickering candle on it. "Make a wish!" Streisand demanded.

"I hope the Dodgers win the pennant!" he replied and blew out the flame.

She laughed, that inimitable sound she made halfway between a snort and a yelp.

He leaned across the table. "Let's get married," he amended.

"Too late. Candle's out," she snapped back. Elliott was disappointed but not despairing, certain that eventually she would say yes.

A few days later they left in a leased car for Lake Tahoe, a picturesque year-round vacation and gambling town high in the Sierra Nevada mountains on the California–Nevada state line. The hotels and casinos almost all overlooked the unbelievably deep, clear lake that is fed by many mountain streams. At every performance she received a standing ovation, always graciously acknowledged by a smiling Liberace, who enjoyed telling the crowd that he was proud of their enthusiastic reception because he had discovered her. Elliott almost never left her side. Neither did he gamble, which he took as a good omen. Streisand counted on his being there when she came offstage, to talk to her about her performance, to hold her in his bear arms when she was tired and needed comforting. He never gave up his entreaties that they get married. After all, he would reason when passion had not won his cause, most people already thought they were married.

Finally, she accepted his proposal and on September 13, 1963, they drove to nearby Carson City, Nevada, the state capital where the Comstock Lode was found in the bluish desert sand in 1859 and scores of men became fabulously rich in silver mined there. Vestiges of the Old West had been preserved, but Carson City was now firmly entrenched in the twentieth century. With Marty Erlichman as best man, they were married by a justice of the peace who had never heard of her and appeared shocked at the passionate kiss they exchanged at the end of his short, no-frills ceremony. Elliott let out a whoop when they were outside again, picked her up, and carried her to the car. She was now Barbra Joan Streisand Gould.

She had earned well up into six figures from *The Second Barbra Streisand Album*. She was richer than she could have ever imagined and wealthy enough for her to get the New York apartment she had dreamed of one day renting. It turned out to be a spectacular seven-room duplex penthouse on the twenty-first and twenty-second floors of the Ardsley, with a view from Central Park West clear across the park to the East Side. It was once the home of the urbane lyricist Lorenz Hart, and anyone who had been anyone on Broadway in the twenty years before World War II had been in this apartment. Streisand claimed she could still feel the vibes of the former occupant. When she and Elliott returned from the West Coast a few days after their wedding, they drove directly from the airport to their new home.

Packing cases were everywhere, as she had been collecting items from England and on her tour. She had encamped like a Gypsy. The kitchen was in a shambles, deep red patent leather (her original idea) was only half applied to the scraped-down walls, scraps of old paper and pots of glue were underfoot. A glorious Aubusson rug that was to adorn the living-room floor was rolled up in brown paper across the foyer, the walls of which were being decorated with flocked red velvet paper. One upstairs bedroom had been made into a sewing room and all her antique hats, shoes, and oddments were stacked in boxes since the wardrobe, where they were to be stored, had not yet arrived. The only room that appeared to be complete was her small dressing area with its built-in vanity, mirrors, and professional hair-dryer set off by a tasseled drape that hung on the one narrow wall with a window.

The first new acquisition she showed Elliott was the fully stocked freezer-refrigerator bulging with TV dinners (Swanson's frozen fried chicken dinners were her favorite), coffee ice cream, green dill pickles, and delicatessen meats — salami, tongue, pastrami. Then she grabbed his hand and marched him through the dining room with its French gilt chairs, to the den, where an ebony Steinway grand piano almost filled the room, and then up to the master bedroom dominated by a huge Jacobean four-poster canopy bed that sat on a raised dais of two steps. The interior of the wood canopy was magnificently carved. She jumped onto the quilted mattress and squealed, "It doesn't get any better than this, does it?"

But it did.

Not only was she rich, she was in love and happy in her work, although she liked it much better when she was off the road and performing at the Bon Soir, which had become her "room." Clubs with featured singers were at their zenith. Top performers drew loyal fans and glittering audiences. Streisand's two bestselling albums had made her a national, much-talked-about celebrity. The Bon Soir was packed whenever she appeared. Mention of her name evoked immediate interest: "*I* saw her at the Lion Club," an apocryphal claim, for the Lion was too small and her engagement too short to encompass the many people who were said to have seen her there. At twenty-one this was pretty heady business. Her time in Hollywood had further fueled her dream of becoming a movie star. She needed a leading role in a big-budget Broadway musical, a showcase for Hollywood to see that she could act as well as sing.

Marty Erlichman kept up with all the shows that were currently in development, but the 1962–63 musical comedy season had been dismal. Even Irving Berlin's *Mr. President* had closed after a disappointing eight-month run. Only one musical, *Oliver!,* Lionel Bart's adaptation of Dickens's *Oliver Twist* had been a hit. Erlichman, despite his enthusiasm for his client's talents, could not have foreseen a lead in a Broadway musical in her immediate future. He was, after all, well aware of her ethnic image, of the lack of roles that might suit her. Dutifully, he put out word that Streisand would welcome a Broadway role again in a part more fulfilling than Miss Marmelstein.

For a year, a musical on the life of the *Ziegfeld Follies* star, Fanny Brice, had been a work in progress. A few years before her death in 1951 at the age of fifty-nine, Fanny Brice had made several unprofessional tapes recording memories, impressions of people, the highs and lows of her private life. The tapes were to be used in writing her autobiography, *The*

Fabulous Fanny, for which she had been paid a $50,000 advance (substantial at the time) by Random House, which expected her to reveal the more scandalous episodes in her life and in those of other celebrities she knew. Brice found herself unable to lay bare her past and never completed the book. Eventually, Ray Stark, Brice's ambitious son-in-law, a former-agent-turned-producer and a man of tremendous tenacity and indomitable moxie, bought back the rights for the original advance.* He hired Ben Hecht and several other top film writers to adapt the book for the screen, with no success.

Stark turned to Isobel Lennart, whose 1945 original musical *Anchors Aweigh,* with Gene Kelly and Frank Sinatra, had been a huge moneymaker for MGM. Her screenplay was also rejected. Studios were not only concerned with the weak script but with how audiences would accept another actress portraying Brice, who remained well remembered and well loved. The original concept was to use Fanny Brice's old recordings on the soundtrack, as had been done with *The Jolson Story.* None of these efforts came to fruition, and Stark then decided to have Lennart's screenplay adapted for the theater.

When playwright John Patrick, who had been the scriptwriter on Stark's first film venture, *The World of Suzie Wong,* turned him down, Lennart was recalled. She was a capable and often inspired writer, but she lacked theatrical experience. However, Brice's story was a good one, a tale that was filled with laughter and tears, a winning theater combination as Brice herself had noted. Fanny Brice made her mark at the age of nineteen when the exceptional showman, Florenz Ziegfeld, signed her as a headliner in his *Follies.* A natural comedienne, she also had a strong contralto singing voice that could be filled with humor or pathos at a turn. She understood a lyric, every song she sang became a self-contained scene, and she could move with a sudden grace that made her audiences wonder why she was considered homely. Brice had fallen in love with Nicky Arnstein, an inveterate gambler and a stylish ladies' man. He quickly became "Mr. Brice" as her star rose ever brighter and his luck

---

* The Fabulous Fanny was later finished and published posthumously.

ran out. When he was accused of fraud and forgery in a bond scandal, she refused to believe the charges.

"Are you sure your memory is as bad as that, Miss Brice?" the district attorney asked her during an investigation into Arnstein's whereabouts.

"Yes, it is very bad," she replied. "I can only remember songs and telephone numbers."

The day Arnstein went to jail, Brice appeared in the *Follies,* dressed not in her usual comedienne's costumes but in a clinging, black satin gown, standing in the light of one bright spot and singing English lyrics by Channing Pollock for the French torch song "Mon Homme."

It cost me a lot but there's one thing that I've got

It's my man . . .

With her poignant rendition of that song, sung in a husky alto voice — which became her signature piece — audiences worldwide fell under Brice's spell, regarding her suddenly as much more than a comedienne. She was now a woman who had overcome personal tragedy with great dignity. Her comedy matched Charlie Chaplin's poor little tramp or Buster Keaton's sad-faced loser. Lennart wrote numerous versions of Brice's life. There were almost as many titles: *Fanny Brice, My Man, The Funny Girl,* and finally simply, *Funny Girl.*

Fran Stark, Ray Stark's wife, watched over the story development with vigilance. Her father, Nicky Arnstein, was still alive, and she wanted him presented in a sympathetic fashion, his culpability in the securities swindle that sent him to prison underplayed. The timing of certain events had to be altered: in no way was Lennart to indicate that her parents had lived together unmarried until after her birth. Nor did the restriction end there: since Fanny Brice's second husband, the composer-showman Billy Rose, was alive and litigious, the story was only to encompass Brice's great love for Nicky Arnstein.* Ray Stark felt he needed an experienced theater man to help transfer the story to the stage and joined forces with Streisand's former nemesis, David Merrick, the theatrical producer of *The World of Suzie Wong.* For the score he turned

---

*Fanny Brice often said, "I loved the man [Arnstein] I didn't like and liked the man [Rose] I didn't love."

to Jule Styne (composer) and Stephen Sondheim (lyricist), who had collaborated on *Gypsy*. After *West Side Story* and *Gypsy,* where he had been limited to writing only the lyrics, Sondheim wanted a show where he could write the entire score. Nor could he imagine Mary Martin, Stark's choice for the lead, as Fanny Brice. When Sondheim refused Stark's offer, Merrick paired composer Styne with lyricist Robert Merrill. After they had written four songs,* Mary Martin decided she did not want to do the role.

Casting around for an alternative, Fran Stark settled on Anne Bancroft, whom she had loved in the original stage version of William Gibson's *Two for the Seesaw* and "had her heart set on this fine dramatic actress to play her mother," Jule Styne once said. "But Merrick was never in favor of Anne Bancroft. He asked me to go down to the Bon Soir and see Barbra Streisand. . . . It was the first time I'd seen Streisand perform in a café, and I saw a tremendous star dimension. . . . I returned to the Bon Soir twenty-seven nights out of twenty-eight in a row. I took several of my friends to see her and got opinions from all sides." One of his friends was Jerry Robbins, at that time thought of as the future director for the show. Both agreed that Streisand would be right in the role, but Stark, with his wife pressuring him, remained adamant in his choice of Bancroft. No one was sure if she could sing well enough, and Stark asked her to audition for Styne and Merrill. She sang numerous songs — ballads and up-tempo numbers — with surprising panache. Everyone thought that she was a good enough performer to carry it off, and the Starks went away certain that she would agree to play the role and that their casting problems were over.

In early summer of 1963, John Patrick and Stark met in his New York apartment. "I pointed out that Bancroft would be miscast and would probably realize that. I remember him saying to me, 'She wouldn't dare turn down a role like this.' The phone rang and I answered it for Ray. It was Bancroft on the line — declining the part."

Patrick was committed to Stark to write two scripts, a contract that

---

*"I'm the Greatest Star," "Don't Rain on My Parade," "Who Are You Now?" and "People."

guaranteed him $1.3 million. He told Stark how sorry he felt, but he could not adapt Lennart's screenplay-cum-playscript because he was not a fan of Fanny Brice. "I thought she was often vulgar and her material sometimes in bad taste." Stark turned the script back to Lennart but asked Patrick to become part of the production team as his assistant or so-called editor.

"A classmate of Ray's from Rutgers came to me and suggested I recommend Streisand to Ray, as he had seen her at the Bon Soir," Patrick recalled. "I went down to see her for myself. She seemed right for the part, and I knew she would do justice to Jule and Bob's score. When I suggested Streisand, I remember his reaction. He thought she was unattractive and showed no enthusiasm. I pointed out to him that Fanny Brice, his mother-in-law, had never been a beauty, but sang 'My Man' like an angel."

Stark would not be convinced. He turned to Eydie Gormé and then to Carol Burnett, who told him honestly, "You need a Jewish girl to play this. It's a whole different quality." John Patrick called Marty Erlichman to inform him that he was going to bring Fran and Ray Stark down to the Bon Soir, but not to let anyone except Barbra know it. Streisand was extremely nervous on the appointed night. This was the opportunity she had been hoping for. The room was packed, a very receptive audience, and she responded with a performance that was one of her best.

"Ray thought she sang well, but Fran hated her and told me, 'I'll never let that girl play my mother.'" Brice's private and public persona differed drastically. Onstage she was the raucous ethnic comedienne; socially she was an elegant, Americanized, well-spoken woman with exquisite taste,* a talented interior decorator whose home was a sophisti-

---

*Born Fanny Borach in New York City on October 29, 1891, Fanny Brice had neither a Brooklyn nor a Jewish accent. Her parents were saloonkeepers in a predominantly Irish neighborhood. In a tape made for her proposed autobiography Brice said, "In 1910 I needed a song to sing to audition for a job in *College Girls*. I raced up to where Irving Berlin had an office and asked him if he had a song for me. Irving sang in a Jewish accent 'Sadie Salome, Go Home,' a song about a girl from the Bronx who became a hula dancer, which he had written the lyrics but not the music for. I had never had any idea of doing a song with a Jewish accent, didn't even understand Yiddish. But I thought, If that's the way Irving sings it, that's the way I'll sing it. If he had sung it with an Irish brogue, I probably

cated showplace and who dressed with great style. Fran Stark saw only Streisand's Jewishness and was vehement that her mother not be portrayed in that light.

Disregarding the Starks' objections to Streisand, Erlichman and Robbins arranged for Streisand to read a few scenes from the play for Merrick, Styne, Merrill, Isobel Lennart, the Starks, and Patrick. "I can't tell you how horrible she looked," Patrick alleged. "She wore a Cossack uniform kind of thing. She read the scene where Fanny's husband, Nicky Arnstein, has just left her. Tears were called for, and she could not manage it." Ray Stark was now as adamant as his wife that Streisand not play Fanny Brice.

Robbins and Styne insisted that she be given another chance. The group gathered for a second time. Again Barbra could not cry. This time she whipped around to Robbins at the end of the scene. "Mr. Robbins," she said sharply, "I can't cry with those words!"

Shortly thereafter, Robbins left the project, and *Funny Girl* looked as though it would be canceled. Then Bob Fosse was hired to replace Robbins, and the show was once again on. A few weeks later, Fosse quit. The producers turned to Sidney Lumet. After telling them that the book needed drastic revision, he was gone. All the time Streisand was in anguish, believing in her heart that this role was her chance to prove that she could be a star.

Fortunately, the show's producers refused to let *Funny Girl* slide into oblivion. They knew the book was the problem; they called Garson Kanin, who had been a close friend of Brice's, and asked him if he would consider collaborating with Isobel Lennart on a rewrite. Kanin, who had successfully collaborated on four films with his wife, actress-writer Ruth Gordon, declined. "Isobel was an excellent screenwriter, but she had no experience in the lyric theater," Kanin explained. "When I met with Stark and Merrick, I told them their difficulty was not that they had a

---

would have become an Irish comedienne. So, Irving is really responsible for the whole thing." Florenz Ziegfeld later hired her for seventy-five dollars a week to appear in his *Follies of 1910* after hearing her sing in dialect. Berlin wrote music and lyrics for "Goodbye, Becky Cohen," also a dialect song, for her. It became a hit. Thereafter, she used the dialect in her comedy skits although not when she sang ballads.

bad book but that they had no book at all." The story was the all-too-familiar backstage drama of the ugly-duckling novice who becomes a star at the sacrifice of the man she loves. Kanin had previously worked with Jule Styne on *Do Re Me,* but they had not got on well, and he was hesitant to go through a similar experience again. Nevertheless, when offered the job as director, he accepted. Stark was pleased because he felt that with both John Patrick and Ruth Gordon (who was always at her husband's side) unofficially overseeing the script along with Kanin, Lennart would be able to pull it off.

Streisand now found her mentor to be none other than David Merrick. His instinct, he told Kanin, was that she should play Fanny. Streisand was currently appearing at Basin Street East. The Kanins found that her act was beautifully conceived, paced well — strong ballads balanced by humorous set pieces — and like Brice, she had the ability to move her audience to both laughter and tears. She was that strange anomaly: a woman who could be called homely by some and stunningly beautiful by others.

The Kanins were convinced that Streisand was the ideal choice and that with Garson's close knowledge of Fanny Brice and his ability to work with strong women (Katharine Hepburn, Carole Lombard, and Ginger Rogers had been the leading ladies of many films that he had either written or directed), he could get a terrific performance from her. A lunch was arranged for them to get acquainted and to see if he could work with her.

Nothing was going to stop Streisand from getting this role. Determined to charm the Kanins, she read as much as she could about them. Ruth Gordon had been one of the great leading ladies of the American stage, as well as a successful playwright and screenwriter. By now in her early sixties, a petite, vital woman, with an expressive rather than beautiful face and a shiny dark cap of hair to frame it, she was quick-witted and merry — and a walking encyclopedia of theater knowledge. She was the first woman of Streisand's acquaintance to be so multitalented, which greatly impressed her. Garson Kanin, a decade younger than his wife, was equally sharp: a short, feisty, spry man with intelligent brown eyes and a smile that slid saucily across his face when he was amused — which was often — who appreciated the turn of a woman's ankle as well as her intelligence and talent.

"I liked Barbra immediately," Kanin recalled. "She was funny, relentlessly ambitious; nothing was going to keep her down. I felt those qualities were very important because they were principal aspects of the Fanny Brice I knew." He went home from their lunch, which lasted several hours, and reread Lennart's libretto. He now could hear Streisand's voice as he read certain lines and had begun to visualize *her,* not *Fanny,* in the role. He was excited and passed along his enthusiasm to Stark, who was still not certain that Streisand could carry a show or that she was attractive enough to please an audience or his wife. He was talking to Shirley MacLaine about the role, he told Kanin.

While Streisand fretted nervously about what was happening and kept nudging Marty Erlichman to do something about getting a decision on whether she had the part, a meeting was called with all the principal players: Merrick, the Starks, the Kanins, Patrick, Lennart, Styne, and Merrill. The Kanins made a lively plea in Streisand's defense. A mesmerizing performer, she had the quirkiness, the Jewish shtick, the stage charisma also possessed by Brice. Styne and Merrill insisted she was the only one to sing the score. The Starks were difficult to convince but finally yielded to the overwhelming majority.

Streisand was asked to meet Stark at his office. Erlichman had already told her she had won the role. Merrick was also there. For Streisand it was an important moment. Fanny Brice was not only the lead of *Funny Girl,* she was the main focus of the story. Streisand had gone from supporting player to star. In playing the role, she could be funny, romantic, tragic, joyous, sexy. She could prove that she could act. Stark remained cool throughout most of the meeting. Merrill thought maybe he had changed his mind. Midway through, Streisand began talking a lot out of sheer irrepressible nervousness. "It wasn't what she said, it was the way she rattled it off," Merrick recalled. "She somehow got under your skin. She was naturally funny. Ray loosened up, and by the time she left, it was agreed. She would play Fanny Brice."

Starry-eyed, she signed a contract with Merrick's company because Stark did not yet have an Actors' Equity agreement (this was his first play). She was flying high. Despite all the problems she had encountered in *I Can Get It for You Wholesale,* Barbra was confident that she and the play would succeed. Stardom was within her grasp.

She left for Los Angeles on October 3 in an euphoric mood to appear on *The Judy Garland Show,* where she planned to announce that she was to play Fanny Brice. Garland's show had been molded into an imitation of other prosaic television variety shows, although the one-woman concert format was where she felt most comfortable. CBS forced her to make chitchat with her guests and to take a backseat while they performed. It was to prove disastrous for Garland, but for Streisand it was a grandstand opportunity to display her talent on a television program watched by millions — and she ran with it. Originally scheduled to sing one solo and one duet with Garland, she doubled her spots with Garland's approval once they were in rehearsal.

A generous performer, Garland was much taken by Streisand's talent. Mel Tormé, musical director of the show, recalled being asked during rehearsals to see Garland in her dressing room. "She was playing Streisand's record of 'Happy Days Are Here Again.' As Streisand's voice came through the speaker, Judy began to sing 'Get Happy' in counterpoint to 'Happy Days.' The result was electrifying."

Tormé went directly to his office and called Streisand. He was sitting at the piano waiting for her when she came in. "Since you sing in any key, try 'Happy Days' in this one," he said. Then beginning the introduction in a key suitable to his own range, he motioned her to start, whereupon he joined in, as Garland had with "Get Happy." "Barbra kept singing as she half-turned to me, a wide smile on her face. When we finished, she exclaimed, 'That's terrific! I mean it! Your idea?'"

"No, Judy's," he replied honestly.

Ethel Merman was taping *The Red Skelton Show* in the adjoining studio and agreed to appear in one segment when she would "accidentally" be discovered in the audience and brought up onstage, where the three women would try to outbelt each other in a rousing rendition of "There's No Business Like Show Business." Merman was the indisputable decibel winner, but the show placed Streisand on a new plateau, equal with the two icons with whom she appeared.

Her high spirits prevailed upon her return to New York as she looked forward to the next step up in her career — the lead in a Broadway show. At this point Stark and Merrick suffered a hard falling-out over who would have final word on production matters. It was a power struggle, and Stark would not give in. "Life is too short to deal with Ray Stark," Merrick said and backed out of the agreement. For a week Streisand was left in limbo. She was near hysteria, constantly talking on the telephone to Erlichman, wolfing ice cream and walking the floors half the night as she worried out loud to a groggy Elliott, refusing to talk to Diana, who kept calling to find out if she had the role or not. One day the show was being abandoned, the next it was back on. Finally Erlichman called her to tell her the good news. Stark was ready to go into production; Marty and Bella Linden, who had become Streisand's lawyer, were renegotiating better terms for her.

Seduced by the lure of her name in lights on Broadway, she hurtled forward, self-absorbed. Elliott had not had an offer for a show since his return from London. She knew he was depressed about it, that she should spend more time and effort with him in working out his problems, but she could not stop or slow down her momentum to do so. Up ahead was the realization of all her dreams.

That is, if she played it right.

12

From the outset she knew that *Funny Girl* was her one-way ticket to fame. Everything in her was now geared toward becoming a star. That brought added responsibility, but it also meant that if she succeeded — and she refused to think otherwise — she would not just be on her way, she would have already arrived.

Fanny Brice was not the usual lighthearted, simpleminded Broadway musical-comedy heroine. Brice was a woman of strong character, outrageously funny as a performer, a real woman with whom audiences could identify. Brice had once said, "People like to feel miserable. You make them laugh, they will forget you, but if you make them cry they will never forget you." The marvelous thing about Fanny Brice was that she could make you do both. Brice also contended that it was her good fortune to have been born homely; it had given her the desperate ambition to become a great star, and she had not settled for less.

"It was scary," Streisand admitted. "I read certain conversations that have never been published [from the transcript of Brice's tapes] and it was very peculiar, we were very much alike in a very deep area, in spirit. I knew that I would do her justice by being true to myself. It didn't interest me to have copied her walk, I was interested in the essence of her.

Her essence and my essence were very similar. That is a little spooky, you know?"

One of the greatest problems she would have with audiences and critics was being compared with Brice, who had died only twelve years earlier and who, as radio's Baby Snooks, had been much loved by the American public during the last twenty years of her life. Every interview that Streisand gave at this time included a denial that she had ever heard or seen Fanny Brice perform, which was likely given that Brice's last movie was released in 1946.* However, according to Barry Dennen, it was not true. He had played numerous Brice recordings when they were living together. Streisand apparently wished to give the impression that she was creating the character from her own perception of the playscript.

On the first day of rehearsal, December 6, 1963, her hair piled high in a huge beehive, bangs falling over her forehead, Streisand arrived an hour late at the Winter Garden (ironically, the same theater where Brice had last appeared in the *Follies*), wearing high brown snow boots and a chic chocolate brown wool suit under a 1920s cocoon-shaped brown caracul coat. She now shopped at Bergdorf Goodman, one of New York City's most fashionable department stores. Although she had not discarded her eclectic thrift-shop wardrobe, she liked to mix new with old. And so with boots that cost over a hundred dollars and a suit for which she had paid three times that amount, she wore a twenty-dollar secondhand fur coat. She was particularly fond of furs, especially striking ones like leopard and pony, and had several of her own designs for suits and coats made up. She realized that, like Fanny Brice, she had a natural flair for design and decoration. Of greater significance were their similar ethnic background, their drive, and their early success — Brice had her big chance at nineteen as a star of the *Ziegfeld Follies*.

---

*Fanny Brice made only sporadic film appearances. But she had a cameo as herself in *The Great Ziegfeld* (1936); was part of the all-star cast in *Everybody Sing* (1938), in which she sang a duet with Judy Garland; and in *Ziegfeld Follies* (1946) did a sketch with Hume Cronyn. Brice debuted in the part-talkie film *My Man* (1928) and headlined in *Be Yourself!* (1930) shortly thereafter.

The cast was gathered on the large stage, where Garson Kanin was discussing procedures with them. He stopped when he saw Streisand and went over to where she was standing by an upright piano. She talked quietly with him for a few moments about some of her scenes but remained fairly aloof from the rest of the company as introductions were made. Ruth Gordon then took her backstage to her dressing room. "She wasn't sure how the star of a show should behave," Gordon said later. "How could she? I thought she was shy and that her coolness was a cover for her nervousness." But her attitude had not been well-received by most of the cast members.

Streisand's situation differed greatly from her last experience, when she had been a supporting player with no major credits, a small salary, and only one song to sing. Now she was the star of the show, and the score was being written expressly with her voice and character in mind. Since November 10, two weeks before rehearsals, she had been working on the songs with Jule Styne and Robert Merrill at Styne's apartment or at Peter Daniels's studio. She was more comfortable with Styne and Merrill than she was with the cast. Styne was an energetic man with a buoyant personality and an incredibly facile ability to compose good, singable melodies. Normally a bright mood prevailed at these rehearsals, but on November 22, President Kennedy was assassinated in Dallas. The whole country was in despair. Streisand wept openly as they went over her songs and smoothed out some of the rough spots. She had been awed by Kennedy when they had met at the White House. Her sense of loss translated into the emotion with which she sang.

Styne and Merrill recognized that they had a singing star of the first magnitude, and the power and meaning that she gave their songs encouraged them to write more numbers for her. Styne would claim that he composed fifty-five pieces of music for *Funny Girl*. In the end there were fifteen songs, some instrumental interludes and dance music (the latter arranged by Luther Henderson). Her rendition of "People" so overwhelmed the song's writers that a decision was made to record it as a single and to release it as soon as possible, with the hope that its success would give the show momentum. Columbia, Streisand's regular label, recorded "People" with "I Am Woman" on the flip side* with Peter Daniels on piano and the orchestra under the direction of Peter Matz. When they listened to the playback after the session, composer and lyricist were certain that the release would be a big hit.

Styne and Merrill were a cohesive team, although they appeared to have little else in common. Of small, neatly compressed stature, Styne seemed to be in perpetual movement, hands gesticulating as he spoke a rapid verbal shorthand of phrases that was often difficult to follow, his short legs carrying him in double time when he walked. Born in the East End of London in 1905, at the age of three he emigrated with his family to Chicago. Before his ninth birthday he was deemed a prodigy and was a soloist with the Chicago Symphony Orchestra. His parents were sure he would be a concert pianist, but his hands were deemed too small by his future piano teacher. Instead, he played dance music and the popular songs of the day, ending up as a teenager playing on an upright in a burlesque house and making his first bet on the ponies. Unfortunately, he won — for he was to be a compulsive, self-destructive gambler for the better part of his life. He started composing for films in the late 1930s and for the musical theater in 1947, careening from one success to another — *Gentlemen Prefer Blondes, Bells Are Ringing,* and *Gypsy.*

Styne should have been a rich man. Instead, he was on the brink of financial disaster and heavily in debt to the IRS (which eventually appropriated most of his earnings from *Funny Girl*). For a time he worked tirelessly on *Funny Girl* and *Fade Out — Fade In,* with Carol Burnett, in tandem. That did not stop him from betting, but it did set an exhausting pace for his lyricist, who was more easygoing.

At six foot two, Merrill towered over Styne. A man of even disposition and of a more conservative nature, he had been writing popular songs until 1957, when he wrote the music and lyrics for *New Girl in Town* and followed up with Jackie Gleason's hit show *Take Me Along* and his finest score, *Carnival,* in 1961, which was still running on Broadway.

---

*"I Am Woman" is the same song as "You Are Woman." In this case it was sung as a solo and with feminine lyrics.

Styne and Merrill were both brilliant at what they did, and Stark trusted their first decision on *Funny Girl* not to include any of the numbers that Fanny Brice had made famous, such as "My Man," "Rose of Washington Square," or "I'm an Indian." Instead, they created new songs — "Private Schwartz," "The Music That Makes Me Dance" — numbers that were original, contemporary, and evocative at the same time.

Funny Girl was to rehearse in New York for three weeks, then play out of town in two cities — Boston and Philadelphia — before coming to Broadway at the Winter Garden on February 27, the planned opening date. Nine days into the cast rehearsals, the schedule looked untenable. Things were definitely not going well. Sydney Chaplin, son of the great Charles, had been cast as Nicky Arnstein and although a gorgeous hunk of man, as required for the role, he was as charmless in his readings as he had been winning in his performance opposite Judy Holliday in the Styne-Comden-Green Broadway hit, *Bells Are Ringing*.

"If we could give him an image to imitate, it might help," Ray Stark told Garson Kanin. "William Powell or Errol Flynn rather than his trying to be Cary Grant." Then, going down a list of other problems in the cast, he added, "Strangely, Barbra doesn't have a sense of humor about herself from her reading. She does things that are funny, but they don't come out of inner humor."

"She was uncomfortable with all the members of the company," Lainie Kazan, who had been cast in a small role and would also function as Streisand's understudy, remembered. "She took herself very seriously, was distant, never able to laugh at herself, relax. Garson exerted great patience explaining where the humor of a scene should come from."

"I don't get it," she would say, looking puzzled. Garson would try another approach.

Having got the starring role she had wanted so desperately, Streisand realized what a tough assignment she had been given. She was expected to be as funny and original as Fanny Brice, but the script did not yet contain material that she could work with. She was insecure and did not want to display her fears to the company, so she kept to herself, with Elliott, Cis Corman, and Marty Erlichman watching her from the back of the theater and conferring with her afterward, much to Garson's irritation.

Throughout rehearsals during the frigid weeks in December, the air in the cavernous Winter Garden was raw with cold, the heat miserly low to save costs. One subzero, blustery day, Ray and Fran Stark — his dark red hair meticulously barbered, her makeup impeccably applied — were seated in the auditorium along with Lennart, Merrill (Styne was up onstage), Gordon, Erlichman, and Patrick ("I don't think anyone in the company knew why I was there," Patrick later said). On the otherwise bare stage, members of the cast sat in straight-back wooden chairs arranged in a circle around Garson Kanin, who was wearing a dapper brown pin-striped suit, with a small brimmed black hat that was his talisman (a gift from Spencer Tracy) cocked on his head. Streisand stood somewhat aloof on the edge of the circle, wrapped in her caracul coat, which she had been wearing almost every day. Kanin was giving a pep talk to his cast, and Streisand seemed impatient for it to end.

"I need your imagination," Kanin told his company. "The best of our show is the unexplored areas. Do not be inhibited. If something tends to come up, then let go. And as you go along, you will begin to anticipate problems. Please bring those problems to me. We're all terribly, terribly kind here."

In an apparent attempt to ease the tension between Streisand and the cast, Kay Medford, who was playing Mama Brice, leaned back in her chair and stage-whispered in a Yiddish accent to Streisand, who was standing behind her, "Did you get the coat honestly?"

Streisand, Medford later said, glanced down at her, unamused.

Styne was bouncing around the stage, talking to the technicians, hands flying. Kanin's assistant gave the order to please clear the stage for the first run-through. The director moved with Styne out into the orchestra and sat down behind a wooden table with a microphone atop it. The order was given for the run-through to start. Streisand entered from the wings still bundled up in her fur coat. She crossed slowly to the stage piano and began to finger the keys. Upstage was a brick wall with painted gray steam pipes running along the bottom half.

The show opens backstage in a theater. Fanny is already a star, with many memories and a broken marriage; after being released from jail, Arnstein has just walked out on her. She sings a song, later cut, and then the story cuts back to her youth. A piano in the orchestra pit starts the song. The musician cannot be seen. It was an eager, eighteen-year-old bespectacled Marvin Hamlisch (who ten years later would compose the score for *Chorus Line*), hired for his first big job as rehearsal pianist. Everyone was edgy. Streisand had moved too slowly. She was not standing where she had been told to stand. Then she began to sing.

"Her voice came off this bare stage and it started to reach around the empty theater," reported Jimmy Breslin, who was seated in the near-empty theater to write one of Streisand's first profiles as a coming star. "She was doing some sort of a dance while she sang and when her voice came on stronger Jule Styne, slumped in his seat, began to nod with the tune. Then there was this sort of growl in Barbra Streisand's voice and now you didn't notice the bare stage or the chairs or the guy carrying the ladder. It didn't matter where you were. She is that kind of a singer."

Kanin's head rocked back and forth with the song. "Yeah," he said out loud and smiled as she sang.

Fran Stark, always smartly turned out and quick with her opinion, was still not convinced that Streisand could or should play her mother, but it was now too late to do anything about it. Marty Erlichman and Streisand's lawyer, Bella Linden, had seen to it that their client was well paid at $5,000 a week, plus a percentage of the gross, and safeguarded: if fired, she would have to be paid off handsomely. The already escalating costs of the show — now upward of $500,000 — seemed to prohibit such a move. Memos flew back and forth between Ray Stark (often dictated by Fran) and Garson Kanin. Putting it simply, Fran thought Streisand lacked class — the element that had always been evident in Fanny Brice's on- and offstage demeanor, even her comedic roles — and how did one teach a performer class? Kanin was sure he could. He called it elegance.

He took Streisand aside. "Elegance is making an art of life," he told her. He went on to explain that an artist's function was to achieve a modicum of order out of chaos. From order came refinement, which in art meant rhythm, tempo, style, form, and "best of all — elegance. Fanny Brice had elegance," he stressed, adding, "There has never been a great comedian who did not have elegance."

For the next three weeks, while they were still rehearsing in New

York, Kanin took her aside whenever he could and worked with her on the matter of elegance. He told her about Chaplin, Brice, Keaton — legendary comedians who had brought dignity to their art. "I want you to stand tall, lift your head, listen to your fellow actors when they are talking to you on stage. Don't make the mistake of believing that the public loves you for yourself when in truth they only love you for your talent.

"Finally, it penetrated," he recalled. "She had more dignity, human nobility, self-respect, and respect for the audience. She left all the common and cheap effect and was on the road."

Streisand was learning things from Kanin that she knew would benefit her immensely — how to move onstage, project her voice, react to what other performers were saying. She lapped up this kind of teaching, pulled more and more from him, wanted to know more about the stars he had worked with, like Katharine Hepburn and Judy Holliday. Kanin kept her as sheltered as possible from the confusion that raged around her. The script was in a constant state of flux, which did not seem to trouble Streisand, who would learn a new scene in a matter of minutes.

The most pressing problems were, and would continue to be, the weak portrait of Nicky Arnstein, the downhill slide of the second act, and the unhappy ending that was totally contrary to what was then expected in musical comedies — even twenty years after Rodgers and Hammerstein's *Carousel* had endowed the genre with a new seriousness of purpose. Lennart would write a new scene according to suggestions given her by the Starks and Kanin. Ruth Gordon privately sent memos of her ideas. John Patrick, meanwhile, confided his comments to Ray Stark, who passed many of them on to Lennart, who wrote and rewrote and rewrote again. Streisand took all these changes with seasoned equanimity. In fact, as she has said, she loved the process of reworking scenes in rehearsals —"week after week being able to experiment, to modify, to change, to discover what worked and what didn't, and why."

No one knew the extent to which Lennart's private life was in upheaval or how much the strain of the pressure exacted on her. She had been an informer for Senator McCarthy's House Un-American Activities Committee hearings during the early fifties, when so many of her former coworkers had their lives ruined and many more were painfully affected and blacklisted.* Wounds ran deep and there were bitter feelings toward those who had informed on friends and colleagues. Many of the executive staff of *Funny Girl* and the cast looked upon her as a pariah, and she felt their scorn. Her son was being treated for drug addiction, her husband was drinking heavily, and, as they were both three thousand miles away in California, her telephone bills were astronomical. She was on edge and quickly dissolved into tears under stress. To bridge this problem, Stark now had Patrick work with Lennart in her hotel suite so that she would not be exposed to criticism at meetings or allow any rumors to spread that Patrick was acting as a play doctor.

Streisand remained detached from the members of the company. "Once in a while I would sit on the floor next to her during rehearsals," John Patrick said, "but we never became close. She was not, in my opinion, a lovable human being, as most actors are. There was a great hostility in the company. [At the beginning] Barbra and Sydney Chaplin, her leading man, hated each other. In the scene where she sits on the doorsteps and sings 'People,' he would look up at her adoringly and whisper out of the side of his mouth, 'You're off-key, you bitch!' Ray tried to fire him, but he had a run-of-the-play contract. Ray used me to talk to him and order him not to invent dialogue of his own. Sydney would reply, 'Well, I don't like the dialogue I'm given, so I'm inventing my own.' Ray devised several funny schemes to make him quit, but Sydney paid no attention to them."

On the few off days that Streisand had, she indulged in her most consuming passion — shopping for antiques. She and Elliott were still in the throes of decorating their duplex penthouse. No longer limited to thrift-shop purchasing, she dragged Elliott to Manhattan's high-priced wholesale antique district with the same avidity. She plunged into vast warehouses, trailed by Elliott and their decorator, dashing from item to item, shouting, "How much?" with the decorator, hired on a friend's

---

*People brought up before the HUAC were asked to name friends and coworkers whose liberal views made them suspected communists. Many frightened witnesses implicated innocent people, guilty of nothing more than a belief in something they considered to be an American right — freedom of speech. It was one of the darkest periods in American history.

recommendation, busily making notes. They would thread from one warehouse to another.

During one such buying orgy, when the two of them were accompanied by *Life*'s Shana Alexander, the hefty owners of a shop specializing in mirrors and glass refused to haggle over price. Suddenly the Goulds fancied that the proprietors of *this* shop didn't like them. "It's a front, Barbra. It's a bookie joint. They're gangsters," Alexander quoted Elliott as saying to soothe his wife's ego before wandering off to investigate on his own. A while later on their way back up the street, Streisand rapped on the window of the supposed "bookie joint" and, waving a sales check from another establishment, shouted: "Yah! You thought I wasn't gonna buy, huh? Well, I spent $3,000 next door."

She had bought five glorious crystal chandeliers and an ornate early-nineteenth-century piano, its interior no longer operative. Once again reunited with Elliott, she excitedly told him about the piano. "How could you buy a piano without consulting me?" he demanded, seriously offended.

"Don't you care about our home?" she countered. "It's the most beautiful piano I've ever seen!"

"It's hideous!" he yelled.

"Elly, it has *painted scenes* on it," she shot back stubbornly.

There followed "a screaming, four-letter fight in the street, hopping in and out of taxis, over curbs, past startled pedestrians, oblivious of decorator, [reporter,] and passersby," Alexander wrote of her eyewitness involvement.

In the weeks since Streisand had started rehearsals, she and Elliott had engaged in a great many verbal battles in less-than-private places — stores, restaurants, the lobby of their building — which would end in a cold silence between them and could last from one day to the next. "Elliott was fighting for what he considered to be his masculine identity. Barbra could not and would not understand that," one friend said. They disagreed about almost every item Streisand bought for the penthouse. Beyond that, they fought about what was to go where, noticeably her decision — which she won — to hang one of the ornate chandeliers in the master bathroom. Their bed was the one exception. Both of them wanted it to approximate a stage setting. "It should be like the place Des-demona got strangled in," Elliott told a bewildered upholsterer commissioned to make the quilted spread and hangings in green brocade. On the bedside table was a gilt-edged photo of Barbra licking a large lollipop and inscribed: "Too Eleot i wuv you Barbrra."

Streisand was undergoing a major upheaval in her career and in her private life. Celebrity and riches had come to her in a span of only three years, and she had not been prepared for the drastic changes they would bring. The newly wedded Goulds seldom had time alone together. Now she was too involved in what was happening at the Winter Garden and in her career to share much else, and she moved in a crowd of people: Erlichman; record producers and representatives; Peter Daniels, who at her request had been made assistant musical director and played in the pit of the show; and staff members, reporters, decorators, drivers, and dedicated fans who were happy to be gofers, running errands and fetching the containers of Chinese food that she greedily devoured.

In rehearsals nothing escaped her critical attention. A costume or wig that did not fit exactly right was rejected. She did not like a song ("I Tried") that Styne and Merrill had written for the finale and refused to sing it. It was cut from the show. Unsure of her dancing ability, she was constantly at dagger's end with Carol Haney, the choreographer. A roller-skate number had been written and choreographed for her, and despite the fact that the logo for the show had been drawn from this number (Fanny upside down with skates in the air), she insisted that it be cut.

Her behavior did not endear her to her coworkers, but by now there was a general consensus that the success of *Funny Girl* was greatly dependent upon her performance and the power of her voice. Kanin sincerely believed no other actress/singer could carry the show and did his best to appease her detractors. "Barbra's just tense," he would say. "She's new at this and she's carrying a heavy weight on her shoulders."

One day during rehearsal Kanin noticed a man — unknown to him — seated in the balcony, apparently taking notes. Outsiders were not permitted into rehearsals, so he went up to confront him. Streisand, nervous about the slow progress she was making in bringing her character to life, had called Allan Miller to come in secretly to observe everything she was doing and work with her on her interpretation. Miller has claimed she also called on him when she was in rehearsals for *I Can Get It for You Wholesale*.

"Who are you?" Kanin asked, "and why are you sitting up here taking notes?"

"I'm Barbra's cousin," Miller said.

Kanin was not taken in. He had heard a rumor that his star was working with a coach in private, a situation intolerable for a director staging a show. "There is only one director here," Kanin insisted. Miller departed, but Streisand made certain that Kanin knew she was displeased. During another rehearsal Kanin had her repeat something numerous times. There were words. It was the star's will against the director's, and it looked for an hour or so that one of them might quit. It ended in a draw.

Her faith in Kanin had been lost, believing that he did not understand the character as deeply as she did or that he could not help her bring more strength and pathos to her interpretation. Frustrated, fearful that her great opportunity might slip her grasp, she became tense and short-tempered.

The day following her standoff with Kanin, Milton Rosenstock, the musical director, arrived early for rehearsal. Streisand — who was usually late — was sitting on a stool, waiting under a single work light. Rosenstock felt "a dread, as if a dynamite fuse had been lighted in the theater." She hardly spoke to him and remained where she was without moving. The cast wandered in. She glared at them with defiance, as if to say, "Goddamit, you didn't expect me today, did you?" Rosenstock noted.

"Okay, let's take it from the top," Kanin ordered when he arrived on the scene.

Rosenstock remembered "an absolute hush in the theater for a few minutes. Then, as the music [to 'People'] started, what Streisand did went purposefully against every instruction Kanin had given her. If she was supposed to stand still, she moved; if she was supposed to move, she stood still. She was running all over the stage, doing crazy things. She was like a maniac, improvising. As I looked back toward the seats, I saw

Garson sitting with his mouth open. Then Jule was on me in a minute, squeezing my shoulder until it hurt. His face was white. He literally snarled, 'Leave her alone, Milt, she's on fire. Just follow, follow . . .'"

Finally, when the rehearsal moved on to "Don't Rain on My Parade," she collapsed into sobs. "I'm so sorry," she cried, "I'm so sorry." No one came forward to comfort her. Rosenstock stopped the orchestra, and she walked off the stage. Kanin canceled rehearsal for the rest of the day.

Rosenstock said she came to him a few days later and said, "I got it now. It's a duet."

"What do you mean, a duet?" he asked.

"I'm not alone up there. I've got you. I've got the whole orchestra. I'm not up there alone."

"Jesus Christ, no, you're not alone," Rosenstock replied with strong irritation.

Nonetheless, she never overcame the sense of "being out there alone," of having only herself to rely upon. A manifestation of her insecurity, her fear that she would fail because of *other* people made her seem aloof, utterly self-centered. Peter Daniels was the one anchor she had. She did not have the close companionship of Elliott or Sheree North, as she had in *Wholesale,* or the empathy of a Jack Kruschen. Lainie Kazan recalled, "It was strange. Although she was the star, Barbra always seemed to be the outsider."

She was further disconcerted when Kazan was signed to be her understudy. Kazan (real name Elaine Levin) had been two classes ahead of her at Erasmus High School. A stunning young woman with enormous dark eyes, gorgeous, thick black hair, a glowing complexion, and a knockout figure, Kazan had majored in theater at college and since graduation had done small roles in two short-lived Broadway shows, *The Happiest Girl in the World* and *Bravo, Giovanni,* as well as appearing in local clubs. She had a powerful show voice, could dance well, and fell into comedy easily. When Ray Stark hired her for the minor role of Vera, a Ziegfeld showgirl and friend of Fanny's, he also signed her to a seven-year film contract. There was talk about the possibility of her playing a role with Elizabeth Taylor and Marlon Brando in *Reflections in a Golden Eye,* a film Stark was developing. Meanwhile, he wanted Kazan to get a little more exposure and gave her fifty dollars extra a week to understudy Streisand, although he made it very clear that he thought she was too beautiful to ever take over the role.

"Fifty dollars a week to me at that time was like — staggering," she recalled. "But I didn't want to be anybody's understudy. I knew in my heart that that was not the gig for me."

Stark, who had broken his leg and had to wear a cast at the time, then committed a fatal error. He asked Peter Daniels to work with Kazan on Fanny's numbers, although Marvin Hamlisch was by this time assistant vocal director and would have been the more likely choice. However, Daniels had done so much for Streisand that Stark felt it was a smart move to have him coach Kazan. With this move, Streisand harbored great resentment toward Stark and Kazan, who was unaware of the ramifications of her new good fortune or how costly her association with Daniels would be for both of them.

"I hadn't met Peter until the first day of rehearsals in New York," Kazan remembered. "He started flirting with me. I said, 'Who's this guy? He's too old for me.' And he wasn't my type. But he was so charming and he had this English accent. Then when Ray signed me as Barbra's understudy and we started working together, he had just separated from his wife and I had just lost my father and he was very comforting to me. He was a fine musician and a wonderful teacher — very patient, very gentle, but sure. He told me he was mad for me from the first day we met. I grew to love him. I knew he was Barbra's conductor and I didn't want to trespass. But it seemed the two things — my growing feelings for Peter and his working with me — did not conflict. And after all, the producer had made the arrangements. We were simply carrying through on our professional commitment. Later I realized that Barbra regarded our relationships as a betrayal by both Ray and Peter."

The tension in Streisand was building. Not only did she fear that Stark might be grooming Kazan to replace her if things did not work out well on the road, but the libretto was in deeper trouble than ever. Streisand and the rest of the company would have to memorize new scenes and complicated song-and-dance numbers on a daily basis. Now even the survival of the song "People," which she had already recorded as a single, was in question. Kanin believed that it was a great number but that it set the wrong mood and did not belong in the show.

"At that moment . . . [Fanny's] just met the fellow [Nick]. Why should she become philosophical?" Kanin asked the song's writers. Kanin had not been the first or only one to think "People" was wrong for the show. Stark agreed, and Styne and Merrill might well have given in, but they were certain that Streisand's recording of it would be a big hit. They promised to write a backup for "People" if Kanin would leave the number in during the Boston tryout and until after the record's release.

"I promise you, Gar, when you put the right light on her opening night and she sings this song, she'll bring the house down," Merrill vowed. "People" stayed in.

A few days before the *Funny Girl* company was to leave for Boston, Elliott was cast as the court jester in a television version of Mary Rodgers's "Once Upon a Mattress," a musical based on the fairy tale "The Princess and the Pea," which starred Carol Burnett as the zany princess, a role she had played in the original Broadway production five years earlier. Since then, Burnett had become a huge television star. Though only two weeks' work, it was the first job Elliott had landed since *On the Town*. Streisand left for the out-of-town tryouts without him. She was given a suite in the Ritz-Carlton Hotel.

Sydney Chaplin was down the hall.

13

Swaddled in a new mink coat, a matching hat pulled down over her ears, Streisand stepped off the train in Boston into the shivery cold. It was late afternoon on January 7, 1964, and in six days *Funny Girl* would open there at the Shubert Theatre. A state of frenzy existed as Carol Haney instituted new dance routines, Irene Sharaff redesigned costumes, Isobel Lennart persistently reworked the second act, and Jule Styne and Bob Merrill put the finishing touches to five new songs that in the end would be cut before the show left Boston. Despite the large company, Streisand kept to herself. She missed Elliott and the carefree times they had shared during the out-of-town tryouts of *I Can Get It for You Wholesale,* shopping for cheap treasures for their walk-up railroad flat. There had been no intermediate stage in her life. One day she lived over a fish restaurant, the next her home was a lavish Central Park West penthouse.

As she was in almost every scene in the show and had to learn new lines with each rehearsal, she had little free time. Allan Miller came up from New York at her request and without Garson Kanin's knowledge and again worked privately with her on her performance, trying to get her to relate what was happening in certain scenes with events in her own life. To infuse more emotional depth into her interpretation, he told her to think about her father and how she would feel if he were in the audience. To bring the role closer to her, he would have done better to point out similarities to Brice: the maturing process of two homely girls, the unerring taste, the penchant for both comedy and tragedy, and even a marriage to an unrepentant gambler. Miller claims a great measure of responsibility for Streisand's effectiveness in the role, but his presence was also detrimental to her relationship with Kanin and her ability to take direction from him. Ultimately, it added to her confusion.

Well aware that she was carrying the show — that if she failed, it would ultimately fail, too — her responsibility was awesome. "She had a killer instinct," one member of the company said, "very sophisticated for someone so new to the theater. Whenever a new scene or song was introduced that could in any way take the spotlight from her, we knew it would get either cut or twisted around to her advantage. And it always did. Syd had a solo, I think the only one he had left at that point, and she began improvising dialogue that she interjected as he sang ['You Are Woman']. Well, her lines were great, and it did help the number when Styne and Merrill turned the solo into a duet with Barbra filling in counter-harmony with comic patter. But since she now had all the gag lines, it quickly became her scene. There was a good supporting character, a beautiful Ziegfeld girl, Georgia, who was the great producer's mistress. The part got whittled down until it just disappeared." Lainie Kazan's Vera now had only four lines. Except for Kay Medford in the role as Mama Brice, no other woman was left in a major part.

Allyn Ann McLerie, a bright, talented dancer and singer who Kanin particularly liked and who had received excellent reviews opposite Ray Bolger in *Where's Charley?,* had been cast as Georgia. McLerie originally had a song and dance called "Baltimore," but by the time *Funny Girl* began rehearsals in Boston, the number first had been shifted to Streisand and then cut.

Kanin was not happy about it, for he felt that Georgia gave Streisand someone to play off in the second act. Streisand did not agree. For Fanny to have a beautiful showgirl as a confidante was not in character. The show was considerably overlong, and McLerie's role was not germane to the plot. Georgia could be cut without additional rewriting. Kanin finally gave in, and the character was sacrificed.*

"It was absolute chaos. The show wasn't right, and we all knew it," Kazan recalled. "People were being fired and replaced left and right. Every day I'd come in and there would be someone auditioning for my small role and for Barbra's. A whole lot of well-known singers arrived one after the other. Eydie Gormé was one I remember. But Jule was really behind Barbra. So was Ray, but he was ultimately a businessman and he had bought out Merrick's financial interest in the show and had a lot at stake."

Kanin was under fire. He and Jule Styne were at loggerheads. Ray Stark was sending memos, several pages long. Fran had her say through her husband in equally lengthy dictated letters. Chaplin was disgruntled, Lennart near collapse, Irene Sharaff and Carol Haney fighting over the dance costumes. Then Carol Haney was fired.

"It was the baby number that got Carol axed," Kazan believes. "There was a number called 'Bye, Bye, Baby Bunting,' which all the showgirls sang dressed in diapers and little bunny ears and snuggy hats. Sydney Chaplin sang to all of us, and we were in cribs and would dance in the cribs while we sang this song. It was so embarrassing that we would just die. We did the number on closing night in Boston. The next thing I know, Carol is fired and Jerry Robbins is there.

"Barbra just did not have the role in her grasp yet. She was nervous, poor baby, the whole show was on her shoulders. But she was shrewd and I knew that. I was in absolute awe of her ability to wheel and deal and usurp the power position. I was staggered by her. I just could not understand how anybody could do that. Ray was anxious to give her a couple

*Garson Kanin's *Funny Girl* files contain an exchange of letters between Kanin and Allyn Ann McLerie regarding this episode. On February 28, 1964, as the show got set for its New York previews, Kanin wrote McLerie, "I would have had it otherwise, Allyn Ann. I believed, then and now, that you brought a note to the show which it needed and needs now. You are wildly attractive and brilliantly talented. You are original and one hell of an actress." McLerie answered that she did not blame him in any way, it was just "the hazards of the trade!"

of days off so that they could find out what they were going to do about her. They were set to try me or someone else in the role, but Barbra was not about to let that happen."

To add to the problems, the cast was having difficulty with the amplification system in the Shubert. Styne was one of the few composers at the time who liked heavy amplification and had even installed hidden mikes in the footlights when Ethel Merman, known for her ability to project, had starred in *Gypsy*. Streisand found her body mike to be offensive. She complied after realizing that some lyrics and dialogue might be lost without it, but the mechanical device slowed her costume changes and was uncomfortable to wear. The microphone was most frequently attached under the front section of her wig beneath either the forehead curls or bangs. The wires ran under the wig, down the back of her neck, and were connected to batteries in a mike pack strapped to her inner thigh.*

"I don't know what happened at this point to change Chaplin's attitude toward Barbra, but about the second week in Boston they suddenly became chummy," Kay Medford said. With Elliott in New York, Streisand was no doubt lonely and in desperate need of someone to turn to for support. She had alienated many members of the cast and crew. Being the "star" was a new experience for her, and perhaps she didn't handle her position well. She distanced herself from those who did attempt to befriend her and was thought to be aloof, cool, always guarded.

Despite Chaplin's physical allure and apparent charm, Fanny and Nicky were not setting off sparks when together onstage, a chemistry that was needed for the story to work. Streisand had much to gain by encouraging Chaplin's attention. She would have a close confidant in the company, and her scenes with him would play better. There was a steady parade back and forth between their rooms. Chaplin arranged some quiet dinners for the two of them, and Streisand was extremely flattered by his attention. In rehearsals he softened toward her. Onstage, new ex-

---

*According to the sound designers T. Richard Fitzgerald and Otis Munderloh, *Funny Girl* was the first Broadway show to use body mikes. *Golden Boy,* which opened six months later, was the second.

citement generated between them. It turned "You Are Woman" into a sensual, sexy number and made the final denouement when the two parted more poignant. Unhappily, rumors began to appear in some Broadway columns. "What new musical comedy star and her leading man are a romantic duet off stage to the fury of the actor's beautiful wife?"* Earl Wilson wrote. Nothing was said about Elliott, but he was no fool. There were accusatory, emotional telephone calls in which he became jealous over Chaplin and she blamed him for upsetting her at a time when she had to be as collected as possible.

Possessing a striking, distinguished manner and good looks that he came by naturally as the son of Charlie Chaplin and his second wife, the enchanting silent-screen actress Lita Grey, Chaplin was a formidable suitor. He told Streisand stories about his father and Hollywood and the stars, and she learned about the shocking effect on the film industry of the McCarthy years, when Chaplin and so many other brilliant filmmakers had been persecuted. She devoured Chaplin's narratives as hungrily as she did their private dinners, often served in her hotel suite. They were both married and, as public figures, in danger of being exposed as lovers at a time when moral standards were rigid. Streisand was also taking a chance of jeopardizing her marriage.

Funny Girl opened in Boston on January 13. The company all waited after the performance in a restaurant next door to the theater for the morning reviews. "For some reason," John Patrick said, "I was given the critics' reviews to read aloud at the table where we all sat. When I read aloud one critic who said, 'Miss Streisand can sing, but she certainly can't act,' Streisand put her head down on the table and burst into tears. I remember saying to her, 'That's nonsense — you can act!' But I don't think she paid much attention. She left the table almost immediately after."

A few days later, *Variety* reported: "*Funny Girl* is a gem of a show which took off at the Shubert [in Boston] and shows considerable box office strength. Barbra Streisand provides brilliance in every scene — singing, dancing, clowning, mugging. She has a wonderful voice and the

*Sydney Chaplin was married to dancer Noelle Adams.

right fizz to carry the Fanny Brice role in high musical comedy style." This should have cheered Streisand, but the critic had added: "Show, however, needs polishing and work in its second act. . . . With some thirty minutes already cut from [a benefit performance the previous night], *Funny Girl* can gain by more editing — especially in the second act."

The length of the show remained a problem. "Our curtain went down at 11:09 Saturday night," Ray Stark advised Kanin, adding that with all the new material Lennart was writing, the curtain would not come down until 11:31. "Do you feel this estimate is reasonably accurate?" he asked. "And is there anything you would like me to do in reference to the situation?" Kanin responded by speeding up the movement and cutting five numbers.*

After a week of performances in Boston, the company left for Philadelphia. It did not take a genius to know that the show was in for a bumpy ride. Playwright-screenwriter and well-known play doctor Norman Krasna flew in from Klosters, Switzerland, where he had a home, to work with Lennart on the libretto, on which John Patrick was still consultant and the Kanins, the Starks, and Styne and Merrill were adding their ideas. "Isobel felt ignored," Patrick recalled, "and once burst into tears at being shunned. Thereafter, I always stood behind her chair [during story discussions] so it would look as if questions being directed to me to take notes on were directed at her."

Everyone was in a stew. There were secret gatherings held in hotel rooms, the ladies' lounge at the theater, the front office, and the music storeroom. "Peter [Daniels] was working separately and privately with both Barbra and me," Lainie Kazan recalled. "He was under ghastly pressure. We were very much in love. He wanted to help me, [but] at the

---

*From the time of its first performance in Boston until it moved on to Philadelphia, at least six songs in all were cut: "Baltimore," "A Helluva Group," "It's Home," "Took a Little Time," "Sleep Now, Baby Bunting," "Bye, Bye, Baby Bunting," and "Absent-Minded Me," which Streisand later recorded as a single. Other numbers that were cut either before Boston or after Philadelphia were "I Tried," "I Did It on Roller Skates," "A Temporary Arrangement," "My Daughter, Fanny the Star," "He's Got Larceny in His Heart," "He," and "Do Puppies Go to Heaven?" Although the majority of these songs were never mounted in the production, the sheer number written for the show is unusual.

same time he felt Barbra would expect his loyalty to be entirely to her. He was under terrible pressure.

"One day, in Philly, I overheard Garson tell the stage manager to fire me, that I was too attractive to play Fanny Brice. I was devastated. So, now they're auditioning more people to understudy, and I'm crazed. I knew I could play the part, but in the sixties somebody attractive just could not be funny unless it was sophisticated comedy or the dumb-smart blonde like Judy Holliday. I ran out of the theater, Peter in pursuit, and I was sobbing.

"Lainie, call Garson, call Jerry Robbins, call them on the phone and tell them that you want to audition for them. Tell them to give you just ten minutes and if they don't like you after that, they can fire you." It took all the courage I had, but with Peter coaching me from the sidelines, I called Garson and pleaded that he give me ten minutes. He agreed and with Peter at the piano, I did 'I'm the Greatest Star' and then one of Fanny's solo scenes. Garson said nothing, not even 'thank you,' and left. But I was never fired."

Kazan's job had been saved, and Streisand's star position had become more secure as she had loosened up and was now both funny and moving, her acting and understanding of the role having greatly improved (there had never been any doubt about the power of her voice). But Stark remained adamant about firing Sydney Chaplin, even if it meant paying off his contract, and both Hal Linden and Darren McGavin (at different times) were brought secretly to Philadelphia to audition privately. Neither had the right chemistry, and Stark dropped the idea. Streisand was comfortable with Chaplin, who she knew would not diminish or compete with her star turn. He was charming and adequate in the role, no more. Her concern was that Kanin would not bring the show together in time for its Broadway opening. Gripped by fear that her great chance for stardom might get sidetracked, or even derailed, she went to Ray Stark and complained, "I think I'm not being directed enough. I need a lot more direction."

Stark was in a quandary. Jule Styne, who had the hotel suite below his in Philadelphia, claimed that one morning Stark lowered a bedspread outside his window, a note attached to the end of it printed with the word HELP! Stark finally turned to Jerome Robbins, who — as he was both a choreographer and a director and had previously been involved in the project — he felt would be able to pull things together. Robbins was not sure he wanted to take on the task and for the moment remained in New York. *Funny Girl* opened on February 4, 1964, at the Forrest Theatre in Philadelphia to glowing notices for Streisand. "All in all, the evening is a Streisand triumph," reported the critic on the *Philadelphia Inquirer.*

"But in dealing with the unhappy marriage between Fanny Brice and gambler Nick Arnstein, who is stiffly played by Sydney Chaplin, *Funny Girl* is unfortunately weighted down by a dull and unimaginative treatment," the critic for the *Evening Bulletin* added. "There are long arid stretches that will have to be eliminated and, no doubt, director Garson Kanin knows exactly where they are."

Apparently, Ray Stark did not think so, because the day before the show closed in Philadelphia, the Kanins received an expensive present of antique china from the Starks, and the next day Jerome Robbins arrived on the scene. Kanin was told that Robbins was not to replace him but to act as production supervisor. From the moment of his arrival, Streisand turned to Robbins for the direction she had asked for. But his appearance at this late date caused a great deal of upheaval in the company.

"Whatever Ray Stark wanted to call Jerry's involvement, I considered that I had been fired," Kanin said. "I did not desert the company entirely, but I withdrew and Jerry took over. The final credit 'Directed by Garson Kanin — Production Supervised by Jerome Robbins' was as confusing to me as it was to everyone else." The Kanins remained in Philadelphia for the show's run and silently attended the pre-Broadway New York rehearsals.

John Patrick left the company as soon as Robbins (who appears to have been kept waiting in the wings by Stark) was hired. "My own impression [of the show in New York] was that he took out a lot of good things that Gar had put in and added a few absurd ones of his own," Patrick commented. The company returned to New York to prepare for a series of previews before the planned opening, which would eventually be postponed four times. Meanwhile, Lennart holed up once again in her hotel room and with Norman Krasna's help began to rewrite part of the second act and the ending once again. This act eventually had forty-one revisions, almost certainly a Broadway record, before the show opened.

Streisand went home to her Manhattan penthouse and to Elliott, her affair with Chaplin over. With no job offers in view, Elliott spent a good portion of his time bolstering his wife and making sure she took care of herself. ("Sometimes, I think Barbra is twenty-two, going on eight," he was heard to comment.) The day began with him shouting to her over the intercom from the floor below their bedroom, where she was still resting, "Come and get your chicken soup!" He made sure that the kitchen was stocked with the foods she liked — almost all high-caloric and fairly indigestible to the majority. Streisand ate like a woman three times her weight, which miraculously remained at 125 pounds. They had installed a small refrigerator in an antique chest beside their bed so that she could dig into a pint of coffee ice cream while watching late night television. On top of the chest was a copy of J. D. Salinger's *Franny and Zooey* and *How to Achieve and Maintain Complete Sexual Happiness in Marriage*. She was, however, more of a romantic than her reading material would suggest.

She ordered two dozen gardenias delivered to the apartment each week. They floated in an urn in the kitchen, a cut-crystal bowl in the dining room, a Baccarat champagne glass in the master bathroom, and a shallow Victorian dish beside her bed. "A gardenia is like a free spirit," she told one reporter. "Its fragrance cannot be captured. It's like it doesn't want to be tied down and destroyed by all the sterility of the modern times." After a short pause, she added, "I think sensory. I always tell Elliott to speak to me sensory."

Ray Stark viewed her in a different light. "She is like a barracuda. She devours every piece of intelligence to the bone," he asserted. One of the actors in the company told a *Time* interviewer, "She is like a filter that filters out everything except what relates to herself. If I said, 'There's been an earthquake in Brazil,' she would answer, 'Well, there aren't any Brazilians in the audience tonight, so it doesn't matter.'"

Streisand *was* self-absorbed when she worked. Everything was geared to succeeding in *Funny Girl,* to becoming a Broadway star. She had added to her performance a dazzling spray of gestures, inflections, and small takes that had made the role distinctively hers. She felt ready to carry the show on her own, and there were many who believed that this had been her intent from the very start. In the fifteen weeks in which the show had made its precarious way to the Winter Garden, she had submitted herself to an intensive education in the art of stagecraft, how to project her speaking voice, move, walk, exit. Miss Marmelstein had been mainly a singing role. Now she had to age, to show many different emotions: love, anger, joy, bitterness. She was seldom offstage and, when she was, had many costume and mood changes to master. If she had not been self-absorbed, she probably would not have been able to rise above the additional and multitudinous problems in the out-of-town tryouts.

Once back in New York from Philadelphia, her relationship with Chaplin moved on to a more professional level. Whatever free time she had was spent with Elliott. They still fought but appeared, like in a Tracy-Hepburn movie, to be fiercely in love. "He looked at her adoringly," one friend said, "and she always lit up when he was near. There was a lot of touching — his arm around her waist, her hand on his arm or chest, her fingers going through his hair. They shared quantities of food, always with mutual gusto, whispered to each other — secret jokes, apparently. Barbra would not be able to control her squeals of giggle-laughter. Elliott was protective, caring and amazingly understanding. She could run hot and cold about people. And she had a quick temper. Very combative. But he knew exactly how to handle her. She could not be diverted or cajoled. You had to stand up to her. She respected that, and I never saw Elliott back down."

Her long hours of rehearsals — and then, as the previews began, the performances and daily changes in the script and music that had to be memorized on short notice — left him extended time alone. His part in the television production of "Once Upon a Mattress" had not generated any potential jobs. Calls to his agent were disappointing. He had worked for only twelve weeks that year and had earned very little money. He found it difficult to be supported by his wife, not to have cash in his pocket. Before her *Funny Girl* involvement, he had collected unemployment. He later said, "I felt like such a failure collecting that fifty dollars. I couldn't justify taking it and I hated waiting in line to collect it." He drifted back to gambling, small bets with a bookie on horses or sporting events. If Streisand was aware of his problems, she was able to block them out as she plowed straight ahead in her consuming passion to make the critics recognize her acting acumen and to make *Funny Girl* a smash hit.

Like many other recording artists who had risen to the top of the charts with shocking suddenness, Streisand did not know how rich she was. Accountants took care of her financial affairs and paid her bills. She has claimed she took a weekly allowance of twenty-five dollars. However, she seldom paid for anything out of pocket. She was living high but certainly not loose. Never would she divest herself of that love of bargaining, an art at which she had already become expert. Whether she was dealing with the butcher or an antique dealer, a discount was anticipated. "Let's see, with twenty percent off that makes —," she would begin. "Whaddaya mean, that's your price?" she would ask with dismay if the answer was negative. "I deserve *something*."

Before going on the road, she had recorded *The Third Album,* which was released in February while *Funny Girl* was in New York previews. A few weeks later she cut the cast album, with a *Life* reporter and photographer chronicling the session. She wore "smudged white Capri pants, knee-high crocodile boots, a flowing, fur-collared cape and a hat like a bishop's miter," *Life* reported. "She was an hour late, but she entered the roomful of irritable musicians with the confidence of Clyde Beatty. You could almost see the cane chair and the whip in her hand. She took no warm-up, and when she sang she was the complete pro."

The *Funny Girl* cast album was number two on *Variety*'s list of best-selling albums within three weeks of its release — before the show opened. *The Third Album* surfaced at number twenty-one and began to make its way up the list while *The Second Album* was still in the Top Ten. Simultaneously, "People" was in the Top Ten on the singles chart. Streisand was making more money from her records than she could ever accrue from the show. Marty Erlichman felt she was actually losing money since he could have booked her for high fees in the best nightclubs in the country. She would think about that at another time. Now her concentration was on her role in a show that was moving inexorably — despite all its postponements — to zero hour, opening night.

She felt additional pressure because *Hello, Dolly!*, starring Carol Channing, had just opened and was being hailed as the biggest musical hit since *My Fair Lady* debuted eight years earlier. Streisand feared her own success would be overshadowed by Channing, who was the toast of Broadway, the darling of the reviewers. Both *Hello, Dolly!* and *Funny Girl* would be compared as period musicals with similar numbers — Streisand's "Don't Rain on My Parade" and Channing's strikingly similar "Before the Parade Passes Me By." Both shows were about strong, controlling women, although Dolly gets her man in the end.

The day before opening night, the first and final scenes still were not set. Jerry Robbins now had Fanny entering with two Russian wolfhounds on a leash. Handling the dogs while crossing the stage, pausing midway to shrug her shoulders and then continuing on, proved — thanks to the misbehavior of the animals — to be more daunting than any of her splashy musical numbers. The scene remained until the last preview, after which — Streisand in a frazzle — the dogs were fired. The next morning the scene was rehearsed with Fanny sweeping across the stage as before, but sans animals. The last scene was rewritten and rehearsed just three hours before the curtain rose on opening night, March 26, 1964.

A state of anxiety enveloped Streisand. Elliott remained with her in her dressing room until her last call. She crushed out the umpteenth cigarette she had puffed on sporadically while she waited. Her dresser gave her costume and hair a final check. The assistant stage manager escorted her across the vast backstage area to the wing from where she would make her entrance.

Milton Rosenstock led the orchestra into the final chords of the overture. The curtain began to rise, and Streisand started onstage for her entrance. There was wild applause the moment she reached midstage, a surprise since she had not realized so many of her record fans would be in the audience. The applause remained thunderous after each one of her solos. Her ability to match Fanny Brice's gifts for hilarity and pathos overrode any objections to the weak book or to the skimpiness of the *Ziegfeld*

Follies numbers that the rising cost of the production had exacted. Her regal descent down a Ziegfeld staircase, dressed as a pregnant bride as a tenor sang "His Love Makes Me Beautiful" was as memorable as Channing's descent down the famous red-carpeted stairway at the Harmonia Gardens. There were no dancing waiters to sweep her off her feet at the bottom of the staircase, but her "Oy vey, am I beautiful!" as she openly advertised her condition by placing her arms around the swollen stomach beneath her lavish wedding gown brought the audience to its feet just the same. It was also clear that the number that was almost scrapped, "People," which she sang standing alone on a stage lit by a summer moon, was the hit of the show and that whatever fate was in store for *Funny Girl,* Barbra Streisand was now a bona fide star.

The standing ovation she received when she took her curtain calls brought this realization smack home to her. She was in a state of high exhilaration when Elliott came backstage directly afterward. He understood, better than anyone, what her personal success meant to her. Although she had always said she wanted to be an actress, her ambition was to become a *star.* Never would she have been satisfied to act without stardom as so many fine professionals do and as Elliott thought would probably be true in his case. Barbra needed stardom as a way to validate her worth, and he was glad for her yet frightened at the same time that her fame might adversely affect their relationship.

A lavish party at the Rainbow Room following the opening had been arranged by Ray Stark. Wearing borrowed diamonds (her own had been stolen the week before from the Stark's palatial East Side apartment), Fran presided elegantly over the party. The cavernous Rainbow Room, sixty-five stories above the streets of New York, its window wall looking out on a brilliantly lit Manhattan night view, was filled with illustrious guests, who for some reason were greeted on arrival by the band with several resounding choruses of "Hello, Dolly!" Former New York governor Thomas Dewey and Dr. Ralph Bunche, who had won the Nobel Peace Prize for mediating the 1948 Arab-Israeli truce, were chatting warmly. New York senator Jacob Javits was talking to an ebullient Sophie Tucker, the last of the red-hot mamas. Greek shipping tycoon Aristotle Onassis was hosting a large table of high-society guests. Bette Davis,

Gary Cooper and his stunning socialite wife, Rocky, and something like three hundred others had gathered and were waiting at their tables, along with those in the company who had already arrived, for the star to appear.

At the stage door of the Winter Garden, with Elliott acting like a football player running interference, Streisand forced her way through the throng of fans, reporters, and well-wishers. Microphones were pushed in front of her, cameras flashed in her face, blinding her. She clung to Elliott. "I can't believe this," she muttered, terrified. People were pawing her even as Elliott and a chauffeur helped her into the rear seat of her newly purchased Bentley. She had just experienced perhaps the single, greatest, personal triumph Broadway had seen in many years. There had been too many curtain calls for her to count. Channing was marvelous in *Hello, Dolly!*, but it was a role many others (eventually including Streisand herself) could and would play. *Funny Girl* would be a hit only because her performance was memorable. Her making the role so very much her own — as Yul Brynner had done in *The King and I* — would impede the success of any other performer doing it.*

She looked elegant as she entered the Rainbow Room on Elliott's arm, he in a handsome tuxedo and she in a dramatic, formfitting black gown. Her hair, cut short for the wigs she had to wear in the show, was coiffed in a gleaming copper helmet around her face. A tremendous ovation greeted her arrival. Everyone stood up, even Bette Davis, who was notorious for her lack of enthusiasm in matters of theatrical protocol. Ray Stark rushed up to his star and guided her through the groups of cheering people while the band played "I'm the Greatest Star" and then segued into "Cornet Man." She finally sat down with Elliott at a reserved table overlooking the dance floor, where the seventy-five-year-old Sophie Tucker plunged into a frenzied dance with a young man a third her age. Champagne was poured, and food was served in great abundance while everyone, including Diana in a designer gown

---

*Although Carol Channing would make a career of playing Dolly Levi in various touring companies and revivals, the black version with Pearl Bailey was a huge success, as were productions starring Ginger Rogers, Dorothy Lamour, and Betty Grable.

bought for her by Streisand, waited for the morning papers with the reviews.

"This is a talent, total, complete, utter and practicing. Vast talent, the kind that comes once in many years. That talent in *Funny Girl* flares and shimmers," wrote Whitney Bolton in the *Morning Telegraph*. "When she is a clown, she is an all-out clown, and when she is young Fanny fetched by handsome, dapper Nicky, confronted by a romance that could lead to more intimate association, she manages first to josh the whole idea, then to hurl herself at their relationship and take it whole to her heart. Miss Streisand, also like Fanny, is no pretty girl, no merely pretty girl. She does not need to be and never will. That talent will flame for a long time. Much longer than the vapid accident of beauty."

That about said it all, but the rest of her notices were nearly as glowing. When the reviews were read, there was much cheering and applauding. Champagne glasses were raised and raised again. A crush of people moved toward Streisand. Elliott held on to her elbow. He knew that crowds petrified her, and he was giving her tangible support. Guests and the press brushed by him trying to get her attention. She was too caught up in the moment to be aware that her husband was being socially acknowledged but otherwise ignored. There was too much else to think about.

She had made it as a Broadway star. The accomplishment was exhilarating. She more than gloried in her fame, she languished in it, reading everything that was printed about her. She confided to the few old friends like Cis Corman (who was now a casting director) that she was glad she had never changed her last name, as all her early detractors now knew she was famous — and there was great satisfaction to be gained from that. And yet, already it was not enough. Broadway stars seldom attained the kind of fame she dreamed about. The great fantasy of her childhood and youth remained out of reach — although closer. Her contract with Ray Stark stipulated that if *Funny Girl* was made into a movie, she would repeat her role as Fanny Brice. Only then would she be truly famous, recognized all over the world — perhaps even immortal. All her considerable energy would now be pressed into service to make that dream a reality.

Part IV

Making It

"I always knew I wanted to be famous. I knew it; I wanted it; I was
never contented. I was always trying to be something I wasn't. I wanted
to prove to the world that they shouldn't make fun of me."
— Barbra Streisand, 1966

14

A day seldom passed without Barbra's name appearing in the press — what she said, what she wore, where she went. The spotlight had caught Streisand in a blaze of stardom. She was "the Face"; she was every-where — the covers of five major magazines, the pages of *Vogue,* the jackets of three bestselling albums, the theater pages of the nation's leading newspapers. She could also have been called "the Voice" since her records were played so frequently on radio and over Muzak in eleva-tors and throughout restaurants. She had made it from the enor-mous, grim society of Nobodies into the small, enchanted circle of Somebodies.

Vogue described her as having an "odd, compelling beauty . . . the length of her neck, the slant of eyes, the round mouth. The way she moves her arms, her hands, with rare grace — but not too much." A few months earlier she had been called a kook for the way she dressed; now she was a controversial fashion leader who by the end of the year appeared on the lists of both the ten best-dressed *and* ten worst-dressed women.

"Some stories make it sound like I used to be an outrageous raga-muffin and now only wear designer fashions," she said shortly after *Funny Girl* opened. "To keep warm I used to wear layers and layers of cloth-ing — boots, leotards, wool dresses, big heavy coats, scarves, the works.

As soon as the first leaf falls from a tree, I'm chilled to the bone. Now I can afford fur, and it's like discovering a whole new world." A ponyskin pea jacket was lined in bleached raccoon, and a matching sailor cap and boots were also made out of pony skins. Jaguar skins were used for a severely tailored, double-breasted man's-style suit. The old cocoon-shaped caracul coat, purchased two years earlier for twenty dollars at a thrift shop, had been copied in white fur. She shopped with Elliott for men's shirts and ties to wear with the menswear suits that she currently favored and that looked especially good with her new boyish bob. She refused to wear the then obligatory girdle because she believed in "a minimum of underwear, so that the body is unconfined."

"What about formal gowns?" a fashion reporter asked her.

"I can always take down the drapes and make a dress!" Streisand said, eying the deep red velvet ones near where she was sitting. Then, with a good imitation of Scarlett O'Hara, she rose from her chair, sidled over to the plush fabric, and drew a corner of it under her chin. "Fiddle-de-de," she trilled in Southern dialect, "who cares!"

There was a Streisand *look,* far-out but fashionable, and a Streisand *sound,* the nasal Brooklyn-Jewish tone. After her performances in *Funny Girl* the rich and famous who were in the audience came to her dressing room to meet and congratulate this new phenomenon. She was invited to, and enjoyed attending, celebrity parties, reveling in the knowledge that she was now one of *them.* The master pianist Vladimir Horowitz confided, "I like listening to Streisand. I don't know why, but I do. I have her records, although I don't listen much to popular music. . . . A recording should have a balanced program — like she does it."

She gave copies of her albums to all the members of her family. "Would you believe my Aunt Muriel and Uncle Larry didn't know it was me when I played my first record for them?" she commented. That her Aunt Anna had died the day she made her debut on television with Orson Bean nagged at her. Family recognition meant a great deal.

Much of the credit for the song selection on her albums belongs to Streisand herself, but the arrangements by Ray Ellis and Peter Matz and the quality of the orchestra under Matz's baton give the records their shining excellence; Peter Daniels played the piano accompaniment. Matz had begun his musical career by creating the orchestrations, vocal arrangements, and dance music for Harold Arlen's *House of Flowers* (the score contains Streisand's favorite song, "A Sleepin' Bee") and the composer's next show, *Jamaica,* which starred Lena Horne. He then wrote the arrangements for Noël Coward's celebrated Las Vegas engagement and his Broadway show *Sail Away.* Matz was expert at working with unique singers and unusual material. His skills were perfectly suited to Streisand's talents.

In his artful arrangements, Matz avoids gimmicks or other crutches. He backs her as a master jeweler positions a precious diamond in a setting to display all the gem's facets and call no attention to itself. Like Streisand, he was a perfectionist. She would insist on many more takes than the record producer asked for and was severely critical of her own performance. She recorded her fourth album, *People,* in August 1964. Released the first week in September, it quickly rose to the top of the charts. Most of the collection is devoted to good songs that were seldom heard or had just come into their own. But it also includes a sophisticated version of Cy Coleman and Carolyn Leigh's "When in Rome (I Do as the Romans Do)," a masterful arrangement of Rodgers and Hammerstein's "My Lord and Master" (from *The King and I*) that recast a pentatonic song into a pop song, and offered a new (and perhaps the best) arrangement of "People"— this time with a quiet, touching ending, her voice soft but steady with emotion.

Less than a month into *Funny Girl*'s run, Elliott left for Jamaica to play a deaf mute, a small supporting role, in his first film, *Quick, Let's Get Married,* starring Ginger Rogers and Ray Milland. It would prove to be an inauspicious movie debut. Nonetheless, it was work *and* it was the movies. "Look what playing a deaf mute did for Jane Wyman," he joked, a reference to Wyman's Academy Award–winning performance in *Johnny Belinda.* He was in Jamaica on April 24, Streisand's twenty-second birthday. As Streisand took her curtain, a member of the audience shouted out birthday greetings, and the rest of the theater took up the cry. Milton Rosenstock led the orchestra in an enthusiastic chorus of "Happy Birthday." An armful of roses was presented to her, and she tossed them one by one over the footlights. Backstage, Ray Stark had arranged a cast party with champagne and a two-tier chocolate cake. Her coworkers gave her an irresistible, fluffy, white miniature poodle with melting brown eyes, the first dog she had ever owned. She named her Sadie and fell in love with her immediately.

After the cast party Marty Erlichman hosted a festive late supper for about twenty guests, including Diana, Shelley and his wife, and the Starks. Streisand seemed *wistful*. It had become more and more difficult for her to appear in public. People rushed over to her for autographs at restaurants, in stores, on the street. She could not even go to the ladies' room in a public place without being approached for an autograph, and several times an overly enthusiastic fan had thrust a piece of paper and a pen under the closed door of the cubicle she occupied. She had lost any semblance of privacy, and she claimed she *still* saw herself as a victim. "Ya know, why me?" To Laurence Grobel, her *Playboy* interviewer, she confessed, "Even my success makes me a victim. . . . I think, Oh, God, don't envy me. I have my own pains. Money doesn't wipe that out." And she told *Life* reporter Shana Alexander, "The only happiness I *know* is real is the happiness I get from eating coffee ice cream."

Stardom had been her dream and there was no way she was going to let it slip from her grasp, but she had discovered early that everything has a price — in many ways, one she hugely resented paying.

She was feeling the pressure and having difficulty getting through her performances each night. A large wall calendar hung in her dressing room, and she would cross off each day at the end of a performance and jot down how many more were left. All the publicity and the massive press coverage had made her crazy. How was she going to maintain the responsibility of fame? What was going to happen next? She didn't want to hurt Elliott, and she thought her celebrity would do just that. She suffered severe stomach pains, and a doctor put her on large doses of Donnatal, a muscle-relaxant prescription drug.

Her relationship with her mother had not improved much. Diana, who still worked in a Manhattan high school, viewed her daughter's extravagant new style with a critical eye and a dire warning that fame and money could disappear as fast as it had come. Diana was unable to say the things that Barbra wanted to hear — that she was proud of her, that she was terrific, that she had turned from an ugly duckling into a silken swan. When Streisand appeared on a magazine cover, it was either "Why were you wearing your bangs down over your eyes?" or "The neckline of your dress is cut too low."

"I wish I could give you the terrible problem I have with my ears!" Streisand once roared at a fan who told her she wished she could be her. And she was aware that unless Elliott's career took off soon, there would be serious trouble ahead in their marriage. At Cis Corman's husband's suggestion, she started therapy sessions three times a week with a psychoanalyst. She would continue therapy on and off (mostly on) for the next thirty years, but these were the sessions when her childhood and youth, so painful to her, were still fresh, smarting wounds, when her resentments toward Diana were constantly dissected and discussed. Unable to shed the past, she carried it around with her like an injured child.

These problems were pushed aside when Erlichman negotiated an astronomical contract in excess of five million dollars for ten television specials for CBS. An even higher fee could have been commanded, but Erlichman had insisted on her retaining complete artistic control and choice of material. She formed Ellbar, a production company that included Elliott as an executive partner. They decided that with no acting offers coming his way, it might be best if he kept an eye on her business interests and helped scout suitable projects that did not necessarily require her appearance. At the Tony Awards dinner in May 1964, she had lost to Carol Channing but the following May received a Grammy (Best Vocal Performance — Female) for the *People* album, for which Peter Matz also won a Grammy for best arranger. Being passed over a second time for a Tony ate away at her competitive nature. Was she *really* not as good as Carol Channing? Did the theater community have something against her? She fretted about such things, turning them over and over in her mind.

On October 10, 1965, Elliott appeared opposite Lesley Ann Warren in *Drat! The Cat!,* a musical with a score that Streisand admired. Two songs, "He Touched Me" and "I Like Him," would become part of her repertory. In *Drat! The Cat!,* a throwback to the mock-melodramas of the

1930s, Elliott played an inept policeman in love with a kooky, criminally minded heiress. It opened to negative reviews, survived a single week, and closed leaving him back where he was before — without a job.

"I thought a lot about what I should do," he recalled. He told Streisand that he wanted to strike out on his own, maybe try Hollywood. "I need you," she cried. "You've got to be there to protect me." It was the affirmation he wanted to hear, and he remained in New York. They were most happy late at night once her entourage had finally departed and when they could have a few quiet hours to themselves. She could be like a child at those times, clinging to him. She harbored many fears. A naked wire hanger in a closet terrified her and had to be removed. Half-lowered window shades resembled lidded eyes and seemed evil to her. These were phobias she was unable to admit to anyone. Elliott was different. He was her one true friend; the only person with whom she felt completely safe and with whom she could be herself, artifice shed, fame of no consequence. The problem was, she did not like the person their absence revealed, and sometimes that made her angry with Elliott for exposing the *nothing* she feared she really was.

The same quest for perfection that she pursued in her recordings was evident in her attention to every detail of *Funny Girl* once it opened. One evening she became incensed because the wax flowers used in a scene had not been dusted; another time, that a spotlight had not been well directed. Her habit was to write notes immediately upon her last curtain, listing what was amiss with the performance, and she would hand them to the stage manager to attend to the next day. She gloried in being the star but did not enjoy the monotony of repeating the same performance eight times a week. Once the show was frozen, she felt frozen, too. "Suddenly, I felt I was expected to do the same things in the same way, night after night. But that's not the way I work," she explained. "When I'm onstage I'm living the moment; no two performances are ever exactly the same. That's the challenge — to make every night as fresh as opening night."

These changes in performance — a pause taken before a line, a new hand gesture or voice intonation — were microscopic to an audience, but to an artist like Streisand they were enormous. Yet, she remained chronically late, arriving about fifteen minutes before curtain, giving Lainie Kazan false hope that she might have a chance to play the show. Kazan and Peter Daniels were now lovers, and although Streisand had not had an affair with Daniels, she was not pleased.

"It was, I guess," Kazan reasoned, "a matter of possession. Peter was supposedly on HER team — and at the time I was too stupid to realize it. I was now mad for the man. I just loved him and wanted to be with him. After the show had been running for a year, Barbra planned a two-week vacation and Ray wanted me to take over, and he set up a whole press thing. I did a run-through of the play with the understudies and Cis Corman was sitting in the back. The end result was that Barbra never took a vacation. I figured I was never going on, although I was always on pins and needles, dressed and ready for that one time she might arrive too late to make the curtain.

"I was very ambitious and I would tell anyone important who I met, 'If I ever go on, can I call you?' My mother and my best girlfriend had a list and they were to telephone everyone on it if that happened. One day [February 2, 1965] I got a call that Barbra was sick [with a strep throat] and that I should come right to the theater so that I could re-hearse with the real cast. Sydney, as foul-mouthed as he was, was simply exquisite to me.

"Well, I was all dressed and ready to go on when Barbra came in ten minutes before curtain. I was devastated. I couldn't even function. I don't know how I got onstage that night, because I had had my mother and friend contact all those people on the list and they had shown up. The headlines on the theater pages of the newspapers the following morning were crushing: SHOW GOES ON BUT LAINIE DOESN'T and IT AIN'T FUNNY GIRL. I had made a lot of people, including Barbra, angry. But around noon I received word from Ray's office asking me to come in early for the Wednesday matinee [that same day]. I was going on. Barbra had wors-ened her throat condition by singing the previous night. 'No phone calls,' the stage manager warned me. 'Just my mother,' I insisted, as I wanted her to see me play the role and he relented. When I spoke to her, I asked her to call all the people on the list. I didn't ask Peter's advice. Maybe

I knew what he would say, but I was not going to let this opportunity go. This was it for me. I thought I might not have the opportunity again.

"I was numb. I had never actually done the role in performance. Sydney dragged me through it. He was phenomenal, and everybody in the cast helped me. The audience was upset when they were told that Fanny would be played by an understudy. Some people left their seats and stood at the back of the theater — ready to leave. But I walked out onstage alone for the opening as the part demands and looked out at that Winter Garden Theatre and I thought about all the great people who had been on that stage, and it worked for me. When I started singing, 'I'm the Greatest Star,' they came back to their seats. It was thrilling. And Peter was there in the pit at the piano. It was very special, and for that evening I dressed in Barbra's dressing room on stage level [her own was five floors up].

"On matinee days the cast remained at the theater for both performances. I was told to return to my own dressing room. They did not tell me until twenty minutes before curtain that I was also playing the evening performance. I now had more confidence, and the show went very well. The laughs came in the right places. I hit all the right notes. Peter was so proud. The next morning all these great notices appeared in the press, and late that day I learned that Peter had been fired; he and Barbra had had an angry confrontation. She thought he was disloyal to her for loving and supporting me. She expected absolute loyalty from her friends. Infractions were not to be tolerated. Within an hour or so he was gone. He had flown to Puerto Rico and hadn't even told me he was going. I was frantic. He left me a note stuck in my Royal typewriter saying he could not handle it anymore, the pressure brought about by Barbra's possessiveness, and his wife who refused to give him a divorce. I went berserk. I took the extra money I had made from going on for Barbra and I left that next morning and flew to Puerto Rico to get him."

Daniels refused to come back but promised Kazan, who left Puerto Rico in time to stand by for the performance the following evening, that he would do so as soon as he had "worked it all out." He returned a month later, at which time Kazan gave her notice. "It was rumored that

I was fired, and has been reported in books that I was, but I never was," Kazan has insisted. "In fact, Ray begged me to stay until they found somebody. And I thought after all this — I mean, it was not very pleasant for me. I was put in my place very quickly for having alerted the press. I was told that I thought more about myself than I did of the show. Barbra cut me. I was treated as something of a pariah. And when I left the show, Ray dropped the option on my film contract with him.

"The sad thing was Barbra and Peter never truly made up. Maybe I was responsible. I don't know. I desperately loved Peter. He did come back, of course, and we were together over twenty years and had a daughter who we both adore. During the years, Barbra called Peter several times to help her out with some arrangements and he did, but it was never a comfortable situation."

A young woman named Linda Gerrard took over the job of Streisand's understudy after Kazan's departure. The show was now well into its second year, and Streisand relaxed her guard enough to take off occasional matinees and let Gerrard do the role. Those performances were never reviewed because her contract contained a clause that she would be dismissed if they were. However, Gerrard was never the threat that Streisand thought Kazan — who had moxie, a powerful voice, good comedic timing, and a star presence — was. Kazan also had stunning looks and not only had she won Peter Daniels's favor but Ray Stark had signed her to a film contract, perhaps to have a backup in case it was decided that Streisand was too ethnic-looking for the movies. It is likely that Streisand had more than a small influence in Ray Stark's decision to drop Kazan from a personal film contract with him. Streisand had learned the meaning of star power and how to exert it.

Her contract with Ray Stark to appear in *Funny Girl* also included the stipulation that she make four films for his company, Rastar. Stark would have to pay her off if it were decided that she could not carry a film, but he was guaranteed her services for the contracted number of movies. She had wanted to do only *Funny Girl,* but Stark refused to make a deal with her unless she acceded to his terms. "I remember Marty Erlichman saying to me, 'Look, if you're prepared to lose it, then we can say, sorry, we'll sign only one picture at a time,'" Streisand has said, adding, "I was not prepared to lose it." This agreement would cause many future problems in her relationship with Ray Stark, which vacillated alarmingly between hate and love, regard for a mentor and resentment because of his hold over her. She called him "a character, an original." He was a smart promoter and a tough businessman who had, in her view, taken more than he had given. Her contract with him guaranteed her star status but it had cost her high — her freedom.

Work began on her first television special when *Funny Girl* was midway through its New York run. Streisand dashed from the television studio to the Winter Garden and back to the studio late at night to listen to playbacks and view the results of the day's filming with Dwight Hemion, her director. She started the enterprise knowing very little about the medium; a week later she was acting like an expert. Her contract with CBS gave her complete artistic control, and she exerted it fully. CBS executives fought her with all their corporate muscle to get her to have guest stars on her show as other television specials did. In the end, her resolve was so strong that they backed down. The show would be a one-woman production, with a full orchestra and an occasional chorus to support her.

The title "My Name Is Barbra" was taken from Leonard Bernstein's song cycle, "I Hate Music."* Peter Matz arranged and conducted the music. The production numbers were conceived, staged, and choreographed by Joe Layton, Elliott's director for both *On the Town* and *Once Upon a Mattress* and recent Tony Award winner for his work on Richard Rodgers's *No Strings*. Streisand was in good hands but never let the control slip from her own. Her involvement in every phase of making the show was intense. Playing to the camera was a thrilling and satisfying experience for her. She fell instantly in love with the medium of film, the process of editing, the ability to refine and correct what she did not like

---

*Leonard Bernstein's "My Name Is Barbara" was previously introduced by mezzo-soprano Jennie Teurel, a noted concert artist of the 1950s and 1960s.

in the way she moved or looked or sang. She learned quickly what angles showed her to best advantage, that her left profile photographed better than her right, and that lifting her chin made her nose appear shorter.

"My Name Is Barbra" was filmed in black and white and aired on April 28, 1965. "There's a play on Broadway," she told her unseen audience, "*Funny Girl*. I kind of like it. In fact, I go there every evening." She instantly established a rapport with the millions of people who were seeing her for the first time. "I can't believe this is my own show!" she told them.

Divided into four musical segments, "My Name Is Barbra" was cleverly set so that commercials would not be obtrusive. One was a view of childhood involving a chorus of off-camera children screaming, "Crazy Barbra! Crazy Barbra!" that recalled Brooklyn and being called "Big Beak." In this personal reminiscence, she wore children's clothes and used giant-sized props that dwarfed her. She then moved seductively among the tuxedo-clad members of the orchestra as she segued smoothly from "Where Is the Wonder" to "People." Next, she took a whirlwind tour of her favorite Manhattan department store, Bergdorf Goodman, modeling outlandish furs and singing a medley of Depression-era songs: "Second Hand Rose," "Brother Can You Spare a Dime?" "Nobody Knows You When You're Down and Out." She saved a stylish concert for last, singing on a dark stage in a single spotlight to spectacular effect: "When the Sun Comes Out," "Why Did I Choose You?" "The Music That Makes Me Dance," "My Man," and closing with "Happy Days Are Here Again."

"The result was a pinnacle moment in American show business, in any form, in any period," wrote the reviewer for United Press International. "She is so great it is shocking, something like being in love. . . . She may well be the most supremely talented and complete popular entertainer that this country has ever produced. She simply dwarfs such contemporary stars as Julie Andrews, Elizabeth Taylor, Judy Garland and Carol Burnett. Anything they can do, she can do light years better. She is alternately gamin-like, sexy, mischievous, innocent, confident, insouciant, girlish, and radiating warmth. So she touches you, to your toes. And then she knocks you out."

The show won two Emmys — outstanding program achievement in

entertainment and outstanding individual achievement by an actor or performer. Ratings were higher than any other variety show released that year. The CBS network's executives wanted her to start almost immediately on a second special that could be released at the beginning of 1966. Streisand could not help but be elated at her instant success in television. Her confidence was bolstered with the knowledge that she could project well on camera and sustain an hour-long program that would be seen by several million people. Her goal — to star in a movie — was closer to her grasp.

Her run in the New York production of *Funny Girl* was about to terminate. "Truthfully, I couldn't wait for it to end," she later confessed. "When it did end, though, on December 26, 1965 [Mimi Hines was to take over for her], I was overwhelmed by the intensity of my emotions; I broke down on stage, and was completely unprepared for the cast and audience singing 'Auld Lang Syne' back to me." The last performance was also the only time Barbra Streisand ever sang Fanny Brice's famous number "My Man" at the Winter Garden. "I did it for Ray," she explained, "because he always loved it. And I did it for Fanny Brice. After all was said and done, it was still her song."

CBS agreed to Streisand's request that her next special be filmed in color, still a novelty in television and employed mostly for variety programs. Called "Color Me Barbra," it was again produced by Ellbar, her company. Her schedule was fierce: not only the television contract to fulfill but her record commitments, a concert tour, the London production of *Funny Girl,* and, she hoped, the film version. As Barbra's income rose dramatically, Elliott was finding it increasingly difficult to adjust to their fast-paced lifestyle and his wife's fame. He was not happy at, in essence, working for her and not at all sure that his job, to look for new projects, was essential. The London production of *Funny Girl* was to open on April 13, 1966, and Elliott would accompany her and stay throughout the run, but for the moment they celebrated New Year's Eve 1965 quietly, Elliott more in love with her than ever — obsessed with her, he would later admit.

"She was so vulnerable, I thought. But I think that was a real trap and, of course, I was taken in by it. She used her vulnerability and insecurities as a seduction, like a laser beam. It was very attractive, and that's part of her art . . . her vulnerability is like one of those snowstorms in a globe that you shake; it's behind glass. She plays vulnerability and has always played it really masterfully.

"She is very cold, smart, and acutely business-oriented. She was that way from the time of *Funny Girl*. Maybe before, but I didn't notice it then. She keeps herself isolated to maintain the status quo of her situation. I told her once, 'Everyone is afraid of you, they tell you only what you really want to hear.' She was so afraid of being hurt that she made herself inaccessible. She lacked trust and faith, and being so successful so young, she could make herself untouchable and unapproachable. Poor baby was miserable. She must be the most miserable person I've ever known. She keeps herself occupied with so many things because she's so afraid to fail, so afraid of the truth."

Sadie, her cherished poodle, went everywhere with her. She cuddled and coddled the small pet. She considered the idea that she and Elliott needed a child. Barbra had no doubt that he would be a good father but was unsure about her own role as a future mother. These thoughts were not far from her mind as she began the New York rehearsals on "Color Me Barbra" the same day that Shelley's daughter, Erica, was born. "Hey, whaddaya know? I'm an aunt!" she announced as she entered the dank studio in the East Seventies, wearing a floppy hat, her mink cape, aquamarine slacks, and matching suede shoes, "with a strip of maroon across the instep," an observer noted. "She was not pretty. It is not, however, the nose. The nose is beautiful. Rather, it is her eyes, set too close together and somehow chilly."

Onboard were all the men she had come to count on — Marty Erlichman, Joe Layton, Dwight Hemion, Peter Matz, and, of course, Elliott. She felt secure. Her mood was phlegmatic. Midafternoon, Sadie arrived fresh from the poodle parlor. Barbra scooped up the small white fluff of a dog that smelled of scented soap, kissed her, and carried her over her shoulder as she walked through the next phase of the rehearsal.

A short while later she was asked to sign for a registered package. It contained a jeweled brooch that she immediately pinned to the sweater she was wearing. "I'm crazy about brooches," she declared. "I pass these things in store windows and I say to an assistant, 'Go call that guy!'" Besides an assistant, she now had a secretary, her agent, a business manager, accountant, lawyer, dress designer, hairdresser, and press agent, all of whom were at the rehearsal along with Elliott, two CBS executives, the sponsor's advertising representative, and photographers and reporters from three newspapers and two magazines. In the middle of the rehearsal hall was a trampoline that she used during one of her production numbers. An instructor who was giving Barbra a demonstration on an intricate leap lost her balance and fell through the springs before finally being able to rise to her feet, stunned but unharmed. This did not daunt Streisand, who tried the flip herself, sprawling awkwardly, crashing to the canvas, and almost bouncing out of control. Sadie, sitting haunched on the sidelines, barked and ran around in circles. The brooch came undone and flew across the floor. Streisand got up and tried the flip again.

"Color Me Barbra" was to be filmed inside the Philadelphia Museum of Art. After six days of rehearsals in New York, Streisand, Elliott, the entire crew, her entourage, Sadie, and the members of the press — about thirty-five people — arrived in Philadelphia on one of the coldest days of the season. With Sadie clutched tightly under one arm, she inspected the hotel suite she was to occupy, pulling up the shades, flicking on the lights, shouting for someone to call room service for a pot of tea and whatever else looked good on the menu. "How about I go get some Chinese?" Elliott offered. She liked the idea but insisted that a staff member be sent.

Food gave her instant gratification. "I'm not comfortable sitting down to a formal dinner," she told one reporter. "I like standing up and eating out of three pots on a stove. I love Cokes and cones and French fries that taste of bacon, like you get in greasy spoons. I love greasy spoons. Recently, after a late party for Princess Margaret — it was a bore — I had the urge for rice pudding without raisins. Some people like it with raisins; I like it without raisins. Well, I had this urge, and every place was closed, but Elliott found a waterfront diner that was open. We could have gone to the Automat, I suppose. I like the Automat. You put in the nickels and get what you want — pies, cakes, sandwiches. But you know, nowadays, it's hard for me to go to the Automat. I mean, people *know* me and inhibit my eating."

In a suite on a lower floor, Rex Reed, the darkly handsome actor-columnist (soon to costar in the transvestite role of Myron in the film adaptation of Gore Vidal's book *Myra Breckenridge*), was waiting with six or eight of Streisand's publicity staff for her to come down for his scheduled interview. He waited three and a half hours. "Okay, you have twenty minutes," she told him when she arrived, sat in a chair, and began to wolf down some fruit in a large basket on a table near her.

She bristled at Reed's first question, What had fame cost her?

"Listen, all my life I wanted to be famous," she replied, a clipped note of hostility in her voice. "I knew nothing about music. I never had a Victrola 'til I was eighteen. I used to buy clothes in thrift shops. Now I don't go there anymore because people bother me. Besides, they've gone up. I always dreamed of a penthouse, right? So now I'm a big star I got one and it's not much fun. I used to dream about terraces, now I gotta spend five hundred dollars just to convert mine from summer to winter. Let me tell you, it's just as dirty with soot up there on the twenty-second floor as it is down there on the bottom." Reed was surprised by her defensive attitude, but with the suddenness of fame had also come some disenchantment. Nothing was ever as perfect as she had fantasized it would be.

Shooting began at 5 P.M., when the museum closed. The doors were locked and manned by security guards. Outside, the local branch of her fast-growing fan club, some forty members, peered through the beaded glass windows carrying a sign that read WELCOME BARB. "Barbra even has a fan club in prison," a woman press agent told Reed. Streisand was ready for the cameras at 7:30. Elliott arrived at about 11:30 P.M. carrying a large brown paper bag and stood on the sidelines as she ran past twelve pillars and up thirty-five stone stairs in the massive front room of the museum singing "Yesterdays." She sighted him, and they both went over to some chairs and sat down as she hungrily dug into the bag and pulled out a hot pastrami sandwich and a container of sour green tomatoes while Sadie danced around her feet and was fed the meat from half a sandwich. At 2 A.M., after a dozen costume changes and scenes played up and down the stone stairs, past walls filled with Cézannes, Picassos, and Matisses, the session ended, to be continued the next day.

Her energy was intimidating to even the hardest workers in the crew. She arrived in the morning for the second part of the shooting, fresh and with a sheaf of notes for everyone from Peter Matz to the property man. "She's not dumb," a CBS official told Reed. "She heads two corporations — one packages her specials, pays her everything, then the profit she makes is the difference between her expenses and what CBS pays her. This includes her salary. It's a one-woman show, so it would be very weird if she was not the boss." She was, of course, but she never permitted herself any liberties. She worked harder than anyone else and never showed exhaustion. "If the star gives up, everybody gives up," she told Reed. "I gotta keep smiling."*

That evening, at 7 P.M., she began an eight-hour recording siege with Matz and a thirty-three-piece orchestra. An exhausted Elliott, who had not left her side, warned her against fatigue hoarseness.

"Hoarse?" she growled, and waved her hands. "Hoarse! I don't get hoarse! What hoarse?" Elliott rubbed her back and held her hand as she listened to the playbacks and selected the ones she wanted to use. She complained only once. Her feet hurt.

She slept until noon the next day, when Diana arrived from New York at her invitation to watch as sequences of the show were being filmed before a live audience. Streisand was singing a camped-up version of "One Kiss." "I made a record of 'One Kiss' once," Diana wistfully told a reporter (who noted that she was "a round-faced, round woman who wears her hair piled youthfully high on her head"). "Of course, I sang it my own way," she added and proceeded to sing a few bars in a thin, trilly soprano.

It was midnight when the audience segments were finished. Streisand then called for a meeting with a press agent and looked over color slides

---

*Streisand was furious with Reed after the publication of his article because of his stress on her cryptic comments and on her eating habits. "She never spoke to me again," he said in 1977. Several years later Streisand's anger subsided and they double-dated — Streisand and Jon Peters, Reed and Streisand's then current agent, Sue Mengers — to the premiere of Streisand's production of *A Star Is Born*.

of publicity photographs with a professional magnifying flashlight while she dictated markings for each picture according to its merits as a reflection of herself.

"Somebody else could do this," she told one of the last lingering reporters, "if only I didn't care so much."

In "Color Me Barbra" she was the only human figure on view. She did acrobatic jumps on the trampoline; sang "Animal Crackers in My Soup" to an anteater (and had the camera superimpose her profile at one point over his); appeared as the Egyptian Queen Nefertiti, whose bust was one of the treasures of the museum, as Marie Antoinette on her way to the guillotine, as a Modigliani lady singing "Non C'est Rien" at a café table; serenaded Sadie (in her television debut) with "C'est Si Bon"; swung from a trapeze, and danced with a chorus line of penguins.

"For Barbra Streisand's second spec of the season," the *Variety* critic wrote, "CBS delivered a true one-woman turn — not another biped in sight the whole hour distance. As it turned out, the exercise in conceit was justified."

Directly after "Color Me Barbra" was shot, Streisand prepared to leave for the London West End production of *Funny Girl*. Elliott had preceded her to find a suitable apartment. He had been offered the role of Nicky Arnstein, and they had lengthy discussions about it before he turned it down. "I'm more talented than all the guys who played Nicky put together," he later said. "I'm not being immodest. Nicky Arnstein was not played. He was never written." However, he rejected the chance, which would have given a great boost to his career, because he did not want to put further strain on their marriage. Jule Styne believed that a husband and wife playing opposite each other did not generate sexual excitement, because everyone knew they shared a bed. In the end, English actor Michael Craig was signed to play Nicky Arnstein.

In Hollywood, Columbia Pictures remained reluctant to approve her in the film version of *Funny Girl*. They were demanding tests be shot in London to see how she looked on a film screen. Television was one thing, they said, but film close-ups would magnify every fault she had. It mattered not that her skin was now nearly flawless, all the old signs of acne miraculously gone, that her hair was groomed and shiny, that the costume department could take care of her figure if help were needed, that her talent was never in question. The bone of contention was her nose. The studio thought she should have it reconstructed. Streisand would not hear of it.

15

Her plane landed at Heathrow Airport in the early morning, the sky still too dark to see more than a flickering of lights as London awakened from the night. Under a mink coat Streisand wore pants and a big sweater. A travel representative met her at passport control. She had not had much sleep, but the activity in the customs hall energized her and she insisted on helping the agent locate her thirty-five suitcases monogrammed BSG. Sighting Elliott, who had arrived ten days earlier, behind the barrier in the waiting area outside the customs hall, she waved frantically and ran toward him. Suddenly, she became aware of the crush of press photographers as flash cameras exploded. She slowed her gait, put on her big sunglasses and pulled down the wide brim of her fur hat to conceal the disappointment on her face. She and Elliott were not going to be allowed a private reunion. They hugged tentatively and then Elliott, his arm protectively about her, bustled her through the pressing crowds led by an airport official and the agent, past a door marked PRIVATE that led to a guarded exit. Not having expected such a large turnout so early in the morning, she was stunned, and her face reflected her fear as she clung to Elliott's arm.

He had rented an elegant townhouse at 48 Ennismore Gardens, behind the Brompton Oratory, that faced a lovely private green oasis with patches of bright early-spring flowers. The weather was mild for February, winter grayness dispelled by short bursts of sun. But with three records on the British charts and the publicity accompanying her arrival, she was unable to go anywhere without being gaped at and besieged for autographs. She and Elliott had two weeks together before rehearsals began, and as Chemstrand, her television sponsor, was paying the bills, they flew first to Paris, where *Vogue* was to do a photo article on her. She had just placed eighth in the list of America's best dressed women (topped by Jacqueline Kennedy), an honor that thrilled her.

In one year she had managed to turn her image around, to prove that her taste for the outlandish was avant garde and not bizarre. "Now I hope people will stop calling me 'kooky,'" she said. She still bought some of her shoes and other accessories secondhand at thrift shops and occasionally drove her Bentley up to Loehmann's in the Bronx to buy cut-rate originals without the designer labels. This did not turn off Parisian haute couture. She had been invited to all the major collections. Designer Marc Bohan gave a luncheon for her with some of the most prestigious fashion figures — Dior, Grès, Cardin, Balmain. She was seated at Bohan's right and never stopped talking. "My husband and I went to le Grand Véfour [a four-star restaurant] for dinner," she told him. "I always judge the cooking by the chocolate soufflé. The cream was sour." She had apparently never had crème fraîche, that classic staple of fine French cuisine.

"I hope you will approve the one my chef has prepared," Bohan smiled drily.

As Bohan's butler went to fill her glass with wine, she asked for a Coca-Cola with a perfect French accent. "I have a good ear," she leaned over to tell Bohan when he complimented her. Actually, she had been studying French with a tutor and had recently recorded a French album *Je m'appelle Barbra* with Michel Legrand that included "Ma Premiere Chanson," a striking song of her own composition. Although a lamentably pretentious album, many of the songs were sung in excellent French, and it sold well if not *as well* as her previous records, her fans not quite sure what to make of a Streisand à la Piaf.

She had something provocative to say about each designer. After the Cardin show in which the clothes all had a look of the twenty-first century, short and angular, she commented, "Those girls didn't have a thing on under their dresses. I could see right through. I was embarrassed." At Grès, watching a large tent dress sway past, she stage-whispered, "You'd never be able to tell *what* was going on under there!" Her only purchases were made at Dior, where she bought day dresses, suits, evening gowns, sportswear, hats, shoes, and coats, at a cost of $20,000. Dior was a very *today* designer, she said. And, indeed, he was.

She posed for the *Vogue* fashion layout in her ocelot coat and a glamorous, body-clinging evening dress and visited the Louvre and several antique shops before Elliott whisked her off to Rome, Florence, and Venice, where, as her records were not yet well known, she could travel with anonymity. The short tour gave the couple a chance to share things without too much outside interference. It was a highly romantic time, and Streisand arrived at the Prince of Wales Theatre (where Elliott had appeared in *On the Town*) on the first day of rehearsals of *Funny Girl* in an exhilarated mood. By day's end her spirits were low. The production would not be up to the standards she had expected.

Kay Medford was the only other member of the original American cast in the London production. The director, Lawrence Kasha, was also American, only thirty-three, and considered to be a bright, new theater talent. Having played over eight hundred performances out of town and on Broadway, Streisand felt she was the only one who knew how the show should go and what worked for her. The auditorium at the Prince of Wales had dead spots, which meant that however well-miked, unless the orchestra could be masked, voices from the stage would be difficult to hear from certain seats. There was also the problem of the British members of the cast who were playing New York and Broadway types with forced accents. Michael Craig — then best known as a British light-romantic film actor — good-looking and capable though he was, seemed fatally miscast as Nicky Arnstein. This was going to be an uphill struggle, and in the end, whatever the outcome, she would bear the consequence.

She remained, as in New York, standoffish with members of the company. She became increasingly testy with the English press, who she found even more forward and invasive in their questions than their counterparts in the States. Ray Stark, battened down for the duration of the rehearsals in a regal suite at the Dorchester, soothed as many of the targets of her verbal assaults as he could by telling everyone what a wonderful performer she was. "The only thing she has not learned is tact," he was quoted as saying.

To a reporter's question as to why she thought she was so successful, she replied, "The only way I can account for it is that whatever ability other performers have, I must have it plus. Onstage I am a cross between a washwoman and a princess. I am a bit coarse, a bit low, a bit vulgar, and a bit ignorant. But I am also part princess — sophisticated, elegant, and controlled. I can appeal to everybody." With this hard-eyed self-perception came her ever present self-doubt. "When I am not performing, however," she added, "I don't think I have that definite a personality. I think maybe I have nothing."

In the first week of April, she learned that she was pregnant. The news was both exciting and frightening. Neither Elliott nor Barbra knew if they were ready to become parents, but they soon got used to the idea. Streisand shopped at Harrods, which was not far from her house, for skeins of fine wool, all in different shades of pink. She knitted like mad for a week on a baby blanket and then stopped, realizing the child might be a boy (she wasn't too fond of the color blue). She bought a book by the Englishman who pioneered the natural-childbirth movement, Dr. Grantley Dick-Read, and became a dedicated follower. Elliott, wanting to share the experience of their baby's birth, agreed to go to natural-childbirth classes with her as soon as they returned to New York.

"To say I love Barbra," he told a reporter, "that's obvious. Otherwise, I couldn't have stood it. I know the traps. I know the wounds, and I've decided it's worth it in the end to wage the battle. People say theatrical marriages don't work. Our battle is especially difficult because we're real people, not just two profiles on a magazine cover. We really love one another."

They did not anticipate that her condition would interfere with her fourteen-week commitment to the London production of *Funny Girl*. But with the baby due on December 15, it was generally assumed that she would cancel her upcoming million-dollar U.S. concert tour from August through October. Following the announcement, the press soon referred to the unborn child as the "million-dollar baby."

"I can't suddenly get poor," Streisand told the American feminist writer Gloria Steinem. "But I don't want a kid who has nothing but toys from F.A.O. Schwarz. Kids like simple things to play with: a piece of paper, a walnut shell, I had a hot-water bottle for a doll," a surprising comment in view of her painful public recall of her own toyless childhood and how she felt at not having a selection of toys. She went on to say, "The most important thing [is] that she feels loved and has *both* parents," obviously still leaning toward the idea that she would have a girl. Filming of *Funny Girl* was almost a year away, time enough for her to get her figure back. Still of concern, however, were these constant demands that she seriously consider having cosmetic nose surgery prior to making her movie debut.

The subject of her nose had come up frequently during the year. Fanny Brice, she was told, had bobbed her nose before going to Hollywood. A list of other famous stars who had "constructive" surgery or cosmetic assistance was rattled off to her. It was said that Marilyn Monroe had breast implants. Rita Hayworth had extreme electrolysis to raise her hairline. Clark Gable had all his teeth pulled and wore a false set to give him a better smile. She consulted noted eye, ear, and nose specialists who agreed that nose surgery might or might not affect her voice. She would be taking a chance. The nasality that so identified her singing voice could be lost. Pictures were drawn to show her what she would look like with the alterations that would be made — the bump removed, the nose narrowed and slightly clipped. She hated it. It simply wasn't her. If anything was done, she wanted only the bump smoothed. She was afraid she would regret the results, and she was terrified of the pain. And certainly she could not have surgery done while she was pregnant.

Under tremendous pressure, she nonetheless energetically pushed on. The English production of *Funny Girl* was beginning to shape up as it went into dress rehearsals. The week before opening night she was frantic. Her nerves frayed, she and Elliott began to fight and the rows grew in intensity. She was, he claims, afraid to trust his love or his judgment.

"She loves from the point of view of a materialist," he has said. "If she doesn't commit to true love, she won't lose anything. She doesn't really give. I told her, 'You destroy what you don't understand and can't control.'" He was determined that she would not destroy him. He was trying to gain leverage, to get her to turn to him for certain decisions, to lean on his strength and save hers. Streisand was that contradictory woman who wanted a strong man whom she could control, itself a paradox. Things had to be *her* way, her word final. Able to respect only a man who could stand up to her, she was compelled to test her power against his. It became a kind of emotional arm wrestling that could spill over into violence if not controlled, a situation both were aware of as fists had flown from time to time, stopped by sheer force of will before any serious damage was done.

One night, neither could govern the anger. An argument had started over Streisand's need to control the people around her, Elliott included. The fact that she could not stop him from gambling infuriated her. Her attacks on his habit only angered him more, making him feel that she was castrating and robbing him of his independence. They were screaming at each other. Streisand said some harsh things framed in expletives, and slammed and locked the bedroom door after herself.

"Open that door!" he shouted. He received no response. "I'm kicking it down if you don't open it up this minute!" he yelled louder. When he saw that she was not going to, he stepped back, ran forward, and rammed the door with his shoulder, breaking the lock — and nearly his arm.

"I don't want your child!" she sobbed, when she saw him hulking in the open doorway holding his injured arm close to his body.

"It was the worst thing she could have said to me," he grimaced, recalling the incident. "Barbra's infantile in some ways, immature in others, no matter how brilliant she may be. But it was wrong of me at that point in her pregnancy to kick the door down."

Arthur Laurents was in London around this time and with Herb Ross and his wife, Nora Kaye, had dinner with Barbra and Elliott. "The conversation all revolved around Barbra, and at one point Elliott got up and excused himself and went across the street to a gambling casino, I think it was Crockford's. He returned about forty-five minutes later and said,

'Well, I just lost twenty-five thousand dollars.' It was more than compulsive gambling. It was getting at her. When she did *Wholesale*, Elliott was the star. Then came *Funny Girl*. She didn't need him. And in the lives of those people, that is very important."

Funny Girl opened in London on April 13 to mixed reviews. She was unprepared for British audiences, who were not as enthusiastic in their response to a performer. The laughs came in different places and were not as hearty, the applause thin. "One of the most nonsensical plots in the history of American musicals," *The Times* (London) reported. "The only reason for seeing this thunderously publicized show is the redeeming presence of Barbra Streisand." Her personal notices were extraordinary. The *Daily Sketch* called her "the most phenomenal creature of strange chemistry ever to set foot on a stage. She sings, and there are saxophones and trumpets and violins in her throat. Her voice takes off on smooth gravel, and soars about in some previously uncharted musical magic land of sweetness."

"She is the heart, the soul, the sound and the music," the *Daily Mail* rhapsodized. "If those magical vocal cords and that insolently sexy frame should temporarily be indisposed, my heart would bleed for the palpitating understudy."*

London was *en fête* with Streisand's success. Princess Margaret came backstage to congratulate her and the rest of the cast on their performances. Streisand joined the receiving line a few minutes late. "Well she isn't *my* royal highness," she commented. In New York she had attended a party in honor of the queen's sister and was accused of being rude and arriving late. "I just could not say, 'Hullo, Your Royal Highness,' to anyone. It doesn't suit me. So I just sort of said, 'Hullo.' Princess Margaret looked at me almost like a fan and told me she had all my records. I didn't know what to say, so I just stood there and replied, 'Yeah?' Then

---

*Streisand's London understudy, Lisa Shane, did take over the role of Fanny Brice for one performance when Streisand was suffering severe nausea due to her pregnancy. Enraged when Michael Craig announced the cast change before curtain, a good section of the audience left for a refund. Shane received good notices the next morning, but the incident convinced the producers that the show would not long survive once Streisand left the cast.

May Britt [the Swedish actress then married to Sammy Davis, Jr.] asked me how come I was so late. I said, 'I got screwed up!' The princess looked bewildered. It was like a scene from a bad movie. I quickly said, 'I mean I got fouled up.' [Another guest claims that what she said was *fucked up*.]

"Tommy Steele [who was in New York, starring in *Half a Sixpence*] looked white and shocked. I didn't know what to do, so I turned to him and asked, 'You two know each other from London, huh?' Tommy was speechless. The princess turned her head away. Nobody said anything. 'I mean,' I said, 'you have worked for her sister?' Tommy answered stiffly, 'I have performed for Her Majesty and Princess Margaret, too.' I said, 'Yeah, that's what I mean.'"

The incident had been widely covered by the press, and here she was once again confronted by the princess, this time in England, where any infraction of manners would be considered not only rude but insulting. "Oh, cripes!" she said out of the side of her mouth to costar Michael Craig, who stood next to her in the receiving line. "You don't suppose she didn't notice I was late?" Margaret glanced her way. She had been talking to the theater manager. She gave him a cordial nod of dismissal and walked directly over to Streisand, smiled regally, and congratulated her on her performance. "Thanks," Streisand replied feebly.

"This is the second time I've seen *Funny Girl*," Margaret admitted. "And I enjoyed it both times — here and New York."

"Yeah? Twice?" Streisand replied uneasily. "Really?" She heaved a sigh of exasperation and touched her hand to her forehead as if to say, "Oy vey! Am I dumb or something?"

Margaret eased her smile and moved on down the line to shake hands with Michael Craig.

On another night Prince Charles came backstage after a performance. He, too, was an obvious fan and, like his Aunt Margaret, an avid collector of her records. Noticeably taken with her, he spoke to Streisand at unusual length about several of her records and the songs on them. She was more relaxed, able to be herself, joke a bit. "How are things at the palace?" she was reported as asking. At the U.S. embassy, Noël Coward toasted her when she was presented with the Anglo-American Award as the best American performer of the 1966 London season, which had also included a badly miscast Mary Martin in *Hello, Dolly!*

Although the British lived in a culture (at that time, at least) not quite as transfixed by celebrity as in the States, the public and the press had warmed to Streisand. There had been some earlier clashes when she was lambasted for her American brassiness. But once *Funny Girl* opened, any transgressions were most often overlooked. She was even forgiven her "American vulgarity" in discussing how much money she made from her records.

When she wasn't at the theater, she roamed through antique shops and art galleries. She bought fourteen paintings from artist Jason Monet, several of them with the artist's pregnant wife as a recurring subject. Streisand was glowing, proud of her own condition, which had been widely reported in the press. She suffered some morning sickness in the early weeks and canceled her two weekly matinees, but her energy level never seemed to drop or to affect the excellence of her performances.

Ray Stark, meanwhile, was continuing negotiations with Columbia Pictures for *Funny Girl*. Along with other Hollywood studios, Columbia was struggling to compete with television. Unable to sustain a large production staff, top directors, and a contract list of stars and supporting players as they had in the past, the studios were becoming used to making deals with independents.

Stark never wavered in his belief that no one *but* Streisand should play Fanny Brice. The question of the photogenic problems that might be caused by her nose had ended, as she had adamantly refused to undergo cosmetic surgery. Ray Stark stood behind her in this decision. He showed "Color Me Barbra" on a full-sized movie screen to studio executives in Columbia's London office to convince them of her photogenic appeal. It was evident that Streisand had one of those faces that loved the camera and came fully alive through its lens. Nonetheless, her looks were so far out of the spectrum of the pert cheerleader or chocolate-box beauty that movie audiences expected of leading ladies that Columbia was still not yet fully convinced she should play the part.

Stark kept all negative reactions to himself, positive that in the end Columbia would see that Streisand *was Funny Girl*. He engaged a European-based scriptwriter to adapt the show for the screen. This was not as strange a choice as it might appear. The House Un-American Activities Committee had purged Hollywood of many of its top writing, directing, production, and acting talents. Unable to ply their craft in Hollywood, many writers crossed the Atlantic to work, albeit most often uncredited and for far less money than was paid to those men and women unscathed and still employed in Hollywood.

Stark approached Sidney Buchman, former vice president of Columbia, who either alone or in collaboration had been responsible for some of Hollywood's most sophisticated comedies and musicals — *The Awful Truth, Holiday, Mr. Smith Goes to Washington, Here Comes Mr. Jordan, A Song to Remember, The Jolson Story*. Sidney had refused to name names before the HUAC and was thus found in contempt of Congress and given a year's suspended sentence. Fired from the studio, blacklisted, and unable to work in Hollywood, he had first gone to London and then established residence in Cannes. Handsome enough in his youth to have starred in his own films, in his sixties he remained a good-looking man of regal bearing with startling china-blue eyes, glistening silver hair, and the nonchalant air of a worldly man who has intimately known prominence, fortune, and numerous beautiful women.

After more than a decade of struggle, Sidney had just made a breakthrough with his successful movie adaptation and production of Mary McCarthy's bestselling novel *The Group*. When Ray Stark rang him in Cannes to ask if he would be interested in writing the adaptation of *Funny Girl,* Sidney said he'd let him know. He then called me. I had also come to London in the fifties from Hollywood and was a member of the clubby group of expatriate writers caught in this treacherous political maelstrom. In order to keep myself and my two children afloat, I had happily worked on numerous screenplays without credit.

Sidney did not like to work alone, and we had found in the past that we were compatible as a team. He flew to London and took me to see *Funny Girl.* Would I work with him on the screenplay? The story was the weakest element of the show, but I was drawn to the classic theme: a woman caught between two great passions — the man she loved and the career that had given her independence and gratification. I agreed. Sidney promised that he would see what he could do about getting me credit. I believed then, and still believe, that he meant it at the time. I knew he was being scrupulously fair financially, but then Sidney had a cavalier attitude toward money. He liked to spend it.

The material we had to work with consisted of the playscript, Isobel Lennart's original screenplay, *My Man* (written before the play), and the lengthy reel-to-reel tapes recorded by Fanny Brice that she had used for her aborted autobiography. The main problems as we saw them were to open the story up for film, give Nicky Arnstein more dimension while keeping Fanny Brice front and center as much as possible. There was also the challenge of creating bridges for the songs so that they would flow smoothly from the spoken dialogue that preceded and followed them. We were still working on the script when Streisand played her last performance of the London production of *Funny Girl** on July 15, the show closing the same night.

Streisand and Elliott returned to New York. Booked into twenty cities for her contracted tour, she had to cancel all but four of them — the Newport Jazz Festival, the John F. Kennedy Stadium in Philadelphia, the Atlanta Stadium, and Soldiers Field in Chicago, which were completely sold out months in advance. In Newport she greeted 117,000 fans, nearly 40,000 more than had attended a recent Frank Sinatra concert there. Because Streisand was a half hour late, John Dupont gave a short organ recital to keep the crowd happy. About nine o'clock the thirty-five-piece orchestra, directed by Peter Matz and concealed behind a scrim on which lighted effects were used for visual interest, played a lengthy overture of Streisand's numbers. She was given a standing ovation when she finally appeared in a glowing orange and gold chiffon gown with one shoe and one earring of each color and a tiny coronet of orange rosebuds

---

Funny Girl was still playing at the Winter Garden in New York with Mimi Hines in the role of Fanny Brice. It closed on July 1, 1967, after a total of 1,348 performances. Hines then went on the road with the show, which traveled across the United States for the next six months. Two summer stock presentations — one starring Edie Adams, the other, Carol Lawrence — were presented in 1968. In 1982 the show was optioned for a London revival, which never materialized.

twined in her hair. She made use of an orange stool as a prop and occasionally came forward onto a special runway built out from the stage for closer rapport with the audience.

Her program would be much the same in each city of the tour: After belting out "Where Am I Going?" and "I Got No Strings," the latter from the Walt Disney film *Pinocchio,* she gave a charmingly whimsical interpretation of Leonard Bernstein's "I Hate Music."

At the end of "Cry Me a River," she stood perfectly still center stage, a brilliant butterfly trapped in the light, her colorful skirt billowing out on both sides of her as a soft breeze blew across the open arena. The audience cheered wildly. Streisand did not react to these mass outpourings of love and admiration as Judy Garland might have. There were no tears, no convulsive hand gestures to indicate emotion, no moves to the edge of the proscenium to touch and be touched by her audience. She remained imperturbably where she had ended the song, looking pleased, patient, accepting — and controlled as she waited for the shouts and cheers to subside. "Thank you," she acknowledged, "thank you," and then sang "Down with Love" to a thumping string bass accompaniment.

Her voice was exquisite in Lionel Bart's "Who Will Buy?" from *Oliver,* the pure and plaintive tone almost unbearably moving. She ended the first half with a stirring arrangement of Harold Arlen's classic "When the Sun Comes Out." After the intermission she reappeared in a shimmering, black sequined Empire evening gown and startled everyone as she launched into a thoroughly unorthodox rendition of "Silent Night"— part carol, part Broadway show tune — that unexpectedly brought wolf whistles from the audience. Included in this section were several songs from her French album, a poignant version of "He Touched Me" and a rousing "Second Hand Rose." She closed with "People" and "Happy Days Are Here Again," which brought the audience to their feet vainly screaming, "More!"

Since the night when Elliott had knocked down the door to their bedroom, there had been a harder edge to their relationship. Streisand had felt fiercely violated by his action, Elliott repentant while at the same time struggling with the emasculation of her terrible oath that she did not want his child, but it was obvious now that both of them did, indeed, look forward to parenthood. As Streisand moved into the last months of her pregnancy, Elliott doted on her, waiting backstage at every performance until she returned to her dressing room, usually a makeshift affair, rubbing her back and her hands. There was always a local doctor on hand, but she seemed in good health and spirits.

In Atlanta rain drenched the outdoor arena the day of the performance, washing out rehearsal plans. That night the field was so muddy that people had difficulty getting to their seats. Many with front row tickets had to be satisfied to sit in the less muddy rear. Streisand sang only a few notes of her opening number and then stopped, complaining of an echo split. Ticket holders had heard it too and began to crawl over seats to move back in the grandstand, where the acoustics were much better. No one left. Streisandmania had swept the country. It was not the same kind of overwhelming public adoration that the Beatles or Elvis evoked. Her fans were somewhat older, more sophisticated. She gave them the best she had to give — which was a great deal — and she did so on every song she sang. Perfect weather the following day hiked ticket sales to over 18,000, and the concert did equally well in Philadelphia.

They reached Chicago for the last week of concerts at the end of September. The stage was erected on the ten-yard line of Soldiers Field. The crowd of 14,220 people sprawled into the end-zone stands. A whistle whined from the neighborhood railway yard. "My god!" Streisand cried into the microphone, "It's got poifect pitch!" She was six months' pregnant and showing noticeably. She patted her tummy when she sang "Happy Days Are Here Again" to thunderous cheers. After more than a dozen bows she retreated to the house trailer that was her dressing room and ordered her hairdresser to cut her hair into a gamin Mia Farrow style. She squealed with delight as she looked at herself in the mirror and then headed back to New York with Elliott in a chartered Aero Commander jet. They were to vacation for a few weeks in a rented beach house at Sands Point on Long Island Sound. "I've got to have time to catch up with the world," she said. "I've had no time to read about Vietnam and Black Power." She had not been able to relax since Paris and their trip on the Continent. She walked barefoot in the sand with Elliott and planned for the baby's imminent arrival.

They returned to New York in October, the baby due in two months' time. Deciding that the penthouse, which lacked a separate wing for a nursery, would hardly be the right environment in which to raise a child, she set out with Elliott in search of a new home. They found what they thought was the ideal apartment for $200,000 in a prestigious West Side building but were turned down by the coop board. The rejection shocked and infuriated her. "I'm not sure it was because I was an actress or because I was Jewish — or both. . . . I am deeply Jewish, but in a place where I don't even know where it is . . . and I thought 'I don't want to live in a city where I can't get a place to live . . . where there is this kind of prejudice.'" For the time being they would remain in the penthouse and redo her sewing room into a nursery.

There were two false alarms before labor began two weeks late at 6 A.M. on December 29, 1966. Streisand, escorted by Elliott, his arm protectively around her, arrived at New York City's Mount Sinai Hospital at 9 A.M. He remained in a labor room with her until shortly before the birth and then went with her into delivery. "It was very traumatic, but Barbra was very brave," he said. "We held hands and talked about a son or daughter. If it was a girl, she was to be called Samantha." At 3 P.M. Jason Emanuel Gould, weighing seven pounds, twelve ounces was born. His father stood close enough to catch a glimpse of him as he entered this life.

"My God, I'm a mother. I'm a little girl myself, and now I'm a mother" were Streisand's first words to Elliott when the nurse handed her the child in her private room, number 507. "He's so delicate," the new mother whispered, tears rolling down her face.

"You know, my baby didn't cry," Elliott bragged when Jason was returned to the hospital nursery. "All the other babies were crying and had their eyes closed, and this woman next to me said, 'Look at that brand-new baby with its eyes wide open,' and it was my baby. He looks like Barbra, only he has a cleft in his chin and dark hair, like me," he added, laughing proudly. "He's got the brightest, bluest, flashingest eyes. Just like her. Exactly. Beautiful." Jason's blue eyes changed to brown a few weeks later.

Their son's birth seemed to have brought his young parents closer together. Although she claimed she was not the maternal type, Streisand was caught up in the excitement and the thrill of having brought a child into the world. There was a nurse and a nanny. The small nursery was decorated in purple and lavender. Streisand's role in the film of *Funny Girl* was now secure. Three months after Jason's arrival, she was to leave for rehearsals and costume fittings in Hollywood. Jason would go with her. Elliott had been cast in Jules Feiffer's *Little Murders* (which was to have a limited New York run) and would join them on the coast when the play, a brilliant but noncommercial vehicle, ended. This had been her dream, to be a Hollywood star. Yet where would Elliott be once she had established herself as she knew she would do?

Their marriage was almost a retelling of the Fanny Brice story. Like Nicky Arnstein, Elliott was a gambler. Intense therapy had not cured him of his habit, and he was unable to earn anywhere near what she did. The library walls of the penthouse were covered with her seven gold records (signifying that each had made over $1 million). She had earned several hundred thousand dollars on the tour, and she would receive $200,000 for her role in *Funny Girl,* which was scheduled to go before the cameras in May.

"I remember two things about this time," Arthur Laurents recalled. "She was giving a party in the penthouse apartment, and she called and said, 'The party's just for friends. Why don't you bring Lena?' Which I thought was odd because she didn't know Lena Horne very well, and I said, 'Well, she really doesn't like to go to parties.' I went up there without Lena thinking it was just going to be friends and there was Ava Gardner and George C. Scott, who at that time [in their affair] were busy beating each other up, and Ava was all black and blue and he was bruised. I remember we all fell on the floor playing 'Spoons'— it's a game like musical chairs except you do it with spoons. Everyone grabs for a spoon when the music stops. And she had a set of new silverware and she screamed, 'Oy! You're bending my silver!'

"Another time, not long before she filmed *Funny Girl,* I went up there and the living room was swarming with men in blue suits — her business manager, her accountant, her attorney, her agent — and I knew it was over." The young woman he had known had become a superstar and more a product than a person. "I said, 'Barbra, I'll see you,' and I left."

In February 1967, before departing for California and her preproduction duties, she recorded an album of standards, *Simply Streisand,* singing straight, no characteristic vocal embellishments. An interesting recording that would eventually form part of the Streisand legacy with songs such as "When Sunny Gets Blue," "Lover Man," and "More Than You Know," it also contained a new suggestive interpretation of the Sigmund Romberg/Oscar Hammerstein II song "Stout-hearted Men," from the operetta *The New Moon.* Streisand sang the number openly imitating Mae West's insinuating, breathy phrasing as she camped her way through it. When released as a single, it became a huge hit in gay bars across the country.

Mae West, the bosomy blond icon of camp, had influenced Streisand since her youth in Brooklyn and would continue to do so for years to come. This star of a bygone age of Hollywood glamour evoked Barbra's empathy and admiration. Mae West was an original; and although Streisand did it well, parodying her was a great mistake since it took away from Streisand's own distinct individuality.

In early March she returned to New York to film her third CBS special, eventually entitled "The Belle of 14th Street." The show was a misguided journey back to the turn of the century. This time Streisand had two guests: the actor Jason Robards and old-time black vaudevillian John Bubbles appearing in a distasteful, blatantly racist song and dance dressed as a chicken. The special misfired, but the concert section, which constituted the last third of the show was classic Streisand at her very best — especially a definitive rendition of "My Buddy." Physically, she was in amazingly good shape considering Jason's recent arrival. She danced, "flew" à la Peter Pan across the stage in one number, and in another did a partial striptease wearing a breakaway costume. She also brought out her Mae West parody again with a provocative rendition of "A Good Man Is Hard to Find."

"The Belle of 14th Street" proved that Streisand had been right in her original determination to appear solo on her earlier television specials. At last, she had yielded to CBS's request for a variety theme. Never an ensemble player, she was unable to enter into the team spirit that was evident with other vocalists on television, stalwarts such as Frank Sinatra, Judy Garland, Dinah Shore, Perry Como, Nat King Cole, or Andy Williams. She was not good at making small talk or cracking jokes that tried to sound unrehearsed. Every word she spoke had to be scripted. And she drew the line when it came to having another singer as a guest, for she recalled all too well how she had been able to appropriate the limelight for herself during her early guest appearances on television with Garland and Shore.

Meanwhile, Ray Stark met with Gene Kelly in Hollywood about his directing *Funny Girl,* but Kelly's schedule would have delayed the production. Gower Champion, a superb dancer and choreographer, was considered. Although he had directed such Broadway hits as *Bye Bye Birdie, Carnival, I Do! I Do!,* and *Hello, Dolly!,* Champion's only directorial film effort had been *My Six Loves,* a syrupy theatrical story starring Debbie Reynolds. Streisand insisted that she needed someone more experienced in film who could help with her acting performance and film technique. Stark turned to Sidney Lumet, the son of a veteran Yiddish theater actor and a director who was known to be sensitive with a serious approach to story. Lumet had directed *The Group,* and Sidney Buchman enthusiastically sang his praises to Stark.

The story of *Funny Girl* was not any easier to adapt to the screen than it had been to the stage. Fran Stark's restrictions still prevailed; Nicky Arnstein would remain one-dimensional. Sidney and I tried to give him more depth of character within these limitations, to make the scenes between Fanny and Nick more confrontational. *Funny Girl* was to be a familiar backstage drama that had been told and retold many times before. It would succeed or fail on Streisand's performance.

Buchman and I had reinstated the role of Georgia, the showgirl and mistress to the great Ziegfeld. The character, who becomes an alcoholic in the course of the film, provides an opportunity for Fanny to show her compassion while at the same time giving her someone understanding to play off and advance the story line. Sidney predicted, "Georgia's scenes will end up on the cutting-room floor. Streisand will shoot down any female competition as quickly as she can." He was right. She would have deadeye aim with the male members of the cast as well.

The first-draft screenplay was completed in August 1966. Sidney flew to New York for script discussions with Ray Stark. Letters (in Sidney's minuscule handwriting), telegrams, and telephone calls went back and forth between us. Everything was all right, Sidney assured me. Not to worry. Then he called, a little less confident, and asked me to fly over. Nicky Arnstein's role was to be drastically pared. A scene that we were particularly attached to was the first to go. In it Fanny visits Nicky in jail, finding him dressed not in prison clothes but as stylishly as ever and playing a high-stakes game of poker with other inmates. Although reminiscent of a Rhett Butler episode in *Gone With the Wind,* the story was based on one Brice had recorded in her autobiographical tapes. Our first draft of the screenplay had started with this scene, played entirely from Fanny's point of view. Realizing that Nicky is never going to change, Fanny leaves the prison in her chauffeured car and, studying her image in the rearview mirror, utters those famous words, "Hullo, gorgeous," and then the story flashes back to her youth.

We also reinstated the roller-skating number, and using the original "Baltimore" number as a basis, a new scene had been created in the Baltimore railroad station, introducing the great black performer Bert Williams as a character (he was in the *Follies* with Fanny). Williams, though a Ziegfeld star, is not allowed to sit in the same car as Fanny and Georgia and the other players with whom he is on tour, which was the unvarnished and ugly truth. Nicky shows up and tells Fanny he is going to Europe to recoup his gambling losses and wants her to go with him. She says no. As she stands in the vast, Victorian-style station waiting to board her train, she changes her mind, leaves the show, goes to New York, takes a tugboat to reach the ship he has boarded, and is helped onto it as it moves out to sea. Most of this sequence survived.

In January 1967, because of a strong personality clash between star and director, Lumet left the project. Within a few weeks, William Wyler was brought on board. Wyler had received three Academy Awards for best director and best picture: *Mrs. Miniver, The Best Years of Our Lives,* and *Ben-Hur*. Four actresses — Bette Davis (*Jezebel*), Olivia de Havilland (*The Heiress*), Audrey Hepburn (*Roman Holiday*), and Greer Garson (*Mrs. Miniver*) — had won an Academy Award for best actress under his direction. Wyler was a Hollywood legend, his work known and admired around the world. A meticulous craftsman, he revolutionized the look of films in the forties by using a deep-focus shot perfected by cameraman Greg Toland that allowed him to film long takes in which characters appear in the same frame for the duration of entire scenes. Called "90-take Wyler," he was a taskmaster, and one of the most innovative of Hollywood's directors. He had never before made a musical, but it was certain that he would be able to turn Streisand into a major film performer if she cooperated with him.

Wyler made it a condition of his contract that a choreographer be placed in charge of all musical sequences. Herbert Ross, who had worked with Streisand as the choreographer on *I Can Get It for You Wholesale*, was signed. Production on *Funny Girl* was now scheduled to start in July, but there would be music rehearsals beforehand. Elliott remained in New York ostensibly on business for one of their companies while Streisand, Jason in her arms and Sadie on a lead, arrived in California on May 2 to settle into a house that had once belonged to Greta Garbo.

16

Dusk was settling as the limousine that met Streisand at the airport cut through Beverly Hills toward Sunset Boulevard. The studio representative sat in the front seat with the driver; the nanny, Jason, and Sadie were with Streisand in back. Most of her baggage was to follow in another car. The day had been one of unusual warmth for early May, and sprinklers whirled and cascaded water over the rich green front lawns of houses they passed. The car turned onto Sunset, drove past the sprawling, gaudy pink stucco Beverly Hills Hotel, its grounds rimmed by palm trees, took an immediate right at the entrance of Benedict Canyon, and then turned into the driveway of 904 North Bedford Drive, one house removed from the corner of Sunset. They paused before the garage gates, where a code was pressed to allow them to pass inside.

The house was set in a pretty white-walled garden, with masses of deep burgundy bougainvillea streaming down one side. Garbo had once cut down most of it with her own two hands, but that was nearly two decades ago. Nonetheless, her celebrity had given the property an aura, and star maps sold by vendors on the Boulevard still listed it as her residence — a curious inclusion, as her address had been kept secret during the years she lived there; even her mail was sent elsewhere.

The inside of the house, built in the Spanish style, was larger than

Streisand had expected. There was plenty of room for herself, Jason, Elliott, and a nanny, although as it had been rented fully furnished, the decoration was not entirely to her taste — a combination of California casual and Hollywood decorator chic. As soon as Jason was settled, she began to rearrange things more to her liking. It was almost impossible to believe. She was here in Hollywood, preparing to star in a movie and living in a house once occupied by Garbo.

Four days later the Starks gave her a welcoming party at their Holmby Hills estate. For the girl from Brooklyn, meeting Hollywood celebrities was a heady experience. The next day she was shocked when the studio demanded she make a screen test. New trepidation had arisen as to how she was going to photograph. She was furious; at first she refused, then — fearful she might lose the role after all — agreed.

"We were all very unsure that Barbra would succeed with a film audience . . . because, at the time the movie was made, her very special qualities were still relatively unfamiliar and certainly nobody in the history of film had ever had that particular combination of — what Barbra did," Herb Ross recalled. "So, we did a very, very careful screen test of her. And once we saw her on the screen — and I was the one who did that test — we knew that she was able to project on film as well as she projected on stage. In fact, the medium was even more flattering to her than the stage." The studio's enthusiasm was greater than Ross has indicated.

On June 16, a Friday, she flew to New York, where she gave a one-woman free concert in Central Park the following evening. The event was televised in a condensed hour version by CBS in September. The Six-Day Arab-Israeli War had ended on June 10 after Israel launched a massive air assault. It now controlled the Sinai peninsula and Jerusalem's Old City and had gained a hold on the strategic Golan Heights. Not surprisingly, Streisand had received several threats and was justifiably terrified to appear before 135,000 people in an open area where she could not be fully protected. The possibility of canceling was discussed, but the Central Park concert had been announced long in advance of the Arab-Israeli hostilities and there were recording and television contracts to be considered. CBS promised Streisand she would receive the best protection they could obtain. CIA and private security personnel were stationed close to the stage and throughout the audience.

She looked especially lovely, a summer breeze causing her voluminous chiffon gowns, designed by Irene Sharaff, to billow gracefully as she glided across the stage and up and down a ramp during the two-and-a-half-hour concert. Although the audience was unaware of her anxiety, her fear never subsided — giving an edge to her spectacular performance. When she walked off the stage after her final bow, she collapsed in sobs into Elliott's arms. This frightening experience would affect her decision not to do concerts again for many years.

Once more Elliott remained in New York to handle business matters when Streisand returned to California the following Monday to resume music rehearsals. The movie would have sixteen songs (approximately one hour of music, 40 percent of the picture). When Fanny was in performance in the *Ziegfeld Follies,* there would be band and period music. In anything apart from the theater sequences, Walter Scharf, the musical director, was using full, contemporary orchestrations and up to eighty musicians. The prerecording sessions were to end on August 3; studio photography was scheduled to start on August 7, a Monday.*

Wyler was demanding more and more revisions. Streisand had her say, Fran and Ray Stark theirs. Sidney and I were off the assignment. We returned to Europe. Ben Hecht and John Patrick were consulted and, finally, Isobel Lennart was called back into service.** For Lennart, it was, according to a letter she wrote to Garson Kanin, "the worst time of my life." She now looked back on the months on the road with the show as "strangely happy."

The casting of Nicky Arnstein remained unsettled. The role had never

---

*Songs cut from the movie of *Funny Girl* were "The Music That Makes Me Dance," "Cornet Man," "I Want to Be Seen With You," "Rat-a-tat-tat" ("Private Schwartz from Rockaway"), "Who Taught Her Everything She Knows," and the chorus number, "Henry Street." Four songs were added: "Roller Skate Rag" (which had its roots in an earlier, similar song) and "Funny Girl" by Styne and Merrill, "I'd Rather Be Blue Over You (Than Happy with Somebody Else)" (written in the twenties by Fred Fisher), and "My Man."
**Isobel Lennart would receive the final screenplay credit.

been allowed to develop. Attracting a star for what was essentially a supporting part had proved difficult, almost insurmountable. However, Wyler was noted for his ability to turn a secondary role into a noteworthy performance, as he had done with Montgomery Clift in *The Heiress*. *Funny Girl* was already well into preproduction and the music rehearsals begun before Wyler cast Omar Sharif, who had starred as *Doctor Zhivago* and was a most unlikely choice, in the part.

Sharif was making a Western in Hollywood, *Mackenna's Gold,* and had lunch in the studio canteen every day at the table next to Ray Stark and William Wyler. "They were getting ready to do *Funny Girl* and . . . were looking for a co-star," he later recalled. "That wasn't such an easy assignment. The screenplay was built around Barbra. What actor would agree to play her straight man? Fanny Brice sang, cracked jokes, fascinated the audiences; Nick Arnstein . . . had to content himself with giving her her cues and looking good in a tuxedo. . . . Apparently it was no cinch to find an actor who could look relaxed in a tuxedo. I just happened to be one of those rare individuals, something that started people in the studio canteen joking: 'Why not Omar Sharif?'"

Sharif, an Egyptian, playing the Jewish Arnstein?

"Well, *why not* Omar Sharif?" countered a desperate Wyler. "Think about it," he said, turning to Sharif. "It's not such a bad idea at that."

Sharif was available and keen to remain in Hollywood. With its $8.8 million budget and the great William Wyler directing, *Funny Girl* would be a major film. Sharif would receive costarring credit equal to Streisand's. "A few days [after I signed my contract,] Arabs and Israelis were locked in the Six-Day War," he recounted. "All the investments in the production were Jewish. The atmosphere [at Columbia] was pro-Israel and my co-star was Jewish. . . . And I was an Egyptian. An Egyptian from Nasser's regime. . . . There was fear of a pro-Israel backlash against me, and subsequently, *Funny Girl.*

"A wave of panic swept over the set. . . . Ray Stark spoke of breaking my contract. Fortunately William Wyler, who was also Jewish, reacted strenuously: 'We're in America, the land of freedom. . . . Not hiring an actor because he's Egyptian is outrageous. If Omar doesn't make the film I don't make it either!'"

Streisand reserved judgment. The dreamy-eyed Sharif possessed a suavely charming manner, and his dark good looks allowed him to pass for Jewish, but as an Egyptian he might feel antagonistic toward Jews — and that would impede their working together. A lunch meeting was arranged. Not only was Sharif an anti-nationalist who disapproved of religious fanaticism and bore only contempt for racism, he had potent seductive powers to which she was not immune.

"You don't become *really* famous until you're a movie star," Streisand had said once. Well, here she was in Hollywood, starring in her first film. The fantasy was now reality. She felt a shivery thrill each time she drove her large Chrysler Imperial through the front gates of Columbia Pictures, heard the guard say, "Good morning, Miss Streisand," and parked in her private space near her specially decorated dressing-room trailer. She was fascinated with every aspect of the studio and claimed she suddenly felt at home. Then there were times, like when she met Marlon Brando at lunch one day, when she became insecure. "How can I be a star when he's a star?" she questioned later. She acknowledged their introduction with a mumbled greeting as she found herself almost unable to speak.

On August 7, when the film first went before the cameras, Streisand treated Wyler not unkindly but with a certain hauteur. "At that point, I think I knew more about *Funny Girl* than Mr. Wyler," she later said. "I had played it a thousand times and had read all the revisions of all the scripts — for the movies and the play." To a reporter during the first week of shooting she explained, "He [Wyler] does things one way, I do them another."

"My principal concern," Wyler confided, "was to present her under the best possible conditions as a new star and a new personality. She was terribly eager, like Bette Davis used to be, to do different and new things. She wanted everything to be the very best. The same as I do." Wyler was a man of infinite patience. He celebrated his sixty-fifth birthday on the first day of shooting but had made his debut as a director at the age of twenty-three, shortly after arriving from his native Alsace. He had directed a plethora of difficult female stars and had even been married to one — Margaret Sullavan. Streisand's *mishegoss,* her compulsive behavior, lateness on the set, her need to be involved in every aspect of the film, barely fazed him; he had been through it all before. Short and feisty with gray-speckled hair, Wyler had a charismatic smile and a merry glint in his blue eyes. Clouds of smoke curled upward from the cigarettes he chain-smoked as he sat in his director's chair watching a scene in progress. When he spoke, he never wasted words. He had lost the hearing in one ear during World War II from high-altitude flying, a disability he had learned to use to his advantage; he turned his hearing aid off when Streisand, or any performer, was being troublesome.

"I don't just expect obedience. I don't like an actor or actress who says, 'Okay, boss, what do you want me to do?'" he said of himself. "I say to them, 'What do *you* want to do? You've read the script and you know what's in it so *you* show *me*.'. . . The actor has to put himself in another person's skin and think like somebody he isn't. I can help and guide but he has to do it finally. . . . Barbra responded to direction very well."

Streisand took another view. "I feel we had a great sort of chemical relationship. Willy can't, um, dissect a scene for you. I mean, he would go, 'Oomph, a little more oomph,' and I'd say, 'Okay, I know what you mean.' And I would give it a little more oomph. . . . He let me see the rushes with him, and I'm supposedly the first actress who's seen them. He knows I'm not destructive. I'm very objective about my work."

She spoke the truth. Able to view herself with cold objectivity, she would often ask to reshoot a scene the next day if she did not like her performance or the technical work caught on film. She saw things in relation to herself. At such times Wyler stood firm. They had battles, more in the first few weeks of shooting than as the production was well underway. He insisted that a Henry Street waif (Fanny) in 1910 would not have two-inch Mandarin fingernails. "Why? Why not?" she kept screaming. "The Chinese have worn them for centuries!" Wyler gave in, which was a mistake because her feline claws present a jarring image on screen with the period costumes.

Wyler admired Streisand, thought she was a true artist, and encouraged her passion to learn all she could about making films as fast as she could. He also knew exactly when to display his sharp edge, but he gave her suggestions serious consideration and often reshot a scene if she showed good cause to do so. A studio worker on the set was heard saying to another, "Willy shouldn't be so hard on her. After all, this is the first picture she's ever directed."

One time, after Wyler had her repeat a scene in rehearsal for the ninth or tenth time, she came over to him, her voice ear-piercing, her hands "going everywhere, like an Italian woman explaining a traffic accident to a cop." Wyler held up an open palm. "'Just tone it down,'" he ordered sternly. "They looked at one another," an observer on the set noted. "Everyone waited for her to explode and say the hell with [you!] Streisand nodded and walked back out onto the cold rehearsal floor." This time she gave Wyler what he wanted, and he flashed a broad smile of approval.

Funny Girl took four months to shoot. Streisand loved making the picture, being the star. She never wanted to leave the studio. She brought Wyler "eleven versions of each scene. Things that we had tried out in Philadelphia and Boston or that had been left out of the show."

This was the living enactment of her dream. "See, Ma, you were wrong. The homely kid from Brooklyn made it to Hollywood and is a movie star." Of course, she loved to see those nightly rushes. There she was in the darkness, watching herself up on the big screen, her image filling it, looking like she always knew she really did look — different but beautiful.

Elliott joined her in Hollywood a few weeks into the shooting schedule. Streisand was having terrible clashes with Ray Stark, who wanted her to commit her next film to his company and go straight from *Funny Girl* into a second film for him, although she had the contractual option of making an outside film first. She did not like the project. Elliott took on the position of mediator. Wyler was privy to some of these rather ugly confrontations and saw how Elliott had dealt with her after she emerged from them, fuming, near hysteria. It reminded him of his marriage to Margaret Sullavan, "But Elliott handled these things a lot better than I did. He came in and sort of straightened things out. He was very good at that." Still, it was obvious that things were not harmonious in the Gould household.

Elliott was trying to develop projects for Streisand's television production company other than those that would star his wife. "I had good ideas that would have worked if they could have been executed," he remembered. "But the television companies were impossible to deal with. I failed completely. I had no track record. I used to deal with all the no men at the networks — a bunch of fucking pigs. I hated them and I hated myself and I hated going someplace with an idea two notches above things that had been done again and again and being strung along and then rejected. . . . I never sold any[thing]. Meanwhile my wife was starring in *Funny Girl* and was the biggest thing in the business and I had all this spare time on my hands. . . . I had more self-respect when I was a teenager, operating the night elevator in the Park Royal Hotel on 73rd Street [in New York]."

His life took an upward turn when, just two weeks after he had arrived in California, he was cast in *The Night They Raided Minsky's*, which would feature Jason Robards, Norman Wisdom, Bert Lahr, Harry Andrews, Denholm Elliott, and Britt Ekland. His role was not large, but it was showy. However, the movie was to go into production immediately in New York. Alone in California with Jason, Streisand felt deserted; she turned — as she had once before — to her leading man. Sharif was married to an Egyptian actress who had not accompanied him to the United States. He had a reputation for having affairs with his costars. He said he worshipped "a certain type of woman. The kind who can use both her intelligence and her femininity." Streisand seemed ideal casting. "As to carnal love," he added, "they've never found a substitute for it." And she was ready for an amorous adventure.

"Barbra . . . who struck me as being ugly at first," Sharif ungallantly recalled, "gradually cast her spell over me. I fell madly in love with her talent and her personality. The feeling was mutual for four months — the time it took to shoot the picture. . . . We spent our evenings, our weekends at her place. . . . We led the very simple life of people in love. . . . We used to cook. When I'd used up all my Italian recipes [learned from Sophia Loren] . . . Barbra would heat TV dinners. . . . [We] would enjoy simple food; then, relaxed in our armchairs, we'd watch television."

Eventually they ventured out to the home of friends like Gregory Peck and his French wife, Veronique. "Like everyone else [in the beginning], Greg knew nothing about the affair Barbra and I were having, and he had invited me over," Sharif remembered. "So I asked him if I could bring somebody with me. I knew he wouldn't let the news out." Sharif was a man who played at life as he would at cards or dice, without counting the cost. He lived in an eternal present. "They say I'm pathologically unfaithful. No. I'm never unfaithful," he argued. "I simply fall in love a lot, often and fast."

"Did I love my wife?" Sharif questioned and then answered. "Yes, in the Middle Eastern way. My marriage wasn't a marriage of love, in the sense of passionate love. It was a marriage of compatibility, affection, friendship." Faten Hamama was ten years older than he, one of Egypt's most famous and beloved stars, the Shirley Temple of the Near East in her youth who had grown into a beautiful leading lady. Eclipsed by his wife's fame in their native country, Sharif sought work abroad, finally succeeding with his role as Ali, the Arabian friend of Peter O'Toole in *Lawrence of Arabia*. He had gone on to play the title role in *Dr. Zhivago*.

When Elliott was in New York, Streisand and Sharif were together most evenings. "He made himself quite comfortably at home," one of Streisand's personal staff said. Members of the *Funny Girl* company were aware that Streisand and Sharif were lovers, although Elliott later claimed he did not know what was going on. He spoke to Streisand every night. She regaled him with her problems at the studio, on the set, with Ray Stark. Despite these complaints she claimed she loved Hollywood — the weather, the space, the studio; Elliott hated it — the artificiality, the false values. "What really got me down was the loss of my second name. As Barbra's husband, I was either Mr. Streisand or Elliott who?"

Not taken in by Hollywood's glamour, Elliott understood, as Streisand did not, the El Dorado lifestyle in which careers and fortunes could shoot up or plummet down on no more than rumors, the hint of scandal, the news that a film was about to bomb. Hollywood is a closed and inbred society that exists and thrives entirely on its own myths. A killer instinct prevails, like the tennis pro who specializes in smashing his opponent's serve. No one believes in playing the game. Winning is all that mattered. Frankly, Hollywood scared the hell out of Elliott and he tried, to no avail, to convince his wife not to make it their permanent home.

Although he flew back and forth to the West Coast, Elliott spent most of the time in New York, which gave Streisand the opportunity to pursue her affair with Sharif, who became progressively more possessive. On the set, his hands rested comfortably on her waist, her shoulder. "A woman mustn't contradict me openly. . . . I can contradict a woman because I'm a man and because arrogance is in the nature of men. . . . I make women happy, with the tenderness, love, and thrills I give them," he proclaimed. "I get any woman I want because I give all of myself. And who can refuse so much human warmth? Giving, consoling, protecting, guiding — these are a man's privileges. Take them away and you take away his male prerogatives. The woman, for her part, must give the impression that she needs the man . . . even if she's perfectly capable of running her own life."

Streisand appeared to find Sharif's macho attitude amusing. She smiled a lot at him, complimented him on a scene or on how he looked. Meanwhile, his role was shrinking on a daily basis. On the set, she would take him aside and they would talk in hushed voices, and she would giggle like a naive adolescent when he whispered something into her ear.

Sharif portrayed Nicky Arnstein as part saint, part Dr. Zhivago, a seductive gaze in his huge dark eyes as he played to Fanny/Streisand, the camera, and any woman who had business on the set. Nicky Arnstein was buried beneath a starched shirt front and a bow tie. What was left was a one-dimensional character. After the first rushes there was talk of replacing him. Streisand would not hear of it. She liked the way she played off him, could feel the sparks, the sexual vibes as Fanny fell in love with him on screen. Wyler agreed that this was true — no dialogue was needed to understand why Fanny was so in love with Arnstein. It was pure carnal desire. More of Sharif's scenes were cut. "If it was Barbra's plan to keep *Funny Girl* a one-star picture, she was being devilishly clever," a member of the cast said. "She got what she wanted and Omar as well."

Sharif was fascinated by American women, "The self-confidence, superiority, and independence of the [American] women! These very beautiful women whom I wanted to seduce and, perhaps, dominate. These women so different from the ones I'd known. These women who dared to breathe without the artificial lung of the male!" He called himself a Europeanized Middle Eastern man. "The bed is the holy table," he confessed. "For me, one love drives away another and the woman who's inspiring that love at the time fills my entire world." Stories circulated among Sharif's many former mistresses of how he could hold an erection for hours using the ancient Arabic mind-control art of *imsák,* also practiced by the well-known playboy Aly Khan.

Caught up in her passion for her lover, the contradiction in Streisand's character was startling. A woman with a fierce streak of independence, she was besotted with a man who demeaned her sex by reducing them to love objects. Yet, at no time during the making of *Funny Girl* did Sharif gain the upper hand. His lust for her gave Streisand a heightened sense of her desirability. It also increased her ability to manipulate and control scenes in which they played together. He was, in fact, the one being used.

Her affair with Sharif stimulated her appetite for European culture. She became a dedicated collector of information, details, facts. "Tolstoy-GogolTurgenevtheGreeksChekhovMolièreRacine," she rattled off at breakneck speed to an interviewer, "I'm reading them *all.* My attention span is very short, I get involved with one book and then I move to another, then I go back to the first. Ya know what I mean?" She shifted from one area of filmmaking to another with this same approach, able to retain only bits and pieces at first, then grasping an amazing working understanding of each field. She was a college student body of one, hand-selecting the top studio expert in lighting, sound, cinematography, and editing as her professors.

The more knowledgeable she became, the more she tested her power. Wyler was amused with her at first, but then he realized she was a genuine force to be dealt with. In Hollywood people did things like robots, she told Elliott in one of their daily coast-to-coast telephone conversations but then added with pride, "I have the courage to talk back."

"Every day, Barbra would see the rushes," Anne Francis, who had been cast as Georgia, recalled, "and the next day my part was cut or something else was cut. Barbra ran the whole show — Ray Stark, Willie Wyler, Herb Ross. She had the Ziegfeld girls' scenes changed — one day she told Wyler to move a girl standing next to her because she was too pretty, and the girl wound up in the background. Eventually, the Ziegfeld girls' scenes were eliminated altogether.

"She told Harry Stradling how to [photograph] her and Wyler how to direct. . . . It was all like an experience out of *Gaslight*. There was an unreality about it. Only the crew was terrific. They were so kind and friendly. . . . I had only one unpleasant meeting with Barbra during the entire five months of rehearsals and production. But the way I was treated, it was a nightmare. And my scenes were whittled from three very good ones and a lot of other ones, to two minutes of voice-over in a New Jersey railroad station."

Although Streisand and Elliott still shared their New York apartment, they appeared troubled and he did not accompany her on location in New Jersey when the company moved to an East River pier near the Manhattan Bridge to photograph the ferryboat scene for "Don't Rain on My Parade."

For that sequence Streisand had to run down the length of the pier several times in her high heels holding two suitcases and a bunch of roses. "Boy, am I going to sue you," she ribbed Ray Stark, who was watching the scene. "My back hurts. My feet hurt. This is the hardest work I've ever done. I'll probably get sick on the tugboat, and I got thorns in my fingers from all these damned roses!"

She returned to Hollywood without Elliott and was reunited with Jason, who had remained there in the care of a nurse and a nanny. It seemed not to disturb her that she was disliked by the majority of the cast. A member of the chorus was heard to say after one difficult day when she was particularly hard to please, "Who does she think she is, Joan Crawford?" Newspaper columnists railed her about being a "girl monster." It was not easy for her to take. But Streisand was fearful that this was her only chance at bat. If she did not make it as a big movie star with *Funny*

Girl, if it bombed and she went down with it, it would be almost impossible to regain the kind of momentum she now had. The smallest detail mattered: a wisp of her hair creating a shadow, an item on a table distracting the eye. She had to be lit perfectly, and having learned which spots flattered her, she kept after Stradling to make sure they were used in all her scenes. No person or object could upstage her in a scene. Her costumes had to be spotless, seamless. She insisted on still another take even when Wyler or Herb Ross was satisfied. She worked with the soundmen and mastered the technique of dubbing. She brought her own makeup kit onto the stage and touched up her face when the makeup men were done.

"I feel like a boxer in the ring," Streisand said. "In Hollywood they have people for everything. If there is a stain on my dress, I'm not supposed to clean it. Then I'm criticized if I stand up and shout, 'Stain person!' until someone from the wardrobe department finally comes. If I didn't shout, a whole half hour could go by before the stain person got there!"

"People were saying she was paranoid," a dancer in the film said, "but I want to be fair. That's a lie. She is, in her own way, the sanest person in the world. A paranoid person is someone who imagines he has enemies. She did not have to invent them. She *had* enemies."

Streisand also had strong supporters. As with the play, *Funny Girl* the movie was fast becoming Streisand's vehicle, the rushes revealing a new, totally original movie personality blazing into incandescent existence. She so lit the film that its success seemed as assured as her own. The studio was pleased, Wyler was satisfied, and Ray Stark, to whom she was contracted to do three more pictures, was ecstatic. "Sure, she's tough," Stradling commented, "but she has an unerring eye."

"You have to understand," Sharif told the *Los Angeles Times,* "she's a kid from Brooklyn. She had a terrible background. She didn't just think she was plain — she thought she was ugly. So no wonder that insecurity. No wonder, when people suddenly start to make a fuss over you, you don't know whether it's for you, or who you are. Those weren't rumors that she caused trouble during the filming of *Funny Girl.* There *was* trouble — in wardrobe, in makeup, and so on. But when the whole film sinks or swims on you, you're in trouble."

What Sharif did not understand was that Streisand thrived on trouble and often was its instigator. Trouble fed her churning mind; it gave impetus to her power of determination and reason for some of her otherwise unconscionable actions.

17

With Elliott increasingly in New York, Streisand's affair with Sharif intensified. She had become the woman she was portraying, madly in love with the gorgeous Nicky Arnstein. From the days when she watched movies from a balcony seat she had fantasized that she was the woman *in* the story, not the movie star portraying her. "I never wanted to be Vivien Leigh," she had said. "I desperately wanted to be Scarlett O'Hara." She had believed that Scarlett and Rhett were real people, and for her the love scenes had an aura of cinema verité, real people in moments of true passion. Wyler saw what was happening and said nothing, as the rushes were incendiary and exactly what he wanted. She glowed onscreen and off. The set buzzed with gossip: *Would she leave Elliott? Would Sharif leave his wife?* The lovers remained discreet off the set until near the end of filming, when they appeared at various social gatherings together. These "sightings" were reported in the press. After they were photographed together at an exclusive charity fashion show at the Factory Discotheque in Hollywood, Elliott telephoned her from New York, hurt and angry.

"Why in hell did you go to the fashion show with Omar?" he screamed across the telephone lines.

"Because the ticket would have cost me $250," he said she replied. Elliott apparently embraced that response at face value, unable to accept the role of the cuckolded husband. Also, it did not sound that unreasonable; Streisand had hung on to many of her old penny-pinching habits and was always pleased when someone else picked up the tab. Then, the following Sunday night she dined alone with Sharif at Matteo's, one of Hollywood's "in" restaurants.

Wanting to avoid a scandal, Elliott told columnist Irv Kupcinet, "Barbra's always been a cheapskate. She accepted those dates with Sharif because she doesn't like buying her own dinners." Cornered by Sheilah Graham, he told her, "I'm furious with Barbra and told her that. She should have known that she is in a very difficult position out there, where the press doesn't like her because she has been uncooperative. I'm just furious with her for putting herself in this kind of position. I'm a very secure person but as a man I have certain reactions."

By downplaying the relationship, he was telegraphing to the public that Streisand had done nothing overtly wrong, that she was simply terribly naive. The situation darkened when Sharif told a reporter with the *Los Angeles Times,* "It's true, I lusted after Barbra."

Such a passionate declaration from a lover who was a handsome leading man known to have had affairs with some of the world's most beautiful women fed Streisand's ego. Chiding remarks about her looks (especially her nose) were always appearing in print, and despite her ability to laugh at them in public, they hurt — deeply. She wanted desperately to be seen as a desirable, attractive woman. Perhaps even more, she longed to feel that way about herself. She saw herself as the great love of two men — her husband and her lover. In such a scenario Elliott would be expected to fly to her side and fight for her.

His reaction to the affair was far different from what she had anticipated. Elliott treated it as if it were an invention of the press and not true, and he remained in New York. Streisand, incensed at his cool attitude, was more outspoken about the significance of her relationship with Sharif. "I know Elliott thinks it's just another Hollywood fantasy," she told a reporter, "but it's not — Omar has told me many times that he loves me."

She quickly learned that Sharif had his own interpretation of love. To him, it was something that could be collected and then left on a shelf.

His scenes completed before Streisand's, he departed Hollywood for Europe a few days later to star with Catherine Deneuve, James Mason, and Ava Gardner in *Mayerling*. Within a few weeks rumors came back that he was having a torrid affair with Ava. Both Streisand and Elliott looked the naive fools in this typically tawdry Hollywood love triangle. When Elliott returned to California, they acted — at least in public — as if nothing had happened. Elliott, who was already having difficulty being the less successful husband of a star, was deeply hurt by Streisand's affair. Streisand, on her part, no longer was sure of her feelings for Elliott.

They were still living together but were seeing separate lawyers in an attempt to work out an amicable trial separation. An announcement was prepared for the press, then yanked back, brought out again, then yanked back again. Their mutual business interests, since Elliott was a partner with her in Ellbar, were complicated, and Jason's custody presented problems. Elliott wanted to have the child with him for a fair amount of time; Streisand was not willing to compromise. She planned to stay in Hollywood while Elliott was in New York, which would have made joint custody difficult with a child so young.

It was not simply the classic story of the price of stardom. Streisand and Elliott both had deep-seated emotional difficulties that predated her rise to fame. Elliott's love and devotion had apparently not been enough to build her self-confidence as a woman. No matter how successful she was, self-doubt remained. Winning the love of her handsome leading man had helped — but just for a time. She needed more freedom to find herself, to experience more in her personal life. Still, she was not sure she wanted to let go of Elliott or that she should. She began therapy sessions anew. Her long investigation into her past, and the reasons for her actions, fears, and insecurities began again. She would spend years speaking about the loss of her father and her painful childhood.

"I don't believe in psychoanalysis per se," she was to say, "but that's what makes up our personality. Only when you get older can you look at things [that happened in childhood] with some distance, and if you have the courage you can feel the pain." She laid much of the guilt for that pain on Diana and Louis Kind. "Even though you — complain — about your parents," she added in a tone of gingerly forgiveness, "you find you're like them in many ways." Fascinated with tales of herself, she would talk about her past to interviewers freely — dogmatically certain she was telling the truth. She was binding her life into a book of her own invention, no doubt based on honest remembrance, but it was *her* truth, a story told from only one point of view — hers. She portrayed herself as a victim of an unhappy childhood, a sexist world. To an extent, this was true. Life, however, is seldom so black-and-white. A case can be put forward that she made herself a victim by believing it was so and that despite the many injustices worldwide toward women, she had suffered fewer than most.

Nothing was done at that time to start divorce proceedings. Elliott still occupied a place in her life. He was a true friend, the father of her child. The one thing that she was sure of was her deep commitment to making movies. She loved the medium, felt "at home" in it, was endlessly intrigued by the camera and the possibilities that film presented. On the last day of production on *Funny Girl,* she gave Wyler an eighteenth-century gold watch inscribed TO MAKE UP FOR LOST TIME. Wyler presented her with a megaphone engraved BARBRA STREISAND — DIRECTOR. It meant a lot to her. She now dreamed of one day producing and directing her own film, one that had a theme that *she* wanted to present, something so good she could feel that it came from her *kishkas,* her gut. In whatever free time she had, she would read — books, manuscripts, playscripts, articles — always looking for the story that she could believe in and embrace.

News travels fast in the powerful front offices of studio executives and long before the filming of *Funny Girl* ended, Hollywood knew that Barbra Streisand was on her way to superstardom. Academy Award–winning producer-writer Ernest Lehman wanted her to star in the movie version of *Hello, Dolly!,* scheduled to go before the cameras almost immediately upon the completion of *Funny Girl.* She had great trepidation about accepting the offer even though the money ($750,000) was enticing and as an outside picture, not involving Ray Stark, she would be the sole financial beneficiary of the fee. She thought, quite rightly, that she was too young for the role of Dolly Levi, the widowed marriage broker who tricks the aging, crotchety Horace Vandergelder into marriage. The press agreed with her. When Streisand finally announced she had accepted the part, the press called her a "role stealer." A divided camp was rooting for either Lucille Ball or Carol Channing to be cast as Dolly.

Stark filed suit and asked for an injunction to prevent her from appearing in a movie for another company while she was contractually tied to his. He submitted two scripts to her, *Wait Till the Sun Shines, Nellie* and a musical version of William Gibson's stage hit *Two for the Seesaw.* * Streisand hated both projects and threatened to go to court to avoid making them. After several fiery meetings between their representatives, Streisand and Stark settled their differences. She would do three more films for his company, but they were to follow two pictures for Fox — *Hello, Dolly!* and *On a Clear Day You Can See Forever,* the adaptation of the Alan Jay Lerner–Burton Lane Broadway musical. She claimed she signed for *Hello, Dolly!* partly out of pique and partly because it presented a challenge to take a familiar character and make it her own. It was to be a greater test than she anticipated.

In the few weeks between the end of production on *Funny Girl* and the recording sessions on *Hello, Dolly!* (which were to be done first then dubbed into the film after the numbers were shot), she returned to New York to appear at a charity concert at Carnegie Hall. She came onstage in a black dress, made memorable by the yards of black lace she had wound into a ruff around her neck, and peered at Leonard Bernstein, the conductor, through a diamond lorgnette "like a diva soprano looking for her pianist." She seemed gentler, less acerbic. She did a small parody of herself, twitching her long gown into place with an exaggerated simper and rolling the whites of her eyes like a turn-of-the-century tragedienne. She sang two songs, Bernstein's "Lucky to Be Me" from *On the Town,* and "People."

While in New York, she engaged a researcher to ferret out information on Yonkers and Manhattan in the 1890s, the two major locations of the film, and information about well-known people of that era — what

---

Wait Till the Sun Shines, Nellie was to be a musical remake of a film of that title made in 1952. *Two for the Seesaw* was adapted as a stage musical retitled *Seesaw* (1973), with a score by Cy Coleman and Dorothy Fields. Neither project reached the screen.

they wore, what they ate, and where they went. She bought antique dresses of the period and wore them during the day to get the feel and look of the period; with the help of her hairdresser, Ara Gallant, and a pair of curling tongs, she re-created a nineteenth-century hairstyle that was most becoming, with tight curls framing her face.

Elliott had moved into a small apartment in the Village, and Barbra occupied the penthouse. He had withdrawn from his involvement in Streisand's career and business interests and was concentrating on his own career. He was fast slipping away from her. But she still did not know what she wanted to do about their marriage. She returned to Jason and California alone.

The talk in Hollywood was that Elliott had exhibited star potential in the yet-to-be-released *The Night They Raided Minsky's*. Elliott was being viewed in a different light. He was funny, irreverent, and almost acceptably antisocial. Although *Minsky's* was a period film, because of the burlesque background, it scored a wickedly comic punch. Elliott had somehow upstaged the rest of the older, highly professional cast. He was offered a leading role in the profane contemporary comedy *Bob & Carol & Ted & Alice,* about sexual freedom and open relationships, in which he was to play Ted, a young man with a confused identity in a neurotic urban world. The prospects for such a film seemed limited, and his paycheck reflected this, but he liked his role of the less sophisticated of the two men and felt a great kinship to the character. More important, he was pleased to be carving out a name for himself and harbored hopes that it would help to resurrect his failing marriage.

Streisand had always seen Elliott as a very funny, special person, a nonconformist who had not found his niche. But had he been held back because she demanded so much attention herself? Did he gamble because he was screaming for her help? And was he now heavily into smoking marijuana to avoid the nowhere reality of their relationship? All these questions pointed to yes, triggering emotions of guilt. And there was Jason to consider. She knew how terribly painful it could be growing up without your father in the house, and she decided to give their marriage another try. Since Elliott so disliked Hollywood, she agreed to compromise and work out a schedule whereby they could live a comfortable bi-coastal life.

On February 13, 1968, with *Funny Girl* not ready for release for another six or seven months, she reported to Twentieth Century-Fox for her first costume fittings for *Hello, Dolly!* Her role was that of a woman old enough to be "Funny Girl's" Yiddish mama. Not only was she too young for the part, but this time she would not be playing a character created in large part for her specific talents and personality. Carol Channing, who appeared as Dolly on Broadway for eighteen months,* had been Ernest Lehman's first choice. But Channing did not photograph well. Lehman had also considered Elizabeth Taylor.

"I talked to Elizabeth . . . and asked her whether she'd ever thought of doing a musical. She got quite excited at the prospect," Lehman said. "When I came to cast the picture, her agent rang me up and told me Elizabeth really wanted to play Dolly. And I must admit I felt very guilty at having ever mentioned it to her, because it was a thoroughly rotten notion of mine. At least I *think* it was. In this business you can never ever tell until after the event."

A slender man in his early fifties with long, graying sideburns and thinning hair arranged artfully across the top of his balding head, Lehman was one of Hollywood's top screenwriters, responsible for the scripts of three of the industry's highest-grossing movie musicals: *The Sound of Music, West Side Story,* and *The King and I*— the last considered by critics to be a landmark film musical. These three films and two of his straight dramas, the original screenplay for the great Hitchcock film *North by Northwest* and the adaptation of Edward Albee's *Who's Afraid of Virginia Woolf?,* had earned him five Oscar nominations. Lehman wore a persis-

*After five years *Hello, Dolly!* was still on Broadway, now restaged by Gower Champion (the original director) with an all-black cast headed by Pearl Bailey and Cab Calloway. Before the glorious Miss Bailey, Dolly had been played by Ginger Rogers. Other Broadway Dollys were Martha Raye, Phyllis Diller, Betty Grable, Eve Arden, Dorothy Lamour, Ethel Merman, and (in London) Mary Martin. The title song was adapted as "Hello, Lyndon!" to become President Johnson's campaign theme music in 1964.

tent look of pain on his narrow face, and on his wrist was a thin gold watch with the letters of his name replacing the numbers. "You've got to have twelve letters in your name or it won't work," he'd tell anyone who asked about it, "and it helps if there are six in the first and the last."

Lehman had been working on the film script of *Hello, Dolly!* over a period of three years, having seen Jerry Herman's Broadway musical adaptation of the 1938 Thornton Wilder play *The Merchant of Yonkers** when Carol Channing was still in the cast, and had found himself "strangely moved, suddenly filled with nostalgia for a New York I never knew — a kind of gay and charming world in which even the wicked were innocent." He saw Dolly Levi as a countrified cousin to the materialistic Lorelei (also played on Broadway by Channing) from *Gentlemen Prefer Blondes*.

Streisand's struggle would be to make Dolly believable. Dolly Levi was a dreadnought, triumphantly sailing the perilous seas of widowhood, using wits, guts, and a surface of supreme confidence. In an age of antiheroes, she was the ultimate heroine. Her victory — over the past, over loneliness, over despondency — radiated hope and much good cheer. And whatever else she was, she could never be dull. Bringing Dolly to full-blooded life on screen was not going to be Streisand's only problem. Three stars had already recorded cast albums: Carol Channing, Mary Martin, and Pearl Bailey. Louis Armstrong had made an outstanding hit record of the title song. Not only would Dolly be onscreen for less than two-thirds of the film, there would be another character integral to the plot, the beautiful, young Irene Molloy (Marianne McAndrew), who had two lovely ballads. She had to move the spotlight directly on herself and tailor Dolly's character to her own concept.

---

*Thornton Wilder had himself adapted *The Merchant of Yonkers* from *A Day Well Spent*, written in 1835 by John Oxenford and produced in London. A German adaptation of the same play by John Nestroy appeared in Vienna in 1842 under the title *Einen Jux Will Er Sich Machen*. First produced on Broadway in 1938, Wilder's version, which starred Jane Cowl, was not a success. Fifteen years later he rewrote the play, which he now called *The Matchmaker*. It opened in London in 1954, starring Ruth Gordon, and was a great success. The following year David Merrick optioned the rights, and Ruth Gordon repeated her performance on Broadway for 486 performances. The play was made into a film by Paramount in 1958, starring Shirley Booth as Dolly Levi.

She began this metamorphosis by influencing Irene Sharaff's design of Dolly's famous Harmonia Gardens costume. The film's key scene is when Dolly struts down the grand, red-carpeted staircase of the restaurant and sings the title song with the waiters who are welcoming her back after fourteen years' absence (which means she could not very well be much younger than thirty-five). Sharaff had designed a startling red gown. Michael Stewart, the librettist of the Broadway show, asserted that Dolly's scarlet gown was symbolic of life returning to her. Photographs of Channing wearing the plush, vivid, figure-molding crimson gown had proliferated the media, and she had sung the title song in costume on several television variety specials. Streisand refused to wear a gown of that color and fought onerous battles with Sharaff and Lehman over the design. One day she refused to leave her dressing room unless it was agreed that a new design in gold would be forthcoming. Sharaff compromised and designed a richly beaded topaz dress that pleased Streisand. The standoff was to be a harbinger of bitter conflicts to come.

Gene Kelly, one of Hollywood's most beloved and admired musical stars, fresh from his success as a director with *A Guide for the Married Man,** was signed up as the director. Like Barbra, Gene "was a 'hot property' and it seemed a smart move. *Was* a smart move," Lehman recalled. There was no one else around whose knowledge of musicals was as wide and varied as his. "He had exactly the qualities we needed on the picture. Tremendous energy, vitality, and a maddening cheerfulness." Later he would add, "Barbra and Gene — they were just not meant to communicate on this earth."

"I'd heard that she was a difficult lady," Kelly said, "so as soon as I agreed to do the picture, I flew to New York [where she had gone to look for a new apartment] and met her with her agent for lunch at the Oak Room in the Plaza Hotel, and I came straight out with it and said: 'Barbra, is there any truth to all these stories that you don't want to rehearse and that you're difficult?'"

---

*Gene Kelly made his directorial debut as codirector with Stanley Donen for *On the Town* (1949). The two men also took codirectorial credit for *Singin' in the Raim* (1952). His solo directorial effort was *Invitation to the Dance* (1956).

"Me?" she replied. "I'm a nervous *chalaria* maybe, but I'm not difficult." All she needed, she told him, was a director to guide her.

She also said she was "dying to do the role, and that I could count on
her," Kelly added. She had actually agreed conditionally, wanting first to
be assured that Jerry Herman would write more songs for her because
the original score gave Dolly Levi only three solos.*

By the time she returned to California, she had changed her mind. She
had read and reread the screenplay and was convinced she was far too
young to play Dolly. An equally serious issue was that the story is not all
that much about the title character. "It devotes as much time to Cornelius and Barnaby and their two young women — all of whom are naive
and childish," Lehman explained, "and there was nothing I could do
about it. . . . It was the nature of the beast. *Hello, Dolly!* is a pretty infantile story. Barbra would telephone me in the middle of the night. 'What
the hell am I doing in this picture?' she demanded to know. 'There is no
way I can play Dolly Levi in a way that makes sense of the woman!' She
wanted out. I assured her that Gene would be able to mold Dolly's ex-
cesses into a workable characterization."

"If only there'd been more time," Kelly defended. "I'd have tried to
help her work out a clear-cut characterization, but we had a tight schedule and I left it up to her. With the result that she was being Mae West
one minute, Fanny Brice the other, and Barbra Streisand the next. Her
accent varied as much as her mannerisms. She kept experimenting with
new things out of sheer desperation, none of which really worked to her
satisfaction. And as she's such a perfectionist, she became terribly neurotic and insecure."

The major interior set constructed for *Hello, Dolly!* on the Fox lot
was the Harmonia Gardens, a combination bar, restaurant, and nightclub
popular in the 1890s. Its decor was suggested by combining elements of
Tony Pastor's in New York, Maxime's in Paris, and London's Crystal

---

*Herman negotiated a new contract for the additional material and quickly supplied "Just
Leave Everything to Me" and a ballad, "Love Is Only Love." When Lehman learned the
latter song was originally written, although not used, for Herman's *Mame,* he was furious
but helpless to do anything about it. The lyrics, however, were new and Streisand approved the songs.

Palace. Built on four levels, it was filled with fountains, candelabra, chandeliers, statues, and greenery; marble, gold, and crystal appointments, and furnishings in mutations of red from scarlet to salmon. "I'd say you've built one hell of a saloon," Lehman told production designer John De-Cuir, who had created much of Rome and Alexandria for *Cleopatra*.

Streisand made an electrifying entrance in her topaz gown, shimmering beneath the blinding lights, and then descended the wide red-carpeted staircase. "What I needed was Rhett Butler to sweep me back up again," she told her stand-in Marie Rhodes. "What I got was Walter Matthau." Rhodes had been Marlon Brando's stand-in for years — the only woman of her profession known to have doubled for both a great male and female star. ("I rather like the change," she said. "At least I don't have to wear pants every day.") Streisand never tired of hearing about her idol from Rhodes.

The topaz gown weighed over twenty pounds, and she was in constant danger of tripping because of the length of the skirt. The scene had to be reshot several times and took two days to complete. The gown did not have the dramatic impact it might have had in red, but it gave Streisand a marvelously voluptuous figure, and the color was a strong contrast against all the red used in the decor. She wore the gown for nearly two weeks as other scenes in the Harmonia Gardens were shot, the most memorable being the sequence in which Dolly, wolfing turkey, dumplings, and beets, rejects, as a ploy, a marriage proposal from Horace Vandergelder, the widower she has been pursuing. While eating heartily, Streisand had to maintain delicacy and attractiveness. By the third take, the dumplings, which were made of egg whites, were hard for her to swallow; by the fifth she almost choked while downing a piece of turkey.

She also wore the unwieldy gown as she made a 360-degree tour of the Gardens accompanied by the elaborately capering, acrobatic, singing waiters and as she sang a duet with Louis Armstrong (making a cameo appearance in the film). Never satisfied with a take, she insisted that scenes be shot over and over, with everyone else seeming to tire but her. She was grateful that Harry Stradling was manning the camera as he had for *Funny Girl*. He was her one ally.

Her chemistry with Kelly was explosive. He expected a certain respect for his position as her director and because of his many years of experience in films. She thought he had an attitude problem. Politeness was not her strong suit. She said what she felt, when she felt it. Kelly was not the only one who had trouble dealing with her. Her leading man, Walter Matthau, found it "painful to adjust to her personality, particularly as she made no attempt to adjust to mine."

Matthau was the complete professional. At the age of forty-eight, he had been in show business for thirty-seven years, having made his debut in the Yiddish theater when he was eleven. As a respected supporting player, he had shuttled between Broadway and Hollywood for years when in 1965 he soared to sudden Broadway stardom in *The Odd Couple* in a role that Neil Simon had written especially for him. He had just costarred with Jack Lemmon in the film adaptation and had won the Academy Award for best supporting actor in 1966 for his role in *The Fortune Cookie,* also with Lemmon. The same slouching posture, craggy face, and growling voice that for years had kept him from becoming a leading man now proved to be his best assets. He was, and would remain for two decades, Hollywood's favorite lead comedian.

"The trouble with Barbra," he contended, "is she became a star long before she became an actress. Which is a pity, because if she learned her trade properly she might become a competent actress instead of a freak attraction — like a boa constrictor. The thing about working with her was that you never knew what she was going to do next and were afraid she'd do it. I found it a most unpleasant picture to work on and, as most of my scenes were with her, extremely distasteful. I developed all kinds of symptoms. Pains in the lower abdomen, severe headaches, palpitations: I was in agony most of the time. . . . I was appalled at every move she made.

"Once I heard her tell Lennie Hayton, our musical director, that the flutes were coming in too soon, and that the first violins were too fast. Then she started telling Gene how she thought I should feed her lines. . . . He should, of course, have told her to mind her own business and do as she was told and not pay so much attention to other people as she had a lot to learn herself. And when she had twenty years more experience, then she should still shut up because she wasn't the director. The poor girl was corrupted by power in her second movie!"

Streisand and Matthau nearly came to blows the day after Senator Robert Kennedy was assassinated. The company was sweltering in 98-degree heat on location in Garrison, a small town near West Point in upstate New York, fighting mosquitoes, and suffering beneath the weight of heavy costumes. Emotions ran high. Another assassination, another Kennedy dead. Streisand was distressed, as everyone was. Kelly considered ending the day early but continued on account of the cost in money and time. The costars were shooting an exterior for "Before the Parade Passes By" involving the entire cast, chorus, dancers, and 2,500 extras. Streisand was determined to "get it right." When she had recorded the song, her final note had been a C-sharp at the top of her range and she held it for ten bars and a beat, longer than she had ever done previously. There was no way she was going to let the scene be less than the song. Streisand wanted to do the scene over. Reshooting such a complicated musical number with all those people was an enormous task, and everyone was tense. Kelly, after a sharp exchange with Streisand, made the decision to reshoot.

She upstaged her own rousing rendition of "Hello, Dolly!" with "Before the Parade Passes By," which starts quietly with Dolly seated alone on a park bench reminiscing about her late husband, Ephraim, and proceeds into an extravagant street parade with several full marching bands, floats, and cavalry troops carrying large flags. In the midst of all this, Dolly struts and weaves through the lines of brightly costumed people and high-stepping horses as she sings, her final note said to be the longest note held by a singer in any movie musical (including Judy Garland's legendary rendition of "Johnny One Note" in *Words and Music*).

"As if contending with [all these problems] were not enough," Matthau said, "Barbra kept asking Gene whether he didn't think it would be better if I did this on this line, and that on the other, etc., etc. — and I told her to stop directing the fucking picture, which she took exception to, and there was a blow-up in which I also told her she was a pip-squeak who didn't have the talent of a butterfly's fart. To which she replied that I was jealous because I wasn't as good as she was. . . . We began a slanging match like a couple of kids from the ghetto. I think Gene thought one of us was going to die of apoplexy or something [in fact, Matthau had

265

recently recovered from a serious heart attack and Kelly was right to be concerned], or that I'd belt her, or that maybe she'd scratch my eyes out — or worse, that we'd just walk off leaving twenty million dollars' worth of movie to go down the toilet."

Things did not get better. "It was not, in retrospect," Lehman recalled, "a happy film. There were things going on that were terrible. The intrigues, the bitterness, the backbiting, the deceits, the misery, the gloom. Most unpleasant. It's quite amazing what people go through to make something entertaining for others."

Matthau's outburst had hurt Streisand more than she wanted anyone in the film to suspect. He had since shouted at her that "everyone in the cast hates you!" She was fearful that it was the truth. No one appeared friendly. Michael Crawford, who would gain fame years later — first as Barnum in the original British production of the same name, then in the title role (in both Britain and the United States) of Andrew Lloyd Webber's musical *Phantom of the Opera* — and who played Cornelius Hackl, the juvenile lead, hardly spoke to her off camera. The same was true of the other young players, who were in some cases actually older than Streisand. Lehman walked around with a dour face. Kelly was cool in his attitude, although he appeared to try harder to appease her than the others did and listened to what she had to say, even if in the end he ignored her advice. This was not the experience she had on *Funny Girl* with Wyler. Suddenly, she had been thrown into a hostile world where she felt like the outsider.

Never able to get Dolly Levi's character in one piece, she nonetheless brought a tremendous vitality to the role and fresh insight into Herman's score (which was not as tailored for her voice as the songs from *Funny Girl*). Her key changes in the "Put on Your Sunday Clothes" number are remarkable, and she added a delightful comic note to "So Long, Dearie"— despite Kelly's arguments with her over a few lines in the bridge of the song where she imitates Mae West. "It's anachronistic!" he insisted rightly. "Mae West wasn't even born in 1890."

"I can't help it," she retorted, shifting into her Westian voice, "I saw *My Little Chickadee* [one of West's most famous movies] last night and it stuck."

Two multimillion-dollar musicals had been constructed around her. Yet, since neither had been released, she did not know if they would succeed and if she would become a bona fide movie star. Her marriage was in eggshell-thin condition, and her mother was pressing her from New York to do something to help her half sister Rosalind, recently graduated from high school. The young woman had changed her first name from Rosalind to Roslyn and decided she, *too,* wanted to become a singer. Diana would fault her again, and Roslyn would hate her for telling the truth — that first she had to prove to herself that she had the talent before anyone, even a famous sister, could help her.

Despite her fame, Streisand was insecure and frightened, and there was no way she could let anyone but her therapist know it. She took Jason and the nanny to the studio with her as often as she could once the *Hello, Dolly!* unit had returned from location. And when she wasn't needed on the set, she would lock the door of her enormous dressing-room trailer and would read to Jason and hold him in her arms. At such moments, her loneliness seemed less acute. Once she was back on the set, she was as feisty as ever, the restless champ fighting all comers and bravely defending her title. "I'm the star of this damned picture," she shouted at Matthau during one of their skirmishes.

"Betty Hutton once said the same thing," he shot back, "and she's just filed for bankruptcy."

18

Klieg lights scraped the sky, eerily turning night into day as an unwelcome October chill nipped the air. Streisand, arriving late as usual, stepped out of a limousine and onto a red carpet that extended from the curb to the entrance of the Egyptian Theatre, to the West Coast premiere of *Funny Girl*. She looked startled as she walked the narrow gauntlet between the cordons of curious, shrieking fans — many of whom had gathered early that morning with their camp stools and lunch bags to assure themselves a position where they could see the stars up close. Elliott held her arm protectively, the two of them flanked by some twenty bodyguards while press cameramen jumped into their path several times to get their picture. Streisand appeared unnerved and Elliott increasingly agitated as they fended off these interruptions with their accompanying flashes of blinding light.

Wearing eye-catching, shocking-pink evening pants, a floor-length lamb's wool embroidered evening coat lined in pink, and a matching pillbox hat, all rather Russian Cossack in appearance, Streisand covered her face protectively, a gesture immediately hostile to Ray Stark's planned media blitz. The photographers complained loudly as she and Elliott pressed forward, the security men having to quicken their step to keep up with the two of them as they crossed the cement forecourt.

On entering the grand foyer, she was greeted by Fran and Ray Stark, who were hosting a benefit postfilm supper party for over a thousand guests under a giant tent in the parking lot adjacent to the theater. Everyone connected with the film (even Streisand herself) already knew that Barbra Streisand was to be a megastar, for the movie had premiered in New York at the Criterion Theatre on September 19, some two weeks earlier, and her personal reviews had been spectacular. Streisand first saw the final cut of *Funny Girl* in a private screening room, then at the New York premiere. Tonight would be her third viewing of the finished product. Always the perfectionist, she still wished she could reshoot some sequences. Despite her optimism for the film's and her own success, she could not calm her nerves. New York had somehow lost its excitement for her, replaced by Hollywood — and it was here that she felt she must be recognized.

She gave new meaning to the words "chronic worrier." When asked by a business manager if she would like to hear the good or bad news first, she said, "Tell me the bad news first. Then when I hear the good news, I'll know what else I should worry about." She had a team of well-paid business advisors. Marty Erlichman diligently worked on behalf of her career. All signs pointed to success, but everything still came back to her ability to become more than just a one-movie, one-role star. She was well aware of the vagaries of the picture business and the men who ran it, whose motto was "You're only as good as the box office returns from your last movie." *Funny Girl* looked as if it would be a hit. She was not that sure about *Hello, Dolly!*

With Ray Stark leading, Streisand and Elliott made their way into the auditorium. Above their heads was the cathedral-like dome ceiling from which hung an enormous chandelier of Egyptian design, all wrought in colors of gold with golden iridescent rays emanating from an ingenious system of concealed lights, giving the effect of a colossal sunburst. She shielded her eyes as she glanced up at it and then, laughing, whispered something to Elliott, who smiled broadly. Possibly she was making a comparison to the chandeliers in their New York apartment. They remained talking with the Starks until almost everyone else had taken a seat, and then were ushered down the aisle to a roped-in section toward the front of the theater. Once she was seated, the lights dimmed and then went out. There was silence. The film began. Barbra Streisand was alone in the dark with a giant image of herself, as she had once shared a similar darkness with her movie idols from the balcony of a Brooklyn theater.

The experience of seeing yourself on a screen in a darkened movie palace with fifteen hundred pairs of eyes watching with you is surreal. Many film actors find the event so painful, they refuse to subject themselves to it. Streisand's reaction was contrary. Guests seated in the row behind her say she leaned forward, watching intently, whispering comments to Elliott on the aisle to her left and to Stark on her right. And she had not removed her hat. The person seated directly behind her, too embarrassed to ask her to do so, angled himself to one side.

When the lights came on again, there was enthusiastic applause, as there always is at the end of a Hollywood premiere — good or bad. People rushed down the aisle shouting their congratulations. A small smile tugged at the corners of her mouth. Otherwise, her face was almost sphinxlike, her pleasure entombed behind steely glances as she slowly made her way toward an exit and, bodyguards and Elliott once again forming a phalanx, went out a side door across to the tented parking lot. Inside the circus-sized tent, the lower East Side New York in the early 1920s, where Fanny Brice had lived, had been re-created. The bar from the Brice family saloon, used in the movie, had been set up on one side. Each corner of the enormous tent had a New York Street sign — Henry Street, Washington Square, Second Avenue, Delancey Street — serving as a guidepost so people could locate their tables. These were centered with potted ferns, each supporting a dozen bagels on a stick, a jarring sight, misguidedly meant to establish a New York deli atmosphere.

As Streisand entered, the band played an obligatory chorus of "Funny Girl," the new song (with the same title, but not the same melody, as one cut from the stage production) added to the film score. Omar Sharif had flown back from location for the premiere and posed with Streisand for the press, Elliott glowering in the background. Sharif, holding hands with his newest lady friend, actress Anjanette Comer, had also attended with the Goulds the New York premiere at the Criterion Theatre and the postmovie fund-raiser held in a similar tent constructed on the parking lot site where the old Astor Hotel had stood. That sumptuous affair had been utter chaos as about thirteen hundred people, including scores of famous people from both the social and entertainment circles, had been invited — over a hundred more than could be seated. Irate guests, having paid a hundred dollars for the privilege of being there, shouted insults at the staff and demanded that other people who were not on the grand list be removed. Men came close to throwing punches. The Starks gave up their seats and wandered from table to crowded table. Some people shared chairs; others remained standing. Escorted by a wary Elliott, Streisand — elegantly garbed in a flesh-colored gown set with sprays of rhinestones, her hair hidden beneath a striking wig that added several inches to her height — was seated with Marty Erlichman and Diana at the table marked #1, but she appeared ill at ease.

There was no such mayhem at the Hollywood postmovie festivities. As the New York critics had already endorsed her performance as a knockout, there was little suspense. For Streisand, the one thing she enjoyed more than being at a party with the movie legends she had so long ago adored was being the toast of it.

"I always wanted to meet Marlon Brando," she recalled. "I wanted to say to him, 'Let us speak to one another, because I understand you. You are just like me.' So . . . somebody comes up behind me and starts caressing my shoulder and nuzzling my neck. And I turn around and there he is! It's Brando! And he says — you know kidding — 'I'm letting you off easy,' and I laughed and said, 'Whaddaya mean easy? This is the best part!' I don't know — what the hell was there to say? It was kind of sad, because he *wasn't* just like me at all. He was a real movie star, a legend and somehow I didn't want him to be real."

When the evening was over, there was no doubt that her performance had scored bicoastally, but she still did not feel like she belonged in that Valhalla of movie idols.

"Bravo!" Pauline Kael, the *New Yorker* critic, wrote. "Streisand has the gift of making old written dialogue sound like inspired improvisation;

almost every line she says seems to have just sprung to mind and out. Her inflections are witty and surprising, and, more surprisingly, delicate; she can probably do more for a line than any screen comedienne since Jean Arthur, in the thirties. . . . It is Streisand's peculiar triumph that in the second half, when the routine heartbreak comes, as it apparently must in all musical biographies, she shows an aptitude for suffering that those clever actresses didn't. Where they became sanctimonious and noble, thereby violating everything we had loved them for, she simply drips as unself-consciously and impersonally as a true tragic muse."

Streisand had evolved into a thoroughly original self-invention, resembling no one else. She was a heroine with "a particular desperation all her own." Much as she decried her Brooklyn roots, she had made them her special territory. To the public she had become "a regular person with a genuine past from a real place. She had this Jewish problem, and this homely problem . . . she was pure oddball," Joe Morgenstern reported in *Newsweek*.

The energy she displayed in her performance was limitless. Yes, some coworkers, like the disgruntled Anne Francis, faulted her for being ruthless, but she had also been courageous and taken artistic gambles without hedging her bets. Although the score of *Funny Girl* had been pre-recorded,* she decided to take the risk of having "My Man" recorded live, which gave the number tremendous presence. After dreadful arguments with Irene Sharaff over a striking wine velvet dress she had designed for the scene, Streisand wore a black gown and stood against a

---

*The original soundtrack recording of *Funny Girl* was released a month in advance of the film but was preempted by Diana Ross's *Funny Girl* album, *Diana Ross and the Supremes Sing and Perform Funny Girl.* To Streisand and Stark's amazement, Jule Styne had assisted Ross with the recording and had written the liner notes, and Peter Matz had helped with the arrangements. "I just don't like the idea of her singing my songs and with my musical arranger," Streisand is reported as saying. "Who the hell does she think she is? The world doesn't need another Streisand!" Ross had an obsessive sense of competition with Streisand, believing that if she had been white, like Streisand, "it would have been a hundred times easier for her." Ross's album was one of her few commercial failures. Streisand's original soundtrack recording, on the other hand, did extremely well, although not as well as the original Broadway cast recording.

Making It

black background so that only her face and two hands were visible as she sang in a soft, poignant voice. At the end of the first chorus, she steps into an arc of light as her voice gains strength and soars defiantly. She has lost Nicky Arnstein but she has sung herself back into being. To hear her sing this song is to believe that she is the character she is playing; and it is that amazing ability that makes *Funny Girl,* with its feeble story, implausibly credible.

"The audience," she ventured, "cannot be lied to. I mean . . . the slightest tinge of falseness, they go back from you, they retreat. The truth brings them closer. They don't know why, they can't intellectualize it, but they know the moment is right or wrong. . . . I guess my best attribute is my instinct. Elliott's grandmother, who is about eighty-five, said she liked me because I was so natural — so *natchel.*" She thought about it for a moment. "Acting is like music," she continued. "I believe in rhythm, you know? Everything is so dominated by our heartbeats, by our pulses, when one goes against certain rhythms it's jarring. . . . I mean I *hear* it! I read a script and I just *hear* and I *see* what the people are doing, and I'll have an idea right off the bat, and it's always my first instinct that I trust."

Perhaps that was true, but *Funny Girl* had occupied four years of her life. She had been able to fashion the character into a clone of herself, very much the same young woman millions of viewers had come to know through her television specials and guest appearances. And she had already familiarized her audience with the album of the show and numerous other recordings where she had included "My Man" along with some of *Funny Girl*'s score. Few in the audience came into the movie theater cold, having to be won over by an actress playing an unknown role. She had the advantage that seasoned and well-loved film stars hold over audiences — that of simply being *who* they are, the character and the performer fusing into one person in their mind. Cary Grant is one such example, but it had taken him years to ingrain his personality so deeply upon movie audiences. The same can be said about Cagney, Bogart, Lemmon, and Matthau, among a score of others. Streisand's experience was unique in that *Funny Girl* was her first picture.

273

The studio's estimates were that *Funny Girl* would gross $65 million in the United States alone.* If it did, Ray Stark would make a huge fortune. "Barbra also stands to make a million dollars from her salary and subsidiary rights [the record and future television and video rights] and she's worth one-half of every cent of it!" he quipped to *Variety,* adding, "I'm only kidding." Streisand did not find Stark's comment amusing. She believed, rightly, that she was as responsible for the success of the film version of *Funny Girl* as she was for the stage production. And although a million dollars was not to be minimized, it nowhere compared with the twenty million dollars or more that Ray Stark eventually stood to make.

Yet had it not been for Stark and *Funny Girl,* Streisand's climb to fame might well have taken considerably longer. When Stark first signed her for the stage version, he gambled on a young woman with obvious talent but who had not yet proved that she could carry a show. It was during the pre-Broadway period of *Funny Girl* that she metamorphosed into an actress of substantial ability. A prototype of the new style of movie producer, Stark was a man who put together star, story, and director as an independent package to make a picture. A friend remembers him as "a little guy who would run up and down Sunset Boulevard, waving a contract and shouting, 'I got a deal! I got a deal!'" Before he returned to California for the West Coast premiere of *Funny Girl,* he told Vincent Canby of the *New York Times:* "I'm making this deal [for another movie] and we have this far-out script. . . . I mean, I read it and frankly I didn't understand it, but it could be fantastic!" He did not reveal the name of the property, but his next picture would be *The Owl and the Pussycat.*

Streisand could be angry at Stark on one level, but the sheer chutzpah of the man appealed to her. He was, she claimed, "the great Oz of Hollywood," and she forgave him many things because this quality so fasci-

---

*In its first domestic release *Funny Girl* grossed $25 million. It eventually did reach the revenues projected by Columbia Studios and Ray Stark in foreign and further releases, television, and video sales. At the figures quoted in the text, Stark received over $10 million by the end of the first year of its release. Barbra Streisand received her $200,000 contracted fee, her royalties from the original soundtrack recording, and the later income generated by her royalties on the film's television and video release.

nated her. Having settled his lawsuit against her (thereby enabling her to make movies independently of his company), they had reached a détente, and she would soon start production without him on her third film (this time for Paramount Pictures), *On a Clear Day You Can See Forever.*

A good portion of the picture was to be shot in England. This meant being separated for eight weeks from Jason, but she could not see taking him with her: they would have so little time together. She had recently bought and moved into a house on Carolwood Drive in Holmby Hills. Jason had settled in and was attached to his nanny. It seemed wrong to uproot him. She called Elliott, and he promised to fly out to California and spend as much time as possible with his son.

The bicoastal lifestyle they had carved out for themselves had failed. Neither seemed able to handle the tremendous pressures on their marriage. They were living separate lives, gathering private memories. Elliott was treading water as he waited for *Bob & Carol & Ted & Alice* to be released. He was finely tuned, frazzled, expectant, fearful, doubtful, on edge, living in an extravagant style paid for by his wife, and gambling again with heavy losses (over $50,000 that year, he was later to admit). He saw other women and felt instantly guilty. Streisand managed to blind herself to her marital problems and to lose herself in her work, in the swift ascent of her career, in her business enterprises, and in Jason. Yet, she remained strongly bound to Elliott. In some way he represented her past, and she was not ready or able to let him go.

Paramount had paid $750,000 for the rights to *On a Clear Day You Can See Forever* and was now contracted to pay Streisand $1 million, astronomical figures for Hollywood in the 1960s. Despite her current popularity, the studio was fearful that they had acted hastily. With period costumes and foreign locations involved, the budget had soared to an unrealistic $20 million, and the story (about a naive young woman, Daisy Gamble, who under hypnosis relives an earlier existence as an English seductress, Melinda Tentrees) was anything but mainstream. The Broadway show placed the flashbacks in the eighteenth century; the film pushed them forward to the early nineteenth century in Regency England to avoid the use of powdered wigs and more cumbersome costumes. Alan Jay Lerner, the author and lyricist of the show, was currently obsessed with the idea of reincarnation. Lerner, who had recently ended his long association with composer Fritz Loewe,* worked this time with Burton Lane, composer of the very successful *Finian's Rainbow.*

"When Alan came to me with *On a Clear Day* I thought the premise simply wonderful," Lane said. "The story in the past was too heavy-handed and not joyful, but it did have such wit and imagination that I finally got excited about it. How that score ever turned out as good as it did is a mystery to me. [It was] the worst two years of my life. Alan was on drugs and I don't know how to deal with people who are on liquor or anything else."

The show, starring Barbara Harris in the dual role of Daisy and Melinda, lasted only 280 performances on Broadway, but Streisand greatly admired the score and viewed the double role as a rare opportunity to display her acting ability. In October 1968, just days after the East and West Coast premieres of *Funny Girl,* Streisand began rehearsals, working closely with Lerner on her role.

Lerner was a tortured man, Stef Sheahan, his secretary, told his biographer, Stephen Citron. "If he was really working hard on a lyric, he could lose about six pounds in a day. You could feel him burning it off in the room. He'd just be there with his white gloves on, which he always wore to keep himself from biting his nails." High-strung, heavily addicted to drugs that kept him in a state of agitation, his marriage to his fifth wife shaky, he was in a perpetual state of nerves. Nonetheless, Streisand was able to get the most from their collaboration. Her voice stirred Lerner; her phrasing of his lyrics gave him new ideas. He held her in a kind of awe, believed she was the greatest entertainer of the twentieth century. He tailored the film script to her special talents, her dialogue as Daisy containing more of the sound of her own manner of speaking — although he was careful to omit any Jewish overtones. He left Melinda as originally created, trusting his instinct that Streisand could, if well directed, project — as Garson Kanin had also believed — the necessary elegance the role demanded.

---

*Lerner and Loewe had written the scores for *Brigadoon, Paint Your Wagon, My Fair Lady, Gigi,* and *Camelot.*

Vincente Minnelli, former husband of Judy Garland, father of Liza, who had directed the film versions of Lerner and Loewe's *Brigadoon* and *Gigi,* was to direct. Arnold Scaasi was hired to do the modern costumes; Cecil Beaton, the period costumes. Scaasi flew out to Los Angeles from New York to consult with Streisand. "We spent a whole day going over the styles she would wear as Daisy," Scaasi remembered. "By eight o'clock I was ready to quit. I had been invited to dinner at the Minnellis', so I stood up and said, 'Barbra, I must leave, I have a previous engagement.' She lifted her eyes from the sketches and very quietly said, 'Arnold, why did you come to Los Angeles?'. . . I immediately realized what she meant and that she was right. I was there on business, not on a social call. I phoned Vincente Minnelli and excused myself from dinner." And he added thoughtfully, "She also has this uncanny eye for detail. Once, when I sent her an embossed invitation to the opening of my collection, she wrote me a note explaining that she would be out of town on that date, and she added a postscript to call my attention to a misprint in the invitation."

Ten days before production was to start, Streisand stopped off in New York on her way across the Atlantic for the London and Paris premieres of *Funny Girl.* To her shock, she learned that Elliott was living with Jenny Bogart, the waiflike eighteen-year-old daughter of director Paul Bogart. Despite her own transgressions with Chaplin and Sharif, knowledge of his affair deeply cut Streisand. She asked Elliott to break off the relationship, to come with her to Europe. Elliott could not see his way to do that. Jenny needed him, he told her, she was so young, so helpless; he thought he had something to give her, a feeling that someone cared. Angry, sad, and in pain, Streisand insisted they draw up a separation agreement and threatened to file for divorce. She left New York for *Funny Girl*'s London premiere deeply distressed. Omar Sharif stood by his leading lady's side, the ashes long cooled on their relationship, and Marty Erlichman was her escort at the gala postpremiere dinner party, also attended by Princess Margaret.

As she prepared to fly to Paris before returning to California to start shooting the studio scenes on *A Clear Day,* she learned she was one of the five nominees for best actress at the upcoming Academy Awards. She had also signed a $5 million contract with the new Las Vegas International Hotel, the highest sum ever paid for a nightclub engagement, and she had just met a fascinating man to whom she was instantly drawn and who appeared to be similarly attracted to her. Pierre Elliott Trudeau, prime minister of Canada, a brilliant, utterly charming, forty-eight-year-old bachelor who had won his election the previous year largely on the youth vote. They met at a small dinner party at the home of a mutual acquaintance the night before her departure. "Sparks flew," a guest recalled.

Sexually drawn to this intense, wiry man with summer-sky blue eyes, Streisand found out all she could about him. In Canada Trudeaumania was at its height. The polls showed that after only one year as prime minister, he had the highest percentage rate of endorsement of any prime minister in Canada's history. Trudeau by nature was a questioner and a listener, but she got him to talk about himself. His mother was Scottish by origin, his father French-Canadian. He was bilingual, educated at the University of Montreal, the London School of Economics, and Harvard. Contrary to this conservative beginning, in his youth he had crossed five continents and twenty countries with a knapsack on his back. His smile was boyish, his charm difficult to resist — and Streisand saw no reason to do so. Since the impressionable time she had met John Kennedy, power and politics had intrigued her. She promised that somehow she would manage to see him again — very soon.

Her life was programmed from the moment she returned to Hollywood, as she plunged into work on *A Clear Day,* which costarred Yves Montand, cast as the professor/hypnotist who, while attempting to cure Daisy's smoking habit, sends her back — in her mind — to her previous life as the temptress Melinda Tentrees. He then falls in love with Melinda during Daisy's hypnotic sessions. Also appearing were Larry Blyden as Daisy's stuffy fiancé and Jack Nicholson in a small but amusing role of her half brother. She got along well with Nicholson, but her working relationship with Montand was strained, although certainly not as difficult as it had been when she played opposite Walter Matthau. This time she had a leading man who was well known as a singer (in his native country, France, at least), the first time this had occurred. A ruggedly attractive man in his late forties, Montand was urbane and a lively individual-ist. Married to the French actress Simone Signoret, he had weathered stormy affairs with Edith Piaf (who had guided him to stardom as one of France's leading chansonniers) and Marilyn Monroe, his costar in *Let's Make Love* (1960). Although he was known primarily as a singing star, his role in Clouzot's classic thriller *The Wages of Fear* (1953) had catapulted him to international fame as a dramatic actor. As a result, he sustained two careers, really — dramatic roles in Europe and more romantic parts in Hollywood, where he could exude his Gallic charm. Seductive though he was, Streisand was not attracted to him.

Wary of Europeans after her affair with Omar Sharif, she concentrated on the film. Vincente Minnelli allowed her great independence; as with *Funny Girl* and *Hello, Dolly!,* she involved herself in everything to do with her character, from costumes, lighting, hair, and makeup to interpreta-tion. Caught up in the art of filmmaking, she was preparing herself for the future — although she was not yet fully aware of it. After *Dolly* and her problems with Matthau, she worked hard to protect her performance, making sure that she was the prime character in the film, that she had the majority of the songs and the full attention of the camera.

"When we commenced *On a Clear Day,*" Montand said later, "I had the mistaken impression that I was the co-star. I was Miss Streisand's first leading man who can sing, even though this was her third musical. I thought she was my leading lady, a partner. I doubt I shall ever choose to work again in Hollywood." He never did.

She flew to New York for location work as the Daisy character and then, a week later, to England for Melinda's Dickensian poorhouse se-quence and the elaborate scenes in the Royal Pavilion in Brighton, the latter to be shot first. Cecil Beaton's costumes for her were spectacular. Beaton was an accomplished author, photographer, and theatrical set and costume designer, known equally well for his portraiture of Britain's royal family, his obsessive pursuit of Greta Garbo, and his wit. He had won two Academy Awards (for his sets and costume designs) for *My Fair Lady,* for which he had also created the original stage decor. Beaton claimed that the memorable white satin Regency gown (which revealed a voluptuous bosom with imposing cleavage) that Streisand wore in the banquet scene of *On a Clear Day* was a shared creation. "It was inspired — and both our ideas, really — to wrap the Streisand features in a glorious white turban, to further accent her strong profile. At the same time, she was totally feminine, beguiling, shamelessly sexual. I tried to stress . . . the physical if not spiritual splendor of the period. On a less gifted actress and model, on almost any American actress I can think of, this would have been wasted and somewhat ludicrous. Barbra has a less monotonously American-type [look] than most actresses of her nationality."

The banquet scene at the Royal Pavilion was the most ornate in the film. Minnelli, who had started his career as a set designer, insisted that every detail be true to the lavish display of the period. Over one hundred extras magnificently costumed in regal Regency clothes sat at an enormous banquet table before mounds of food — all real and prepared by leading English chefs. Streisand sat across the table from languid-eyed John Richardson, playing Robert Tentrees, Melinda's future husband. Close shots would be filmed later of their sexual wooing as they ate and drank in a powerfully seductive manner. For now, they were simply guests at the royal banquet. "Eat up!" Minnelli shouted, as the cameras began turning. "Devour everything in sight! Shove it all in. You're gourmets." Streisand did as requested.

That night she had a date with George Lazenby, an Australian actor who had just made his film debut as James Bond in *On Her Majesty's Secret Service*. They had dinner at a kosher restaurant. Unable to resist some of her Jewish favorites — knishes, dill pickles, latkes — Streisand gorged herself and fell ill by the end of the evening. Early the following morning (Easter Sunday and double time for the crew, but Minnelli wanted to limit his days of foreign production) she had to report to the studio to shoot the scene as Melinda in the royal kitchens. The set was decorated with great sides of beef, game and geese, baskets of fish, trays of game and sweet pies, rounds of pungent Stilton cheese, and a suckling pig on the fire. "Not the most congenial atmosphere for someone with a weak stomach," Cecil Beaton commented. "The smell of food, now becoming a little high, had to be sweetened by atomizer sprays." Streisand, though obviously ill, persisted. Beaton marveled at her stamina after what must have been "a night of much vomiting."

15

15. Her affair with Omar Sharif (note
misspelling of his name on chair) during
the filming of *Funny Girl* sent her marriage into a tailspin.
AP/Wide World

16

17

18

16. "Hullo, gorgeous," she shouted when she received the Oscar for her performance in *Funny Girl*. Her shocking see-through trouser suit stunned the audience.
UPI/Bettmann

17. She flew to Europe, where Elliott was making a film, in a failed attempt to save her marriage.
AP/Wide World

18. With her son, Jason Gould, the baby she had never wanted to be a child of divorce.
Press Association Photos

19

20

21

19. "Political Streisand." Here with presidential candidate Eugene McCarthy. She appeared in a fund-raising concert to help his campaign. McCarthy lost.
AP/Wide World

20. However, New York congressional candidate Bella Abzug won her race. Streisand opened her townhouse for a fund-raiser and was overwhelmed by the crowds who attended.
UPI/Bettmann

21. At the London film premiere of *Funny Girl*, with costar and former lover Omar Sharif, she is congratulated by Princess Margaret. As an American, Streisand did not think she should curtsy. "Well, she is not my royal highness," she told a colleague.
AP/Wide World

22. With Prince Charles in Hollywood. He came to hear her record for her film *Funny Lady*. "I could have been the first Jewish princess," she later joked. *AP/Wide World*

23. At the royal command performance of *Funny Lady* with costar James Caan. Her new love, Jon Peters, can be seen directly behind Streisand. Veteran actor James Stewart views the scene with a small smile. *Syndication International*

24. In a wistful mood, celebrating her thirty-fifth birthday with Peters. Tulips and gardenias are her favorite flowers. *AP/Wide World*

25. On her way to Europe to film *Yentl* after her traumatic breakup with Peters. *Syndication International*

22

23

25

24

26. There were and would be other men in her life. But perhaps none had as strong an influence as Peters. Here, with Canadian prime minister Pierre Trudeau, who she considered marrying if he had asked her—he did not.
UPI/Bettmann Newsphotos

27. Richard Baskin, lyricist and heir to an ice cream fortune.
Tammie Arroyo/Retna Ltd.

28. Macho television star Don Johnson.
AP/Wide World

29. Tennis great André Agassi (center, here seen with Michael Bolton).
AP/Wide World

26

27

28

29

30

30. With brother Sheldon Streisand and half-sister Roslyn, who had just opened at the Persian Room in New York in a solo singing act.
UPI/Bettmann

31. Peter Daniels was one of her earliest musical advisors and arrangers; Lainie Kazan, her ambitious understudy in *Funny Girl*. Their affair and subsequent marriage caused an irreparable rift.
Lainie Kazan

31

32. She appeared opposite Robert Redford in one of her most successful movies, *The Way We Were*.
AP/Wide World

33. Jon Peters coproduced *A Star Is Born* with her. It put him in the league of powerful Hollywood operators.
UPI/Bettmann

32

33

34

35

34. She had worked on *Yentl* for nearly sixteen years and fought her greatest movie battle to get it made. Here, with Robert Evans, on a studio lot in England.
Time-Life

35. Her most provocative role has been as the call girl who proves her mental competence to stand trial for murder in *Nuts.*
Warner Brothers

36. She produced, directed, and starred in *The Prince of Tides,* with Nick Nolte and Jason Gould portraying her real-life son.
Academy of Motion Picture Arts and Sciences

36

37

38

39

40

37. Posing her mother, Diana, for the camera at the premiere of *The Prince of Tides*. Jason peers over the head of his grandmother, and half-sister Roslyn, a new glamorous blonde, smiles brightly.
Peter C. Borsari

38. With Jason at the 1992 Academy Awards. She was bitter at the industry's lack of recognition of her directorial work on *The Prince of Tides*.
Albert Ortega/Roy Gallela Ltd.

39. Cis Corman (center), her oldest friend, has become her much relied upon business partner. Here they attend the Golden Globe Awards together, escorted by Richard Baskin.
Retna Ltd.

40. On the set of *The Prince of Tides*, Cis was always nearby to offer help and advice.

"Barbra is one of two kinds of superstars: the coolly detached and the fanatically involved," he professed. "Barbra is the latter. Barbra and I talked our way into everything, and I trusted her judgment, something I seldom do with any actor, especially a relative neophyte. I had never met anyone so young who had such an awareness and knowledge of herself. Both Audrey Hepburn's wardrobe for *My Fair Lady* and Barbra's for *A Clear Day* contained before-and-after outfits. Both women are very different, yet they're both regal, and that came through in the clothes I designed for them. Melinda [in early scenes] came from lower-class origins and was dressed in a rather grubby, unflattering manner, much as Eliza Doolittle during her Covent Garden days. Both women were marvelous at conveying this earthiness, and seemed to relish the chance to wear rags and carry on like craven guttersnipes. But as grand ladies, dressed to the hilt, they were truly in their element, aware that everything had been building up to that moment — neither had a lack of confidence in their ability to act regal and look monumental, despite their widely varying types and images."

Beaton claimed, as did Minnelli, that there were no great contests of will between them during production, although he was somewhat perturbed that Streisand would only approve his still photographs "when lines, marks and a spot on the chin had been brushed out." When she returned to the States, he wrote in his diary: "I like B.S. very much: she is a good, fine girl and if we do not speak the same language we are at any rate in sympathy with one another. She is very clever — and meticulous."

Her romance with Lazenby was short-lived. She left London without ties, but not without romantic thoughts. The good-looking prime minister of Canada had unsettled her. Not only had she found him sexually exciting and intellectually challenging, she was confident that he felt the same way about her.

19

Three dates with Warren Beatty — a "fling," she called it — proved disappointing. She demanded more than good sex from a man. She expected commitment. She romanticized about Trudeau — the intellectual father figure — respecting the power he wielded, the world stage he occupied. Their affair was moving slowly. They spoke on the telephone. She read up on Canadian history and current political leaders. They met briefly in New York: he was there on official business, and she once more was looking for a new Manhattan residence.

The world did not yet know that Barbra and Elliott were going their separate ways, and for the moment they both preferred to keep the press guessing. He came out to California to discuss the divorce and, to keep up appearances, escorted her to the forty-first Oscar presentations on April 14, 1969, held in the Dorothy Chandler Pavilion in the new Los Angeles Music Center. The long drive down to the auditorium in a chauffeured limousine was rife with tension. They both made a concerted effort to avoid personal issues. Seeing him again, watching his tenderness with Jason, had touched her. Elliott was a good father and Jason adored him, and she could not dismiss her own confused feelings about him, which made her question her decision to obtain a divorce.

She had been nominated for the best actress award alongside four exceptional performers: Katharine Hepburn, for *The Lion in Winter;* Patricia Neal, for *The Subject Was Roses;* Vanessa Redgrave, for *Isadora;* and Joanne Woodward, for *Rachel, Rachel.* Her competition was formidable; all four women were known for their roles in dramatic films. *Funny Girl* was a musical, and she had played Fanny Brice in such a spontaneously natural manner that the critics had not viewed her performance as "acting." For many, it was hard to distinguish between the actress who played the role and the woman in real life.

The Academy Awards ceremony was to start at exactly 6 P.M., and all the participants had been notified that the doors to the pavilion would be locked at that hour since the show was being televised. At 5:45 Streisand and Elliott were tied up in gridlocked traffic. She became agitated, her voice — as she railed against the traffic jam — high-pitched, strained. Elliott attempted to calm her. The driver assured them both that they would make it in time. Other guests were jumping out of nearby limousines stalled in the pileup of cars and were making swift tracks toward the front doors of the pavilion.

Streisand refused to make a running entrance and eventually, with about two minutes to spare, walked gracefully toward the auditorium, Elliott close by her side, and smiled at several of the press photographers.

Beneath a tent-shaped, black taffeta evening coat, she wore a revealing see-through, black chiffon pajama outfit with starched white Puritan cuffs and collar that had traces of black jet. Designed by Scaasi for Daisy in *A Clear Day,* the outfit had been rejected as too revealing for the character to wear. Shocked faces turned to stare at her as she entered the packed wood-paneled auditorium with its gleaming crystal chandeliers. One row of the audience applauded as she walked past them down the aisle. For all the costume's seductive design and revealing sheerness, it did not lack style, and she looked especially lovely: her skin glowing; her hair coiffed beautifully in a loose, casual manner with blond streaks highlighting it; eyes bright; smile radiant, bravely masking her inner anxiety.

The Oscars are an especially long ceremony, and the awards for best actress, actor, and film are at the end of an often tedious evening. Streisand sat stiffly as all the nominated members of the *Funny Girl* company were passed over; *Oliver!* won the larger share of the evening's Oscars:

best picture, best musical score, best art direction, and best direction. Ruth Gordon won best supporting actress for *Rosemary's Baby* over Kay Medford's performance as Mama Brice.

Ingrid Bergman, looking luminously beautiful, opened the envelope containing the winner for best actress of 1968. For a moment a look of astonishment came over her lovely face. In a stunned voice, she cried out, "It's a tie!" and then read off the names: "Katharine Hepburn for *The Lion in Winter,*" and then waiting until the applause abated before adding in a strong and pleased voice, "and Barbra Streisand for *Funny Girl!*"

Streisand rose briskly from her seat, ran up the aisle and the steps to the wide stage — gargantuan golden Oscars standing sentinel at the rear — and stood beaming beside Bergman. Hepburn was in New York, and her director, Anthony Harvey, accepted the award in her name and then stepped away from the podium. "Congratulations!" Bergman said to Streisand, who grasped the gold Oscar in her hands and in strident Brooklynese exclaimed, "Hullo, gorgeous!" There was a wave of laughter, then wild applause. When the audience quieted, she graciously declared, "I am honored to be in such magnificent company as Katharine Hepburn."*

The next day Streisand called Diana. "Well, Ma, what do you think about the award?" she asked.

"What kind of a dress was that to wear in public?" was her mother's reply.

Despite Streisand's intense therapy, she remained unable to deal rationally with her mother's negativism. The rejected child she harbored inside her refused to let go. As with so many areas in her life — her career, her male-female relationships — Streisand wanted things on her terms, which were often founded on unrealistic demands. In her late fifties by then, Diana was not going to change. Plumpish, resigned to life without a partner, she remained much the same as she had always been, harboring old-world Jewish fears and superstitions that to speak well of things,

---

*Hepburn and Streisand were the first cowinners of an Academy Award since 1932, when Fredric March (*Dr. Jekyll and Mr. Hyde*) shared the best actor honor with Wallace Beery (*The Champ*).

to be too optimistic, was to court disaster. She was no less pessimistic with Shelley, but he was better able to cope with his mother. Content in his career, very much the family man, he did not have the need to seek Diana's approval. Nor did his sister's success and fame threaten or overwhelm him. He and Barbra remained close in spirit. Streisand knew Shelley would be there for her if she needed him, and the reverse was true. But their lifestyles, friends, and interests were far apart. She would see him and his family when she was in New York — a family visit, welcomed but disconnected from her everyday life. With Diana, it was quite a different matter. Open wounds still festered.

At the time, Diana was caught up in Roslyn's career, which was not moving along at any great speed. She was defensive when the press claimed the half sisters did not get along. "Barbra loves Rozie very much," she told a reporter. "But Roz was a little shy and didn't know how to approach a big sister who had gotten so famous. When Barbra was in *Funny Girl* on Broadway, Roz went to forty matinees and stood through them all. At home she would play the *Funny Girl* album day and night, lip-syncing and imitating Barbra. She was really her best imitator." Which was Roslyn's immense failing, for she was not as gifted.

Asked for her advice on child-rearing, Diana replied candidly, "Never give your kids too much praise. In fact, I try to tone them down if I see they have an exaggerated opinion of themselves. I just kind of make a remark that calms them down."

Roslyn entered the room at this point. "She says something like, 'Don't forget you got it from me; you didn't fall out of a tree.'"

"Yeah. My voice comes from my mother," Streisand says. "How else can I explain it?" Yet, even this acknowledgment of Diana's talent was spoken with an air of disaffection.

Neither woman understood the other. Diana's life had been one of compromise, which she both accepted and resented. Pragmatic and lacking drive or the desperation to learn, absorb, improve, Diana's character was at complete odds with that of her famous daughter and of the image Streisand nurtured of her father, the intellectual scholar, the man who refused to compromise his ambitions, who was so supportive of the young people he taught.

Her father, she was told, had spoken several languages — English, German, Yiddish. She was now studying French and Italian and had started private instruction in music theory. "That was fascinating: to create sound and tone from a mathematical concept, to be able to say that something I hear in my head is an F-sharp minor chord with a flatted fifth," she mused. "I studied piano till my teacher said I had to cut my nails. I said, 'I'm not going to be a concert pianist — so what if I do make some clicking noises on the keys?'" Yet, she realized that a flat-fingered position was no way to play the piano, and the lessons soon ended.

Valiantly, she tried to keep up with the stacks of political journals to which she subscribed. "There is so much more to learn, so much more to do," she said excitedly. "I love the movies — life is so tentative and short that I want something to remain as proof that I existed. I think that's why I like antiques — because they have proven their immortality. They know something I don't." Antiques were survivors like herself.

The insistent buzzing in her ears that made her so sensitive to sound remained a constant source of distraction. Maybe sometimes, she said, it made her walk around "like a *farbissener*— which means kind of depressed [more literally, "soured"]. I get these letters from kids telling me that I am 'different' just like them. I write back. 'Do you have a buzzing in *your* ears?'"

Her success did not ease her acute insecurity. She suffered immense fear that she could — if not protective — lose her status. She wanted, and sought, greater control in the movies she would make in the future. There was a strong indication that the musical as a popular art form was in crisis. The common Hollywood practice of adapting a hit musical for the screen might soon be obsolete, and her hold could loosen if she did not make the transition — which she had always yearned for, anyway — into a straight dramatic actress. This was easier said than done since studio executives were doubtful that the moviegoing public would accept her in a new image. To her, this left only one alternative. She must form her own film production company, a costly and perilous adventure, for the possibility had to be considered that she might fall flat on her face.

At that time the greater part of her income came from records and concerts, not from movies. Her last five albums, the film soundtrack of

Funny Girl, A Happening in Central Park, A Christmas Album, Simply Streisand, and *Je m'appelle Barbra,* may not have reached the top of the charts, but her immense earnings on all her records, which included her previous album hits, were estimated as being over $3 million annually. Her albums, released twice a year, kept her constantly before the public, the records played consistently over radio. She more than realized how important it was for her to keep in step with the changes in the music world. The music she sang in movies, the Broadway sound, was fast losing its hold on young people, and she did not want to become set in the concrete past.

Just after the Academy Awards, she recorded a new album, her sixteenth, *What About Today?,* her first pop album. The songs on it — from Jim Webb's antiwar elegy "Little Tin Soldier" to other compositions by Paul Simon, Paul McCartney/John Lennon, and Buffy Saint-Marie — were mostly protest songs. She had accomplished an amazing feat: she made the crossover on record to a contemporary sound without losing the dramatic, distinctive quality for which she was famous. It would be this remarkable ability she had to move vocally with the times while still maintaining her skill with a show tune or classic that would sustain her recording career and win her throngs of new young fans with each release.

Flower children and student violence were the mark of the two last years of the 1960s. In the summer of 1968, American antiwar protesters had fought a pitched battle with 11,900 of the Chicago police force, 7,500 National Guardsmen, and 1,000 FBI and Secret Service men. There had been over two hundred university demonstrations since then. American participation in the Vietnam War was dividing a nation. Draft-card burning, flag burning, bra burning, and the women's movement all gripped the nation. Student radicals had been a powerful force in Eugene McCarthy's bid for the presidency, which Streisand supported. They won the media contest but could not get McCarthy the nomination, nor could they prevent the man Streisand hated most, Richard Nixon, from becoming president.

She was in a time warp, trying desperately to break loose. She celebrated her twenty-seventh birthday on April 24, 1969. For nearly a decade she had lived and worked in a world composed of much older people.

She had few young friends and now thought she was in love with a man, Pierre Trudeau, over twenty years her senior — an affair that must, because of the seriousness of his purpose and her marital status, be kept hidden from the public. It meant catching a day or a weekend together in a secret liaison. Trudeau was fascinated by her. Her fame was a potent attraction, but she also brought something fresh into his life. He confided to friends that he thought she was one of the most beautiful women he had ever known, that she possessed innate majesty. He was amazed at the sharpness of her mind. They were a curious match — a Jewess and a devout Catholic, a movie star and the Canadian prime minister. Yet, a strong sexual attraction was fueled by these very differences. Always a paradox, she fantasized about marrying the older and more conservative Trudeau at the same time as she explored youth-oriented music, smoked marijuana, and contracted to appear at the new International Hotel in Las Vegas, an establishment whose primary objective was to attract customers to the hotel's gambling tables. Returning to Las Vegas, where she had been so unhappy, had more to do with money than morals. Despite the high sums she earned, she always feared that one day she might not have enough.

The International Hotel was two and a half times the size of the splashy reigning favorite, Caesars Palace. Every feature of the hotel was elephantine; its height of thirty stories (the tallest building in the state of Nevada), its pool (second-largest body of water in the state, behind only Lake Mead), its casino (the largest in the world, with over a thousand slot machines), and its three enormous entertainment facilities — a lounge, a legitimate theater, and the showroom — each starring a well-known personality in productions to rival, in glitz at least, whatever Paris or New York could offer. Streisand's engagement began on July 2, and in the summer the desert heat could exceed 120 degrees. But there was no need for a hotel guest ever to leave the air-conditioned gilded palace where there were no clocks in the gambling rooms to remind players of the lateness of the hour.

However, the International was still under construction when Streisand arrived, and it appeared that the hotel would not be complete in time to open the showroom. While she was rehearsing, curtains were being draped, light fixtures installed, and plaster fell like snow over a stage large enough to accommodate both the Ziegfeld and Goldwyn Girls as well as the Radio City Music Hall Rockettes. In addition to her fee, her contract included twenty thousand shares of stock in the hotel, each worth fifty dollars by opening night. Expectations for her twice-nightly, four-week stint were high. She had just won the Academy Award, and *Funny Girl* was now breaking movie-house records across the country.

For her much-heralded Vegas opening she wore a gauzy, gold crea-tion of Scaasi's, her hair coiffed into a chic upsweep, and she sang into a handheld jeweled microphone. Backed by a sixteen-piece band con-ducted by Peter Matz, sometimes she stood center stage, sometimes near the piano or perched on a high, shocking-pink stool. Unlike other Vegas cabaret shows, there was no opening act, no beautiful, pony-legged showgirls in scanty, colorful costumes, no backup singers, no lavish sets — none of the things Las Vegas audiences expected. At the top of her form, her program was almost identical to her Central Park appear-ance the previous year, with two new numbers: "In the Wee Small Hours of the Morning" and "When You Gotta Go" in a "stunning exhibition of stylistic and vocal virtuosity." Yet, as word of the lack of produc-tion values in her act spread, reservations dwindled. Her instincts — that audiences would want to see and hear her, not showgirls in a flashy show — had betrayed her.

She became restive. Fear plagued her. She would forget her lyrics. When columnist Joyce Haber visited her dressing room during her en-gagement, she showed her a calendar with each day she had already ap-peared crossed out. "Only thirty-nine performances to go," she sighed. She hated the repetitive nature of the show, any show — having to do the same thing twice a night. Accustomed now to the business of making films, a staff to cater to her every need, the absence of a live audience who could boo as well as cheer her, and the ability to perfect her perfor-mance in a cutting room, she felt trapped. Onscreen she could sell her image; onstage she had to sell herself.

Elvis Presley was to follow her into the showroom. He slipped into the back of the balcony to watch her work during the first week of her engagement. "He pointed mutely to all the empty seats around him," one of his biographers, Albert Goldman, wrote. "Then, he settled down to listen to the program. He gave no signs of pleasure. . . . When it was all over, he turned to [an assistant] and said two words: 'She sucks!' Then, he went downstairs to the dressing room to tell Barbra how much he had enjoyed her performance. When he was admitted . . . he was astonished to find the great star alone. Elvis had never been alone for one moment in his entire life. Two or three men always accompanied him even to the bathroom. Streisand made no bones about her disgust with the audience and the hotel. 'This place isn't even built yet!' she fumed. 'I wouldn't be surprised if some night while I'm out there working some schmuck doesn't walk by with a ladder on his shoulder!'"

She vowed to him that she would never work Vegas again. (Later she admitted, "I really didn't enjoy performing live anymore.") The two shook hands, she wished him more luck than she had had, and they parted.*

In order to ease her nerves at other times in Las Vegas, she took several drags of marijuana just before she stepped out onstage and she stowed several joints in the pocket of the black jeweled jacket of one of her gowns. At one point she took out a joint to light it. "First, just faking it," she later told *Rolling Stone* magazine. "Then I started lighting live joints, passing them around to the band — you know. It was *great*. It relieved all my tensions. I ended up with the greatest supply of grass ever. Other acts started sending me the best dope in the world. I never ran out." However true or exaggerated that claim was, drugs were not a part of her life. She smoked a joint to relax, a habit she had shared with Elliott.

Many of the Vegas performers who were paid huge salaries lost most of it at the gambling tables. Gambling never intrigued her; it brought Elliott to her mind, and she desperately wanted not to think about him. Elliott had suddenly become a huge star in his own right. The bang-up

*Elsewhere it has been written that Elvis made a sexual overture to Streisand at the time and, picking up a bottle of nail varnish from her dressing-room table, knelt before her to paint her famous finger talons. Streisand has told friends, "When have you ever heard of a man painting a woman's fingernails as an ode to seduction? It would stick to *everything!*"

acting job he had done as the square, bumbling lawyer who succumbs to an affair in *Bob & Carol & Ted & Alice,* a satire of Southern California sex, sensitivity and spouse-swapping, was talked about as the best of the year, a shoo-in for an Oscar. He was natural, unmanicured, good-looking, but nothing like a movie star, all of which made him a new kind of sensation, "a hero for an uptight generation," *Time* wrote. By October 1969, he had made three more movies in which he played a lead: *M*A*S*H* (as Trapper John), *Getting Straight,* and *Move.* And he was contracted to star in three more films the following year — *I Love My . . . Wife, The Touch,* and *Little Murders.* He had been steamrolled into stardom. "I always knew there were things going on in me, that I had something to express," he told Judy Klemsrud of the *New York Times.* "However, I don't take success seriously. But I'm pleased for my friends. There are a lot of people I want to be able to help — actors, writers, and directors. And now I'm in a position to do so."

Streisand was happy for his success, to validate her early belief in Elliott and for what it would mean to Jason. It also set her to wondering if she had done the right thing in splitting up. Then reality would set in. Fame, she knew, did not change the basic person. She was still carrying around her bag of insecurities, and Elliott his. What had brought them together had also driven them apart. Streisand had believed that with success in her career and Elliott's love and support, she would overcome her insecurities. When that had not occurred, she turned away from him, searching elsewhere for an elusive panacea to happiness.

Elliott, on his part, wanted success and yet at the same time, was uncomfortable with both his own and Streisand's. Success meant responsibilities that he feared he could not carry out. He felt that he had failed in his marriage, that they both had let Jason down, and he was unsure of what he wanted from life. He was "something of a paradox," one interviewer wrote. "At times you detect flashes of shyness and vulnerability. But mostly, he comes across as just plain tense. . . . When he's not pacing the floor, he sits on a couch cracking his knuckles, gulping water and chain-smoking cigarettes." He was also using large amounts of uppers and downers, had lost through gambling almost all he had earned in the past year, and was seeing a psychiatrist five days a week. He was willing to admit in print that he still cared earnestly for Barbra. "We have a very deep personal relationship. I chose Barbra and Barbra chose me because we fell in love. . . . We have a great son. He's like a little tiger — beautiful. He looks like both of us. He is the best thing that either of us could ever hope to do. I want Jason to have the kind of mother Barbra wants to be, and she wants for him what I want for him.

"Maybe we'll get back together again, maybe we won't. I know that I'll never take her out in public again, like I did to the Academy Awards last spring [where he had felt ignored]. When I see her now, we go to little out-of-the-way places where no one sees us."

They were dating from time to time, private dinners to talk about Jason or discuss their current problems, things they found they could not talk about with others — their families, their fears, their self-doubts. However, one subject not discussed was her attraction for Trudeau.

She was living a dual life, dating Trudeau secretly and being seen at grand openings and galas amid a crush of the curious and admiring. *Hello, Dolly!* premiered at the Rivoli in New York on December 16 before a black-tie socialite audience. Marty Erlichman accompanied her, Streisand exotically dressed in a fox-fur-trimmed embroidered coat, high boots, and a pillbox hat, her hair drawn back smoothly from her face, "looking like an elegant Nefertiti." Two blocks from the theater they were trapped inside their black Rolls-Royce limousine by about fifty overenthusiastic fans who ran alongside the vehicle, slowed it to a crawl, and then started rocking it. Streisand, terrified, let out an ear-splitting scream. The zealots drew back, allowing the driver to reach the theater. Frightened to get out, fearing she might be attacked, Streisand remained inside the vehicle for several minutes. When she finally emerged, Erlichman, the driver, and several security and police officers (the premiere was ironically for the benefit of the Police Athletic League) formed a semicircle around her, but the fans broke through and she was swept up in a shoving, elbowing crowd that converged from all directions. She was in a panic when she reached the lobby. Erlichman had been hit in the head by a camera, punched, and knocked to the ground in the melee.

"Oh, my God, what's happening?" Streisand cried as he was helped inside, spurting blood. A doctor among the invited guests took Erlichman, Streisand refusing to leave his side, into a private office to clean the wound, which looked more serious than it was. The showing of the film was delayed for a half an hour until both of them finally took their seats, Streisand next to Louis Armstrong. After the showing, she was whisked away in a different car, parked at a side entrance. Fans caught sight of her and ran after the vehicle for a few feet and then fell back.

The after-theater supper dance was held at the Pierre Hotel, and Armstrong sang a lusty chorus of "Hello, Dolly!" with the band and then did some smart hoofing with a dance group to entertain the guests. Streisand looked pale through the entire evening and fretted over Erlichman's injuries, even though he was well enough to join her.

"I will never go to another premiere," she vowed afterward. "It's inhumane."

"She is one of the few mysteriously natural, unique performing talents of our time," Vincent Canby wrote in the *New York Times*. "She has become a national treasure. Casting her as Dolly Levi is rather like trying to display Yellowstone National Park in a one-geyser forest preserve."

But the film did not work, and no one knew that better than Streisand. All the problems she had first seen remained. She was too young for Dolly Levi, and both she and Matthau were too often off camera, at which time the movie featured young members of the cast in some truly silly plot devices. The sets were certainly spectacular. Lehman and Kelly had been reverential to history and architecture to the point of idiocy. By preserving a slim and often witless musical on a large movie screen, they had inflated its faults to giant proportions. She was criticized in most of the major reviews for her "Mae West" inclusions, although it did work well for her in what was probably her best number in the picture, "So Long, Dearie." But the movie looked good and so did she. Matthau was droll and crusty, as required, and there were moments of great joy — Louis Armstrong's appearance was one of them, as was her arrival scene at the Harmonia Gardens.

Despite protestations to the contrary, Streisand, swathed in white mink, did attend the glittering Hollywood premiere of the film and the postmovie supper dance in the huge adjoining tent. Matthau gave her a wild greeting when he caught sight of her, grabbing her up in his arms and kissing her — much to her surprise and others' who knew how volatile their relationship had been on the set of the film. Later, asked by a reporter how it was to work with her, he replied diplomatically, "Barbra had moments of likability."* She came down the aisle of the theater with Erlichman flanked on all sides by security guards, who took their post outside the ladies' room during intermission, allowing no one in until she reappeared.

Her romance with Pierre Trudeau was still very much alive. He had flown to New York shortly after the premiere there, and they had ventured out to a restaurant, where he was photographed smiling intimately at her across the table. She appeared shy in his company, quieter — but glowing. Once she returned to California, they spoke frequently by telephone. On his invitation, on January 25 she flew to Ottawa, where over the next three days they spent as much time together as he could spare. It was the first time that she played a supporting role in a relationship.

She sat in the visitors' gallery of the imposing Canadian House of Commons and listened intently as he brilliantly parried questions from his colleagues while stealing glances up at her. At one point he appeared not to have heard a question. "If the prime minister can take his eyes and his mind off the visitors' gallery . . . ," the MP who had the floor remonstrated. Trudeau smiled sheepishly as the house members laughed. After the session he was detained but then ran to her car as she was leaving, helped her inside, and held her hand for a long moment before pulling away and returning to his job.

She believed she was in love. At least, she confided to others that this was the case. There was a strong physical attraction, a great excitement when they were together. She was proud that so prominent and intelligent a man found her attractive, and she was in awe of his mind, his grasp of world situations. Still, she was unsure how they would ever make it as a couple. There were so many things she still had to prove to herself. She now wanted to produce her own movies and to establish her place as a dramatic actress, and Hollywood was the best place for those ambitions.

---

*Asked the same question by the author, Matthau replied, "I take the Fifth [Amendment]!"

Then, too, she would have trouble taking a backseat to such a powerful husband. And there was Jason. How would such a marriage affect him? Would Elliott remain a strong presence in their son's life, as she wanted him to be? There was their religious differences. Then, too, Trudeau had not proposed marriage; she had no guarantee that he would, that he wanted any more from her than a brief affair might offer.

On Manitoba Night, a yearly Canadian celebration, he escorted her to a gala celebration at the National Arts Center. She looked especially lovely, very dramatic with a tallish white mink hat, her hair again parted in the center and drawn back from her face, her ensemble trimmed in white mink on the collar, cuff, and hem, her long, angular hands with their polished extensions plunged deep in a muff of the same fur, in a kind of "Greta Garbo as Anna Karenina" look. All through the evening Trudeau gazed lovingly at her while she remained restrained, cool, somewhat diffident. Doubts had continued to assail her during the day, and Trudeau's public recognition of them as a couple made her situation difficult.

The following evening they dined alone at the prime minister's residence. She was ushered into an austere reception room, "heavy Victorian ornaments, dour, unsmiling family portraits, gray everywhere," and told, "The prime minister will be down shortly." This sober introduction into his private lifestyle was in direct contrast to the man she thought she knew and whose informal approach to politics, which included wearing sandals in Parliament on humid summer days, was debated with lively enthusiasm in the press.

For two years before becoming prime minister, Trudeau had been minister of justice in the Lester Pearson government and had brought sweeping reforms to Canada's judicial system. As a champion for human rights, he became "the beloved black sheep of the Liberal Party," but there was also the private man with a reputation as a heartbreaker. In the words of Margaret Sinclair, with whom he was soon to be romantically involved, Trudeau "had a silky, warm, charming manner that eased any initial awkwardness a woman might be feeling." It has been said that "charm is the power to please by force of personality and intellect, an instinct for the persuasiveness of sympathy, the indefinable effect of an enchantment." Trudeau possessed these things, and Streisand was moved and captivated by him at turns.

He joined her almost immediately upon her arrival. According to a servant's report, they dined by candlelight at a table set up before a roaring fire. The food was bland but the conversation was spirited. Trudeau possessed a gentle, teasing way of speaking, "a sort of old-fashioned gallantry." After dinner they took a walk in the garden. The air was cutting cold as they wandered briskly by the river that bordered the property, the lights of the city reflected on its surface. Then they returned to the residence. Backstairs reporting went no further. The servant left the two alone in the house to retire to her own quarters.

For all his phenomenal success, Trudeau was a solitary man who had never lived with any woman very long, but he had reached an age when he wanted children, a family. Exactly how Streisand fitted in with his scheme for his future is cloudy. Known to be attracted to women in the public eye, his affairs were invariably short-lived. Reason overcame passion, and he would move on rather than become inextricably entangled in a relationship that was not to his liking or that might be injurious to his political career.

She left the next day for New York (where she was to begin shooting *The Owl and the Pussycat,* her first nonmusical movie), confused, not sure what she should do — break it off before she was too deeply involved or continue to see him.

"Oh, yeah, I thought [being first lady of Canada] would be fantastic," she later acknowledged. "I'd have to learn how to speak French. I would do only movies made in Canada. I had it all figured out. I would campaign for him and become totally politically involved in all the causes, abortion and whatever," obviously forgetting in her enthusiasm that as a Catholic, Trudeau could not covenant abortion and that her status as a divorced woman, if marriage was ever proposed, would become an almost insurmountable obstacle.

Still, the old self-doubts prevailed. "I was always concerned with being looked down upon as an actress," she admitted. "I always felt that certain people thought, Oh, you're an actress, ah. Cheap. Vulgar. Loose. Immoral. Amoral. . . . People want to be friendly with actresses, they're so *charming*, so *amusing*. It's all so condescending, like having a clown, having this toy."

"Is it love?" a reporter asked Diana Kind, a most unlikely person to know her daughter's heart, since Streisand discussed nothing of a personal nature with her mother. "Who knows?" Diana replied, offering her customary platitudes. "Barbra has a lot of interesting friends."

In late February her relationship with Trudeau came to a sudden end. He had fallen in love with Margaret Sinclair, a nineteen-year-old Canadian who, Streisand learned, he was seeing when she was visiting him in Ottawa.* She was hurt and confused. For years she had turned to Elliott at such troubled times. He was in Sweden making *The Touch* with one of the world's greatest directors, Ingmar Bergman, and had been nominated for an Oscar for best actor in *Bob & Carol & Ted & Alice*. Maybe the time when they had first met and married had just been too premature. Now, with both of them enjoying fame, they could do fantastic things together. She had always believed in him, as he had believed in her. She had a short break in her shooting schedule. Taking a wild chance, she flew to Stockholm to talk with him.

"Barbra wanted us to get back together immediately," Elliott recalled. She brought up Jason, their history together, her continuing feelings for him, her sense of loss without him. "I didn't know that was my last opportunity, and I don't know if it would have made a difference if I had," he said. "I told her, 'If that's what you want, then that's what I want, but I can't just disregard Jenny.'" He suggested that they wait before moving back together so that he could have a chance to see that Jenny did not feel deserted, that she had someone to help her make the transition to

---

*In her memoirs, Margaret Sinclair Trudeau wrote: "He flew Barbra Streisand up to Ottawa to accompany him to a gala at the Arts Center. . . . It was a romance. Every paper carried it. For the next few days my pique and jealousy was such that each time Pierre rang, I slammed down the phone: 'Go back to your American actress!' I yelled at him." The future Mrs. Trudeau converted to Catholicism and married the prime minister eighteen months later. Despite her religious conversion, she eventually divorced Trudeau.

being on her own again. "But Barbra needed immediate validation," and he could not give it to her. Nursing her injured feelings, she returned to New York.

Although unable to surrender all her ties to Elliott, she knew now that their marriage was really over. She suspected she would never want to remarry. "Jason already *has* a father," she told a close friend, "I have a special destiny to fulfill." She had felt that way since childhood. Then, she believed it meant she would one day be a great Hollywood star. Having achieved that wish, she set her goal higher.

"After she *schlepped* through *Hello, Dolly!*," Barry Dennen said, "I wrote her a telegram with just three words, 'What a pity.' But I never did send it."

He did not have to. Streisand agreed. She had caught her second wind and was ready for the onset of a different phase in her career — to succeed as a dramatic actress, to direct and produce her own movies — and then? Her life was like an ocean, wave lapping against wave — and always there was deeper water to tread beyond.

20

Streisand entered films at a time when strong women with powerful screen personalities were an endangered species. The industry was male-dominated, with a profusion of macho stars and adventure films. Good female roles were almost nonexistent, and women in executive positions unwelcome. Welcomed or not, she intended to break through the male bastion that controlled Hollywood. *Look out world, here I come!* was her attitude. *That* world was making movies, now her world, her life, and she intended to make of it what she wanted.

The days of gutsy actresses such as Joan Crawford, Bette Davis, Katharine Hepburn, Susan Hayward, Carole Lombard, and Rosalind Russell were over. Marilyn Monroe was dead, and with her had died the Hollywood sex queen. In 1970 there were only two major female American film stars — Barbra Streisand and Jane Fonda. Streisand was offered, and refused, the role of the marathon dancer in *They Shoot Horses, Don't They?* (1969) and that of the brittle New York call girl in *Klute* (1971). Both went to Fonda, the latter winning her an Academy Award. Neither role appealed to Streisand. Too downbeat.

Shortly after *Klute,* Fonda plunged into a plethora of anti-establishment causes, championing the Black Panthers and a campaign to end the war in Southeast Asia — activities that ensured Streisand was left virtually without competition. She had the power; now she must decide how to use it.

Possessing a strong screen presence even when miscast, as she had been in *Hello, Dolly!,* finding a role to fulfill her potential was a rough-and-tumble struggle. If she wanted good roles in interesting films, Streisand would have to become her own producer. In Hollywood, however, the more a woman used her energy, her brains, and her talent, the more she was resented. A woman like Streisand, who fought for every inch she gained, was a threat.

Although called a castrating, hard-driving bitch by some of the men she worked with, a man in the same circumstances would have been respected for his drive and ambition. All around her she saw male stars — Kirk Douglas, Burt Lancaster, John Wayne, Jack Lemmon — organizing their own production companies, receiving the profits that had hitherto gone to their employers. She decided that was what she must do and was also smart enough to know that she could not go it alone.

Marty Erlichman still functioned as her personal manager, overseeing her career, but her agent at the time was the high-powered, supersalesman Freddie Fields, who in 1961 with his ex-partner David Begelman had started a talent agency, then called Creative Management Associates (later to become International Creative Management). Streisand had signed with CMA during her 1963 engagement at the Coconut Grove, realizing that to make it in movies she had to have a knowledgeable and established Hollywood agency behind her. Fields, a man with a ready smile, sharp wit, and a penchant for grand gestures — extravagant gifts, chauffeured Rolls-Royces to take his stars to their public engagements — had renegotiated, with attorney Bella Linden's considerable help, Streisand's original *Funny Girl* contract.

Freddie Fields was a genius at putting together package deals — star, property, director — but Streisand was the agency's only bankable star. Determined to overtake William Morris, then the top Hollywood talent agency, Fields came up with an idea that he felt certain would attract other talent of her caliber (necessarily men; there were no other female stars in her orbit) to his agency list. Sue Mengers was his prime talent-acquisition agent. Fields put together the idea of a company that would be owned partially by the stars, who would be partners in the company, and partially by the public. He needed Streisand as bait to bring in performers in her stratum and promised her the world: artistic freedom, a chance to do her own projects, whatever she wanted to do, virtually no strings attached. She would get 10 percent of the gross and would agree to deliver three pictures to this company. Streisand, feeling this was just the opportunity she was looking for to have control over her films, agreed. Mengers then went all-out to woo other candidates away from their current agents. It did not take long before she had convinced Paul Newman and Sidney Poitier of the viability and advantages of such a company. On the surface the three stars seemed a good match; all were serious performers, and each had a strong social conscience.

Agents Fields and Mengers, a formidable duo, set up a press conference on June 11, 1969, in New York at the Plaza Hotel, where, at a table in one of the ballrooms, the three stars signed incorporation papers for the First Artists Production Company, Ltd., in front of over three hundred press photographers, reporters, and television news film crews. Each of the three stars had made an initial commitment to produce and appear in three films. Additionally, the company planned to engage in television production, music publishing, recording, and other ancillary activities.*

Speaking first, Streisand said in a clear, authoritative voice that she saw the new company as "a natural development, a logical progression. I have always had to be free to play the roles and sing the songs I felt strongly and instinctively were right for me. We'll be making many diverse films and we're determined that every one of them — drama or comedy or musical — will reach the very high standards we demand of ourselves."

Newman added that the purpose of their company was "not necessarily to economize, but to put film production on a more efficient basis."

---

*Forty years earlier film stars Mary Pickford, Charles Chaplin, Douglas Fairbanks, Jr., and William Hart formed United Artists to distribute their own independent productions. Hart dropped out two weeks later, but United Artists became a major film distributor in Hollywood and earned sizable profits from the release of its movies. The precedent, therefore, had been set for Streisand, her star partners, and First Artists.

Poitier spoke more about the new era of the motion picture industry. "You either lead it, or move with it, or follow it. We have opted for leadership."

After the announcement the stellar triumvirate adjourned to a private suite, where they drank champagne and talked glibly among themselves and their representatives, but there was a curious lack of chemistry between them. On Streisand's part, she had "a cool suspicion of the others," a staff member who was present at the gathering recalled. She was the lone woman in a company with two powerful men who were both as valuable at the box office as she was. Although they parted amiably, a competitive spirit was unleashed. Plans for the company moved forward, guided in those early months by Fields and Mengers, who managed not long after to snag Steve McQueen from William Morris as a fourth member of First Artists. Warner Brothers, along with a British merchant bank, Arbuthnot Latham & Co., Ltd., was to supply the financing.

One of Streisand's prime reasons for becoming a partner in First Artists was to chose her own projects. The one closest to her heart was an Isaac Bashevis Singer story, "Yentl, the Yeshiva Boy," which had been sent to her by producer Valentine Sherry in 1968 just after she had completed *Funny Girl*. Having read it, she called Fields to tell him that she wanted to do it as her next movie. Fields tried to convince her that she should not do another ethnic role so soon after playing Fanny Brice. Streisand was persistent and took an option on the property.

Set in nineteenth-century Poland, the story centered on Yentl, only child of a widowed talmudic scholar who had instilled his daughter with a love of learning. After his death, and as girls were denied an education in talmudic law at that time, the teenaged Yentl disguises herself as a boy, cuts off her hair, straps down her breasts, adopts male clothing, renames herself Anshel, and runs away to another town. There, accepted as a boy, she attends a yeshiva and falls in love with an older male student, Avigdor, to whom she does not dare confide the truth. Finally, she is pressured into a marriage to the beautiful young woman Hadass, who Avigdor loves but cannot marry. Yentl eventually reveals her true identity and embarks for America, where to continue her education she will no longer have to pretend to be male.

The story appealed to Streisand on several levels. It was about a girl who had lost her father, a man of learning; it dealt with equal opportunity and education for women; and it was rooted in the history of the Jewish people. She approached the Czechoslovakian director Ivan Passer, the son of wealthy Jewish parents who had survived the Holocaust. He seemed exactly the right choice to develop *Yentl*. He struggled with the story for a while and then backed out, telling Streisand that she was too old and too famous to play the part. Also, women masquerading as men had never been accepted on the screen. He reminded her of Katharine Hepburn's disastrous film in which she donned masculine attire, *Christopher Strong* (1933), a movie that was a failure at the box office and earned Hepburn the wrath of critics. Apart from that, he could see no way to overcome the climactic wedding night scene between two women, Hadass and Yentl. Nor, for that matter, had Paramount when she approached them originally seeking financing.

"I would think, 'I can never make this movie. Maybe Ivan was right; I'm too old. Maybe I'm too famous.' I was so scared that I would talk to everyone about it and after a while I began to really hear myself, and hear this person talking about this dream they had, but being too frightened to go after the dream." She continued to talk about it but went on with her commitment to star in the film adaptation of Bill Manhoff's *The Owl and the Pussycat,* a whimsical version of the Pygmalion myth that had been more successful as a play on Broadway than in the West End. She played Doris, a luckless, brassy, fast-talking prostitute, an overbearing character who was nonetheless vulnerable and likable — a sort of ethnic, apolitical Billie Dawn from *Born Yesterday.* Doris was Streisand's first straight comedy role, and she began shooting on location in New York with great enthusiasm.

Originally conceived for two characters, a black woman and a white man, the Broadway production of *The Owl and the Pussycat* had starred Alan Alda and Diana Sands, with whom Streisand had appeared in *Another Evening with Harry Stoones.* Streisand's costar was George Segal. They worked magically as a team. In a farcical inversion of the movie cliché, Segal played the reticent maiden to Streisand's incorrigible seducer. As one writer astutely noted, they illustrated "Schopenhauer's theory that the ideal couple is the one in which the man's feminine components equally match the woman's masculine traits."

In the story Segal's character, Felix, a bookstore clerk with pretensions of becoming a writer, is distressed by the late-night sexual activity of his neighbor, Doris, a hooker who calls herself a model and actress. Felix reports her behavior to their landlord. Doris is evicted and, with no place to go, brazens her way into Felix's apartment, refusing to leave. Verbal battles lead into sexual seduction. The dialogue is fast and witty; the romantic ending as Doris abandons prostitution and Felix accepts his future as nothing more than a bookstore clerk is thoroughly satisfying.

Except for the sudden death of her much-relied-upon cinematographer, Harry Stradling,* during the making of *The Owl and the Pussycat,* Streisand's first film for Ray Stark since *Funny Girl* was a happy working experience. She was thrilled to be cast in a straight romantic comedy, to prove that she could succeed without singing a note. And she liked and understood the character she played. This time she and Stark got on well. Her old friend Herbert Ross directed the film. Robert Greenhut, who would go on to produce most of Woody Allen's movies, was production manager and always helpful. And she had an exceptional rapport with George Segal, whose offbeat personality appealed to her. Segal was not only an actor who could move deftly from drama to comedy and from stage to film, he was a dedicated jazz musician, singer, and conductor (under his baton, his Beverly Hills Unlisted Jazz Band would perform in 1981 at Carnegie Hall).

The movie, which began shooting on October 6, 1969, was filmed entirely in New York using the city streets, Doubleday Bookstore on Fifth Avenue, Riker's Restaurant, Club 45, and Central Park for locations, and a small studio on West Fifty-sixth Street for all other scenes. Fearing Streisand might create problems if she did not have a luxurious dressing room, Stark had the film's production designer John Robert Lloyd create a suitable one for her. Lloyd completely mirrored the walls

---

*Harry Stradling died on February 14, 1970, shortly after completion of photography on *The Owl and the Pussycat;* cinematographer Andrew Laszlo took over to supervise all retakes and second-unit work.

and "put in thick white carpeting, and all kinds of funny things — bean-bag chairs, things that were faddish. And [he] made her a special dressing room table with those three-fold dressing room mirrors with lights around them like the old-fashioned dressing rooms used to have. And [he] put a star on the door." Streisand was pleased with the result and except for one scene, in which she was to be filmed topless, was never difficult.

"She only calls me 'Herbie' when she's uptight," Herbert Ross explained. "Otherwise, I'm Herbert. For that scene, as soon as I heard 'Herbie, I gotta talk to you,' I knew she had big reservations even though I thought we'd worked them all out. She got me into a corner and said, 'Herbie, I can't. I've got goose bumps and they'll show. Herbie, I just can't. What would my mother think?"

Arguments went back and forth for nearly an hour. "Oh, what the hell. I'll do it once!" she finally exclaimed, disrobed, and crossed the set barebreasted to where Segal waited on the bed.

"Cut and print! Beautiful!" Ross shouted.

When she saw the rushes, although her nudity revealed a splendid, sensual body, she insisted the scene be cut, claiming it destroyed the impact of the scene that followed. Reluctantly, Ross acquiesced and turned over, at Streisand's request, the negative frames in which she had been topless.*

This was during her romance with Pierre Trudeau, which more than possibly influenced her decision. Her association with the prime minister deepened her interest in politics and provided her with another stage on which to exercise — not just her ego but her enormous intelligence. None of her films had allowed her to express her concern for social ills or dissatisfaction with the status quo. In her first two years in Hollywood, her main efforts had been to establish herself as a superstar. Having

---

*Ten years later the magazine *High Society* somehow got ahold of either the original negative frames or pirated copies of Streisand's discarded topless scene and published several stills. Streisand attempted to block publication and sued for five million dollars in damages. The judge ruled against her, although he ordered the publisher to notify wholesalers to tear the offending pages from the magazines before putting them on newsstands. There is no way of knowing how many wholesalers obliged.

accomplished that, she was now feeling intellectually dissatisfied. She detested the loss of privacy that fame had extracted. She was followed by paparazzi wherever she went. Fans seemed to feel they had the right to intrude on her private time — attending a children's movie with five-year-old Jason or dining with friends. Becoming more actively involved in politics afforded her the opportunity to use her celebrity to validate her beliefs.

So much had happened to her and the country since she had first gone to Hollywood in 1967 that it hardly seemed possible that only three years had intervened. An American spaceship had landed on the moon. Richard M. Nixon, a man she loathed, was president. Unrest spread on college campuses as the Vietnam War dragged disastrously on. There were over 44,000 American casualties, another 300,000 men had been wounded, bombing had intensified, Cambodia was invaded, and a unit of the U.S. Army in Vietnam had massacred 347 civilians, women and children included, in the tiny village of My Lai.

Vigorously antiwar, she became involved in the congressional campaign of Bella Savitzky Abzug while she was in New York making *The Owl and the Pussycat*. Abzug, a stocky, middle-aged lawyer with a forthright style, belting voice, and a taste for large, slouchy hats, was not only staunchly antiwar but a dedicated proponent of women's rights. Abzug was a true original, employing a New York confrontational style with a talent for outsized theatrics. As a young woman she had been in the Stalinist wing of the Democratic party. Although her views had mellowed, she was a fighting liberal — as, in fact, were all three Democratic congressmen from New York City, Ed Koch, Ed Ryan, and Leonard Farbstein, whose thirty-year tenure as the representative for the Nineteenth Congressional District she was challenging in the June 23 (1970) primary.

The Abzug-Farbstein contest grew ugly. Farbstein accused Abzug of being, among other things, a communist and anti-Israel (neither accusation was correct). Abzug charged him with being against the women's movement and more hawk than dove (also not exactly the truth). Streisand met Abzug through Cis Corman. The two women hit it off right away. "They shared a kind of mirror image," one close observer said.

"Bella nursed fantasies of being a great performer, and Barbra of political power."

Streisand's views were to the far left, but certainly not radical in a time when Leonard Bernstein hosted fund-raisers for the Black Panthers and when some of the most prestigious universities in the country were erupting into violence. Seldom neutral, Streisand was a sometime antagonist, meaning that she believed in the liberal issues, lent her celebrity, donated money, and helped raise funds, but her career and personal life took precedence. She was also not against the publicity value and the means to attract new fans that her association with such meaningful, newsworthy causes generated. The ideal of female equality was, however, deep-rooted in her consciousness. And as new role models such as Bella Abzug, Gloria Steinem, and Betty Friedan (who asserted, "This is not a bedroom war. This is a political movement.") came on the scene, she joined with them in a spirit of community.

Reacting to the excitement of the city during political campaigns, Streisand decided she wanted to return to New York but not to her old apartment. On March 31 she bought a townhouse for $375,000 (the asking price had been $420,000) at 49 East Eightieth, circumventing board approval on co-op apartments. But she was quickly disenchanted with the house. "I would much rather have the seventeen rooms horizontally than vertically — or on two instead of five levels," she admitted only weeks later, adding that she would sell "if a buyer could be found and I could purchase a suitable co-op in an apartment building where I am welcome."

The house on East Eightieth Street was built in 1929, when art deco was moving into high gear. The residence was an impressive stone structure entered through an iron-and-glass front door from a walled courtyard. Streisand had the front windows replaced with lead-glass panels from a Victorian gazebo that she had bought from the set of *On a Clear Day*. She took the Russian-born well-known art deco artist Erté on a tour of the house and incorporated some of his ideas — a twenties period mural in the dining room and indirect lighting, which had been popular at that time. The decor, however, incorporated Regency, Victorian, art nouveau, art deco, *and* contemporary influences, to include the furnishings from the penthouse and to showcase the many stored pieces of antique furniture, paintings, and objets d'art she had been collecting over the years.

Working with an architect and a decorator, she redesigned the new house to her needs and liking. Jason would have a suite of rooms. His bedroom was to be fashioned around a colorful, contemporary Frank Stella painting and be filled with white furniture. The adjoining play-room would contain the Victorian shop furnishings she had bought when she was filming *On a Clear Day* in England and would include an ice cream parlor bar, a gum machine, and penny candy and toy cabinets. The library was to be a repository for her art nouveau furniture, turn-of-the-century art glass, German expressionist artworks by Gustav Klimt and Egon Schiele, and Czech artist Alphonse Mucha's celebrated art nouveau posters. She was having structural work done in the kitchen — "everything in stainless steel, white and red — I love red," she said. "I hate the kitchen being in the basement. Well, I'll have to leave a supply of cupcakes on every floor." Her own suite was to be in shades of rose. The bed that she and Elliott had once shared was to be replaced by a 1920s satin-tufted model.

While all this was being prepared, she remained with Jason at the Ard-sley. By the middle of May it became evident that the renovations would take longer than planned. As the house would have to remain empty for the workers, she agreed to open it to the public Tuesday evening, June 9, for a fund-raising party at which paying guests would meet Democratic congressional hopeful Bella Abzug.

Three thousand invitations were sent out urging all who wished to contribute twenty-five dollars to the cause of "sending to Washington next January that very special lady running for Congress who is dedi-cated to peace" to drop in between 5 and 8 P.M. "There will be stars of stage, screen and radio! — drinks, canapés but *no* furniture!!" Bella-Boosters, as campaign helpers called themselves, worked for a week to clean up the house, scrubbing and waxing floors, washing windows. "Hey! Now I can see the sycamore out front!" Streisand exclaimed as she came by to see how things were going.

Wearing a bright yellow pantsuit, her hair loose and soft about her face, and very little makeup, Streisand appeared in high spirits the evening of the open house, although she remained fortified in a corner of the walled garden. Numerous staff members and Bella-Boosters were on hand, so very few of the guests could make their way through to greet her, and there was tight security at the doors. About two thousand people came to support Abzug and to see Streisand and her house; as the premises were not large enough to accommodate such numbers, lines formed at the front door and queued down the street. Waiting supporters complained loudly, especially when well-known personalities were seen to circumvent the lines and enter through a side door. Nonetheless, the publicity given the event was tremendous, and there could be no doubt that Streisand's endorsement of Abzug was strategically successful. Photographs of the two of them together appeared in all the New York City newspapers.

For as long as Hollywood has existed, politicians have been aware that movie personalities create deeper and more immediate bonds with the public than they can, that seeing the stars whom they admire respect a candidate is a great vote-getter; and the more famous the celebrity or cultural icon — as Streisand was now — the better the politician's chances of claiming a large block of votes. Abzug garnered a comfortable lead at this stage over Farbstein. The election in November would present Abzug's next challenge, and Streisand agreed to lend her name and to appear at a preelection concert to be held on Sunday evening, November 1, at the Felt Forum at Madison Square Garden.

The same week that Abzug won the Democratic nomination, *On a Clear Day* premiered. Initially envisioned as a three-hour road-show presentation, the film had been cut mercilessly. Any narrative flow Vincente Minnelli's direction had given it was lost in the elimination of fifty minutes of footage. Jack Nicholson's character was so abbreviated that it was hard to know what he was doing in the picture. Yves Montand was charming but strangely unpersuasive as the psychiatrist who falls in love with Daisy's former incarnation, and he sometimes spoke lines and sang lyrics as if he were doing so phonetically. And yet, Streisand was delightful as Daisy and mesmerizing as Melinda, and I have to agree with Vincent Canby of the *New York Times* that the high point of the picture, and one of the most graceful Streisand moments ever put on film, is the royal dinner "at which Minnelli's camera explores her in loving, circling close-up while her voice is heard on the soundtrack singing 'Love with All the Trimmings.'"

"She looks grand as Melinda, stroking her breast with a cool crystal goblet of white wine to arouse a man ogling her at dinner (the gambit would work equally well with red wine)," the critic at *Newsweek* wrote. "She's a thoroughbred clothes horse for Cecil Beaton's costumes. She flashes lightning-like between Melinda's airs and Daisy's earthiness and when her Daisy admits to possession of various psychic powers she does so ruefully, as if it were a curse and she were Mrs. Job."

The picture, one of the last of big-budget Hollywood musicals, is beautifully filmed. Streisand is hypnotic at times, pure joy at others; she looks spectacularly beautiful as Melinda. Despite the butchery that took place once it was in the cutting rooms, *On a Clear Day* is a visual delight. The score is not up to the standard of either Alan Jay Lerner's or Burton Lane's best shows, but it has some fine songs, tailor-made for Streisand's voice. However, the public was simply not interested in a movie about hypnotism, psychics, and reincarnation — even if it starred Barbra Streisand. Her fans were content to buy the original soundtrack album, on which they could listen to her sing in her distinctive voice in more intimate surroundings; and the film had a poor return at the box office.*

Elliott had met with Streisand in New York shortly before the open house for Bella Abzug and had taken Jason to his first circus. Elliott's film *M*A*S*H* had taken the top prize at the Cannes Film Festival. His career at this moment lapped Streisand's. Elliott was, in fact, number five and Streisand rated in ninth position — the only woman — on the Top Ten box office stars for 1970. She was having renewed thoughts about a reconciliation and asked him the status of his relationship with Jenny Bogart. He told her that Jenny was pregnant with his child.

The news of his mistress's impending motherhood shook Streisand,

---

*On a Clear Day would later recoup its losses when it was released to television and sold as a videocassette.

and much distressed, she asked Elliott to file suit for divorce as soon as possible.

He flew to the Dominican Republic, which had recently passed a law permitting foreigners to obtain a divorce in seven days. Jenny, now five months' pregnant, accompanied him. On July 6 the deed was done. Streisand was a divorced woman. "I remember the various court officials in their donnish robes and hats," Elliott later recalled. "They said in Spanish, 'Are you sure you want to go through with it?' My better self thought no, I don't. But I had to follow through. I did it for Barbara's sake, it was what she wanted"— a cold and cavalier attitude toward Jenny considering her condition, and not entirely true.

Streisand, and even Elliott himself, did not realize how serious his drug addiction had become. "I didn't know how dangerous acid was," he said. "I never tried to kill myself but I think I came close. Acid opened up a lot of things. Maybe it opened my mind up too much." Almost immediately following his trip to the Dominican Republic to obtain their divorce, he started a film under the aegis of Warner Brothers, *A Glimpse of Tiger,* an original screenplay by Herman Raucher, on which he was both producer (with Jack Brodsky) and star. The story was about a big bear of a man, on drugs, who is growing progressively mad, but funnily so. He works the subways pretending to be blind and meets a prim young woman who is taken with his far-out humor and his daring. The two are drawn into a bizarre affair, and in the end the man murders the woman. Despite its dark subject, the script was crisp and funny, and even the denouement was more black comedy than horror.

As shooting progressed, the times Elliott was on acid increased. He became impossibly aggressive, and Anthony Harvey, the director, quit. To ease the tension and believing he was being funny, Elliott came onto the set the next morning "wearing his *M*A*S*H* helmet, a stocking over his face and sucking on a baby's [pacifier]." When Harvey returned, lured back by the film company executives, Elliott became enraged and had to be restrained from attacking the director.

Kim Darby, his costar, was terrified that he had gone mad and demanded security guards be hired by the movie company to protect her in case he became violent. A week later the film was canceled. Worse was to follow. The company, to collect its insurance, had amassed a file on Elliott's bizarre behavior during the weeks of production. He was examined by two psychiatrists who certified him mentally unbalanced, permitting the company to collect $1.5 million in insurance.

Although *M*A*S*H* and *Getting Straight* were in general release and *Move* and *I Love My . . . Wife* being readied for production, Elliott's meteoric rise to fame, a matter of two years and six major award-winning box-office successes, would come to a numbing and almost sudden end. He was no longer financeable. Two years later he was able to return to work and would star as Raymond Chandler's fictional detective Philip Marlowe in *The Long Goodbye* and in 1976 with James Caan in the farcical *Harry and Walter Go to New York,* but his short reign as a cult hero and box-office star was over. He was, he says, "skirting insanity, skating through it."

Streisand was devastated over Elliott's condition and his fall from grace. "Oh, my God," she sobbed to a friend, "not Elly."

Adding to the strangeness of the situation, Streisand had a financial interest in *A Glimpse of Tiger.* John Calley, president of Warner Brothers, called Raucher (whose adaptation of his own novel *Summer of '42* was also a Warner Brothers film) to tell him that Streisand liked the story and that he thought the project could be salvaged if he could reverse the roles and write an upbeat ending. Raucher went to see her. "She made chicken soup and was extremely helpful," he recalled. "But after two meetings and several dry starts on the new approach I decided it wouldn't work." Warners, whose investment had been considerable in the failed project, did not agree and turned to other writers.

Meanwhile, Streisand had been taken by Anne Richardson Roiphe's novel, *Up the Sandbox,* and optioned it for development. But there was no film in her immediate future. She was at odds with herself, having to cope with the impact that Elliott's breakdown and illness might have on her son's life and her own. Elliott had been more than her lover and mate, he had been her friend and protector.

In October 1970, much saddened and concerned, she moved into her New York townhouse. The tree-lined street glowed autumnal red. Light glimmered brilliantly through the deep red stain-glass window panes she had put in some of the ground-floor windows. Sliding glass doors led from the kitchen to the walled-in garden, where Jason did somersaults on the grass and learned how to catch a ball. Yet, the house depressed her. New York brought back too many memories. She decided to sell the East Side townhouse and return to the Ardsley, having not yet given up her lease.

She was scheduled in late November and December to undertake two concurrent engagements at the Riviera and International Hilton Hotels in Las Vegas. First, however, she was committed to the fund-raising, vote-rallying evening concert for Bella Abzug being held just two days before the November election. A lot of mud had stuck to Abzug from the bitter campaign she had fought with Farbstein, and she was not a shoo-in by any means. About four or five weeks before the concert, Streisand announced that she could not take on an entire evening. "It seemed as though she really wanted to back out," Madeline Lee, the producer of the concert recalled. "Marty Erlichman met with me; the director, Stanley Prager; Hal Prince, who was guiding the event; and the rest of the executive staff, all of us doing our jobs without compensation. He said Barbra now wanted to do the second half of the program and only then if for the first act we could get three performers — specifically Zero Mostel, Godfrey Cambridge, and Woody Allen. [They had to be of that caliber and not singers.] I think that Marty was hoping that the whole thing would go away and that these conditions would let Barbra off the hook. Tickets had already been sold for a concert of Barbra Streisand for Bella Abzug. This was a terrible setback. I tried but none of the three men was available on that night. When I reported this back to Marty, he seemed very happy because it would free Streisand of her obligation.

"We just couldn't afford to lose Streisand's name value. Bella had been under vitriolic attack. Rocks were thrown through the windows of her campaign headquarters by militant supporters of Israel who thought she was anti-Israel. We were rather desperate. I came up with an idea called 'Broadway for Bella,' where in the first half top Broadway stars would sing and perform numbers from current hit shows. Most theaters were dark on Sunday night, and I thought I had a good chance of getting the stars. Marty was not too enthusiastic, but he agreed to have Barbra wait for a week to see if it could be accomplished."

At week's end, Lee had signed up Joel Grey, Jack Gilford [Lee's husband], Lauren Bacall, James Coco, Rita Moreno, Phyllis Newman, Donna McKechnie, Alan Alda, George Segal, Tammy Grimes, and the entire cast of *Hair*. Erlichman agreed to go forward, but all advertisements and the program itself had to read 'Broadway for Bella' starring BARBRA STREISAND." An unflattering caricature of her as Fanny Brice by Al Hirshfield was chosen for the program. She hated it but in the end allowed it to be used.

"The place was jammed — I don't know — maybe twenty thousand people," Lee continued. "Lauren Bacall was one of the guest hosts. She was starring in *Applause* at the time. She came out and in a husky, cigarette voice (about two notes deeper than Bella's) said, 'I guess you don't know why I'm here tonight. Well, I'm Bella Abzug's vocal coach!' The first half was sensational. Then Barbra appeared in a slimlined, black evening gown with spaghetti shoulder straps. Her hair was simple and back in a plain little chignon, and she had a red chiffon scarf. She looked stunning. This was during a period when they were dressing her up in films and in Las Vegas with wigs and costumes and *ongepotchket* [overly decorated] evening outfits. We had a twenty-three-piece orchestra, and she sang seven songs and an encore, I believe. A beautiful Russian lullaby that had been cut out of *Funny Girl* (she tied the scarf under her chin like a babushka for that one), 'People' and numbers that she was planning to use in Las Vegas. She was so good, she was chilling. She never sang better, she never looked better. Much to our horror people ran up the aisles wanting to touch her. She looked terrified. I think it was Alan Alda who came out onstage and helped her off." The coverage was enormous, and Abzug was duly elected to Congress two days later.

The Owl and the Pussycat opened the following week. "Barbra Streisand's delicate snarl is the voice of New York tuned to a parodist's sensibility," Pauline Kael wrote in the *New Yorker*. "It's the sound of urban character armor; she rattles it for a finely modulated raucousness. . . . She is a living, talking cliff-hanger. . . . Though she doesn't sing in this picture, she's still a singing actress; she makes her lines funny musically, and she can ring more changes on a line than anybody since W. C. Fields, who was also a master of inflection." The film was a huge success at the box office and was in the black within a few weeks of its release. Streisand had proved that she did not have to sing in a movie for it to be profitable. She pressed forward on the nonsinging stories she was developing — *Up the Sandbox, Yentl,* and *What's Up, Doc?*

She no longer enjoyed performing live, and her return to Las Vegas was fraught with dissatisfaction. Stage fright plagued her. The late hours and gaudy ambience of the hotels and of Las Vegas annoyed her. She could not wait to honor her contracts and return to California. Her impatience and irritation did not affect her performance. The rooms she played were packed, and there were standing ovations after each show, which ended with "In the Wee Small Hours of the Morning" and "When You Gotta Go." "The lyrics," she claimed, "with their 'Auld Lang Syne' sentiment, seemed like a fitting way to bid farewell to a decade full of dreams, challenges and adventures."

Her last performance was on New Year's Eve. It was 1971, a year into a new decade, destined to be the most tempestuous time in her life.

Part V

Making Movies, Making Love

"One of the reasons I care about being a movie actress is to be remembered, to be slightly immortal; because I think life is so short that by the time we get to see things with some sense of reality and truth, it's all over. So I'm sure that's why I care so much about making movies: It prolongs your life."

Barbra Streisand, 1977

"People say I got this strange hold over Barbra. I do. It's called love."

Jon Peters, 1976

21

Being a movie star was no longer enough. Life was incomplete without a man by her side. Her closest friends — Cis Corman and lyricist Marilyn Bergman, whom she had met since coming to California — seemed to be happily married. Streisand was sensitive to their supportive, loving relationships. Every man she dated was viewed by her as a prospective life partner. They all failed her standard. She wanted *poifect,* nothing less.

"Actually, I believe women are superior to men, I don't even think we're equal," she professed. "Among many other things, women are stronger than men. . . . [Men] have more heart attacks, ulcers, nervous breakdowns and suicides. Their façade is killing them." Thoughtfully, she added, "I have enormous compassion for men, which really came into focus with the birth of my own son. This little boy who wanted to be held and comforted and soothed has to grow up in a world where he cannot cry because it is 'unmanly.'"

Tender sentiments; yet, it is doubtful that she would have welcomed into her life a man who would not be able to control such emotions. She had only recently confided to friends that she was tired of being "the man around the house, of making the money and all the decisions." Ambiguity, thy name is Barbra.

The house in New York was put up for sale and sold swiftly. After all the years of renting, she bought the Central Park West penthouse and set about redecorating it, removing all the Louis XVI influences, the red flocked wallpaper, and large mirrors in highly decorated gilt frames. "Look, this was my first real home," she told an interviewer for *Architectural Digest*. "Let me tell you. I wanted Louis, Louis, Louis — as much as I could lay my hands on. And I got it: chandeliers, bronzes, porcelains, satin. Now I've become far more sophisticated."

She was in what she called "my burgundy era . . . Art Nouveau, Art Déco — all those rusts, mauves and greens, and those swooning fin-de-siècle colors and sinuous shapes!" She had become so knowledgeable about these two early-twentieth-century design periods that she could have given a concise lecture on their roots and differences. Her tastes had changed, but not her penchant for setting fashion trends. Hot pants, platform shoes, polyester, and Day-Glo colors were the current vogue. The young seemed determined to express themselves in what they wore. Their clothes had a certain tackiness to them that Streisand disliked. She led the way with designer blue jeans and tie-dyed shirts for relaxation; long slinky gowns in black, gray, or white for evening. The elaborate coiffures she had endorsed after *On a Clear Day* were replaced by long, straightened, flaxen-bleached hair. Motivated by a desire for youth and some of the fun she might have missed earlier in her life, she strove to keep fit. Her ice cream binges occurred less often; her passion for delicatessen food was disciplined. She jogged on the beach in the mornings and played tennis with Burt Bacharach, who was working with her on a proposed album. On March 14, 1971, she made her first television appearance in three years (the much-delayed broadcast of the concert in Central Park, which had been taped just after she had made *Funny Girl*) on Bacharach's CBS special, joining him at the piano to sing "(They Long to Be) Close to You" and several other Bacharach-David songs.

Her old albums continued to sell at a steady rate. American record sales had tripled in the last decade. To the shock of their millions of horrified fans, the Beatles, rock music's reigning superstars, went their separate ways. But the Rolling Stones, Temptations, Fifth Dimension, Blood, Sweat and Tears, and the Doors were all in the Top 40, and Streisand was one of the few solo singers with them. The Turtles and the

Temptations played the Nixon White House. ("Me? Never!" she had commented.) In England, an LP called *Empty Sky* introduced a young Elton John. Elvis Presley was still a force, but new faces and sounds were emerging — Marvin Gaye, James Taylor, Carole King. At the height of their fame, Janis Joplin and Jimi Hendrix died tragic deaths — victims of living in the fast lane. The music world was going through a transitional time with great contrasts. Streisand was determined to keep up with the changing market and explore new material with the same deep scrutiny she had given to Arlen, Styne, Merrill, Lerner, and Lane.

Afraid the public might not want a "different" Barbra Streisand, she recorded eight songs for an album titled *The Singer,** which was to combine old and new music. When Clive Davis, the president of Columbia Records, heard the tracks, he was concerned that she was walking the line too cautiously and asked her to consider putting aside work on *The Singer* to collaborate with a new producer (she had been working with Wally Gold), Richard Perry, on a more contemporary album. When she and Perry met, he played her some of the songs he wanted her to sing if she agreed to do the replacement album with him. One of them was Laura Nyro's "Stoney End"; others were Randy Newman's "I'll Be Home," Harry Nilsson's "Maybe," and Joni Mitchell's "I Don't Know Where I Stand." She agreed to go ahead with the album, which became *Stoney End.*

The venture was to be one of the few times she would not have Peter Matz as her musical arranger or conductor, the first time that she would have a backup group (three female singers), and also the first time that the musicians and technicians were either her age or younger. "Richard was always trying to get me to sing on the beat," she recalls, "which I found very hard to do." She was skeptical about the album's acceptance. Although not yet thirty, she considered herself part of the old guard of singers, her sound more Broadway than rock. Now Barbra Streisand proved that she was a singer for any day. Each number is sung beautifully,

---

*The title song of the abandoned album, "The Singer," written by Walter Marks and arranged by Peter Matz, had its inspiration in French singer Edith Piaf. The music is very Gallic, the lyrics suited to cabaret. Streisand later released it on *Just for the Record* . . .

with tremendous energy and with lyric attitudes that brought the songs to a brilliant polish. She happily lost a bet to Perry that the record would not be a hit. Released only a week before her "Broadway for Bella" concert, it was number one on several national charts by the time she returned to Los Angeles after her Las Vegas engagements.

Suddenly, she felt younger, gayer, more energized. She made a second album with Perry, *Barbra Joan Streisand,* designed to appeal to a wider audience with the inclusion of some rock-and-roll numbers. At best, the album is a mixed bag. She tried hard to pump drama and give some stature to the lyrics of "Space Captain" and belted out a grating primal shriek in John Lennon's "Mother," failing in both cases to add anything to the original material. Yet, a Burt Bacharach–Hal David medley and a fuguelike duet with herself, both vintage Streisand, vindicate the less-successful numbers. The album wavered at the bottom of the charts, but it did reveal that she was not afraid of new music trends.

Making movies, her *own* movies, remained her top priority. *Yentl* was at a complete halt; *Up the Sandbox* was taking time to develop. Her contract with Ray Stark for two more movies would bring her a tenth of what she would have been paid elsewhere. She had a genuine fear of doing concerts. Records were the greatest source of her income.

In Hollywood, where money is more highly valued than anything else, it is earnestly believed that the larger the budget of a picture, the more successful it will be. How the money is spent — on the highest-paid stars, expensive writers, superlavish settings — does not much matter. Streisand did not subscribe to that philosophy. She had been overwhelmed with the amount of money lavished on the sets and costumes for *On a Clear Day.* She saw nothing inherently bad or wrong about artists' making millions of dollars. She was, however, wary of sacrificing creativity for money — they were not interchangeable.

By nature frugal and a tough bargainer, during the early days of her success she had been extravagant, spending quantities of money on furs and furnishings. Still, she was never wasteful. "I can't throw away a half a yard of material or four inches of satin ribbon or a button or . . . or a left-over slice of roast beef or a spoonful of peas!" she once said. She still had the clothes she had bought when she was appearing at the Lion and the

Bon Soir. The most exotic hung on padded hangers decorating her dressing room. Others she had remade or used the fabric elsewhere for throw pillows or to decorate container boxes for her dressing room. Leftover food was recycled or frozen. Streisand still delighted in getting something for free, being taken out to dinner or given special perks such as a chauffeured car paid for by the studio. Yet, her funds were (as they had been for years) handled by others. Although doing well, she was not making the great sums of money from films that were reported in the press. She insisted that "I have never made as big a salary as many secondary male stars do today. The things you read in the paper about million-dollar this and million-dollar that, that's all bullshit. That's not true." She was referring to the pictures she had made under her Rastar contract. She had, of course, drawn a star salary for her two Fox pictures.

Managers, agents, and financial advisors took a considerable percentage of her earnings (at least 25 percent), and the investments on her behalf in the stock market had not proved successful. She claims she "never knew what was really going on . . . never really read the contracts . . . understood the deals. I didn't care!" What she wanted now was to feel responsible for her own actions.

Divorced from Elliott, a free woman, able to date openly, she met through friends blond, boyishly handsome Ryan O'Neal, who had just separated from his second wife, Leigh Taylor-Young, with whom he had costarred for five years on the popular *Peyton Place* television series. Streisand's affair with O'Neal was a light-hearted, California-oriented relationship — days at the beach where O'Neal had once been a lifeguard; casual parties with friends; and on chill, damp evenings, romantic tête-à-têtes before a roaring fire in the comfortable den in his beach house. O'Neal had two children, Tatum, eight, and Griffin, six, from his first marriage, so on weekends when he had custody, Jason, five, had companions,* which pleased her. Her inability to spend much time with

---

*Ryan O'Neal's first wife was actress Joanna Moore. Both their children, Griffin and Tatum, became actors. Tatum starred in her first movie at the age of ten with her father in *Paper Moon* (1973) and became the youngest person ever to win an Academy Award.

her son in these formative years distressed her. With the pressures of her career and her active social life, it was often difficult. And although Jason was now in private day school in Santa Monica, he was an only child surrounded by a large female staff. Elliott objected to this, but his life was in too much turmoil to offer an alternative. Weekends spent with his mother, O'Neal, and the two O'Neal children seemed a viable and thoroughly pleasant arrangement.

Ryan was Hollywood's newest and most promising leading man, having just been nominated for an Academy Award for his first major role, in the highly successful film adaptation of Erich Segal's bestselling novel *Love Story*. Why shouldn't Streisand and O'Neal make a movie together? They met with Sue Mengers, who represented them both. John Calley was still hopeful that Streisand would do *A Glimpse of Tiger,* Mengers told them. Maybe that was the way to go.

About this time the young writer-director Peter Bogdanovich, who had just made the critically acclaimed *The Last Picture Show,* entered the scene. Bogdanovich read the script of *A Glimpse of Tiger* and did not think it could work even with a reversal of roles. A movie buff since childhood, when he said he "used to live inside films and act out all the parts all week long," one of his favorite genres was the screwball comedy, which had starred the likes of Carole Lombard, Katharine Hepburn, and Jean Arthur. Although *A Glimpse of Tiger* had gone awry, it did have its roots in those madcap movies of the thirties. Using this as a springboard, borrowing quite blatantly from the classic Katharine Hepburn–Cary Grant 1938 picture, *Bringing Up Baby,* and "stealing from everything you could imagine including Feydeau farce, vaudeville, and silent film comedy," Bogdanovich helped to transform Elliott's bête noire into a spirited romp with the help of writers Buck Henry (who had done a superb job of adapting *The Owl and the Pussycat*), Robert Benton, and David Newman. *A Glimpse of Tiger* went into production on August 16, 1971, and was immediately renamed *What's Up, Doc?*

The story is set in San Francisco, where an absentminded young musicologist (O'Neal) has come in pursuit of a grant accompanied by his dominating fiancée (hilariously played by Madeline Kahn). In the hotel drugstore he meets an anarchic and disaster-prone polymath (Streisand). All three are caught up in a wildly complicated subplot involving mixed-up suitcases, missing jewels, spies, and gangsters, moving far away from the original concept. The verbal and visual gags are fast and funny. There is an inventive chase up and down the switchback streets of San Francisco, ending with a cavalcade of vehicles hurtling like lemmings into the Bay.

With Ryan, Jason, and his nanny, Streisand settled into the exclusive Huntington Hotel while they were on location in San Francisco. She was in high spirits, glowing from Ryan's attention when an unidentified telephone caller threatened to kidnap Jason. All her old fears returned. Under stress and justifiably concerned, she insisted on tighter security and took the youngster with her to the set every day. Her relationship with Ryan suffered with her nervous agitation, and she threw all her energy into making the comedy, a genre she was expert at and her costar a novice, relying on her to set the timing.

She was in her element, and the pace of the picture zinged along. Although not a musical, she sang a sizzling version of Cole Porter's "You're the Top" behind the titles. She also sang Herman Hupfeld's classic "As Time Goes By" in a scene of the movie where she seduces Ryan as he accompanies her on the piano upon which she first sits, then slithers across. Warners was confident they had a hit — which proved to be the case — but during the filming, the relationship between the two stars cooled. Ryan turned out not to be quick enough or bright enough to sustain her interest. By the end of the production, he had reconciled with his wife, although they later divorced.

The breakup of her affair with Ryan did not disrupt her life. She returned to Las Vegas in December for the last of her contracted appearances and swore all over again that she would not do concerts or nightclub work ever again. Fear and anxiety were her excuse, but there was more to it. Film and recordings, where she performed in a professional atmosphere, were her chosen arena of expression. They were immeasurably safer. A song could be recorded over and over and then edited until it was exactly the way she wanted it to sound; and there were no outsiders, no one but herself to please. When making a movie, lighting, makeup, and the work of some of the industry's top camera crews ensured that not only would she look her best, she could be made to be beautiful or sexy or sophisticated. She had grown up living within the fantasy of the screen, imagining herself as any of the great beauties she had admired. Now that she could be one herself, she was mature enough to understand that much of what a moviegoer thinks is real is illusion. Still, she was in love with herself on film, and insecure about her looks in true life and fearful — *yes* — that a terrorist or a crazy person could bring her harm or that exuberant fans could injure her or crush her to death as they tore at her clothes or pulled her hair. Just recently, Diana Ross had had a wig painfully yanked from her head in an emotional attack by fans who appeared to have just wanted to touch or take away something that belonged to her. Unfortunately, the wig had been attached for security with an inordinate amount of hairpins. Streisand, the perfectionist, was equally terrified at the thought of forgetting lyrics, of mild applause or, worse, jeers or hecklers.

As soon as she returned from Las Vegas, she enthusiastically set to work on *Up the Sandbox*. The film's strongest appeal to her was its theme of women's equality with men. She played Margaret, a woman torn between her needs to strike a blow for female independence and her love of being a wife and mother of two small children. She escapes into fantasy — daydreams in which she is the heroine of garish adventures. She has a bizarre affair with Fidel Castro (who turns out to be a lesbian in male attire), attacks her obnoxious mother with a baked meringue, joins a group of black revolutionaries in a plot to blow up the Statue of Liberty, and goes on an African expedition to learn the secret of painless childbirth.

The shooting schedule was to start in Los Angeles in early March, then move six weeks later to New York for a month of location work before continuing on to Uganda in East Africa, where — after a recent coup d'etat the previous year — the country was in the hands of Major General Idi Amin and the Ugandan army. Border clashes with Tanzania were being reported, diplomatic arguments with the United States and Israel were heated, and Amin was engaged on a reign of terror that would within a few years take the lives of 250,000 Ugandans. It hardly seemed like an intelligent location for a Hollywood movie, despite the promised savings in location costs (because labor was cheap and there were no unions to set a minimum wage).

Up the Sandbox was nominally Streisand's film, and as it was her initial venture for First Artists, she could have been expected to take full control. Instead, she stepped cautiously into the baptismal waters and let her producers, Irwin Winkler and Robert Chartoff, hold the reins, although she retained artistic authority and supported herself with close associates and friends — Marty Erlichman as associate producer, Cis Corman as casting director. She worked on the screenplay with playwright-screenwriter Paul Zindel. *Up the Sandbox* put her in touch with herself, her feelings, her viewpoints on the difficulty of being a woman in a male-dominated world; and she was able to include these ideas in the script.

Despite her vow to never again appear before the public in a large concert, she was convinced by Warren Beatty and his sister, Shirley MacLaine, that she should do so one more time to help get Democratic presidential nominee Senator George McGovern elected, and in so doing remove Tricky Dick Nixon from the White House. Every move that Nixon made seemed to pull the United States deeper into the Vietnam War. In 1970, less than a week after Streisand's twenty-eighth birthday, Nixon announced that he was sending American soldiers into Cambodia. The Vietcong sanctuaries had to be cleared, Nixon declared, "the world's most powerful nation cannot afford to act like a pitiful, helpless giant." Something had to be done to stop the madness of supposedly shortening the war by escalating it. Nixon had to be routed from office, and Beatty was enlisting all the power stars he could to help.

In the two years since their brief affair, Beatty had emerged as a high-profile political advocate. For all his renown as Hollywood's Don Juan, Beatty was and is an intelligent man with strong political viewpoints. In 1968, following his huge success in *Bonnie and Clyde,* he campaigned for Robert Kennedy in the presidential race. After Kennedy's assassination, he stopped filming for two years and devoted his energies on behalf of gun-control legislation. He had enlisted early in McGovern's 1972 dark-horse candidacy, as had Shirley MacLaine, who in 1969 gathered Hollywood's liberal elite at her Encino home to meet Senator McGovern, a spokesman for antiwar and environmental sentiments, women's activities, and civil rights.

McGovern had one fatal flaw for a politician. As a speaker, he was so boring "he made your skull feel like it was imploding," and he spoke in a tired whine. MacLaine, "who could talk to anybody about anything," and Beatty, who was a compelling speaker, traveled with the candidate, introduced him, knocked on doors, and spoke in living rooms, union halls, and college campuses in an attempt to mitigate this shortcoming.

Nixon's celebrity entourage, made up of aging luminaries such as Jack Benny, John Wayne, Lawrence Welk, Art Linkletter, and Jack Warner, was wryly called the "Hollywood Wax Museum." Beatty helped to surround McGovern with predominantly young, hip, irreverent stars. After the Florida primary, with the campaign low on funds, Beatty proposed to raise money with a series of coast-to-coast rock concerts beginning in Los Angeles in April and concluding two months later in New York. He talked Streisand into appearing in the opening fund-raising concert on April 15 at the Los Angeles Forum, promising her that the security would be tighter than Fort Knox and that she could record the concert for commercial sale.

Although the show also featured James Taylor, Carole King, and Quincy Jones (though not mentioned or included on the subsequent album, giving the false impression that it had been a solo Streisand concert), she received star billing. Eighteen thousand people bought tickets that cost up to a hundred dollars a seat, raising $300,000 for McGovern's campaign. As with the concert two years earlier for Bella Abzug, Streisand occupied the entire last half of the program.

"If I would have known there would be so many people on the two sides of me, I would have had my nose fixed," she quipped when the applause finally quieted at her entrance. There were shouts of, "Don't do it, Barbra!" and she said huskily into the microphone, "Never!"

She appeared more relaxed than ever before in concert. She opened with Joe Raposo's "Sing," one of Jason's favorite songs from *Sesame Street*. She was in top form, and her renditions of "Starting Here, Starting Now" and Jimmy Webb's "Didn't We" displayed her great control in the use of voice dynamics. What distinguished this concert from earlier ones was her tremendous rapport with the audience. In the middle of the first act she took time out to engage in a five-minute monologue. Holding a glass of iced tea (supposedly booze), she took a loud slurp.

"Ya know — to conquer their fears, some performers drink," she said, taking another noisy swallow. "I really hate the taste of liquor. Some take pills. I can't even swallow an aspirin. I believe performers should be strong. We should face our problems head on." She withdrew from the skirt pocket of a black evening dress what looked like a joint and took a long drag. "Is it still illegal?" she asked, and was answered by a loud "Yes!"

"The way to conquer fear is to talk about it freely, get it out in the open, and discuss it," she went on conversationally, inhaled deeply, and turning to David Shire, the conductor, added in a mock stoned voice, "Ya know that wonderful chord you just played? What was it? An F minor seventh with a demented pinky on the fifth? It was really — high." The audience roared their approval. Then, having milked the moment for what it was worth, she became sober, although not yet entirely serious. "As I spend a lot of time in L.A. I thought I'd dedicate the next song to [smoggy] L.A." And she launched into a masterful arrangement of "On a Clear Day (You Can See Forever)." Marijuana, although she did smoke it occasionally, was not really part of her lifestyle. Bringing it into her performance in such an open manner was a calculated move to create an immediate rapport with the younger and freer members of the audience. The concert ended with a contemporary rendition of "Happy Days Are Here Again" (arranged by Don Hannah, complete with a female backup group) that brought the audience to its feet and raised vociferous cheers.

Nixon placed her on his list of "political enemies" following the concert, and doomsayers claimed that "this enforced hollering" was destroying her voice and that she was relying too much on cannabis and would probably go "the Judy Garland way" in a couple of years. None of this greatly disturbed her. With Jason and his nanny, she flew to New York two days after the concert, happy to be back in the newly refurbished penthouse.

With filming in Manhattan completed on May 19, she had her staff pack more than forty suitcases (supplies, clothes, gifts for the natives) and made the long flight that would take her with shocking swiftness to Africa and a completely alien culture. At first the women of the Samburu tribe in the section of Uganda where the film company for *Up the Sandbox* set up their cameras refused to be photographed and had to be cajoled to play bit parts in the movie. They were suspicious, slow, and sometimes unknowingly destructive — moving things about, interrupting shooting.

Irvin Kershner, the director, was an urbane and witty man; balding, tall and lean, he was a student of Zen and a man with some mystery about his early background. His most recent films, *The Luck of Ginger Coffey* (1964), *A Fine Madness* (1966), *The Flim Flam Man* (its U.K. title, *One Born Every Minute,* 1967), and *Loving* (1970) had established his reputation as a director of great originality and sensitivity, but he was not bankable. Although the members of the cast were all competent actors, Streisand was the only star in the movie. Once again, she was carrying a project on her back. This weakened any power Kershner might have had over her performance and the script. *Up the Sandbox* did not succeed as a film, either critically or commercially, but there is something in her performance — "a deeper and warmer presence," *New Yorker* critic Pauline Kael called it — that for the first time on film revealed a great undeveloped actress. "She hasn't the training to play the classical roles that still define how an actress's greatness is expressed," Kael added. "But in movies new ways may be found."

Streisand was determined that such would be the case. She was happier, far more comfortable, making movies than she had ever been appearing on the stage or in concert. Even bad reviews did not sting as sorely, as they came so long after the completion of a movie, usually when she was already engaged in another production, hopes soaring — *This will be the one, the movie that will say all I want to convey without sacrificing commerciality.* She could not imagine herself ever giving up acting to sing in concert. "I'm very fragile emotionally," she said at the time. "I'm not strong; I take it all so seriously, so hard, it becomes painful to me. I get palpitations, I get ill, I get sick to my stomach, I get terrible headaches. I just become a mess. I say, What do I need this aggravation for? It's much easier just to act." By that she meant in movies, where there was no au-dience except herself and a director to please, and an atmosphere that was calculated to help her perform her task to its best advantage in every pos-sible way.

Acting met a deep personality need for her. It was a way of living, not just a means of earning a living. Having reached the top, she maintained a fierce drive to become better, to improve. That meant never repeating herself. Her great problem was finding suitable roles in a script that ex-cited her interest and in which she saw social overtones, something mean-ingful. She also needed a gifted director who was not too arrogant to accept her input but who at the same time was strong enough to provide the necessary perspective, experience, and professionalism — someone who fully understood what it was she was after even though she often felt that she held the tail of a tiger that was swinging her into uncharted country.

She also possessed an equal need for a man who could bring these same qualities to her personal life. Streisand could grandstand as often as she liked about women's independence, sexual freedom, and equality with men, but that was not what she really longed for. What she wanted — *what she had always wanted* — was a man who could stand up to her, who did not feel intimidated by her fame and her strength, who would love her unconditionally with raw sexual passion and not feel threatened by her intelligence and ambition, who would be the masculine to her fem-inine, the feminine to her masculine: a perfect match. But what man in her circle *was* such a person? So far, she had not met one.

She was ready for a relationship, was desperately seeking one. This was a time of sexual freedom, pre-AIDS and post-Pill. There were flings, short affairs that bored her and fizzled out after only a few meetings. She feared that they went to bed with her just *because* she was Barbra Strei-sand, that they might never have been attracted to her otherwise. On April 24, 1972, she celebrated her thirtieth birthday. Diana retired from her job in New York and moved out to California with Roslyn. They were living in a two-bedroom apartment in Beverly Hills. Although Streisand had provided the funds and encouraged the move, she suddenly had misgivings. Her mother's proximity brought back painful childhood memories.

Believing *Up the Sandbox* was a well-made, major movie, she was shocked when it was received badly during its first sneak preview in San Francisco. After reediting, the film was released a week before Christmas 1972, to audience apathy and bad reviews.

"Barbra was baffled by the failure of *Up the Sandbox*," Arthur Laurents recalled. "She had been told that she was star insurance and she believed it. . . . [She] could blame the financial fiascos of *On a Clear Day* and *Hello, Dolly!* on the mistakes of overproduction combined with a shrinking market for big musicals. But *Sandbox* was her own little picture. She had thought it would be a fine film and a valuable statement on the theme of women's liberation. Now her pride and joy was rejected. She was as depressed and belligerent as the mother of a whiz kid who had flunked the spelling bee over p-s-y-c-h-o-l-o-g-y."

Arthur Laurents had written a film treatment for Ray Stark (which would later evolve into *The Way We Were*) that encompassed all the facets of the Streisand he had seen evolve, from feisty Brooklyn girl to somewhat disillusioned Hollywood movie star in her prime, and encapsulated them into Katie Morosky, the story's protagonist. After reading the fifty-page treatment, she called Laurents and shouted into the telephone, "That's me! You've got it!"

22

Haunted by the past, unable to shed it, the therapy sessions in California continued. Streisand could not let go of her father's death, still feeling deserted and cheated by it. She always imagined that her childhood would have been much different had he lived; she dwelled on it, fantasized what it would have been like. She viewed her early years in a negative light, the cause of great unhappiness and pain. In one session when her early past was under discussion, the analyst touched her hand and she broke down and sobbed, leaning against the woman's shoulder. But the ache did not go away; she held it close to her like an injured child. We are often formed by what was missing in our childhood, not what we had. Manny Streisand's tragic early death could well have been responsible for his daughter's desperate need to achieve, to be someone, to make the name *Streisand* one to be remembered and respected. Her extraordinary success was a tribute to her father's too-brief life, but it never seemed to satisfy her own needs.

Things might well have been different for Streisand had her father lived. She might have been content to be daddy's girl, another man's wife, a mother to their children, or she might have felt deprived of her independence, of the right to fulfill her own ambitions. She was wise enough, in touch with herself enough, to know that, and still she could not let go. It was not as though Manny Streisand's death and her personal loss were all that was on her mind. She was caught up in the snares of stardom, surrounded — as Arthur Laurents commented — "by those blue-suited men."

"Ray was looking for a property for Barbra," Laurents recalled of this time period. "She wasn't mad about him and she wanted to get out of their contract, and he was getting desperate. He came to see me in New York. He had an idea, a sort of combination of *Sound of Music* and another movie — you know, the way Hollywood producers do. It was impossible, but I told him I'd think about a story. I'm very good at whipping up something, and I did get an idea. On my way up to see Barbra [at the Ardsley] I thought, 'This is terrible.' When I got there I said, 'I'm not going to tell it to you. It's awful.'

"'Well, what are you going to do?' she asked.

"'Oh, I don't know, if I think of something, I'll write it.' She then asked me to give her a list of books to read, and I wrote out a list which included some books by Solzhenitsyn [author of *The First Circle* and *Cancer Ward*]. Later, he got the Nobel Prize [1970], and she called me and said, 'Hey! Your guy won!'

"'Did you read any of them?' I asked.

"'No. Too big a mountain to climb,' she replied.

"Anyway, the story that finally came to me was *The Way We Were*. I knew a girl at Cornell, whose name was — believe it or not — Fanny Price, who was rather like Barbra and she was in the YCL [Young Communist League]. I dabbled in that and I knew a lot about the Hollywood witch-hunts.* Then I was very attached to Jigee Viertel,** and I combined the two women. I wrote a treatment of one hundred twenty or so pages and gave it to Ray, who was still in New York. He got on a plane

---

*Arthur Laurents had been blacklisted during the early years of the hearings of the Hollywood Un-American Activities Committee.
**Virginia Jigee Viertel, author and screenwriter Peter Viertel's wife, previously married to Budd Schulberg (*What Makes Sammy Run*), who was active in Hollywood political life during the 1940s.

and called me when he arrived in Los Angeles. 'It's wonderful. I want to do it!' he said.

"Ray sent it to Barbra to read—she was well under the influence of Cis Corman by then." Corman was working closely with Streisand, reading scripts, helping to develop properties. They remained good friends. "I think Cis had a great influence in what Barbra chose to do. Anyway, Barbra made a curious remark. There's something in that treatment that Katie never used four-letter words until she went to Hollywood, and Barbra said, 'That's me!' She can be surprisingly prudish, but that hardly seemed the case. I've always thought she sort of invented herself.

"She loved it. I suggested Sydney Pollack as a director, although I didn't know him at the time, because I had just seen *They Shoot Horses, Don't They?*, which I liked. Pollack was very close to Robert Redford [who he had directed in the adaptation of Tennessee Williams' *This Property Is Condemned* (1966)], and so that was the way they eventually got Redford, but not without a struggle.

Streisand had changed considerably since she and Laurents had last worked together. She was now a star and worked hard at keeping the image. She was concerned with every small facet of a script she might be considering: the time span of the story, the kind of clothes she would have to wear, the number of scenes she was in, and the other female roles. Never an ensemble player, she had fallen easily into the power of stardom.

Laurents's relationship to Streisand was on an entirely new level here — star and screenwriter, the latter a replaceable commodity in Hollywood, whereas a performer of Barbra Streisand's bankability was not. On reading Laurents's first draft, Stark had doubts about the script. "Sydney called me and said that he had bad news, that Ray was firing me. 'But you're the director,' I replied. Sydney said he could do nothing. A half hour later Ray called and said Sydney was firing me, and he, the producer, could do nothing." They brought in eleven writers in all, including well-known Hollywood scribes Dalton Trumbo, Francis Ford Coppola, Judith Rasco, Alvin Sargent, and David Rayfiel. Paddy Chayefsky and Herb Gardner, both from New York, were consulted. "They told Ray they wouldn't touch it, it was wonderful, to leave it alone," Laurents added. "But Ray and Sydney started to muck around with it. It was really painful because I cared a great deal about that story. Much of it was from my own life and was about the witch-hunt, which they knew nothing about. A lot of the rewriting was to make Redford's part bigger.

"Sydney would never let me meet Redford. It was very odd." Pollack gave Laurents a tape of a conversation they had about the script. Redford's chief concern was that the film was basically geared to the woman's role. Laurents warned Pollack, 'I know how you feel about Redford, but the story is hers. No matter what you do, you can't change that; but you can hurt it.

"They started shooting and got into trouble, and Ray called me. By then I was over the pain, but I was also over the Walter Mitty dream. It wasn't pleasurable. It was uncomfortable and, of course, I really *wasn't* over it. I still cared about it. I asked for a lot of money. I also said, 'I'll come out there and tell you what I think and if you don't like it, I'll come right back. It was an armed truce." Laurents returned to the project and received full credit.

"The person who was terrific was Barbra," he asserted. "She's like a pack rat, you know? She saves every line of every script. She kept saying, 'What about this? What about that?' She fought to keep meaningful things in the script [the political viewpoints, shadings in the relationship between the two main characters]. Redford glared at me the whole time. I thought the reason was that I was not building his part up. He behaved badly, but that goes with the territory. You can't expect decent behavior from a movie star or anyone else in the industry who stays and lives in Hollywood. They stop being human beings. They're too insecure. They're afraid. You have to make the first move. You're not saying, 'Hello,' I'm not saying, 'Hello.'"

At the story's center are two Cornell University classmates, impassioned radical Katie Morosky, a Jewish activist with the Young Communist League from New York, and a WASP jock from Virginia, Hubbell Gardiner, who is a writer — two people ill-mated but drawn to each other, Katie sexually, Hubbell not. She is attracted to the fairy-tale prince in Hubbell; he is mesmerized by her energy, moral conviction, and drive.

They marry and Katie pushes Hubbell, who has shown a natural talent for the written word, to become the best writer he can be\. They move to Hollywood when he signs a contract to adapt for the screen a novel he has written. Once in Tinseltown, he destroys his original work while turning it into a commercial movie. Katie becomes more deeply involved in left-wing politics. Disillusioned, she returns to New York with their infant daughter, divorces him, and eventually remarries a Jewish lawyer and works for liberal causes while Hubbell goes on to write for television. They meet one more time and realize that they cannot return to the past.

Close comparison could be made between the love relationship of Katie and Hubbell and Fanny and Nicky Arnstein; the man being more attractive than the woman, who is the brighter of the two.

Extremely selective in his acting roles, the bronzed, square-jawed, sky-eyed Redford was Hollywood's current top heartthrob.* When first approached by Pollack, Redford adamantly refused the part. The character, he claimed quite correctly, was a man lacking conviction or purpose. The film belongs to Katie, and Redford was concerned about it.

"He didn't like the script, he didn't like the character, he didn't like the concept of the film, he didn't think the politics and love story would mix," Sydney Pollack said. "There was nothing about it he liked and, in fact, he kept saying to me, 'Pollack, you're crazy! What are you doing this for?'" But Redford's trust of Pollack's instincts was strong. "Maybe he sees something I don't see," Redford told his wife, Lola.

"It had to be those two together [Redford and Streisand]," Pollack continued. "Barbra understood that. They were so prototypical of what the story was about."

Pollack badgered Redford for six months to play Hubbell. He agreed to revise the script to strengthen the Hubbell role so that it was as germane as Katie's to the picture. Ray Stark, realizing the marquee value of

---

*Redford had recently costarred with Paul Newman in *Butch Cassidy and the Sundance Kid* (1969) and had starred in *Downhill Racer* (1969), *Tell Them Willie Boy Is Here* (1969), and *Little Fauss and Big Halsy* (1970). He was soon to make *The Candidate* (1972) and would be nominated in 1974 for his performance in *The Sting*, in which he again costarred with Newman.

Streisand *and* Redford, offered Redford a salary that exceeded Streisand's (the first and only time a costar would receive more than she did) and a profit percentage of the film. Redford still waffled. Stark finally gave Pollack an ultimatum: if Redford did not agree by midnight June 10, 1972, he was making a deal the following day with Ryan O'Neal, actually Streisand's first choice for the role and for whom she briefly rekindled her affections. A half hour before the deadline Pollack was on the telephone with Stark to tell him that Redford had agreed to play opposite Streisand.

At the end of August, Streisand flew to New York, Jason in tow, and then drove up to the film's first location, Union College in Schenectady, New York, where they would remain for a month. By the time principal photography began on September 18, mother and son were settled in a large, comfortably furnished Victorian house near the campus. Redford and Pollack had suites at the local Holiday Inn. Although there was no friction between the stars, Redford is rather laid-back as a personality and was often unnerved by Streisand's inability to just relax and *do it*. They had opposite acting styles. She likes to talk about a scene and rehearse it several times before the cameras roll. Redford, an instinctive actor, prefers to create the scene on camera. Her relationship with O'Neal once again cold, she formed a crush on Redford. He was America the Beautiful, and she carried that inner glow with her onto the set and before the cameras. But Redford was a dedicated family man; his attitude toward her was reserved. This gave an edge to their performances that resulted in a highly charged sexual chemistry between them.

"I think with any small encouragement from Redford, Barbra would have had an affair with him in those early weeks of shooting in Schenectady," a close member of the crew said. "When we left Schenectady and set up in New York for the exteriors we shot there, she seemed edgy. Maybe it was her attraction to Redford, maybe just her concern with the progress of the picture. She is a compulsive worrier. By the time the company landed in L.A. for the West Coast and interior scenes, they [Redford and Streisand] seemed more . . . connected, I guess. Which didn't seem to alleviate Barbra's constant agitation about the rightness or wrongness of a scene that they had just played or were about to play together."

She was in awe of Redford, Laurents said. "She was simply mesmerized because she found him so beautiful, and he was ever so pleasant because he thought he was stealing the movie away from her."

That never did happen. Streisand held her ground, memorably in the early scene when Katie, naked, crawls into bed next to a drunk and almost comatose Hubbell, slowly inching near him until she is in his arms. He has sex with her as if on automatic. Then after climaxing, he falls back asleep. "It's me, Katie," she says in an agonized whisper to the snoring, inert beautiful man whom she adores. The scene has great erotic power. Here is the insecure, unglamorous girl who seduces the golden man of her dreams and then realizes he may never know he has made love to her.

Katie's character has sympathetic vulnerability: the feminine part of her nature always betraying her need to stand by her man; the masculine, to march to her own drummer. This dichotomy in the character she was playing carried over into Streisand's own attitude on the set. She was more unsure than usual, calling Pollack late at night in an apprehensive state to discuss the day's footage: Did she play a particular scene right? Should they reshoot it the next morning? The angle of a close-up was too unflattering. How could Hubbell love such an unattractive woman? At the end of the picture she gave Pollack a gold watch engraved "For all those 11 o'clock phone calls."

Pollack admired her insatiable need to understand the character she was playing. Originally intending to become an actor, he had studied with the New York theater coach Sandy Meisner and in the 1950s appeared in several plays and television dramas. His first directorial work had been on television, where in five years he directed eighty shows. Then in 1965 he directed *The Slender Thread,* a feature film starring Anne Bancroft. A traditionalist of sorts, his movies are mostly conventional in form, but not necessarily in point of view. He calls himself a romantic, and certainly *The Way We Were* reflects that temperament. His major film career took off with *They Shoot Horses, Don't They?* The picture firmly established Pollack as belonging in the front ranks of American directors, but his early acting experience (from time to time he still appears in his own films, most memorably as Dustin Hoffman's agent in *Tootsie*) gives him a special knack for eliciting great performances from his actors. Streisand felt comfortable with him and respected his opinion, although it did not stop her from harassing him.

Pollack had retained much of the political debating that went on between Katie and Hubbell in Laurents's script. Then, at the sneak preview at the Northpoint Theater in San Francisco, Ray Stark decided the audience was bored during a six-minute scene that Laurents calls "the entire motivation for Katie's leaving Hubbell," and told Pollack to cut it.

"I didn't even have the negative with me. I just made the cut with a razor blade on the positive print before previewing it the next night," he said. The second preview was more successful. "You could just feel it. The chunk that came out was never missed and the audience remained alert," Pollack insisted.

Laurents disagreed. "It was all wrong. The climax of the picture is absolutely missing. It was cut. What you see now is Streisand and Redford at the beach house [in Malibu] and she has some line about how willy-nilly circumstances make one come to a decision, in her case to get a divorce. The audience seemed to have bought it. But it had originally been preceded by a scene where Hubbell came home from the studio and said, 'The studio says they are going to fire me because I have a subversive wife.' And Katie replies, 'So if we get a divorce and you don't have a subversive wife?' She won't inform, even for him. They took it out and nobody noticed. Yes, the marriage was rocky. But they needed that scene. That's where the two stories came together. Barbra knew that," Laurents explained. "Katie could never betray her friends or her beliefs. And she would have to leave Hubbell after he made such an unconscionable request of her. They took the earlier scene out, and nobody noticed. Nobody cared."

Cast as a character modeled after extreme-right-wing gossip columnist Hedda Hopper was former child star Marcia Mae Jones (*These Three, Heidi, The Adventures of Tom Sawyer, The Little Princess*), now in her fifties and considering a comeback. When she came on the set, everyone — including Pollack — was kind to her. "It was curious," she recalled, "at first, I felt like I was home again. It was great. I was wearing this marvelous hat in the scene. Hopper was famous for her outrageous hats. She was also bitchy, dangerously so. It was a good bit, nothing more — although I received sixth billing even *after* being cut from the film. Streisand never came over to speak to me — the usual courtesy when an older performer is in a film. Nor did she ever speak to me. Very cold. The set had a chilling feeling. I had never experienced anything quite like it. I was relieved when it was over."

Sometimes the set was like that, usually not when Redford was on hand. Streisand was serious about her work and did not waste time with niceties. Redford had said, "Working with Barbra was just that — *work.*" Pollack added, "Barbra wanted precision; Redford, spontaneity. Barbra likes lengthy rehearsals and multiple takes, Redford is better in his early takes. After that, he just gets bored."

The film is filled with illogical plot devices, a confusing chronology, and blatant tear-jerking emotion. Yet, it not only works, it has a life of its own — not unlike *Casablanca,* in which the chemistry that exists between two charismatic stars sustains a familiar story. Not only does *The Way We Were* have a memorable, lushly romantic title song by Marvin Hamlisch, it is a three-handkerchief love story. Sentimental tales, such as *An Affair to Remember, Seventh Heaven,* or *A Star Is Born,* are never highly regarded by the critics, although they are the movies that often survive as classics.

The Way We Were would become one of Streisand's most memorable films. Something about it reaches out and touches you. "It flows like velvet," Rex Reed, one of a minority of critics who liked the movie, wrote. "That's why the movie is so likable. We lost a lot of innocence in the dark movie palace of our youth. *The Way We Were* reclaims it for us. Years from now, in some futuristic movie museum, it just might be one of the movies we'll be looking at and remembering with fondness." He turned out to be prophetic.

Although there was every reason for the film — "a torpedoed ship full of gaping holes" — to be a disaster, the chemistry between the two stars, so seemingly mismatched, kept it mystically afloat. "Redford's the best leading man she's ever had," Marilyn Bergman recalled, "and she knew it. Alan [Bergman, her husband and co-lyric writer] and I sat with her when she first saw the movie. She kept nudging me and saying how great *he* was."

A tremendous bonding had occurred between Streisand and the Bergmans during the work on *The Way We Were*. Thirteen years Streisand's senior, Marilyn Bergman had become the older sister she never had. Calm, intelligent, her soft voice persuasive, sure, Bergman was a woman of uncommon good sense, supremely talented, able to handle smoothly her creative partnership with her husband, motherhood (the Bergmans were the parents of a teenage daughter), political activism, and friendship with even-handed intensity. Streisand admired her talent and her opinions and felt easy in her company.

In 1968 the Bergmans had won the Oscar for their lyrics to "The Windmills of Your Mind" from the Steve McQueen–Faye Dunaway film *The Thomas Crown Affair*. They were now contracted to collaborate with Hamlisch on the title song for *The Way We Were*. Hamlisch, who scored the background music as well, had employed the melody as a love theme throughout the film, musical advice that had contributed much to the picture's mood and cohesion. The first concept of the song was written in the minor mode. Hamlisch quickly shifted it into the major. "If I'd left it in the minor mode, it might have told you too much in advance that Streisand and Redford were never going to get together," he said. "So I wrote a melody that was sad but also had a great deal of hope in it." The song was originally to be sung by Streisand over the last scene, where Hubbell and Katie run into each other in front of the Plaza Hotel in New York and realize that they have no future — only the past. Believing the lyrics would dilute the impact, it was not recorded over the scene and titles.

This songless version was shown at the first sneak preview, and when Hamlisch looked around and saw how unmoved the audience was when the lights came up, he begged Columbia to let him rescore the ending, with Streisand singing the Bergmans' lyrics. The cost of a rerecording session was prohibitive as it involved fifty-five musicians, and Columbia was now in a situation in which it was approaching insolvency — its

stock, because of failed films, high costs, and impropriety in management, had fallen two-thirds of its value since the start of principal photography on *The Way We Were*. Finally, after much discussion, Columbia
relented. Then Hamlisch had to convince Streisand, who thought the
song was too sentimental. "So is 'My Funny Valentine,'" he told her. "I
hate "My Funny Valentine," she snapped back.

Hamlisch and the Bergmans wrote a second, more complicated and
less romantic number. Streisand made tracks of both songs, which were
separately scored over the last scene and the final titles. Both versions
were shown to Stark, Pollack, and the Columbia executives, and a vote
was taken. Streisand was the only one who voted against "The Way We
Were," one of the few times that her musical judgment was wrong. The
song, with its rueful lyrics, longing to replay the past, coupled with Hamlisch's moving melody, makes a memorable, poignant ending to the film.
It is the long moment when Hubbell rushes across the street to hold
Katie, seemingly forever — oblivious to his fiancée waiting nearby —
breaking our hearts as his own is so obviously shattered. Katie's we know
has been broken long ago. And although we feel both of these two lovers
go on with their lives, it is the way they were that they — and we — will
remember.

The Way We Were placed Streisand in her own romantic time warp.
Elliott was now married to Jenny. His finances shaky, he had moved back
to the small Village apartment on Morton Street, and Jason now had a
half brother. Pierre and Margaret Trudeau were the parents of two children. Streisand was that loathsome cliché — the great star who came
home to an empty bed. She turned her concentration, as she always did,
to work. Five years had passed since her last television special, and in the
spring of 1972, CBS insisted she honor her final commitment. Ken
and Mitzie Welch, who had been responsible for her classic rendition of
"Happy Days Are Here Again," contributed the concept of the show —
"Barbra Streisand . . . and Other Musical Instruments"— and would
supply the special material and musical arrangements. The original design had been to team Streisand with some of the world's greatest musi-

cians — Pablo Casals, Isaac Stern, James Galway. CBS rejected this idea but agreed to a format that included musicians and music from various countries. The network also demanded that Streisand have either one guest from what they submitted as List A, or two from List B, or three from List C — "like a Chinese menu," Mitzie Welch quipped. Streisand and the Welches quickly agreed on Ray Charles, so there was no need to go any further.

Streisand first rehearsed some of her solos in the living room of the Carolwood Drive house. Mitzie Welch remembered "an antiques dealer who kept calling her and coming over and showing her things. Right in the middle of a phrase she would jump up and go look at things and come right back to the exact place where she had left off. It was amazing. When you work with Barbra, you work with a true artist. She has ears like nobody else has. She seems to hear sounds more acutely. Nothing slips past her.

"One day she came down to the beach [where the Welches had a home]. Jason was friends with our daughter. Barbra had a bathing suit on, and I stood and watched her as she ran across the sand. She moved in almost a poetic rhythm, not of this world, unbelievably sexual, not like other people. Her physical presence was tremendous. I said to Ken, 'She's really beautiful,' and he agreed."

They recorded and scored a few numbers in Los Angeles before going to London, where the show was to be televised. "We hired all kinds of ethnic musicians — Ghanian, Indian, Irish bagpipers, Turks, and an eleven-year-old British pianist [Dominic Savage]. It was really wild," Ken remembered. "Some of them didn't speak English, but it was wonderful how we managed to communicate. The two numbers that stand out in my memory are 'I Got Rhythm' with the Irish bagpipers — their beats are not the same. It's not 4/4 time! — and a symphony of household appliances: washing machines, sewing machines, orange juicers, vacuum cleaners, and Barbra with an electric toothbrush. Very hard. You had to dial a note and if you had it once you might never get it again. We went an inch at a time. Barbra, dressed as a Turkish belly dancer, sang 'People' with a group of Turkish musicians playing their national instruments. Ray Charles did a magnificent job of 'Look What They've Done to My Song,' and he and Barbra sang 'Cryin' Time Again' together. Larry Gelbart, Mitzie, and I wrote the continuity."

The show took eleven grueling weeks to film. Midway through, Streisand entered into an intense affair with a wealthy American, married and the father of two children, who was in Britain promoting his business interests there. They had met through one of her financial advisors. Vital, Jewish, about fifteen years older than Streisand, he had no connection with the entertainment industry. He visited the television set several times, but the press were kept from knowing his name, and their liaison was conducted in an otherwise secret fashion.

One of Streisand's English friends recalled that she was so in love that "she glowed with it. I think he was very important to her. He was a strong personality, a take-charge sort of man, extremely intelligent. He owned a chain of stores, masses of real estate, sat on the boards of several large companies — very impressive. He had a painful family situation that made divorce unconscionable — at least for him. I think Barbra admired that trait in him, although it was not easy for her to accept. She spent almost all of her free time with him while she was shooting in London, and I know they rendezvoused often when she first returned to the States. I understood her attraction. He was a charismatic personality, very, *very* sexy. But she was really in love, and that could only have been self-destructive because he had no wish to leave his family and it seemed sheer madness for Barbra to be in a relationship where she could not even be seen in public with the man she loved.

"We were quite friendly at that time, went shopping together — things like that. She was truly in love. But as the time came for both of them to leave Britain, she was — well — troubled. She was afraid that once they were back in the States where his wife and children lived and where her celebrity would be more inhibiting than abroad, it would be difficult for them to continue their affair. I felt great sympathy for her. At times, she possesses this great vulnerability. There's something — *wistful* — about her, and you think here is one of the most famous, richest women in the world and underneath there is such sadness. Through the years she has renewed this affair but nothing changed — he remains married and Barbra, her fame has never diminished."

Work was the answer to a broken heart, and what better than to be engaged in a comedy? She began filming *For Pete's Sake* shortly after her return to Los Angeles. The film, written by Stanley Shapiro and Maurice Richlin, was produced by Shapiro and Marty Erlichman for Ray Stark and Columbia and was directed by Englishman Peter Yates (*Bullitt* [1968], *Murphy's War* [1971], *The Hot Rock* [1972],* *The Friends of Eddie Coyle* [1973]). Streisand's role is that of a hard-up Brooklyn housewife who falls into the clutches of a loan shark and finds herself involved with a call-girl racket, the Mafia, and urban cattle rustling, all enacted with farcical humor: outrageous disguises, pratfalls, wisecracks, and corny, old-time comedic setups (hiding a man in a closet when a husband returns home unexpectedly). Since *What's Up, Doc?* was proving to be one of Streisand's top moneymakers, Columbia and Erlichman believed another madcap comedy was in order. However, *For Pete's Sake* turned out not to have the same winning elements of humor.

For her role as Henry (short for Henrietta), Streisand wanted a short, gamin hairdo that would also be comfortable under the many wigs she had to wear. Just before the picture went before the camera, she attended a games party at the Welches, who both loved puzzles, charades, and wordplay. "Julie Andrews, Blake Edwards, Carol Burnett, Tony Perkins — all good games players were there," Mitzie recalled. "I would have had Stephen Sondheim if he was in town! And there was Harvey Korman and his wife, Donna. Well, before the party I had had my hair done at a chic beauty salon in Beverly Hills owned and run by Jon Peters. So had Donna Korman. When Jon did my hair, he said, "I know you work with Barbra. I have to meet her. I want to know where her head's at." I laughed at that, and he said, "I mean it. Fix me up. Let me do her hair or something."

"I told him I didn't have anything to do with her personal life. So a few days later she comes to our house for the party and she sees Donna

---

*In Britain called *How to Steal a Diamond in Four Easy Lessons.*

with this very short, wonderful haircut and she said, 'Who did that?' to me. Barbra sometimes speaks in staccato sentences, not explaining a lot. I said, 'Did what?'

"'That haircut. That's what I want for *For Pete's Sake.*' Actually, it then had the awful title *July Pork Bellies.* 'I want that kind of hair.' 'Oh well, the guy that did that wants to meet you,' I told her. And I gave her his number. The next thing I know, they call us from Mexico — 'Hi. We're here together.' I said, 'I guess you liked the haircut!' She laughed. The next time I saw her, she looked marvelous, hair cropped short, very gamin — and she was head over heels in love."

23

She had never met anyone quite like Jon Peters. Forget any stereotypical ideas of a hairdresser. Peters, with his wolfish smile, sharp eyes concealed behind dark shades, and a stallion's mane of thick, black hair, looked more like a young mafioso. He drove through the imposing front gates of her Carolwood Drive house in a flashy red Ferrari. The car was well known in the high-priced hills above Sunset Boulevard. His fee for a haircut and styling ran into the hundreds, but he seldom made a house call to a first-time client. Streisand was different. She was important to him. He could have more women than he wanted. He was rich enough — worth several million dollars with his three salons and the beauty products that bore his name. What he wanted was class-A entry into the film industry. Once he had that, he planned to make important pictures. He saw his future as being a contemporary Darryl Zanuck — a moviemaker with power and pizzazz. He never doubted his ability to take the precarious jump from hair impresario to movie mogul. All he needed was the right connection.

He left the car on the curved driveway just below the front doorway of Streisand's house and slung a Gucci bag with his equipment over his shoulder. He wore tight designer jeans that left little doubt about his attributes. When she joined him in the living room twenty minutes later, he was about to leave. She apologized for being late. "Don't ever do it again." He grinned and removed his sunglasses. She noted that his dark, quick eyes took full inventory of the measurements of her body. "You know, you're a cute little thing with a very foxy body and a great ass," he said as she turned to lead him to her dressing room, where he was to cut her hair.

He was testing. She could throw him out. She did not.

Three years younger than Streisand, Peters had dropped the *h* in John the same way she had excised the middle *a* in Barbara. He was smart, quick, and charismatic. Women were drawn to him by his arrogant charm, hormonal appeal, and frank regard for sex that promised an experienced and adventurous lover. In and out of trouble in his youth, he was also streetwise and tough. "You do not want to fight this guy, period," his cousin Silvio Pensanti warns. "Shoot yourself in the leg and have the ambulance come get you, 'cause I guarantee you'll be better off. Jon's fights lasted about four seconds. Boom! Boom! Boom! The guy's down — it's over!"

Born June 2, 1945, in Burbank, California, to a Cherokee father, a short-order cook who died when Jon was ten, and an Italian mother whose family owned Pagano's, a well-known Beverly Hills beauty salon, Peters was proud of his rugged reputation. "My father . . . made me a warrior. I learned to fight, to defend myself. I was Cochise's son," he liked to brag. Sighted by a casting director who was scouting for darkhaired, dark-complected youngsters to be extras in Cecil B. DeMille's *The Ten Commandments,* he "rode a donkey into the Red Sea" in one scene. "I saw DeMille with a whip and boots and a hat," he would excitedly recount. "There must have been 5,000 extras, and there was this incredible man directing traffic. The image stayed with me."

Power energized him. He became the younger Silvio's protector in grade school and dominated the older, bigger boys in his neighborhood. "Nobody messed with Jon Peters, ever," Silvio says. "Because the harder you hit him, the madder he got. You want to take Jon on? You and what army? I'm dead serious — this man has no fear."

After his father's death, his mother remarried. Peters hated the man and ran away from home several times, fell in with a group of toughs like himself, was picked up by the police for car theft when he was eleven, and was placed on probation in his mother's care. He drove her car and nearly wrecked it, played truant from school, and refused to take any orders from his stepfather, who he claimed beat him. Unable to cope with her wayward son, who at twelve was now running wild, Helen Peters Bairo turned him into the police, her betrayal fueling his sense of outrage. He did time in a reform school for petty larceny, the youngest juvenile in his group. During the day he did roadwork — digging ditches, helping to lay pipes, clearing out fallen branches and trees — under armed supervision. At night he was shackled to his bed.

None of his youthful trials had broken his spirit; instead, they powered his drive to show the world he was someone to be reckoned with. Upon his release, his uncles gave him a job in their beauty salon, washing hair and sweeping up the cuttings. "I'd come in and see all these women," he recalled, "and I thought, 'Wow! this is it!'" A year later, in 1959, at fourteen, he borrowed $120 from his mother, dropped out of school, and made his way by Greyhound bus across the country to New York.

His macho manner and dark good looks made him appear older. With some fast talking (his special talent) he got a job in a sleazy all-night hair salon, where his specialty became dyeing the pubic hair of whores to match their poodles'. He learned quickly how important hair is to a woman, how intimate and reliant her relationship can be to a person who can make her look better than even she thought possible. He studied styling, paying for his lessons by boxing quasi-professionally, married "an older woman" of fifteen, and then began salon-climbing — from good to "in" to tony to top.

He returned to the West Coast alone (the marriage was not annulled until five years later), went to work as a stylist for Gene Shacove (the model for Warren Beatty's hairdressing lothario in *Shampoo*), and wooed a client, actress Lesley Ann Warren, who had appeared with Elliott Gould in *Drat! The Cat!* and was the lead in the Rodgers and Hammerstein 1965 television production of *Cinderella*. Slim, dark, perky, with a pleasant singing voice and manner, Warren had dreams of becoming a film star, which Peters encouraged. They were married by a rabbi (Warren was of Jewish heritage) in 1967 shortly after she was cast in a supporting role in the Disney musical *The Happiest Millionaire*, which starred

Fred MacMurray, Greer Garson, and Tommy Steele. Peters became her manager, promoter, and agent. He believed he could make her into another Judy Garland, overlooking the obvious — that her voice was not memorable — and forgetting that Garland *was* a star when she married Sid Luft, who went on to promote her later career. Warren gave birth to their son, Christopher, in 1968; her career, despite Peters's constant promoting, merely ambled along. It was clear that though she had talent and was likable, she did not have star quality.*

In 1970 the decade of the hairdresser entered in full swing. Peters became an entrepreneur. Two years earlier Peters, who by now had traveled to London and Paris, and a partner, Paul Cantor, had opened a salon on Ventura Boulevard in Encino. Influenced by London hair stylist Vidal Sassoon, Peters favored sleek bobs and geometric haircuts. A specialty was his "bad girl" look, hair cut in layers "to make you look like you'd just been romping around in bed." Decorated with pop art, the salon — where stylists, sans drab uniforms, wielded blow-dryers with the speed and grace of fencing experts — quickly became well known. He managed to raise $100,000 and opened two sleekly modern salons in upper-middle-class San Fernando Valley sections, a thirty-minute drive over the canyons from Beverly Hills. He became, in his words, "the American Vidal Sassoon, cutting, cutting, *cutting*," which he claimed "reached in me a creative side that had never been explored."

"Jon is smart, fucking smart, big-time smart," a friend elaborated. "He's a fucking genius with money. He knows just how to parlay a small investment into a gold mine, how to raise money without putting a dime up himself. He was a college-of-one, self-taught. His mind is always working, never placed on hold."

It did not take him long to see where the blow-dry action would pay the most. He opened the Jon Peters Salon on glamorous Rodeo Drive, one of the most famous high-rent streets in the world. His clientele were the young, the beautiful, the rich, the famous, the idle divorcees, and the

---

*Lesley Ann Warren made a stunning "comeback" in *Victor/Victoria* (1982) in the comedic role of James Garner's Chicago showgirl mistress, for which she was nominated for an Academy Award as best supporting actress.

neglected wives of Hollywood CEOs. *Have blow-dryer, will travel* was how he was described by many of his friends and peers. He became known in the short span of a year for his sexual prowess as much as for his chutzpah and business ability. Rumormongers barked at his heels like hungry dogs (most of them clients he had not romanced), saying he was "having it off" with many of the alluring actresses, models, and Hollywood wives he attended. With three salons, a wig factory, and two beauty-supply companies, he was, at twenty-seven (although he claimed to be two years younger), the head of a ten-million-dollar empire with three hundred employees, and estranged from a less-than-patient Lesley Ann Warren.

An old friend of Peters's claimed, "He comes out of the Hugh Hefner paradigm. Girls are sort of like, 'I can have all this, so why not?'"

Walter Yetnikoff, who was head of CBS Records, put it more crudely. "We're both equally crazy, but Jon is a better penis lapper than me — or so the reputation goes."

Streisand took to Peters right away, but she was wary. "Stop coming after me," she told him shortly after their first encounter. "You're not my type." When he asked to see her the following Sunday, she told him she was playing tennis. He had never played the game before but showed up with a racquet and, not even knowing how to score, beat her. "Then I told him I liked more distinguished men," she later recalled. "Men who smoked pipes. So he comes over wearing a velvet jacket over a T-shirt and jeans, glasses, and a pipe. He even traded in his Ferrari for a Jag. Jon never lets up." And constantly he told her how great she looked; why didn't she show her body more in the movies? He dug her body, thought she had a sexy ass, terrific legs. No one had told her that before.

Their sexual draw was powerful; her need to feel young and desirable — strong. She did, indeed, like the haircut he gave her and asked him to design the wigs she had to wear in *For Pete's Sake,* agreeing he would get screen credit.

"How about Mexican food?" he asked after making a dinner date.

"Swell. Love it," she replied.

"Be ready at five."

"I usually don't eat that early," she responded.

"You usually don't have to fly to Mexico first," he countered.

It was a bold move — very theatrical — and she accepted. They flew down in a private chartered plane to a picturesque beach resort near Acapulco. That was when she called Mitzie and Ken Welch.

With amazing swiftness their relationship moved from fling to affair to live-together lovers. Streisand was besotted. Sex played a major role, but there was more. She was ready for an affair that did not have to be hidden from the world. In the beginning she was rebelling against the restrictions of her recent relationship with a married man. After all, why should she — Barbra Streisand, independent woman and star — align herself with a man who could never be fully hers? The survivor in her fought for better and won. Peters was one of the few men who was her emotional, if not her intellectual, equal. And even though she knew that she could never dominate him, that they were certain to wage a power struggle if they became a couple, she sensed that under the bravado, the prima donna theatrics, the hustler's moves, and the streetwise patter, lay insecurity — and that was something with which she could closely identify.

"I came from off the street, from jail and all that," he once said. "I'd go into the salon and see ladies with diamonds, sophisticated people from good families. . . . I used to throw up before work every morning because I was so frightened." He'd been that way in the boxing ring, and he still fought a tough fight, winning most of his bouts. Outsiders did not see him as insecure, any more than they saw Streisand in that light. Like her, he was the ultimate survivor, armor-plating his vulnerability with brassy self-promotion.

They spent whatever free time she had during the filming of *For Pete's Sake* on his ten-acre Paradise Cove ranch in Malibu, a hybrid mixture of frontier crudeness and Bel Air chic. Expensive country fabrics covered the large custom-made couches. There was a state-of-the-art sound system and hand-rubbed pegged-wood floors. A Jacuzzi whirlpool bath was constructed from an old wine vat. There were two corrals and a large riding paddock for jumping horses. Streisand, an urban creature who had hated camp and outdoor life as a child, learned to ride Cupid, the lively horse Peters had given her as a present. Spending less and less time in her Holmby Hills home, she grew orchids in the garden he had set aside for her at the ranch, wore T-shirts and dungarees, helped to feed his pet lion (which he kept in a cage but took for walks around the ranch on a chain lead), did her own laundry, baked bread, and went on day trips to the public beach in Malibu with Jason, now seven, and Peters's son, Christopher, who was five.

"He makes me happy," she replied when asked Why Peters? by close friends who perceived him as a master con man, albeit one with certain appeal and quick intelligence. Some observers who believed they detected an undercurrent of violence in his character were fearful for Streisand. But there was no denying how much more relaxed, natural, and content she appeared. She seemed transformed by an inner shine. "Jon is a very macho man," she proudly declared. "He's got scars all over his hands from fighting." His seeming lack of fear and brazen disregard for social decorum filled her with admiration. He once carried her, propped on his shoulders, out of a party that he wished to leave, refusing to let go of his hold on her despite her laughing but insistent protest.

He accompanied her on location to New York, where *For Pete's Sake* began shooting in September 1973, taking a suite at the Plaza Hotel while she officially occupied the Central Park West penthouse. Although separated, legally he and Lesley Ann Warren were still married. Professionally, he was responsible for Streisand's wigs and hairstyles. Privately, he took charge of her appearance, choosing younger, sexier clothes for her, advising her on projects, playing new music, new sounds for her to consider recording. They conferred a great deal on and off the set, and the gossip columnists picked up on it. By the time they returned to Hollywood, their affair was an open secret and they gave a press interview at which they admitted they were in love and were to be regarded as a couple. Streisand was glowing, happy, and let him do most of the talking.

Having successfully taken over her private life, Peters moved in to pilot her professional endeavors. Unlike in her relationship with Elliott, she relied on Peters's business and creative judgment. It would not be long before he would sell out his hairdressing empire at a good price and engage his talents for hustling and promotion in the film business under Streisand's aegis. He warned her from the outset about *For Pete's Sake*'s poor potential. The story was ridiculous. In the early rushes, which he attended with her, it was obvious that there was no onscreen chemistry between Streisand and Michael Sarrazin, her leading man. She had turned down the strong leads in *Klute* and *Cabaret* that had won Academy Awards for Jane Fonda and Liza Minnelli, respectively. Clearly, Peters suggested, she needed guidance that she was not getting from Marty Erlichman, her agents Freddie Fields and Sue Mengers, or Cis Corman. The reviews when the film was released the following June proved his instinct about *For Pete's Sake* was sound.

"Streisand looks like Jerry Lewis with cleavage as she runs through the kind of silly plot that Lewis thrives on. But Lewis *is* a genuine crazy," Paul Zimmerman of *Newsweek* wrote. "Streisand, saddled with a script beneath burning, comes out an abrasive wise-mouth who cannot plead comic insanity."

With Peters at her side, Streisand had been striving to navigate her career into forward action since the previous December. He had sat in on the recording sessions for her solo "The Way We Were" single and the album with the same title,* helping her decide which tracks were best and offering suggestions that she respected and incorporated. Released in November 1973, the single reached number one on the charts by mid-February 1974 and remained in the Top Ten for five months. By March 1974, the album was also number one. The single won Streisand *Billboard*'s award as the top single of the year. The song was also given a Grammy as Song of the Year and in April earned Marvin Hamlisch an Academy Award for best film song.**

On Valentine's Day 1974 Streisand and Peters bought a rustic eight-acre property in Ramirez Canyon, a gorge in the Santa Monica Mountains that rises out of the Pacific at Malibu. "It had aluminum sliding

---

*This album was later retitled *Barbra Streisand Featuring "The Way We Were" and "All in Love Is Fair"* when Rastar Productions, producers of the Columbia film, filed suit against Columbia Records, charging breach of contract as it was in direct competition with the soundtrack album and maintaining that record buyers would be mislead into buying Streisand's solo album under false premises. The suit was settled out of court, and the album title changed.

**Hamlisch was the first individual ever to win three Oscars in one night — best song and best original score for *The Way We Were* and best score adaptation for *The Sting* (arranged from music by Scott Joplin).

doors and it was white stucco. In other words, it was really crummy," she said in describing the original house. The place did have beautiful views and seemed to offer them privacy, which was impossible at the house on Carolwood Drive, where fans peered over the gates trying to catch a glimpse of her. In a major renovation campaign to improve, enlarge, and personalize the new jointly owned property, Peters hired a professional group of toy makers from Mill Valley, near San Francisco, to work on the inside construction because of their wood-carving talents. They lived in the guest house (which would later also be restructured) as they worked, paneling the walls in old, scorched, and oiled wood, adding clear and stained lead-glass panels to many of the windows, and building beds, cupboards, and cabinets. In a short time, the house took on the appeal of Geppetto's workshop.

"The kids' rooms were all built-in, which was so great," Streisand recalled. "Both boys had ladders to climb, one to a loft, one to a bunk bed. Each room was different. My son's was in red velvet with the wood. And Christopher's was done in an Aztec print."

She was in a deeply romantic mode. At night she lit the house with dozens of candles, and she and Peters curled up on an upholstered mattress that occupied the space opposite the twelve-foot stone fireplace wall in the living room. Lush bouquets of fresh garden flowers scented all the main rooms in the house. They made love, talked endlessly, and fought fierce battles — Streisand almost always ending up in tears and apologizing the following day. Friends who witnessed these scenes were surprised to see her be the one to give in. She listened to Peters's advice, trusted his opinions on film scripts that were submitted to her, and discussed the possibility of his producing her next record and their both becoming involved in the production of her second film for First Artists. Jon Peters was now in the Barbra Streisand business.

A small theater production of *Yentl* in Brooklyn that she read about renewed her interest in the project, but no studio was yet ready to back an ethnic period picture with transvestite undertones, even with Streisand in it. She still owed one more film to Ray Stark, who sent her over a sequel to *Funny Girl,* titled *Funny Lady,* written by Jay Presson Allen, who had won an Academy Award for her adaptation of *Cabaret*. "He'll have to drag me to court before I do this," she declared, refusing at first to read the script. Finally, when she did, and Peters had as well, she agreed to appear in the film. "This is much better than *Funny Girl*," she said, reversing her decision. Unlike the earlier rejected version, Allen's screenplay depicted an independent woman valiantly struggling in a man's world, a theme with which she identified.

Principal photography would begin in the spring of 1974, just when she was settling into the remodeled house, now called the Barn. For the first time she felt resentment at having to be a hard-working mother and "wife."

Moving into the Barn with Peters and the two boys gave her a seductive taste at what really being "Sadie, Sadie, married lady" could be like. At heart she was an extremely private person, not much of a partygoer, terrified of crowds. Strangely, although it might seem that she had one of the most recognizable faces in the world, usually when she took the boys shopping or to the public beach, people did not know her. "They think I'm too small or too short, or what would I be doing on a public beach?" she said. "If I were Barbra Streisand, would I be on a public beach? So they look at me kind of funny, or they say, 'Boy, you look a lot like her.' They don't even ask me if I *am* her. And I say, 'Yeah, yeah, I've been told that before.' Sometimes I do these elaborate lies: 'No, I'm not her. What would I be doing here if I were her? I wish I had her money. Ha, ha, ha.' Sometimes it's easier to just tell the truth. 'Yes, I am her.' But it *is* a pain in the ass to have to sign things."

She had a small clique of close friends: Marilyn and Alan Bergman; Cis Corman and her husband; Marty Erlichman and his wife; Shirley MacLaine. They drove out to the Barn, and she helped cook for them with her "beloved Grace" — the housekeeper who had lived in her household since Jason was an infant and whose laughter and good nature filled her home with a sense of well-being. There was a Steinway in the large open living-room area, but she never sang when people were there; it embarrassed her. "I feel them listening so hard, I feel my power, and it frightens me," she explained. "Somehow, in a big place, when the lights are on you and it's total blackness out there, you're singing alone, it seems like it's the place to do it, to do the thing I do. But I no more could sing a song in a room with my friends than jump off a bridge."

Seaside picnics and domestic dawdling ended in April when *Funny Lady* went before the cameras. Once again, as with her first three film musicals, this was to be a big-budget movie, and as she was the star and major asset, the studio's investment would be on her shoulders. Where once marquees had glittered names such as Garbo, Hepburn, Dietrich, Hayworth, Turner, and Crawford, in 1974 Streisand stood alone. Liza Minnelli, despite her Academy Award for *Cabaret,* had not proved reliable at the box office, and Jane Fonda, with her antiwar protesting, was politically incorrect and currently off the screen.

"Blame it on Vietnam," *Funny Lady* scenarist Jay Presson Allen theorized. "Anytime there's a war, society concentrates on its masculine qualities. For the past few years female audiences have been lost because there've been no stars they could identify with in a positive way — except Streisand."

With Peters at the wheel of the car, on April 1, 1974, she drove through the gates of Columbia for the first day of production on *Funny Lady*. Budgeted at $7.5 million, the film would have a fourteen-week production schedule with locations in Atlantic City, Philadelphia, and New York. Musical rehearsals had begun several weeks earlier. Herbert Ross — who was functioning as dramatic and musical director with his wife, Nora Kaye, former prima ballerina, as his assistant — had devised a drastic budget-cutting system. Fourteen musical numbers were filmed by multiple cameras in sixteen days.* Columbia was still undergoing such financial difficulties that it was on the brink of bankruptcy; David Begelman, Streisand's former agent, and Alan Hirschfield were brought in to reorganize the company. Four years later Begelman would be forced to leave in the wake of an embezzlement scandal that rocked the industry. For now, Streisand believed in him and in the theory that having once

---

*The major songs recorded were "So Long, Honey Lamb," "Blind Date," "I Found a Million Dollar Baby in a Five and Ten Cent Store," "Clap Hands, Here Comes Charley," "Am I Blue," "How Lucky Can You Get?," and the "Crazy Quilt" sequence (the latter a series of show scenes in which the sets deconstruct as Streisand and the chorus perform).

looked after her interests, he would protect them in his new position. Time proved otherwise.

James Caan, who had shot to near-stardom with *The Godfather,* was cast opposite her as songwriter-producer-entrepreneur Billy Rose. Omar Sharif returned as Nick Arnstein. The team of John Kander and Fred Ebb, composers of *Cabaret,* wrote the new songs in the score, and Peter Matz was back onboard as both arranger and conductor.* Veteran cinematographer James Wong Howe, winner of two Academy Awards, came out of five years' retirement to photograph the picture. And Streisand's personal designer choice, Bob Mackie and Ray Aghayan, did her costumes. The story steamrolls through the years when Fanny divorces Nick; moves on to romance, marriage, and divorce to supershowman Billy Rose; and finally builds to her enormous hit as radio's "Baby Snooks."

Streisand and Stark fought constantly, mostly over her interpretation of Brice. Stark, still struggling to protect the image of his late mother-in-law, wanted her played more sympathetically. Streisand saw Brice rather as "a tough lady who hid her inner softness under a carapace of flinty wisecracks and never aimed to be lovable at the cost of her own personality." She added, "I'm not playing me anymore. I'm completely relaxed." Peters was standing nearby to smile his agreement.

She also fought with her opinionated leading man. "I'd yell at her," Caan recalled, "put her down and call her a spoiled rotten thing, and she would call me this or that and we'd carry on. . . . I remember for some reason, it was very important to Herb Ross to get a shot where we both get covered in talcum powder. Barbra [was wearing] this beautiful green-spangled dress and made up just right. She said, 'I don't think that Jimmy should hit me in the face with this powder. That powder is toxic, you know, and I'll get it in my lungs.'" Caan, sensing that a big argument was brewing, took matters in his hands. "Barbra, I think you're right," he said. "Maybe I shouldn't hit you with the thing. Maybe you'll hit me and then I'll pick it up and I'll go to hit you with it and then I won't.' She

---

*Marvin Hamlisch also contributed a couple of "thematic" musical cues linking *Funny Girl* with *Funny Lady.*

said, 'Oh, that's terrific. That'll be great!' I said, 'Now, mind you — if you blink or back off when I start to raise my hand, I'm gonna whack you with it . . . 'cause it's only the idea that you're ready to accept it that'll stop me.' She said, 'Okay. I won't blink.'

"So we set the scene up and did it. She hit me in the face with the powder. I picked it up and drew my hand back and she just stood there. She did not blink. I hit her square in the face with it. I'm telling you I went to the floor laughing, I couldn't stop, and she looked at me . . . I mean, I really felt bad. . . . She called me names. She said, 'You lied to me!'" Caan couldn't stop laughing, and finally Streisand saw the humor in it and laughed with him. "He had his fingers crossed so God shouldn't strike him dead, and then he let me have it," Streisand added good-naturedly.

Ross, of course, had worked with Streisand before but found her quite a different person than previously. "Her commitment was not one thousand percent to the film. *Funny Lady* was virtually a movie that was made without her — she simply wasn't there in terms of commitment." Her main concern was always Peters: where he was, what he thought of what she was doing. The crew was often kept waiting while she located him by telephone. There is no doubt that her relationship with Peters was more important to her than the film she was making. It was as simple as that, but she never gave less than was required of her.

Peters, watching from the sideline, felt that Streisand should "be playing hotter, sexier, younger roles." And, of course, she was making this movie (because of her old contract with Stark) for far less than she would be paid elsewhere. Streisand was torn. She had truly liked the script; she had even enjoyed being able to play in scenes with Sharif and show him how little their affair now meant to her. Her mind, however, was on Peters and a project that they had decided to do together for First Artists with Jon producing — an updated version of *A Star Is Born*. One day Peters arrived on the set of *Funny Lady* with a jewelry box containing a diamond-and-sapphire butterfly. A week later it was announced in the press that he would produce her next album, *Butterfly*.

Columbia Records balked. There was no way they were going to allow her lover, who had no music experience, to produce an album.

Streisand persisted. "Do they think I would let Jon produce a record if I wasn't absolutely sure he could do it?" she defended. "I believe in imagination. I believe in taste. These are the important ingredients, and they're all things he has." Despite Columbia's displeasure, Peters began work on the *Butterfly* album before shooting ended on *Funny Lady,* and Streisand did double time, recording for *Butterfly* the contemporary sounds he had chosen for her and performing for the cameras the old-time tunes of *Funny Lady.*

The executives from Columbia Records were unhappy from the first playback session. Peters had chosen the title *Butterfly* to reflect the many moods Streisand could affect in her music. He had wanted her to sing "God Bless the Child," the Billie Holiday standard, and a medley of "A Quiet Thing" from the Kander and Ebb score of *Flora, The Red Menace,* and a song dropped from Stephen Sondheim's *Anyone Can Whistle,* "There Won't Be Trumpets." ("Recording that medley is what first got me thinking about doing a Broadway album," Streisand later claimed.) The record company did not think the songs were contemporary enough, and they were cut — but not without a fight on Streisand's part.

Most of the songs that Peters had chosen (and she had approved) presented her in a different light. This was going to be a whole new Barbra. Gone was the romance, the nostalgia of "The Way We Were." Gone was the funny girl, the funny lady. She was into Woman — not just Woman but avant garde Woman, always liberated (well, *almost*) and with very little sense of morality and absolutely no remorse for blatant promiscuity. The songs were delivered in a gospel rock, either with a backup group or with Streisand overdubbing herself. Two selections, "Love in the Afternoon" and "Guava Jelly" (which would eventually be released as a single as well) contained fairly explicit sexual lyrics. "Love in the Afternoon" is prescient of *The Bridges of Madison County* in that the lyrics tell the story of a country woman, bedded once so memorably by a man just passing through — oral sex is implied — that she never forgets him.

The effect of "Guava Jelly" is even more startling. The lyrics concern a woman's desire to have "it" rubbed on her belly. The comparison is to guava jelly, and the metaphor pulls no punches as Streisand, over and over, more and more breathlessly, pleads, "rub it, rub it." Tom Scott, who had worked with Joni Mitchell, arranged and conducted. Columbia Records insisted on some more staple cuts. The finished album is eclectic in a way that none of her previous albums had been. Side one reflects more of what Peters and Streisand were trying to accomplish. At one point in "Jubilation" she achieves a true revival-meeting style that equals Mahalia Jackson in full gospel voice. Side two presents some of the old Barbra with "I Won't Last a Day Without You," which qualifies as one of those "doormat" songs — women who can be strong only with and through their men — that she has always professed to hate. Then, with "Let the Good Times Roll," she winds up back where she began — raunchy — no longer talking about good times but gratifying, orgasmic sex.

Before the album's release the press warned that it was going to be a disaster and that Peters was the culprit. "This is possibly the best singing I've ever done," she replied. "For the first time in my life . . . my work [referring to recording] has become fun for me, and it used to be a drag. My attitude has changed toward people. I'm less afraid. That's Jon. It kills me to have him put down more than to have me put down."

The album sleeve was a photo collage of Streisand and Peters: her looking at him worshipfully, playful shots of them touching, clowning, embracing. His dark, piercing eyes and black beard gave rise to sinister press descriptions of him as "Streisand's Svengali" and "Film Empress' Rasputin." The lovers, now turned musical partners, waited anxiously for the critics to speak. To their jubilation, the *New York Times* review was a rave. "Beyond the fashionable cracks at Peters' profession [as a hair-stylist] — and there have been many these past months — his role as record producer certainly has enhanced this album. *Butterfly* is one of Streisand's finest albums in years." Not all the critics agreed, but most thought it *was* her most daring; and Columbia was not displeased when *Butterfly* hit the charts at a lucky thirteen and remained in the top twenty for the next five months.

The final weeks of shooting on *Funny Lady* in early August were a time when everyone on the set, along with the rest of the nation, was gripped by the Watergate hearings, the impeachment articles, and Nixon's resignation on August 9. Streisand sat in her dressing room between takes watching the House Judiciary Committee solemnly and cautiously go about the business of trying to remove a president from office. "Expletive deleted" became a joke on the set as committee members kept everyone in suspense about whether they were going to indict Nixon.

Her gift to Stark when filming ended was an antique mirror upon which she had scrawled "Paid in Full" in blood-red lipstick. A few days later she sent him a plaque engraved with the words "Even though I sometimes forget to say it, thank you, Ray. Love, Barbra."

However unhappy she might have been working for Stark or displeased Peters was that she was playing an older woman out of touch with the *now* generation, *Funny Lady* is warm and funny and gorgeous. She looks sexy, sings at top form, and brings a mature freshness to the role of Fanny Brice. Her reviews were raves and the picture, a huge success; but she was less interested in *Funny Lady*'s triumph at the box office than she was with the projects she was working on with Peters. Her ambitions for him were sky-high. Instinctively, she understood his gnawing hunger for fame and riches. He talked about becoming one of Hollywood's top producers. He could see himself quite clearly as the head of a great studio. She took him seriously, believed in his visions, and became furious when members of the press referred to him in a derogatory manner as "a hairdresser." "He's not using me," she defended him to friends. "He gives much more than he takes." Her drive for his success was as strong as for her own, maybe even more at this moment — for the lady was in love and she wanted the world to know how wisely she had chosen.

24

On Christmas morning 1974 she rose at dawn and made bagels and hot chocolate in the kitchen of the Barn for Jason and Christopher when they came down to the living room to open their gifts, stacked under a towering nine-foot tree decorated with pinecones and candy canes. It was the first time she had ever celebrated the Christian holiday. The bagels were her bid for interfaith. She viewed this as a time for family. She and Peters were now on such good terms with Lesley Ann Warren that the three of them attended Gestalt therapy sessions together in which the analyst encouraged them to release their emotions and to recognize them in response to one another. To those close to her, Streisand appeared less tense, more open. She laughed more easily, luxuriating in her maternal role and domestic responsibilities.

The boys became friends, collaborating on monster movies with an 8mm camera that was a present to Jason from Elliott. Streisand was supremely happy. She oversaw the selection of every flowering bush, tree, and stone for the path that led to the stable, which was being converted into a multilevel villa eventually to contain guest quarters, a gym, and a projection room. With time to indulge her passion for collecting, the Barn was quickly filling up with newly found pieces. As a couple — Peters with his platform saddle shoes and hip-hugging corduroys worn without underwear, Streisand in tight jeans tucked into high boots, her hair bleached blond and worn straight and loose — they looked cool, sexy, *with it.*

He made her feel young; she made him a movie producer. He had gone from no status as "a kid with dirty underwear going to beauty school" to millionaire emperor of hair to the producer of Barbra Streisand's next movie, a five-million dollar musical, the fourth version of *A Star Is Born.** And in January 1975, with *Butterfly* still on the charts, Streisand and Peters were trying to convince Warner Brothers, which was putting up the money for First Artists, to hand him the directorial reins of the movie as well. In a very short time he would become Streisand's manager, receiving 15 percent of her earned income and replacing Marty Erlichman.

The original concept of what would eventually be called *A Star Is Born* as conceived by husband-and-wife novelists John Gregory Dunne (Dominic Dunne's brother) and Joan Didion in the fall of 1973 had only a fleeting connection with the earlier versions made under that title. A love story about two rock singers, one on the way up, one on the way down, the background is the contemporary, rat-pack world of groupies, rock concerts and tours, drugs and psychedelic flip-outs — far from the artificial, unhip glory of Hollywood in its golden years. Still, the up-and-down professional careers of the two lead characters bore enough similarity to the much-reprised Warners' classic that Dunne and Didion went to their ex-agent, Dick Shepherd, now head of Warner Brothers, to see whether they could do it under the studio's aegis. (Warners owned the rights to all three previous versions.) Shepherd liked the idea and agreed to their writing a contemporary rock version of the film. Dunne and Didion were not aficionados of the *A Star Is Born* movies, but they were

---

*The original story upon which all four versions of *A Star Is Born* are based was written by Adela Rogers St. Johns. *What Price Hollywood?* (1932), directed by George Cukor, stars Lowell Sherman as an alcoholic movie director who helps waitress Constance Bennett achieve film stardom while he sinks into drunken ruin. *A Star Is Born* (1937), directed by William Wellman, has Fredric March as an alcoholic actor and Janet Gaynor as the movie hopeful he grooms into stardom as he self-destructs. *A Star Is Born* (1954), with George Cukor back at the helm, presents Judy Garland and James Mason in a musical version of the same story.

avid rock enthusiasts and had just returned from traveling around with the rock groups Jethro Tull and Uriah Heep. They were also highly respected literary authors of the contemporary scene. By the following spring a script was completed and submitted to director Peter Bogdanovich for consideration. Bogdanovich thought it was awful.

The script passed next to actor-director Mark Rydell, who loved the screenplay, which he called "a savage look at the rock world." Refusing to pay Rydell anything near the price he was asking for his services, Warners instead agreed to let him develop the project without payment and gave him three months to work with Didion and Dunne on the script, line up two stars, "and get some of those spectacular concert scenes off the drawing board." If he succeeded, Warners would then sign a lucrative contract for him to direct the film. At the end of this time the heavy-handed screenplay — glaringly raw-boned and with two characters who were not sympathetic — was in deep trouble. Liza Minnelli, Elvis Presley, Carly Simon, James Taylor, Cher, and Diana Ross all turned down one or the other of the two leading roles. Rydell went to Kris Kristofferson, a top country-and-western star who had become an increasingly popular film personality after playing Billy in *Pat Garrett and Billy the Kid* and the romantic star of *The Sailor Who Fell from Grace with the Sea,* a sleeper movie that became a cult film. Kristofferson possessed a commanding presence — tall, lean, crusty, wary-eyed: a macho man who could become surprisingly tender and vulnerable. He liked the script and committed himself to the project; but without a female star, Warners would not bank it. When Rydell's three-month free period elapsed, Warners took him off the project and handed it to director Jerry Schatzberg. In June 1974 Sue Mengers received the script as a submission for Streisand. First Peters read it.

"*I* discovered this project," he later insisted. "*I* was the one who found it for Barbra, and convinced her to do it." He neglected to add that he let her know how much he wanted to produce it. Later he was to say, "The character in *my* movie is a guy who's fighting all the time and hitting all the time. And he can't relate. It's the macho guy, which is very much like me."

He saw the story from a personal angle and offered changes before

Warners, Schatzberg, Dunne, or Didion even realized he was to be involved if Streisand accepted the female role. "Two people fall in love," he explained. "She becomes a super-superstar by realizing what the most important thing to both of them is: communicating. Wanting to have children. Not the thousands of agents and press agents and all that stuff that controls their life. He's a guy who spent the first thirty years of his life fighting — very aggressive — and then met this woman and fell very much in love and realized that this was his chance to live. But he accidentally dies. For us [he and Streisand] the understanding of it — through film — was a very heavy thing. Do you know what I mean? That's why the script had to be perfect. Because it has to be right for us."

The press treated Peters's bid through Streisand to produce as a joke. She was devastated by their jibes and sarcasm — "Hair today and gone tomorrow!"

"Anyone who wonders how a first-time producer can make a $5-million film with the top female star in the country just has to take a look at the way I produced Barbra's album. Or how I run my beauty salons. I employ 300 people. I'm a businessman, man, that's all," Peters defended.

As a First Artists film,* Streisand had creative control. She was unhappy at this point with Kristofferson, with whom she had once had a brief affair ("one of her flings," as she called them). It had been after her divorce and the end of her romance with Trudeau. After a few dates, Kristofferson had essentially dropped her. She was too demanding, too needy, for where he was at that time in his life. Except for her respect for his musicianship Streisand had not given him much thought since then, but when she was told he had been cast as the declining rock star in the film, she agreed he was a good choice. No innuendo was meant. Kristofferson was at the height of his popularity.

In the one truly farcical time before Kristofferson signed on, Streisand called Schatzberg and suggested that Peters play opposite her. The director dismissed it as a gag but quickly found out she was serious. "Can you

---

*Warners would now get the distribution rights, reimbursing First Artists for two-thirds of the film's negative cost upon delivery of a finished film. Streisand would receive 25 percent of the gross returns.

sing?" Schatzberg asked Peters sensibly. After all, the male lead as written was a famous rock singer. "No," Peters told him, "but you can shoot around me and dub." Schatzberg refused to cast him. Dunne and Didion were off the script after finalizing a deal that gave them 10 percent of the film, and Jonathan Axelrod, a bright, young scenarist was rewriting. By this time Dick Shepherd had been replaced at Warners by John Calley.

"I'd never met Peters before," Calley recalled. "He came in and said that in his and Barbra's view, the screenplay was moving away from being suitable for Barbra. I agreed with them. Forget about whether the screenplay was good or not, the issue was 'Is it right for Barbra?' Peters said, in effect, 'It's very simple, either we get to take over the screenplay and make it work for Barbra or we take a walk. It's entirely up to you. Do whatever you like.'" Calley had no alternative. Warners did not want to lose a Streisand musical. Axelrod became a casualty, and Schatzberg soon followed.

Peters, flying in the face of his detractors, was determined to direct. "Why not?" he shouted at one reporter who ignited his temper. "Directing is a thing I've done my whole life! It's getting people to do what I want them to do!" He was showing the press around his Malibu ranch, kicking rocks out of his path with the steel toe of his expensive boots. "When I started this place, it was all dirt. Look at it now," he said with a sweep of his hand that indicated his vast domain.

The week before Christmas 1974, Peters gave a party for the employees of his hairdressing empire to tell them that Jon Peters, Inc., would soon be in other hands. His interest was now fully focused on the movie he was about to produce. He walked out of his offices without a second glance. That part of his life was over. For the next month he and Streisand spent their evenings in front of the fireplace at the Barn tearing the script apart. "We're going to make this a love story," he told Marie Brenner of *New Times*. "They're the most beautiful people and the love they have for each other is the same feeling as Barbra and I have for each other. . . . We're going to make it much closer to the 1936 version, the one with Janet Gaynor. That was magic. That's what we want to achieve."

Streisand agreed. They were a team, but it appeared that Peters had taken the lead. "She was ecstatic, really," one friend said. "Very proud of him, strongly believing in his ability, gaining a new kind of strength, more womanly, through his." Brenner was prescient in observing that "what Jon Peters appreciates very well is that he is living with a large entertainment corporation and that the merger looks permanent . . . [but] that kind of power is rarely benign. It is not enough for Jon Peters to mastermind the career of his private conglomerate. He is not satisfied with a minor role as Barbra's shield, giving her the privacy she says she now wants. Yes, he sees himself as the take-charge guy in her business life . . . but even more, he sees himself as the lead in their larger-than-life real-life movie. He believes he is on the way up, all the way up. The only question now is the quality of the ascent."

Streisand, Newman, Poitier, and McQueen had come into First Artists giving the impression to outsiders and the press that they were all big buddies and were going to work together and do these great projects. This was not the reality. Streisand harbored resentment that her partners would be participating in the profits from her film. "That became sort of the attitude," recalled Ed Holly, who had joined the company as senior vice-president in charge of finance and would in two years become president. "When Barbra and Jon were preparing the picture, the company was at the poorhouse steps. All the partners were behind in their pictures.* Barbra had delivered only one, *Up the Sandbox,* which was not a commercial movie, but it showed the kind of thing she wanted to do. It expressed a new spirit, a new thinking. Warners literally forced her not to drag her feet on *A Star Is Born,* as they were at the courthouse steps

---

*The way the company was organized, each of the First Artists founders agreed to make three films for the company. In 1971 Steve McQueen had joined the company. A year later Dustin Hoffman agreed to produce films independently through First Artists but never exercised his option to buy stock and had been feuding with them from that time (although he was later to make *Agatha* and *Straight Time* under their aegis). Paul Newman produced and starred in *The Life and Times of Judge Roy Bean, Pocket Money,* and *The Drowning Pool,* which were not successful at the box office. Sidney Poitier made low-key and limited-interest ghetto movies with all-black casts (First Artists had expected him to replicate highly commercial movies like *In the Heat of the Night*). Streisand's *Up the Sandbox* had lost money. First Artists' only successful film for the company at this time was Steve McQueen's *The Getaway.*

[with First Artists]. They agreed to an expanded budget of six million dollars. It created problems. This was a higher budget than the other partners could expect and would also lower profits or raise losses, whichever was the case. The stars just could not be in bed together. The egos were too big. Even those nice, easy-to-deal-with people — Sidney and Paul — could not work with Barbra.

"Jon came on the board of directors of First Artists. From a business standpoint, the execs of the company did not deal directly with the stars. We dealt with whomever they put on the board, and in Barbra's case it was Jon. We had some pretty hard fights along the way. Jon could only see things from Barbra's standpoint, so we were in conflict in that what might be best for Barbra might not necessarily be best for the company and the stockholders. So immediately, we had a fight on our hands. He was a tough fighter, a hard negotiator, and not always fair. But that's Jon. Barbra used him as a buffer and a go-between. She did not like to deal with people except on a creative basis."

The script remained a difficult problem, and Streisand called Arthur Laurents and asked for his help. She had four different versions and sent them to him. "After I read them," he recalled, "I told her she should play the other part [the role of the star on the way down], which was much more interesting, and that only one of the scripts was really good. 'Which?' she wanted to know. 'The one written by Joan Didion and John Dunne.' And I added, 'But you're not going to do that one.' And she asked, 'Why not?,' and I said, 'Because it's tough.' Barbra wanted what I guess all insecure women want — to be romantic princesses."

By the summer of 1975, with Streisand and Peters still working on the screenplay, Warners issued an ultimatum: *A Star Is Born* would have to go before the cameras by January 2, 1976. They had at this point (because of conflicting commitments) lost Kristofferson, and Warners had refused to go along with Peters's replacing him. "What about Brando?" Streisand proposed during one meeting. "I always wanted to play with Brando. Why does it have to be a musical?"

Peters leaped up from his chair, exclaiming that they had recently talked to Brando at the studio. "The son of a bitch, he wanted to fuck

Barbra! I was ready to kill him! I take him off, and I kiss him! He's beautiful! I love him, the bastard! They'd make a great pair. Imagine. Streisand and Brando!"

Eventually, Kristofferson — upon winning a co—above-the-title credit shared with Streisand — came back on the project. What was now needed was a deft writer who could take the forty pounds of script and revisions and turn it into a workable screenplay with a believable, strong role for Streisand. "It would be nice if the picture was good," one Warners executive said when Frank Pierson was asked to work on yet another revision, "but the bottom line is to get her to the studio. Shoot her singing six numbers, and we'll make sixty million dollars."*

Pierson had written the screenplays for *Cat Ballou* (1965), *The Anderson Tapes* (1972), and *Dog Day Afternoon* (1975) and directed one film, John le Carré's *The Looking Glass War* (1969). He was keen on directing and played his cards carefully. He presented Streisand and Peters with a fresh approach to the story that they both liked. But he did not wish to rewrite the script unless he was also hired as director. Peters nodded his agreement. He had decided he would not direct after all, he told Pierson. "Why?" Pierson asked.

"How could I direct Barbra and keep our relationship? I had to decide which was more important, our love or the movie." One sensed this had been an issue that they had chewed over for a long time. Streisand had, in fact, grown fearful that if Peters were to direct, the stress would be too much for her. What if they fought bitterly? "You and Barbra make the picture," he told Pierson. "I'm here [as producer] to expedite. You need somethin', I'll kick ass to get it."

Pierson, a benevolent-looking bespectacled man, prematurely gray (he was thirty-eight), his broad chin hidden by a neatly clipped beard, planned to keep the basic story line: the man going steadily downhill and self-destructing as the woman keeps ascending. The real change that he

---

*No less than thirteen writers, including Streisand and Peters, had worked on the screenplay leading up to Pierson's involvement. They were Joan Didion, John Dunne, Jonathan Axelrod, Bob and Laura Dillon, Jay Presson Allen, Buck Henry, Arthur Laurents, Renée Taylor, Joseph Bologna, and Alvin Sargent.

envisioned was in the relationship between the lead characters. In earlier film versions of *A Star Is Born* and in the Dunne-Didion progenitor, her success and his failure were seen in terms of a competition that he lost, because she won. Pierson dropped that approach on the basis that in the seventies, working women contributed a large share of the family income and husbands no longer found this humiliating. In Pierson's screenplay the tragedy is that the woman's deep love was not enough to keep alive an artist whose career — which was the measure of his manhood — comes crashing down around him.

Next came the issue of the ending. "I hate him if he kills himself and leaves her all alone, this little girl," Peters told Pierson, who reminded him that Garbo threw herself under a railroad car in *Anna Karenina,* Ronald Colman had his head lopped off in *A Tale of Two Cities,* and Ali MacGraw died of a sudden illness in *Love Story* — all phenomenally successful pictures. Nonetheless, Pierson compromised, revising the script to have the man die in an auto accident — although, as he is drinking beer while driving 140 miles an hour in blinding sunlight, his death still evokes suicide.

Weekly conferences were held with Pierson, as Streisand and Peters contributed to the creation of the characters. More and more Pierson realized how autobiographical the fictional lovers were becoming. "People are curious," Streisand told him, "they want to know about us. But I don't want you to use too much. I don't know if I should tell you this or not, because someday they'll want to do my life story, and I don't want to use it up." She then shared some of her Brooklyn childhood memories with him, along with stories of the passion and growing violence in her relationship with Peters. She was confident that no two people had ever loved as ardently as they had. Theirs was a historic affair. They were each contributing a greatness to the other's development. There had been no other show business couple to compare them with. Maybe Elizabeth Taylor and Mike Todd, if he had lived. They were unique, and their experiences were profound.

Peters was anxious to incorporate details of their life together, "how we make love, fight and love again. A fight can be an intimate thing between two lovers, can really strip them naked, lead to an ultimate sexual experience. Hate and love are the two most passionate emotions we feel. Put them together and — *wham!*" The scene where the rock star, now named John Norman Howard, and Esther Hoffman meet ended with the line "You've got a great ass," one of the first things Peters said to Streisand. And Esther snaps at the press who dog her trail, "When is it ever enough, goddamn it!" — words she shouted at reporters who would not leave them alone.

"It's not our life," Streisand interjected. "You don't want to make it too real." However, a love scene in a bathtub encircled with burning candles, the only light in the room, was taken from their personal experience, as was the romp in the open field on the fictional antihero's ranchland. And when it came time to create the sets, Streisand had the fictitious Esther's apartment decorated as though it were hers, bringing carloads of furniture, fabrics, and other things from her attic and cellar storerooms (many from the walk-up over the fish restaurant that she and Elliott had once shared) to make the set feel as though it were once someplace where she had lived.

While Pierson was working on the script, Streisand was supervising the Barn's transformation from its rustic past into an *Architectural Digest* vision of country life. The mattress that doubled as the living-room couch was now covered in fur and antique Victorian pillows, the bathtub in the master bedroom was rebuilt from natural stones cemented together. The house was all earth tones, and the wood artfully aged. Every wall, nook, and cranny was overflowing with objects — art deco statuary, collections of startling variety, antique throws and shawls, Tiffany lamps, mammoth tropical plants, objets d'art of every description and "in such profusion only an impression of magnificence is generated. . . . It is like a magical attic, in which every trunk and old discarded hat rack or moose head has a sentimental history, printed on a card." Hats and boas were draped on hangers for display on the backs of doors. Period shoes with marquisette buckles and satin bows were lined up on open shelves.

Outside you could hardly walk without tripping over construction material, as a natural rock swimming pool (a larger version of the bathtub) was in the throes of work; a double tennis court was underway;

and two houses on abutting property, which they had just bought as additional guest houses, were being rebuilt and redecorated — one in art deco style, the other in art nouveau — for her to furnish and decorate as authentically as possible. Streisand was relishing her time away from the cameras *potchkeeing,* as she called it. Peters had gained ten pounds and strutted around "like Nixon eyeing improvements at San Clemente." With revisions still being made on the script of *A Star Is Born,* he joined forces with Marty Erlichman to produce a film for Barwood, Streisand's company, based on the life of Bruce Lee, the diminutive Chinese-American martial arts expert who had died a sudden and mysterious death two years earlier.

Streisand was learning to play the guitar for a scene in the film and "drove everybody crazy playing it morning, noon, and night." She also wanted to write a song and plucked away on the melody, trying to get the right chords. She cried in the bathroom after a guitar lesson because her teacher wrote songs and she thought she could not. Peters followed her into the john. "You can do it," he insisted, "you can do anything you set your mind to. *Try* to write a song! Go on, try!" One day when Paul Williams, who with Kenny Ascher (also the musical conductor) had been signed up to write the score for the film,* drove up to the Barn for a conference, Streisand played the melody she had been working on. Williams was knocked over. It was "wonderful" he said. "She was like a little girl . . . kind of shy. She had been taking guitar lessons, and she was watching her fingers to make sure that she got the chords right."

Williams jubilantly told her that she had composed the love theme and promised to have words for the song shortly. To her irritation, these were the last lyrics he wrote before they went into the prerecording sessions, but she felt newly confident when she played and sang the song, now titled "Evergreen," for Marty Erlichman (not yet aware that Peters

---

*In the end Paul Williams wrote the lyrics for "Evergreen" (music by Streisand); "With One More Look at You/Watch Closely Now," and "Spanish Eyes" (music by Kenny Ascher); and "Everything" (music by Rupert Holmes). Additional songs were "Queen Bee" (words and music by Rupert Holmes), "Crippled Crow" (words and music by Donna Weiss), "I Believe in Love" (words by Alan and Marilyn Bergman), and "Lost Inside of You" (words and music by Barbra Streisand and Leon Russell).

would soon usurp his position as Streisand's manager), who was certain it would be a big hit — as big as "The Way We Were."

Despite Streisand's optimism, all did not go well on the scoring stage the day they recorded "Evergreen." Ed Holly recalled that when Phil Feldman, who preceded him as president of First Artists, "a strong, hard-hitting man whose main function at the time was as a troubleshooter," got word midmorning that the conductor was quitting, they both hurried down there. "Barbra was yelling and screaming — really out of control — but she couldn't define anything. We decided to send everyone out for a long lunch break. An hour later she returned and spoke to Howard Klein, the vice-president in charge of production. 'By three o'clock when I return to the scoring stage, I want this many violins [more],' she ordered. She had figured out in her head during lunch what was wrong. So, immediately the call went out to get the additional musicians that she wanted. At three o'clock she was back — highly energized — additional musicians onboard, and within an hour they were recording. The difference from the morning session was dramatic. She had whipped the musicians into a frenzy, and the final effect had been good. The orchestra had not been full. She is such a perfectionist. She can't stand things not coming out exactly right and not being terribly articulate, it frustrates her. She hears things that no one else hears, has terrible fights with everyone she works with. She doesn't seem able to discuss and reason. She is a yeller — and it grates on people with whom she is working. 'Perfect' usually means doing things *her* way."

After legally extending the start date by one month, *A Star Is Born* went before the cameras on February 2, 1976, still budgeted at $6 million. After the preproduction recording chaos on "Evergreen," Peters insisted that the music in the film be recorded live and had Streisand sing "Queen Bee" live in a local club that had been redecorated to look like an Arizona bar. "We screened it at Warner Brothers and the thing worked," said Phil Ramone, the music producer. "And most of the people who were skeptics were astounded that Barbra really came off the way one would want her to, free to sing and react to the people, and not having to lip-sync."

Peters was getting his feet wet in the picture business and loving every bit of it. "He was just like a feisty sponge," Holly said. "He could absorb anything that was going on and was a quick study, but his attention span for anything other than the picture was zilch. None of us knew how to handle him other than to just accept the fact that he and Barbra were a couple and that he was there and if you accepted Barbra, you had to accept Jon; and we formed ways of working with him. He was sort of adopted by Howard Klein, who really taught him what picture-making is all about. Jon's ambition exceeded even Barbra's. He uses people and burns them out."

"I know I'm not an easy person to work with," Peters admitted. "I know what I want and I'm going to get it. I was terrified, but I couldn't show them that, could I? I had to get things done. I was the producer . . . so I walked through people. I had to."

Seldom did a day go by without reports appearing in the press on their affair and the problems on *A Star Is Born*. The Streisand-Peters merger was the Jackie Kennedy–Aristotle Onassis love story of that time — everyone seemed tuned in, espousing opinions, predicting the outcome (mostly negative, that the affair would end with shooting on *A Star Is Born*). The media, fans, and the just plain curious had made their way up the narrow mountain road, overhung with great oaks and eucalyptus, to the gates that led to the front gardens of the Barn. Streisand and Peters hired private guards and bought two attack dogs.

The scenes with fans and press in the picture took on a greater sense of reality, imitating her own experiences as flashbulbs exploded in her face when she drove out of her own driveway, the way people grabbed at her, tore at her clothes, tugged at her hair as she tried to go into a restaurant or attend a public affair. All of them wanted a piece of her, believed they were entitled to it, and grew angry if she yelled obscenities at them. Her affair with Peters had tossed her into an arena of pit bulls. She could no longer go to the beach with the boys and count on not being recognized, even though she now employed wigs and disguises — big glasses, Garbo hats that shaded her face. She was the *now* woman, newly found by the young twentysomethings. She hated it all and when she was not at the studio, she remained cloistered behind the gates at the Barn with her gun-toting guards and attack animals.

Frank Pierson was finding his task as director fraught with danger. He was a man caught in the middle between the producers of the film and the studio whose money he was overspending.

"I don't feel you want to love me," Streisand told him one day when shooting was not going well. "All my directors have wanted to make me beautiful. But I feel you hold something back; there's something you don't tell me. You never talk to me." Pierson apologized, adding that he was just not the demonstrative type.

"You fight like hell with Jon, you fight like hell with everyone you lean on," he told her.

"I know," she answered. "But Jon is so strong! I never had a father; I was always in charge of myself. I came and went as I pleased. I can't stand for someone to tell me what to do." Then, her voice grew strident with sudden venom. "Ray Stark always used to bully me, the son of a bitch. You'll pay for every lousy thing Ray Stark ever did to me!"

One of the most important locations in the film — the retreat in the desert that John Norman Howard, the fictional rock star, builds — became a bitter struggle between the director and his star. Streisand did not want to spend so much time in such bleak, unfriendly open spaces. She had convinced Peters that they should use the Barn as a location: the rock star's fatal accident could occur on the Pacific Coast Highway. Finally, she gave in, and an area near Tucson, Arizona, was chosen. As they waited to move the crew and cast there, Peters flew with her to New York to watch a Muhammad Ali fight on closed-circuit TV in Madison Square Garden. As they came down the aisle of the packed arena to take their front-row seats, a man broke through their protective entourage and reached out to grab Streisand by the arm. Peters took a swing and connected.

This was the reality of her life, the cost of fame. She was viewed by some as a public possession to be grabbed at and touched at will, an invasion of her privacy that infuriated and disgusted her. Why *her?* Other celebrities were not subject to such bruising attention. Top singers were almost always singled out — Garland, Sinatra, the Beatles. Music made a connection, incited people where straight drama did not. The incident with the overenthusiastic fan brought the role of Esther Hoffman into closer focus.

"Pow! I let him have it!" Peters told Pierson on their return. "He made a motion like he's gonna touch, maybe he's gonna hit, Barbra: He's gonna hit my woman! I go crazy! Bam! Pow! They're pullin' me off him. The cops come take him away. You can't go anywhere with her! That's the meaning of 'star'! We gotta get that in the picture!"

Peters had a streak of inner violence that not only could be used to protect her but could also be turned against her. Ugly fights between Paul Williams and Peters, where the two men came close to blows, caused Williams to walk out on a live recording session. Tensions did not ease as the picture got underway. Pierson reported a fierce fight between Streisand and Peters over a scene she had just played to his disapproval. When Pierson went for his car, Barbra darted out of the hedges where he was parked, "For God's sake, take me home!" he claimed she cried, jumping inside and huddling in a dark corner of the vehicle. "He gets so furious. I don't know what to do!" She sat huddled and silent as they drove out to Malibu. When they arrived at the Barn, Peters was already there, lights illuminating the entire property. He stood hulking in the doorway as she got out of the car. There were an awkward few minutes in which neither moved toward the other. Then Peters went inside and Streisand followed. Pierson remained parked there for a short time. Hearing nothing, he left.

The two stars worked in different ways. Kristofferson had a more direct approach to acting. To play drunk, he *got* drunk. When he was to be high in a scene, he got stoned. She hated that. He was also slower than she was in getting a scene down and required more time to rehearse. However, one time, when the script called for them both to cry, Kristofferson was able to do so, while Streisand needed menthol blown in her eyes to cause them to tear.

"Jesus, Barbra," Kristofferson apologized, "I wish I could do something to help you. It's my fault, I'm not giving you what you need."

Streisand fumed as she walked away and drew Pierson to one side. "Did you hear what he said — the *ego?* He thinks what he does controls what I do!" she sneered.

Kristofferson, realizing he was in an undeclared sparring match with

Streisand, tried to duck the wild blows. (He later was to say that making the film was "an experience worse than boot camp!") A man of great personal strength and sex appeal, there was about him the legendary aura of the lonely, wandering American, rootless, searching. He had that hungry, sensitive look that had made Gary Cooper a star; and his music and lyrics had the particularity and intellect that had brought Bob Dylan to the front. The son of an army general, he was born in Brownsville, Texas, a border town where Mexican-American feelings were rife. It was a tough background and he wanted to be able to write about the injustices he had witnessed. He majored in creative writing at Pomona College, then went to Oxford as a Rhodes scholar. To please his father, he joined the army, went through officer's training, served in Germany, and ended up as a major teaching English at West Point. All the while, he wrote songs and sang them to his own guitar accompaniment, bursting onto the music scene in the late sixties to become a top country-and-western concert and recording star — singing his own message-filled lyrics, which he also did in several early films.

The enigma of *A Star Is Born* is that Kristofferson was playing a singer-composer, which he was, and yet someone else wrote his music. This became a grating matter, one with which he was at odds with Peters. There was also concern that his performance as a music star on his way down might seem too realistic to the public, a fear that was not without substance.

The bathtub love scene between Kristofferson and Streisand became another cause of dispute. Kristofferson came on the set nude under his bathrobe. Peters insisted he wear flesh-colored shorts. "What the hell are they afraid of?" Kristofferson shouted, but he acquiesced. When they rehearsed the intimate scene, the doors to the rehearsal room were kept open, on Peters's orders, so that Kristofferson would not be alone with Streisand. Peters ran around the set screaming obscenities, yelling that the "fucking bastard is going to pee all over Barbra!" Pierson tried to calm him down as Streisand kept shouting, "It's okay! It's okay!" Finally, the scene was shot and Peters dashed over to the tub and helped Barbra out.

All their differences grew into news events reported in *Time, People,* and the tabloid press. A massive live concert with 55,000 people was a major scene in the movie. It was shot at Sun Devil Stadium in Tempe, Arizona, and even though the concert was being used for the company's purpose, the audience had to purchase tickets at $3.50 apiece. The crowd waited for over two hours in blazing ninety-degree heat as the cameras and stars got ready. Shouts and jeers became insistent; Streisand, in the outfit she wears in the filmed sequence, a crocheted hat and coat over some tight pants, took over the microphone, working to calm the audience, amazingly getting them to laugh, telling them what was going to happen when the cameras began to roll, singing a song from the movie to appease them as the technicians worked madly behind the cameras preparing for the shot.

"Look at her directing the crowd!" Peters told *Village Voice* reporter Arthur Bell as they stood on the sidelines. "Seventy thousand people [somewhat of an exaggeration], they'd do anything she'd say. It's like Brooklyn, you know what I mean? She's got balls. She's telling that crowd what she wants. I give to you, you give to me. See her working that crowd? See that?"

"If this film goes down the drain," Streisand told Pierson later when they watched the rushes, which she felt had missed what she wanted captured, "it's all over for Jon and me. We'll never work again."

Her love for him was obvious to all. The big question was whether they would get married when the film was completed. "Perhaps," she told one interviewer. "I hope so — but marriage is not the most vital issue in our lives right now. He talks about it. I talk about it, but not at the same time. I'm all for women's liberation: do it because you feel it. All women should call their own shots, not in a militant manner but with the conviction that they've got a helluva lot to offer other than looking pretty and passive."

Nonetheless, looking sexy for Peters was one of her high priorities. Onscreen and privately, she had never dressed more provocatively, tight pants caressing her well-rounded buttocks, clinging fabrics and deep cleavage revealing her shapeliness. And for the first time in her life someone else's success meant as much to her as her own. Their fights and vehement disagreements contributed to the power of their mutual attraction. Streisand firmly believed Peters's promise to make her the greatest star in the world.

But Peters also kept his keen, brown eyes set on his own future and a time when his star might eventually outshine hers. His hunger for power in the industry was insatiable, equal to Streisand's. Maybe, after all, he was the one, the *poifect* match she had sought for years to find, the man to be the masculine to her feminine.

25

Streisand was at Frank Pierson's shoulder every inch of the way. No decision was made without her. She made sure of that. There was hell to pay if she was not consulted. She was executive producer and Peters, the producer, a step below. They could not be ignored. No matter what she, as an actress, contributed to her films, the end result was a reflection of the directors, their vision, and the ability to see it through. That is where the ultimate control is, for film is a director's medium. That was what she wanted — to direct her own films. She could taste the power, the ability to fulfill her personal visions, the scenes she saw so clearly in her head. But studios were resistant to give women the opportunity to direct, another example of Hollywood's "boys' club" mentality, and she was going to need ammunition.

"You lay it out and it's shit," she told Pierson as they were setting up a scene toward the last week of production on *A Star Is Born.*

He led her away from members of the crew with whom they had been working. "You're rude," he told her. "There's no reason to talk that way to me, so don't do it anymore. You're in a rage. What's that about?"

"Because I should have codirector credit," she replied. "I've directed at least half of this movie. I think I should have the credit for it, don't you?"

"Well, I'll tell you," Pierson answered, after fielding his surprise, "I've contributed a lot to your performance. So, it's a deal. I'll split my director's credit with you and you can share costarring credit with me."

She stared at him with cold appraisal.

"Why didn't you fight to direct it from the start?" he asked.

"I wanted someone to be a buffer between Jon and me." Her ice blue eyes scrutinized his face for a reaction. "What about the credit?" she persisted. "I don't think I can insist on it. People criticize me enough as it is; they're always waiting to attack. I think it's something you have to give of your own free will."

It was mid-April. That week Pierson won the Oscar for his screenplay of *Dog Day Afternoon*. Neither Streisand nor Peters congratulated him. About midnight Peters came to his hotel room. "You don't listen," he shouted at Pierson and went over a long list of things he (and presumably Streisand) saw as infractions. Pierson went into the bathroom to urinate. Peters kept yelling at him. Pierson suspected that Peters wanted him to resign, but he never came to the point. Suddenly, he blurted out, "I'm not afraid of your Oscar!" and departed.

Their battle with Pierson continued straight through to the end of production. As soon as Streisand received the tape copy of his cut of the film, she set up a $500,000 editing room in the pool house at the ranch where the editor, Peter Zinner, and a group of assistants worked under her constant and critical eye as she had them cut Kristofferson's footage. "Primarily, she felt that her character needed more time on the screen," Zinner recalled. "She felt that some of the sequences were too heavy with Kristofferson. I would say that she made major changes, not so much with the story line, but as far as the characters were concerned. Her character became much more pertinent."

No scenes were to be left of Kristofferson's character before his decline, when his great strengths as a performer, his emotionality, the sensitivity, the intimacy he created with an audience, explained his stardom and Esther's respect for him. This remains a major flaw in the movie, one Streisand refused to recognize in her determination to focus the story on Esther, to make it a Streisand film despite Kristofferson's costar billing.

Fourteen-hour days, seven-day weeks, she sat on a hard high stool laboring with complete concentration as she studied the strips of film on the small eight-inch-wide Moviola screen. She had learned how to operate the KEM editing equipment, which allowed her to fast-forward, reverse, and freeze-frame the footage. She was alone at last with her image, able to inject her vision on Pierson's cut, not an easy task, for as director Sidney Lumet insists, "No movie editor ever put anything up on the screen that hadn't been shot." During the scoring process she fiddled incessantly with an electronic control board, bringing the drums up, the guitars down, her voice out. She would stop the film and have it run backward. She would hear things no one else could, finding fault with a certain beat, a missed stress. She remained after all the engineers had left and worked until exhaustion overtook her. With Cis Corman, Sue Mengers, Marilyn Bergman, and some other close friends as advisors, she supervised the editing for five months on a final cut "like a crazy person," one of her staff said.

Streisand was too involved with her career and the fate of *A Star Is Born* to devote much time to her role as mother. Plans had been made for Jason to join Elliott, Jenny, and their two young children for the summer in Holland, where Elliott was filming. But for the time being, she had Jason, nine, and Christopher, seven, both in her care, and she found the responsibility of two active boys difficult. Television producer Bob Shanks, the man who had given her the chance early in her life to appear on national television with Orson Bean, and his wife, Ann, vividly recalled the day they spent at the Malibu complex filming a Barbara Walters interview with Streisand. They arrived early in the morning with Cis Corman, Walters, and the crew. Streisand told Jason and Christopher to play outside. About 2 P.M. Peters asked Streisand, "Where are the boys?" She shrugged her shoulders. "Did they have lunch?" he prodded. She said she hadn't seen them since morning. "That's fucking great!" Peters exclaimed and went out in search of the boys.

"By that time," Ann Shanks reconstructed, "we thought we had about two-thirds of the interview done. Barbra has a propensity for drawing people into what seems at the time to be minor decisions. She picks someone outside her closest circle. On this day it was me." Shanks, a former actress, talented photographer, and theater producer, has a distinct style — chic bohemian, you might call it. She is outgoing, very, *very* funny, a natural comic, and an irrepressible mimic. Streisand immediately appeared to bond with her.

"Barbra had chosen a pink sweater for the interview. 'Whaddaya think?' she asked me. 'Good, good,' I said. 'Pink is good.'

"'For me?'

"'Yeah. Especially for you.'"

Sue Mengers had joined the group earlier, and Streisand turned to her. "'See, Ann says pink is good for me.'" (Apparently, Mengers had not approved of the choice.)

"So she wore the pink sweater in the interview section Bob and the crew had already finished. Now, suddenly, she wanted to look at what had been shot. 'Ya *still* think pink is good for me?' she asked in this kinda half-quetchie, half-coy voice. 'Yes, I still do,' I replied.

"'Naaaaw,' she drawled. 'I don't think so.'" She changed the sweater, and there was nothing that could be done but scrap four hours of work and reshoot. Walters was not too happy but gamely went through the interview a second time.

One section, shot late in the day, included Peters. When it was shown to her, Streisand became quite upset. "I hate it!" she protested. "I look awful."

"You may *think* you look awful, but I know *I* look great," Peters shot back. There was some sharp bickering between them. Streisand made the crew rerun the film that had been shot. "See — stop it! Right there! That's a bad angle for me." It was agreed that the offending shot could be edited out without any problem, and she was satisfied.

The discussion then led to the editing of *A Star Is Born*.

"I just saw the end credits," Mengers announced. "I couldn't believe that you had taken both an editing and a wardrobe credit." Mengers is a woman with a strong personality and a strident voice, and her tone made it perfectly clear that she soundly disapproved.

"Why shouldn't I have those credits?" Streisand snapped. "I picked out all my clothes. It's my taste that you see reflected onscreen. And I have worked hard on the editing of the picture. I deserve the credits, and I'm taking both of them."

"You can't do a thing like that in Hollywood," Mengers reprimanded. "There are unions. You'll have an ugly fight on your hands *and* you'll be the laughingstock of the town!"

"Well, I did the work and I want the credit!" Streisand shouted.

Mengers stormed out. The argument was not settled until shortly before the film was released. Streisand did not receive film credit for either category.*

Peters finally invited Pierson to view Streisand's cut of the film. Pierson wrote later, "All night the film ran over in my head. Kris's character often seems an unpleasant drunken dangerous bore; she seems silly — why would she love him? I see she has speeded up the film by cutting his establishing scene, moments of boyishness, of feeling the pain of his existence, that makes us feel for him and with him; she has cut his reactions . . . the sadness, the wonderful wasted quality Kris brought the part, the exhaustion and the playfulness with which he courts her . . . is diminished or gone."

Streisand had been successful on centering the story entirely on her character. The other players are plastic. Kristofferson's songs are tuneless; his voice and delivery show no sign of having once been of the caliber to make him a rock idol. One wonders what Esther ever saw in him. She is, in fact, irritated by him from their first encounter, and only after that candlelit bath together, now sexually involved with him, does she change her attitude. Also, there is an inherent age problem: Streisand — though dressed young — appears to have outgrown her clothes and her role.

Then there is the score. Kristofferson's songs (not of his composition) are painful to hear, and although Streisand is supposed to become a rock star of the magnitude of a Janis Joplin, the songs that make an impression are closer to the old Streisand mold — "Evergreen," "Woman in the Moon," and "Lost Inside of You." The most puzzling question is how she allowed herself the self-indulgence to sing for nearly eight minutes, in concert, at the end of the film — completely obfuscating the impact of the climactic scene that follows Kristofferson's death and the Grammy

---

*The final credit for film editor was Peter Zinner, A.C.E.; for wardrobe, Shirley Strahm and Seth Banks.

Awards ceremony at which she is announced as Esther Hoffman Howard, taking on her husband's name professionally for the first time. In the medley that follows, one assumes the segue from the poignancy of "With One More Look at You" to the hard-rock up-tempo of "Watch Closely Now" is to telegraph the message that Esther is on her own and is going to be all right. However, she is just dandy before Kristofferson is killed in the car crash, and the audience has no doubt that after a proper period of mourning, she will be just dandy again, for she has displayed great inner strength and determination for the majority of the picture.

Nonetheless, Streisand's performance is commanding. The camera work is extremely good and there are times when the story tugs at your heart. Still, Streisand's *A Star Is Born* is not just a flawed film, it is travesty, turning legend into pulp fiction.

None of these criticisms are meant to diminish Streisand's elephantine efforts to make what she believed would be a great film. She knew by instinct what was missing from the previous versions of *A Star Is Born,* both in their statements about female suffering and in their emotional architecture. She did not want to make herself a victim in the same way that Gaynor and Garland had been in their renderings, and in that she succeeded. But there are deep flaws in the story structure, poor character development, and weakness of dialogue that undermine the picture.

"You have to understand the way she saw it," John Gregory Dunne explained. "It was her life on the line. If the picture went down, she went down with it. She just had to do what she thought was right."

"*A Star Is Born* was the beginning of Barbra's examining her own power," Peters added. "It was a discovery period for her. And she started to realize that she could do it, she could take control of her life. I was the tool, in a way. The halfback. I was the one who ran interference for her — because there were a lot of changes she wanted to make, but she couldn't always articulate it."

So consumed was she with getting everything right as she saw it that even when the finished picture was shipped for exhibition, it was accompanied by the following note: "In setting your usual level of sound, please make sure that Reel 1 and Reel 2 are allowed to play *as loud as pos-*

sible. The color is also at its best at 14½-foot candlepower. . . . Barbra Streisand."

The film premiered on December 18, 1976, at the Westwood Village Theatre in West Los Angeles; the first reviews from the Hollywood trades were laudatory. Streisand and Peters basked in glowing optimism, certain *A Star Is Born* would validate her dedication to the project and diminish any effect from the bad publicity that ran rampant during the making and cutting of the movie. None had wounded her as much as a lengthy vitriolic article written by Frank Pierson and published in *New West* and *New York* magazines disclosing personal conversations between them.* Pierson did not attend the preview but did comment that he liked what Streisand had done to the final cut. One thing has to be said regarding Pierson's position as director: he knew from the outset that Streisand and Peters had the definitive word on all decisions and on the final cut. This was bound to create problems unless he accepted this weakened position.

When the largely negative critical response appeared nationwide, Streisand and Peters were unprepared. A STAR IS BORN: DEAD ON ARRIVAL, bannered *Rolling Stone,* which summed up its critique by saying, "If only the music had been better, if only Streisand and Kris Kristofferson were rock singers, if only his role had been developed. If only . . . it might have been good."

"*A Star Is Still-Born,*" Rex Reed wrote. "They haven't remade *A Star Is Born,* they have buried it six feet under." "*A Star Is Shorn,*" jibed the *New Times.*

Streisand was in shock. People she knew who had seen the movie had called it brilliant. Both she and Peters believed the reviews were personal attacks. She felt bitter, and although *A Star Is Born* was an immediate box office success, grossing $9.5 million in the first nine days of its release (eventually to earn over $140 million, Streisand's greatest moneymaking picture), she never forgot any of the words written by the critics castigating the film. Even the huge (five million) album sales did not mitigate

---

*Some of those conversations are quoted in this chapter.

her resentment. What did please her was having her song "Evergreen" become such a huge commercial hit.

With the success of *A Star Is Born*, Peters's career as a producer was now guaranteed. "[Most of my life] I've fought for what I believe in and was not above using violence. Now, though, I've found different ways to communicate emotionally," he commented. "Since being with Barbra, I have gotten it together. She has shown me that things can be different. I've evolved as a person. My desires and passions are the same, but I don't feel as threatened." He paused and added, "You know, James Dean lived my kind of frantic life."

They were working on another project about a clown — Streisand was wild about clowns. They did not actually have a story, and they brought Arthur Laurents out to the West Coast to see if he could offer some help. The project never took off, but they spent a lot of time together and their early closeness was somewhat recaptured. "Peters taught her to have fun," Laurents said.

One day as Peters and Laurents were driving together in and around Los Angeles, he turned to Laurents and asked, "Would you speak to your friend for me?"

"About what?" Laurents inquired.

"The kid's gay. She should face it now."

"Jason was only twelve," Laurents recalled, "and I said, 'How do you know?'

"And he said, 'He's interested in antiques.'" It was crazy. There is no connection, but he had an instinct and he wanted to save "his woman," as he often called her, any pain that might be waiting for her, oblivious to his own possible contribution to that pain.

Peters was now spending more time hustling and promoting himself than he was for Streisand. Even before *A Star Is Born* went before the cameras, he had formed his own company, Jon Peters Organization (JPO), leased a posh suite in Burbank, decorated it in a combination of art deco and antique Asian, signed a three-picture deal with David Begelman at Columbia, and optioned *Eyes* (to become *The Eyes of Laura Mars*), a thriller screen treatment by John Carpenter with voyeurism as its theme. Columbia hoped that Streisand would agree to play the lead, a photographer specializing in sex-and-violence compositions. Despite the fact that Irvin Kershner, who had directed *Up the Sandbox,* would direct and that she would be working with Peters, Streisand refused to accept the role of the psychic Laura Mars, who could "see" the future murders of some of her friends as well as her own. It was not a role she wanted to play, and the trials of *A Star Is Born* had exhausted her. She needed time to recharge, time to be with Jason, and to have some space for a spell without Peters, whom she alternately battled with and passionately loved. To Columbia's disappointment, Peters did not pressure her to join him in his project.

"The truth was, Jon wanted to make it this time on his own and felt he was perfectly able to do it," a friend recalled. "I don't doubt that he led Columbia to believe Barbra would come onboard. It helped him close the deal. But *Star* was a big winner, he had brought it in on budget and Hirschfeld and Begelman [at Columbia] knew he was a helluva lot smarter than the public had been led to believe. Begelman — this was before the shit hit the fan and he was caught up in those embezzlement charges — stood behind him, and he was a strong power at the studio those days. They did insist that he come up with a big star."

Blond, cool, green-eyed Faye Dunaway, who had just won the Academy Award for best actress in *Network,* was cast as Laura Mars. Dunaway was one of the most sought-after female stars, having also been nominated for best actress twice before, in *Bonnie and Clyde* and *Chinatown.* Peters was determined to make a stylish thriller. *Laura Mars* was shot almost entirely on location in New York "to capture that disturbing New York contrast between haute couture chic and dangerous street decay that Laura's photography reflects," he said.

After the script was completed and preproduction set, Streisand remained in Malibu while Peters went off to New York. She threw herself into the work of designing and decorating the three additional separate houses (making a total of five dwellings, the smallest being 3,500 square feet), each self-contained on two acres of land, which were now part of their Malibu complex. They had fought fiercely when the first guest house was under construction. In terms of decorating taste, they were decades apart and stylistically at odds. Peters leaned toward either a *now* or a ranch look; Streisand, to art deco, art nouveau, Victorian, and American primitive. Sometimes their fights ended with them sleeping in different houses for a night. "I hate that lamp! Jon bought it," she told a reporter. "And the glass doors in the dining room, too. I keep threatening to tear them out. They should be stained glass."

"They were very competitive with each other," a staff member recalled. "At times, it seemed that they enjoyed in a strange way yelling at each other and the drama that went along with this type of behavior."

Peters was not a man whom she could control; and although that appeared to be what she wanted, it was also most often the reason that they fought. He would not be governed by a woman, and she was unable to do anything else. Compromise was simply not a part of her character. "Well, I guess you'd say she was hooked on him," a close observer noted. "I'd say they were obsessed with each other. Jon was turned on by the fights they had. He liked an element of danger, of risk. They were like teenagers sometimes, teasing, daring."

Peters now had his own team working for him, although Streisand was never far in the background. After her experience with Pierson and the publication of his article on the shooting of *Star,* with its vivid uncompromising descriptions of Peters and herself, Streisand became adamant that anyone who worked for them either on their domestic or business staff sign a document vowing never to talk to anyone publicly or otherwise about them. This created a row between Streisand and Peters, who refused to have anyone working for him sign such a paper. Michael Meltzer, a young man and former CPA hired as a general assistant to Peters, recalled that one day when they were driving to the studio in his employer's specially built black Mercedes convertible, Peters said to him, "Michael, one day soon I'm going to own a studio."

Meanwhile, Streisand always got what she wanted. Once it was a garage near their offices at the studio. It happened to be leased and occupied. Within an hour of her request, it was emptied and the lease turned over to her. "You had to handle Barbra and Jon with kid gloves," Meltzer recalled, "because you couldn't tell when something would explode in your face. Working for them was a tough environment. Both of their lives were dedicated to work. They argued a lot. His ego was as healthy as hers. The staff knew how to get out of their way when they were on a tirade. Barbra was suspicious, insecure. She worried that Peters was unfaithful. One night she called me at two A.M. Jon was to have arrived on a flight earlier that evening from New York and he had not. She wanted to know if I knew where he had gone. She called back in a half an hour to say he had arrived home bearing gifts."

Although ostensibly Meltzer was working for Peters, it was his job to renegotiate prices for things Streisand wanted to buy. There was one store in Los Angeles where she bought many of her art deco pieces. After she picked them out, Meltzer was sent down to haggle price with the owner. "No matter what price I got, she wasn't satisfied. I had to try another time to get it cheaper. She had this fetish about money. She was generous in terms of large amounts — big charities, things like that — but absolutely mean and niggardly about the salaries of the working people she hired. I recall once that Jon had hired some young Mexican workers who had no green cards and paid them three-fifty an hour [scale at the time], but the work wasn't getting done fast enough. Barbra wanted them to work overtime. They asked for an additional twenty-five cents an hour overtime. She told me to fire them and have them replaced. It killed me, but I did it. Another time I had to fire an older domestic couple who had been with her since she first came to Hollywood. They seemed to have outlasted their usefulness. She gave me orders that the couple had to be out by Saturday of that same week, as she and Peters would be away and return then. With Barbra, when she's done with you, she's done with you. When your employment was over, so was the relationship. It didn't matter that you were working for Jon. Barbra had to be in control. You had to absorb her passions and lose your own initiative. At the end of the tunnel, where does it leave you?

"I quit after eighteen months. When one works for Barbra, you become sucked up into her life, you have no life of your own. I was on call twenty-four hours a day. Because both Barbra and Jon were terribly demanding, the slightest error could result in severe verbal tirades. I found this to be very difficult. One always had to be thinking about the consequences of every act, for you never knew when you could get tripped up. Yet, whatever her failings, I was in awe of Barbra, blown away by being in her presence. Being with both of them was like being in the center of a high-energy field."

A Star Is Born received four Academy Award nominations: cinematography, sound, original song score and its adaptation, and original song — "Evergreen," which Streisand sang to thunderous applause at the awards ceremony on March 28, 1977. After all five nominated songs had been presented, Neil Diamond opened the winning envelope and jubilantly called out, "The winner is . . . 'Evergreen.'" Paul Williams, the song's lyricist, accompanied Streisand onstage, whereupon she said teary-eyed into the microphone, "In my wildest dreams I never thought I would win an Oscar for writing a song."

"I was going to make a comment about, 'Isn't it nice they gave *me* one too," Williams candidly recalled, "but I kept my mouth shut about that. What I *did* say was, 'I'd like to thank all the little people,' then I remembered I *am* the little people [he is on the short side]. I was far from sober." At the Grammys a few weeks later, when they won for Song of the Year, he thanked "Barbra for writing a beautiful melody, and Dr. Jack Wallstader for the Valium that got me through the whole experience." Her relationship with Williams had been difficult from the outset, but as he fully admitted later, he was heavily on drugs and alcohol at the time and not easy to work with.

Since the release of *A Star Is Born* and the incredible success of the soundtrack recording, the "Evergreen" single, and the album *Streisand Superman,* which went platinum, more fans than ever made their way up the narrow road leading to the complex. Streisand reached a point of near paranoia. The property was now encased by an eight-foot metal fence with concealed television scanners and electronic gates. There were three guards who rotated eight-hour shifts. Signs posted on the fence and gates declared DANGER. BEWARE. GUARD DOGS TRAINED TO ATTACK. Twice one of the three Dobermans thus trained bit guests, and one person sued (the case was settled out of court). In attempting to protect herself, to keep the prying and the uninvited out, Streisand had merely placed restraints upon herself. She was, in effect, locked in. She also found herself to be bored and lonely with Peters away, and flew to New York with Jason to join him. Loneliness was not her only impetus. Rumors that Peters and Dunaway were having an affair had filtered back to her.

Jason was enrolled at Dalton, a private day school on the East Side; Peters moved into the Central Park West penthouse in the Ardsley with them as he worked on the film; and the Dunaway threat was dispelled. Then she was faced with another problem. First Artists, saved by the financial success of *A Star Is Born,* was pressing Streisand to honor her contract and make the third film owed to them very soon so that the momentum would not be lost.

"There was a script that was originally meant for Steve McQueen and Ali MacGraw," Blossom Kahn, who was director of new projects, recalled. "Neither one of them wanted to do it, and I was sent to New York with the express purpose of convincing Barbra to do the film. It was set in the Midwest and was about a young farm gal who lived near a small town and this city man comes through and sweeps her off her feet (an early *Madison County*). Straight romantic drama. I thought it was not right for her. I was there doing something I did not believe in, but I was determined to give it a good try.

"For about two weeks I was at her apartment day and night. Jon was there almost every evening. They were at each other all the time. Terrible fighting. Love-hate. It embarrassed me but didn't seem to bother them that I was there. I'd take a scotch and sit it out until things cooled or they were suddenly lovers again. She was terribly worried about the possibility of someone kidnapping Jason. She didn't want the car to take him through Central Park when he was driven to and from school. She was afraid of everything. Neurotic to the nth degree. One day she asked me to accompany her to the doctor for a tooth extraction. She had an abscess that had kept her up all night. When we got to the dentist's office, she kept insisting that I come inside with her while the deed was being done. Thank God, the dentist and nurse finally cajoled her into letting me stay in the reception room.

"Phil Feldman, then the president of First Artists, called me every day — 'How're you doing?' he'd ask. I'd repeat, 'I'm not getting anywhere.' Then toward the end of the second week she told me, 'There's

no use in your wasting your time here, Blossom. I'm not going to do it.'
I liked Barbra but was intimidated by her. She has a tremendous presence. It's an attitude, but there's also something mesmerizing about her eyes — so blue, and when she talks to you, often unblinking. Jon was *shrewd.* He wanted to be Svengali. And [with her] there is that little girl who wants to come out and be loved, who uses her vulnerability. I'll never forget the scene in the dentist's office. She was so childlike, terrified. You felt you wanted to hold her hand to keep her from being scared."

Capitalizing on First Artists' eagerness for her to make a film, Streisand applied pressure on them to advance $200,000 for story costs to develop *Yentl.* "We all were doing everything we could to get Barbra to work, and *Yentl* was all she wanted to do," Ed Holly said. "We did not feel the project would be commercial. Even the Jewish community would be upset [because of *Yentl*'s cross-dressing and wedding-night scenes]."

At about that time Sue Mengers received a script entitled *The Main Event,* written by two TV-comedy writers, Gail Parent and Andrew Smith, to be submitted to her client, Ryan O'Neal. He liked the battle-of-the-sexes forties-style story — about a perfume executive who loses all her money to an embezzler but is left with the contract of a washed-up fighter and is determined to turn him into a moneymaking champion. The real battle is a sexual one between the woman manager and the male fighter, reminiscent of old Tracy-Hepburn movies.

Ryan suggested Mengers send the treatment to Diana Ross, who was Ryan's Malibu beachfront neighbor and lover. "Ryan used to jog in the nude," Ross recalled. "He wasn't easy to ignore." Mengers decided it would be better to reunite the team that had made *What's Up, Doc?* so successful at the box office, and she sent the script to Streisand. Peters read it first and, with his background in boxing, decided it would be a good picture for him to produce with Streisand as the star. She was reluctant. *Yentl* remained her top priority, and *The Main Event* did not immediately appeal to her, so she wavered for several weeks.

"Why am I not working?" she rhetorically asked Sydney Pollack, who remained a good friend. "What am I saving myself for? This is stupid. I should be out here, Sydney. So, every picture won't be great. I mean, I haven't done a picture in so long [just over a year]. I sit here and wait and wait and wait — for what? For Chekhov to come along? For Shakespeare to come along? I'm getting older, and there are a million things I want to do," she rationalized. "*What* am I saving myself for? And yet I say to myself, Why would I want to go and do something that I'm not really stimulated by? And then I argue with myself. I talked to Truffaut once, who said, 'You do your work and at the end you have a body of work. Some of it is good and some of it is not good, but the stuff that's good will override what isn't good — that's what a body of work is. You can't just sit and wait for the perfect script.'"

Although it was a superficial project, she did have enormous trust in Peters's instinct that *The Main Event* would be a commercial success — and it would also fulfill her contract with Columbia. And so her sabbatical ended. After numerous rewrites on the script, on October 2, 1978, the film went into production at the Main Street Gym in downtown Los Angeles under the direction of Howard Zieff, who had recently had a box office hit with the Walter Matthau–Glenda Jackson comedy *House Calls*. Zieff signed on with much the same restrictions as Pierson had had in his contract. Streisand was to have the final word. Once again, a director would be cast as middleman between her and Peters.

One time Peters and Zieff were watching the Muhammad Ali–Leon Spinks fight on television. Around the fifth round, Streisand suddenly jumped up and began to do vigorous exercises dancing back and forth in front of the screen. Peters demanded she sit down. "I just can't sit and watch Muhammed Ali, who's always been a winner, lose," she said.

"Then leave the room," Peters ordered. She did after the next disastrous round for Ali, who after fifteen rounds lost his heavyweight championship title to Spinks. For Streisand, losing was never an option for herself or for those whom she considered winners.

Seven years had passed since Ryan and Streisand had worked together and been lovers. They had remained friends. "You like the fights?" she asked him one afternoon at the Barn. Reflecting on the recent match, she added mistily, "My stepfather liked the fights. I always wanted his approval. He never liked me. He used to sit in his undershirt, drinking beer and watching the fights on television. And, you know, one time I crawled underneath the TV picture when I went by so I wouldn't interfere with his view. He never even noticed. He would *never* see me. He just stared at the fights.

"When he went off, I thought it was my fault, and so did my mother," she continued. Ryan recalled that her glance was somewhere off in the distance. "Then one day, when I was in *Funny Girl* on Broadway, I scratched the cornea of my eye and my understudy [Lainie Kazan, but this was not the same incident that had caused her to be fired] was getting ready to go on in my place. Everyone was telling me not to go on because I might hurt my eye. Then I got this card and a little dish of candy from my stepfather — he was out in front, in the audience. So I said, 'I'm going on.' The doctor anesthetized my eye so it wouldn't tear. I never did a show like that. It was the best performance I ever gave. After the show, I waited in my dressing room for him, but he never came back." She was silent for a moment. "I still have the candy dish. I've never been able to part with it," she added quietly, suddenly giving a new insight into her relationship to the man she always claimed she hated but whom she wanted desperately to love her and whom she appears to have been more willing to forgive than she has ever admitted.

"Am I cool about Barbra and Ryan playing love scenes? Hell, no!" Peters admitted to a *Los Angeles Times* reporter. The two men had gone three rounds in the ring together, presumably for publicity and fun, but Peters was seen as the better boxer and twice let go a couple of hard punches that caught Ryan unprepared and sent him reeling.

As she had done with *A Star Is Born,* at the end of principal photography, Streisand took over the editing of Zieff's final version and "cut the film to her own purpose." She had worked out fastidiously for all the roadwork and exercise scenes, and there are an overabundance of close-ups of her body parts, particularly her rear, that smack of self-indulgence. But the movie scoots merrily along, the jokes are funny, and Streisand and Ryan — although they are *not* Katharine Hepburn and Spencer Tracy or Rosalind Russell and Cary Grant — *are* engaging. Made on a comfortable $7 million budget, with an extraordinary $8 million advertising budget,* *The Main Event* would gross over $80 million, of which Streisand would receive $1 million as her fee and 10 percent of the gross — a whopping additional $8 million. (She would make upwards of $15 million on *A Star Is Born*.)

The most surprising thing about Streisand's association with *The Main Event* is the compromise the script made to her avowed principles. The character she played was a woman of stubborn independence and liberated individuality. Yet, in the end, she surrenders her fighter/lover's championship and the money that will save her from financial collapse in order to get her man. This is not the message of a woman who spoke so high-mindedly about women's need to be treated as equals and to be given the same opportunities as men. Peters was later to say, "*The Main Event* was my fault. I pushed Barbra into that. It was time to do a movie, and I wanted her to do a comedy. But it was material she really didn't like." It appeared that passion had won over conviction.

She recorded the title song as part of her *The Main Event — A Glove Story* album, and it hit the charts within two weeks of release in January 1979. Shortly thereafter, she became embroiled in the problems at First Artists. She had no more pictures to deliver under the terms of her contract, but she owned a large number of stock shares in the company. The foundation upon which First Artists had been formed had been shaky from the start. None of the stars had worked to make the whole as good as the parts, or even the parts as good as they should have been. And by the time Streisand had completed her last commitment to the company, as had the other partners, it was obvious that none of them cared to continue their involvement.

Ed Holly had replaced Phil Feldman as president, and it was his thankless job to try to work out a sale of the company's assets.** When the sale

---

*Advertising budgets for films are usually set at no more than 20 percent of the total production cost.

**"An Australian firm got interested and offered a full price for the company, and there was general agreement that this would be a reasonable price and everybody at that point sort of wanted to get their money and run," Ed Holly remembered. "The Australians, sensing that they had a good chance of getting forty percent of the stock just with stars' shares, went to them individually and got agreements with three of them, Barbra being one, to sell their stock. Newman would not sell. I decided to fight the Australians — if was completed, Streisand was suddenly free to make whatever film she chose as long as she could get backing and distribution. There was no doubt in her mind that the film she *must* do was *Yentl* and that now no one would stop her from directing it, even if she had to finance the project entirely with her own money. She began work on the script, seen then as a straight dramatic film. The story took possession of her. The relationship of Yentl and her father filled her with envy; his death brought her renewed pain over the loss of her own father.

On a trip to New York in the fall of 1979, she accompanied Shelley to their father's grave in a Jewish cemetery in Queens. She had been seven the last time she was there. Upon her father's tombstone was written the words "Beloved Teacher and Scholar." Shelley took a photograph of her standing beside it. When it was developed the following day, she was surprised to observe that the name ANSHEL was carved on the tombstone of the grave adjoining that of Manny Streisand. "I couldn't believe it," she said. "That's a very unusual name. Not like Irving. And right there next to my father's grave was a man named Anshel, who was Yentl's dead brother, whose name she takes when she disguises herself as a boy. To me it was a sign, you know, a sign from my father that I should make this movie."

This discovery had such an impact that she asked Shelley to go with her to visit a medium, "a nice, ordinary-looking Jewish lady," Streisand recalled. "We sat around a table with all the lights on and put our hands on it. And then it began. The table began to spell out letters with its legs. Pounding away. Bang, bang, bang! Very fast, counting out letters. Spelling M-A-N-N-Y, my father's name, and then B-A-R-B-A-R-A. I got

---

they owned one hundred percent of the company, fine, they could do what they wanted, but I wasn't going to let three of the star stockholders sell control of the company. I simply was not going to let this happen when there would be two thousand small public stockholders who would then be out their investment.

"So I filed lawsuits in both federal and state courts against the Australian company under the loophole law, and the three star stockholders — Barbra, Sidney Poitier, and the estate of Steve McQueen, who had just recently died. This forced the hand of the Australians, who came back and bought the whole company — and that was how it was resolved. But it is a strong indication of how little First Artists meant to the stars themselves. They were willing to sacrifice their autonomy — their ideal — for financial gain."

so frightened I ran away. Because I could feel the presence of my father in that room. I ran into the bathroom and locked the door. When I finally came out, the medium asked, 'What message do you have?' and the table spelled out S-O-R-R-Y. Then the medium asked, 'What else do you want to tell her?' And it spelled S-I-N-G and P-R-O-U-D. It sounds crazy, but I knew it was my father who was telling me to be brave, to have the courage of my convictions to sing proud! And for that word S-O-R-R-Y to come out . . . I mean, God! It was his answer to all that deep anger I had felt about his dying. . . . And I thought . . . life is going by so fast. I have to stand up for what I believe in. I can't be frightened anymore. I don't want to be some old lady saying 'I shoulda made that movie *Yentl.*'"

She and Peters had bought back the rights from First Artists just before the company was sold. Her plan was to direct and star in the film while he produced it. Peters tried every means possible to talk her out of going forward, especially since every major studio in Hollywood had turned it down. Not only was he certain that, if filmed, *Yentl* would be a dismal failure at the box office, he was not convinced that she could be persuasive as a young boy. One night he was greeted as he entered their home by a slim young man. "She came out dressed as a yeshiva boy with a pipe and a hat, and I thought it was a guy robbing the house," he said. "I was going to punch him in the mouth."

Peters, now flying on his own and seeing his star rising, did not have as much time to devote to Streisand or her projects as she would have liked. They fought bitterly. She was determined to go forward with *Yentl.* "It was a time in my life when I needed to be really independent, both personally and professionally," she said. "I thought to myself: I have to make this picture, and I have to also be the producer."

It was a scary time for Streisand. She was nearing her fortieth birthday. Peters was away a good deal of the time, surrounded by some of the most beautiful young women in the business. She drew her small circle of close friends tighter to her and joined in efforts to raise funds through celebrity galas to help reelect President Carter and defeat Ronald Reagan. She was back in therapy, but prime in her mind was *Yentl.*

After many weeks of trying to discourage her, Peters reluctantly placed an announcement in *Daily Variety* that Streisand would direct *Yentl* for his company. Rusty Lemorande, Peters's executive in charge of creative development, was sent to Eastern Europe to photograph authentic locations in Hungary, Austria, Czechoslovakia, Romania, Poland, and Yugoslavia. When he returned, Peters had another change of heart.

"You're not going to do it!" he recalled telling her. "We're going to do something else together.' I was a little domineering, I guess, and I remember her looking at me and saying, 'Just because you said that, I'm going to do the movie *no matter what.*'"

Whether Peters was involved or not was no longer important to her. She was determined to make *Yentl,* and when she left the room, eyes brimming with angry tears and determination, she knew the end of their affair was imminent. There could be no room in her life for a lover who, despite the passion she still felt for him, did not support her one hundred percent.

26

A mink coat held closed over a plaid wool shirt tucked into belted designer jeans, her head down, Streisand slipped out of her building on Central Park West and into the waiting limousine before the two reporters stationed outside her door reached her side. The day was gray, one of damp, penetrating cold and intermittent spells of freezing rain. Her hair was frizzy, falling in corkscrew ringlets on her forehead. She looked preoccupied, perhaps in pain. She was meeting Peters for lunch. It was over. Had been for a month, since New Year's Eve — the turn of the decade, 1980, the first in seven years that they had not spent together. She was going to try to be civil about it, but it was no less painful than her divorce from Elliott and just as complicated, for they had mutual business interests and owned property together. Peters still had a stake in *Yentl*. They did not see eye to eye about its future, and although he had been persuaded to go on with the project, he was fighting hard to have the film shot on location in New York State around Lake Placid and not in Czechoslovakia, where costs could accelerate without his supervision. Streisand wanted all rights — which meant she would have to find other financing.

They were lunching at Cafe des Artistes, little more than a mile's drive from the Ardsley straight down Central Park West. The energy of the city was mightier on such cold, windswept days. People walked faster, the upper halves of their bodies breaking through the layers of cold. Even the skyscrapers that faced the park seemed to be in violent motion as the wind whipped around their pyramidical, ziggurat towers. It was two o'clock, an hour chosen because they expected the chic West Side restaurant to be emptying out. She had thought their meeting place had been kept a secret, but photographers accosted her the moment the driver helped her out of the car.

"Go to hell!" she shouted at *New York Post* photographer Martha Cooper, who was snapping away close to Streisand's face as she headed for the front door, which swung open the moment she approached and then closed immediately after she was inside, two employees now barring the press from entering. Peters stood to greet her from a table off to one side, standing beneath one of the restaurant's famous colorful art nouveau murals. Once her fur coat was removed, the contrast between them was glaring: Peters — post-Beatle haircut and rabbinical beard impeccably groomed, recently custom-made Savile Row suit, white shirt, and Sulka tie with a perfect Windsor knot; Streisand — hair flying, California casual.

They talked for about an hour. Neither ate very much. When they rose to leave, Peters had a wistful look in his unusually dense dark eyes. Both of them wanted to make their parting as amicable as possible. Neither was actually sure why it was ending. For Streisand, it had been the most consuming relationship of her life; for Peters, certainly the most important. Their impact on each other had been immense. They had had — as Stephen Sondheim wrote in a lyric —"a good thing going." Sure, it had been a bumpy ride, but never dull, and both of them had moved forward, grown. She looked at him now and she was proud. He had made it into the big time, the *very* big time. "Look at you," her expression said. "You're a mensch, a real mensch!" They reached the front door and made a decision to get into her car and dismiss his. She dropped him at his New York offices and rode back home alone. She had succeeded without much struggle to reclaim the rights to *Yentl*. She would now be on her own — producing, directing, and starring in the film if she could raise the required capital, which she estimated at this stage to be $13 million. And she would not have Peters to help her.

Their giant egos had overwhelmed the great passion they had shared. They were terribly competitive, and she seemed to fear that Peters's rise to power diminished her own. Peters had evolved from film apprentice to studio mogul. He no longer needed Streisand to lead him down the corridors of power, nor did he want her presence to lessen his own accomplishment. He also could not resist the attention of a beautiful woman, and Streisand was too proud, too liberated, too much her own woman, to deal with a lover's adultery, especially one no longer under her thumb.

This last year, 1979, she had taken an emotional journey back to her roots. Never a fully practicing Jew, she nonetheless strongly felt her Jewishness. To understand more thoroughly the culture and motivations in *Yentl,* she had painstakingly researched the period, the history of the Eastern European Jews, and the laws and social structure that formed their world in the late nineteenth and early twentieth centuries. She sought out specialists in the field, rabbis from the three branches of the faith — Orthodox, Conservative, and Reform.* At the same time, Jason was to celebrate his thirteenth birthday in December and was studying for his bar mitzvah. The ceremony, held in a synagogue or temple, is not a sacrament or a sacramental ritual. It simply signifies the arrival of a Jewish boy at the age when, presumably, adult reason and responsibility commence. It is usually held on the Saturday closest to the boy's birthday — in Jason's case, January 5, 1980.

Both Streisand and Elliott, who was separated from Jenny at the time, had met Rabbi Daniel Lapin of the Pacific Jewish Center. "I explained to her," the rabbi recalled, "that in order for the bar mitzvah to have any meaning, in a deeper sense, for her son, he would have to know and see that it meant something to her, too." Rabbi Lapin recommended that

---

*Streisand did much of her research at the Hillel Foundation at USC, to which she later bestowed funds for a Jewish performing arts center. The Pacific Jewish Center, where Jason Gould was bar mitzvahed, had been cofounded by TV critic and writer Michael Medved. In April 1981, following a significant contribution by Streisand, the center's grade school in Santa Monica was renamed and rededicated the Emanuel Streisand School.

she study Judaism along with Jason. This coincided beautifully with her research for *Yentl*. Once a week she would meet with the rabbi and discuss what she had learned and pose tough theological questions.

The intense study of their faith and heritage brought her closer to Jason, who had developed into an intelligent young man with a sense of humor and a curiosity about many things. He liked to write, and his school essays show that he had a flair. He seemed pleased to be sharing more private time with his mother, engaging in a project with her. During her seven years with Peters, they had not been able to manage as much time together as either one of them would have wanted.

The impending bar mitzvah also brought her in closer contact with Elliott, although not in a romantic sense. That had been over for many years, but there was a strong feeling of family as Elliott and his aging father Bernard, as was the custom, stood on the *bima* with Jason, and she, in her front row seat in the small synagogue, watched the passing of ancient tradition from father to son to his son. The bar mitzvah is a ceremony of joyous celebration, and so, a party following the ritual is appropriate. Three tents were erected at the Malibu compound. Kosher and Chinese caterers were hired. Streisand danced with Jason and a nimble Bernard and managed a turn around the floor with Elliott, who also danced with Diana. Later her mother got up on the bandstand and sang "One Kiss." There was exultant Jewish, Russian, and popular music, the latter so that Jason and his friends could dance, although most of the young people were too shy.

With Jason's bar mitzvah behind her, and her business arrangements with Peters settled, she began the ignominious task of pitching *Yentl* yet again, this time along with film taken of the location sites in Czechoslovakia that she wanted to use and a screenplay by Ted Allen. Warner Brothers and Columbia Pictures passed. She went to United Artists, the budget at this point up to $14.5 million. They said they *might* consider the project if she were to sing in the film. Ted Allen claims he had suggested this from the outset and, as Streisand did not want to do a "Ray Stark–Herbert Ross musical," that Yentl sing her thoughts. Streisand saw this as a viable compromise. *Yentl* could be "a realistic fantasy . . . a film with music." Late evenings were spent in her living room with Michel

Legrand at the piano, Streisand jumping up from her cross-legged position on the floor and going over to the piano as a thought came to her, and the Bergmans nearby scratching out words to proposed songs by Legrand.

She was now working on the screenplay with help from the venerable author Isaac Bashevis Singer. Ted Allen mused that the script he had written and she had discarded "gave indications of the anti-Semitism in Eastern Europe that drove the Jews to America, and I don't think that Barbra liked that. She had another concept." What she had always seen in the story was Yentl's burning need to study the Talmud,* and perhaps become a *talmid chachem,* a learned scholar, an expert on the Talmud. The *talmid chachem* is the most honored figure in the life and culture of traditional Jewry, but women were denied access to the Talmud and its learning. Yentl does what she does because she believes women should be equal to men and that equality can be achieved only through education. It is also a story of unrequited love, of a young woman who loses her father, the one kindred spirit she has in life, and how she must come to terms with this terrible loss.

As soon as Legrand and the Bergmans had a number of the songs that would express Yentl's feelings, Streisand recorded them on tape and made another attempt to interest the studios. This time around, United Artists came forward. A film with Streisand singing was quite another matter, but they fought to get a deal that would protect them if Streisand the director should fail. They wanted her to give them the right to approve the final cut. Streisand struggled to retain her power.

While these negotiations were in progress, Sue Mengers brought her a lucrative proposition. Mengers was married to Belgian director Jean-Claude Tramont, who, four weeks into production on the film *All Night Long* for MCA/Universal, had fired Gene Hackman's costar, Lisa Eichhorn, an intelligent American-born actress who had attended

---

*The *Talmud* is a massive and monumental compendium of sixty-three books: the learned debates, dialogues, conclusions, commentaries, commentaries upon commentaries, commentaries upon commentaries *upon* commentaries, of the scholars who for over a thousand years interpreted the Torah (the first five books in the Bible, also known as the five books of Moses) and applied its teachings to problems of law, ethics, ceremony, and traditions.

London's Royal Academy of Dramatic Arts. The role of Cheryl Gibbons, the neglected wife who finds her sexuality with the night manager of an Ultra-Save drugstore, an establishment with a particularly weird clientele, called for an earthiness that Eichhorn did not exhibit in the rushes. Production was halted, and Mengers asked Streisand to replace the fired actress.

The film is really about Hackman's character, the frustrated George Dopler, who hates his job, is in an unhappy marriage, and finds himself in love with a married woman (Gibbons) whose ambition is to write country-and-western songs and who is having an affair with his son. Cheryl Gibbons originally had only five or six scenes, but the chance to stretch herself and play a Marilyn Monroe, waiflike blond temptress appealed to Streisand. An added inducement was the offer of the $4 million fee *plus* 15 percent of the gross. For this stipend — the highest Hollywood had ever paid to a performer at that time — she would have to take only six weeks from her work on the screenplay of *Yentl,* and the money would help her finance the film.

After a four-week hiatus, when her role was being developed, production on *All Night Long* was resumed on June 9, 1980, and remained on location in and around Los Angeles for the next six weeks in a heat wave that brought temperatures above 100 degrees and in the last week, a major strike by the Screen Actors Guild involving residuals on video, cable, and pay television. Streisand had only one more scene to shoot, in which she was to slide down a fire pole (her husband in the film was a fireman). It was not until late October, the strike settled, that she returned to do the remaining shot. "Uh-uh," she said, terrified as she stood on the edge of the second-floor perch where she was to grab the pole for her descent. "I don't think I can do it. I have a weak stomach." After several of the crew and Hackman himself went down to prove that she would be all right, she did the slide in one take.

All Night Long is not a film that Streisand fans shout about. She plays her blowzy, sexually awakened housewife exactly on key, in character, without any razzle-dazzle or Streisand mannerisms, and she *supports* Hackman in several of his strongest scenes. Although not for everyone, the gritty American working-class world it portrays (as seen by Tramont's unique foreign eye) is gripping; Hackman gives an indelible, moving performance, and Streisand proves how good an actress she really is. But all her energies were now turned to *Yentl*.

"I constantly had to give up everything," Streisand recalled of her dealings on *Yentl* with United Artists. "I didn't get paid for writing, I got paid Directors Guild scale for directing, which I think is something like $80,000, and I got paid much less [$1 million] as an actress than I did in *All Night Long*. And then I had to give back half my salary if we went over budget [now at $16.5 million]. But it didn't matter to me. Nothing mattered to me except getting this movie made."

By this time, there had been numerous rewrites of the screenplay, including Singer's, one by Elaine May, and several by Streisand. Finally, English television writer Jack Rosenthal, author of *The Bar Mitzvah Boy*, which Jule Styne had transformed into an unsuccessful musical, was hired. Streisand and Rosenthal worked together. Unaware that the financing of the film depended largely on her soundtrack album, Rosenthal kept trying to cut Streisand's numerous songs, mostly ballads that seemed to stop the flow of the story. They had "great rows" over this issue and Streisand always won out in the end.

Yentl took her on a long journey, and during this odyssey she had been forced to face many of the demons in her life: her sense of desertion, being a woman in a man's world, perceiving herself as ugly, guilt at not being the daughter she believed would have pleased Diana. "I've lived so many years feeling guilty," she said. "Jewish guilt. And I'm finding out about life, talking to people, hearing what they feel and think. They've got the same *mishigas* as I do. . . . People are afraid of their own feelings. Their own sexuality. . . . The other day, while I was driving to my [group therapy session], I was having an anxiety attack. Couldn't breathe. I was in a rage . . . feeling miserable, upset, like I was going insane. Like, maybe I *am* insane. I'm such a terrible person and maybe I really am these awful things you read about and how do I deal with that and live with myself?

"[But when I got to the session] the therapist said, 'Look, you're all mad, and so am I; there's only one difference: I respect my madness.' He stripped half of my anxieties away. Because it was OK to be crazy, we're all crazy, and if you can respect your own madness — far out."

Her "craziness" manifested itself in her intensity about things that mattered to her. She was in a state of constant turmoil. She wore people down, desperate to endow them with her sense of urgency; and *Yentl* had become her raison d'être. Although finally forced by United Artists to surrender approval of the final cut, she was rigid in her determination to maintain control over all major elements of the film.

She had won her battle to film *Yentl* in Czechoslovakia and at Lee International Studios just outside London, where she arrived in February 1982, two months before the start of principal photography. One major issue with United Artists remained unresolved. Her original contract had not included an agreement that she supply a completion bond, a form of Hollywood insurance, in which a private company agrees to pay any amount over the budget that the producer spends on the film.

"The day before we were going to start shooting," she recalled, "United Artists said they would close down the production if I didn't give in and take on the completion bond. It was ridiculous, because they paid the company $700,000, which I needed in making the movie [which meant she would have to supply the deficit out of private funds or raise it elsewhere]. They didn't trust me. Not in that way, I suppose."

"The night before the first scene was shot, I prayed to my father. 'Tell me what to do.' I didn't know what to do. I felt as though I had too much power. You want it desperately for so long, and then you want to give it away." Actually, financial considerations had already diminished her power — she had very much wanted to hire the brilliant Italian cinematographer Vittorio Storaro (*Reds*) but could not, because his $250,000 fee was beyond the budget allowed by United Artists.

"I had to tell Storaro that I couldn't afford him, and three days later I woke up in my insanity. . . . *My* insanity. I had just given away a half a million dollars to set up a chair in my father's name for cardiovascular research at UCLA. I thought to myself, 'I just gave away $500,000 but I didn't treat myself to a $250,000 gift of Storaro?' It taught me a lesson about my own lack of love for myself. And *Yentl* is really about that, too. Yentl finally learns to appreciate herself, too."

On April 14, 1982, just ten days short of her fortieth birthday, Streisand walked terrified onto the sound stage where she would shoot *Yentl's*

41

41. Jon Peters (sans beard) remains a
close friend and confidant.
Walter McBride/Retna Ltd.

42. She became godmother to Peters's adopted daughter, Caleigh, seen here with Streisand as they exit the Palace Theatre, New York, after attending a performance of *Beauty and the Beast*.
Walter McBride/Retna Ltd.

43. Recording the *Back to Broadway* album, she said, brought her closer to her roots in theater.
Walter McBride/Retna Ltd.

44. The album featured numerous Stephen Sondheim songs. They worked beautifully together, one of her most successful musical collaborations.
Gary Gershoff/Retna Ltd.

42

43

44

45. Her involvement with politics intensified with time. With Anita Hill, she received the 1992 Bill of Rights Award presented by the American Civil Liberties Union of Southern California. *AP/Wide World*

46. She was active in Clinton's first presidential campaign and introduced him at the presidential gala at the Capital Centre the night before his inauguration. *AP/Wide World*

47. And he gave her a big bear hug. *Reuters/Bettmann*

45

46

47

48

48. She attended the state dinner at the White House with news anchor Peter Jennings. For a time it seemed they might be a romantic item.
Reuters/Bettmann

49. Talking to the chairman of the Joint Chiefs, General Colin Powell, at a dinner for the White House correspondents. She was escorted by ex-lover Richard Baskin, seen behind her.
AP/Wide World

50

51

50. The star-studded opening-night performance at the MGM Grand Hotel, Las Vegas, December 31, 1993. *AP/Wide World*

51. Streisand looks out her dressing room shortly after her sensational concert at Wembly Stadium, London, April 25, 1994. *Richard Open/Retna Ltd.*

52

53

54

52. Prince Charles was in the audience cheering every song she sang. Here, he smiles his approval backstage, where Marvin Hamlisch (fourth from left, with tortoiseshell glasses) takes in the scene. *Richard Open/Retna Ltd.*

53. Waving to fans in London. She was now headed back to the States and a concert tour that would break all records. *AP/Wide World*

54. AIDS activist/playwright Larry Kramer's *The Normal Heart* was a project she was determined to film. After ten years, she lost the rights and she and Kramer (seen here at a reading of the play to raise funds for AIDS) had a public dispute. *Anthony Savignano/Galella Ltd.*

55

56

55. Smiling but nervous as she begins her
speech "The Artist as Citizen" at
Harvard University, defending the
involvement of entertainers in political
activism.
Reuters/Bettmann

56. In *The Mirror Has Two Faces* she plays
a Columbia professor. Here she prepares
for the next scene.
Bill Davila/Retna Ltd.

57

58

57. Streisand and costar Jeff Bridges
clowning on the set of *The Mirror Has
Two Faces.*
Joseph Marzullo/Retna Ltd.

58. At the premiere of *The Mirror Has
Two Faces* with actor and current love
James Brolin.
Bill Davila/Retna Ltd.

opening shot. Cast and crew applauded, and she was presented with a director's chair, her name printed on it. She made the rounds, shaking hands with everyone. A prop man was embarrassed by his sweaty palms. "Believe me, there's no one more nervous than me. We're all going to make mistakes, especially me. I will make most of them. So I need you," she assured him.

Not long before filming began, her old friend William Wyler died. His wife, Tally, sent her a note: "You never got a chance to talk to Willie about *Yentl*. But I know there were things he would have liked to have told you. So when you're on the set and there's a moment when you don't know what to do — just be very quiet and maybe you'll hear Willie whisper in your ear." Often Streisand would go off to one side and seem as though she was silently communing with either Willie or her father.

Her need to get things right led her to expect the cast and crew to research their respective areas. Just prior to production she had given Mandy Patinkin (who was playing Avigdor, the man Yentl loves but to whom she can't reveal her true identity) a seven-volume set of books entitled *The Legends of the Jews;* and to Amy Irving (cast as Hadass, the young woman Avigdor loves but who marries Yentl disguised as a boy) several books on keeping a kosher kitchen.

"To get the feel of the music, movement, and crowds, and also because of the wedding scene in the film, Barbra would try to attend as many Hasidic weddings as she could possibly find," Jeanette Kupferman, the film's historical consultant, remembered. "'Can you find me a wedding?' became a familiar request. . . . Needless to say, Barbra was a great hit with all the gorgeously attired Hasidic matrons, who were greatly flattered by her interest in them. . . .'Is that really a *sheitel?*' she would inquire, sticking one finger under the elastic of a magnificent upswept coiffure. 'You must give me your wigmaker's name,' or 'Say, could you tell me about Havdala candles?'"

She claimed she was sick every day on her way to work because it was all so overwhelming. "I kept remembering that a friend of mine, Irvin Kershner, said, 'One day at a time.' I don't know how I survived it, but I'm proud I did. I didn't think I would at times."

At one point the English tabloid papers claimed she was having trouble with her cast and crew, who resented her arrogant and autocratic style of direction. To quash these allegations, the crew sent a letter with the signatures of all involved to the newspapers calling the accusations lies. "She has captivated us all with her dedicated professionalism," the letter stated.

"She'd fix my hair ribbons, brush an eyelash off my cheek, paint my lips to match the color of the fruit on the table. I was like her little doll that she could dress up," asserted Amy Irving, barely five foot four, her physical delicacy accentuated by the gauntness of her face and the startling contrast of her pale skin and vivid blue eyes to her dark hair. "For the scenes where I had to laugh," Irving added, "she'd stand behind the camera pulling the strings of an imaginary Hadass doll, making it burp and cry until I'd completely crack up."

The most difficult scene in the film — the kiss by Hadass in her seduction of Anshel/Yentl — was done in one take. "I had asked Amy to be very maidenly before that scene," Streisand explained, "and she did it beautifully. But then in the bedroom, where she comes on erotically, I asked her to let all her sexiness out, and wow! did she let it out."

Yentl's cast and crew, led by Streisand, left London in early July for Prague, where they would then travel to the small village of Roztyly, a two-and-a-half-hour journey, to begin shooting on the first exterior scenes in Czechoslovakia. Heavy rains had deluged the small village, turning all the roads into rivers of mud. Despite the unexpected weather conditions, Roy Walker, the production designer, with the help of the Czech crew that had joined the company, managed to create Yentl's village of Yanev out of a section that had formerly been a few wooden houses and a pig farm. The smell of sewage and urine pervaded the area, and there were flies the size of beetles.

The Soviet-dominated country, once celebrated for its experimental theater work and its many fine films, had been in a period of heavy-booted repression since the democratically inclined Alexander Dubček was replaced as party leader in 1970. Now, twelve years later, conditions had worsened. Efforts were continually made to stamp out dissent, including mass arrests, union purges, and religious persecution. However, Czechoslovakia's economy was in serious jeopardy, and officials had been attempting to woo Western film companies that needed old-world locations for their projects, offering lower production costs and the use of the film studio in Prague.

Diana was half-crazed over the idea of her daughter's making a movie in an unstable country behind the Iron Curtain, where people were murdered or just disappeared. Then there was the lack of healthy food, the distance from home — or even a Western hospital — should something happen. "She was a typical mother crying on the phone," Streisand told Canadian talk show host Brian Linehan, a strong sense of pride in her voice as she added, "She didn't want me to go; she was scared." That Diana cared she might be in jeopardy mattered a great deal to her. However much she had felt cheated by the loss of her father's love, her need to be reassured of her mother's love was even stronger.

She flew in vegetables and fruit, two items in severe shortage, to make sure her company remained in good health. Not until she arrived in Roztyly could she have known what faced her. Across from an unlovely square was a small hotel that she took over to provide rooms for the cast and key people in the company. Czech members boarded with local families. Her room was unprepossessing: a bed up against the wall, in the middle a small table with one chair, next to the bed a table with a mirror, and a cracked washbasin. Threadbare curtains covered the windows, which looked out onto some grubby buildings, but in the distance were gardens filled with flowers, and giant poplars and firs, a river with a bridge that was built during Yentl's time.

Never before had she made a film outside the embracing paternalism of a studio, a controlled environment in which she knew everything would be weighted to her best advantage. She dug in, nails cut stubby-short, a great sacrifice on her part, and was never heard to complain about the conditions. The scenes that were the most difficult for her to shoot were those in which she was both actress and director. She had to learn how to get the best out of her fellow players and whether the camera was placed right, to splinter her concentration without losing it, so that she was aware of what was happening around her.

"I had to make all the decisions," she said, a residue of awe in her voice at her own accomplishments. "I had a coproducer who handled the day-to-day budget stuff, but I had to make all the other decisions — where we shoot, how long we remain in one place." Her intent was to make *Yentl* a *realistic* fantasy. "Just by having the music, you make it a fantasy," she explained. "Music is not real. People don't stop to sing. . . . *Yentl* was beautiful pictures, fairy-tale images. I wanted it to be a romantic film.

"I trusted my instincts a lot. I had to constantly remember that I was wearing four hats [director, producer, writer, and star]. I found the experience very humbling. I was very moved by it. That power is very humbling. And I found myself being very soft-spoken, feeling even more feminine than I have ever felt. More motherly, more nurturing, more loving. I had patience I never dreamed I would have. I never wanted people to feel that I was so powerful. . . . I wanted people to be able to come up to me and give me a suggestion. Because if they can make it better, then I'm gonna use anything they can offer me."

"She was an American woman directing her first film in a European and Eastern European film culture, yet she was able to react as the situation required," her coproducer, Rusty Lemorande, commented. "My respect for her grew enormously."

Jon Peters showed up in Roztyly just before the company was to move on to their next location, the old Jewish quarter of Zatec, in Bohemia — the northeast section of Czechoslovakia. In the summer of 1980 Peters had formed a partnership with Peter Guber in PolyGram Pictures, where he had soon become the dominant force. In January 1982 the partners had left PolyGram and established the Guber-Peters Company, with offices at Warner Brothers' Burbank studio; they were on their way to becoming one of the richest, and most controversial, partnerships in film history. Peters was in Europe on business and made the detour to see Streisand. There were issues that needed settling, papers that they had to agree on to sign, but this could have been done through lawyers and the mail. The truth was, he still cared deeply about her and wanted to make sure that she was all right.

"She treated him like any good friend and, as such, expected him to realize that she was working under stress and did not have time to do much shmoozing," a crew member recalled. "In Europe shooting ends at seven P.M., and Barbra had a buffet table loaded with fresh vegetables and other things not easy to obtain in Roztyly. All the townspeople would gather and take things, but they were very polite, careful not to take too much. Jon was terribly impressed with the way Barbra was handling the whole scene, but he didn't have the stomach for a place like that — the smells, the bugs, the mud roads. He left the next day. I remember seeing her walk with him to the car that was to take him to the nearest railroad station. Her hair was cut in a boy's bob and she looked gamin, truly young, no more than the sixteen years old she was supposed to be in the film. It was a miracle how young she looked. Jon couldn't take his eyes off of her. They had a long clinch, bear hug–style. She turned away the moment he was seated in the car and started calling out orders to a member of the crew who was nearest to her. I caught her looking back once — just as his car slipped out of sight around a bend in the road."

The exteriors for Bashev, the village where Avigdor and Yentl/Anshel study, were shot in Zatec before the company moved back to Prague. In that ancient city she filmed a scene on the famous Charles Bridge, which had been closed so that the film company could replicate a time when only carts and horses crossed its giant span.

She preferred to film in long, continuous takes rather than short, choppy scenes that could be put together in the editing room. The camera movements were graceful, rhythmic, inspired by the music. "I had only nine days to do the musical rehearsals for this film," she recalled. "In *Funny Girl* I had six months. But I had done a lot of my work on tape. And I couldn't have somebody like Herb Ross stage the musical numbers. I didn't want *Yentl* to be that kind of musical." She even choreographed the dancing.

Once back in London, the film almost complete, her problems began. By the time she had dubbed the soundtrack, both dialogue and music, she had gone $1 million over budget. Completion Bond, the company insuring the film, gave her an ultimatum. Either she finish dubbing *Yentl* in six weeks or it would take the movie away from her and hire another filmmaker to complete it. "I need ten weeks and I'll put up $1.7 million of my own money," she told the United Artists representatives who had flown to London. They insisted that it be handled through their offices for tax purposes.

"It was all about money," Streisand said. "I kept saying, 'Please, we're going to ruin the movie. I'm going to die from the pressure. This is supposed to be a joyous experience.' I did anything to get it done so that they could never take it away from me. And in the end UA didn't touch my movie. Not a frame."

She likened her directing approach to her natural talent in singing. "It is very rare when a moment of inspiration hits you. It's when things come from your unconscious. They pass through your cerebral state, coming from your guts, your soul, the place that's in the very core of you. You can't think about it too much — if you do, it's gone."

Making *Yentl,* and the sixteen years that she had devoted to its development, had a tremendous impact on her life. She was not a "born-again Jew," but she had gone deeply into her Jewishness. "I talked to all the rabbis I could talk to, searching for different points of view from the Reform, Conservative, and Orthodox rabbis. It's a complex thing. It's men through the centuries who have found a way to use Jewish law to enslave women. That was a fascinating thing for me to find out. Part of me, my whole life, I've always been very desperately curious about knowledge. . . . I love knowledge. . . . What Yentl learns by the end of the film is that if you really care about yourself, then you don't settle. You go on to find more of what your dreams are about, what you want out of life."

Jon Peters returned to Hollywood with a new attitude toward *Yentl.* He had never felt *Yentl* was a property Streisand should film. Now, he did and he talked up the film whenever he had a chance. She welcomed his support, but it changed little between them. "*Yentl* was Barbra's way of saying kaddish for her own father," he said. "She created him on film so she could love him and say goodbye to him. She buried her father in the movie and dedicated it to him. I cried when I saw the movie. I sobbed, actually. I wish I had produced it," he confessed later.

That would have been a great mistake. *Yentl* is uniquely Streisand's movie, and until the last half hour of the film, it is a personal triumph. The musical soliloquies work beautifully; her performance is impeccable.

The picture has a lyrical glow to it. She *is* sixteen in this movie, whereas she never seemed young in *A Star Is Born*. She achieved what she set out to do — make a romantic fantasy. It is also a film about human freedom, male as well as female. It fails in the last section; Yentl/Anshel's marriage to Hadass *after* the blundering wedding night simply does not ring true, and the last song — when Yentl is aboard ship for the United States — breaks the spell that has so marvelously been cast, for suddenly the viewer is faced with exactly the kind of musical number Streisand said she wanted to avoid.

Yentl premiered on November 16, 1983, at the Cinerama Dome in Hollywood. "I ran out and bought all the chocolate-covered marzipan and walnut cookies I could carry and sat there and stuffed myself," she admitted. "That's how scared I was." She was desperate for "her child" to be accepted, and the early trade reviews assured her this was the case.

"To put it succinctly and at once, Barbra Streisand's *Yentl* is a triumph — a personal one for Streisand as producer, director, co-author and star, but also a triumphant piece of filmmaking," the *Hollywood Reporter* lauded. "At long last . . . she has realized her dream. Magnificently."

It had cost her a lot, and unlike the lyric from the old Fanny Brice song, there was one thing she *hadn't* got, and that was her man. Jon Peters had entered into a volatile relationship with Christine Forsyth, a glamorous blond interior decorator whom everyone thought he might be grooming for a film career. Jason was almost seventeen and about to leave home for New York, where he would be attending New York University Film School, which he had chosen over the equally fine film school at the University of Southern California. Sure that he wanted to be involved in some aspect of films — acting, writing, directing — he also had a need to go out on his own, to be his own person, and perhaps to place some distance between himself and his mother. She had sacrificed precious time at his expense to make *Yentl*. There was no new man in her life — at least, no one who mattered — and no new project that excited her.

She went to the Bergmans for Thanksgiving and came home alone to the house on Carolwood Drive. She spent very little time at the Barn anymore. "She denies her unhappiness," Elliott said. "But she is *so* unhappy. She doesn't have a life — not a *real* life — and it remains to be seen whether she will ever be capable of love."

Vehemently, she denied it; but most of her life she had loved a phantom father. And what chance had Elliott or Jon or any man against one created to perfection by a grieving daughter's dreams? Like Yentl, wasn't she now free? She remained hopeful that the right man would enter her life. She had picked up the threads of her relationship with the married man whom she had been seeing before she met Jon, but his situation had not changed. She would concentrate on finding another story that grabbed her by the heart. Meanwhile, she would go back, once again, into therapy.

Streisand met Richard Baskin, the Baskin-Robbins ice cream heir, at a small social gathering at Christmastime, and they were mutually attracted. A bearlike man over six foot four, his imposing size, his Samson-like dark curly hair, and his protective manner brought out the deeply feminine woman inside her; and her vulnerability was answered by a soft spot in him. He had seen *Yentl* and told her how good it was, that its ethnic roots had touched him. He played the guitar, wrote songs, and had been the musical director on a low-keyed film, *Honeysuckle Rose,* about a country music star that featured Willie Nelson. Like Barry Dennen, his had been a privileged childhood and youth. A decade younger than Streisand, a self-contained, cerebral man, proud to become her lover — which he soon was — he moved into the Carolwood Drive house in February. A Streisand whim, friends said. It wouldn't last. Where were the crashing symbols, the explosive scenes that so marked her serious love affairs? She would soon get bored with *compatibility* and trade it in for a more stimulating *combative* relationship. Two years later they were still together.

27

"She should only live and be happy," Diana said to one of her neighbors who commented harshly on Streisand's live-in relationship with the much younger Baskin. The old wounds would not heal, but Diana seemed to have mellowed, become less critical. Roslyn, who had moved out of her mother's apartment but still lived in Los Angeles, was not having much luck in her career. Although she had a pleasant voice and was attractive, she did not have Barbra's drive or her exceptional talent. The half sisters had a delicate relationship — their hostilities, resentments, and jealousies not yet resolved. Roslyn had thought Streisand would help in her quest for a career in movies. What she got were nonspeaking parts as an extra in two of her sister's films: in *A Star Is Born* she sat at Streisand's table during the Grammy Awards scene, and in *The Main Event* she is one of the women working out in the aerobics class with Streisand at the beginning of the picture. Streisand was at a loss at what else she could or should do for Roslyn. But the guilt lingered.

"Everyone wants a small piece of me," she complained to an intimate. "I *have* to be protective." She worried about Jason. He seemed to be having a difficult time finding himself, and they did not communicate well. Telephone conversations were unsatisfactory, and when he came home for holidays, she seemed always to be involved in a consuming project.

Baskin remained in residence, but friends noted a difference in their relationship. Where once there had been harmony, there was evidence of backbiting, of a crumbling romance. "All the men in my life have said, 'Can't you stop working at seven o'clock?' I never understood what they meant," Streisand has said about the failure of her relationships.

Work filled her life and she was once again following in her earlier footsteps — bringing the man in her romantic life into her work, placing him in a position of power but having to deal with her as the ultimate authority, setting a standard that he felt he must live up to or his masculinity would be compromised. Baskin understood music and recording techniques, and so she teamed up with him in that area of her career.

In the late summer of 1985, no movie on the horizon, she decided to return to her roots to do an album of Broadway songs. "It's time I did something worthwhile," she told Stephen Holden, music critic for the *New York Times*.

She felt she had to stop recording songs "that any number of other people" could sing as well if not better than she could. She yearned to do something she truly believed in. "Broadway music is the music I love, it is where I come from, it is my roots," she stressed. Although she had recorded dozens of songs using rock rhythm sections, she felt out of her "element singing music with a strong, regular backbeat. . . . Because I am a singer who believes in the moment I do each take of a song differently. You can't do that with rock and roll because everyone says that you have to sing on the beat, and that's very hard for me."

She joined forces once again with Marty Erlichman. Erlichman went to Columbia Records with her wish to do a Broadway album. "Barbra's contract with them says she has to deliver X albums," he explained, "but they have to be approved albums — meaning most of them have to be contemporary. Columbia would not approve this album. It was not considered to be a pop album. Therefore, she didn't get the advance she was entitled to, and it wasn't going to count as an approved album contract, except if it sold 2.5 million copies, at which point it would automatically become an approved album, whether they okayed it in advance or not."

She went ahead with her plans even though she did not think Broadway songs were mainstream any longer. Originally, she had wanted to make a double record, but agreed to a single LP under pressure from the record company. Never too proud to eat crow, she called Peter Matz, with whom she also had not worked in a long while, and asked him if he would agree to coproduce, arrange, and conduct the orchestra. Matz, who had done the orchestrations for most of her early albums and certainly was at least partially responsible for their success, agreed. They would produce the majority of the songs. Baskin, with David Foster, would handle the production on the other cuts.* The four of them (Streisand immediately and totally immersed) began "marathon listening sessions to find a blend of obscure songs and standards."

After weeks of listening to show scores by Kern, Hammerstein, Rodgers and Hart, Bernstein, Berlin, the Gershwins, and other legendary Broadway tunesmiths, she focused on the one composer she had all but completely ignored throughout her early recording and concert career — Stephen Sondheim. "It's like growing into a part like Medea or Hedda Gabler," she remarked. "It's not good when you're twenty. You need to be older." For an unreleased cut in 1974 from the *Butterfly* album, she had recorded Sondheim's "There Won't Be Trumpets" from *Anyone Can Whistle* and then changed her mind as Columbia had wanted her to do more contemporary songs with simpler lyrics. Now she appreciated their complexity and was drawn to Sondheim's sophistication and intellectualism.

The song that particularly attracted her was "Putting It Together" from Sondheim's then-current show, the 1985 Pulitzer Prize–winning *Sunday in the Park with George*. She called him at his home in New York, although they hardly knew each other. "I told him of my conversation with my record company . . . that I wanted to do an album of Broadway songs. And they were very resistant and unhappy, and they said, 'Barbra, you can't do a record like this. It's not commercial. This is like your old records. Nobody's going to buy it.' Every word they said only encouraged me. I wanted to put all their comments into this song. And I thought, 'What a great way to open this album.'"

---

*Richard Baskin ended up producing two of the cuts, "Not While I'm Around" and "Something's Coming."

The actual lyrics of the song related to the art world (the French painter George Seurat was the main character in the show). "She wanted to make [the song] relevant to the music business," Sondheim remembered, "so she asked me if she could fix one word to replace 'lasers,' and I said, 'Why not use "vinyl" instead?' and she leaped at it and thought that was wonderful. And I said, 'Let me look at the rest of the lyric, if you want to personalize it. I'm sure I can make it more record-oriented and less art-related', which is what it was in the context of the show. Once you get into it, then it becomes fun to do, and that's why I did it."

"I would talk to him for hours," Streisand added. "I felt I couldn't ignore the truth . . . you don't hide it; you use it. So I told him, 'Here I am, a very successful recording star and yet I have to fight for everything I believe in. I'm still auditioning after twenty-three years.' I asked him if he could encompass that thought and he wrote, 'Even though you get the recognition/Everything you do you still audition.' You see what I mean?"

Sondheim had never been known to custom-tailor a song for a singer. "Barbra Streisand has one of the two or three best voices in the world of singing songs," he explained. "It's not just her voice but her intensity, her passion and control. She has the meticulous attention to detail that makes a good artist. . . . Although every moment has been thought out, you don't see all the sweat and decisions that went into the work. It is as though she just stepped out of the shower and began singing at you."

"He believes as I do," Streisand said about Sondheim, "that art is a living process, that it's not set in stone, that it breathes and it grows and it changes. It blew my mind when I said things to him like 'I never understood "Send in the Clowns." What would you think about writing a second bridge that would kind of tell us more about this relationship?' And no problem. I've asked him to make a lot of changes like that, and at first we'll be on the phone and he'll say, 'Wait a minute. You can't do that.' And then he says, 'Let me call you back,' and in two hours he calls me back and it's done. I don't know quite how he does these things. He's very, very organized."

The Broadway Album became a predominantly Streisand-sings-Sondheim album as in addition to "Putting It Together" she does "Send in the Clowns" (*A Little Night Music*) "Somewhere" and "Something's Coming" (*West Side Story,* music by Bernstein), "Not While I'm Around" and "Pretty Woman" (*Sweeney Todd*), and "The Ladies Who Lunch" and "Being Alive" (*Company*).

Working with Sondheim was, she has asserted, "one of the most exciting collaborations I've ever had, because we both talk fast, we think fast; so it was like shorthand half the time . . . we practically didn't have to finish sentences. It was so exhilarating, there were moments I was screaming with joy over the phone."

Sondheim came out to California and worked alongside her in the recording sessions. Here were two of the truly towering talents in the music world, both intense personalities, both perfectionists. Sondheim, in sweatshirt and sneakers, sitting on one chair, his feet up on another, would pull at his close-cropped salt-and-pepper beard as he labored over each word he scratched out on a pad of music paper. Streisand, comfortably dressed in a jogging suit, hovered nervously nearby. Much in awe of Sondheim, she considered him one of the twentieth century's greatest theater composers. His mind was as quick as hers, and there was an instinctive knowledge of how to adapt his lyrics and music for her needs.

"Everyone in the studio knew that they were part of something important," claimed Alan Bergman, who with Marilyn attended most of the three-week session. "The musicians, rather than escaping to the halls, stayed in their chairs and listened to the playbacks. Every take was different — a fresh meaning to a phrase, a new bend to a note."

The album, which soared with full-bodied, tender bel canto renditions of the Broadway songs she had chosen, was released in early November 1985, shot right up to number one on the *Billboard* chart (there had been an amazing 800,000 advance sale), and proved to be one of the most thrilling of Streisand's career. She had always believed in it but had not expected it to be such a big hit, and it renewed her faith in the public's taste for good music. She had the conviction that if she followed her intuition on what was best for her, she *would* succeed; and she had proved, as she once had with *Funny Girl,* that she was right.

"Listen, I cried, I was so moved," she bellowed long-distance over the telephone to Larry Kramer. It was spring 1986. He was in New York; she was in Los Angeles. "I gotta make the movie of your play," she insisted. Could you come out here?"

The play that had so aroused her emotions was Kramer's devastating drama *The Normal Heart,* which had recently opened on the West Coast after a highly lauded run in New York. Kramer agreed to fly to Los Angeles to discuss the adaptation of his work for the screen. Streisand's enthusiasm, her strong feeling for the play, greatly energized him. He did not know what her background or orientation was to the subject of AIDS, and he understood that she wanted to produce, direct, and star in the film. The latter was worrying because it is not as much Dr. Emma Brookner's story (the only female member of the cast) as it is about the men whose lives were in mortal jeopardy with the advent of the plague.

Her ten-month odyssey in Europe directing herself in *Yentl,* shortly before Baskin entered her life, had strongly affected Streisand's professional attitudes and goals. She now possessed a broader view of what she wanted to achieve: to make a statement with her talents; to break through the barriers for women in film. Making *Yentl* had been a rite of passage. She felt almost grown-up now, although that vulnerable child she was always trying to subdue occasionally gained the upper hand. The wonder was that after twenty-three years of glittering stardom, fame equaled by only a tiny few — Marilyn Monroe, Marlon Brando, Elizabeth Taylor — with a notoriety that never dwindled or showed signs of fading, she remained excited about life, people, ideas. Ambition had once possessed her — being someone, being rich. Now it was accomplishing things that mattered, contributing to a better understanding of a few of the world's problems.

The house on Carolwood Drive, high atop Holmby Hills, a short distance from Sunset Boulevard, had become her home and workplace in the past few years. Her meeting with Kramer was for half past one in her ground-floor study, and she was nearly two hours late. Kramer and Cis Corman were waiting anxiously for her to join them. Cis was now involved with all her production plans. A born mediator, a woman of classic understanding, Cis had early on become a substitute maternal figure to Streisand, a totally nonjudgmental "mommy" to whom she could reveal her worst feelings and fears, let everything hang out, so to speak, knowing that Cis would not castigate her for her honesty and would instead offer her some clearheaded guidance.

Her friendship with Cis has remained the one constant in Streisand's close circle, as lovers and business partners have moved in and out of her life with traumatic impact. The simple truth is that she trusts Cis as she does no one else. Cis was the first person to encourage her to sing. They have shared their dreams, gone through much together. Their relationship transcends ego and the usual built-in power struggle endemic to a partnership in which one member is a star of tremendous voltage and the other dependent upon that person for his or her career.

Streisand knew Cis would be discussing with Kramer the story problems that they had outlined together and that he would be well occupied. Still, she felt contrite about being so late. She was always suffering Jewish guilt for something or other. Just being late, as often happened and as she was now. Nobody understood. She had to give *everything* to a meeting like this. She could not talk to a writer about such a personal work as *The Normal Heart,* a play about AIDS that she knew was at least partly autobiographical, without doing her homework. So, she had remained in her upstairs bedroom suite, studying the text of the play, a screenplay that Kramer had adapted before her involvement in the project, and several scientific articles on the ravaging disease that was decimating the gay community.

For her to succeed with the project, she needed to understand as much as she could about AIDS. Like *Yentl,* this was a story with great personal meaning to her because so many men she had known and worked with had died of the disease, but as she started down the staircase in her home that dim, foggy afternoon in early March 1986, she had no idea that she had just taken her first steps to another years-long odyssey.

She continued down the curved staircase and past the living room on the way to her study. When you looked around the rooms on the spacious ground floor of the Carolwood Drive house, there was no sign of Baskin's three-year tenancy, so distinctly was her personality ingrained and so overwhelmingly had his seemed to have been ignored.

With the exquisite pieces of art nouveau that she had been collecting through the years, the house had begun to look like a museum. Maybe it *was* a museum. Maybe all of her homes had become museums: this one, the five-house complex in Malibu, the West Side penthouse in New York.

Kramer, a kinetic, dark-haired man with a winsome smile who wore his fiftysome years with youthful panache, stood when she entered the all-white study decorated in what she called "Hollywood forties glamour." Before her arrival, the room had been dominated by a white grand Steinway and two white overstuffed sofas. In her presence everything diminished in size. Not that she is large. She is, in fact, a rather small woman, slim and about five four. That day she was dressed in a soft peach pastel jogging suit, with immaculate white sneakers, and clutched in her arms Kramer's play, a pad of notes, and a tape-recorder. Her highlighted ash-blond hair framed her angular, well-chiseled face in a mass of Medusa-like curls. Her nose may be her best known feature, but it is her startling blue eyes and the delicate translucence of her skin that hold one's attention and admiration. Not beautiful by accepted nonethnic standards, she possesses a *presence* polished to an awesome glow by celebrity. By instinct, Streisand knows where to stand so the light will be the kindest, how to position her head to lengthen her neck and shorten the image of her nose; when she held out her hand, it was like an exotic flower with crimson-tipped petals unfolded.

"When my agent told me that Barbra Streisand was interested in *The Normal Heart,* we were in a restaurant in New York and I lay down on the floor like a nut and began hitting it and shaking my legs," Kramer recalled. "God knows what people thought. I was just so fucking thrilled. I wanted her to do it because I knew that if she did, a lot of people would see it. The play meant a great deal to me. It was my life; at the same time it was a play that I knew could make a difference to the gay community if it were given wide commercial exposure. Once I contained myself, I made it clear that there had to be a proviso that I write the script. I thought everything was settled when I flew out to meet her. She had a screenplay that I had done earlier, before her involvement, and we were going to talk about it and where we should go from there."

Kramer was a screenwriter long before his success as a playwright. During Britain's film renaissance in the 1960s he had been transferred by Columbia from its New York offices to the story department in its London branch. By the end of the decade he had formed his own company and wrote and produced the brilliant adaptation of D. H. Lawrence's *Women in Love,* with Glenda Jackson, for which he received an Academy Award nomination. "The only reason I did *The Normal Heart* as a play was that I didn't think I could get a movie done on the subject and that a play was much faster. It was a story that had a message and had to get out fast. I believed it would change the world, and Ronald Reagan would behave [regarding help to inaugurate government research into the AIDS virus]."

Streisand and Kramer immediately set to work on a revised screenplay the morning after their first meeting. "I was so impressed with the way she worked," Kramer said, "like a Trojan. We would start at nine A.M. in the study and we would work until midnight. We never stopped to eat. She had food brought in, lots of it, well prepared. She could talk and eat at the same time without any problem. She never lost her train of thought; it was amazing. Kim Skalecki, her secretary/assistant, would come in with important papers and things for her to sign, calls that had to be made. She handled it all in a thoroughly professional manner. She had converted a garage [at the Carolwood Drive house] into separate quarters for offices for Kim and three other assistants.

"We were figuring out the sequence of the scenes mostly, the structure and what would happen within scenes, and she asked me a lot of questions about the characters and a lot of questions about homosexuality. I suspect that she knew about Jason's homosexuality, but it was not a subject that we talked about. Only later did she try to educate herself about homosexuality. She would talk to various people in the industry who were out of the closet and ask them what made people gay. I gave her a pretty graphic book about gay sex and I'm sure it disturbed her, but I felt if she was going to direct *The Normal Heart,* she had to understand something about the physical side of homosexual love."

Day after day, for a period of two weeks, spring rain tapping at the windows, she sat with Larry Kramer in her dazzling white study and read with him all the parts in the script out loud and then voiced her comments on changes she thought should be made — a line of dialogue that was too raw, a speech that was overly wordy, a point that required more emphasis.

"What I found difficult was — maybe because I had always loved her as a performer — getting beyond the fact that I was actually sitting with *her,* Barbra Streisand," Kramer confessed. "I was in awe of her — the talent, the fame. We all grew up with her. It's like a member of the older generation being in a one-to-one situation with Judy Garland. It took a while before I felt free to say what I actually thought. It's not that you edit what you think, but you do in a way. And if she would say something that I didn't agree with on the script, I would speak out and she would say, 'Well, let's try it this way.' Sometimes she would give in and sometimes she would say, 'I want it this way.' How much of a fight can you have? Not much."

Kramer went back to New York believing he was to start work on the screenplay. He brought with him a sheaf of notes on changes to be made — scenes to be included or excluded, speeches to be cut, parts to be developed and enlarged (the doctor she was planning to play had to be more germane to the story). The contract was waiting for him to sign. There was no mention of his writing the final screenplay. "I confronted my agent and told him he had not done what I wanted him to do. That I had to write the screenplay. I called Barbra on the phone and she got very angry with me, and I said, 'You don't understand. This is my life story. I have to write the final screenplay. No one else can be brought in.'"

"Well, that is something I can never give up," Streisand told Kramer. "I simply have to have my power and my control over the story."

Kramer broke the deal. Streisand had lost *The Normal Heart.* Kramer could not have known how difficult this was for her. The play would haunt her for years, become an obsession in the same way that *Yentl* had. Still, he should have realized with his studio background how impossible it would be for her to guarantee him the lone, final credit on a screenplay yet to be written. *Control* was the operative word. Streisand's need was to express *herself, her* views along with those of the author. In the end it would be Barbra Streisand, not Larry Kramer, who would be judged by the work presented on the screen. The media was always accusing her of being a control freak. The phrase rankled.

Although Kramer's *The Normal Heart* now seemed lost to her, nagging thoughts on what *was* normal remained and were partially responsible for her decision to proceed immediately with *Nuts,* a film she would produce but not direct and in which she plays the idiosyncratic, high-priced call girl who murders a client in self-defense.

Dim echoes of Streisand's own childhood permeate the story with its background of an abusive stepfather and a mother's silence. Always striving for a deeper understanding of herself and of her many anxieties and resentments, she was ceaselessly engaged in attempts to come to terms with her past; and the projects she chose reflected this.

With the approach of summer, Streisand, accompanied by Cis, who was to be the coexecutive producer on *Nuts,* and Martin Ritt, the director with whom she would collaborate, began the strenuous task of researching neuropsychiatric hospital facilities to help in her interpretation of the tormented, incarcerated psychotic Claudia Draper. On these field trips, which took her to Bellevue Hospital in New York City and the Mental Health Court in the San Fernando Valley, she spoke to several dozen schizophrenic, seriously disturbed female patients. Afterward she confessed, "I felt totally comfortable with them."

"I don't believe any of the women Barbra met with knew who she was," Cis observed. "She could be herself. It must have been a refreshing feeling."

Being herself was no easy matter. She was by now a cultural icon, presented by a good portion of the media as a controlling, vainglorious woman who at the same time just happened to be one of the greatest singers and personalities of the twentieth century. Very few people are able to be natural when confronted with such celebrity. It intimidates them. Streisand also has an abrasive manner and no patience with people whom she does not consider up to her standards in intelligence. She can make even very knowledgeable people feel inadequate. It is not an ingratiating character trait and has kept her coterie of close friends rather limited. Most of them, like Cis Corman and lyricist Marilyn Bergman, have known her from the early days of her success. "It is fascinating to me that she is so put down by the media," Cis Corman criticized. "People who know her love her."

That was obviously not enough for Barbra Streisand, who after twenty years of therapy was still trying to find good reason to love herself. Right now, she took a respite from therapy sessions to concentrate fully on the development and production of *Nuts*. Her top priority was to break through the "old boy" monopoly in Hollywood with a picture that would be praised for its content and her performance as well as its production.

Marty Ritt had sincere concern over social issues and a skill to elicit strong performances from his actors. From 1948 to 1951 he had directed over 150 live dramas for the newly emerging television medium and acted in some 100 more until he was blacklisted for his past "suspected" communist affiliations. He had taught at the Actors Studio for the next six years, coaching such future stars as Paul Newman, Joanne Woodward, Lee Remick, and Rod Steiger. His foothold in films was gained in 1957 with *Edge of the City;* he had made many notable films* and had recently been named Distinguished Director in Residence at UCLA's College of Fine Arts. Streisand could not help but admire his work. At the same time there was a conflict because Ritt believed there could only be one director on a film, and Streisand was not willing to relinquish her control.

"Marty and Barbra didn't always agree," Maureen Stapleton, who gave a shattering performance as Streisand's mother in *Nuts,* said. "But there weren't any big scenes between them — no flying off the handle or stomping off the set. I loved Barbra. We had good chemistry. She's such a professional. Sure, she's a perfectionist, but that's swell with me. I'm sure Marty respected her opinions. It's not a good thing for a director to lose control. I don't think he ever did. Everyone was very close while we made the picture. Of course Eli [Wallach, who played the court psychia-

---

*A partial list of memorable movies directed by Martin Ritt (1914–90) include *No Down Payment* (1957), *The Long Hot Summer* (1958), *The Sound and the Fury* (1959), *Hud* (1963), *The Spy Who Came In From the Cold* (1965), *Hombre* (1967), *Sounder* (1972), *The Front* (1976), and *Norma Rae* (1979).

trist] is an old friend. Karl Malden, too [the fictional stepfather who has sexually abused Streisand's character]. When I think of it, except for Richard Dreyfuss [the beleaguered court-appointed defense attorney], everyone on the film was ages older than Barbra, but somehow she seemed the most serious person around."

The role of Claudia Draper was exhausting both emotionally and physically. The script went through numerous revisions, with as many writers — six in all — and Streisand was deeply involved in the writing of each. The basic themes of the story — the lack of communication and understanding between a young girl and her mother and the abuse of a stepfather — stirred emotions that ran brutally deep. Her conversations with mental patients and visits to the women's wings of prisons and mental hospitals were disturbing. There was the realization of how lucky she was that she had been both talented and ambitious, that she left home as early as she did and won fame so soon after. It was critical to her that the final screenplay by Alvin Sargent and Darryl Ponicsan not only make a statement that was meaningful but also explore the myth of accepted mores and what was deemed normal behavior. She stressed to Marty Ritt the importance of making the film as real as possible, gritty and ugly when necessary. What she did not want was a glossy *Spellbound*.

The script, approved by Warner Brothers with a cost budget of $21,584,000 (production costs having escalated greatly from the time that *Yentl* was made), went before the cameras on October 20, 1986. Ritt was not too well and did not have the patience with which Streisand's first film director, William Wyler (*Funny Girl*), had been endowed. A stocky, powerful-looking man with a massive and intelligent face that suggested an odd alliance between Charles Laughton and Mister Magoo, Ritt had at seventy-two an encyclopedic and unorthodox knowledge — he could casually quote Chaucer and Goethe alongside Al Capp and Charles Schulz. He told one intimate that he had "learned my own judgment is the only one I can trust."

"How old are you?" he asked Streisand at one of their early meetings. She never blinked an eye. "Forty-five," she shot back.

"I think you're too old to play Claudia Draper. She's a much younger woman, still in her twenties. Tough from the vicissitudes of her career as a hooker, but young enough to pull in big bucks for her favors." Later Ritt recalled the scene: "I had to admire [Streisand]. She took it like a trouper. She could have thrown me off the picture. After all, she was the boss. Her body stiffened. I noticed that. There was fire in her eyes. 'You're wrong,' she said, 'and I'm going to prove it to you!'"

The statement became a challenge, and during the shooting a competitive atmosphere often existed between them. Ritt, like Streisand, was a scrupulous craftsman with an exact and exacting sense of place and period. Although they were not destined to become friends, they both retained great respect of each other's ability.

Production ended on February 3, 1987. Ritt worked for ten weeks on the editing while Streisand hired herself to compose the picture's score. ("Who else would hire me?" she has quipped.) As the film was a courtroom drama, it did not require much music, but she had dreamed of scoring a movie (Charles Chaplin being perhaps the only other actor, producer, and director who had accomplished this formidable task) for a number of years. "The end title music," she explained, "was written to convey a sense of freedom and personal triumph [as Claudia is judged sane and competent to stand trial.]" Later Alan and Marilyn Bergman added lyrics to it and the song became "Two People," recorded for her *Till I Loved You* album released the following year.

Ritt, like other directors who had worked with Streisand since she formed her own company,* had not succeeded in winning approval on the final cut. His hope had been that she would like what she saw when she ran his version and it would stand. He felt confident that this would be the case. He had, in fact, confessed to her that he thought she had done a magnificent job of Claudia. He left believing the picture was finished. To others he confided that he thought she would be nominated for an Academy Award.

As soon as she received Ritt's cut of the film, Streisand went into vir-

*Streisand had signed a multifaceted contract with Warner Brothers in June 1984 to develop a full range of motion picture projects on which she would work on all levels — as star, director, or producer, or all three — under the auspices of her own company, Barwood. *Nuts* was her initial venture. Cis Corman was named president.

tual seclusion in her private editing room at her Malibu ranch estate, with its separate editing cottage filled with half a million dollars' worth of the latest and finest professional equipment. For three weeks she worked night and day impressing her own stamp and personality on the film. She cut some of Stapleton's footage and the courtroom scenes, and reworked the flashbacks that led to the murder sequence. Her role was always major. Now it almost overpowered the film and would have but for Dreyfuss's forceful performance. She worked, shut away, food brought to her, immersed, possessed by her need to achieve as near perfection as seemed possible.

With such dedication to her labor, there was little time or place in her life for Richard Baskin. He had accompanied her in February to the Grammy Awards, where she was presented with an award for *The Broadway Album*. As she came offstage one of the show's producers touched her on the shoulder. She turned. Beside him was a handsome blond man whom she recognized. "I'd like you to meet Don Johnson," the producer introduced. Johnson smiled boyishly. "Congratulations," he offered, his china blue eyes locked momentarily with hers. "Yeah. Thanks," she grinned and moved away.

"There's one damn sexy lady," Johnson, at the time the reigning American male sex symbol and star of the television adventure series *Miami Vice,* murmured as he watched her go.

Streisand glanced back over her shoulder, catching a fleeting glimpse of Johnson as Baskin and two security men led her to an exit door.

28

"I'm at a place in my life where I'm almost realizing my dreams," she had told an interviewer a few years earlier. "The other day, I was so anxious about it, I started to cry when I said the words, 'Oh, my God, I'm almost getting everything.' It was a total emotional experience. Because I am so used to complaining, to being negative, that to be in a happy place is a whole new way of life for me." She had been deeply, *deeply* in love with Peters, believing that she had found her life partner. That dream had evaporated, but she was once again in a happy place. Baskin was a charming, intelligent man, supportive and loving, and he was undemanding of her. Still, he lacked Peters's charisma, the vital life force. There was no strong conflict of wills and egos, no speedway curves or roller-coaster emotions in their relationship. She was free to concentrate on her career, on developing projects in which she believed, and on causes she cared to support.

She closely oversaw the Barbra Streisand Foundation, which distributed over a million dollars yearly to various causes that ranged from funding AIDS research, abused children programs, and battered women shelters, to endowing university medical chairs (in her father's name), to supporting environmental and civil rights, to supplying musical instruments to elementary schools so that young students could play in a band.

But in none of these had she taken an active part. Then along came the catastrophic explosion of the nuclear power plant at Chernobyl to thrust her actively back into two more rings of activity — live concerts and politics — that she had shied away from for over a decade.

"It was April 26, 1986," Marilyn Bergman recalled. "Barbra and I were talking about the disaster at Chernobyl. She called me that morning, and she was absolutely horrified at what happened. The question was, What can be done about this? And the answer was, The only thing that I know to do about it is to take back the Senate for the Democrats." Bergman was a founding member of the Hollywood Women's Political Committee, formed two years earlier, spawned from strong anti-Reagan sentiment. The HWPC aimed to influence the vote by raising large sums of campaign money for the candidates of their choice through gala dinners and balls and operated "on the explicit conviction that politicians could learn from listening to their Hollywood donors." The movie industry had proved to be a vital campaign aid. At the time of the Chernobyl disaster, there were six Democratic senatorial candidates in close races.

Streisand was not a member of the HWPC, although she would soon join. Bergman was suggesting she do a concert to help raise funds for Democratic antinuclear candidates. Streisand was reluctant. "I'm still not comfortable singing in public in front of a large audience," she countered.

"It became a discussion of what is more frightening: performing in front of an audience or nuclear annihilation?" Bergman explained.

The months that followed might be called "the political awakening of Barbra Streisand." A few days after Bergman's conversation with Streisand, Bergman had lunch with Stanley Sheinbaum, an ardent liberal activist, and told him that her friend wanted to learn more about nuclear issues. Sheinbaum accepted the challenge. Dinners were arranged at his home and at Carolwood Drive to meet policy experts who would brief her on the subject. Leading scientists such as Marvin L. Goldberger, then president of the California Institute of Technology, and Disney Drell, from Stanford, were drafted as tutors.

Sheinbaum provided Streisand with literature, books, and articles on the Reagan administration's nuclear policy. She was an avid student. "She started with very little knowledge," Goldberger recalled, "and a great deal of suddenly awakened concern. . . . I had two roles: one was that of someone who knows a great deal about nuclear power, nuclear reactors, and has also spent an awful lot of time worrying about strategic weapons and international security. So, in a sense I was a resource person that tried, when necessary, to separate for her fact from fiction and [could help her to find] the appropriate vehicle to make the maximum contribution in this area about which she was so greatly concerned."

"Marilyn realized the way Barbra Streisand could help win back the Senate [for the Democrats] was to raise money," the HWPC treasurer, attorney Bonnie Reiss, said, "and the way she could do that was to sing."

Streisand was not easily convinced. The many years she had absented herself from concert work had increased her trepidation. Finally, in midsummer, with the election only three and a half months away, she agreed to do a concert, but the event would have to be limited to invited guests and presented in the safe and comfortable setting of her secluded, well-protected Malibu ranch (which she had retained during her split with Peters). Tents were raised over tables set for formal outdoor dining. To transform the grounds of the ranch to a professional outdoor auditorium necessitated the logistical task of carving out an amphitheater from a stretch of flat lawn and wiring it for sound and lights in three weeks' time. Nonetheless, everyone at the HWPC was enthusiastic, for not only would Streisand be performing live for the first time in many years, she would be doing it in her own home, a great enticement to potential ticket buyers who were being asked to pay $5,000 to see the concert.

No one was more excited about the event than Streisand. "After all of my insistence that I didn't want to sing in public anymore, I sang," she said. "Chernobyl had erupted in lethal radiation. The arms race was bankrupting the nation and the world. And I wanted to add my one voice to demands for action." The dinner concert was called "One Voice," which had a double meaning: a solo concert (although Barry Gibb sang two songs with her) and the message that each person could make a difference in the fight against the proliferation of nuclear energy. Baskin joined forces with her as musical producer; Randy Kerber was the musical director; Streisand and Erlichman, producers (with Marilyn Bergman as executive producer); and Gary Smith and Dwight Hemion, who had presented most of her television shows, were to produce the live concert for Home Box Office, with the proceeds going to the Barbra Streisand Foundation for distribution to the various charities she supported. The funds raised directly from the concert would be used to help in the campaigns of the six liberal Democrats.

Streisand oversaw the transformation of her property into a professional outdoor arena, wrote the script with Marilyn and Alan Bergman, prepared and rehearsed seventeen songs, and recorded on audiocassette hundreds of individual, personalized invitations, "which," one observer wrote, "landed on the desks of Hollywood's most powerful men and women like a summons." Within a few days, over three hundred people, the capacity audience, sent in their checks.

The night of the concert, September 6, 1986 — a warm evening tempered by a soft Pacific breeze — Streisand was flushed with nervous excitement as she waited for her entrance music in the newly constructed, temporary dressing-room area behind the stage. Robin Williams, seemingly awed by the star-studded audience, opened the concert with some humorous patter. Seated in impeccable white chairs set up in semicircular rows on the grass skirt facing the stage were some of Hollywood's greatest stars (and liberal Democrats): Shirley MacLaine, Warren Beatty, Sally Field, Bette Midler, Jane Fonda, Goldie Hawn, Walter Matthau, Jack Nicholson, and Chevy Chase, among others, and in a grand show of solidarity, ex-husband Elliott Gould, ex-lover Jon Peters, and Jason. Streisand would be judged by her peers, but they were also her friends — people who held the same political views as she did. They were here to support a cause they all believed in, so she was guaranteed a receptive audience — not that she would ever give anything but her very best.

Her entrance in a flattering white beaded turtleneck sweater, white evening skirt slit to the knee, was met with thunderous applause. "You're nice. You're all friends. Thank you for being here." She smiled and waved and threw kisses. The sheltering sky was starlit. A soft breeze made wisps of her frizzy blond hair, worn loose and to her shoulders. Rather than the usual thirty-five-man orchestra she was accustomed to, she had engaged a versatile group of mostly synthesizer instrumentalists — "Eight guys and some big electric bill!" she told her audience. Randy Kerber conducted from his position at the keyboards.

Her songs were geared to the theme of the evening — helping to save and protect the environment, our love for others, pride in our country — which gave the concert a soft, often sentimental edge, although there were some satirical gibes at the Republicans in specially written lyrics by the Bergmans. She made a beautiful segue from a short speech about nonproliferation of nuclear energy into "People," sung with more wisdom than passion and imparting new meaning to the lyrics. "Over the Rainbow," which she proclaimed "the greatest movie song ever written," was dedicated to Judy Garland, who was so identified with it. Streisand sang it against an exquisite backing by Kerber as a song of great hope. The bridge was especially youthful and carefree. She was Dorothy on the road to Oz, a young girl touched with wonder, her dreams still intact. Garland's underlying plea for love and protection, the vulnerable voice and misty eyes that had mirrored severe human suffering, were stifled. Streisand had made the song her own, and it was a tour de force. She had even improved Yip Harburg's somewhat saccharine coda by changing "if happy little bluebirds fly" to the more universal "if all those little bluebirds fly."

Two duets with Barry Gibb, "Highway to the Sky" and "Who's Sorry Now?," were the least successful of the evening's program. Then came an especially moving rendition of "Papa, Can You Hear Me?" from the score of *Yentl,* sung as the darkness of night encroached in the flickering light of a single candle: "in memory of those great father figures — Abraham Lincoln, John F. Kennedy, Gandhi, Sadat." This was followed by "The Way We Were," which had a much more contemporary sound than any previous arrangement along with numerous mellisonant sections. For an encore she ended the evening with a stirring interpretation of "America the Beautiful," beginning a cappella and eventually asking the audience to join in. As they did, they clasped hands and swayed as though moved by the night wind.

Streisand was visibly affected by the emotion generated by her audience. Tears filled her eyes as she left the stage after her final bow. Much as she had grown to fear public appearances, she had missed the instant gratification and the outpouring of love she received from a live audience.

The dinner concert raised $1.5 million, an amount that exceeded by $500,000 the proceeds from a Republican fund-raising dinner for President Reagan the following night. This caused much jubilation among HWPC members and a certain pride for Streisand, especially as the concert ultimately helped the Democrats regain the Senate, as five of the six senators who were the benefactors of the event won their seats. Streisand's political consciousness had been fully awakened (her social consciousness had always been apparent), and there would be no backsliding for her from this point.

In the fall of 1987, when she was mired in the final work before the release of *Nuts,* Richard Baskin moved out of the Carolwood Drive house. "One day he was there, the next he was gone," a friend said. "I was surprised. She really liked him a lot." Streisand had harbored great hopes for this relationship; she seemed desperately to need the stability it brought to her life. But the relationship lacked that depth of feeling she had felt for Elliott and the passion she had had for Jon Peters. Let no one be misled. Barbra Streisand is a romantic, and one whose view of love was formed by her early passion for movies and the great cinematic love affairs that she avidly watched unfold on the screen as she, an awkward, unhappy youngster, sat in a balcony seat in a darkened theater in Brooklyn. Being in love still meant that special magnetic pull between two people, the sound of trumpets, the flash of fireworks; and she had not felt this with Baskin.

Her separation from Baskin during the long weeks of discomfort as *Nuts* went before the cameras had been the breaking point. Days spent filming inside a woman's prison, dressed in prison drabs, her hair a tangled mass of curls, taking on the terror of the real women dealing with madness and horrors she could only imagine, had not made her easy to deal with. Although it was Baskin who made the final decision, the parting was not acrimonious. Still, it hurt — and she was alone, a condition with which she never dealt well. Jason had gone back to New York to study at the NYU Film School to better prepare for his future as an actor and a moviemaker. She was happy that he had found what it was he wanted to do, but his departure had come at a time when they had not worked through their problems. She did not doubt Jason's love; it was their inability to communicate, to discuss the deeper issues that might be troubling him — his homosexuality, his being the son of such famous parents and wanting to follow their careers in either theater or films.

Her impasse with Jason was all the more troubling because of her own struggle as a young woman to relate to *her* mother and how much pain her inability to do so had given her. She had meant things to be different for Jason. She loved him dearly, wanted only the best for him, and was exceptionally proud of the fine person he had become. She had not been a mother in the way a woman without a career of the magnitude of hers might have managed, but she had tried to compensate with the quality of time they spent together.

With Jason and Baskin gone, she fought depression, went back into therapy, and held on to the thought that *Nuts* would be a great success and that she would finally be recognized as a serious actress. The movie opened on November 20 to mixed reviews and strong criticism that she was miscast in the role of Claudia Draper. In retrospect, it can only be assumed that the critics could not overcome their own strong image of Streisand. They viewed the film with a clichéd idea of women in prostitution, and Streisand's ethnic looks and intellectual approach to the character was not it. They were wrong, for Claudia Draper is one of Streisand's finest performances: chilling, moving, and especially *real*. It is shocking that she was overlooked in the Academy Awards for that year, a blow to Streisand, who thought her performance should have been acknowledged (she was not even nominated). It did not ease her resentment that the film came in at $6 million over budget and did not do well at the box office, the latter of which she blamed, at least partly, on the press.

Streisand, the ultimate survivor, now threw all her energies into acquiring a new project, *The Prince of Tides,* a bestselling book by Pat Conroy, author of *The Great Santini* and *The Lords of Discipline*. A big, sprawling novel about a dysfunctional Southern family with a dark secret of rape and murder at its center, *The Prince of Tides* consumed Streisand's interest. Without doubt it was a filmic story, the characters were all well defined and interesting. Once again, it is about a wounded family and those members who are fighting to keep their sanity and survive. And it had a role she wanted to play, Dr. Lowenstein, a dedicated psychiatrist, unhappy in her own private life, who falls in love with her patient, Tom Wingo, whose twin sister, Savannah, is also her charge. Dr. Lowenstein was not the main character in Conroy's novel but becomes the catalyst in the film script and the feminine half of the movie's love story.

As Christmas approached, Streisand decided to spend a few weeks at the ski resort in Aspen, Colorado, which had in the past decade become the American Mecca for snow sports, the very rich, and the glitterati of the entertainment world. Although not an expert skier, she liked the sport and the relaxed ambience of the resort. Aspen is also breathtakingly beautiful, circled as it is by rugged, ice-sheathed peaks but with plenty of gentle, rolling slopes for the intermediate skier. The Bergmans and numerous other friends would be there. Lyricist Marilyn Bergman, a blond woman with a lovely face and the girthy look of an opera diva, and her soft-spoken, sparsely built husband, Alan, always helped Streisand to ward away the blues. Warmth, good music, and engaging conversation abounded in their company, and so Aspen seemed like a good place to spend the holidays.

At a Boxing Day (the day after Christmas) party at the Bergmans, Streisand once again saw Don Johnson. He had grabbed hold of her arm, pulled her off into a private corner, and then left early with her. "If I want to meet people, I have to talk to them first because so many are intimidated by me," Streisand said. "So if a guy does make the first move [as had Peters and Johnson], he is already a step ahead."

Johnson had lived his life fast and claimed he had no regrets. "I have done everything I've ever taken a fancy to. The only things I haven't done are things I haven't thought of," he boasted. He could be called tough but, as friends and coworkers avouched, "he could have charmed Hitler." He was the natural fantasy man for any Jewish woman with Streisand's background — the blond, bronzed, macho gentile man with the physique of a beach lifeguard and a smile that could light up a funeral. By New Year's they were lovers; by February 1987 — just four weeks later — they were a couple.

"I'm happy, very happy," Streisand declared to the press. "And I have never been very happy, so it's something I'm learning. It's as if I were a child again." She had expressed similar sentiments in the early days of her affair with Peters. In truth, the two men stood comparison. Both were younger, cocky, and streetwise; had spent time in juvenile reformatories (where Johnson also learned how to defend himself); and were aggressive both in business and sex. Johnson was also a good athlete, bordering on the professional in golf, tennis, skiing, and powerboat racing. There was another side, however, to his swaggering, macho, womanizing reputation. He was intelligent and sensitive and — having suffered a great sense of loss with his parents' divorce when he was a youngster — wanted to settle into a close family situation so that his son (whom he had with former lover Patti D'Arbanville) would have a real home with him. But he did have an inner violence that flashed occasionally. And Peters had been a close and protective father as well.

"That character he played in *Miami Vice* was an extension of things Don had done," his longtime media consultant, Elliot Mintz, confided. "He drove fancy cars when he was broke and wore fancy clothes when he couldn't afford them . . . and he always had a strong effect on people. When he walked into a room, women — especially — reacted and sometimes in the most unabashed way . . . and I'm talking long before *Miami Vice*."

A very sexy man who appealed to both men and women in the same way that movie idols like Tyrone Power and Robert Redford had before him, Johnson had an aura of invincibility, a vitality that was instantly appealing to Streisand. He glowed with good health, and his looks, tousled gold hair streaked almost platinum in places by the sun, and strong, handsome well-proportioned features were distinctive. Whatever the camera made of his appearance, in person there was something of the Fitzgerald antihero Gatsby in his looks, the once-rough diamond polished to a shine but still showing small, giveaway imperfections.

Born Don Wayne in Galena, Missouri, Johnson was a rebellious youth from a working-class family, who as a teenager landed in a detention school for car theft. Shortly after his release, eighteen months later, he hustled his way into a drama course after being thrown out of his high-school class for obstreperous behavior. Bright and street-smart, he possessed incorrigible charm. Encouraged by a teacher, he went on to achieve a scholarship to the University of Kansas, followed by a stint at the American Conservatory Theater in San Francisco. His theater career was nearly throttled when he got hooked on drugs, alcohol, and "enough partying and casual sex to fuel the most hedonistic episode of *Miami Vice*."

"I lived with Don Johnson, I discovered him, put him in a play set in prison with a gay theme [*Fortune and Men's Eyes*]," the actor Sal Mineo once said. "People imagined all sorts of things. . . . I'll put it like this: Yes, I'm bisexual and blond guys are my favorite type, and I did enjoy seeing Don nude on the stage [in the play] and [bare-chested] on the silver screen, for that matter. Who wouldn't?" Mineo was stabbed to death in 1978 in what appears to have been a homosexual attack.

Before he was thirty-two, Johnson had been married and divorced three times (actress Melanie Griffith, then only sixteen, was his third wife), and in 1982 had fathered his son Jesse with D'Arbanville, a tall, well-built comedic actress who had a small role with Streisand and Ryan O'Neal in *The Main Event* (1979) as O'Neal's gum-chewing, earthy girlfriend.

Fame had not come as suddenly or as early to Johnson as it had to Streisand, but his hard-knock years had not suppressed his natural exuberance. He talked easily, laughed heartily, and had more in common with Streisand than first appearance might reveal. Knowledgeable musically, he had been singing all his life and had recently cut a successful single, "Heartbeat," which had hit the charts. "I have this persona as an actor and as a person of being this sort of street-smart tough guy. Tough guys don't sing or dance, do they?" he told *Playboy* magazine. "So here was a chance [to make a record] and say 'Fuck you!'"

A perfectionist in his work, a workaholic by his own admission, a serious actor who wanted to direct, Johnson was not afraid to say what he felt or to go after what he wanted. He spoke with a candor that ranged "from downright dangerous to outright playful," and he was going through a period in his life when he was trying to make some sense of his past.

"Nobody got higher than I did for longer than I did," he admitted. "I look back now and say, 'What the fuck was I doing?' — waking up in a joint with a bunch of people lying around with needles in their arms." Off drugs, in control of his addictions, Johnson was hell-bent for international success, but he had not lost his lust for life.

For Streisand, at that moment, Johnson was just the right man. He made her feel younger, more alive, and self-confident — as once Jon Peters had done.

"I don't think Barbra ever got over being a wallflower as a kid," a member of her close family confided. "Until she left Brooklyn when she was seventeen or so, she didn't date much. I remember that she didn't go to her senior prom. It's always been important to her to be seen with a good-looking guy, a man other women also find attractive. Barbra always had to prove her own worth to herself, both in her work and the men she chose to love."

With Johnson she looked like a woman in love. They exchanged intimate glances in public, held hands, laughed at each other's jokes. They were a good fit, able to mix sex, work, and enthusiasms. Johnson wasted no time. He claimed he was in love with Streisand and believed he had "run into the woman who could be *it*." It was apparent to Streisand's close circle and the media alike that she reciprocated his passion. Wherever they were, they seemed unable to keep their hands off each other.

Johnson had gained twenty-five pounds to play a small-town building contractor who's depressed about the state of his marriage and growing old in *Sweet Hearts Dance*, the movie he had just completed, and was on a physical-fitness regime to lose the weight, and Streisand joined in with the sports she at least liked. He played a competitive game of tennis. "He has a killer instinct," one of his opponents in a tournament in Aspen said. "He can slam a ball with ferocious power." He was less fierce when hitting the ball with Streisand, who was not anywhere in his league, but she worked hard to improve her game. She even responded to his enthusiasm for boating — he had won several major races — fighting seasickness to ride the waves in a small craft with him.

No sooner had Johnson lost his excess weight than he was called in to reshoot the end of *Sweet Hearts Dance* and he had to regain some of it. Streisand went on an eating spree with him, somehow managing to stay slim while he ballooned once again. They talked about his role, his interpretation, what he would do if he were directing the movie. Robert Greenwald was the director of the film but Johnson had directed several episodes of *Miami Vice* and hoped to do a feature as soon as possible. "One day," Greenwald remembered, "Don said to me, 'You know, Barbra may come out while we're shooting; is that okay?' And I said, 'Sure, it's fine.' But she never came." When they later met, he asked Streisand why she hadn't come. "She looked at me, smiled and said, 'Well, I decided there were enough directors on the set as it was!'" She viewed the rough cut of the film with Johnson and made "some very, very good suggestions," Greenwald added.

They retained separate residences. Streisand was not yet ready to bring a man into her home again, although she spent all the time she could with Johnson. They were a couple but held on to their individual identities. She looked truly happy — laughed and clowned a lot — her eyes shone, her skin glowed. Wherever she was photographed, Johnson was right there with her. He supported her dedication to getting *The Prince of Tides* into production, not an easy task because she wanted to produce, direct, and star in the film and the budget was high. "Barbra not only makes me laugh, she makes me think," he told an interviewer, adding; "the possibilities are limitless!"

"Don makes me feel very feminine," she told a member of her close circle. "I have to be so strong for everyone — Mom, Jason, my staff — that it's nice to have someone be strong for me." Her skin was bronzed from the sun, her body trim, and she wore clothes that showed off her new streamlined figure to its best advantage. Suddenly, she seemed to have shed ten years. Dining out, going to the movies, shopping with

Richard Baskin, had been painful, for he had not been someone who was accustomed to stares and attention that celebrity attracts. With Johnson it was entirely different. He was at the height of his fame, a raunchy sex symbol. Female fans went wild whenever they caught sight of him. Streisand, who had never been cooperative about signing autographs in public, now did. She was able to enjoy her fame, the attention of fans, when she was in Johnson's company because he received as much adulation as she did.

The ranch he owned in Colorado gave them time together out of the limelight. The house was on a large spread of land that looked out on a breathtaking vista of mountains and plains. Dawn was spectacular; night, chillingly beautiful. There was something magical about the place. Johnson liked to mingle with his neighbors and fellow ranchers, so they spent considerable time in Colorado riding horseback, spending quiet evenings together at his ranch house before a roaring fire, or relaxing in the company of close friends. Johnson's six-year-old son, Jesse, sometimes rode with them and played golf at the local club alongside his father with a set of specially made small irons. Streisand could relive some of her happiest days when Jason was a small boy and she and Elliott took time out to be with him. Those times had not been often enough, she realized now.

By the end of the golden summer of 1988, he looked like a Greek god and she was glowing with health and the kind of beauty that shines when a woman is in love. The intimacy between them was such that she was able to talk about her past, to explore her feelings. As she did, *The Prince of Tides* began to take on more meaning for her.

The character she wished to play, Dr. Lowenstein, is described in Pat Conroy's book as "one of those go-to-hell New York women with the incorruptible carriage of lionesses." Conroy's Dr. Lowenstein was a fictional blood cousin to Kramer's Dr. Brookner in *The Normal Heart*. With childhood abuse and murder at its center, *The Prince of Tides* contains overtones of *Nuts*. Streisand was searching through her work for answers to her own nagging psychological problems, carryovers from childhood that neither success nor a loving relationship could obliterate. Several studios rejected the project, which only steeled her determination. As the rejections mounted, she grew frantic and turned to Jon Peters, now a powerful studio head at Columbia, who took it on. "It helps to have an influential ex-boyfriend," she joked. But her ties to Peters were not really severed. It was one more relationship with which she had to make peace, not an easy task — for despite her attachment to Johnson, she still felt in some way tied to Peters, who had married Christine Forsyth. She saw Peters frequently, would discuss her projects with him, and would come away from a meeting with him feeling unnerved, perhaps just a little less sure of her commitment to Johnson. Peters remained on a roll in the industry, and he and Guber were each amassing huge fortunes. If she needed Peters, all she had to do was yell for help and she felt confident that he would be there.

"When I first read *The Prince of Tides* I knew I had to make it. [It] was about coming to terms with the people in our lives . . . our parents . . . our children . . . our mates . . . and even more important than that," she said, "as I am learning myself, it's about coming to terms with ourselves by accepting, loving and being in harmony with the child who still lives inside us."

In mid-September 1988 she and Johnson recorded a single, "Till I Loved You," together. It turned out to be their farewell song. Ten weeks later, Johnson and Melanie Griffith (one of his three ex-wives) announced, to Streisand's shocked disbelief (she claimed that she had no indication of it), that they were going to be remarried. Griffith had spent several months in a rehabilitation center for alcoholism after completing her acclaimed performance in *Working Girl*. Streisand knew that Johnson had been seeing Griffith but solemnly believed him when he told her that it was out of concern for her health and her struggle against addiction.

The world suddenly came crashing down around her. She had somehow failed once again to sustain a meaningful relationship. This time she was the spurned woman, and she was furious at Johnson for ending their affair in such a cold, public manner. For weeks she brooded about him and the cruel press coverage that made her out to look a fool.

She was ready once again to go back to the beginning, to try to make some sense of it all, to hold her life in her arms and learn to give it the love she believed she had never had. And yet, could she ever let go of the anger she felt for the bruises she bore? "My mother could never make up for the part in my childhood that I never got," she said bitterly at the time. The journey back would coincide with the making of *The Prince of Tides*. Always Barbra Streisand would see her life in terms of the drama and romance that was found in movies.

29

As Jason's parents, Elliott and Streisand now had something to face together. In 1989, Jason then twenty-four, neither he nor they had discussed the matter of his homosexuality in public or, it seems, in private.
Elliott has admitted having had a total block on the subject, and it was not
until five years later — after Jason himself went public — that his father
told English journalist Corinna Honan, "Yes, [Jason] is gay. That's his
preference, his business. It's something that's new to me and it's an acutely
delicate subject. But I'm more than just empathetic. Whether it has been
a problem for Barbra, I don't know. It's really important not to be preju-
diced and both of us are devoted to him.

One thing that had brought Streisand and Jason closer was his intense desire at this time to be an actor. She had seen him in several local
amateur productions and thought he possessed a true gift. He had also
played bit parts in three unreleased movies that year. When Streisand
first read *The Prince of Tides* about the Wingos, a South Carolina family
whose children grow up repressing nightmarish traumas, Streisand recalled thinking, "Jesus, I'm perfect for this part [as the middle-aged Jewish psychiatrist]. I identify with the woman completely, even to the line
in the book that says she is in the middle of aging extraordinarily well."
She also saw part of herself in the traumatized Wingo children and in the

relationship between Dr. Lowenstein and her sullen, teenage son, Bernard. When she started to cast, Jason was living away from home in a small West Hollywood apartment, pursuing his acting career.

"Jason has never asked me for anything. He has never been ambitious," she later said. "He doesn't have a desire to be famous or anything like that, because, you know, it's complicated being my son and Elliott's son, problems of competition and all that. But here my kid calls up one day and he says, 'Mom, about that role, I hear you're getting ready to cast someone else. I thought you thought I'd be good for it.'"

Streisand had cast another actor in the part, Chris O'Donnell (later to make a name for himself in *Scent of a Woman* with Al Pacino), who was a star quarterback for his high-school football team. "Barbra showed me this kid that she had cast for the role of her son," Pat Conroy, the author of *The Prince of Tides,* remembered, "a very handsome blond kid. Of course, everyone looks wonderful in Hollywood, but I said, 'That ain't the kid.' So she said, 'I already hired him.' I still said, 'That still ain't him. This kid Bernard is not a good athlete, that's the point. 'So she sort of flipped through other kids she'd auditioned. She finally came to this one kid. I didn't know it was her son. But he showed a snarling, wonderful teenage quality [and looked like Streisand, which had to have some bearing on the casting]. I said, '*That's* the kid, right there.'" Streisand recalls this happening when Conroy saw a picture of Jason on the piano in her living room. Memory is like that, often elusive, finding its place in other than original surroundings. Whoever is correct, the point is that Conroy saw Jason as Bernard before Streisand and when she was resisting what to others seemed both logical and right. Even when Jason was finally signed to play the role, the news was kept from the media and not announced until months later when the film was already in production and on location. "I thought, deep down, 'Well, it's dangerous. We could both get attacked for this,'" she confessed.

"Every film she directs involves a working-out of a part of her own life," Marilyn Bergman added.

"I think she read *The Prince of Tides* seven times," said Cis Corman, who was to be executive producer on the film. "She knew the book so well, she would tell Pat what he had written on page 376. I mean after

Yentl, she could have become a rabbi. Look, it's a painful process for her but with moments of joy."

Making a film with Streisand means feeding her insecurities. "You have to keep saying 'You're beautiful, you're wonderful,'" Corman admitted. Nonetheless, most of the actors who have worked under her direction will tell you how sensitive she is to their problems, perhaps because she is so conscious of her own.

Streisand said at the time, "A lot of this movie is very meaningful to me because it's about not blaming your parents. We've all come from some type of painful childhood. But if you blame your parents, it keeps you the victim. The mother in me makes me possibly a better director. Women can bring a certain kind of nurturing quality to a film," a point Amy Irving had affirmed about Streisand as a director during the making of *Yentl.*

Three weeks before leaving for South Carolina, where the film was to begin shooting, and only days before April 24, 1990, Streisand's forty-eighth birthday, Diana, now eighty-two, was rushed to the hospital with severe chest pains and underwent bypass heart surgery. Streisand was in a panic. Work was put aside as she stayed with Roslyn by their mother's side. "It changed my whole perspective of the importance of the film," Streisand confessed. "The film became non-important. The relationships with people I love began to matter more than the movie."

Diana was now an elderly woman. She had been much maligned publicly by her elder daughter and had never had any means of refuting or ameliorating Streisand's constant barbed statements of the emotional abuse she had suffered at her hands. She had not been a demonstrative or, at times, a supportive parent, but she had done what she thought was best. She was not equipped either to handle the situation she found herself in after her husband's death or to nurture a daughter's "fancies." But neither had Diana ever turned her back on her daughter, no matter how bitter and cutting Streisand's statements were about her to a press eager to exploit celebrity-revealing comments. Diana had inherited her own pain, an unsympathetic mother, the fear that she could not make it on her own. She had been born into a time when women had much less chance for achievement unless they were beautiful, which she was not;

she had lost the husband she loved and been humiliated by the man she believed would make a home for her children and herself. She was a victim of her era and her inadequacies.

Streisand had been fighting her mother all her life. Underneath, there was an unseverable cord. She loved Diana, always had. She had clung to her, slept in her bed for years after Manny's death, had wanted to make things good for her from the time of her first success, needed affirmation of Diana's approval and love more than that of any one other person in her life. She had a lot to think about now and was determined to make sure Diana knew she loved her before it was too late.

With Jason and about one hundred members of the cast and crew, she took the company on location to the small town of Beaufort, South Carolina. Beaufort was where Pat Conroy had spent his teenage years and where he would later teach English and coach football at his high school like his alter ego Tom Wingo. In the book the town is named Colleton, but Conroy has described it unmistakenly. Beaufort is in the low country where warm white sands meet the south Atlantic. The town boasts a beautiful natural harbor. Offshore there are dozens of inlets and waterways where small fishing boats troll for sweet Gulf shrimp. High bluffs, densely wooded with subtropical growth, rise to the north of town, and some of the surviving older houses are made of crushed oyster shells. Others, built high for coolness, have wide front porches and old-fashioned gardens where jasmine, oleander, and wisteria mingle with oak trees bearded with Spanish moss. From above comes the sound of seabirds and the drone of heat-drawn bugs; in the evening cool, what Streisand called, "a quiet, mystical quality."

It took time building the required sets, so it was not until June 18 that the film went before the cameras. The first scene to be shot would be one of the last in the picture, with Tom Wingo reunited with his wife and three daughters after his affair in New York with Dr. Lowenstein, walking with them on the beach, although fifteen endings would be shot before that one was chosen.

Nick Nolte had been cast as Tom Wingo, deeply Southern, a man of great outer strength and inner turmoil, born into a dysfunctional family.

His twin sister, Savannah, is a famous, gifted, troubled poet, and a suicidal patient of Dr. Lowenstein. Caught up in her own difficult family situation — a philandering husband and a difficult teenage son — the middle-aged Lowenstein persuades Wingo to come to New York and help her fill in the missing information that she hopes will unlock the mystery to Savannah's deep depression. During these voluntary, nonpaying sessions, he reveals the hidden secrets of the Wingo family, which include an abusive father, murder, and rape. Dr. Lowenstein and Wingo fall in love and enter into a relationship that helps both of them resolve their personal situations.

Both Warren Beatty and Robert Redford were previously discussed as possibly playing Tom Wingo, but neither was right for the character, who requires a strong macho appearance, sensitivity, and the ability to "unleash torrents of raw emotion." Nolte, at six foot one, 210 pounds, had a brawny, bruising physique. He is rugged, blond, and raspy-voiced, and his background had been rough-and-tumble. Raised in Omaha, Nebraska, he had gone to Arizona State University on a football scholarship and transferred to three other schools because of poor grades and a low tolerance for alcohol. He turned to acting, supporting himself in the beginning as an ironworker. Fourteen years later he was still in touring companies, taking college courses whenever he had the time to obtain the credits he lacked for his diploma and joining in the antiwar demonstrations that proliferated during the Nixon years. He was arrested and placed on five years' probation for counterfeiting draft cards and married and divorced twice before, in 1976 at the age of forty-two, he made his first breakthrough as the costar of the Irwin Shaw television miniseries *Rich Man, Poor Man*. He quickly became a popular Hollywood star known as "a tough guy with soul and a natural acting ability."

Nolte had not fared well in his relationships with women and was at the time of *The Prince of Tides* caught up in a hostile divorce with his third wife. Streisand had to consider seriously whether he might have difficulty taking direction from a woman. She decided to chance it, as Nolte projected just the right blend of grit and tenderness required for the role. "In the movie, Wingo would have to come to trust a female therapist, while in real life he was going to have to trust me, a female director," Streisand later said. This did not become the problem she anticipated. Nolte had a great respect for her.

"Barbra likes to explore," he said. "We shot some key scenes in several different ways. We also had long discussions about male-female relationships. It was the first time I had worked with a woman director. In working with male directors, I've found that the male actor and director have a kind of collusive attitude about the emotional points of scenes. With Barbra, there is a lot of continued exploration."

Their love scenes ignited sparks. "I don't find it that easy to bare my soul, to do intimate things in front of a camera," she admitted. "I'd rather do it in private. I had to yell, 'Cut!' when things got too hot [with Nolte]. His makeup was all over my hair. You couldn't see my blond streaks." She had even more difficulty with appearing nude. She wears a scant nightdress in one scene (after a great deal of discussion about it with Nolte and Cis Corman). "I just find it rather sexier to wear sheer clothes in bed," she defended. The love scenes she found most satisfying in the film were those that dealt with deep, mutual affection, Lowenstein cradled in Wingo's arms in a chair. "The woman going back to the safety of childhood again, being held by the father or someone who loves you," she explained.

The act of touching people's faces, their hands, or being held, comforted by someone in his or her arms, had great meaning to her. In her direction of the scene where Wingo has his final catharsis, she re-created her own visual memory of the time the touch of her therapist's hand on hers had caused her to open the floodgates of her emotions and weep. In a two-hour documentary laser disc on the making of *The Prince of Tides,* which she narrates, Streisand illustrates what she wanted Nolte to experience when Lowenstein takes Wingo in her arms, his head on her breast, as he weeps after revealing the hidden secrets in his family. "Oh, this is interesting, this is what it feels like to be held by your mother."

The documentary is all about her directorial approach to the making of the film and, while fascinating and insightful as to the reasons behind many of her choices, reveals the strikingly egotistical manner in which she thinks of her work, the way she takes total possession of its creative process. "I did this to the script," "I wrote that scene in my mind over and over," "I rewrote," "I improvised," are used throughout. One could easily surmise that she was the sole author of the screenplay. Never once does she say that she is working from a script adapted by Becky Johnston and Pat Conroy from his novel.

Despite their differences on *Yentl,* she had brought Jack Rosenthal to Beaufort from London to "humanize the dialogue." One evening when they were working over dinner in a Chinese restaurant, he bit down on the thighbone of a roasted duck, smashing his molar to fragments inside his gums. It was, he said, "the least painful part of the three weeks I spent working with Barbra on the script."

She refused to let things go and would spend hours on the smallest detail, driving her coworkers as hard and as long as herself. Yet, difficult as she is in any work situation, as a director Streisand is unquestionably sensitive to mood, to frame, to moment. She has caught some extraordinary images in the film, which she points out in the documentary — the Wingo house rising in morning mist from the marshes, the grace of the land, the view from Lowenstein's skyscraper terrace looking down on nighttime New York City — but Stephen Goldblatt, the picture's cinematographer, is never mentioned.

Then there is the music by James Newton Howard. Streisand once mentions "Jim" in relation to the music, but clarifies no further of whom she is speaking. She had a brief affair with Howard during the time he was scoring the movie. They had been working closely together. Howard is a sensitive, attractive man and there was a musical union of ideas, a time — placed in musical context — when they were "breathing" together. It is something that an accompanist and a singer can have. With the work done on the scoring, the affair ended simply, seemingly no resentments on either side. Howard delivered a lovely score that fully captures the mood of the picture and often helps to define the action — the atonal reverse of a theme to indicate a character's alienation, the balletic section that takes Wingo and Bernard through their football sessions.

Film is undeniably a director's medium. "I like to see my visions come to life," Streisand often says. If a director does not have a vision, he or she should not be one; but without all the glorious technical, artistic, and creative talents that contribute to the final film, a director would be paralyzed, unable to bring that vision to life, a world of its own. Streisand's inability to share or give credit to her coworkers has to do with her complete absorption in the movie she is making and her inability to think of it as anyone else's but her own.

She does, however, give full credit to the great violinist Pinchas Zukerman, heard dubbing the solos for Dr. Lowenstein's virtuoso husband, Jeroen Krabbe (who brilliantly managed the difficult fingering). Jason had one scene in which he also had to be seen playing Fritz Kreisler's difficult violin piece "Praludium and Allegro," and doing so in a manner that would show a tremendous gift. ("If I could play the violin like that, I'd never touch a football," Wingo tells him.) He had three months to accomplish the fingering and body movements. After three lessons he played "Twinkle, Twinkle, Little Star" on the instrument. "I couldn't stop laughing," Streisand confessed. "I know I hurt him and I hate that, but he was so awful. However," she added proudly, "by the time he had to play it in the scene, he was able to do it like a young prodigy. His hands were so stiff from practicing, he had to soak them every evening. I *knew* my son could master it."

Directing her son presented some problems. Jason was always prepared, always professional, and almost always good-natured. "There's not a bad bone in his body," Streisand said. But he is his mother's son and has strong opinions. They clashed more than once. Streisand had him playing one scene over and over, to his irritation. "You've told me what you want, now tell me what you don't like!" he snapped at her. She attempted to do so, and finally he did the scene as she envisioned it. In the last scene he has with Wingo, set in Grand Central Station, the script called for him to walk off briskly to catch his train, sadly leaving behind the man who was a father figure to him and had helped him become an acceptable athlete. After several takes, Streisand shouted at him, "Walk like a man! Walk like a *man!*" meaning this was the moment in the film when he would become an adult, but it sounded like a put-down to members of the company.

While they were in Beaufort, mother and son came to a deeper understanding and appreciation of each other. Jason acquitted himself well in the part of Bernard, giving a real and sympathetic performance. He is always right on, believable. He bears a close resemblance to his mother; although like Elliott, his eyes are dark, his hair brown and curly, his prominent nose and full mouth mark his Streisand lineage. Slim at the time, fairly small of stature, possessing a winning boyish smile, he never appears to be too old for the role.

Jon Peters, then separated from Christine, visited Beaufort during the location shooting. During their short on-again, off-again marriage they had adopted a little blond girl they named Caleigh. Streisand had been asked to be the child's godmother, and she accepted. Peters was retaining shared custody and by every sign was devoted to the child. Nonetheless, Streisand was concerned about Caleigh's welfare as a child of divorce. Marriage and adopting a child herself — preferably a girl, she asserted — seemed a feasible idea to her, although there was no man of any importance in her life. *The Prince of Tides,* however, had numerous children in the cast, and by her own admission she enjoyed working with them more than with any of the other actors. Wingo had three young daughters, played by talented children with whom she spent much time. There were also the flashback scenes of the young Wingo, his sister, and brother. The three child actors cast in the parts went on to California with the company to shoot in an indoor tank the beautifully choreographed underwater swimming scene that has such a magical look in the picture. Streisand spends over half an hour on her documentary discussing the auditions and screen tests of these children, as proud of their natural acting ability and their attractiveness as she would be if they were her own.

"[I've been] thinking about how I want to spend the rest of my life," she said at the time. "I want to work with children. I feel a lack of children in my life. My son is very grown-up. I was thinking of adopting a child, but I'm not too sure I want to do that as a single parent. It wasn't too hot for me, and I don't particularly want to do that to another child."

It was clear in viewing the rushes of the film that she was getting a spectacular performance out of Nolte and the other actors. It is Dr. Lowenstein who does not thoroughly satisfy. There is a strained seriousness to Streisand's performance that often interferes with believability. She is stiff, mannered, and in many two-shot or group scenes lit too importantly, almost hammering home the point that she is in the shot. This is particularly true of the scene in which Nolte sees her across the room at an art exhibit and she appears to be standing in an aureole glow, making it impossible for anyone to miss her. "I don't think about acting much," she said defensively. "It is easier if the part is very much you. And this character I understood very well." The dual role of director and actor was a challenge that she had been extremely successful in handling with *Yentl,* but much less so on *The Prince of Tides.*

"It's Barbra's talent for performing that works against her abilities as an actress," Nolte contended. "It's really a lonely job to be a singer, a totally different mentality. As an entertainer, it's all about *me.* The lights have to be right for *me.* [Entertainers] come on the set, and they don't know how to share. They don't want to stick around for off-camera work. They have not grown up with a sense of teamsmanship. It makes it very hard for them to be taken seriously in the acting community. Barbra's much more tolerant as a director. You really don't have time to focus on yourself, and in that position she works real fine."

Streisand acknowledged the difficulty of directing herself. "When I direct, I become very patient, very compromising, for a perfectionist," she said. "There is a certain kind of acceptance of things you cannot change that would be very helpful in life. I live my life when I'm directing the way I would like to live my life when I'm not directing."

Photography was completed on *The Prince of Tides* in late September. Now she spent long hours in the dubbing room and on the editing, like an artist working on a canvas —"Finishing a Hat," "Putting Things Together," as Sondheim had written. It would be fifteen months before it was released, her work done and judgment made. She always said she liked the times between projects to *potchkee* around, shop, redo her houses, read, read, *read,* and plan her next adventure in moviemaking. She was redecorating both the Carolwood Drive house and the New York apartment with Frank Lloyd Wright and Gustav Stickley furniture. New paintings by Gustav Klimt and Egon Schiele hung on the walls. She was restless.

She saw Caleigh whenever she could in California, keeping her overnight. The little girl with her sunny smile and golden hair had fully won her affection. Caleigh was in some way the winning child she would have liked to have been and the daughter she would have wanted to have. Caleigh was so pretty, so feminine, so receptive to and giving of love. Streisand cared deeply for this outgoing youngster. Her instinct was to protect Caleigh from any insecurities she might suffer. She wanted to be there for her, remembering that she had had no such support and perhaps feeling that she had not been there as she would have liked with Jason. Thus, on the days and nights, usually once or twice a week, when Caleigh was with her, she made sure that her calendar was clear of other appointments. In the evening she would read to Caleigh and stay with her until it was time for the child to go to sleep.

Her relationship with Caleigh was curious. After all, the child was the adopted daughter of her ex-lover. But through Caleigh a solid link with Peters was maintained. Also, Jason's homosexuality left little hope that she would ever have a grandchild. "I don't know," one of her close friends offered, "I think Barbra feels somehow she can relive her life through Caleigh — that is, the life she would have liked to have had. She's become with Caleigh a part of a fairy tale. Caleigh's world is all pink and beautiful — or at least Barbra is trying to make it so. You know she is always reliving the so-called pain of her childhood. And yet, that is exactly what has made her strong. Pain does that for people. Cuts the chaff from the wheat. Separates the people with guts from those who are weak. Barbra *had* to make it — and she did. And one thing — she has never been ashamed that she was once poor and has always been proud of her heritage."

Streisand has always strongly felt the connection between herself and her Jewish roots. Her work on *Yentl* further strengthened them, along with her pride in the heritage of the Jewish people. Perhaps the only Hollywood star in its history who has been so publicly proud of being a Jew, she has never been given enough respect for her decision to portray Jewish women who could be admired — Fanny Brice, Katie Morosky, Yentl, all seminal roles, and soon in *The Prince of Tides,* Dr. Susan Lowenstein. Culturally, it has meant that whatever the public does not accept about Streisand, it has had no problem with her Jewishness and implicit in that acceptance is respect for her ethnic pride. It is a great part of what has made her the enormous icon that she is. The other quality that endears her to the public is her vulnerability. She can make all the tough statements in the world, but she fools nobody. Beneath the sometimes rigorous facade is a soft-hearted, emotional woman.

Elliott has claimed that her vulnerability is her secret weapon. But then Elliott himself also exudes a pervading aura of vulnerability that draws immense sympathy. What Streisand lacked was the ability to forgive what she believed to be transgressions against her. She carried a certain sense of injustice around with her, which has often been mistaken for vulnerability.

Shortly after the completion of *The Prince of Tides,* she learned that Peter Daniels had died of cancer. "Late one night the day after he died," Lainie Kazan remembered, "I received a telephone call. A woman on the line said in a rather shrill voice, 'Did you get my flowers?' Peter had been seriously ill for two years and I had given up everything else to care for him at home, and with his death I was exhausted, emotionally and physically. I didn't recognize the voice and I said sharply, 'Who's calling?'

" 'Barbra.'

" 'Barbra,' I said, 'I was just getting ready to send you a thank-you note.' She had sent me a tree of gardenias, and with it had come a most beautiful note. Finally, she had come around to recognize the importance of Peter in her life. It was too late. The last time we had spoken, I had seen her on the street and run up to her. She had just looked at me blankly. 'Barbra, it's Lainie,' I said, and she had replied in a totally bizarre manner, 'Oh, yes, Erasmus [referring to the fact that they had both attended the high school].' But [this night] we talked for over an hour about Peter, our children, life. We really had a meaningful conversation — for me, at least. Then she said, 'Where do you live?' I said, 'I live in the [Pacific] Palisades [near Santa Monica].'

" 'I never have been in the Palisades,' she responded, I guess her kind of humor. 'Why don't you invite me over for dinner?'

"I had, after all, just lost my husband and I said, 'Barbra, as soon as I gather my pieces together, you will be the first person I'm going to call. So I did call her later and never got a response."

While she waited for the December 11, 1991, premiere of *The Prince of Tides,* she put together a four-disc autobiographical album, *Just for the Record . . . ,* a compilation of previously recorded released and unreleased songs that allowed her briefly to tell her life story in the liner notes, giving her reasons for their inclusion and explanations about how they came to be made. The design divided her career into three decades: the sixties ("dedicated to the memory of Peter Daniels, who became my first accompanist"), the seventies ("to my beloved Gracie [Davidson, her late dedicated housekeeper who had been with her since the time Jason was a youngster], whose laughter I still miss and to Howard Jeffries [sic], who would have liked this record"),* and the eighties ("to my mother, who is 82 years old and still has a beautiful voice. And to Cis Corman, who's been my best friend through the 60s, 70s and 80s.").

Putting together this album was a highly emotional experience. It begins with that first private recording she made of "You'll Never Know" at the age of thirteen and includes numerous previously unreleased recordings of songs that she felt best told the story of her career as a singer. During the process of making it, she had Marty Erlichman contact Barry Dennen to see if he would give her the tapes that they had fought so bitterly over thirty years earlier. Dennen remained reluctant.

Just for the Record . . . has been deemed by several critics as an egotistical trip down Streisand's memory lane. It is, in fact, a remarkable album giving the listener a rare chance to listen to the development, changes, and maturing tastes of one of the world's greatest contemporary song stylists. It also allowed — via the lengthy written notes interladen with over 150 pictures from her own private collection — Streisand to tell things from her point of view.

"She throws a lot of stories around," reporter Hilary de Vries wrote of an interview with her shortly before the premiere of *The Prince of Tides.* "[Most of them] designed to portray Streisand as the victim triumphant,

---

*Howard Jeffrey became a "working buddy" of Streisand's during the filming of *Funny Girl* when he was assistant choreographer to Herbert Ross. They became friends. He also worked with her on most of her subsequent musical films. He died of AIDS in 1988. His name is misspelled in the dedication.

one who creates art in the face of a deprived childhood, dictatorial directors and an anti-woman industry. The effect, however, is of someone anthologizing her life as she lives it, studying herself from a slight remove, with the lighting just so."

"I'm just interested in the truth," she told de Vries, who was interviewing her for the *Los Angeles Times*. It is, of course, a question about whose truth. Streisand's? Elliott's? Diana's? Jason's? Peters's? The men and women who worked with her during her long career, who shared her early years? She has told the same stories frequently to the media — fictionalizing, embellishing, replaying the memories over and over in her mind to react anew, analyze, free herself of guilt, or in some cases, learn to take it. Then, the truth had often been obfuscated, distorted, or dramatized, not an unusual occurrence for the creative or self-involved or for those people who simply want to charm, impress, or shock to gain attention. If you tell a story enough times, it begins to have its own truth — and that is how it was with Streisand. By constantly repeating stories about her deprived childhood, her unhappiness as a child became a solid foundation on which she, and the public, could understand where she came from, why she did some of the things she has done. It also allowed her audience their own vision of the woman they were watching, which added another dimension to her performance, as it had done with two of her vocal predecessors, Billie Holiday and Judy Garland.

She has the habit of telling stories when she does not want to talk or answer questions. "The other day I went to the theater to see the trailer of *The Prince of Tides*. And when I'm in New York, I, like, take a cab," she began the de Vries interview. "I don't have a twenty-four-hour-a-day-limousine. I grew up in a poor family, and you don't think of hiring cars, but [I suddenly found myself terribly late] and in a sweatsuit — schlocky — the way I'm dressed most of the time, to tell you the truth. Well, not schlocky . . . So I started to run, and could *not* get a cab. And it reminded me of when I first started on Broadway and the nights when I couldn't get a cab to my own show [*Funny Girl*], and I would plead with people on Central Park West — tears running down my face — to take me to Broadway. . . ." Always with such stories there were references to the past and never to the amazing highs in her astounding life —

always to the pathos, the defenseless experiences that were a part of her history.

The Prince of Tides met with good reviews upon its general release on Christmas Day; almost all the critics extolled her talent as a director able to draw superb performances from her cast. Her own performance was consistently panned, a great disappointment to her. She had, perhaps, taken on too much. *The Prince of Tides* would have been even better had she directed another woman in the role of Dr. Lowenstein.

Her fiftieth birthday on April 24, 1992, found her impatient with herself. The redecorating was completed, and there was no one special man in her life. She was beginning to feel her age, although she still looked a decade younger. And the men she was attracted to grew younger as she aged. "Poor baby is miserable," Elliott said. "She makes herself occupied with so many things because she's so afraid to fail. So afraid of the truth."

One of her closest old friends sighed deeply as he added, "It's the mirror that she has to face each morning, unadorned, makeup-free, no flattering pink spots, no chance to cut and edit. That's at the core of Barbra's great sadness. She can only be what she wants to be — that Hollywood image of glamour — by artificial means. She is not a great beauty. I don't think she is able, or ever will be able, to accept that. She sees the homely Jewish girl from Brooklyn, *crazy Barbara, the girl with the big beak,* looking back at her. She does not, and cannot see what *we* see — the rare beauty that is under her public disguise. She's an original species, a one-and-only, and she has no way to judge. Barbra's greatest tragedy and her greatest blessing is that she was not born beautiful. That is something with which she may never come to terms."

30

People were talking. Streisand was smitten with a young man, a twenty-two-year-old tennis star, several years younger than Jason, and twenty-eight years her junior. Even blasé Hollywood was in a fit about the news. His name was André Agassi, the "King of Grunge," and that year, 1992, he would earn several million dollars. On the court, his dark ponytail falling from the back of a black cap, his clothes scruffy and black socks scrunched down over his tennis shoes, gold hoops dangling from his ears, a Che Guevara beard framing his striking face with its sharp features, bushy brows, and quick-shifting eyes, he was a shaggy antihero to the young people who came to see his showman style and killer skill. Adult tennis buffs often greeted him with sneers, treating him like a bad Las Vegas lounge act. He had broken tennis's "Mr. Clean," all-white dress code. He was a maverick and a valuable commodity in a sport in which adult participation and viewership were on the decline. "Agassi is tennis's marketing tool for its next generation of fans," Harvey Araton of the *New York Times* wrote. "He comes MTV-ready, and if he turns the stomachs of a few parents, he also induces their kids to ask, 'Can we get tickets for the Agassi match?'"

"He's very intelligent," Streisand said in his defense, "very, very sensitive, very evolved — more than his linear years. And he's an extraordinary human being. He plays like a Zen master. It's very in the moment."

Agassi was *today, tomorrow* — and that is where she wanted to be. She was fifty, middle-aged, but she thought of Agassi as being older than his given age and of herself as being younger. That narrowed the gap. He was vital and strong, moved like a gale wind, talked up a storm, and was cocky, self-assured, and utterly irrepressible.

They had met briefly at Aspen during the Christmas holidays, shortly after the release of *The Prince of Tides,* and began seriously dating in the spring of 1992. "I've been learning about the sweet mysteries of life and this is one of them," Agassi confessed to Maureen Dowd of the *New York Times* when asked about his relationship with Streisand. "I'm not sure I can fully explain. Maybe she can't either. But it doesn't matter. We came from completely different worlds, and we collided, and we knew we wanted to be in each other's company right then."

Streisand appeared happy, animated. Her close friends respected her right to live her life as she chose. Jason was supportive. She was accustomed to Diana's disapproval, and she cared little for what Hollywood thought. The relationship was not as all-consuming as her more serious affairs in the past had been, and while Agassi was off on the tennis circuit, she involved herself intently in "minding the store."

The Prince of Tides was doing exceptionally well at the box office, already having made back triple its cost, and promised to be one of her biggest moneymaking movies yet. Although it was one of the five films nominated for best picture, she felt she was personally snubbed at the sixty-fourth Annual Academy Awards, her successful directorial efforts not included as one of the five nominated directors.* She complained that it was because she was who she was, that she was a woman, that Hollywood would never open its mind to her.

---

*Nominated for best picture were *The Silence of the Lambs* (winner), *Beauty and the Beast, Bugsy, JFK,* and *The Prince of Tides.* Nominated for best director were Jonathan Demme (*Silence of the Lambs,* the winner), Oliver Stone (*JFK*), Barry Levinson (*Bugsy*), John Singleton (*Boyz N the Hood*), and Ridley Scott (*Thelma and Louise*).

She was quick to respond to the reputation she had gained in the industry as a "ball breaker," "a control freak." "Well, control means artistic responsibility, being completely dedicated to a project, having a total vision, being interested in all aspects down to the copy on the radio commercials," she countered. "I want to be responsible for everything I do in my life, whether it's good or bad. I have visions in my head. I hear music; I dream. It's very rewarding to have them materialize." She thought for a moment. "If a man did what I did, he would be called thorough. While a woman's called a ball breaker. I resent that."

Her rejection by the industry raised a good deal of controversy. "Barbra was the first woman to really wield power," said Lynda Obst, producer of *The Fisher King,* which was nominated for five Academy Awards (it received one — best supporting actress for Mercedes Ruehl.) "Barbra raised too much confusion in the beginning of her career. She threw her weight around. People are grudging in their admiration. There's so much commercial respect for her, but they also withhold a certain kind of embrace."

Considering that the film was not only nominated for best picture, but received seven other nominations (including Nolte's performance and that of Kate Nelligan as his mother, but not Streisand's portrayal of Dr. Lowenstein), it is surprising that she was overlooked entirely. But there are just five directors nominated and, as one Academy voter ventured, "she was sixth good." Nonetheless, she took it as a personal rejection and went public with her feelings. The final five directors chosen were all men, a point that she stressed. They were also worthy nominees. *The Prince of Tides,* though beautifully photographed and well acted, was a flawed film; Streisand's directorial hand is sure in all scenes in which she does not appear, and as her role is major, that is not the greater percentage of the picture.

The awards and the controversy over Streisand's not being nominated bolstered the box-office receipts of *The Prince of Tides.* She remained bitter even when in June, just two months after the Academy Awards, Sony (which now owned Columbia Pictures) completed negotiations with her for a $60 million multimedia entertainment contract, one of the largest deals ever made in the industry. Recent record contracts, with equally high figures, were made by Michael Jackson and Madonna with Time Warner, but Streisand's involved both records and movies and included gross percentages, which greatly increased the base amount.* Sony was also to continue to maintain distribution rights to her lucrative thirty-seven-album catalog, which had accounted for more than 60 million album sales since 1964, the largest number for any recording artist during that period.

"An artist like Barbra Streisand comes along once in a generation, so you hold on to her," said Al Teller, former president of CBS Records (now Sony Records). Mega entertainment attorney Peter Dekom added, "Few artists have a proven track record that they can sing, act, write, direct, and produce. Barbra is a multiple threat in every category." And Irving Azoff, then chairman of Time Warner's record business chimed in, "There are few entertainers who ever create an audience demand across both the music and film entertainment spectrum the way that Barbra does. She typifies taste and elegance, not only commercial success."

The industry believed that she was being recognized and acknowledged for her achievements. Streisand did not see it that way. She would never forgive the Academy and remembered too well how hard she had to fight for stories she believed in, how record executives always made her feel like she was auditioning the songs she wanted to include on her albums. Power was complete autonomy, and it was doubtful that she would ever be able to command that. She had been the most powerful *woman* in Hollywood for years, but the industry remained an exclusive men's club. It was a barrier she was unable to break.

---

*Under the contract components of Sony's deal with Streisand, she was guaranteed $5 million advance per album for six albums plus an unprecedented 42 percent royalty rate on the wholesale price of each unit sold (approximately $2.90 on each album sold at 1992 prices). She also was granted what is referred to as a "favored nations" clause that guaranteed her a royalty rate that exceeded any other artist on the company's roster. On the film end of the contract, which did not require her to deliver a specific number of pictures, she was to receive a $4 million advance against 10 percent of gross revenues for every movie in which she appeared and $3 million for her services as director. Sony was to commit $2 million a year over an estimated ten years for development funds and operating expenses to Streisand's Barwood Production Company to hire writers and executives to create film properties that she would direct, act in, or produce.

"Language gives us an insight into the way women are viewed in a male-dominated society," she said on June 12 when she accepted the Dorothy Arzner Award, named after the moldbreaking director-filmmaker. She went on to illustrate:

"A man is commanding — a woman demanding.

"A man is forceful — a woman is pushy.

"A man is uncompromising — a woman a ball breaker.

"A man is a perfectionist — a woman's a pain in the ass.

"He's assertive — she's aggressive.

"He strategizes — she manipulates.

"He shows leadership — she's controlling.

"He's committed — she's obsessed . . .

"If he acts, produces, and directs, he's called a multitalented hyphenate. She's called vain and egotistical.

"It's been said that a man's reach should exceed his grasp. Why can't the same be said for a woman?"

She ended by telling the group of professional women in film, "We are a remarkable breed. We are the girls in the 'hood — sisterhood, that is. . . . Nature designed us to be creators — to give life. . . . Let's create images that show life, not only as it is, but how it could be. Let's use our collective female energy to make films that reflect our nurturing instincts and put that out into the world. Because the world surely needs it."

Streisand and Robert De Niro's Tribeca Films purchased rights for the book *To a Violent Grave: An Oral Biography of Jackson Pollock* by Jeff Potter, published in 1985, about the tumultuous relationship between the famed abstract artist and his wife/manager, Lee Krasner. De Niro's late father was a painter, and the story had two strong costarring roles for him and Streisand. She optioned a story about Lt. Col. Margarethe Cammermeyer, who was forced to resign from the Washington State National Guard when she acknowledged that she was a lesbian. A screenplay, *The Mirror Has Two Faces,* written by Richard LaGravenese, who had been responsible for the script of *The Fisher King,* was submitted to her, and after reading it she became immediately involved. Nonetheless her wish to make *The Normal Heart* remained strong.

Within the activist gay community there were rumblings that she, as one of Hollywood's biggest stars, had not done enough for AIDS. Elizabeth Taylor had already stepped forward and become the AIDS spokesperson for liberal Hollywood. Where was Streisand, they asked? They complained that she had given *only* $350,000 in 1991 for AIDS research and treatment, and most of that delegated for children afflicted with the disease. But this is an unjustified and uncharitable criticism. Streisand had endowed academic chairs in women's studies at the University of California, cardiovascular research at UCLA, and another at the Environmental Defense Fund. Her Streisand Foundation continues to grant over a million dollars a year to civil liberties, environmental causes, and AIDS. And she often was moved to add large sums for other causes and catastrophes, like the Valdez oil spill, as they came along. She believed she could accomplish more as an advocate for the gay community by being able to make a commercial film that would reach a large audience and show them as being like everyone else in their need for and their right to love. She also had personal motivations: Jason's homosexuality, of course, but also Stan Kamen, a close friend and her agent at William Morris (since she and Sue Mengers had parted several years earlier), had recently died from AIDS, and she had been intensely upset by his death and the frustration of knowing there was no medical cure for the plague and that resources for research were limited.

This was a couple of years before the film *Philadelphia,* starring Tom Hanks in an Academy Award–winning performance, broke the Hollywood standoff on stories about AIDS patients. *Philadelphia,* however, focused on an AIDS patient's right to continue a career in the workplace rather than on the character's right to love. Hollywood was not yet ready to explore this theme. Streisand would continue to walk in the face of gale winds with *The Normal Heart.* Renegotiations with Kramer for the rights were set into motion in the spring of 1990. Things went much more smoothly this time. Both gave in a bit; a compromise was reached. Kramer would write the script, but she would still retain the last word. Once again he flew to California for story conferences at her house. Both had changed. "She was a softer person, also more conscious of how hard she had been on herself in the past," Kramer reflected. "She talked a lot about it, about not trying to be the perfectionist all the time. She had been in the kind of therapy where you get in touch with the inner child. She was more considerate, somehow gentler.

"I had known for two years that I was HIV positive, and I thought I was shortly going to die. Literally the first week I started work with her, I got an emergency call from my doctor in New York. How he got Barbra's number I've never known. But my blood work had just come in, and he called to tell me that he had to put me on AZT right away and wanted the name of a pharmacy in Los Angeles so that I could start immediately. I was very upset, and Barbra was marvelous, comforting and organizational at the same time. I'll never forget it — or her. She put her arms around me, she contacted the pharmacy, and we talked.

"I was violently anti-AZT. There were different schools of thought about whether it was good or not, and until we had more medical details, I was reluctant to take it. So this was a big emotional thing. Also, AZT can have scary side effects on your body, and I thought, Holy shit! I was afraid that I would have these skin lesions and not be able to work so well, and this was what I had been wanting for years — for Barbra to come back on the project."

Kramer recalled that when his doctor rang from New York, Streisand sensed it was something serious. "She said if you want to talk privately to take it in the bathroom, which adjoined her study. When I came out, I was shaken and she said, 'What's the matter?' And I told her. Then she put her arms around me and hugged me close to her, very maternal. I was terribly moved. I couldn't hold back my tears.

"From then on it was, 'How are you feeling? How's it going? Are you having any side effects?' There was great warmth. Much different than in 1985, when I felt more like a hired hand. Fortunately, the medication did help, and I did not have any side effects, so I carried on working.

"Barbra writes in the old-fashioned way, in which every shot and every angle is described. She wants a sense of what the camera is doing, what you start to focus on, where does it move, what's the action so that she can follow. She is a person who questions everything. If you had a comma there yesterday, and you don't have one today, why has it been removed? And she knows and she remembers that there was a comma there. She has a low file cabinet, really an open drawer, that has every scene of every version of the script that I have written, she has written, and anyone else has written. It is broken down by scenes, and she will remember which one had what and constantly compare them. Then she will record on tape exactly the sequence she wants so that there will not be any chance of a slip-up. I would then bring it in to her the next day, sort of polished.

"We'd work from three-thirty in the afternoon often until eight or nine in the evening. The rest of the house had undergone redecoration. There was new art, a great deal of mission furniture, but the study remained basically the same. She always looked lovely. She has such beautiful skin — unbelievable skin, her eyes are such a clear blue and her hair always seems right, even when it's just hanging. She wore the same kind of clothes to work in — designer-type jogging outfits.

"There is something about her that is very touching. She is very vulnerable. You can feel it, and whether she is opening it up to you or not, you are in the presence of it. Maybe that is what the great singers have. They can sing these songs about how the world has touched them, or love has touched them, and you want to say, 'It's all right.' And she remembers all the bad things the press ever said about her. I asked her why she held on to things for so long, why didn't she let it go, and she replied, 'I can't seem to help it. How do you do it? You've been criticized so much. Why doesn't it bite the shit out of you?'

"'Well, it used to,' I told her, 'but you cannot take a strong opinion about something and not know that you are going to offend somebody, somewhere. Let it go, let it go,' I kept telling her. She's trying so hard to be everything. To be the most perfect person, the most admirable person. People talk about her lust for power, her need for control. Control is a very harsh word for the way people use it against her. She wants to run her company her way, she has that right. A case in point. 'There are things you write that I can't put on the screen,' she told me. 'Give me an example,' I asked.

"'Well, the scene where the two men make love believing they have engaged in safe sex and there is a spot of semen on one of the guy's chest, and they don't know whose it is and one of them indicates that it could be poisonous.'

"'That is what I wanted to show. That a slip like that could kill you. I think it's very moving.' And she replied, simply, with finality, 'You can't show semen on somebody's chest.'"

Her affair with Agassi came to a sudden end. She had gone to Wimbledon to watch him play Pete Sampras in the quarterfinals in June and cheered him on wildly, to no avail. Agassi lost the match. By September he was dating a younger woman and soon after would pair up with the actress Brooke Shields, who was closer to his own age. At this point there was no other man in Streisand's life. Jason was in New York attending film classes at New York University, where he had made a short movie (in which his father and his grandmother, Diana, appeared) that was highly praised. He was now concentrating not on acting but on a career as a writer and director. Streisand remained for a while in Manhattan. She was lonely, "very lonely," close friends say. Jason suffered from a fear of heights, a phobia that had been a fairly recent development, and could not take the elevator up to the penthouse apartment. This meant they met at more impersonal locales — restaurants, other people's homes.

"I think, strangely enough, that Barbra wants to make *The Normal Heart* for Jason," Kramer said. "I believe it's her way in fighting for his acceptance and his right to love whom he wants and be proud of who and what he is. It's the ultimate gift, the utmost. If she's nervous about anything, that's where the nervousness comes. It is not easy to do a film about homosexuality when your son is involved in it. Also, I suspect that when the movie is finally made, it will come out more about Jason because he wants to work on it. He has exceedingly good taste and I think Barbra, and Cis Corman, too, respects his ability."

Jon Peters and his wife, Christine, were now divorced. Streisand's concern was Caleigh, only three years old at the time. She identified closely with the child and felt her bewilderment at being the victim of a broken home. Her friendship with Peters remained solid. Both he and Christine saw Streisand's involvement with Caleigh as a stabilizing force in the little girl's life. Streisand decorated a bedroom in the Carolwood Drive house for her; a storybook room in pink and white with crisp organdy curtains and shelves filled with books and dolls. The child was closely attached to Streisand and was visibly happy to be with her. Peters had the responsibility of her care, but Christine also shared custody. Caleigh was still too young to know how she would be affected by Streisand's involvement in her welfare and rearing. Affectionate by nature, Caleigh hugged and kissed Streisand a lot. Caleigh called her "Baba," and Streisand doted on her. "I want only the best for her, the most love and affection that it is possible to give her," she told close friends, who noted the happiness Caleigh brought to Streisand. "She sees Caleigh as her own. It's amazing how much she loves that child," one commented.

She had always been a champion of children's problems in a world where they had so little control over their lives. Caleigh brought this issue closer to home.

"One night when I was putting [Caleigh] to sleep," she recalled, "I started to sing her a lullaby. 'Rock-a-bye-baby on the tree top/ When the wind blows the cradle will rock/ When the bough breaks the cradle will fall . . .' 'The cradle will fall???' " she exclaimed. "What was I supposed to tell her? I mean really that's a frightening thought [to tell a child.]"

She created garden space for a proper play area with a sandbox and slide and a playhouse where Caleigh could have lemonade and cookies with a friend in the afternoon. She made sure Caleigh had playmates, inviting children from her preschool to the house; took her to the beach, where they built sand castles together; went shopping with her for clothes, allowing the child's taste to guide her purchases; and accompanied her to the pediatrician for her regular checkup, holding her hand so she would not be frightened. One could read many things into her close attachment to the engaging blond child whose blue eyes and wide smile were so appealing. She was the child she would have wished to have been, the girl she always wanted, the tie that would keep her bound to Peters, the granddaughter she might never have. But, perhaps, the most obvious explanation was that Caleigh satisfied a need in Streisand for a continuing bond with another person.

Streisand reentered the political arena when Bill Clinton won the Democratic nomination in the summer of 1992. She had not been energized by Michael Dukakis in the previous election. Now, along with the Bergmans, she joined wholeheartedly into working for his election, as impressed with Hillary Rodham Clinton as with her husband. Finally, there was an especially intelligent potential First Lady, reminiscent of one of her longtime idols, Eleanor Roosevelt. Mrs. Clinton seemed to understand the domestic issues at stake — AIDS research, health care, a woman's right to abort, the state of the environment — and would not be hesitant to raise her voice to bring them to the attention of the country.

She met the Clintons the night of September 16 at an HWPC fundraiser held on the expansive lawns of the $39 million, forty-nine-acre Beverly Hills estate of reclusive film producer Ted Fields, one of the five top national Democratic donors. It was the first time in six years that she sang in public — this time not as a solo performer but on a program crowded with Hollywood's Democratic supporters — among them Warren Beatty, Annette Bening, Goldie Hawn, Whoopie Goldberg, Steven Spielberg, Candice Bergen (wearing glasses), Jack Nicholson (in shades), Michelle Pfeiffer, Dustin Hoffman, Richard Dreyfuss, Danny DeVito, Rhea Perlman, Dionne Warwick, and Mike Nichols and Elaine May, who did a rare stand-up comedy routine. Beatty introduced Clinton, who appeared somewhat overwhelmed by the stellar gathering and their eloquent outpouring of support.

"Warren Beatty said he hadn't known me a long time," he said during his speech, "but I was sitting there thinking I have known many of you a long time. I have seen your movies or sung your songs and just imagined that life could be as it seems to be in the lyrics or up on the screen." He added, "I have always aspired to be in the cultural elite that others condemn."

Streisand, simply dressed in a black scoop-necked, long-sleeved Donna Karan gown, her hair casually brushed loose to frame her face, commanded a huge ovation as she stepped up to the microphone. "Six years ago," she told the Hollywoodites who had raised over a million dollars that evening, "I was motivated by the disaster at Chernobyl. Now I'm motivated by the possibility of another disaster: the reelection of George Bush and Dan Quayle." The crowd roared, and she sang "On a Clear Day (You Can See Forever)," followed by "Happy Days Are Here Again."

Maybe they were. A dedicated Democrat, it seemed that for the first time in sixteen years someone she could identify with had a good chance of making it into the White House. She liked the man a lot. He had the kind of charisma that she admired, and he *listened* to his wife, to *women*, to what just plain people had to say. He was the kind of man to whom she could easily have become attracted. They spoke for a while later that evening. Others present while they conversed say he told her his father had died before he was born and that he understood she had lost her father at a young age. "It has a way of affecting your whole life," he said.

"Yes," she replied. "It's a tough thing to overcome. I'm not sure you really ever do. It hurts to think mine never got to know I became famous, that I achieved some good things. But that you are on your way to becoming president, that's a tough one not to share."

Clinton smiled down at her from his great height and nodded his head, then they were joined by several others who wanted to shake the hand of the man they hoped would soon be president of the United States.

31

"How come nobody attacked the Republican White House for their involvement with Arnold Schwarzenegger, Charlton Heston, and Bruce Willis?" Streisand shot back at a reporter who asked her views on the media accusations that the supposed Hollywood-Clinton connection was a threat to "the very fabric of this republic." Her man had won, and this time she was a part of the pre- and postinaugural celebrations as well as having a front-row seat when he took the oath of office. A huge Hollywood contingent had come to Washington for the final gala of Clinton's inaugural week, attended by 19,000 guests at the cavernous Capital Centre. The gigantic celebration was nastily referred to in the press as a "Hollywood-Washington production." Streisand sang "Evergreen" as the president and the First Lady held hands. Then, an enthusiastic audience thundering their approval, she gave her all to "On a Clear Day (You Can See Forever)" and "Happy Days Are Here Again," the latter to five ovations that did not stop until she introduced the president-elect, at which point the vast crowd stood up, all at once, all whistling, all hurrahs and clapping.

Streisand handed the microphone over to Clinton, who stood onstage beneath the glare of a white spotlight, a black stool used in her act behind him. "Thank you for sharing with me my last night as a private citizen," he told them and turned to Streisand, who was still standing on the podium, and gave her a warm, tight bear hug.

One staff member, who had also worked on the Reagan and Bush preinaugural galas, found the Democrats "much more fun, much more casual. Everybody is in a party mood. No prima donnas. No ozone layer of spray over everything. Four years ago all the gowns seemed to be red, white, or blue. This year — solid sequins — the brighter and funkier, the better." Streisand wore, in contrast to the glittery evening dresses chosen by Goldie Hawn and others, a striking three-piece pinstriped Donna Karan suit, the floor-length skirt slit to the thigh, referred to in the *Washington Post* as "the peek-a-boo power suit."

The highly successful Karan, America's leading woman designer, and now one of Streisand's closest friends, had created a new, daring, sophisticated look for her. The two women not only shared a love of fashion, they had many of the same views and social commitments. They were part of "the sisterhood"— those women who, like Streisand, compete in a man's world. Karan, a tall, dark-haired, handsome, comfortably built — trim, but not model-thin — woman, runs a spectacularly high-profile fashion house. But the financial backing for her enterprise came from businessmen who were interested more in the profit column than the designer's need to express herself creatively, a situation that Streisand also dealt with in making movies.

Once again Streisand was under attack by the *Washington Post,* which was particularly vituperative in its assault on what it called "Clinton's wooing of entertainment royalty," adding that film stars were "incapable of serious involvement with the politics industry of Washington." Streisand was singled out as a prime target and referred to demeaningly as "*La* Streisand."*

"When I directed a movie," she replied to a *Los Angeles Times* journalist, "it was as if I was being told how dare I attempt to infiltrate a man's

---

*Jack Valenti, president of the Motion Picture Association of America, Inc., immediately wrote a letter to the editor of the *Washington Post* in Streisand's defense. "Barbra Streisand has read deeper and absorbed more about what ails this society than most of the bureaucrats who inhabit the higher reaches of our government," he stressed.

domain. Now, it's: How dare I be interested in politics. Forgive my tone if I sound angry but I am!"

The extraordinary meanness of the press did not stop Streisand from enjoying the thrill and excitement of the historic occasion. She stayed at the Mayflower Hotel, instantly renamed in the press as "the power hotel of the week," as other guests included President Clinton's mother, Virginia Kelley; her husband, Dick; Clinton's brother, Roger; Mrs. Clinton's two brothers, Tony and Hugh Rodham; Vice-President Al Gore and his family; political guru James Carville; Barbara Walters; and a long list of top film, concert, and television performers. Streisand was also being called "the woman fast becoming the top celebrity."

The following day, January 20, she sat teary-eyed at the stirring inauguration ceremony, the weather crisp and cool, a winter sun lighting the podium as Bill Clinton, his broad, usually smiling face somber on this occasion, was sworn into office. The new president seemed enveloped in an aura of youth; he was, after all, only forty-seven, a year older than John F. Kennedy had been when he was assassinated. This is truly what Streisand had come to Washington to witness, the central simple reality. A man she believed in was taking the oath of office as president of the United States. It was a moment that signaled the turning of a great page. She had soaring hopes for the future of the country. She who complained so much, who suffered such heavy Jewish guilt, who nurtured a negative approach, who saw the black side rather than the white, the half-empty glass instead of the half full, who claimed to feel threatened and frightened so much of the time, felt optimistic. The Clinton administration was one with which she could personally identify. She felt an insider, like somehow she belonged.

This was to usher in a new phase of her life in which she would speak up and out, become an activist. "We [Hollywood executives and stars] have the right to be taken as seriously as automobile executives," she told an interviewer after one of the media sneeringly addressed her as "the princess of tides." "No one would question the president of G[eneral] M[otors] talking to people in Washington."

Streisand carried away many memories from the day: "a cheerful thumbs-up and wink from out-going President Bush through a limousine window as the car pulled away from the White House; Mrs. Clinton and Mrs. Bush chatting amicably as they raced through Capitol corridors toward the West Front; Clinton stooping to pet Millie [the Bushes' dog] when the Clintons arrived at the White House; young First Daughter, Chelsea, unable to suppress a yawn even during the very peppy singing of the national anthem by Marilyn Horne." She was mesmerized by these personal recollections and in awe of the history that she saw at every turn. She had become in these few days a part of that history. The thought thrilled her, whipping up a deep sense of patriotism that was equal to her pride in her gender and her heritage.

And she had a handsome escort to the various activities, ABC-TV anchorman Peter Jennings, a distinguished-looking news reporter with a self-assured air and great popular appeal, who had recently separated from his wife. Streisand perhaps saw in him some of the same attraction that once had drawn her to Pierre Trudeau: the intelligence, the grasp of political and worldwide issues mixed with good looks and considerable charm. There were eleven official inauguration balls. Streisand, in a gray jersey Karan gown ("cut down to here and slashed to there"), briefly attended the most high-profile one, the Arkansas Ball at the Washington Convention Center, with Jennings, departing shortly after the Clintons moved on.

Streisand held court, according to the *Washington Post,* at what was called *the* after-the-ball Inauguration Day party at the chic Jockey Club. Jennings had to report back to work, so she came with Donna Karan. The only persons missing were the president and First Lady. Jack Nicholson could be heard laughing his diabolical laugh. Warren Beatty and Annette Bening passed around a picture of their new baby daughter. Lauren Bacall cha-cha-ed. Jack Lemmon, Kathleen Turner, Chevy Chase, Shirley MacLaine, Robert De Niro, and Richard Dreyfuss were there along with a host of Kennedys and well-known politicians. At 1:30 A.M. Streisand, "wearing a long black hooded cape which made her look like Marie Antoinette fleeing revolutionary Paris," made a getaway through the kitchen, past the bar, and out the front door, with Karan close on her heels.

Streisand's relationship with Jennings would remain on the basis of "just good friends," although she relied on him for inside information on many of the topics that interested her. They spoke often and met whenever she was on the East Coast. Her obvious and ongoing public comment on issues caused the media once again to proclaim that she was about to declare herself for political office. She made it as clear as she could that she was not interested in running for anything, she was merely an involved citizen. A lot of press was given to the supposition that she had the ear of the president, which she hotly denied. In mid-May 1993 she was invited to the Washington White House correspondents dinner and then "granted 5 minutes with Clinton. I talked with him about what was being done for AIDS research," she averred. "The month before, some of us from the entertainment industry were invited to the health-care meeting. We didn't even have dinner with Clinton. We saw him afterward. We had dinner with his mother — whom I adore because she's this resilient, optimistic woman.

"There was all this criticism that Hollywood people were getting into areas that they are not expert on, but we were asked to come to the White House for communications ideas — we were called there for them to tap into our communication skills — how to get a message across to the American people. We've been called 'air-heads' and 'nitwits.' This is so unfair. And it's smearing the main industry in our community. It's saying there isn't a brain around. Did the entertainment industry create the national debt?

"The media are in a Hollywood-bashing mode these days. They reported contemptuously that Janet Reno and I had dinner and 'hashed out issues.' Why two prominent, hard-working women, isolated by their position, should not want to talk to each other is beyond me. Why such venomous response toward people from Hollywood? Why are we so threatening to the media? We have the right as an industry, as people, as professionals, to be taken as seriously as automobile executives — an industry that is having trouble selling its products abroad. On the other hand, we make something that the whole world wants to buy, it improves our balance of payments, creates jobs and pays a lot in taxes."

She wandered the capital on this trip as a tourist, visiting the Smithsonian and Monticello. "The most moving moments were being at the National Archives," she confessed, "and holding the Emancipation Proclamation and Louisiana Purchase and seeing the film at the Holocaust Museum about the survivors who were reaffirming the preciousness of life, struggling to maintain their dignity, helping one another to gather strength to survive. They didn't surrender to cynicism — which is killing our country and preventing our pulling together."

Nothing was going to stop her from speaking her mind. She was, and always had been, pro-choice, for the equality of women, for the protection of the environment — a dedicated liberal. "That's why I have a foundation to fortify my beliefs," she told Robert Scheer of the *Los Angeles Times*. "That's how I give back. That's how I raise my voice. And whether the right-wing conservatives like it or not, I will keep on raising it."

In the early days of January 1994, she got Sammy, a fluffy white bichon frise with dark button eyes and an affectionate nature. She had been without a dog for many years. Sadie, whom she had adored and whom she did not think she would ever replace, had died before she made *A Star Is Born*. Sammy followed at her heels wherever she went in the house.

On the morning of January 17, the devastating earthquake she had always feared would come to Los Angeles arrived. She awoke in her room in the house on Carolwood Drive to a sudden shifting of the bed beneath her and the sounds of breaking glass, wood creaking, the house groaning and shaking. The first thing she did was get out of bed, carefully avoiding the glass from a nearby broken window, and went in search of the young puppy, frantically calling his name. When she found him sitting under her dressing table, "he was so calm he calmed me," she said. She then called her mother, who was frightened but unharmed. When Diana assured her that she was fine, she checked the damage to the house. The fireplace in the living room had collapsed and there was plaster dust everywhere. Miraculously the Tiffany peony lamp had survived without a chip. A large mirror had smashed, along with many porcelain and antique treasures and a great deal of pottery. In a major catastrophe of 6.7 intensity that took the lives of fifty-seven people and seriously injured thousands more, her losses seemed inconsequential, but it did convince her that she must have her more valuable and breakable possessions either shipped to New York to be placed in storage or be sold.

She had recently finished work on a new album, *Back to Broadway,* that included many of the songs she had not been able to record for the first Broadway album. Sondheim theater music was well represented with "Everybody Says Don't" (*Anyone Can Whistle*), "Children Will Listen" (from *Into the Woods,* and perhaps Sondheim's most important song), "Move On" (*Sunday in the Park with George*), and "I Have a Love" and "One Hand, One Heart" (*West Side Story,*) a duet with Johnny Mathis. But this time Sondheim did not have as great an influence over the recording sessions. She included two songs, exquisitely rendered, from Andrew Lloyd Webber's yet-to-be seen *Sunset Boulevard,* "As If We Never Said Goodbye" and "With One Look."

Sunset Boulevard was in rehearsal for its West Coast premiere, and Don Black and Christopher Hampton, the English writers who shared credit for the lyrics, were in Los Angeles. She wanted some small changes to be made to adapt the lyrics of "With One Look" and "As If We Never Said Goodbye" to her needs (as Sondheim had done with "Putting It Together" on the earlier album), and she asked Black and Hampton to meet with her at the Carolwood Drive house to discuss it.

"It was the highlight of my professional career," Black, who also collaborated with Webber on *Song and Dance* and *Aspects of Love* and wrote the lyrics for "Born Free" and many other hit songs, stressed. "She is a great storyteller with phenomenal instinct into the proper phrasing and interpretation of a lyric. It was what every songwriter dreams of — to have a song sung by Barbra Streisand.

"Christopher, myself, and David Caddick, who is Andrew's musical director and was also on *Sunset,* went together. Christopher couldn't stay long, as he had another engagement, but he wanted to meet her. The three of us went to her house. It looked a very modest house as we drew up to the gates. It wasn't that long driveway that you have in your fantasy as the approach to a home belonging to a star of her caliber. Inside it was another matter, marvelous taste, but again not what you would expect. What would that be? Shangri La, I suspect.

"She was late. There was a problem that had suddenly developed with a tooth, and she had gone to the dentist. This was midmorning, an especially bright autumn day. Her secretary greeted us and made us comfortable in the living room, where a piano occupied one corner. We waited about a half an hour. Christopher was about to leave when she came in, her attitude sisterly. 'Hi, hello everybody,' she greeted, very familylike. I was struck with how ordinary she looked. Nothing starry about her — casual clothes, almost no makeup, tennis shoes. 'How are you guys for tea, coffee?' she asked. There was no feeling at all that you were in the presence of such a famous woman. It was quite amazing. After about five or ten minutes of chitchat, Christopher left and there was just me and David Caddick seated at the piano. He said nothing for hours on end — he wasn't asked to.

"She sat down opposite me and kept offering snacks — little potato latkes, olives, nuts. She'd push a dish closer to me on the table between us. Meanwhile, she dissected the lyrics with forensic precision. Her main concern was 'With One Look.'

"'Will people know what I'm talking about?' she asked. 'As written, it's about a silent movie star. People are going to hear it on the radio or by record and if they haven't seen the show they won't know what I'm talking about.'

"She wanted to put a few words of explanation in the verse. I didn't agree with that. 'Songs from musicals are specific,' I told her. We talked about it for a long while. There was nothing argumentative about it or dictatorial or demanding. She was flexible, but we went over every comma and crotchet of the song. At the end I did say, 'Well, let me think of something.' Her secretary then interrupted with some papers she had to sign, and sandwiches were brought in, and I took the time to write some lines for the front of the song. I think they were something like — 'They don't want me anymore, they all say I'm through, but it's time they knew/ With one look and so on.' My intention was to set up right away that this was a star past her prime but still defiant.

"There is a line — 'One tear from my eye,' and she wanted 'one tear *in* my eye makes the whole world cry.' I admired her intense involvement. She cared so much about every detail. There was a comfortable collaborative feel to the session. Very affable. This went on for hours with David still at the piano, very respectful, just poised there. Finally she said, 'Well, maybe we should try it.'

"She was now seated next to me on the couch having a cup of tea, and she puts the cup down and without rising and without the piano sings the opening lines of 'With One Look.' This remarkable voice came out. After the first few bars David found her key and backed her, and it was just unbelievable. Here was this most ordinary-looking woman having a cup of tea and singing liquid diamond in my ear. I ran out of goosebumps.

"'Well, what do you think?' she asked. 'Is it okay? I haven't sung for years. You know I haven't done a concert in so long. You really think it's okay?'

"She was so insecure, very uncertain about it, and really it was just wonderful. There was no pretending. I had the highest respect for her. Then when we stopped the session, she played some of the tracks she had already recorded for the album and told me how Sondheim rewrote everything for her. I could understand why he did it. She gives a lyric new meaning, fresh interpretation. She is simply the greatest singer of our time. Still, as she played the tracks she would ask, "Does it sound like it's mixed right here? Could you hear the breath?"— more like a singer just starting her career. There was no doubt in my mind why she has stayed at the top. Because she doesn't release a record — she *unveils* it.

"Andrew had agreed that I should work with Barbra, but I was still apprehensive and showed him what I had done. You're dealing with two icons. How many people are there in their strata? It would have been terrible if Andrew hated it but Barbra loved it. It would be a nightmare that doesn't bear thinking about. But Andrew thought the lyrics were right for her purpose. In the end he produced the songs and worked on the arrangements for the recording."

Black was also with her when she recorded the two songs from *Sunset Boulevard*. He was ecstatic with the first take, more so with the second. She went on to do about twenty more. "I thought, 'Oh my god! Don't keep singing because this voice can't last!' But it did. Then she has the engineer play back the same line from each of her takes. She has a sheet and ticks off which phrase or word she likes the best of each. Then she has them put together. It's a miraculous job of stitching, a surgical skill. 'I like the breath on take twenty-two,' I heard her say. And you're sitting there and it's simply mind-boggling.

"She wanted various musical phrases, and she would sing them to the trombonist or the trumpeter and say, 'You know, it would be very nice if you could play something like — 'Then she would *la-la* a few notes that took on an instrument sound. She is unique."

Back to Broadway went onto the charts almost immediately upon its release, and it is the great success of the album that sparked Streisand and Marty Erlichman to the idea that the time was right for her to return to the concert stage. Her past appearances before a live audience had always put her through "great misery . . . every night I was terrified." Then, as she explained it, on April 24, 1993, "Donna Karan gave me a wonderful birthday party, and Liza Minnelli got up to sing, and I am sitting there thinking, 'How does she do this? How does anyone get up in front of people and sing?' I could never get myself to sing at parties . . . with people looking at me. I can sing onstage because it is a black curtain out there. I can just see a few people and even that disturbs me. So, I was fascinated just watching her, and it became a challenge. I didn't like accepting that fright. I am frightened about a lot of things, but what I hope is good about me is that I go through the fear.

"'Why can't I do this?' I thought. Besides, so many fans wanted me to sing live. People were saying, 'You owe it to them.' It was starting to get to me."

"I had returned to London," Don Black remembered, "and Alan Bergman rang me up and said Barbra wanted to open with 'As If We Never Said Goodbye' and would I make some changes [that had not been made for the record], make it more relevant to a singer who was coming back after being away from the concert stage for a long time. 'I don't know why I'm frightened/I know my way around here/ The cardboard trees, the painted sea . . .' That's Norma Desmond. I changed it to 'the band, the lights, familiar sights . . .' and various little bits throughout, and then I faxed it to Alan, and he faxed back Barbra's suggestions. There were six or seven phone calls as well. Again, the minutest details."

The song had personal meaning for Streisand, who had begun her career in live venues — cabaret and the stage — and had grown steadily fearful of maintaining these appearances. That fear had not disappeared, but a concert tour would greatly enhance her recording potential. A record album and a pay-per-view TV special (later scrapped in favor of a Home Box Office special) would be the natural spinoffs and should generate tremendous revenues.

Money was much in her mind. She was rich, but not rich enough to do all the things she wanted to do without concern for her future. There were the films she wanted to make that did not appear to be commercial, and there was her foundation and the various deeply felt causes they helped support that could be increased to more significant contributions. And on a more personal level, she was refurnishing her New York apartment with priceless American eighteenth-century antiques and paintings — this time responding to a private tour of the White House that remained vivid in her mind, with priceless American eighteenth-century antiques and paintings.

As far back as December 15, 1991, she had told Tom Shales of the *Washington Post* that she was considering doing a tour for financial reasons. "I actually am running out of money, because I don't work very often," she told him. "I've bought all this land [California beachfront property] and I can't sell my other land [the Malibu ranch], so I might have to go out and sing just to pay for my house." The ranch was proving to be a tremendous drain on her resources. The taxes were exorbitant, and the maintenance — with the vast grounds and the five houses — was enormous. Also, the estate had served its purpose in her life. The decoration of each house had been like making a movie. Once finished, she wanted to go to the next project. Art deco and art nouveau were no longer her passion. She wanted money to buy primitive and early American art as well as furniture of the Arts and Crafts period. Negotiations were begun with Christie's auction house for a public sale of some of the contents of the ranch houses.

In August 1993 Kirk Kerkorian, the owner of the new billion-dollar, five-thousand-room MGM Grand in Las Vegas, not aware that Streisand was even considering a return to the concert stage, called Erlichman and proposed to donate $3 million to her favorite charities if she would make a one-time appearance at his hotel. The date was to be New Year's Eve, less than two weeks after the opening of the world's largest hotel-casino project. The offer came at a propitious time. Her movie projects were at a temporary standstill, "plus," as she said, "the show was to be on New Year's Eve. I hate New Year's Eve. It is a very lonely night for me . . . never a happy time. There is such an obligation to be happy. So, I thought: What a great way to escape New Year's Eve . . . doing a show."

Kerkorian's offer was the perfect opportunity for Streisand to initiate a live concert performance. She did not, however, intend to appear without private compensation. Erlichman offered Kerkorian a deal whereby she would perform at the MGM Grand for two nights, December 31 and January 1, which could earn Streisand close to $10 million for each performance;* additionally, the shows would be filmed (the best performance of each song being used) for television. Kerkorian, who knew that Streisand's appearance could well be the entertainment coup of the decade, swiftly agreed to the new terms. Other name acts such as Paul McCartney or Michael Jackson might well draw the crowds, but their appearance — since they had toured widely in recent years and been seen on cable television — would not be as newsworthy.

Everything else in Streisand's life was put on hold as she began work with the Bergmans on the concept for her appearance. Her idea was to make the concert an autobiographical trip through her life and career, using music and film clips as the milestones. Not only would she write most of the script, she would also direct; but she wanted to be surrounded by people whose judgment she could trust — Erlichman, Cis Corman, the Bergmans, Dwight Hemion.

She approached Marvin Hamlisch, who twenty-one years earlier had worked with her on *The Way We Were,* to take on the job of conductor. Since they had made *The Way We Were,* for which he had won two Oscars, Hamlisch had received a third Academy Award for his adaptation of

---

*The $20 million estimate included the expense and payroll of producing the concerts, which would be deducted from that amount as well as the $3 million Streisand still planned to turn over to her foundation for charitable distribution. Kirk Kerkorian rightly gambled on the fact that she had rarely performed in public for more than twenty years and that the two concerts would be sold out quickly.

Scott Joplin's music for *The Sting,* won four Grammys, a Tony, three Golden Globes, and had composed the music for the Pulitzer Prize–winning show *A Chorus Line,* as well as that of *They're Playing Our Song* and *The Goodbye Girl.*

"I didn't need the job," he said, "but I would never have said no to it. I thought it was the right thing to do. I also thought it would be a very historic kind of event for her to come back to the stage after twenty-seven years, and I wanted to be part of it. I just thought I was made to do this. When I was asked to think over the situation — conducting for Barbra — to me that was a privilege. We are talking about a great voice . . . a great lady."

Tickets went on sale for the two New Year's concerts at the MGM Grand in early October. Erlichman has claimed that the telephone company did not want the Las Vegas tickets to be on sale during the week—they were afraid incoming calls would overload the system. Over a million requests were clocked in the first Sunday, only the earliest callers able to purchase tickets. Streisand was overwhelmed with the response. An idea brewed now that Las Vegas could be the launch of an international tour. She was petrified of the enormity of such an undertaking, of the possibility that she would suffer terrible stage fright, of forgetting her lines and lyrics.

For years she had been accustomed to scripted dialogue filmed in short pieces and of knowing that if she misspoke, it could be reshot or edited later. Finally, she agreed that it would help if she was superbly prepared and if she could use some kind of TelePrompTer system large enough for her to see from the stage, but the musicians, technicians, and venues had to be the very best. Erlichman went off on a lengthy trip to view the arenas and concert halls in some of the major cities he thought would prove the most viable, and she went into rehearsals on the largest soundstage at Columbia Pictures, the same one on which she had recorded the songs for *Funny Girl* and *Funny Lady.*

Her first ambition was to have the sound for her live performances controlled as perfectly as it was when she was in a recording studio. For this task she hired one of the top acoustical technicians in the country, Bruce Jackson, who had worked for six years with Elvis Presley and ten with Bruce Springsteen. "I had heard that she was impossible to work with," Jackson said. "She definitely kept everyone on their toes. If you disagreed, you had to stand your ground. She would listen and try to rattle you. If you showed you were rattled and gave up ground, you were dead. She *was* demanding, but I found if you give her what she wants, she is in fact a great pleasure, very stimulating."

"She knew what she wanted, but she didn't know how to get there," said Tom Gallagher of Aura Systems, the company that was manufacturing a special speaker system for the concerts. "It was our job to keep experimenting until we got it right."

Streisand wanted an intimate, controlled sound — and in the size of the arenas where she would be singing, this was not easy to achieve. After many ideas had failed, Jackson finally came to her with the suggestion that carpet be laid on the floor and heavy drapes hung on the walls of the concert venues. "I knew this would be hugely expensive, but when I mentioned it to Barbra and Marty, they both said, 'Yes, do it.'"

She was to be backed by a sixty-four-piece orchestra. Donna Karan was designing the two gowns she would wear in the two sections of the concert so that she would not only look marvelous but be able to move largely unrestricted. To keep herself as calm as possible, she listened to meditation tapes when she was not needed. The entire effort was as concentrated and as carefully choreographed as a Broadway show. The rehearsals at Columbia were her out-of-town tryouts. Nothing was left to chance. Every comment she was to make onstage was drilled over and over to achieve near perfection.

"Barbra would tell me these stories [about her life]," Hamlisch recalled, "and I would say, 'Put it in the show.' She has a wonderful way of putting the truth out there almost with a little bit of whimsy, and that way you realize she is one of us. She is this person who has this great talent, but she is talking to us like she really cares. A very important thing about the concert was to have her fans see her as she is."

The last few days before the first show, Friday night, New Year's Eve 1993, were mayhem. The immense MGM Grand Hotel's Garden arena seated over 13,000. All the doors except one leading into the arena were sealed for security reasons, which meant that 13,000 people would have to line up single-file, airport-style, and pass through metal detectors. (Specified VIPs were ushered through a rear door.) Tickets were astronomically priced from fifty to a thousand dollars with four thousand seats at the top level, the average price per person being more than $500, and some fans had paid brokers three and four times face value for choice seats. Would they now be in a rage at having to stand in line for up to an hour to take their seats? And would this create a disgruntled audience that would be difficult to woo in the first few songs of her program? Streisand weighed all sides of the question and decided that she could not appear unless she felt secure and, therefore, would take the risk.

Wild expectation spread through the crowd as they waited to pass through the security check and enter the arena on New Year's Eve. The performance had been scheduled for 8 P.M. Around half past eight numerous white stretch limousines drew up to the curb. As each celebrity occupant stepped out, cheers went up from the crowds. There was Liza Minnelli, the president's mother (an inveterate gambling and Las Vegas enthusiast), Coretta Scott King, the widow of slain civil rights leader Martin Luther King, Jr., Prince, Quincy Jones, Michael Crawford, Alec Baldwin, Kim Basinger, and Streisand's former directors Peter Bogdanovich and Sydney Pollack. No one appeared disgruntled that the luminaries did not have to wait in line. "Never in my life did I think I would see her live," one woman who had paid $500 for her ticket and had been waiting since 6 P.M. said. Another agreed. "I had to be here. What if she doesn't feel comfortable onstage and decides to never do another concert?"

As soon as she stepped out on the stage at the MGM Grand, she would hear the thunderous roar of the crowd and come face to face with the reality of her life. There was no one in the entertainment world to equal her, not Frank Sinatra, Michael Jackson, or Madonna. She was no longer just a superstar. She was a living icon.

32

She arrived back in Los Angeles after the two Las Vegas concerts in high spirits. Not only had the shows and the concession sales netted her after-production revenues of more than $13 million, there had been an overwhelming demand for tickets — over a million calls logged on November 8, the day they were put on sale. Convinced now of the public's wish to see her perform live, she enthusiastically entered into plans for the tour that Erlichman was arranging. London's Wembley Stadium was set as the kickoff on April 20, 1994. She had fifteen weeks to institute the small changes to the program, rehearse, and get her life in order before departing for England. The latter was a tall order.

Long before the Las Vegas concerts, she had listed the Malibu ranch property for sale with a real estate broker for $19 million, the price was reduced a year later to $11.9 million when it had not sold. Finally, she made the decision to donate the land and houses on it (unfurnished) to the Santa Monica Mountains Conservancy, which allowed her a $15 million deduction on her taxes. The overwhelming inventory of furnishings and collectibles that had filled the houses now had to be carefully gone through. She would keep very little. The more valuable pieces, along with some things from the Carolwood house, 535 lots, would be placed at auction on March 3 and March 4 at Christie's Manhattan. A charity preview of twenty-five of the prized pieces — the large Tamara de Lem-picka oil that had hung in the art deco living room in one of the houses at the ranch, a magnificent Jacques Lipchitz bronze sculpture from the same room, the art nouveau desk that she had bought on the install-ment plan while appearing in *I Can Get It for You Wholesale* on Broad-way, and the Tiffany peony lamp from the living room of the Carolwood house among them — was held on February 17, at the St. James's Club on Sunset Boulevard, cost of admission $250 (proceeds to go to the UCLA Breast Cancer Center). A second auction, to be held in June in Com-merce, California, would feature nearly three hundred additional lots of the contents of the Malibu ranch houses, toasters, waffle irons, coffee makers, linens, dishes, and many items that would seem more likely to be found in a garage sale but — because of the appeal of owning some-thing of Streisand's — would be offered at Tiffany prices.

She was at home in Los Angeles when she learned that she had made over $6 million from Christie's auction. Her financial problems seemed to be behind her, but giving up the Malibu ranch and divesting herself of so many possessions that were deeply tied to her most meaningful memories had not been easy. Now she was facing the unknown — her first concert tour in twenty-eight years — and from the moment it had been announced in the press that top ticket prices would be $350, the media had been merciless in their attacks on her. Her fans did not seem to object. All performances in the six-city tour (London, Washington, D.C., Detroit, San Jose, Anaheim, and New York City) were almost com-pletely sold out within a matter of hours.

Before Streisand arrived in London, Erlichman added two more con-certs at the 12,000-seat Wembley Stadium to satisfy the demand for tick-ets. The English press ran banner headlines about "the selling of Barbra Streisand." Never had there been a concert appearance with as much preperformance publicity, most of it centered around the astronomical price of tickets and the fact that a week before the first concert many had changed hands at ten times their face value. Selfridges, the Oxford Street department store, constructed a Barbra Streisand Boutique, with every-thing from a £10 coffee mug to a £300 wool-and-leather embroidered jacket; in between there were watches, posters, scarves, purses, totes,

T-shirts, polo shirts, baseball caps — almost all with her picture and the concert logo that she helped design with graphic arts representatives from Sony Music, her merchandising agent. To add to these obvious moneymakers, stores stocked reissues of most of her albums. Wembley Stadium would also have several boutiques with the same merchandise, and the program for the concert, composed with her help, would cost £13 ($20), of which she received a 45 percent royalty.

Marty Erlichman, Cis Corman (Marvin Hamlisch had arrived earlier to rehearse the orchestra), and several members of her staff — secretary, hairstylist, makeup artist, dresser, and a bodyguard, accompanied her to London on the Concorde, arriving late Sunday evening, April 17, 1994, a momentous date for her, as she had never before appeared in concert in Great Britain. Dressed comfortably but in less-than-elegant fashion in a brown leather jacket, baggy pants, wedgie scuffs, and a wool beret, she emerged sleepy-eyed behind her tinted glasses and was met by an entourage of police, senior airport officials, airline VIP representatives, and concert promoters, as well as more than fifty members of the press and a host of fans. With her hefty guard in front of her, Erlichman at her side, she munched an apple as they made their way through the crowds to a waiting Daimler limousine that would take them to the Dorchester Hotel where she had a thousand-pound-a-day suite filled with the white and yellow flowers she so loved (especially tulips) and prestocked with the queen's and her own favorite bottled water, Malvern, boxes of Reese's Peanut Butter Cups, and Hershey Mint bars.

On early-morning television the following day she told her interviewer, "I don't like to be famous. I don't like the press to follow me. I don't like to talk about myself and I want to be remembered for the work I do, not the articles about me or what people think about me. It's just not a thing I get off on — the applause, the roaring applause of the crowd. It doesn't affect my being. I want to please people, I want to give them what they want, but I feel I'm doing that now through the movies and the albums I make." She had, however, been greatly affected by her reception in Las Vegas, which had left her on a high for several days afterward.

Nothing, even her previous stays in London, had prepared her for the

British media. It was not so much the considerable numbers that stalked her every move—she was used to that—but their derisive, scornful attitude. She was front-page news in all the daily papers except the *Financial Times,* and the articles featured every possible negative: she was pampered, difficult, money-hungry, "the most steely woman on earth," dressed "decidedly down-market," and had Wembley Stadium fully carpeted because she thought it would be "too draughty" (no member of the press having thought to ask the real reason for the last "idiosyncrasy"). She took it as good-naturedly as she could.

"You have got to get this right," she admonished one journalist gently. "The British always say Strei-*sunned.* My name is pronounced with a soft *s,* like the stuff on the beach. *Stry-sand.*" On Tuesday afternoon, between rehearsals at Wembley, she took time out to appear in the parking lot for a charity event, to hand over the keys to one of fifty Variety Club Sunshine coaches (her personal donation) to be used to transport disabled children to holidays and events they otherwise could not afford to attend. She accepted flowers from a lovely dark-eyed child. "Flowers, oh, flowers," she exclaimed with tears in her eyes. She would, in fact, contribute $10.2 million from her tour revenues to charity.*

She was too busy rehearsing, making sure there were no glitches in the first concert, Wednesday night, April 19, just twenty-four hours away, to nurse her usual preshow jitters. Whenever she did have a moment free, she would meditate alone. She feared the British critics would be hard on her, that there was some kind of general group response to her American brashness, her feminist positions, and her money. They would come to hear her, bringing their "attitude" with them. She could not change, nor did she care to do so. She was who she was and what she was, and that was that. Take it or leave it. But she could do everything in top form — sing, perform, look her best. She rehearsed until the orchestra was too exhausted to go on. Relentless activity kept her from thinking

---

*In the United States Streisand's charitable contributions from the tour included $25,000 each for musical education — instruments, equipment, and teaching staff — to schools across the country, including her old high school, Erasmus Hall. Sony Music matched each school donation.

about the moment she would step out onstage for the first concert. Stage fright once again assailed her. She listened to meditation tapes, trying, as she said, "to have a positive attitude because I easily get sidetracked into this abyss of fear and I have to get myself out of it." The scathing pre-concert articles in the press had greatly upset her.

What she perhaps did not realize was that the more vilified by the media — both American and British — the more her grip on the public strengthened. "She is not just a singer," a fan who had bought tickets for all four Wembley concerts insisted. "She is a role model — the living proof that if you believe in yourself, you can do anything you want. She had a terrible childhood, but she was determined to succeed. She is an inspiration to us all." Another added, "Her mother told her she was ugly and couldn't sing. The press always criticize, but she is a born survivor."

She represented a woman's triumph over adversity, and her constant tales of her unhappy childhood, her perception of being homely, her unstable love affairs, the media abuse, made her seem vulnerable and reduced the distance between her and her fans. "She is living proof that you can do anything," one said of her. "She would have been a secretary if she had listened to her mother," Giles Coren of *The Times* concurred. "That early rejection is of great importance to English fans and [Wembley] will be as much a show of solidarity as an entertainment. They will come in their droves to show Barbra's mother just how wrong she was."

The day of the concert Streisand took precious minutes out to call Diana. "She said she hoped I'd be able to see the show when it comes to Los Angeles," Diana told reporters. "I said I hoped so, too." These were not the words her daughter sought to hear. Her drive to succeed, her insatiable ambition, her need to be famous, recognized as *somebody,* had always gone hand in hand with her hunger for her mother's applause, a show of maternal hubris. She would never feel she had succeeded until she received it. The irony was that Diana's apathy had driven her to become a star of the greatest magnitude and was why she was never satisfied with what she achieved and always feared that with one misstep, everything she had accomplished would vanish.

Before she sang a single note, she was given a standing ovation that lasted five minutes. In a rare public display of emotion, she brushed tears from her cheeks with the back of her hand. Finally, the audience sat down again, and she sang her opening number. The show was almost identical to the Las Vegas concerts, although she inserted some chitchat about England and the English, not spontaneous — every word projected in clear view of the audience on the TelePrompTer.

As she said, "This is a very special night, very special to me," the words rolled across the prompt screens. "People ask me why I'm on the road for the first time in twenty-seven years," she began. "Hey, if you came from California with the earthquakes, mudslides, and the fires, *you* would hit the road, too." She took a sip of the herbal tea she preferred. "I love England, especially cucumber sandwiches with the crusts cut off," she exclaimed to a few titters. Some video footage was shown of Princess Margaret at the opening of *Funny Girl* twenty-eight years earlier, as well as additional clips of Prince Charles greeting her backstage, all of them looking incredibly young. "Who knows, if I had been nicer to him I might have been the first real Jewish princess . . . Princess Babs," she joked. "I can imagine what the newspaper headlines might have been. 'Blintzes Princess Plays the Palace' and 'Barbra Digs Nails Into Prince of Wales!'" This time, there was the sound of genuine laughter.

An ardent, spirited audience, they seemed not to mind the Tele-PrompTer as she told them at every performance, "I could never be here otherwise. I have a fear of forgetting the words, which I once did in front of 135,000 people [the Central Park concert in 1968], and it's a fear."

She was welcomed back to London with great emotion. The audience kept rooting her on. "Thank you, thank you," she repeated over and over. At the close of her last song, a curiously chosen anticlimactic interpretation of "For All We Know," they watched her go offstage and jumped to their feet applauding for her to return. When she did, they grew silent, expecting her to sing an encore. With disarming hesitancy, she said, "I didn't think you'd get all my jokes and stuff," bowed, and to audible gasps of disappointment, did not return. Nonetheless, as people filed out, the general feeling was that this had been an experience of a lifetime and worth every pence.

A stellar list of British celebrities had attended — Elton John, Michael

Caine, and Shirley Bassey among them. Don Black was there at her special invitation. "What did you *really* think?" she asked.

"You were wonderful," he replied. "But all that psychiatrist thing doesn't work. Over here we don't go to psychiatrists so much. What we do is sit down and have a nice cup of tea and a chat with somebody, and we sort ourselves out that way." After the concert she entertained her personal guests at the small, exclusive Blakes Hotel. Streisand appeared almost giddy at the lively celebration, which did not end until 4 A.M. The reviews the next morning were mixed, many of the critics still deploring the price of the tickets, the psychobabble of the script, the TelePrompTer, even the £28 bottles of champagne during intermission (which had not seemed to bother the general audience). Nonetheless, there were only glowing accolades for the greatness of her voice.

"She is the supreme communicator," wrote Tony Parsons in the *Daily Telegraph*. "Streisand has an ability to talk directly to an audience's heart that is surpassed only by Sinatra. When [she] takes flight, she makes music that is full of memories and a sense of loss. . . . She is unquestionably the last of the great romantics."

London hailed her as "the ultimate pop diva." It was difficult to turn on a radio music station that was not playing her records. Almost every newspaper edition carried some story about her; Elton John was giving her a £200,000 party (a figure much inflated, but it did cost almost half that) on Sunday, April 24, her fifty-second birthday, at his country estate. She had refused to attend the "celebrity-packed" publicity party Sony had planned (and canceled) for the previous night, to her record company's chagrin, because she was not given control of the guest list, which would have allowed her to exclude much of the media. Prince Charles was attending the concert on Monday, the twenty-fourth; Diana gave an interview from California; a full-page color layout of Streisand and Caleigh appeared in one daily; and there were a constant barrage of stories with headlines similar to "Barbra Strident strikes up the band's anger" (*Daily Mail,* April 22), an example of the Englishman's penchant to use a play on words. Hamlisch had brought only twelve of his key musicians with him to London. The remainder of the orchestra was local and was furious when asked to sign the day before the first concert an agreement of confidentiality binding them not to discuss anything having to do with Streisand's appearance to the press. In fact, such letters were distributed to the employees of the Wembley Stadium, as they were to those at the MGM Grand, and would be at every place that she would appear.

The stage crew was barred from watching rehearsals. One person said, "I was told by my boss that I must look away if I see Streisand because she doesn't like people staring." A member of the orchestra complained, "It's the principle I object to — the assumption that we are going to leak material about her. I have played for some of the finest opera singers in the world but I have never come across anything so reminiscent of a prima donna."

Still, no one in the orchestra refused to sign the agreement, which bore a great similarity to the ones the queen's staff were required to sign. Had they not signed, they were warned that they would be replaced. This was all part of Streisand's driving need for both privacy and control, most difficult to obtain when she so prominently placed herself in the public eye. She hated not being in control of what was written about her, certain the truth would not make its way into print. She wanted it *all* — the power, the glory, the fame, *and* the privacy accorded nonpublic figures. Times had changed since her early years as a star; the media were in command. Gone were the days when studios and publicity representatives fed the press at their will. The press was voracious for stories about the famous, and for a time Streisand became a competitor to Princess Diana — pictures and stories about her, however insignificant, in overwhelming demand. It was as though the media thought she were just too talented, too famous, too rich, too outspoken, not to take her down for it.

Her authoritarian demand of employees to sign papers that bind them to silence, to threaten the loss of their jobs if they discuss their work with her, is at extreme odds with all her professed liberalism. And although such tactics are not unconstitutional unless they emanate from a government agency, it is a gag order, an infringement on the right of the free speech of others while she enjoys a platform for all her comments, ideas, and positions on various issues. The double standard here is both shocking and disappointing. One expects more of a woman like Streisand, who is always out there fighting for her own personal rights.

Monday night's concert was also a fund-raiser, a percentage of the revenues (estimated at £150,000) to be donated to the Prince's Trust. Streisand had last seen Charles in 1974 during his visit to Hollywood. He had arrived at the studio where she was filming *Funny Lady* as she was recording the song "So Long, Honey Lamb." During that twenty minutes they chatted, Streisand shared her mug of tea with him.

Charles is a great fan of hers and seemed truly taken with her as a person. Members of the recording orchestra remembered observing the intense eye contact between the two. "Sparks flew," one musician (who did not want his name revealed) observed. They met again at a champagne reception before the concert, and she warmly clasped his hand in hers twice during their five minutes of conversation, neither seeming inhibited by the others present (Marvin Hamlisch, Marty Erlichman, Charles's equerries, members of the management staff of Wembley Stadium, and several photographers). During her performance Charles, dressed conservatively in a dark blue suit, sat rapt with attention in a reserved balcony area thirty yards from the stage with celebrities including Joan Collins and Priscilla Presley. In the section of the program where Streisand usually showed video footage of Caleigh and herself and then sang "Some Day My Prince Will Come" for the child, she introduced the Disney song and remarked on her fondness for songs featuring imaginary princes. "What makes this song extra special is that there's a real one in the audience tonight," she announced.

When she had finished singing, Charles rose to his feet with the rest of the audience and joined in a two-minute ovation that ended with the crowd's stamping their feet and demanding more. She returned to sing "Somewhere." Charles jumped to his feet again and applauded vigorously when she was done. Smiling broadly, Streisand waved at him and made a gesture of a bow.

The sound of applause did not appease her great sense of loneliness at being away from Caleigh. "I am devoted to my goddaughter," she told anyone who asked about the inclusion of Caleigh's photographs in the printed program. She called California often to speak to her. Although only on the first engagement of her tour, Streisand was already missing the child, and after the fourth and last show in London (each separated by several days, as she did not like to give concerts back to back) she returned to Los Angeles expressly to see her. Then, after a joyful but short reunion, she and Erlichman rejoined Hamlisch, the orchestra, and her technicians in Washington, D.C., where the president and the First Lady attended her first night concert there. She was fighting the beginnings of a cold but after her Washington appearances continued on to Detroit for two shows at the Palace of Auburn Hills arena. "In Detroit," she said, "I thought, *I don't know how I'm going to get through the next fifteen shows.* It's very exhausting physically. It's a lot of breathing; you have to be in pretty good shape. And I don't work out vocally. I don't practice. It's the most boring thing you can imagine, doing scales. So I just said, 'Fuck it, I can't [do scales]. I'm too tired the day after a concert.'"

Her next venue was to be the Arrowhead Pond in Anaheim, the home of the Mighty Ducks hockey team and with 19,200 capacity the largest of all the arenas in which she had performed. By the time she arrived in Los Angeles, her cold had worsened. She was suffering from viral tracheolaryngitis, was placed on antibiotics, and was told by her doctor that she must rest her voice.

Originally scheduled for Wednesday, May 25, the first of the six southern California concerts was postponed to Thursday, June 2, to give her a chance to recover sufficiently. The show was also scheduled to go to San Jose in northern California. A glittering array of celebrities (Michael Jackson, Warren Beatty, Goldie Hawn, Walter Matthau, among others) attended opening night along with some of the most important people in her life — Elliott and Jason, Jon Peters and Caleigh, André Agassi, Don Johnson, Ray and Fran Stark, and in the front row, Diana and Roslyn. As she ended her first number and came down the steps from the balcony set and walked across the front rim of the stage, she glanced down over the footlights. Diana, eighty-five and severely arthritic, was on her feet applauding with the rest of the delirious crowd. Streisand leaned forward.

"Mom, you stood up. Take it easy, Mom. Sit down. I'm glad you're here. I love you," she said, straightened, stood still for a moment, and then motioned with her hands for the audience to be seated.

There was no sign of laryngitis as she launched into her program, which now included a ten-minute *Yentl* sequence —"a masterly staged affair that proved to be the most crowd-pleasing sequence of the show." She received even greater acclamation at the finish. "One sensed it was for more than the music," Robert Hilburn of the *Los Angeles Times* wrote. "It was also in admiration of the independence and determination Streisand has shown over the years in such pursuits as film directing."

Since London she had also changed the ending of the concert, which had been the melancholy song "For All We Know," about the possibility of two people never meeting again, to the brighter more uplifting "Somewhere," from *West Side Story*.

"If there's such a thing as a concert ticket that's worth the money, this might be the one," *Daily Variety* declared. She played the second concert on June 4, but — her throat still giving her problems — the last four shows were canceled. As the Arrowhead Pond was booked ahead for several weeks, it was decided she would return to Anaheim after San Jose and New York to end the tour with concerts there, on July 10, 18, 22, and 24.

Her throat problems were cured by the time she opened at Madison Square Garden on Monday night, June 20, for the first of her five American venues. The majority of theaters are dark on Monday, so almost all the performers who were then on Broadway turned out to welcome her home. She was, after all, a Brooklyn girl, one of their own. Attending her triumphant return were Liza Minnelli, Chita Rivera, and the casts from almost every show along the Great White Way. She seemed relaxed, looked marvelous (she had fresh copies of her two gowns made for each city on the tour), and was in magnificent voice. She had returned to the New York concert stage the same week that the city played host to the Gay Games. "One of the best things about the games," she told her enthusiastic audience, "is that I can walk down the street and not be recognized because there are so many impersonators."

After singing "The Man Who Got Away," she told Liza over the microphone, "Your mom sang that great." Rex Reed commented that it was the ultimate in chutzpah, but Liza laughed and did not appear to take the remark as an affront.

Reed was not as completely won over as the cheering, stamping aggregation in the Garden indicated they all were. "There's no denying her talent," he said, "but it's always the voice that gets to you, not the interpretation. Every inflection, every modulation, every supersonic high note, seems canned on vinyl. You could be home listening to records. She doesn't have the vulnerability of Garland or Piaf, or the kind of moment-to-moment self-discovery that breeds the art of spontaneity. She's such a perfectionist . . . she's not about to open the doors and let you in."

Reed was in the minority. It is almost impossible to compare Streisand with Garland and Piaf. They are cut from a different cloth. Both victims, exposing their bruised, fragile selves to their audiences who listened to them in quite a different way than Streisand's audiences listen to her. Streisand's fans are not sharing her pain, they are celebrating her strength to overcome all the obstacles that they perceive she has overcome — turning homely into beautiful, making ethnic mainstream, daring to cross over into a man's world as director, producer, and business executive. She is a dignified feminist, a liberal proud of the word and never afraid to voice her opinion. And she has maintained uninterrupted stardom and popularity for more years than any other entertainment figure except perhaps Sinatra. She is far more intelligent than either Garland or Piaf and approaches her work in a more intellectual way. They were unique, most certainly, and could move you to chills and tears, making you want to run up onstage and hold them in your arms, to save them. And especially in Garland's case, to forgive anything and everything — even when she could not hit the notes or remember the lyrics. Much more is expected of Streisand, and she makes sure that, to the best of her ability, she lives up to her own high expectations.

The tour, coupled with her multimedia projects, had given her more star power than anyone, rock star or opera diva, on the concert circuit. By the time she completed all the performances, with two shows added to her Madison Square Garden appearances, it would be the biggest money-making tour in entertainment history. The previous December, before appearing in Las Vegas, she had told Barbara Walters, "Let me say this, I have a long way to go. I have a lot to learn. I'm still sensitive to criticism. I go through periods when I can just laugh at it, you know? And periods when I think it's just plain mean. You have to accept life for what it is. The pain and the joy; the hate, the love. My musical director [Hamlisch] came to see me and he gave me a book called *Life Is the Message*, about changing the world. Well, we cannot change the world. It's such an overwhelming feat, but yet by changing ourselves each of us in a very small way *can* change the world."

The tour had helped her battle her fear of appearing before a live audience, although the demons remained (if less active), but had she changed the world even a little by doing it? Hardly, although throughout her long career she had changed the public's taste, the view of beauty, the idea that without a formal education you cannot walk as an equal with intellectuals, the concept that women are not emotionally equipped to stand toe to toe with male power brokers. The concerts, including Las Vegas, had grossed over $64 million by doing things *her way.** All the final decisions were hers — from music to script to performance, set, sound, merchandising, and road arrangements. There was a totality in her efforts, the only way she knew how to work. She dealt always from strength to strength. This had not been a "comeback" tour as so many of Garland's had been. Streisand was a greater star for having been unavailable to the public for so many years.

"She's God's bell," said exercise guru Richard Simmons, one of her most steadfast admirers. "In the eighth grade I was two hundred pounds. And I saw her emerge from not the most beautiful girl in the world to the most beautiful woman that I've ever seen in my entire life. She helped my self-image."

Her own self-image was another matter. Nothing was ever enough. She had to prove herself over and over and *over* again. It was an obsession. Something ate at her from the inside, drove her on. No one who worked

---

*That figure does not include the money earned from concert merchandise, the HBO special, and the royalties from the concert album. However, the expenses of the tour were high — $20 million on the road and $4 million in Las Vegas, Streisand has claimed.

with her could ever match her pace. In mid-July of 1994, she returned to Los Angeles to complete the four concerts at Arrowhead Pond. Rumors had preceded her that she might cancel. The weather was unduly hot and humid. She was once more having some trouble with her throat. She did, indeed, appear to the overwhelming enthusiasm of her audiences. On the final night Hollywood turned out in force, a great many of those who had already attended the Las Vegas, New York, or earlier California concerts, returning to hear her again. She received standing ovations from the moment she stepped out onto the stage. After the final number she asked the audience if they cared to remain while she performed for the television cameras. There was a scramble as the majority raced back to their seats.

While the taping ensued, friends and VIP guests had been escorted backstage to an airless, white-walled room to wait for Streisand and pay her homage. They sat restlessly as they watched her on the large monitor, hearing again "that crystalline voice rising, rising — and then, at the break where almost every other singer goes reedy, blazing higher so that you feel [as Marvin Hamlisch puts it] that she's *pulled you through*." Warren Beatty placed his arm around an exhausted, very pregnant Annette Bening. Elliott and Jason were there with Diana, seated in a wheelchair, and Shirley MacLaine squatted, Indian-style, as she talked to her. Caleigh stood patiently beside her father despite the lateness of the hour. It is rare that Beatty and MacLaine, though brother and sister, ever attend anything together. Finally, the screen went blank. The filming session was over and it was very late. A chosen few of those waiting were escorted into Streisand's adjoining white-carpeted, heavily mirrored dressing room, where silver-framed photographs of Jason and Caleigh were displayed.

"You did good," Diana said grudgingly. "I'm proud of you."

Still looking glamorous and appearing fresh, Streisand replied, "Thanks, Mom," her words spoken so softly she could barely be heard.

The next morning she was at Sony Studios by ten o'clock, editing footage for the television special and mixing tracks for a projected album of the concert (actually, an accretion of several of the concerts). Home Box Office expected that the televised concert would, like the tour, break viewer records. She swore she would never do a tour again. "You have to put makeup on, comb your hair. You have to wear high heels. My feet get cramps!" she complained.

As soon as she came off the road, Streisand immersed herself in work once more on the Margarethe Cammermeyer story, now planned as a made-for-television movie, under the title *Serving in Silence*. She had begun *Serving in Silence* in the fall of 1992 after reading a newspaper article about Lieutenant Colonel Cammermeyer, a highly decorated army nurse for twenty-six years who had been discharged for revealing in a security-clearance interview that she was a lesbian. The highest-ranking military official ever discharged for homosexuality, she had become a leader in the fight to overturn the military's ban on homosexuals.

"Barbra had a passion about wanting to do this project," Cis Corman said. "It was such a blatant case of discrimination and prejudice." Convincing the colonel to have a film made of her story was not easy, not even for Streisand. Finally, she conceded, and Streisand pressed forward with Craig Zadan (a former close associate of Stephen Sondheim) and Neil Meron, who had produced the Emmy-nominated *Gypsy* with Bette Midler, as producers, while she remained the executive producer. What the project needed was a star to play the colonel. In the spring of 1994, Glenn Close had just left the Los Angeles cast of *Sunset Boulevard* and had time in her schedule before preparing for the November opening in New York. Streisand was about to depart for England. She believed that Close would be superb in the role, bringing to it both the strength and the feminine qualities of Cammermeyer. Close, one of the screen's finest actresses, thought so, too, and agreed to become part of the project, both as star and as coexecutive producer with Streisand. The two women had immediate rapport, a writer was hired, and the enterprise set in motion.

Presenting a major story about lesbians to the small screen seemed on the surface to involve insurmountable problems. Advertisers were reluctant to buy time; there was concern over a possible viewer boycott. But the potency of the involvement of Streisand and Close was enough for Lindy DeKoven, NBC's senior vice-president of miniseries and motion pictures for television, to accept the project.

"What the network ordered and what it got were two different things," Craig Zadan recalled. "The network assumed it would be predominantly courtroom scenes. But what evolved in the writing was a love story. Glenn told us, 'Under no circumstances are you to take out any of this love story. Otherwise, as an actress I'll have nothing to play.'" The script was not as graphic as what was suggested for *The Normal Heart,* but it did contain impassioned scenes of two lesbians embracing and kissing.

The movie was being shot on location in Vancouver when she ended the tour. A group in New York called the Family Defense Council had already raised the specter of an advertiser boycott unless the lesbian kiss was cut. Close's costar, Judy Davis, was threatening to quit, fearing her role would be sacrificed to satisfy the hostile group. Not only was Streisand working on the controversial *Serving in Silence,* she was engaged once again in rewrites with Larry Kramer on *The Normal Heart* and with Richard LaGravenese on *The Mirror Has Two Faces,* the more commercial property. Dedicated though she was to *The Normal Heart,* she desperately wanted to be able to show a studio that she could make a simple commercial film and bring it in on budget and on time. But time was the very thing that Kramer, battling HIV, did not have. If *Mirror* should go into production first, he would be difficult to deal with. She did not want this to happen, nor to lose *The Normal Heart.* She was going to have to juggle the two in such a way that Kramer could be appeased. It appeared that Streisand had walked right into the eye of a hurricane.

33

"I'm a shy person," Streisand told an interviewer for the *Los Angeles Times* who asked whether she had plans for another tour, "and I don't *have* to go out on the road again. I lost weight and sleep. I thought I would disappoint people, that I wasn't good enough. It all worked out. It was right for me to gain this confidence to feel absolutely at ease onstage, to feel I belonged there and deserved to be there, that I could give and receive the love of those audiences. I really *am* grateful to those people. For too many years I didn't appreciate my own singing. . . . But it's not my love; my love is making movies."

Columbia was pleased that she had chosen to work on a commercial project such as *The Mirror Has Two Faces.* LaGravenese had sent her his first revised draft while she was on tour. She thought it took a wrong turn and asked him to rewrite. When she received the second version, she decided she liked the first one better, although it required more work. After several weeks of unsatisfactory story meetings with LaGravenese, she called in Carrie Fisher, who had successfully adapted for the screen her novel *Postcards from the Edge,* believing Fisher might give her character sharper focus. Fisher's fee for the work was higher than the budget allowed, so Streisand went back to LaGravenese with more detailed suggestions and he began work on what would become the final shooting script.

The Normal Heart was once again placed on a back burner, and she was caught between Kramer's wrath and her own guilt. Not only did she love the project, she had great sympathy for Kramer's physical situation, his fear of dying before the film was made. Kramer had also become a close friend of Jason's, and as one of the country's leading gay activists almost always got press coverage when he chose to speak out on any related topic. She knew he would be furious that she was yet again delaying the project and would not be silent in his protest. She anticipated trouble, and it came just as soon as it was announced that *The Mirror Has Two Faces* was to be her next film.

"Why are you doing this piece of shit?" Kramer, unable to contain his anger, yelled at her when she told him her plans.

"It's not a piece of shit!"

"It is a piece of shit. Everyone I know says it's a piece of shit."

"Who said it's a piece of shit?"

"Well, Jason said it's a piece of shit."

"Jason says it's a piece of shit?"

"Yes. He did."

"She seemed suddenly reflective and I pressed my point," Kramer recalled. "'This is the peak of your life. You don't have two years to waste your time and your energy and your intelligence making a piece of shit,' I continued. 'That's not how you create a great body of work.' She was troubled and I hated having to hurt her.

"'I've already created a great body of work!' she defended. 'I've tried so hard not to be so hard on myself. Why are you doing this to me? I want to try to make a movie without going through so much Sturm und Drang. I want to do it as an exercise to show I can go in, make a movie fast, not drive everyone nuts, including myself, and get out and on with the next one. Anyway, everyone is pressuring me to do it.'

"'No one has more power than you.'

"'That's what you think. It's not easy. I've said I'd do [*Mirror*] — and Jeff Bridges will kill me [the actor who was to play opposite her].'

"'Why don't you send him the script of *The Normal Heart?*'"

"'Oh, he'd be wonderful, but I couldn't do that!'"

"In Hollywood, they don't live in the real world," Kramer commented after telling this story. "And so, she scheduled *The Mirror Has Two Faces* first and *The Normal Heart* was to be delayed until after it was finished."

Meanwhile, *Serving in Silence* was being prepared for television release, and she was directly involved in the final work. Ironically, in view of her expressed feeling at a previous time that there were great differences between heterosexuals and homosexuals, she now offered an altered opinion to the press, "I would like people to identify with the people in the story [the colonel and her lesbian lover]. We're basically more similar than different." She worked extremely well with Glenn Close, whom she greatly admired for her "dignity and integrity." The show was not to be aired for ten weeks, but the press was already publishing caustic articles about the project, proclaiming that the network took it on only because of Streisand and Close's involvement and because they would then get the right to re-air Streisand's HBO concert special.

"Why is it," Colonel Cammermeyer inquired, "that every time I see something written about her [Streisand], it's never without some negative connotation. What *is* it about the fact that she's talented, enriching, caring, gives of herself emotionally and financially to the things she believes in — what is it about her that is so offensive to people?" A parallel, Cammermeyer believed, existed between her "own experience as a lesbian in the military; both worlds are ruled by boys' clubs that close ranks against women who don't toe the line."

Serving in Silence was aired on NBC on February 6, 1995, to generally good reviews and high ratings and was nominated for several Emmys, including Best Original Film Made for Television and Best Actress in that category, but did not receive an award. Streisand was always disappointed and bitter when her work with film was overlooked for awards. But her energy and enthusiasm had been channeled into the development of *Mirror,* although she continued working with Kramer on *The Normal Heart* and attempting to find financing and a star to play opposite her to enable her to schedule the film to follow *Mirror.* For the time being Kramer, whom she genuinely respected and cared for, was appeased.

In November 1994 she was occupied with fund-raising in support of California Democrats running for state or national office — no concerts but luncheons and galas at which she was, along with numerous others, a celebrity guest. She took time out from her political activities to attend an event honoring Prince Charles when he arrived in Los Angeles, his first visit in twenty years. They had only a brief opportunity to talk, but a close observer once again noted their "terrific eye contact. It was like POW!" Charles was staying at the elegant, secluded Bel-Air Hotel situated in Stone Canyon, which weaves through the mountains above Sunset Boulevard in West Los Angeles. With its enchanted gardens, eleven acres of private parkland, ancient trees, and its graceful artificial lake — home to a wedge of swans — the hotel resembled a French country château and the stunning accommodations mirrored this theme. A few days after Charles and Streisand spoke at the gala, he arranged a private meeting in his luxurious suite of rooms, where they spent an hour alone together.

A bevy of pressmen, having picked up word of her visit, gathered at the front gates. Hair flying in the cold November wind, head down, huge dark glasses hiding her face and wearing a belted coat and high boots, Streisand hurried into a waiting car that whizzed her away. The idea of Streisand and Charles ever being romantically involved seemed bizarre enough somehow to make sense. Charles is a fan, that is true, and they had got on well when they had seen each other, however briefly, in London during her tour. But there was a breath of romance in the secrecy and the lack of other participants attending the encounter. Charles, following in the footsteps of his philandering father, Prince Philip, has never been entirely faithful to either his wife or his mistress, although he has maintained a long-standing extramarital relationship. It is unlikely that Charles and Streisand ever had an affair, but it does seem that the prince was strongly attracted to her.

As Christmas 1994 approached, there was still no one special man in Streisand's life. She remained in close contact with Peter Jennings and sought out his advice on political matters that concerned her or items she read about in the newspapers and wanted to hear about in greater depth. Jennings has charm, warmth, a fine intelligence, and his own sphere of

fame. But he was also dating a younger, very attractive television producer — Katherine Freed.

Why was she not able to find a soul mate, a man who would love her
deeply and to whom she could return the depth of that love? She was no
longer the fame-hungry girl who had married and divorced Elliott, or the
besotted woman who had given herself so completely to Peters. She had
met, worked with, and had affairs with some of the most powerful, vital,
intelligent, and sexy men in the world. Whatever man she was drawn to
had to measure up to the best of those gentlemen; so far, none had. The
man she wanted could not be intimidated by her immense fame, her
ironclad dedication to everything she attempted. He must share her enthusiasms, her convictions, her expectations, as well as have a career of
merit on his own. In addition, he had to be sensitive and understanding
when necessary, strong and protective when required. He could not be
married or have "a roving eye." Such a man was not easy to find. But she
never abandoned the possibility that he was out there.

Streisand had agreed to give a lecture on February 3, 1995, at the
John F. Kennedy School of Government at Harvard on "the artist as citizen" and was jotting down notes all the time on what she wanted to
say — which mainly was a defense of the right of Hollywood celebrities
to speak out on politics. Having experienced the prejudice of the media
toward the politically active members of the film community during the
presidential election, the subject was one that she had been agitating over
for many months. The week before the speech was to be presented, she
flew to New York to consult Jennings. Her fear was not so much the
speech itself, but the question-and-answer period that would follow, at
which she might be called upon to respond to subjects or matters on
which she was not sufficiently knowledgeable. Jennings acted as a consultant but did not do any rewriting on her speech.

Ivied academia was in a frenzy of excitement at the prospect of her
forthcoming appearance at Harvard, much more attention being paid to
her than to a recent visit by Secretary of State Warren Christopher. The
university had to hold a lottery, so great was the demand for tickets in the
seven-hundred-seat auditorium. Arrangements were made for a camera
newspool to be set up to cover her televised appearance. Special machines

were installed to check for counterfeit tickets, and Cambridge police were stationed at every door and stairwell. Streisand remained terrified of an attack or a shooting by some crazy person, even though no incident of suspected violence had occurred during her concert tour.

She arrived by private jet in Boston with her secretary, Kim Skalecki, two days before her talk and was driven to the Charles Hotel, where she was given the presidential suite. That night she holed up in her rooms rewriting her speech yet one more time. The following day she had a "wonderful lunch" with John F. Kennedy, Jr., and twenty-five intense, serious, idealistic students, at which she discussed issues from welfare to defense spending. She grew misty-eyed when the youthfully handsome Kennedy met her and accompanied her on a tour of Harvard. Thirty-one years had passed since her treasured meeting with his father. Later she audited a class on constitutional law, for which she even did the homework after a run-through on her speech in the deserted auditorium.

Her nerves increased as the time for her to speak approached. After the audience was seated, she stood in the wings waiting for a lengthy laudatory introduction by Harvard University's interim president, Albert Carnesale, to end. When she finally stepped out on the stage that had previously played host to the likes of Mikhail S. Gorbachev, Newt Gingrich, Al Gore, and a plethora of presidential hopefuls and administration officials, she was "*really* nervous." Wearing a conservative charcoal gray pinstriped, severely tailored Donna Karan dress, a single strand of pearls, her nails "seriously sculptured," she clasped and unclasped her hands, hugged her knees, rocked backward and forward, and clenched the arms of her chair as Carnesale went on about her accomplishments.

"You heard of *shpilkes?*" she asked in a Brooklyn accent, to a chorus of laughter and vigorous applause when she finally stepped up to the microphone. Standing in front of a large wall hanging that read HARVARD UNIVERSITY — JOHN F. KENNEDY SCHOOL OF GOVERNMENT and the school's emblem emblazoned, she sounded much like the impassioned Katie Morosky in *The Way We Were* as she told the students "I must admit I'm confused by [Speaker of the House Newt Gingrich's] thinking. He proposes taking children away from poor mothers and placing them in orphanages. If that's an example of mainstream culture, let me say I'm happy to be a member of the counterculture. I am also proud to be a liberal. Why is that so terrible these days? The liberals were liberators — they fought slavery, fought for women to have the right to vote, fought against Hitler, Stalin, fought to end segregation, fought to end apartheid. Liberals put an end to child labor, and they gave us the five-day work week! What's to be ashamed of?" With a shrug of her shoulders, she spread her hands palm up in a gesture that indicated *you know what I mean?*

Defending the right of a celebrity to be involved in politics, she asked, "What is the sin? Is it caring about your country? Why should the actor give up his role as citizen just because he's in show business? For his role in the movie *Philadelphia,* Tom Hanks had to learn quite a bit about being a gay man with AIDS. Should he have remained silent on this issue? For thirty years Paul Newman has been an outspoken defender of civil liberties and a major philanthropist. Would it be better if he just made money and played golf? Or is Robert Redford a bubblehead because he knows more about the environment than most members of Congress? . . . Most artists turn up on the humanist, compassionate side of public debate because . . . we have to walk in other people's shoes and live in other people's skins. This does tend to make us more sympathetic to politics that are more tolerant," she proudly acknowledged.

Eyes glancing down to check her notes from time to time, she went on to castigate the far right for "waging a war for the soul of America by making art a partisan issue." She suggested that the arts programs were minimal — "the Public Broadcasting System costs each taxpayer less than one dollar a year — they hardly could be under attack for the money's sake. Maybe it's about shutting the minds and mouths of artists who might have something thought-provoking to say." She reminisced about her childhood with stories about how her father had walked home from his teaching job to put the money he saved in the *pushke,* the charity box that many Jews had in their homes. She pointed to her own experience as a member of the Choral Club at Erasmus High School, stressing how important it was for children anywhere to "find solace in an instrument to play or a canvas to paint on," a plea that the government not cut such necessary funds.

During the fifty-minute speech she appeared at turns ardent and edgy. She gestured a lot, brushed her shoulder-length, blond-streaked hair back from her face, wet her lips, drank water when she paused. After her closing remarks, she was given a standing ovation. Carnesale came forward and announced that there would be a short recess and then their guest would answer questions. Backstage, Streisand appeared excruciatingly anxious and had to be calmed. The feared question period was next.

A round of applause greeted her return to the podium.

A Harvard senior, Christopher Garcia, asked the first question. "Why are you being so defensive?" adding that it sounded like the artistic community was "out of touch with society."

He was barraged with hisses, and Streisand raised her hands in a gesture that seemed to mean: *I'll answer that.* "Why are you a Republican?" she countered.

Her discomfort in this section of the program only grew as the questions became more technical than philosophical. Several times she fended these with an honest "I don't know enough about that to give you an answer." When asked if she had plans in politics, she replied, "Political ambition and political fervor are two different things." Finally, with only one more question allowed, a young woman praised her as articulate, wealthy, and intelligent. Streisand gave her a crooked Fanny Brice smile. "You've got a guy for me?" she asked.

She had put herself on the front line. She was always setting tough goals for herself, a higher mountain to climb, a new set of obstacles to overcome, critics to win over. The press was generally positive to her appearance and her speech, but arch-conservative author Arianna Huffington wrote a stinging rebuttal in the *Washington Post*. "Barbra, how could anyone hear anything over the din of such high-pitched melodrama?" she charged. "Why do you insist on characterizing conservatives' wish to curtail tax-payer subsidies for the arts as motivated by 'disrespect' for art and artists? Is your wish to cut the defense budget motivated by 'disrespect' for our military and its servicemen?" Her suggestion was that the private sector raise the $167 million annual budget necessary to sustain the arts.

Holding scant regard for Huffington's opinion, Streisand was not upset by her diatribe. She had spoken out on issues that were meaningful to her and believed she had a right to public address.

By the end of summer her attention was consumed by preproduction pressures for *Mirror,* which would go before the cameras in and around New York in late October. Casting had been a relatively simple matter. With Jeff Bridges now definitely signed to costar, Pierce Brosnan, the suave, handsome Irishman, fresh from his role as James Bond in the most current 007 movie, was cast as the devilishly attractive other man (in this case Streisand's movie brother-in-law), Dudley Moore as Bridges's drinking buddy, and Lauren Bacall — in what would turn out to be a stroke of ingenious casting — as Streisand's glamorous mother.

"Everyone was optimistic on the first day of shooting," a member of the crew recalled. "I've worked with Barbra on several other film projects, and she seemed calmer, more assured. Having known her for thirty years or more, I've watched as she has changed. All of us do over such a span of time, of course. But with Barbra the change has been as dramatic as everything else in her life. She's lost touch with the real world, sees things only from her point of view. She has always been self-involved, demanding, a workaholic. But she once had a marvelous zest for life, wanted to eat up the whole world. That's not there anymore. What I feel she's lost is her sense of humor, the ability to laugh at herself. She's so damned serious these days.

"She's always been like that little girl with a curl in the middle of her forehead — one day she's very good, the next day she's horrid. She can be your best friend and sympathetic supporter. Then the wind changes and she can cut you off in the most appallingly cold, cruel manner. In recent years I've seen it happen with scary frequency. On the set of *Mirror* it became a common occurrence. I was terrified that what I was watching was the total unwinding of someone I had loved and admired very much. The filming process itself was like a bad movie. I began to wonder, 'Where is all this going and what is it all about?' She became paranoid. There was no contradicting what she said. She was the only person in the world. It was megalomania to the nth. One night I came back to the apartment I was using while we were in New York and I cried. It was as though I had lost someone very near and dear to me."

She had gone into this project believing that it would be far less complicated or emotional than *The Normal Heart*. It was going to be the movie that would show the studios that she could make a nonmusical, commercial film on budget, prove that she was a reliable, bankable director. One week into the filming she knew she had made a mistake in casting Dudley Moore in his role. He was too comedic, too much the drunk from *Arthur,* which changed the focus of the scenes he was in.

"It was hard to tell if he was playing an inebriated character or if he *was* one," a member of the crew commented. "One thing was sure — Barbra and Moore were incompatible and *she* was the producer, star, and director."

Moore was quickly replaced by George Segal, whom Streisand had worked with so well years before in *The Owl and the Pussycat*. Then right before Christmas the director of photography Dante Spinotti and his eight-man crew were replaced by Andrzej Bartkowiak — who had worked with her on *Nuts*— and new technicians. This was a major change. The director of photography sets the tone of the picture. Streisand was not happy with the way she looked in the daily rushes or with the shots that Spinotti had filmed. "She had been complaining about the camerawork almost from the beginning of the production," a member of the fired camera crew said. "There were too many gauzes around the lens. Her eyes — one of her best features — got very soft."

Two days later she dismissed Alan Heim, an Oscar-winning film editor, replacing him with Jeff Werner, who had also worked with her before. The winter months were brutal. Exterior shots had to be postponed, interior sets constructed on overtime. A movie that had originally been budgeted at $35 million quickly escalated by many millions, to the shouts and fury of the studio executives. Streisand was on edge, and the set was bristling with palpable tension. Cis Corman, who was coproducer, was more diplomatic than Streisand and did her best to smooth relations between the major cast and crew members and Streisand. Even Jeff Bridges, who has a reputation as being easygoing found her difficult. "[She] can piss you off, but if I get pissed off, I can't work. So I don't allow myself to get there," he said at the time.

The set was closed, no outsiders allowed. When they were on location, shooting a scene in a store or a restaurant, the area was blocked off and guards patrolled with walkie-talkies. "The whole team [cast, director of photography, crew, security] is a walking thermometer for Youknowwho," one observer reported. "The word would pass — she's feeling okay . . . she's getting makeup . . . she's left the trailer . . . she's due momentarily . . . she's coming."

On one rare occasion in January, *New York Post* entertainment reporter Cindy Adams, whom Streisand had known for years, was permitted on the set, an indoor antiques and collectible bazaar with a hundred booths on Twenty-fifth Street that had been transformed into an "annual antique spring market" for the scene being shot. (Streisand had cased it earlier and bought numerous pieces for the penthouse.) This meant that in the middle of New York's winter freeze — the coldest, snowiest January in fifty years — the cast had to wear light spring clothes. The crew arrived at 5 A.M. to set lights and camera angles, dress the walls with early American quilts "which they'd brought in, and reposition merchandise and cases," Adams related. "The director/star made her entrance at nine A.M. in a little pink cardigan and promptly rearranged the lights, camera angles plus whatever else could be rearranged. Renata, her handsome assistant with the long blond hair, at her side."

The scene to be shot had Streisand studying an early American patchwork quilt in a wall showcase as, a short distance away, Segal asks Bridges about his sex life with his mousy wife, "So, did you do it already?"

When lunch was called, the scene had not yet met with Streisand's approval. At 9 P.M. that evening, having munched on a sandwich for dinner, she was watching the dailies and making notes for the following day's work, obsessed with the movie she was making, struggling to bring it to realization as she envisioned it. *Mirror* now belonged to her, possessively. She was totally immersed. She returned to her apartment about 11 P.M., studied her lines for her next day's scenes, and was up and working on them again by 7 A.M.

So consumed was she on the production of *Mirror* that she had allowed the option on *The Normal Heart* to lapse. Although she had never stopped believing in the project, it had expired on January 2, 1996, several weeks earlier. When Kramer's representative pressed for a decision on her part to either renew her contract or allow Kramer to take it elsewhere, she made no reply. Finally, as April approached, *Mirror* still shooting and overages mounting, Streisand insisted she would make *The Normal Heart* once her present commitment was complete and she had been able to sign a male star and a director, having decided she would not direct herself. Jason called Kramer and suggested that he (Jason) would be up for director if Kramer could convince his mother that he could do it. Kramer was hoping for a more experienced director and thought this might not be a good idea.

Then, on April 8, Kramer, who still had no further word on whether Streisand would pick up her option, was interviewed by *Variety* in an article that was reprinted and excerpted widely: "This woman has had this play since 1986. She doesn't own it anymore and my health is deteriorating and I would very much like to see the movie made while I'm alive. She was all set to make *The Normal Heart* about a worldwide plague, and at the last minute she switches to a film about a woman who gets a facelift. I didn't think that was decent of her to do to me, her gay fans, and the people with AIDS she talks so movingly about." And he added, "My ten-year journey of futility with Barbra to make *The Normal Heart* has been almost as long as my fight as an AIDS activist to end this plague."

Streisand then issued a public statement: "I am painfully aware of [Kramer's] ticking clock. Therefore, I am now stepping aside and will no longer be involved with the project. I wish Larry only success in getting *The Normal Heart* made. I personally have a strong commitment to projects that reflect and further the needs of the gay community."

"Barbra was deeply hurt by Larry's attitude and the harsh coverage she received in the press over the now abandoned property," a close friend confided. "I think *The Normal Heart* was almost as important to her as *Yentl* had once been. And Larry had made a great impression on her, brought her a special awareness of both the plague and the gay community. But once he went public, she went ice-cold on him. She felt she had put in almost as much in the project as he did, that he should have understood how much she cared, what it meant to her. She took it as a personal stab."

On April 15 she sent Kramer a fax accusing him of being self-destructive, of having acted unreasonably, of demanding too much for himself when she had not received compensation for the many years she had worked on the movie. "I love this project — and I was trying to get it made . . . for your sake as well as mine. . . . I have to finish *Mirror* as you would have wanted me to finish *Heart*." She then asked him to stop making statements that *Mirror* was a movie about a woman with a face-lift, requesting that he read the script before making "unjust judgments."

Things grew worse on the set of *Mirror* after the fracas over *The Normal Heart* and anonymous interviews given to the press by at least two members of the crew about Streisand's frenetic behavior, tantrums, and all-around ill humor. Ultimatums were levied. No one was to speak to any member of the press or his or her job would be on the line. "This is my first major film," one associate told me. "I'm scared shitless. She has the power to make it difficult, if not impossible, for me to do another film with TriStar, and with the manic way she has been acting, I have little doubt she would do so if she knew I was talking to you. Every day I walk out on the set and I can't believe what I am seeing and hearing. There is a dark cloud of fear, of apprehension, of wanting the filming to end. But now, just when we all thought that was about to happen, she has decided she must reshoot a major sequence. That's another five to seven days' work. . . . I'm going to turn off my phones and my pager and sleep for four days when the last shot is in the can. I'm on the verge of a breakdown. Barbra? She has a summer of supervising the editing ahead of her, then the advertising and publicity campaign, working out the release and distribution. And she is not going to let go of this film until she drives everyone and herself working on postproduction crazy."

But Streisand is an enigma, admired by some as defensively as she is castigated by others. "I love Barbra," Richard LaGravenese said. "She is terribly maligned, misunderstood." And Kramer might have lost the shimmering awe in which he once held her, but despite his harsh public criticism of her, and her angry, cutting fax to him, still feels bonded to her. "She is often misguided," he explained, "but she is never passive."

A lover added, "The most wondrous thing about Barbra is how deeply feminine she can be. It is the key to her tremendous personal sex appeal. She has a way of making the man in her life feel greatly protective of her, needed, despite her ability to scrap her way through one of the toughest businesses for a woman that there is — filmmaking. And there is her wide-eyed wonder of so much in the world, her curiosity, her intelligence, her *caring*. Barbra *cares* and that's important. She's always felt guilty about Elliott. She was very young then, self-centered, working through her own demons. That guilt, I believe, has made her especially sensitive to the needs of the man who might currently figure in her life. It's her great fame that gets in the way, the constant demands made on her and those she inflicts upon herself that make loving Barbra complex and often frustrating. You want to protect her not only against the world but against herself, and the latter leads to resentment and a destructive, contradictory 'I'll show you!' attitude on her part. The funny thing is that the end of an affair with Barbra can be the beginning of a lifelong friendship. She makes an important mark on your life. She has on mine."

Shortly after the filming of *The Mirror Has Two Faces* was completed, she began dating the very manly looking James Brolin, who in 1976 had portrayed Clark Gable in the film *Gable and Lombard*. Brolin — tall (six foot four), his handsome, broad-boned face now framed by luxuriant silver hair — is two years older than Streisand. He was born in Los Angeles and had a comfortable, middle-class childhood; attended UCLA, where he majored in theater; and almost immediately after graduation was cast in the *Bus Stop* television series. Then came his long association on the popular *Marcus Welby, M.D.* show as Robert Young's youthful assistant (for which he won an Emmy.) After a succession of costarring film roles including *Skyjacked* (1972), *Westworld* (1973), *Capricorn One* (1978), and *The Amityville Horror* (1979), he returned to television as the leading man in the successful series *Hotel*.

Brolin possesses a calm persona, great charm, intelligence, and striking good looks, his resemblance to Gable still strong. Perhaps he succeeded in making Streisand realize her fantasy of *becoming* Scarlett O'Hara. The early months of their relationship were fraught with the problems of the final editing on *The Mirror Has Two Faces*. When the movie was released in November, the vehemence of the overwhelmingly disparaging reviews was a terrible shock to her. She had thought she had made a romatic screwball comedy that would easily repay her investors despite the huge amount that the film had gone over budget, and she expected Academy attention for her direction and performance. But at the first showing for Oscar voters, there was total silence, disbelief, no applause when it ended. "It was embarrassing," one voter said. "I was glad she had not attended."

The plot has Rose Morgan (Streisand), a self-effacing ugly duckling, marry handsome math professor Gregory Larkin (Jeff Bridges), agreeing to a platonic union. When Rose, panting with lust for her celibate husband, finally demands sex, he goes off on a European lecture tour, allowing her time to work out diligently at a gym, bleach and perm her hair, buy a sexy wardrobe, and have her mother (Lauren Bacall), cosmetician, give her a makeup makeover — all to bring the professor's sexual temperature to boiling. He returns to a superavailable Cosmo Girl with frizzy blond hair and provocative cleavage who now has men in a frenzy of desire. The great flaw is that Rose was warmer, funnier, and prettier *before* her *Fatal Attraction* rebirth, and one cannot help but wonder why men are now wild about her and the professor is baying like a dog under her bedroom window.

Streisand had refused to listen to anyone's advice. No one dared tell her, as star, producer, and director, that what had started as a smart, amusing comedy had turned into an egocentric psychodrama that becomes mean-spirited and vengeful toward the secondary female characters — Rose's mother and her younger sister. The press was relentless in its attacks on her, and her image was not helped when she went from one talk show to another repeating her old, well-worn stories about how ugly Diana (now defenseless, in her mideighties, and in the early stages of Alzheimer's) had made her feel as a young woman.

Bruised and hurting from the critics' harsh treatment of the film and the poor performance it was having at the box office, she turned to Brolin for solace and he proved to be solidly there for her. Her experiment with "commercial" filmmaking had proved a failure. It seems doubtful that *The Mirror Has Two Faces* will ever pay its investors much of a profit. But in a sense the hard knocks she received because of it has made her more vulnerable to settling into a close, loving relationship.

Streisand has always wished for more than what she has — be it career, money, achievement, love. She wished to be a great star and it happened, but not without her constant attention to how she could achieve her goal. She has not had to fight drugs, weight problems, multiple divorces, tragedy, and severe and frequent illness. She does not move her fans to tears or her friends into becoming protective shields. But without the spectacular beauty of other stars, she was forced to invent herself, make herself over, always refusing to accept the fact that without her musical genius she would have never made it into films.

Pushy, hungry, grasping, brilliant, possessor of one of the greatest popular voices in her lifetime, dazzling in her accomplishments, infuriating in her absolute refusal to alter her personality or beliefs to please anyone other than herself, Streisand is nonetheless a living kaleidoscope of the last half of the twentieth century as she represents so many touchstones in our lives. She was the homely girl who became beautiful when she sang. She remains the dreamer, the wonderer, the believer in most of us that anything can be won, against the worst odds, if you have the guts and the vision to see it through.

Chutzpah, guts, strength — call it what you may, Streisand defines it. She has also dared — off- and onscreen — to hazard beyond ordinariness into the adventurous extreme. She made ethnicity a great advantage, turned style around so that it mimicked her own, and has a voice that has never grown reedy or dropped into tobacco or alcoholic huskiness. It is a voice that takes us with it as it soars. It comes from somewhere deep inside her, given to her by her special god, perhaps to make up for the things she did not have—a father, beauty, inner peace: a voice that can only happen once.

Acknowledgments

I have this theory that the more we learn about the men and women we choose as our icons and our heroes, the more we learn about ourselves. Each biography I write is a self-journey in that discovery. The writing of this book has taught me much about our admiration for people who are great survivors, perhaps because so few of us know their strength. It has brought me close to what it can cost to become rich and famous, but even more to be different than most other people, a one-off, unique.

I often think of myself not as a biographer but as a literary detective. But no one can make his or her way alone through the maze of truths and half truths, the real and the imagined, that constitutes the days and years of someone's life. To be a good literary detective, one needs the help of other attuned ears, expert witnesses, confidants, coworkers, contemporaries, family and friends — loving as well as injured and resentful — lovers, admirers, critics, and fans. I have been most fortunate in having representatives from each of these categories in the writing of this book. I wish I could thank every contributor personally. In the majority of my biographies I have been able to do so. Occasionally, the subject of the biography creates a climate of fear that promises banishment from his or her good graces and perhaps loss of employment if associates decide to tell the biographer a part of their own lives that also happens to involve the subject. That has occurred in the writing of this book. Nonetheless, well over a hundred people have chosen to discuss with me the part they played in the life of Barbra Streisand, many of them requesting that their names not be revealed. I have honored their choice and thank them here anonymously. I have already done so privately.

My special appreciation to Garson Kanin, who not only gave freely of his time but allowed me access to his extensive files on the stage production of *Funny Girl;* to Marian Seldes, who added to this trove with files of her own; to Arthur Laurents, whose insights and recall added greatly to my understanding of many areas in which this story had to travel. And to Larry Kramer, whose honesty and forthrightness was a gift that I shall treasure.

Of the many who gave so liberally of their time, allowing me to spend hours with them, interviewing them in depth, talking on the telephone, filling out questionnaires, and tediously searching files for information and who made the writing of this book such a vital experience, I would like to thank Peter Matz, Don Black, Lainie Kazan, Jack Kruschen, Ken Welch, Mitzie Welch, the late John Patrick, the late Jule Styne, Luther Henderson, Barry Dennen, Bob Schulenberg, David LeVine, Milton Mensch, Marcia Mae Jones, Madeline Lee Gilford, Anthony Newley, Ira Howard Levy, Ann Shanks, Bob Shanks, Herman Raucher, Rex Reed, Thomas Z. Shepard, Billy Barnes, Ed Holly, Pat Holly, Blossom Kahn, Rose Tobias Shaw, Alan Shayne, Kathleen Brady, Martha Wilson, Harry Medved, Martha Weinman Lear, Louise Kerz, Al Hirschfeld, Jackie Sedeli, Sharon Palmer, Carl De Milia, Millard Vine Clark, Cindy Bouton, Ray Rominger, Nathan Clark, Joan Rivers, Maureen Stapleton, Eli Wallach, Judy Horgan, Michael Edwards, Michael Smith, Kristine Krueger, Michael Meltzer, Lila Burkeman, Alice Weiss, Richard LaGravenese, Dwayne Manwiller, Amy Rosenfeld, Bella Linden, Jocelyn Clapp, Kelly Vencill, Barbara Dunlap, Catherine Craco, Arthur Gelb, Graig Simpson, Tom Gates, Stanley Brassette, Angela Corio, Debra Cohen, Paul Arbor, Walter MacBride, and Don Bowden. And although he has been gone for many years, I must thank Sidney Buchman, who taught me a great deal about making movies and the men and women who make their living at it.

I would like to single out with special gratitude Sally Slaney and Terence McCarthy, who were invaluable aids in my London research, Polly Brown in my Washington, D.C., research, and Jeffrey L. Carrier in Brooklyn; the staffs of the Academy of Motion Picture Arts and Sciences, the Billy Rose Theatre Library at Lincoln Center, the British Film Institute, the Recording Industry Association of America, the Museum of Broadcasting, and the Screen Actors Guild.

To my English and American editors — Ion Trewin and Fredrica Friedman — my many thanks. My gratitude to my fine copyeditor, Stephen H. Lamont, and to Cary Holcomb and Holly Rapport.

I have had the good fortune to have two supportive agents — Mitch Douglas in the United States and Gill Coleridge in Great Britain. In the twenty years we have worked together, Mitch has always been there when I needed him, help offered without request (including his encyclopedic knowledge of theater, films, and recordings) and friendship given freely. We have had a unique relationship, and I am grateful for it. I want to add my thanks to Richard Aieli, Cassia Joll, and Liz Cowin, and to the ever cheerful Lilia Mejia, who brings so much special care to my working days.

And last but always tops — my love, admiration, and utmost gratitude to my husband, Stephen Citron, whose musical expertise and knowledge as respected historian of the musical theater added immeasurably to my work on this book and whose love and good companionship has lighted my life.

I thank you all.

Anne Edwards
Blandings Way
1996

Appendix

Theater Credits

Another Evening with Harry Stoones
Gramercy Arts Theatre   *Opened October 21, 1961*
Producer: Jeff Harris; Director: G. Adam Jordan; Music: Jeff Harris;
Music director: Abba Bogin
Cast
Susan Belink (later known as Susan Belling),
Dom DeLuise, Barbra Streisand, Sheila
Copelan, Virgil Curry, Diana Sands, Kenny
Adams, and Ben Keller.
Songs: "Jersey" and "Value" (sung by Streisand)
Closed October 21, 1961

I Can Get It for You Wholesale
Shubert Theatre   *Opened March 22, 1962*
Producer: David Merrick; Director: Arthur Laurents; Book (based on his novel):
Jerome Weidman; Music and lyrics: Harold Rome; Orchestrations: Sid Ramin;
Musical direction: Lehman Engel; Choreographer: Herb Ross; Dance arrange-
ments: Peter Howard; Costumes: Theoni Aldredge; Sets and lighting: Will
Steven Armstrong; Production supervisor: Neil Hartley
Cast
Harry Bogen   Elliott Gould
Mr. Pulvermacher   Jack Kruschen

Mrs. Bogen (Momma)   Lillian Roth

Martha Mills   Sheree North

Ruthie Rivkin   Marilyn Cooper

Teddy Asch   Harold Lang

Miss Marmelstein   Barbra Streisand

Blanche [Maltz]   Bambi Linn

Tootsie Maltz   James Hickman

Meyer Bushkin   Ken LeRoy

Sheldon [Maltz]   Steve Curry

Songs: "I'm Not a Well Man," "The Way Things Are," "When Gemini Meets Capricorn," "Momma, Momma," "The Sound of Money," "Too Soon," "The Family Way," "Who Knows?" "Ballad of the Garment Trade," "Have I Told You Lately?" "A Gift Today," "Miss Marmelstein," "A Funny Thing Happened," "What's In It for Me?" "Eat a Little Something," "What Are They Doing to Us Now?"

Closed December 8, 1962— 300 performances

Funny Girl

Winter Garden   *Opened March 26, 1964*

Producer: Ray Stark in association with Seven Arts Productions; Production supervisor: Jerome Robbins; Director: Garson Kanin; Book: Isobel Lennart; Story: Isobel Lennart; Music: Jule Styne; Lyrics: Bob Merrill; Choreography: Carol Haney; Musical director: Milton Rosenstock; Orchestrations: Ralph Burns; Dance orchestrations: Luther Henderson; Scenery and lighting: Robert Randolph; Costumes: Irene Sharaff; Vocal arrangements: Buster Davis; Associate director: Lawrence Kasha

Cast

Fanny Brice   Barbra Streisand

Nick Arnstein   Sydney Chaplin

Rose Brice   Kay Medford

Eddie Ryan   Danny Meehan

Mrs. Strakosh   Jean Stapleton

Florenz Ziegfeld, Jr.   Roger DeKoven

Tom Keeney   Joseph Macaulay

Heckie   Victor R. Helou

Mrs. Meeker   Lydia S. Fredericks

Mrs. O'Malley   Joyce O'Neil

Ziegfeld tenor   John Lankston

Vera (also understudy)   Lainie Kazan

With: George Reeder, Royce Wallace, Robert Howard, Buzz Miller, Alan Weeks, Dick Perry, Joan Cory, Rose Randolf
Songs: "Sadie, Sadie," "Find Yourself a Man," "If a Girl Isn't Pretty," "I'm the Greatest Star," "Cornet Man," "Who Taught Her Everything?" "His Love Makes Me Beautiful," "I Want to Be Seen with You Tonight," "Henry Street," "People," "You Are Woman," "Don't Rain on My Parade," "Rat-tat-tat-tat," "Who Are You Now?" "The Music That Makes Me Dance."
Closed July 1, 1967   1,348 performances

Funny Girl (London Production)
Prince of Wales Theatre   *Opened April 13, 1966*
Production directed by Lawrence Kasha
Musical director: Milton Rosenstock
Cast
Fanny Brice   Barbra Streisand
Nick Arnstein   Michael Craig
Rose Brice   Kay Medford
Eddie Ryan   Lee Allen
Closed July 15, 1966

Film Cast and Credits

Funny Girl

Columbia/Rastar   1968

Producer: Ray Stark; Director: William Wyler; Screenplay: Isobel Lennart; Musical sequences director/choreographer: Herbert Ross; Photography: Harry Stradling; Art director: Robert Luthardt; Set decoration: William Kiernan; Songs: Jule Styne-Robert Merrill; Music director: Walter Scharf; Sound: Charles J. Rice; Film editor: Robert Swink; Costumes: Irene Sharaff

Cast:

Fanny Brice   Barbra Streisand

Nick Arnstein   Omar Sharif

Florenz Ziegfeld   Walter Pidgeon

Rose Brice   Kay Medford

Eddie Ryan   Lee Allen

Georgia James   Anne Francis

Academy Award: Barbra Streisand (best actress, shared with Katharine Hepburn)

Academy Award nomination: Best picture, Harry Stradling (cinematography), Kay Medford (supporting actress), song, "Funny Girl" (Jule Styne and Robert Merrill), Walter Scharf (score)

Hello, Dolly!

Twentieth Century-Fox   1969

Producer: Ernest Lehman; Associate producer: Roger Edens; Director: Gene

Kelly; Screenplay: Ernest Lehman; Book (musical): Michael Stewart; Based on *The Matchmaker* by: Thornton Wilder; Photography: Harry Stradling; Production designer: John DeCuir; Set decoration: George Hopkins, Walter M. Scott, Raphael Bretton; Art direction: John Martin Smith, Herman Blumenthal; Music direction: Lennie Hayton and Lionel Newman; Costumes: Irene Sharaff; Songs: Jerry Herman; Choreographer: Michael Kidd; Dance arrangements: Marvin Laird; Sound: Jack Solomon, Douglas Williams, Murray Spivak, Vincent Vernon; Film editor: William Reynolds

Cast:

Dolly Levi   Barbra Streisand

Horace Vandergelder   Walter Matthau

Cornelius Hackl   Michael Crawford

Barnaby Tucker   Danny Lockin

Irene Molloy   Marianne McAndrew

Minnie Fay   E. J. Peaker

Academy Award: Score, art direction

Academy Award nomination: Best picture, Harry Stradling (cinematography)

On a Clear Day You Can See Forever

Paramount/Koch/Lerner   1970

Producer: Howard W. Koch; Director: Vincente Minnelli; Screenplay: Alan Jay Lerner; Photography: Harry Stradling; Production designer: John DeCuir; Set decoration: George Hopkins, Raphael Bretton; Songs: Burton Lane-Alan Jay Lerner; Music supervisor/arranger/conductor: Nelson Riddle; Choreography: Howard Jeffrey; Sound: Benjamin Winkler, Elden Ruberg; Film editor: David Bretherton

Cast:

Daisy Gamble/Melinda Tentrees   Barbra Streisand

Dr. Marc Chabot   Yves Montand

Warren Pratt   Larry Blyden

Dr. Mason Hume   Bob Newhart

Tad Pringle   Jack Nicholson

Robert Tentrees   John Richardson

With: Simon Oakland, Pamela Brown, Irene Handl, Mabel Albertson, and Leon Ames

The Owl and the Pussycat

Columbia/Rastar   1970

Producer: Ray Stark; Director: Herbert Ross; Screenplay: Buck Henry; From the play by: Bill Manhoff; Photography: Harry Stradling, Andrew Laszlo; Music: William Saracino; Music director: Richard Halligan; Production designer: John Robert Lloyd; Art direction: Robert Wightman, Philip Rosenberg; Set decoration: Leif Pederson; Sound: Arthur Piantadosi, Dennis Maitland; Film editor: John F. Burnett

Cast:

Doris   Barbra Streisand

Felix Sherman   George Segal

Barney   Robert Klein

Eleanor   Roz Kelly

Landlord   Allen Garfield

What's Up, Doc?

Warner/Saticoy   1972

Producer: Peter Bogdanovich; Director: Peter Bogdanovich; Screenplay: Buck Henry, David Newman, Robert Benton; Photography: Laszlo Kovacs; Production designer: Polly Platt; Art director: Herman Blumenthal; Set decoration: John Austin; Music director: Artie Butler; Music supervisor: Ray Phelps

Cast:

Judy Maxwell   Barbra Streisand

Howard Bannister   Ryan O'Neal

Eunice   Madeline Kahn

Frederick Larrabee   Austin Pendleton

Hugh Simon   Kenneth Mars

Mrs. Van Hoskins   Mabel Albertson

Up the Sandbox

First Artists/Barwood   1972

Producers: Robert Chartoff, Irwin Winkler; Associate producer: Marty Erlichman; Director: Irvin Kershner; Screenplay: Paul Zindel; From the novel by: Anne Richardson Roiphe; Photography: Gordon Willis/Andy Morton; Art director: Harry Horner; Music director: Billy Goldenberg; Set decorator: Robert De Vestel; Sound: Keith Stafford; Film editor: Robert Lawrence; Casting director: Cis Corman; Costumes: Albert Wolsky

Cast:

Margaret Reynolds   Barbra Streisand

Dr. Beineke   Paul Benedict

With: David Selby, Ariane Heller, Jane Hoffman, John C. Becher, Jacobo Mo-

rales, Barbara Rhoades, Stockard Channing, Isabel Sanford, Conrad Bain, Paul
Dooley, Anne Ramsey

The Way We Were
Columbia / Rastar   1973
Producer: Ray Stark; Director: Sydney Pollack; Screenplay: Arthur Laurents;
Novel by: Arthur Laurents; Photography: Harry Stradling, Jr.; Music director:
Marvin Hamlisch; Songs: Marvin Hamlisch, Alan and Marilyn Bergman; Pro-
duction design: Stephen Grimes; Set decoration: William Kiernan; Sound: Jack
Solomon; Film editor: Margaret Booth; Costumes: Dorothy Jedkins, Moss
Mabry
Cast:
Katie Morosky   Barbra Streisand
Hubbell Gardiner   Robert Redford
Carol Ann   Lois Chiles
George Bissinger   Patrick O'Neal
J. J.   Bradford Dillman
Paula Reisner   Viveca Lindfors
Columnist   Marcia Mae Jones
Rhea Edwards   Allyn Ann McLerie
Bill Verso   Herb Edelman
Brooks Carpenter   Murray Hamilton
With: Sally Kirkland, Diana Ewing, Eric Boles, Don Keefer, Dan Seymour,
George Gaynes, James Woods
Academy Award: Marvin Hamlisch (score), song, "The Way We Were" (music
by Marvin Hamlisch; lyrics by Alan and Marilyn Bergman)
Academy Award nomination: Barbra Streisand (best actress), Harry Stradling, Jr.
(cinematography)

For Pete's Sake
Columbia / Rastar / Persky-Bright-Barclay   1974
Executive producer: Phil Feldman; Producer: Martin Erlichman and Stanley
Shapiro; Director: Peter Yates; Screenplay: Stanley Shapiro, Maurice Richlin;
Photography: Laszlo Kovacs; Music director: Artie Butler; Songs: Artie Butler,
Mark Lindsay; Film editor: Frank P. Keller; Sound: Don Parker; Costumes:
Frank Thompson; Hairstyles: Jon Peters
Cast:
Henrietta Robbins   Barbra Streisand
Pete Robbins   Michael Sarrazin

Mrs. Robbins   Estelle Parsons

Fred   William Redfield

Mrs. Cherry   Molly Picon

Nick   Louis Zorich

Loretta   Vivian Bonnell

Bernie   Richard Ward

Judge Hiller   Heywood Hale Broun

Funny Lady

Columbia/Rastar/Persky-Bright/Vista   1975

Producer: Ray Stark; Director: Herbert Ross; Screenplay: Jay Presson Allen, Arnold Schulman; Story: Arnold Schulman; Photography: James Wong Howe; Music director: Peter Matz; Original songs: John Kander, Fred Ebb; Production design: George Jenkins; Costumes: Ray Aghayan, Bob Mackie; Film editor: Marion Rothman; Sound: Jack Solomon

Cast:

Fanny Brice   Barbra Streisand

Billy Rose   James Caan

Nick Arnstein   Omar Sharif

With: Ben Vereen, Roddy McDowall, Carole Wells, Larry Gates, Heidi O'Rourke, Samantha Huffaker, Matt Emery, Joshua Shelley, Corey Fischer

Academy Award nomination: James Wong Howe (cinematography), Peter Matz (score), song, "How Lucky Can You Get" (John Kander and Fred Ebb)

A Star Is Born

Warner Brothers/First Artists   1976

A Barwood/Jon Peters Production

Executive producer: Barbra Streisand; Producer: Jon Peters; Director: Frank Pierson; Screenplay: John Gregory Dunne and Joan Didion, Frank Pierson; Story: William Wellman and Robert Carson; Photography: Robert Surtees; Film editor: Paul Zinner; Production designer: Polly Platt; Musical concepts: Barbra Streisand; Music producer: Phil Ramone; Music underscore: Roger Kellaway; Music supervision: Paul Williams; Music conductor: Kenny Ascher; Set decorator: Ruby Levitt; Art director: William Hiney; Choreography: David Winters; Sound: Robert Knudson, Dan Wallis, Robert Glass, Tom Overton; Wardrobe: Shirley Strahm and Seth Banks

Cast:

Esther Hoffman   Barbra Streisand

John Norman Howard   Kris Kristofferson

Bobby Ritchie   Gary Busey
Gary Danzinger   Oliver Clark
The Oreos   Vanetta Fields, Clydie King
Quentin   Marta Heflin
Bebe Jesus   M. G. Kelly
With: Sally Kirkland, Joanne Linville, and Paul Mazursky
Academy Award: Song, "Evergreen" (music by Barbra Streisand, lyrics by Paul Williams)
Academy Award nomination: Robert Surtees (cinematography), Roger Kellaway (score)

The Main Event

Warner Brothers/First Artists/Barwood   1979
Producer: Barbra Streisand/Jon Peters; Director: Howard Zieff; Screenplay: Gail Parent, Andrew Smith; Photography: Mario Tosi; Production designer: Charles Rosen; Music: Michael Melvoin, Paul Jabara, Bruce Roberts; Music supervisor: Gary Le Mel; Music editor: William Saracino; Film editor: Edward Warschlika; Set designer: James Payne; Costumes: Ruth Meyer; Original Songs performed by Barbra Streisand: "The Main Event" (Paul Jabara and Bruce Robert), "Fight" (Paul Jabara and Bob Esty)
Cast:
Hillary Kramer   Barbra Streisand
Eddie Scanlon (Kid Natural)   Ryan O'Neal
David   Paul Sand
Percy   Whitman Mayo
Donna Rochester   Patti D'Arbanville
Leo Gough   James Gregory
With: Chu Chu Malave, Richard Altman, Joe Amaler, Seth Banks, Lindsay Bloom, Earl Bowen, Roger Bowen, Sue Casey

All Night Long

Universal   1981
Producer: Leonard Goldberg, Jerry Weintraub; Director: Jean-Claude Tramont; Screenplay: W. D. Richter; Photography: Philip Lathrop; Production designer: Peter Jamison; Music director: Ira Newborn, Richard Hazard
Cast:
George Dopler   Gene Hackman
Cheryl Gibbons   Barbra Streisand

Freddie   Dennis Quaid

Bobby Gibbons   Kevin Dobson

Helen Dopler   Diane Ladd

With: Ann Doran, William Daniels

Yentl

MGM/UA   1983

Executive producer: Larry De Waay; Producer: Barbra Streisand, Rusty Lemorande; Director: Barbra Streisand; Screenplay: Jack Rosenthal, Barbra Streisand; Story: Isaac Bashevis Singer; Photography: David Watkin; Production designer: Roy Walker; Film editor: Terry Rawlings; Art direction: Leslie Tomkins; Set director: Tessa Davies; Music director: Michel Legrand; Music: Michel Legrand, lyrics by Marilyn Bergman and Alan Bergman; Costumes: Judy Moorcroft; Casting director: Cis Corman; Musical sequences staged by: Barbra Streisand

Cast:

Yentl/Anshel   Barbra Streisand

Avigdor   Mandy Patinkin

Hadass   Amy Irving

Papa   Nehemiah Persoff

Reb Alter Vishkower   Steven Hill

Shimmele   Alan Corduner

Academy Award: Michel Legrand (score)

Academy Award nominations: Music direction, song, "Papa, Can You Hear Me?", art direction, Amy Irving (best supporting actress)

Nuts

Warner Brothers   1987

Producer: Barbra Streisand; Director: Martin Ritt; Screenplay: Tom Toper, Darryl Ponsican, Alvin Sargent; Play: Tom Topor; Photography: Andrzej Bartkowiak; Art director: Eric Orbom; Set director: Ann McCully; Film editors: Rick Spare, Jeff Werner; Sound editors: Julia Evershade, Virginia Cook-McGowan; Music arranged and conducted by: Jeremy Lubbock; Music: Barbra Streisand

Cast:

Claudia Draper   Barbra Streisand

Aaron Levinsky   Richard Dreyfuss

Arthur Kirk   Karl Malden

Rose Kirk   Maureen Stapleton

Judge Murdoch   James Whitmore

Dr. Herbert Morrison   Eli Wallach
With: Leslie Nielson, William Prince, Dakin Matthews, Robert Webber, Hayley Taylor Block

The Prince of Tides
Columbia Pictures   1991
Producer: Barbra Streisand, Andrew Karsh; Director: Barbra Streisand; Screenplay: Pat Conroy, Becky Johnston; Novel: Pat Conroy; Photography: Stephen Goldblatt; Production designer: Paul Sylbert; Music director: James Newton Howard
Cast:
Tom Wingo   Nick Nolte
Dr. Susan Lowenstein   Barbra Streisand
Lila Wingo   Kate Nelligan
Sallie Wingo   Blythe Danner
Bernard Woodruff   Jason Gould
Herbert Woodruff   Jeroen Krabbe
Savannah Wingo   Melinda Dillon
Eddie Detreville   George Carlin
Henry Wingo   Brad Sullivan
Academy Award nominations: Best picture, Nick Nolte (best actor), Kate Nelligan (best supporting actress), music, cinematography, sound

The Mirror Has Two Faces
TriStar Pictures in association with Phoenix Pictures   1996
A film by Barbra Streisand/Barwood Films Production
Executive producer: Cis Corman; Producer: Arnon Milchon, Ronald Schwary; Producer/director: Barbra Streisand; Photography: Dante Spinotti/Andrzej Bartkowiak; Screen story and screenplay: Robert LaGravenese; Production designer: Tom John; Set decorator: Alan Hicks; Film editor: Jeff Werner; Costumes: Theoni V. Aldredge; Sound: Tom Nelson; Assistants to Barbra Streisand: Kim Shalecki, Renata Buser, Ari Sloane; Love theme composed by Barbra Streisand; Music composed and adapted by Marvin Hamlisch
Cast:
Rose Morgan   Barbra Streisand
Gregory Larkin   Jeff Bridges
With: Pierce Brosnan, George Segal, Mimi Rogers, Brenda Vaccaro, Elle Macpherson, Lauren Bacall

Television Credits

The Jack Paar Tonight Show
NBC   *New York City, April 5, 1961*
Black and white
Host: Orson Bean
Streisand sang "A Sleepin' Bee."

PM East
Group W Television   *New York City*
Black and white
Host: Mike Wallace
Streisand did thirteen shows from October 1961–January 1962.

The Joe Franklin Show
Channel 11   *New York City*
Black and white
Host: Joe Franklin
Streisand did three late-night talk shows in the autumn of 1961.

The Garry Moore Show
CBS   *Los Angeles, May 29, 1961*
Black and white

Host: Gary Moore

Streisand sang "Happy Days Are Here Again."

The Tonight Show Starring Johnny Carson

NBC   *New York City, November 1962–February 1963*

Black and white

Host: Johnny Carson

Streisand made four appearances.

The shows were live, and very few of the early shows were taped. On one taped show she sang "Spring Can Really Hang You Up the Most."

The Ed Sullivan Show

CBS   *New York City, June 9, 1963*

Black and white

Host: Ed Sullivan

Streisand sang "When the Sun Comes Out."

On other Sullivan shows Streisand sang "Lover, Come Back to Me," "My Coloring Book," and "Cry Me a River."

"The Bob Hope Show"

CBS   *1963*

Black and white

Streisand did a hillbilly routine with Hope and sang "Miss Marmelstein."

The Judy Garland Show

CBS   *Los Angeles, October 6, 1963*

Black and white

Host: Judy Garland

Guests: Barbra Streisand, Smothers Brothers, Ethel Merman

Musical director: Mel Tormé

Streisand sang a duet with Garland ("Be My Guest"); medley with Garland ("Hooray for Love/Lover, Come Back to Me/After You've Gone/By Myself/How About You/You and the Night and the Music/It All Depends on You"); another duet with Garland ("Get Happy/Happy Days Are Here Again"); a trio with Garland and Ethel Merman ("There's No Business Like Show Business"); and two solos ("Down with Love," "Bewitched [Bothered and Bewildered]"). (There is also a video release *Judy (Garland) and Friends* containing the complete Streisand appearance, with the exclusion of the "Be My Guest" duet.)

"My Name Is Barbra"

CBS   New York City, April 28, 1965

Black and white

Host: Barbra Streisand

Executive producer: Martin Erlichman; Directed by Dwight Hemion; Choreographed by Joe Layton; Music arranged and conducted by Peter Matz; Set designs: Tom John

Songs, Act 1: "My Name Is Barbara," "Much More," "I'm Late," "Make Believe," "How Does the Wine Taste?" "A Kid Again/I'm Five," "Jenny Rebecca," "My Pa," "Sweet Zoo," "Where Is the Wonder?" "People."

Songs, Act 2: Medley: "Second Hand Rose/Give Me the Simple Life/I Got Plenty of Nothin'/Brother, Can You Spare a Dime?/Nobody Knows You When You're Down and Out/The Best Things in Life Are Free."

Songs, Act 3: "When the Sun Comes Out," "Why Did I Choose You?" "Lover, Come Back to Me," "I Am Woman," "Don't Rain on My Parade," "The Music That Makes Me Dance," "My Man," "Happy Days Are Here Again."

"Color Me Barbra"

CBS   New York City and Philadelphia, March 30, 1966

Color

Host: Barbra Streisand

Executive producer: Martin Erlichman; Produced by Dwight Hemion; Directed by Joe Layton; Music arranged and conducted by Peter Matz; Set designs: Tom John

Songs, Act 1: "Draw Me a Circle," "Yesterdays," "One Kiss," "The Minute Waltz," "Gotta Move," "Non C'est Rien," "Where or When."

Songs, Act 2: Medley: "Animal Crackers in My Soup/Funny Face/That Face/They Didn't Believe Me/Were Thine That Special Face/I've Grown Accustomed to Her Face/Let's Face the Music and Dance/Sam, You Made the Pants Too Long/What's New, Pussycat?/Who's Afraid of the Big Bad Wolf?/Small World/Try to Remember/Spring Again/(Have I Stayed) Too Long at the Fair?/Look at That Face."

Songs, Act 3: "Any Place I Hang My Hat Is Home," "It Had to Be You," "C'est Si Bon," "Where Am I Going?" "Starting Here, Starting Now."

"The Belle of 14th Street"

CBS   New York City, October 11, 1967

Color

Host: Barbra Streisand

Costars: Jason Robards, Jr., John Bubbles, Lee Allen and the Beef Trust Girls
Executive producer: Martin Erlichman; Produced by Dwight Hemion; Directed by Joe Layton; Arranged and conducted by Peter Matz; Art direction: Tom John
Songs: "I Don't Care," "Alice Blue Gown," "We're Two (Three, Four, Five) Americans" (with Robarts and Allen), "Liberstraum," "Mother Machree," "Hark! I Hear Them" (adapted from Shakespeare's *The Tempest*), "My Melancholy Baby," "Everybody Loves My Baby (But My Baby Don't Love Nobody But Me)," "A Good Man Is Hard to Find," "Some of These Days," "How About Me?" "I'm Always Chasing Rainbows," "My Buddy," "Put Your Arms Around Me, Honey."
Sung by others: "You're the Apple of My Eye," "I'm Going South."

"A Happening in Central Park"
CBS   *Filmed live on June 17, 1967, in New York City*
Released September 16, 1968
Color
Executive producer: Martin Erlichman; Produced by Robert Shereer; Associate producer: James S. Stanley; Music director: Mort Lindsay; Art director: Tom John; Costumes by: Irene Sharaff
Songs: "The Nearness of You," "Down With Love," "Love Is Like a Newborn Child," "Cry Me a River," "I Can See It," "Love Is a Bore," "He Touched Me," "I'm All Smiles," "Value," "Marty the Martian," "Natural Sounds," "Second Hand Rose," "People," "Sleep in Heavenly Peace (Silent Night)," "Happy Days Are Here Again."

"The Burt Bacharach Special"
CBS   *Los Angeles, March 14, 1971*
Color
Host: Burt Bacharach
Special guest: Barbra Streisand
Music arranged and conducted by Burt Bacharach
Streisand sang "One Less Bell to Answer" and "A House Is Not a Home" in a duet with herself, and with Bacharach at piano and in duet, "(They Long to Be) Close to You" and "Somewhere in this World."

"Barbra Streisand . . . and Other Musical Instruments"
CBS   *London, November 2, 1973*
Color

Guest stars: Ray Charles, Dominic Savage

Executive producer: Martin Erlichman; Concept: Ken and Mitzie Welch

Songs: "Piano Practicing," "I've Got Rhythm," "Johnny One Note," "One Note Samba," "Glad to Be Unhappy," Medley: "People/Second Hand Rose/Don't Rain on My Parade," "Don't Ever Leave Me," "By Myself," "Come Back to Me," "I Never Has Seen Snow," "Auf dem Wasser zu Singen," "The World Is a Concerto," "Make Your Own Kind of Music," "The Sweetest Sounds," "Look What They've Done to My Song," "Cryin' Time Again."

"Dick Cavett Special"

CBS   *1975*

Host: Dick Cavett

Guest Stars: Barbra Steisand, James Caan

Songs: "The Way We Were," "Don't Rain on My Parade," "My Man," "The Man I Love" (duet with Caan from *Funny Lady*), "It's Only a Paper Moon," "I Like Him (Her)," "How Lucky Can You Get."

"The Stars Salute Israel at 30"

ABC   *Los Angeles, May 8, 1978*

Color

Host: Barbra Steisand

Special Guest: Prime Minister Golda Meir (interviewd by Streisand via telephone and satellite)

Songs: "Hatikvah.

"22nd Grammy Awards"

CBS   *February 27, 1980*

Color

Streisand sang a duet with Neil Diamond: "You Don't Bring Me Flowers."

"One Voice"

HBO   *Originally filmed September 6, 1986*

Color

Guest stars: Robin Williams and Barry Gibb

Executive producer: Marilyn Bergman; Produced by Martin Erlichman and Barbra Streisand; Coproducer: Ellen Krass; Directed by Dwight Hemion; Written by Barbra Streisand and Marilyn and Alan Bergman; Musical producer: Richard Baskin; Musical director and conductor: Randy Kerber; Production designer: Rene Lagler

Songs: "Somewhere," "Evergreen," "Something's Coming," "People," "Send in the Clowns," "Over the Rainbow," "Guilty" (duet with Barry Gibb), "What Kind of Fool" (duet with Barry Gibb), "Papa, Can You Hear Me?" "The Way We Were," "It's a New World," "Happy Days Are Here Again," "America the Beautiful."

"Putting It Together — The Making of the Broadway Album"
HBO — CBS Fox Video   *April 1986*
Filmed October 29–November 12, 1985
A Barwood Film
Interviewer: William Friedkin
Guest artists for "Putting It Together": Sydney Pollack, David Geffen, Ken Sylk
Executive producer: Barbra Stresiand; Produced by Joni Rosen; CBS coordinator: Jeanne Mattuissi; Edited by Tom McQuade; Conductor-arranger: Peter Matz
"Somewhere" musical video directed by William Friedkin
Songs include "Putting It Together," "Pretty Women," "Send in the Clowns," "Something's Coming," "If I Loved You," "Can't Help Lovin' That Man," "Somewhere."

"Barbra: The Concert"
HBO   *April 1995*
Repeated on NBC   September 1995
Color
Production conceived and directed by Barbra Streisand; Executive producer: Martin Erlichman; Written by Alan and Marilyn Bergman; Musical direction and arrangements by Marvin Hamlisch; Production designer: Marc Brickman and David George; Sound designer: Bruce Jackson; Clothes by BSDK [Barbra Streisand/Donna Karan]; Editor: Tom McQuade
Special appearance: Mike Meyer
Voice-overs: Steven Susskind, Judith Gordon, Phil Austin
Songs: "As If We Never Said Goodbye," "I'm Still Here," "Everybody Says Don't," "Don't Rain on My Parade," "Can't Help Lovin' That Man," "I'll Know," "People," "Lover Man," "Will He Like Me?" "He Touched Me," "Evergreen," "The Man That Got Away," "On a Clear Day (You Can See Forever)," "The Way We Were," "You Don't Bring Me Flowers," "Lazy Afternoon," Disney medley: "Once Upon a Dream/When You Wish Upon a Star/Someday My Prince Will Come," "Not While I'm Around," "Ordinary Mir-

acles," Medley: "Where Is It Written?/Papa, Can You Hear Me?/Will Someone Ever Look at Me That Way?/A Piece of Sky," "Happy Days Are Here Again," "For All We Know," "Somewhere," "What Are You Doing the Rest of Your Life."*

"Serving in Silence"
The Margarethe Cammermeyer Story
NBC   *February 6, 1995*
A production of Barwood Films Ltd., Storyline Productions, Inc., and Trillium Productions, Inc., in association with Tristar Television
Executive producers: Barbra Streisand, Glenn Close, Craig Zadan, Neil Meron, Cis Corman; Producer: Richard Heus; Screenplay: Alison Cross; Director: Jeff Bleckner; Music: David Shire; Production consultant: Margarethe Cammermeyer
Cast:
Col. Margarethe Cammermeyer   Glenn Close
Diane   Judy Davis
Far   Jan Rubes
Mary Newcombe   Wendy Makkena
Capt. Bonnie Kern   Susan Barnes
Agent Coleman   William Converse-Roberts

---

*There were two recorded versions of the concert; the video release was *Barbra the Concert Live at the Arrowhead Pond* Anaheim, July 1994 (the laser disc of which includes a bonus track "What Are You Doing the Rest of Your Life" but excludes the Disney medley. The audio version on Columbia CD and minicassette includes the Disney medley and was recorded at Madison Square Garden. The network telecast of the concert includes the Disney medley along with other additional material.

Streisand also has given extensive interviews on televison programs, including the Dick Cavett and Barbara Walters shows, *60 Minutes with Mike Wallace, Larry King Live,* C-SPAN, and the *Today Show.* There is also a laser disc narrated by Streisand on the making of *The Prince of Tides.*

Discography

The Recording Industry Association of America sets the standard for gold and platinum discs. From 1958 to 1974 the basis for a gold record or album was $1 million in *wholesale* revenues. In 1975 the standard was changed to 500,000 units sold *and* $1 million wholesale revenues. The platinum standard was created in 1976 and certifies one million units sold *and* $2 million in revenues. United Kingdom and foreign album sales are not included in these figures.

All albums with the exception of those designated with an asterisk (*) are available on compact disc.

I Can Get It for You Wholesale (Original Cast Recording)
Columbia   *April 1962*
Produced by Goddard Lieberson; Music and lyrics by Harold Rome; Musical direction and vocal arrangements: Lehman Engel; Orchestrations: Sid Ramin
Barbra Streisand sings one solo: "Miss Marmelstein." She is also heard on "I'm Not a Well Man," "Ballad of the Garment Trade," and "What Are They Doing to Us Now?"

Live at the Hungry i*
An in-performance album that was sold and circulated heavily until Streisand placed a restraining order on it.

Pins and Needles
Twenty-fifth Anniversary Edition
Columbia *May 1962*
Produced by: Elizabeth Lauer and Charles Burr; Under the supervision of: Harold Rome; Music and lyrics by Harold Rome; Musical direction: Stan Freeman; Vocal arrangements: Elise Bretton
Singers: Barbra Streisand, Jack Carroll, Rose Marie Jun, Alan Sokoloff, and Harold Rome with Stan Freeman at the piano.
Barbra Streisand sings five solos: "Doing the Reactionary," "Nobody Makes a Pass at Me," "Not Cricket to Picket," "What Good Is Love?" and "Sitting on Your Status Quo."
She can also be heard with Harold Rome, Jack Carroll, and Alan Sokoloff on "Four Little Angels of Peace."

The Barbra Streisand Album
Columbia *February 1963*
Produced by Mike Berniker; Music arranged and conducted by Peter Matz
Songs: "Cry Me a River," "My Honey's Loving Arms," "I'll Tell the Man in the Street," "A Taste of Honey," "Who's Afraid of the Big Bad Wolf?" "Soon It's Gonna Rain," "Happy Days Are Here Again," "Keepin' Out of Mischief Now," "Much More," "Come to the Supermarket (in Old Peking)," "A Sleepin' Bee."
Barbra Streisand's first album in the Top Ten on the charts. Made gold.
Grammy Awards: Album of the Year; Best Female Vocal Performance.

The Second Barbra Streisand Album
Columbia *August 1963*
Produced by Mike Berniker; Music arranged and conducted by Peter Matz; Additional material by Peter Daniels
Songs: "Any Place I Hang My Hat Is Home," "Right as the Rain," "Down with Love," "Who Will Buy?" "When the Sun Comes Out," "Gotta Move," "My Coloring Book," "I Don't Care Much," "Lover, Come Back to Me," "(Have I Stayed) Too Long at the Fair," "Like a Straw in the Wind."
In the Top Ten on the charts. Made gold.

The Third Album
Columbia *February 1964*
Produced by Mike Berniker

Songs: "My Melancholy Baby,"[†] "Just in Time,"[††] "Taking a Chance on Love,"[†] "Bewitched (Bothered and Bewildered),"[‡] "Never Will I Marry,"[‡‡] "As Time Goes By,"[†] "Draw Me a Circle,"[††] "It Had to Be You,"[†] "Make Believe,"[‡‡] "I Had Myself a True Love."[††]

In the Top Ten in the charts. Made gold.

[†] Arranged and conducted by Ray Ellis

[††] Orchestrated and conducted by Sid Ramin

[‡] Arranged by Peter Daniels

[‡‡] Arranged and conducted by Peter Matz

Funny Girl (Original Cast Recording)

Capitol   *April 1964*

Produced by Dick Jones; Music by Jule Styne; Lyrics by Robert Merrill; Musical director: Milton Rosenstock; Orchestrations: Ralph Burns; Vocal arrangements: Buster Davis; Featuring: Barbra Streisand, Sydney Chaplin, Kay Medford, Danny Meehan, and Jean Stapleton

Songs sung by Barbra Streisand: "I'm the Greatest Star," "Cornet Man," "His Love Makes Me Beautiful," "I Want to Be Seen with You" (duet with Chaplin), "People," "You Are Woman" (duet with Chaplin), "Don't Rain on My Parade," "Sadie, Sadie," "Rat-tat-tat-tat," "Who Are You Now?" "The Music That Makes Me Dance."

Other Songs: "If a Girl Isn't Pretty," "Who Taught Her Everything?" "Henry Street," "Find Yourself a Man."

People

Columbia   *May 1965*

Produced by Robert Mersey; Piano accompaniment: Peter Daniels; Arranged and conducted by Peter Matz and Ray Ellis[†]

Songs: "Absent-Minded Me," "When in Rome (Do as the Romans Do)," "Fine and Dandy,"[†] "Supper Time,"[†] "Will He Like Me?"[†] "How Does the Wine Taste?" "I'm All Smiles,"[†] "Autumn,"[†] "My Lord and Master," "Love Is a Bore," "Don't Like Goodbyes," "People."

Number one in the charts. Made gold.

Grammy Award: Best Female Vocal Performance.

My Name Is Barbra

Columbia   *1965*

Produced by Robert Mersey; Orchestrations and arrangements by Peter Matz

Songs: "My Name Is Barbara," "A Kid Again/I'm Five," "Jenny Rebecca," "My Pa," "Sweet Zoo," "Where Is the Wonder?" "I Can See It," "Someone to Watch Over Me," "I've Got No Strings," "If You Were the Only Boy in the World," "Why Did I Choose You?" "My Man."

In the Top Ten on the charts. Made gold.

Grammy Award: Best Female Vocal Performance.

My Name Is Barbra, Two . . .

Columbia   *October 1965*

Produced by Robert Mersey; Conducted and arrranged by Peter Matz and Dan Costa

Songs: "He Touched Me," "The Shadow of Your Smile," "Quiet Night," "I Got Plenty of Nothin'," "How Much of the Dream Comes True," "Second Hand Rose," "The Kind of Man a Woman Needs," "All That I Want," "Where's That Rainbow?" "No More Songs for Me," Medley: "Second Hand Rose/Give Me the Simple Life/I Got Plenty of Nothin'/Brother, Can You Spare a Dime?/Nobody Knows You When You're Down and Out/Second Hand Rose/The Best Things in Life Are Free."

In the Top Ten on the charts. Made platinum.

Color Me Barbra

Columbia   *March 1966*

Produced by Robert Mersey; Conducted and arranged by Peter Matz

Songs: "Yesterdays," "One Kiss," "The Minute Waltz," "Gotta Move," "Non C'est Rien," "Where or When," Medley: "Animal Crackers in My Soup/Funny Face/That Face/They Didn't Believe Me/Were Thine That Special Face/I've Grown Accustomed to Her Face/Let's Face the Music and Dance/Sam, You Made the Pants Too Long/What's New, Pussycat?/Small World/I Love You/(Have I Stayed) Too Long at the Fair/Look at That Face," "C'est Si Bon," "Where Am I Going?" "Starting Here, Starting Now."

In the Top Ten on the charts. Made gold.

Harold Sings Arlen (With Friend)

Columbia   *March 1966*

Produced by Thomas Z. Shepard; Arranged and conducted by Peter Matz; Music by Harold Arlen

Streisand sings a duet with Arlen, "Ding Dong! The Witch Is Dead," and a solo, "House of Flowers."

Je m'appelle Barbra

Columbia   *October 1966*

Produced by Ettore Stratta; Arranged and conducted by Michel Legrand

Songs: "Free Again," "Autumn Leaves," "What Now, My Love," "Ma Premiere Chanson" [the first song of Streisand's own composition to be recorded], "Clopin Clopant," "Le Mur," "I Wish You Love," "Speak to Me of Love," "Love and Learn," "Once Upon a Summertime," "Martina," "I've Been Here." In the Top Ten on the charts. Made gold.

Simply Streisand

Columbia   *October 1967*

Produced by Jack Gold and Howard A. Roberts; Arranged by Ray Ellis; Conducted by David Shire

Songs: "My Funny Valentine," "The Nearness of You," "When Sunny Gets Blue," "Make the Man Love Me," "Lover Man," "More Than You Know," "I'll Know," "All the Things You Are," "The Boy Next Door," "Stout-Hearted Men." Hit number twelve on the charts. Made gold. (Richard Rodgers wrote on the back of the album one of Streisand's most treasured accolades: "Nobody is talented enough to get laughs, to bring tears, to sing with the depth of a fine cello or the lift of a climbing bird. Nobody, that is, except Barbra. She makes our musical world a much happier place than it was before. Sincerely, Richard Rodgers.")

A Christmas Album

Columbia   *October 1967*

Produced by Jack Gold; Numerous arrangers.

Songs: "Jingle Bells," "Have Yourself a Merry Little Christmas," "The Christmas Song (Chestnuts Roasting on an Open Fire)," "White Christmas," "My Favorite Things," "The Best Gift," "Sleep in Heavenly Peace (Silent Night)," Gounod's "Ave Maria," "O Little Town of Bethlehem," "I Wonder as I Wander," "The Lord's Prayer."

One of Streisand's largest-selling albums, it hit number one on the charts and made triple platinum.

Funny Girl

Columbia   *July 1968*

Motion picture soundtrack

Produced by Jack Gold; Arranged and conducted by Milton Rosenstock; With Omar Sharif, Kay Medford

Songs sung by Streisand: "I'm the Greatest Star," "I'd Rather Be Blue Over You (Than Happy with Somebody Else)," "His Love Makes Me Beautiful," "People," "You Are Woman, I Am Man," "Don't Rain on My Parade," "Sadie, Sadie," "The Swan," "Funny Girl," "My Man."
Sung by others: "If a Girl Isn't Pretty," "Roller Skate Rag."
Hit number twelve on the charts. Made platinum.

A Happening in Central Park
Columbia   September 1968
Produced by Jack Gold; Arranged by Peter Matz; Musical director/conductor: Mort Lindsey
Songs: "I Can See It," "New Love Is Like a Newborn Child," "Folk Monologue/Value," "Cry Me a River," "People," "He Touched Me," Medley: "Marty the Martian/Sound of Music/Mississippi Mud/Santa Claus Is Coming to Town," "Natural Sounds," "Second Hand Rose," "Sleep in Heavenly Peace (Silent Night)," "Happy Days Are Here Again."
A number of songs from the live concert were not included on the record. Although it rose only to number thirty on the charts, it made gold.

What About Today?
Columbia   1969
Produced by Wally Gold
Songs: "What About Today?" †† "Ask Yourself Why," † "Honey Pie," † "Punky's Dilemma," † "Until It's Time for You to Go," ‡ "That's a Fine Kind of Freedom," † "Little Tin Soldier," † "With a Little Help from My Friends," ‡ "Alfie," ‡ "The Morning After," †† "Goodnight." †
† Arranged and conducted by Peter Matz
†† Arranged and conducted by Don Costa
‡ Arranged and conducted by Michel Legrand
This album went up only to number thirty-one on the charts.

Hello, Dolly!
Twentieth Century-Fox Records   December 1969
Motion picture soundtrack
Produced by Lennie Hayton and Lionel Newman; Arranged and conducted by Lennie Hayton and Lionel Newman; Music by Jerry Herman
Others on record: Michael Crawford, Danny Lockin, Marianne McAndrew, Walter Matthau, and Louis Armstrong
Songs sung by Streisand: "Just Leave Everything to Me," "Put on Your Sunday

Clothes," "Before the Parade Passes By," "Love Is Only Love," "Hello, Dolly" (sung with Louis Armstrong), "So Long, Dearie," "Finale," (entire cast).

Other songs: "Ribbons Down My Back" (sung by Marianne McAndrew), "Elegance," "It Takes a Woman," "It Only Takes a Moment."

Rose to only number thirty-two on the charts; remained on the charts for forty-six weeks. Made double platinum.

Barbra Streisand's Greatest Hits
Columbia   *December 1969*

Composed of song tracks extracted from previous records, both albums and singles, and includes "People," "Second Hand Rose," "Why Did I Choose You?" "He Touched Me," "Free Again," "Don't Rain on My Parade," "My Coloring Book," "Sam, You Made the Pants Too Long," "My Man," "Gotta Move," "Happy Days Are Here Again."

Hit number thirty-two on the charts; remained on the charts for forty-three weeks. Made double platinum.

On a Clear Day You Can See Forever
Columbia   *July 1970*

Motion picture soundtrack

Produced by Wally Gold; Arranged and conducted by Nelson Riddle; Music by Burton Lane; Lyrics by Alan Jay Lerner; Other artist: Yves Montand

Songs sung by Streisand: "Hurry! It's Lovely Up Here!" "On a Clear Day (You Can See Forever)," "Love with All the Trimmings," "He Isn't You," "What Did I Have That I Don't Have," "Go to Sleep." Songs sung by Montand: "Melinda," "Come Back to Me," "On a Clear Day (You Can See Forever)."

The album did not make it onto the charts.

The Owl and the Pussycat*
Columbia   *December 1970*

Motion picture soundtrack

Produced by Thomas Z. Shepard; Performed by Blood, Sweat and Tears

Streisand does not sing on the record, which does include dialogue (both Streisand and her costar George Segal are heard) and incidental music from the picture.

Stoney End
Columbia   *February 1971*

Produced by Richard Perry

Songs: "I Don't Know Where I Stand," "Hands Off the Man (Flim Flam Man)," "If You Could Read My Mind," "Just a Little Lovin'," "Let Me Go," "Stoney End," "No Easy Way Down," "Time and Love," "Maybe," "Free the People," "I'll Be Home."

Hit number ten on the charts. Made platinum.

Barbra Joan Streisand
Columbia   *August 1971*
Produced by Richard Perry
Songs: "Beautiful,"[†] "Love,"[†] "Where You Lead,"[†] "I Never Meant to Hurt You,"[‡] Medley: "One Less Bell to Answer/A House Is Not a Home,"[‡‡] "Space Captain,"[††] "Since I Fell for You,"[§] "Mother,"[§] "The Summer Knows,"[‡] "I Mean to Shine,"[§§] "You've Got a Friend."[§§]

[†] Arranged by Nick De Caro
[††] Arranged by Fanny
[‡] Arranged and conducted by Dick Hazard
[‡‡] Arranged by Ken Welch, orchestrated by Peter Matz
[§] Arranged and conducted by Gene Page
[§§] Arranged by Head

This album went up only to number thirty-one on the charts.

Live Concert at the Forum
Columbia   *October 1972*
Produced by Richard Perry
Songs: "Sing/Make Your Own Kind of Music," "Sweet Inspiration/Where You Lead," "Sing/Happy Days Are Here Again" (arranged by Don Hannah); "Don't Rain on My Parade," "On a Clear Day (You Can See Forever)," "My Man," "People" (arranged by Peter Matz); "Starting Here, Starting Now" (arranged by Don Costa); "Didn't We" (arranged by Claus Ogerman); "Stoney End" (arranged by Gene Page).

Hit number nineteen on the charts. Made platinum.

Barbra Streisand . . . and Other Musical Instruments
Columbia   *October 1973*
Produced by Martin Erlichman; Arranged by Ken Welch
Songs: "Piano Practicing," "I Got Rhythm," "Johnny One Note/One Note Samba," "Glad to Be Unhappy," Medley: "People/Second Hand Rose/Don't Rain on My Parade," "Don't Ever Leave Me," Monologue, "By Myself,"

"Come Back to Me," "I Never Has Seen Snow," "Auf dem Wasser zu Singen," "The World Is a Concerto/Make Your Own Kind of Music," "The Sweetest Sounds."

Barbra Streisand Featuring "The Way We Were" and "All in Love Is Fair"
Columbia   *January 1974*
Produced by Tommy LiPuma; Arranged by Marvin Hamlisch
Songs: "Being at War with Each Other," "Something So Right," "The Best Thing You've Ever Done," "The Way We Were," "All in Love Is Fair," "What Are You Doing the Rest of Your Life?" "Summer Me, Winter Me," "Pieces of Dreams," "I've Never Been a Woman Before," Medley: "My Buddy/How About Me?"
Hit number one on the charts. Made platinum.
Grammy: Song of the Year ("The Way We Were," music by Marvin Hamlisch, lyrics by Marilyn and Alan Bergman)

The Way We Were
Columbia   *January 1974*
Motion picture soundtrack
Produced by Fred Salem; Arranged by Marvin Hamlisch
Includes the one song from the movie, "The Way We Were," sung and reprised by Streisand.
It hit number twenty on the charts. Made gold.
Grammy: Song of the Year (Hamlisch/the Bergmans); Best Original Motion Picture Score (Hamlisch)

Butterfly
Columbia   *October 1974*
Produced by Jon Peters
Songs: "Love in the Afternoon," "Guava Jelly," "Grandma's Hands," "I Won't Last a Day Without You," "Jubilation," "Simple Man," "Life on Mars," "Since I Don't Have You," "Crying Time," "Let the Good Times Roll."
Hit the charts at number thirteen. Made gold.

Funny Lady
Columbia   *March 1975*
Motion picture soundtrack.
Produced by Peter Matz; Arranged and conducted by Peter Matz

Songs: "How Lucky Can You Get?" "So Long, Honey Lamb," "I Found a Million Dollar Baby in a Five and Ten Cent Store," "Isn't This Better?" "Me and My Shadow," "If I Love Again," "I Got a Code in My Doze," "Great Day," "Blind Date," "Am I Blue," "It's Only a Paper Moon/I Like Him/Her" (duet with James Caan), "More Than You Know," "Let's Hear It for Me."
Sung by Ben Vereen: "Clap Hands, Here Comes Charley."
Hit number six on the charts. Made gold.

Lazy Afternoon
Columbia   *October 1975*
Produced by Rupert Holmes and Jeffrey Lesser
Songs: "Lazy Afternoon," "My Father's Song," "By the Way," "Shake Me, Wake Me," "I Never Had It So Good," "Letters That Cross in the Mail," "You and I," "Moanin' Low," "A Child Is Born," "Widescreen."
Hit number twelve on the charts. Made gold.

Classical Barbra
Columbia   *February 1976*
Produced by Claus Ogerman
Songs: "Beau Soir," "Brezairola," "Verschwiegene Liebe," "Pavane," "Après un Rêve," "In Trutina," "Laschia ch'io pianga," "Mondnacht," "Dank sie Dir, Herr," "I Loved You."
It is worth noting that Streisand received a Grammy nomination for this album: Best Classical Vocal Soloist Performance.

A Star Is Born
Columbia   *February 1976*
Motion picture soundtrack
Produced by Barbra Streisand and Phil Ramone; Arranged and conducted by Kenny Ascher
Songs: "Watch Closely Now," "Queen Bee," "Everything," "Lost Inside of You" (arranged by Pat Williams), "Hellacious Acres," "Evergreen" (arranged by Ian Freebairn-Smith), "Woman in the Moon," "I Believe in Love," "Crippled Crow," "With One More Look at You/Watch Closely Now," "Evergreen" (reprise).
Hit number one on the charts. Made quadruple platinum.
Grammy Awards: Best Female Pop Vocal, Song of the Year ("Evergreen," music by Barbra Streisand, lyrics by Paul Williams).

Streisand Superman

Columbia   *June 1977*

Produced by Gary Klein

Songs: "Superman," "Don't Believe What You Read," "Baby Me, Baby," "I Found You Love," "Answer Me," "My Heart Belongs to Me," "Cabin Fever," "Love Comes from Unexpected Places," "New York State of Mind," "Lullaby for Myself."

Hit number three on the charts. Made platinum.

Songbird

Columbia   *May 1978*

Produced by Gary Klein

Songs: "Tomorrow," "A Man I Loved," "I Don't Break Easily," "Love Breakdown," "You Don't Bring Me Flowers," "Honey, Can I Put on Your Clothes," "One More Night," "Stay Away," "Deep in the Night," "Songbird."

Hit number twelve on the charts. Made platinum.

Eyes of Laura Mars*

Columbia   *July 1978*

Motion picture soundtrack

Numerous producers.

Songs: Streisand sings only one song, "Prisoner."

Barbra Streisand's Greatest Hits Volume 2

(Volume 1   *December 1969*)

Columbia   *November 1978*

Numerous producers and arrangers.

Songs: "Evergreen," "Prisoner," "My Heart Belongs to Me," "Songbird," "You Don't Bring Me Flowers" (duet with Neil Diamond), "The Way We Were," "Sweet Inspiration/Where You Lead," "All in Love Is Fair," "Superman," "Stoney End."

Hit number one on the charts. Made quadruple platinum.

The Main Event

Columbia   *June 1979*

Numerous producers.

Songs: Streisand sings the title song and reprises it. The rest of the album includes vocal and instrumental work of various artists.

Hit number twenty on the charts. Made gold.

Wet

Columbia   *October 1979*

Produced by Gary Klein; Numerous arrangers

Songs: "Wet," "Come Rain or Come Shine," "Splish Splash," "On Rainy Afternoons," "After the Rain," "No More Tears (Enough Is Enough)" (duet with Donna Summer), "Niagara," "I Ain't Gonna Cry Tonight," "Kiss Me in the Rain."

Hit number seven on the charts. Made platinum.

Guilty

Columbia   *September 1980*

Executive producer: Charles Koppleman; Produced by Barry Gibb, Albhy Galuten, and Karl Richardson; Arranged by Barry Gibb, Albhy Galuten, and Peter Graves

Songs: "Guilty" (duet with Barry Gibb), "Woman in Love," "Run Wild," "Promises," "The Love Inside," "What Kind of Fool" (duet with Barry Gibb), "Life Story," "Never Give Up," "Make It Like a Memory."

Hit number one on the charts. Made quintuple platinum.

Grammy Award: Best Top Vocal by Duo or Group (with Barry Gibb)

Memories

Columbia   *November 1981*

Includes songs recorded on earlier albums.

Songs: "Memory," "You Don't Bring Me Flowers" (duet with Neil Diamond), "My Heart Belongs to Me," "New York State of Mind," "No More Tears (Enough Is Enough)" (duet with Donna Summer), "Comin' In and Out of Your Life," "Evergreen," "Lost Inside of You," "The Love Inside," "The Way We Were."

Hit number six on the charts. Made quadruple platinum.

Yentl

Columbia   *November 1983*

Motion picture soundtrack

Produced by Barbra Streisand, Marilyn Bergman, and Alan Bergman; Arranged by Michel Legrand

Songs: "Where Is It Written?" "Papa, Can You Hear Me?" "This Is One of Those Moments," "No Wonder," "The Way He Makes Me Feel," "No Wonder" (reprise), "Tomorrow Night," "Will Someone Ever Look at Me That Way?"

"No Matter What Happens," "No Wonder" (reprise), "A Piece of Sky," "The Way He Makes Me Feel" (a second version recorded separately), "No Matter What Happens" (a second version recorded separately).

Hit number nine on the charts. Made platinum.

The Legend of Barbra Streisand: The Woman and Her Music in Her Own Words
A two-record LP that includes a one-hour interview. This is a demonstration-only recording released for radio play as publicity for the movie *Yentl*.
Executive producer: Norm Pattiz; Produced by Westwood One for Columbia Records; Written and produced by Bert Kleinman; Hosted by Phil Hendrie; Interview by Mary Turner
Songs: Segment one: none (introduction). Segment two: "People," "Minute Waltz," "Where Am I Going?" Segment three: "Second Hand Rose," "My Man," "He Touched Me." Segment four: "Free Again," "Sam, You Made the Pants Too Long." Segment five: "The Way We Were," "All in Love Is Fair," "Evergreen." Segment six: "My Heart Belongs to Me," "You Don't Bring Me Flowers," "Songbird." Segment seven: "No More Tears (Enough Is Enough)," "Woman In Love," "Guilty." Segment eight: "Papa, Can You Hear Me?" "The Way He Makes Me Feel." Segment nine: "Where Is It Written?" "A Piece of Sky."

Emotion
Columbia   *October 1984*
Executive producer: Charles Koppelman; Produced by Barbra Streisand, Richard Perry, Maurice White, Jim Steinman, Albhy Galuten, and Richard Baskin
Numerous arrangers
Songs: "Emotion," "Make No Mistake, He's Mine" (duet with Kim Carnes), "Time Machine," "Best I Could," "Left in the Dark," "Heart Don't Change My Mind," "When I Dream," "You're a Step in the Right Direction" (music by John Mellencamp, lyrics by Barbra Streisand), "Clear Sailing," "Here We Are at Last" (music by Barbra Streisand, lyrics by Richard Baskin).
Hit number nineteen on the charts. Made platinum.

The Broadway Album
Columbia   *November 1985*
Produced by Barbra Streisand, Peter Matz, David Foster, and Richard Baskin; Arranged by Peter Matz and David Foster
Songs: "Putting It Together," "If I Loved You," "Something's Coming," "Not While I'm Around," "Being Alive," Medley: "I Have Dreamed/We Kiss in a

Shadow/Something Wonderful/Adelaide's Lament," "Send in the Clowns," Medley: "Pretty Women/The Ladies Who Lunch," "Can't Help Lovin' That Man," Medley: "I Loves You, Porgy/Bess, You Is My Woman," "Somewhere." Hit number one on the charts. Made triple platinum.

Grammy Awards: Best Female Pop Vocal, Best Arrangement Accompanying Vocal ("Putting It Together," Peter Matz).

One Voice
Columbia   *April 1987*
Live performance
Produced by Richard Baskin
Songs: "Somewhere," "Evergreen," "Something's Coming," "People," "Send in the Clowns," "Over the Rainbow," "Guilty" (duet with Barry Gibb), "What Kind of Fool" (duet with Barry Gibb), "Papa, Can You Hear Me?" "The Way We Were," "It's a New World," "Happy Days Are Here Again," "America the Beautiful."
Hit number nine on the charts. Made platinum.

Till I Loved You
Columbia   *November 1988*
Songs: "The Places You Find Love," "On My Way to You," "Till I Loved You" (duet with Don Johnson), "Love Light," "All I Ask of You," "You and Me for Always," "Why Let It Go?" "Two People," "What Were We Thinking Of," "Some Good Things Never Last," "One More Time Around."
Hit number ten on the charts. Made platinum.

A Collection ... Greatest Hits AND More
Columbia   *October 1989*
Many of these tracks first appeared on other albums.
Songs: "We're Not Makin' Love Anymore," "Woman in Love," "All I Ask of You," "Comin' In and Out of Your Life," "What Kind of Fool" (duet with Barry Gibb), "The Main Event/Fight," "Someone That I Used to Love," "By the Way," "Guilty" (duet with Barry Gibb), "Memory," "The Way He Makes Me Feel," "Somewhere."
Hit number twenty-six on the charts. Made platinum.

Just for the Record ...
Columbia   *September 1991*
A four-disc boxed set that includes seventy-seven tracks culled from released and

unreleased recordings made by Barbra Streisand over the past thirty-one years of her recording career, along with some material from her private archives, early television appearances, and nightclub performances. The set also comes with a booklet of her own album notes and photographs.

Produced by Barbra Streisand and Martin Erlichman; Coproduced by John Arrias; Project coordinator: Karen Svenson

Songs from disc one: "You'll Never Know" (recorded by Streisand in December 1955 at the age of thirteen); "A Sleepin' Bee" (April 1961); "Moon River" (January 1962); "Miss Marmelstein" (December 1962); "Happy Days Are Here Again" (May 1962); "Keepin' Out of Mischief Now," "I Hate Music," "Nobody's Heart (Belongs to Me)," "Value," "Cry Me a River," "Who's Afraid of the Big Bad Wolf?" ("I Had Myself a) True Love," "Lover Come Back to Me" (from *Live at the Bon Soir,* previously unreleased material, recorded November 1962, that was to have been Streisand's first album); "Spring Can Really Hang You Up the Most" (February 1963); "My Honey's Lovin' Arms" (February 1963); "Any Place I Hang My Hat Is Home" (August 1963); "When the Sun Comes Out" (June 1963); "Be My Guest" (with Judy Garland and Ethel Merman), medleys with Garland: "Hooray for Love/After You've Gone/By Myself/ 'S Wonderful/(I Like New York in June) How About You?/Lover, Come Back to Me/You and the Night and the Music/It All Depends on You/Get Happy/ Happy Days Are Here Again" (from *The Judy Garland Show,* October 1963).

Songs from disc two: "I'm the Greatest Star" (March 1964); "My Man/Auld Lang Syne" (closing night of *Funny Girl,* Winter Garden Theatre, December 26, 1965); "People" (September 1964); "Second Hand Rose" (sung by Diana Streisand Kind, a home recording made April 1965); "Second Hand Rose" (as part of Act 2 medley of TV show "My Name Is Barbra," April 1965); "He Touched Me" (October 1965); "You Wanna Bet" (December 1965); "House of Flowers/Ding, Dong! The Witch Is Dead" (April 1966); "(Have I Stayed) Too Long at the Fair/Look at That Face/Starting Here, Starting Now" (from TV show "Color Me Barbra," March 1966); "A Good Man Is Hard to Find," "Some of These Days," "I'm Always Chasing Rainbows" (from TV show "The Belle of 14th Street," October 1967); "Sleep in Heavenly Peace (Silent Night)" (from TV show "A Happening in Central Park," September 1968); "Don't Rain on My Parade," "Funny Girl" (October 1968); "Hello, Dolly" (July 1969); "On a Clear Day (You Can See Forever)" (August 1969); "When You Gotta Go," "In the Wee Small Hours of the Morning" (previously unreleased, recorded at the International Hotel, Las Vegas, July 1969).

Songs from disc three: "The Singer," "I Can Do It" (previously unreleased from aborted album, March 1970); "Stoney End," "(They Long to Be) Close to You" ("The Burt Bacharach Special" March 1971); "We've Only Just Begun" (previously unreleased, April 1971); "Since I Fell for You" (August 1971); "You're the Top" (with Ryan O'Neal, March 1972); "What Are You Doing the Rest of Your Life?" (home recording, summer 1972, previously unreleased); "If I Close My Eyes" (December 1972); "Between Yesterday and Tomorrow," "Can You Tell the Moment?" (previously unreleased, April 1973); "The Way We Were" (soundtrack version); "Cryin' Time" (November 1973); (unreleased tracks, March 1974); "God Bless the Child," "A Quiet Thing/There Won't Be Trumpets"; "Lost Inside of You" (spring 1976); "Evergreen" (November 1977); "Hatikvah" (May 1978).

Songs from disc four: "You Don't Bring Me Flowers" (with Neil Diamond, February 1980); "The Way We Weren't/The Way We Were" (June 1980); "Guilty" (October 1980); "Papa, Can You Hear Me?" "The Moon and I," "A Piece of Sky" (audition tape, spring 1981, for *Yentl*); "A Piece of Sky" (November 1983); "I Know Him So Well" (previously unreleased, August 1985); "If I Loved You," "Putting It Together" (November 1985); "Over the Rainbow" (September 1986); theme from *Nuts* (composed by Barbra Streisand, released December 1987); "Here We Are at Last" (music by Barbra Streisand, lyrics by Richard Baskin, June 1984); "Warm All Over" (April 1988); "You'll Never Know" (April 1988).

Hit number thirty-eight on the charts. Made platinum.

The Prince of Tides

Columbia   *December 1991*

Motion picture soundtrack

Produced by Barbra Streisand and James Newton Howard; Arranged by James Newton Howard

Songs: "For All We Know" and "Places That Belong to You." (The rest of the album is instrumental music.)

Back to Broadway

Columbia   *July 1993*

Produced by Barbra Streisand, David Foster, Andrew Lloyd Webber, and Nigel Wright

Songs: "Some Enchanted Evening" (arranged by Johnny Mandel and David Foster), "Everybody Says Don't" (arranged by Barbra Streisand and Bill Ross), "The Music of the Night" (duet with Michael Crawford, arranged and conducted by Andrew Pryce Jackman for the London Symphony Orchestra), "Speak Low" (arranged by Johnny Mandel and David Foster), "As If We Never Said Goodbye" (arranged by Andrew Lloyd Webber, John Cameron, and David Cullen), "Children Will Listen" (arranged and conducted by Jonathan Tunick), "I Have a Love/One Hand, One Heart" (arranged by David Foster and Bill Ross), "I've Never Been in Love Before" (arranged and conducted by Jeremy Lubbock), "Luck, Be a Lady" (arranged and conducted by Jeremy Lubbock), "With One Look" (arranged by Andrew Lloyd Webber and David Cullen), "The Man I Love" (arranged by Johnny Mandel), "Move On" (arranged and conducted by Michael Starobin).

Hit number one on the charts. Made double platinum.

Duets

Capital   *October 1993*

Executive producer: Charles Koppelman, Eliot Weisman, and Don Rubin; Produced by Phil Ramone; Coproduced by Hank Cattaneo

This is a Frank Sinatra album on which he sings duets with other singers. Streisand paired with him on "I've Got a Crush on You."

Barbra: The Concert

Columbia   *September 1994*

Two discs

Produced by Barbra Streisand and Jay Landers; Numerous arrangers; Conducted by Martin Hamlisch

Songs on disc one: "As If We Never Said Goodbye," "I'm Still Here/Everybody Says Don't/Don't Rain on My Parade," "Can't Help Lovin' That Man," "I'll Know," "People," "Lover Man," "Will He Like Me?" "He Touched Me," "Evergreen," "The Man That Got Away," "On a Clear Day (You Can See Forever)."

Songs on disc two: "The Way We Were," "You Don't Bring Me Flowers," "Lazy Afternoon," Medley: "Once Upon a Dream/When You Wish Upon a Star/Someday My Prince Will Come"; "Not While I'm Around," "Ordinary Miracles," Medley: "Where Is It Written?/Papa, Can You Hear Me?/Will Someone Ever Look at Me That Way?/A Piece of Sky," "Happy Days Are Here Again," "For All We Know," "Somewhere."

Hit number ten on the charts. Made double platinum.

Special Grammy Award: Lifetime Achievement Award

The Garland Duets

Paragon 1001

A collection of duets from the Judy Garland television show, which includes the Garland-Streisand "Be My Guest" and two medleys: "Get Happy/Happy Days Are Here Again" and "Hooray for Love."

This material — minus the "Be My Guest" duet but containing a medley sung by Garland, Streisand, and Ethel Merman — is available on the home video release *Judy Garland and Friends.*

Streisand has also recorded a myriad of singles, some of which, including the original deleted title song from the stage version of *Funny Girl,* have never been otherwise released.

Notes

Part I: The MGM Grand Garden

Chapter 1

Much of the concert, backstage and onstage was re-created from the several video-tapes that were made, as well as from interviews with several of the participants.

"with Andrew's happy compliance": Black, interview.

"When Streisand sings": Kael, *For Keeps,* p. 872.

"Good!": Anonymous interview.

"There's food": Anonymous interview.

"The Beatles have to divide": *Daily Express,* April 7, 1966.

Chapter 2

My gratitude to Larry Kramer and the staffs at *Architectural Digest* and at Christies Manhattan for their help with the material in this chapter.

"I lost weight and sleep": *Los Angeles Times,* May 23, 1993.

"Perfection is": *Playboy,* October 1977.

"Yes! Yes!": Kramer, interview.

"as the ultimate gift": Ibid.

"I think Jason's": *Daily Mail,* November 1994.

"I think I'm always drawn": Christie's catalog, Streisand auction March 3–4, 1994.

"I didn't grow up": Ibid.

"with the mosaics": Ibid.

"Sometimes when it's been hard": Ibid.

"I don't put a black vase": *Architectural Digest,* December 1993.

"She was in a terrible state": Anonymous interview.

Part II: Roots

Chapter 3

Camp Cascade and Fleischmanns were reconstructed through numerous personal interviews with attending campers and instructors and through archival records of the area.

"There was something about Manny": interview.

"Many of his students": Clark, interview.

"He was, I think": Ibid.

"It was terrible": *Daily Mail,* April 23, 1994.

Chapter 4

Much of the material on Streisand's family, Brooklyn, and the various schools described was obtained through interviews with neighbors, schoolmates and co-workers of the Rosen-Streisand family and through school, city, and state records and the archives of Columbia University, George Westinghouse Vocational High School (formerly Brooklyn High School for Specialty Trades), and the Brooklyn Historical Society. Life at Erasmus Hall was re-created with the help of former students, teachers, and archival material at the school, to which I was given access.

"Couches to me": *Playboy,* October 1977.

"It was so strange": *Playboy,* February 1984.

"The children on the street": *Daily Mail,* April 23, 1994.

"I remember their taking": *Playgirl,* February 1984.

"I hated those men": Ibid.

"You're not leaving": *Playboy,* October 1977.

"He never talked to me": *Playgirl,* February 1984.

"Why do you take *his* side?": Ibid.

"Barbra was a very complex child": *Daily Mail,* April 23, 1994.

"Ever sleep on a couch": *Life,* December 1983.

Chapter 5

"He was really mean to Barbra": *People,* December 12, 1983.

"When she came home": *Daily Mail,* February 1994.

"When I was nine years old": *Playboy,* October 1977.

"She was critical of me": *Playgirl,* February 1984.

"I was a character in the movie": Interview with Barbara Walters, 1976. Museum of Television and Radio.

"Somehow, it made me think": Interview with Barbara Walters, 1977. Museum
of Television and Radio.

"a smart-ass remark": Anonymous interview.

"That's the kind of school": Ibid.

"In every other high school": Ibid.

"I never knew how big": Frommer, *It Happened in Brooklyn,* p. 178.

"between the kids from the poor part": Ibid., p. 36.

"I was never asked out": Interview with Mike Wallace, *60 Minutes,* November
24, 1991.

"Some of the kids": Jordan, *The Greatest Star.*

"She often appeared lonely": Anonymous interview.

"great echo sound": *Larry King Live,* February 6, 1992.

"It's only wind and noise": Ibid.

"My mother went first": Liner notes, *Just for the Record . . .*

"At first, I was awfully disappointed": Ibid.

"It was a thrilling experience": Riese, *Her Name Is Barbra,* p. 45.

"I was so sure": *Daily Mail,* April 23, 1994.

Chapter 6

Malden Bridge was re-created from interviews with former members of the
company and from archival material.

"I was this absolute misfit": Interview with Barbara Walters. Museum of Television and Radio.

"If only looks mattered": Anonymous interview.

"he would sit there [Bobby Fischer]": *Playboy,* October 1977.

"Ma, look, it's $105": Ibid.

"I wouldn't just take stuff": *Saturday Evening Post,* July 27, 1963.

"Incidentally": Patrick, interview.

"Can't you just see me": *"Seventeen" Interviews Film Stars and Super Stars,* p. 147.

"There's *something* about her": Riese, *Her Name Is Barbra,* p. 48.

"It was the single *worst* audition": Ibid.

"I never meant to neglect": *Daily Mail,* April 23, 1994.

"She was extraordinary": Rifkin, interview.

"A week or two later": Riese, *Her Name Is Barbra,* p. 53.

"It was a scene of sexual exploration": *Playboy,* October 1977.

"The poor guy in the scene": Riese, *Her Name Is Barbra,* p. 53.

"I had never been exposed to literature": *Playboy,* October 1977.

"At sixteen, he wrote about": Jordan, *The Greatest Star.*

"I learned a lot in Brooklyn": *Los Angeles Times,* March 16, 1965.

"I would read magazines": *Playboy*, October 1977.

"I was feeling this strange power": *Los Angeles Times*, March 16, 1965.

"When I sing": Ibid.

"It's not the best production": Rivers, *Enter Talking*, pp. 67–68.

"The place seemed furnished": Ibid., pp. 68–69.

"a skinny high school girl": Ibid., pp. 69, 71.

"carrying at her age": Ibid., p. 71.

"The actual performance": Ibid., p. 73.

"It's closed": Ibid., p. 76.

"*She* was going to be a big star": Riese, *Her Name Is Barbra*, p. 49.

"She was waiflike": Mensch, interview.

"We lived in total poverty": Jordan, *The Greatest Star*, pp. 40–41.

"He was strumming a guitar": Jordan, *The Greatest Star*, p. 43.

Chapter 7

The author conducted interviews with Bob Schulenberg and Barry Dennen for this chapter. Schulenberg and Dennen were also given copies of their previous interviews with René Jordan for his 1975 book *The Greatest Star*. They corrected and amended all quotes used from the book attributed to them in this chapter. Interviews were also conducted with several others who were close to Streisand during this formative time in her career.

"swathed in cloaks and veils": Jordan, *The Greatest Star*, p. 43.

"But I also hear this noise": *Playboy*, October 1977.

"The whole production": Dennen, interview.

"We spent the afternoon": Ibid.

"Trying this, trying that": Ibid.

"Barbra *was* my creation": Ibid.

"small, but modern . . . apartment": Ibid.

"What a smart girl": *All About Barbra*, undated. Academy of Motion Picture Arts and Sciences archives.

"We would do an entire review": Levy, interview.

"Barbra had fully moved in": Ibid.

"The first time I saw her": Schulenberg, interview.

"Whew! It's hot in here!": Kazan, interview.

"Great talent but a dog!": Anonymous interview.

"a five-by-five singer": Gavin, *Intimate Nights*, p. 246.

"It looks good": Jordan, *The Greatest Star*, p. 50.

"Little girl": Liner notes, *Just for the Record* . . .

"Hey!": Anonymous interview.

"It's curious": Schulenberg, interview.

"I liked him very much": Ibid.

"She had great eyes": Ibid.

Chapter 8

I am most grateful for the interviews granted me by Arthur Laurents, Lainie Kazan, Bob Shanks, and several other people involved or witness to this period in Barbra Streisand's life who have helped me to reconstruct the scenes in this chapter.

"[as if] she were announcing": *All About Barbra,* undated. Academy of Motion Picture Arts and Sciences archives.

"When she got off the stage": Ibid.

"I knew that this was a STAR!": Ibid.

"A few days later": *Life,* January 9, 1970.

"Did you like the way I sang": Anonymous interview.

"At the Bon Soir": *Life,* January 9, 1970.

"What do I do?" Dennen, interview.

"Weighing in": Private tape of show.

"songs of unrequited love": Ibid.

"That old fart!": Dennen, interview.

"She would just *do* things": Ibid.

"He really cares about me": Schulenburg, interview.

"There was a certain date": Jordan, *The Greatest Star,* pp. 55–56.

"They never hit it off": Schulenberg, interview.

"So, who's this dame": Riese, *Her Name Is Barbra,* p. 86.

"The tapes were like children": Dennen, interview.

"I made her walk": *Time,* April 10, 1964.

"She was half exhilarated": Schulenburg, interview.

"I said no to Barbra Streisand": Shanks, interview.

"This is so exciting": Private tape of show.

"We went over them": Dennen, interview.

"Barbra loved Barry": Schulenburg, interview.

"a repentant lover": Dennen, interview.

"When I sang that": *Life,* January 9, 1970.

"When she's done with you": Anonymous interview.

"Usually at the end": Gavin, *Intimate Nights,* p. 248.

"Do something!" *Life,* January 9, 1970.

"I was pretty hard to reach": Liner notes, *Just for the Record . . .*

"I can't stand it": Schulenberg, interview.

"When Barbra left": Anonymous interview.

"I wrote that I was born": *Wall Street Journal,* May 14, 1993.

"generally had to scrape": Jordan, *The Greatest Star,* p. 63.

"I remember [Barbra]": Ibid., pp. 63–64.

". . . a bad Twentieth Century-Fox musical": Ibid., p. 64.

"this kook on t.v.": *New York Post.*

"The part I liked best": Liner notes, *Just for the Record . . .*

"People like you": Private tape of show.

"Now, let's be honest": Ibid.

"Hey, I'm sorry": Kissel, *The Abominable Showman,* p. 237.

"I had never seen her": Laurents, interview.

"I sang": *Saturday Evening Post,* July 27, 1963.

"How many times": Kissel, *The Abominable Showman,* p. 237.

"When I returned": *Life,* May 22, 1964.

"The moving chair came later": Laurents, interview.

"This strange-looking": *Life,* May 22, 1964.

Part III: Broadway Baby

Chapter 9

This chapter has been helped enormously by interviews with Arthur Laurents, Jack Kruschen, Peter Matz, Garson Kanin, John Patrick, Luther Henderson, Lainie Kazan, numerous members of the companies of *I Can Get It for You Wholesale* and *Funny Girl,* and Arthur Gelb of the *New York Times.* I was also given access to the private *Funny Girl* archival files of Garson Kanin.

"felt bad for Barbra": Kruschen, interview.

"I was tough on Barbra": Laurents, interview.

"She scared me": *Playboy,* November 1970.

"We'd play things": Ibid.

"This child was too good to be true": Ibid.

"He'll never dance": Ibid.

"That meant everything": Ibid.

"When an entertainer": Ibid.

"He was always doing bits": Ibid.

"I used to hear her warm up": Kruschen, interview.

"I spent weeks": *Los Angeles Herald-Examiner,* November 13, 1983.

"Nobody remembers": Laurents, interview.

"Two singers": Gelb, interview.

"I couldn't believe": *All About Barbra,* undated. Academy of Motion Picture Arts and Sciences archives.

"mousey-colored hair": Ibid.

"Can you become": Jordan, *The Greatest Star.*

"We were walking around": *Life,* May 22, 1964.

"About four A.M.": Ibid.

"I didn't care": Ibid.

"The only window": *Playboy,* November 1970.

"All those stories": Laurents, interview.

"Get rid of it": Jordan, *The Greatest Star,* p. 69.

"I knew no one": Laurents, interview.

"She knew how": Anonymous interview.

"I told her": Laurents, interview.

"I have dealt with revolting people": *Holiday,* November 1963.

"This could have meant": Anonymous interview.

"Once she was onstage": Anonymous interview.

"She really hit her stride": Anonymous interview.

"The evening's find": *New York Times,* March 23, 1962.

"Miss Streisand possesses": *Theater Arts,* April 1, 1962.

"So she came to me crying": Laurents, interview.

"Barbra decided": *Daily Mail,* September 26, 1994.

Chapter 10

"It was my love": *Daily Mail,* September 26, 1994.

"I don't think she even": Ibid.

"It was a difficult thing": *All About Barbra,* undated. Academy of Motion Picture Arts and Sciences archives.

"I was very friendly": Laurents, interview.

"It was hell": *Saturday Evening Post,* July 27, 1963.

"They brought in a paid audience": Jordan, *The Greatest Star,* p. 182 (paperback ed.).

"You could smell the air": Anonymous interview.

"I hear that first record": *Playboy,* October 1977.

"My mate was making it": *Playboy,* November 1970.

Chapter 11

"long, lean and galvanically fit": *Daily Telegraph,* May 28, 1963.

"A new apartment": Anonymous interview.

"Elliott even looked happy": Anonymous interview.

"I liked Ed": Liner notes, *Just for the Record . . .*

"And I've had to wait": *HBO: The Concert.*

"I didn't have it to pay." *Playboy,* November 1970.

"Make a wish!": Ibid.

"It doesn't get any better": *Life,* May 22, 1964.

"Are you sure": Tape made by Brice for her memoir.

"had her heart set": Jordan, *The Greatest Star,* p. 109.

"I pointed": Patrick, interview.

"I thought she was": Ibid.

"a classmate of Ray's": Ibid.

"You need a Jewish girl": Ibid.

"Ray thought": Ibid.

"I can't tell you": Ibid.

"Mr. Robbins": Ibid.

"Isobel was an excellent screenwriter": Kanin, interview.

"I liked Barbra immediately": Ibid.

"It wasn't what she said": Kissel, *The Abominable Showman,* p. 274.

"She was playing Streisand's record": Edwards, *Judy Garland,* p. 209.

"Life is too short": Kissel, *The Abominable Showman,* p. 274.

Chapter 12

For this chapter, interviews were conducted with Garson Kanin, Marian Seldes, John Patrick, Luther Henderson, Lainie Kazan, Peter Matz, and various other people. Mr. Kanin also kindly allowed me to go through and use material (including letters) in his files from the stage production of *Funny Girl,* which he directed.

"People like to feel miserable": *New Yorker,* November 1929.

"It was scary": *Playboy,* October 1977.

"She wasn't sure": Kanin archives.

"If we could give him an image": Kanin, interview.

"She was uncomfortable": Kazan, interview.

"I don't think anyone": Patrick, interview.

"I need your imagination": Kanin archives.

"Her voice came off": Jimmy Breslin, *Daily News,* December 1963.

"Elegance is making an art of life": Kanin, interview.

"I want you to stand tall": Ibid.

"week after week": Liner notes, *Just for the Record . . .*

"Once in a while": Patrick, interview.

"It's a front, Barbra": *Life,* May 22, 1964.

"How could you": Ibid.

"a screaming, four-letter": Ibid.

"Elliott was fighting": Anonymous interview.

"It should be like": Ibid.

"Barbra's just tense": Kanin, interview.

"Who are you?": Ibid.

"an absolute hush": Taylor, *Jule: The Story of Composer Jule Styne,* p. 244.

"I got it now": Ibid., p. 245.

"It was strange": Kazan, interview.

"Fifty dollars a week": Ibid.

"I hadn't met Peter": Ibid.

"At that moment": Ibid.

"I promise you": Ibid.

Chapter 13

Many of the quotes in this chapter came from the same source interviews and archival material as in previous chapters. The author also had access to several of the scripts in progress used during the out-of-town try-outs and final production of *Funny Girl.*

"She had a killer instinct": Anonymous interview.

"It was absolute chaos": Kazan, interview.

"It was the baby number": Ibid.

"What new musical comedy star": *New York Post.*

"For some reason": Patrick, interview.

"*Funny Girl* is a gem": *Variety,* January 17, 1964.

"Our curtain went down": Kanin archives.

"Isobel felt ignored": Patrick, interview.

"Peter [Daniels] was working": Kazan, interview.

"All in all": *Philadelphia Inquirer,* February 5, 1964.

"But in dealing": *Philadelphia Evening Bulletin,* February 5, 1964.

"Whatever Ray Stark wanted": Kanin, interview.

"My own impression": Patrick, interview.

"Sometimes, I think Barbra": Anonymous interview.

"A gardenia is a free spirit": *Time,* April 10, 1964.

"She is like a barracuda": Ibid.

"She is like a filter": Ibid.

"He looked at her": Anonymous interview.

"I felt like such a failure": *Playboy,* November 1970.

"smudged white Capri pants": *Life,* November 6, 1964.

"This is a talent": *New York Morning Telegraph,* March 27, 1964.

Part IV: Making It

"I always knew": *Look,* April 5, 1966.

Chapter 14

This chapter owes a great deal to two members of the Smith-Hemion production team who chose to be anonymous and to Rex Reed.

"odd, compelling beauty": *Vogue,* June 1970.

"Some stories make it sound": *New York Herald Tribune,* September 6, 1964.

"I can always take down": Ibid.

"I like listening to Streisand": *New York Herald Tribune,* March 1, 1964.

"Even my success": *Playboy,* October 1977.

"The only happiness I know": *Life,* May 22, 1964.

"It was, I guess": Kazan, interview.

"It was rumored": Ibid.

"There's a play on Broadway": Tape of show.

"Truthfully, I couldn't wait": Liner notes, *Just for the Record . . .*

"She was so vulnerable": *Daily Mail,* September 17, 1994.

"Okay, you have twenty minutes": *New York Times,* March 27, 1966.

"She's not dumb": Ibid.

"Hoarse?": Reed, interview.

"I made a record": Ibid.

"For Barbra Streisand's second spec": *Variety.*

Chapter 15

Material in this chapter was gathered from the author's own involvement in the adaptation of *Funny Girl* to the screen, correspondence with Sidney Buchman, interviews with Arthur Laurents and members of the London company of *Funny Girl,* and archival material.

"My husband and I": *Daily Telegraph,* March 3, 1966.

"I hope you will approve": *New York Times,* February 2, 1966.

"Those girls didn't have a thing on": Ibid.

"The only thing she has not learned": *Look,* October 15, 1968.

"The only way I can account": *Life,* March 18, 1966.

"To say I love Barbra": *Look,* April 5, 1966.

"I can't suddenly get poor": Ibid.

"She loves from the point of view": *Daily Mail,* September 19, 1994.

"Open that door!": Ibid.

"The conversation all revolved around": Laurents, interview.

"One of the most nonsensical": *The Times* (London), April 14, 1966.

"the most phenomenal creature": *Daily Sketch,* April 14, 1966.

"She is the heart": *Daily Mail,* April 14, 1966.

"Well, she isn't": Riese, *Her Name Is Barbra,* p. 211.

"Oh, cripes": Anonymous interview.

"I'm not sure it was because I was an actress": *New York Herald Tribune,* October 17, 1966.

"My God, I'm a mother": *Ladies' Home Journal,* August 1966.

"You know, my baby": Ibid.

"He's got the brightest": *Newsweek,* January 23, 1967.

"I remember two things": Laurents, interview.

"Georgia's scenes": Letter from Sidney Buchman to the author, July 9, 1966.

Chapter 16

"We were all very unsure": Madsen, *William Wyler,* p. 381.

"the worst time of my life": Kanin archives.

"They were getting ready": Sharif, *The Eternal Male,* pp. 73–74.

"At that point I think": Madsen, *William Wyler,* p. 387.

"He [Wyler] does things": *Los Angeles Times,* November 27, 1967.

"My principal concern": Madsen, *William Wyler,* p. 390.

"I just don't expect obedience": Ibid., pp. 391–92.

"I feel we had": Ibid., p. 392.

"Why? Why not?": Anonymous interview.

"Willy shouldn't be": Anonymous interview.

"going everywhere": Madsen, *William Wyler,* p. 389.

"eleven versions of every scene": *Los Angeles Times,* September 17, 1967.

"But Elliott handled these things": Madsen, *William Wyler,* p. 394.

"I had good ideas": *Playboy,* November 1970.

"a certain type of woman": Sharif, *The Eternal Male,* p. 77.

"As to carnal love": Ibid., p. 76.

"Barbra . . . who struck me": Ibid., pp. 79–81.

"He made himself": Anonymous interview.

"What really got me down": *Playboy,* November 1970.

"A woman mustn't contradict me": Sharif, *The Eternal Male,* pp. 77–78.

"If it was Barbra's plan": Anonymous interview.

"The self-confidence": Sharif, *The Eternal Male,* p. 34.

"The bed is the holy table": Ibid., p. 77.

"Every day": Francis, interview.

"I feel like a boxer": *Los Angeles Times,* September 17, 1967.

"People were saying": Anonymous interview.

"You have to understand": *Los Angeles Times,* October 27, 1968.

Chapter 17

"I never wanted to be": *Look,* April 5, 1966.

"Why in hell": *Chicago Tribune Magazine,* August 27, 1967.

"Barbra's always been a cheapskate": Ibid.

"I'm furious with Barbra": *Hollywood Citizen News,* August 28, 1968.

"It's true I lusted": *Los Angeles Times,* October 27, 1968.

"I know Elliott thinks it's just": Ibid.

"I don't believe": *Los Angeles Times,* July 3, 1967.

"Like a diva soprano": *Vogue,* June 1970.

"I talked to Elizabeth": Hirschhorn, *Gene Kelly,* p. 252.

"strangely moved": *Hello, Dolly!* archives, Academy of Motion Picture Arts and Sciences.

"Like Barbra": Hirschhorn, *Gene Kelly,* p. 253.

"I'd heard": Ibid.

"dying to do the role": Ibid.

"It devotes as much time": Ernest Lehman Collection, USC Cinema-Television Library.

"If only there'd been": Hirschhorn, *Gene Kelly,* p. 254.

"I'd say you've built": Ernest Lehman Collection, USC Cinema-Television Library.

"What I needed": Interview.

"painful to adjust": Hirschhorn, *Gene Kelly,* p. 254.

"the trouble with Barbra": Ibid., pp. 255–56.

"As if contending": Ibid., p. 256.

"It was not, in retrospect": Ibid., p. 257.

"It's anachronistic!": Ernest Lehman Collection, USC Cinema-Television Library.

"Betty Hutton once said": Hirschhorn, *Gene Kelly,* p. 295 (paperback ed).

Chapter 18

I am much indebted to the archival material at both the Academy of Motion Picture Arts and Sciences and the British Film Institute for all the chapters in this book dealing with the making of an individual film. Special interviews for this chapter included ones with friends and coworkers of Alan Jay Lerner.

"I always wanted to meet": *Playboy,* October 1977.

"Bravo! Streisand has the gift": Kael, *For Keeps,* pp. 182–84.

"a particular desperation": *Newsweek,* January 5, 1970.

"The audience . . . cannot be lied to": Ibid.

"Barbra also stands to make": *Variety,* October 8, 1968.

"a little guy": Anonymous interview.

"When Alan came to me": Citron, *The Wordsmiths,* p. 221.

"If he was really working hard": Ibid.

"We spent a whole day going over": Jordan, *The Greatest Star,* p. 192.

"Sparks flew": Anonymous interview.

"When we commenced": *Paris Match,* November 23, 1970.

"It was inspired": Teti and Moline, *Streisand Through the Lens.*

"Eat up!": Vickers, *Cecil Beaton,* p. 533.

"Not the most congenial atmosphere": Ibid.

"Barbra is one of two kinds of superstars": Teti and Moline, *Streisand Through the Lens.*

"I like B.S.": Vickers, *Cecil Beaton,* p. 534.

Chapter 19

"Well, Ma": *New York Times,* February 23, 1970.

"Barbra loves Rozie": Ibid.

"That was fascinating": Ibid.

"There is so much more to learn": Ibid

"like a *farbissener*": Ibid.

"He pointed mutely": Goldman, *Elvis,* p. 441.

"a hero for an uptight generation": *Time,* October 13, 1969.

"I always knew": *New York Times,* October 5, 1969.

"something of a paradox": Ibid.

"We have a very deep personal": Ibid.

"heavy Victorian ornaments": Trudeau, *Beyond Reason,* p. 47.

"the beloved black sheep": Ibid.

"had a silky, warm . . . manner": Ibid.

"Charm is the power": Lord, *Picasso and Dora,* p. 45.

"a sort of old-fashioned gallantry": Trudeau, *Beyond Reason,* p. 42.

"Oh, yeah": *Playboy,* October 1977.

"I was always concerned": Ibid.

"Is it love?": *Los Angeles Times,* January 31, 1970.

"He flew Barbra Streisand": Trudeau, *Beyond Reason,* p. 42.

"Barbra wanted us to get back": *Daily Mail,* November 1994.

"Jason already *has* a father": Anonymous interview.

"After she *schlepped*": Dennen, interview.

Chapter 20

I am especially indebted for the help on this chapter from Ed Holly and Blossom Kahn (both formerly executives of First Artists), Madeline Gilford, producer of "Broadway for Bella"; Michael Edwards, a key figure in the opposing camp of two of Bella Abzug's later campaigns for the Senate; author and screenwriter Herman Raucher; and the access given me by Warner Brothers Studios to their archives.

"a natural development": Transcript of statement, Warner Brothers archives.

"a cool suspicion": Kahn, interview.

"I would think": *Playgirl,* February 1984.

"Schopenhauer's theory": *The New Yorker,* November 14, 1970.

"put in thick white carpeting": Riese, *Her Name Is Barbra,* p. 310.

"She only calls me 'Herbie'": Ibid., pp. 310–11.

"They shared a kind of mirror image": Madeline Lee, interview.

"I would much rather have": *New York Times,* June 5, 1970.

"everything in stainless steel": Ibid.

"There will be stars": Invitation for June 9, 1970, fund-raiser to send Bella Abzug to Congress.

"Hey! Now I can see": *New York Times,* June 5, 1970.

"I remember the various": *Playboy,* November 1970.

"I didn't know how dangerous": Ibid.

"wearing his *M*A*S*H* helmet": Ibid.

"She made chicken soup": Raucher, interview.

"It seemed as though": Lee, interview.

"The place was jammed": Ibid.

"Barbra Streisand's delicate snarl": *New Yorker,* November 14, 1970.

"The lyrics": Liner notes, *Just for the Record . . .*

Part V: Making Movies, Making Love

"One of the reasons": *Playboy,* October 1977.

"People say": *Los Angeles Times,* November 7, 1976.

Chapter 21

"Actually, I believe women": *Playboy,* October 1977.

"Look, this was my first real home": *Architectural Digest,* May 1978.

"my burgundy era": Ibid.

"Richard was always trying": Liner notes, *Just for the Record . . .*

"I can't throw away": *Ladies' Home Journal,* August 1966.

"I have never made": *Playboy,* October 1977.

"never knew what was really going on": Ibid.

"used to live inside films": Wakeman, ed., *World Film Directors,* vol. II, p. 133.

"stealing from everything": Ibid., p. 134.

"he made your skull": *The Power and the Glitter,* p. 241.

"If I would have known": Concert, April 15, 1972.

"Ya know — to conquer": Ibid.

"a deeper and warmer presence": Kael, *For Keeps,* p. 477.

"I'm very fragile emotionally": Interview with Mike Wallace, *60 Minutes.*

"Barbra was baffled.": Jordan, *The Greatest Star,* p. 227.

"That's me!": Ibid., p. 229.

Chapter 22

Interviews for this chapter were conducted with Arthur Laurents, Marcia Mae Jones, Mitzie and Ken Welch, among others.

"Ray was looking": Laurents, interview.

"They were insecure": Ibid.

"They told Ray": Ibid.

"The person who was terrific": Ibid.

"He didn't like the script": *Premiere,* July 1980.

"Maybe he sees": Ibid.

"It had to be": Ibid.

"I think with any small encouragement": Anonymous interview.

"She was in awe of Redford.": Jordan, *The Greatest Star,* pp. 229–30.

"the entire motivation": Laurents, interview.

"I didn't even have": *Premiere,* July 1980.

"It was all wrong": Laurents, interview.

"It was curious": Jones, interview.

"Working with Barbra": Riese, *Her Name Is Barbra,* p. 337.

"It flows like velvet": *Daily News,* October 19, 1973.

"a torpedoed ship": *New Yorker,* October 15, 1973.

"If I'd left it in the minor mode": Gilbert, *The Top Ten,* p. 229.

"like a Chinese menu": Mitzie Welch, interview.

"an antiques dealer": Ibid.

"We hired all kinds": Ken Welch, interview.

"she glowed with it": Anonymous interview.

"Julie Andrews, Blake Edwards": Mitzie Welch, interview.

"That haircut": Ibid.

Chapter 23

"You know you're a cute little thing": *Woman,* November 5, 1978.

"You do not want to fight": Griffin and Masters, *Hit & Run,* p. 25.

"My father . . . made me a warrior": Ibid., p. 12.

"rode a donkey": Ibid., p. 13.

"Nobody messed": Ibid.

"I'd come in": *Los Angeles Times,* November 7, 1976.

"Jon is smart": Anonymous interview.

"He comes out of the Hugh Hefner": Ibid.

"We're both equally crazy": Yetnikoff, interview.

"I came from off the street": *Woman,* November 5, 1978.

"Jon is a very macho man": Anonymous interview.

"It had aluminum sliding doors": *In Style,* June 1994.

"The kids' rooms": Ibid.

"He'll have to drag me to court": Jordan, *The Greatest Star,* p. 238.

"They think I'm too small": *Playboy,* October 1977.

"I feel them listening so hard": Ibid.

"Blame it on Vietnam": *New York Times,* April 16, 1991.

"a tough lady who hid": *Los Angeles Times.*

"I'd yell at her": Swenson, *The Second Decade,* p. 136.

"Her commitment was not 1000 percent": Archives of the Performing Arts, Special Collections, University of Southern California.

"Do they think I'd let Jon produce a record.": Ibid.

"Recording that medley": Liner notes, *Just for the Record . . .*

Chapter 24

This chapter has been greatly helped by material in the Archives of the Performing Arts, Special Collections, at the University of Southern California, and in the archives at Warner Brothers, the Academy of Motion Picture Arts and Sciences, the British Film Institute, and the special film archives at the University of Wisconsin, Madison. In addition, the author conducted numerous interviews, including those with Anthony Newley, Arthur Laurents, and Ed Holly and Blossom Kahn of First Artists.

"a kid with dirty underwear": *Woman,* November 5, 1978.

"a savage look at the rock world": *New Times,* January 24, 1975.

"and get some of those": Ibid.

"*I* discovered this project": Ibid.

"Two people fall in love": Ibid.

"Anyone who wonders": Ibid.

"Can you sing": Anonymous interview.

"I'd never met Peters": *New Times,* January 24, 1975.

"Why not?": Ibid.

"We're going to make this": Ibid.

"She was ecstatic": Anonymous interview.

"what Jon Peters appreciates": *New Times,* January 24, 1975.

"That became sort of the attitude": Holly, interview.

"After I read them": Laurents, interview.

"What about Brando?": Anonymous interview.

"The son of a bitch": *New York,* November 15, 1976 (reprinted in *New West,* November 22, 1976).

"It would be nice": Ibid.

"How could I direct": Ibid.

"I hate him": Ibid.

"People are curious": Ibid.

"how we make love": *Village Voice,* April 26, 1976.

"It's not our life": Ibid.

"in such profusion": *New York,* November 15, 1976 (reprinted in *New West,* November 22, 1976).

"like Nixon": *People,* April 26, 1976.

"drove everybody crazy": Anonymous interview.

"You can do it": Ibid.

"She was like a little girl": Swenson, *The Second Decade.*

"a strong, hard-hitting man": Holly, interview.

"We screened it": Swenson, *The Second Decade.*

"He was just like a feisty sponge": Holly, interview.

"I know I'm not an easy": *New York,* November 15, 1976 (reprinted in *New West,* November 22, 1976).

"I don't feel you want to love me": Ibid.

"Pow! I let him have it!": Ibid.

"For God's sake": Ibid.

"Jesus, Barbra": *Village Voice,* April 26, 1976.

"an experience worse than boot camp": Ibid.

"What the hell": Ibid.

"Look at her directing": Ibid.

"If this film": *New York,* November 15, 1976 (reprinted in *New West,* November 22, 1976).

"Perhaps . . . I hope so": *People,* April 26, 1976.

Chapter 25

The material in this chapter was gathered from the same sources as the previous chapter, with the addition of interviews conducted with Michael Meltzer, Bob Shanks, Ann Shanks, and others.

"You lay it out": *New York,* November 15, 1976 (reprinted in *New West,* November 22, 1976).

"You don't listen": Ibid.

"Primarily": Riese, *Her Name Is Barbra,* pp. 380–81.

"No movie editor": Lumet, *Making Movies.*

"Where are the boys?": Ann Shanks, interview.

"By that time": Ibid.

"I hate it!": Ibid.

"I just saw the end credits": Ibid.

"All night": *New York,* November 15, 1976 (reprinted in *New West,* November 22, 1976).

"You have to understand": Swenson, *The Second Decade,* p. 186.

"*A Star Is Born* was the beginning": *Los Angeles Times,* January 2, 1977.

"A STAR IS BORN: DEAD ON ARRIVAL": *Rolling Stone,* January 1977.

"[Most of my life]": *Los Angeles Times,* January 2, 1977.

"Peters taught her": Laurents, interview.

"Would you speak to your friend": Ibid.

"The truth was": Anonymous interview.

"I hate that lamp!" *In Style,* June 1994.

"They were very competitive": Meltzer, interview.

"Well, I guess": Ibid.

"Michael, one day soon": Ibid.

"No matter what price": Ibid.

"I was going to make": Riese, *Her Name Is Barbra,* p. 387.

"There was a script": Kahn, interview.

"We were all doing everything": Holly, interview.

"Ryan used to jog in the nude": Taraborrelli, *Call Her Miss Ross,* p. 349.

"Why am I not working": Swenson, *The Second Decade,* p. 191.

"I just can't sit": Meltzer, interview.

"When he went off": Swenson, *The Second Decade,* p. 193.

"Am I cool?": *Los Angeles Times*, January 2, 1977.

"*The Main Event* was my fault": Swenson, *The Second Decade*, p. 192.

"An Australian firm": Holly, interview.

"I couldn't believe it": *Los Angeles Times*, October 16, 1983.

"a nice, ordinary-looking Jewish lady": Ibid.

"It was a time in my life": *Playgirl*, February 1984.

"You're not going to do it!": Ibid.

Chapter 26

"I explained to her": Riese, *Her Name Is Barbra*, p. 410.

"gave indications": Ibid., p. 408.

"I don't think": Swenson, *The Second Decade*.

"I constantly had to give up everything": *Playgirl*, February 1984.

"I've lived so many years": *Playboy*, October 1977.

"The day before we were going to start shooting": *Playgirl*, February 1984.

"I had to tell": *Los Angeles Times*, October 16, 1983.

"You never got a chance": Swenson, *The Second Decade*, p. 250.

"To get the feel of the music": Ibid., p. 245.

"I kept remembering": *Los Angeles Times*, November 1, 1983.

"She'd fix my hair ribbons": Swenson, *The Second Decade*, p. 248.

"I had asked Amy": *Los Angeles Times*, October 16, 1983.

"I had to make all the decisions": *Playgirl*, February 1984.

"She treated him like any good friend": Anonymous interview.

"I had only nine days": *Los Angeles Times*, October 16, 1983.

"It was all about money": Ibid.

"It is very rare": Ibid.

"I talked to all the rabbis": Ibid.

"*Yentl* was Barbra's way": Swenson, *The Second Decade*, p. 251.

"I ran out and bought": *Playgirl*, February 1984.

"She denies her unhappiness": *Daily Mail*, September 17, 1994.

Chapter 27

This chapter was especially enhanced by interviews with Stephen Citron, Peter Matz, and numerous other fine musicians and musicologists.

"all the men in my life": *Wall Street Journal*, May 14, 1993.

"Broadway music": *New York Times*, November 10, 1985.

"Barbra's contract": Swenson, *The Second Decade*, p. 273.

"marathon listening sessions": Zadan, *Sondheim*, p. 289.

"It's like growing": Ibid.

"I told him": Ibid.

"She wanted to make": Ibid.

"I would talk": Ibid.

"Barbra Streisand had": Ibid.

"He believes as I do": Ibid.

"one of the most exciting": Liner notes, *Just for the Record* . . .

"Everyone in the studio": Liner notes, *The Broadway Album.*

"Listen, I cried": Kramer, interview.

"When my agent told me": Ibid.

"The only reason": Ibid.

"I was so impressed": Ibid.

"What I found difficult": Ibid.

"I felt totally comfortable": Interview with Gene Shalit, November 1987.

"It is fascinating to me": *Los Angeles Times,* December 8, 1994.

"Marty and Barbra didn't always agree": Stapleton, interview.

"learned my own judgment": Martin Ritt Collection, Academy of Motion Picture Arts and Sciences.

"How old are you?": Ibid.

"The end title music": Ibid.

"I'd like you to meet Don Johnson": Anonymous interview.

Chapter 28

This chapter benefited from numerous personal interviews, including one with Maureen Stapleton.

"I'm at a place": *Playboy,* October 1977.

"It was April 26, 1986": *Wall Street Journal,* May 14, 1993.

"on the explicit conviction": Ibid.

"It became a discussion": Ibid.

"She started with very little knowledge": Ibid.

"Marilyn realized": Brownstein, *The Power and the Glitter,* p. 310.

"After all my insistence": Liner notes, *Just for the Record* . . .

"You're nice": "One Voice" transcript.

"the greatest movie song": Ibid.

"in memory of": Ibid.

"If I want to meet people": *Cosmopolitan,* September 1995.

"I have done everything": Ibid.

"he could have charmed": Ibid.

"I'm happy": Ibid.

"That character": *Los Angeles Times,* August 24, 1995.

"enough partying": *Playboy,* 1988.

"I have this persona": Ibid.

"from downright dangerous": Ibid.

"Nobody got higher": Ibid.

"I don't think Barbra": Anonymous interview.

"run into the woman": *Playboy,* 1988.

"He has a killer instinct": Anonymous interview.

"One day": *US,* October 3, 1988.

"Barbra not only": Ibid.

"Don makes me feel": Anonymous interview.

"It helps to have": Anonymous interview.

"When I first read": Liner notes, *Just for the Record . . .*

"My mother could never make up": Ibid.

Chapter 29

The laser disc "The Making of *The Prince of Tides*" was invaluable in the work on this chapter. I was also fortunate to have the cooperation of several of the staff and technicians on the film.

"Yes [Jason] is gay": *Daily Mail,* September 17, 1994

"Jason has never asked me": *Cosmopolitan,* October 1991.

"Barbra showed me this kid": *Los Angeles Times,* December 26, 1991.

"I thought deep down": Ibid.

"I think she read": *Los Angeles Times Sunday Magazine,* December 8, 1991.

"You have to keep saying": Ibid.

"A lot of this movie is very meaningful": Ibid.

"It changed my whole perspective": *New York Times,* December 22, 1991.

"a tough guy": Katz, *The Film Encyclopedia,* p. 1016.

"In the movie": Laser disc "The Making of *The Prince of Tides.*"

"Barbra likes to explore": *New York Times,* December 22, 1991.

"I don't find it that easy": Laser disc "The Making of *The Prince of Tides.*"

"Oh, this is interesting": Ibid.

"The least painful part": *Daily Mail,* July 9, 1995.

"I couldn't stop laughing": Laser disc "The Making of *The Prince of Tides.*"

"There's not a bad bone": *Cosmopolitan,* October 1991.

"You've told me": Ibid.

"[I've been] thinking about how": *New York Times,* December 22, 1991.

"I don't think about acting": Ibid.

"It's Barbra's talent for": Ibid.

"When I direct": Ibid.

"I don't know": Anonymous interview.

"Late one night": Kazan, interview.

"She throws a lot of stories": *Los Angeles Times Sunday Magazine,* December 8, 1991.

"The other day": Ibid.

"Poor baby is miserable": *Daily Mail,* September 17, 1994.

"It's the mirror": Anonymous interview.

Chapter 30

"Agassi is tennis's marketing tool": *New York Times,* October 4, 1992.

"He's very intelligent": Ibid.

"I've been learning": *New York Times,* July 1, 1993.

"Well, control means": *Playboy,* October 1977.

"Language gives us": Transcript of speech.

"She was a softer person": Kramer, interview.

"I think, strangely": Ibid.

"I want only the best for her": Anonymous interview.

"She sees Caleigh": Anonymous interview.

"One night when I was putting": Concert program, London, April 1994.

"Warren Beatty said": *Washington Post,* September 17, 1992.

"Six years ago": Transcript of appearance.

"It has a way": Anonymous interview.

Chapter 31

This chapter owes a great debt to the perceptive interviews given to me by Larry Kramer, Don Black, and various others.

"How come nobody attacked": *Los Angeles Times,* May 23, 1993.

"much more fun": *Washington Post,* January 20, 1993.

"Clinton's wooing": *Washington Post,* September 17, 1992.

"Barbra Streisand has read": *Washington Post,* January 30, 1993.

"When I directed a movie": *Los Angeles Times,* May 23, 1993.

"We . . . have the right": Ibid.

"a cheerful thumbs up": *Washington Post,* January 21, 1993.

"cut down to here": Ibid.

"wearing a long black-hooded": *Washington Post,* January 22, 1993.

"granted 5 minutes": Ibid.

"The most moving moments": Ibid.

"That's why I have": *Los Angeles Times,* May 23, 1993.

"It was the highlight.": Black, interview.

"I thought, 'Oh, my God!'": Ibid.

"great misery . . . every night I was terrified": *Los Angeles Times,* May 23, 1993.

"Donna Karan gave me": Ibid.

"I had to return to London": Black, interview.

"plus . . . the show was to be": *Los Angeles Times,* May 3, 1993.

"I didn't need the job": *Los Angeles Times,* August 21, 1994.

"Barbra would tell me": Ibid.

Chapter 32

This chapter owes a great deal to several of the backstage people involved in the Concert and who asked for their names not to be included in my acknowledgments.

"I don't like to be famous": *BBC Morning Show,* April 18, 1994.

"You have got to get this right": *Daily Mail,* April 20, 1994.

"to have a positive attitude": Ibid.

"She is not just a singer": *Daily Mail,* April 17, 1994.

"her mother told her": Ibid.

"What did you *really* think": Black, interview.

"I was told by my boss": *Daily Mail,* April 22, 1994.

"In Detroit": *Vanity Fair,* November 1994.

"Mom, you stood up": *HBO: The Concert.*

"If there's such a thing": *Daily Variety,* June 3, 1994.

"There's no denying her talent": *New York Observer,* July 4–11, 1994.

"Let me say this": Interview with Barbara Walters for ABC, December 13, 1994.

"She's God's bell": *New York,* April 15, 1994.

"that crystalline voice": *Vanity Fair,* November 1994.

"You did good": Ibid.

"You have to put makeup on": Ibid.

"Barbra had a passion": *Wall Street Journal,* February 3, 1995.

"What the network ordered": Ibid.

Chapter 33

This chapter was especially helped by interviews with Larry Kramer, Richard La-Gravenese, and members of the staff and crew of *The Mirror Has Two Faces,* as well as Amy Rosefeld and other political science students who attended Streisand's appearance before them.

"I'm a shy person": *Vanity Fair,* November 1994.

"Why are you doing": Kramer, interview.

"Why is it": *Wall Street Journal,* February 3, 1995.

"Hollywood": Ibid.

"I must admit": Harvard University archives.

"Why are you": Ibid.

"Barbra, how could anyone": *Washington Post,* March 10, 1995.

"Everyone was optimistic": Anonymous interview.

"It was hard to tell": Ibid.

"She had been complaining": Ibid.

"[She] can piss you off": *W,* July 1996.

"The whole team": Anonymous interview.

"which they'd brought in": Ibid.

"This woman has had": Kramer, interview.

"Barbra was deeply hurt": Anonymous interview.

"This is my first major film": Ibid.

"I love Barbra": LaGravenese, interview.

"She is often misguided": Kramer, interview.

"Yet, the most wondrous thing": Anonymous interview.

Bibliography

Bach, Steven. *Final Cut: Dreams and Disaster in the Making of Heaven's Gate*. New York: Morrow, 1985.

Beaton, Cecil. *Cecil Beaton's Diaries, 1963–1974*. London: Weidenfeld & Nicholson, 1978.

Bordman, Gerald. *American Musical Revue*. New York: Oxford University Press, 1985.

————. *American Musical Theatre*. New York: Oxford University Press, 1978.

Brady, Frank. *Barbra: An Illustrated Biography*. New York: Grosset & Dunlap, 1979.

Brownstein, Ronald. *The Power and the Glitter*. New York: Pantheon Books, 1990.

Carrick, Patrick. *Barbra Streisand: A Biography*. London: Robert Hale Ltd., 1991.

Citron, Stephen. *The Wordsmiths: Oscar Hammerstein & Alan Jay Lerner*. New York: Oxford University Press, 1995.

Conroy, Pat. *The Prince of Tides*. Boston: Houghton Mifflin, 1986.

Considine, Shaun. *Barbra Streisand: The Woman, the Myth, the Music*. New York: Delacorte Press, 1985.

Crist, Judith. *Take 22: Movie Makers on Movie Making*. New York: Viking, 1984.

Dunne, John Gregory. *Studio*. New York: Farrar, Straus & Giroux, 1969.

Edwards, Anne. *Judy Garland: A Biography*. New York: Simon & Schuster, 1975.

Engel, Lehman. *This Bright Day*. New York: Macmillan, 1974.

Friedrich, Otto. *City of Nets*. New York: Harper & Row, 1987.

Frommer, Myrna Katz and Harvey. *It Happened in Brooklyn*. New York: Harcourt Brace, 1986.

Gavin, James. *Intimate Nights*. New York: Limelight Editions, 1992.

Gilbert, Bob and Gary Theroux. *The Top Ten — 1956–1981*. New York: Simon & Schuster, 1982.

Goldman, Albert. *Elvis Presley*. New York: McGraw-Hill, 1981.

Griffin, Nancy and Kim Masters. *Hit & Run: How Jon Peters and Peter Guber Took Sony for a Ride in Hollywood*. New York: Simon & Schuster, 1996.

Harvey, Stephen. *Directed by Vincente Minnelli*. New York: Harper & Row, 1989.

Hirschhorn, Clive. *Gene Kelly*. London: W. H. Allen, 1974.

Holt, Georgia, and Phyllis Quinn with Sue Russell, *Star Mothers*. New York: Simon & Schuster, 1988.

Jordan, René. *The Greatest Star*. New York: G. P. Putnam's Sons, 1975.

Kael, Pauline. *For Keeps: 30 Years at the Movies*. New York: Dutton, 1994.

Kantor, Bernard, Irwin Blacker, and Anne Kramer. *Directors at Work*. New York: Funk & Wagnalls, 1970.

Katz, Ephraim. *The Film Encyclopedia*. New York: HarperCollins, 1994.

Kimbrell, James. *Barbra — An Actress Who Sings*. Boston: Branden Publishing Co., 1989.

———. *Barbra — An Actress Who Sings, Volume II*. Boston: Branden Publishing Co., 1992.

Kissel, Howard. *The Abominable Showman*. New York: Applause Books, 1993.

Knepp, Donn. *Las Vegas*. Menlo Park, Calif.: Lane Publishing Co., 1987.

Laufe, Abe. *Broadway's Greatest Musicals*. New York: Funk & Wagnalls, 1977.

Laurents, Arthur. *The Way We Were*. New York: Harper & Row, 1972.

Lerner, Alan Jay. *The Musical Theatre — A Celebration*. London: Collins, 1986.

———. *The Street Where I Live*. New York: W. W. Norton, 1978.

Lennart, Isobel, with lyrics by Bob Merrill and music by Jule Styne. *Funny Girl*. New York: Random House, 1964.

Liberace. *Liberace: An Autobiography*. New York: Putnam, 1973.

Lord, James. *Picasso and Dora*. New York: Farrar Straus & Giroux, 1993.

Lumet, Sidney. *Making Movies*. New York: Knopf, 1995.

McClintick, David. *Indecent Exposure*. New York: Morrow, 1982.

Madsen, Axel. *William Wyler*. New York: Thomas J. Crowell Company, 1973.

McCullough, David. *Brooklyn . . . and How It Got That Way*. New York: Dial Press, 1983.

Miller, Allan. *A Passion for Acting*. New York: Backstage Books, 1992.

Miller, Edwin. *"Seventeen" Interviews Stars and Superstars*. New York: Macmillan, 1970.

Minnelli, Vicente. *I Remember It Well*. New York: Doubleday, 1974.

Monti, Ralph. *I Remember Brooklyn*. New York: Birch Lane Press, 1991.

Morris, Jan. *Manhattan '45*. New York: Oxford University Press, 1987.

Pogrebin, Letty Cottin. *Deborah, Golda and Me: Being Female and Jewish in America*. New York: Crown, 1991.

Reed, Rex. *Do You Sleep in the Nude?* New York: New American Library, 1968.

Riese, Randall. *Her Name Is Barbra*. New York: Birch Lane Press, 1993.

Rivers, Joan, with Richard Meryman. *Enter Talking*. New York: Delacorte Press, 1986.

Sharif, Omar, with Marie-Thérèse Guinchard. *The Eternal Male*. New York: Doubleday, 1977.

Spada, James. *The First Decade — The Films and Career of Barbra Streisand*. New York: Citadel Press, 1974.

———. *The Woman and the Legend*. New York: Doubleday, 1981.

———. *Streisand: Her Life*. New York: Crown, 1995.

Suskin, Steven. *Opening Night on Broadway*. New York: Schirmer Books, 1991.

Swenson, Karen. *Barbra The Second Decade*. New York: Citadel Press, 1986.

Taraborrelli, J. Randy. *Call Her Miss Ross*. New York: Birch Lane Press, 1989.

Taylor, Theodore. *Jule: The Story of Composer Jule Styne*. New York: Morrow, 1979.

Teti, Frank, and Karen Moline. *Streisand Through the Lens*. New York: Delilah Press, 1983.

Tormé, Mel. *Judy Garland: The Other Side of the Rainbow*. New York: Morrow, 1970.

Trudeau, Margaret. *Beyond Reason*. New York: Paddington Press Ltd., 1979.

Uslan, Michael and Bruce Solomon. *Dick Clark's the First 25 Years of Rock & Roll*. New York: Crown Publishers, 1981.

Vickers, Hugo. *Cecil Beaton*. Boston: Little, Brown, 1985.

Wakeman, John, ed. *World Film Directors,* Vols. I and II. New York: H. W. Wilson, 1988.

Willensky, Elliot. *When Brooklyn Was the World 1920–1957*. New York: Harmony Books, 1986.

Zadan, Craig. *Sondheim & Co.,* second edition. New York: Harper & Row, 1986.

Zec, Donald, and Anthony Fowles. *Barbra*. New York: St. Martin's Press, 1981.

Magazines and Periodicals

Architectural Digest: May 1978; December 1993

Cosmopolitan: April 1969; October 1991; September 1995

Esquire: October 1976; October 1982

In Style: June 1994

Ladies' Home Journal: August 1966; August 1969

Life: May 22, 1964; November 6, 1964; March 18, 1966; January 9, 1970; December 1983

Look: April 5, 1966; March 18, 1966; October 15, 1968

McCall's: April 1975

Newsweek: January 5, 1970

New Times: January 24, 1975

New West: November 22, 1976

New York: April 15, 1976

New Yorker: November 1929; November 14, 1970; October 15, 1973

People: April 26, 1976; December 12, 1983

Playboy: November 1970; October 1977; 1988

Playgirl: February 1984

Premiere: July 1980; December 1987

Redbook: July 1965

Saturday Evening Post: July 27, 1963

Showmusic: Spring 1995

Time: April 10, 1964; August 19, 1966; October 13, 1969; September 7, 1970

TV Guide: October 1, 1994

US: October 3, 1988

Vanity Fair: October 1991; November 1994

Village Voice: April 26, 1976

Vogue: June 1970

Woman: November 5, 1978

The Hollywood Reporter

New York Times Magazine

Rolling Stone

Variety (daily and weekly)

Archives

The Academy of Television Arts and Sciences, North Hollywood

Beaufort Chamber of Commerce, Beaufort, South Carolina

Erasmus Hall High School, Brooklyn

Brooklyn Chamber of Commerce

The Billy Rose Theatre Collection, Lincoln Center Library for the Performing Arts, New York City

William Wyler Collection — University of California at Los Angeles

Archives of the Performing Arts, Special Collections, University of Southern California, Los Angeles

Special Collections Film — University of Wisconsin
Special Collections Theater and Arts — Harvard University
Screen Actors Guild of America
Directors Guild of America
Academy of Motion Picture Arts and Sciences
British Film Institute
Brooklyn Historical Society
Frances Howard Goldwyn Library, Hollywood
Museum of Television and Radio, New York
National Academy of Recording Arts and Sciences, Burbank
Warner Brothers Studio Archives

Index